Psychology

ROSS STAGNER

University of Illinois

T. F. KARWOSKI

Dartmouth College

Psychology

NEW YORK TORONTO LONDON

McGRAW-HILL BOOK COMPANY, INC.

1952

PSYCHOLOGY

Library of Congress Catalog Card Number: 52-6004

THE MAPLE PRESS COMPANY, YORK, PA.

FOR MARGARET AND EILA

Preface: To the Student

This book offers an introduction to the scientific study of psychology. For most of you, it will be the first contact with such an approach to human behavior. What rewards can you expect, what satisfactions can you obtain, from this study?

For many students the most pressing problem in any course is to be able to pass examinations on the content of the textbook. However, there are other rewards which can be got from the study of psychology. These may include purely practical goals, such as proficiency in salesmanship or advertising. The most productive orientation, the one which will maximize learning and memory for psychological principles, is the desire for a broader understanding of yourself and others.

Learning without motivation is virtually nonexistent. Learning related to strong motives is rapid and permanent. If you can establish connections between the ideas we have presented in this book, and your own long-term desires, you will be a successful student.

What purposes of your own would be relevant to the study of psychology? They are, after all, the same as those of thoughtful men and women who have studied man and his nature throughout the centuries. What are the aims which you share with previous thinkers? We believe that the three following are most significant:

1. *Man's continuing interest in the great ideas of his predecessors.* What we are today, and the knowledge we have today, depend on what our parents knew a generation ago. Interest in the "Great Books" and study of the historical development of ideas testify to the importance of this trend.

2. *The need to get a new conception of the world in terms of new discoveries.* No sooner is a new experiment performed, a new principle established,

than there is a rush to change our picture of the world to fit the new facts. Nuclear physics and modern medicine have forced us to progress from old to new conceptions of the world and of man. Psychology seems well on the way to doing likewise.

3. *The appreciation of facts and their practical applications.* While some scientists are truly "impractical," most research ultimately throws light on practical problems. Many major scientific investigations have been motivated by concrete, everyday needs.

You, as a student, show these same three trends in your personal development. Consciously or unconsciously, you are a *historian*. You cling to knowledge based on your past experience; you will resist learning some of the ideas contained in this book because they will seem to conflict with what you "know" from your own observations. You are also a *philosopher*, even though the thought seems strange to you. You have a strong need to "make sense" out of what you study; you want to get a picture which "hangs together" and presents a systematic pattern. Isolated fragments, which do not relate to one another, annoy you. Finally, you are a *technician*. You want to know how this works, how it can be useful in controlling the real environment in which you live and function.

No textbook can educate you or anyone else on all these levels. Indeed, the best book and the best instructor can only offer an opportunity to learn. Effective education is self-education. The really sound way to use this text, consequently, is to treat it as presenting some facts and ideas which you want to organize into your own personal picture of man and his behavior. Do not abandon such efforts on the ground that they are "mere theorizing." Whether or not you wish to do so, you *will* develop a viewpoint on psychology—you will have a "theory" about people. Your problem is to make that theory as sound as possible. We have tried to organize this book so as to help you achieve this.

The development of a personal conception of human nature can be rewarding; it is one of the exciting outcomes of the study of psychology. Mere memorizing of facts offers little to arouse enthusiasm; but fitting facts about behavior into a picture which explains your roommate, your friends, or yourself makes a fascinating detective story. As you develop this understanding, you also get satisfactions far beyond those of remembering facts. Needless to say, the facts must be learned for this understanding to develop.

Effective learning is exciting. If you are intrigued by some point in this book, go and read more about it. Perhaps our discussion of animism will make some students want to read more on magic and primitive sorcery, as in Frazer's *The Golden Bough*. Others may be stimulated to learn about color, or about anxiety, or about childhood influences on personality. Every good student will find some topics that arouse his interest, something that he will want to study in more detail; it is an important part of the educative process that he pursue these topics and learn about them on his own initiative.

We shall not pretend that you can learn psychology from this book without effort. All good things are obtained by working. The real question is, are the rewards worth the effort? We believe that the satisfactions derived from a real comprehension of psychology will be far greater than the energy you expend.

This book, and the workbook which accompanies it, have been planned to help the student in realizing the three factors in significant learning. At the close of each chapter, we offer a list of collateral readings, which includes some of the great experiments in the field, and the thoughts of pioneer explorers on some major problem. You should make use of these in following up the interesting topics in the chapter. The workbook presents simple experiments by which you can get concrete experience to illustrate the principles stated in the text. We have also included various kinds of questions designed to help you locate the key facts and principles of each chapter.

But we have worked hardest to provide the student with something we consider absolutely vital. This is the broad, over-all view, the organized picture of man and his nature. Students inevitably develop—apparently, they *must* get—this broad, general conception of psychology. Rather than leave this development to chance, we have deliberately written into the book a systematic organization of psychological facts around the principle of homeostasis.

Homeostasis is a relatively new concept in psychology. New experimental work may prove that it is not the key explanatory principle we have represented it as being. But, in order to avoid facing the student with a bewildering array of disorganized facts, we have used homeostasis as the organizing concept around which a systematic picture of human behavior can be developed. Learning makes sense—psychology makes sense—when the facts are fitted into patterns defined by a few basic and consistent ideas. This we have tried to do.

Psychology is today the most vigorous of the sciences. It is young, dynamic, expanding. Writing this book has been, for us, an intellectual adventure. We have been compelled to abandon some of our old notions, develop new ideas. You can share in this adventure without accepting our book as dogma. By observing, by testing, and by thinking about human behavior, you can develop your own conceptions of psychology. From the very fact that they are your own, they will be learned, remembered, and used more effectively. This is the significant goal for you, the student of psychology.

At the conclusion of such a long and involved task as the writing of this book has been, we feel indebted to many of our colleagues for stimulating and helpful criticism. The ideas around which our treatment of psychology has been organized were clarified and structured in discussions with too many people for their names to be listed here. For specific advice on the manuscript, however, we want to thank our colleagues at Dartmouth—Irving Bender, Shammai Feldman, A. H. Hastorf, and Francis King; and at Illinois—W. G. McAllister, Charles E. Osgood, and L. I. O'Kelly. We also wish to acknowledge the aid of our students, both undergraduate and graduate, whose reactions have guided us in both formulation and expression of psychological principles.

Ross Stagner
Theodore Karwoski

Urbana, Ill.
Hanover, N.H.
   February, 1952

Contents

CHAPTER 1

Orientation

"The Proper Study of Mankind"

Virtually all of us find the observation of our fellow man to be a fascinating activity. The gossip of sewing circles, the small talk of cocktail parties, and the sensational stories of the tabloid newspapers all attest to the focusing of interest on our friends and our neighbors, if not on ourselves.

It is, furthermore, necessary that this should be so. In our complex society, each individual must have some awareness of others, some understanding of their behavior, in order to adjust at all. The wife who complains, "My husband doesn't understand me" and the employees who organize a union and go on strike against an unsympathetic employer indicate clearly the urgent need for better knowledge of the roots of human actions. The term *human relations* extends to education, business, politics, friendship, marriage, and parenthood. Mere comfort, not to say success, in these spheres, calls for some understanding of human beings.

Moreover, it has always been so. As far as we can dig into man's life in the past, man's concern about himself and his relation to others has been an intense preoccupation. Psychology is an ancient study. The earliest recorded history and the observations on savage mentality from all parts of the world reveal an elaborate theoretical conception of man's place in the universe in what is known as primitive *animism*, or the theory that the whole world is animated by a "spirit" or soul. The essence of animism is that every material body—plant, animal, lake, and star—contains a second being, a kind of a demon, which is of a substance different from the material body. Thus medicine and astronomy, in which the primitives have made some advances, were aspects of psychology. The primitives, to be sure, were primarily interested in the practical business of exorcising the demons that infected the soul. The medicine men were masters in the techniques of suggestion, hypnosis, and mental relaxation long before the dawn of modern science. Their practical bent did not preclude theorizing. Animism is always accompanied by a systematic conception of various demons and their relations to each other and an elaborate ritual to control them. The details varied with various people, but the demonological presence of a spirit world within the material world was universally held by all (Fig. 1:1).

Modern psychology is not indifferent to animism. The child's early attempts to understand his environment show animistic tendencies which we shall refer to as animistic thinking. Occultism is still a force in

FIG. 1:1. Are psychological processes controlled by demons? Primitive psychology held that the soul was something different and separable from the body. Psychological illnesses (and physical disease as well) were related to "possession by demons." The witch doctor, usually a shrewd practical psychologist, "cured" many ailments by his rituals. Modern psychology attempts to get away from this animistic formulation of problems to a scientific way of thinking. (*Courtesy of National Film Board of Canada.*)

our civilization. Parapsychology is a search by scientific methods for evidence of thought transference across time and space. The psychoanalysts see in their own results the vestiges of what seem to be unconscious attachments to savage totems and taboos in dream symbols which have an ancient lineage.

Müller-Freienfels, in an inspired passage, conveys the feeling of this heritage of animism in our history.

A stately train of pioneers blazed the trail for modern psychology! Painted Indians and tattooed Polynesians; pious Brahmans and worthy Greeks; Dominicans in black robes and Franciscans in brown robes; men of the baroque period in proud wigs; braided men of the age of enlightenment—all had attempted to fathom that mysterious essence which men, ever since men existed, have called their soul. What they so glibly called the "soul" was an extremely variable entity. Like Proteus of the Greek legend, it always changed its form as soon as

one attempted to grasp it. . . . And still all these interpretations of the mystery called soul were not arbitrary whims, for each attempt captured some essential quality of the soul, no matter in what fantastic disguise. This is reflected in the fact that most of these soul concepts reappear in some form or other in modern psychology.[1]

Against the background of this long history, psychology as a science is seen as an infant, still in its swaddling clothes. Psychologists cannot brush aside this heritage even though they would like to, because in the course of time keen men isolated problems which still live today and simply have to be coped with. Although the thinkers of the past knew very little if anything about the physiology and internal structure of the organism, their inferences based on objective observation of the behavior of men and things often are strikingly modern.

[1] *The Evolution of Modern Psychology*, pp. 19–20. Reprinted by permission of Yale University Press.

This is especially true of the Greeks. Though they did not have the factual information we have, their analysis of the events as they saw them set up critical issues in psychology for the next two thousand years. This is what William James meant when he wrote: "I say at once that in my humble opinion there is no new psychology worthy of the name." We might add that to the historical philosopher there is nothing new under the sun.

For thousands of years, the proper study of mankind has been man. This long history has included constant observation, discussion, checking, and hypothesizing. Scientific psychology is less than a century old, but this modern approach has been profoundly affected by these earlier analyses. Particularly this historical background is effective in determining what are considered to be the major problems of psychology.

The Nature of Psychological Reality

What are the key problems of psychology? The amazing Greeks propounded many questions with which scientific psychology is still concerned. One of these problems can well be titled "the nature of psychological reality." Here is the way it arises: if I touch a piece of iron, I become aware of the object as having a certain shape, hardness, temperature, and so on. In short, I have a little replica of the object somewhere within me; I can describe it from memory, treat it as if it were present, and solve problems involving its use. Now it is obvious that the physical object has not been "taken into" my mind; but something is there which was not there before. What is this something, and how is it related to the physical object?

This is the essential question in the nature of psychological reality. It can be restated in terms of memory and imagination: what is the nature of the picture I see when the object is not present, or when it

has never existed? It was precisely because they grasped the central stem of this problem and formulated a rational solution that the Greek philosophers diverted the development of civilization away from the course of animism and demonology.

Plato and Aristotle made their great contribution to the development of a scientific psychology by stating this problem correctly and offering a solution in terms of a relationship. They both realized that the external object and the experienced object are not identical. The physical object does not get into the eye and crawl up the optic nerve to be deposited in the brain. Today such a statement is too obvious to be made, but to the primitive mentality it was by no means obvious. The Greeks knew nothing about the nervous system, but Plato and Aristotle were sure that external reality affected something inside the body, to produce a correlated phenomenon, the object as experienced. To bridge this gap they used the concept of *form*. Experience preserves the form of an object, but not the total object. Thus, the footprint of a shoe on the sandy beach is not the shoe, but it is a replica of the shoe as to form. Aristotle seems to have had something like this in mind when he wrote of a *tabula rasa* within the body, a clean waxy surface upon which external stimuli left imprints. Today we say that experience involves a modification in the nervous system in response to external and internal stimuli. *Tabula rasa* is of course an analogy—the assumption was that some peculiar substance existed within the body which had these properties. This substance was called the *soul* or the *mind*.

This meticulous formulation of the problem tended to get fuzzy as it was handled by various writers. There was a tendency to reify the soul substance; it became a kind of agent, or person within a person, having an independent existence of its own, apart from the total individual. When this led to the notion that "physical" and

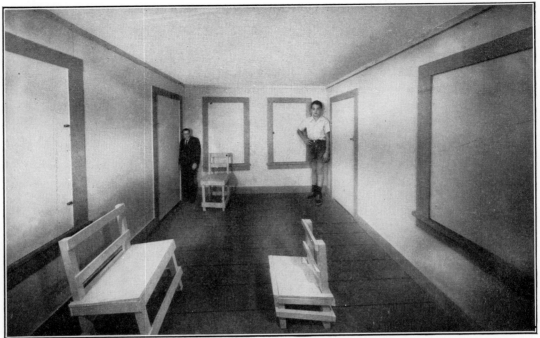

FIG. 1:2. How do we know the nature of external objects? The primitive is likely to think of memory pictures as somehow replicas, small duplicates of the original object. The Greeks realized the fallacy of this; particularly, their observation of illusions proved that perception does not give us an exact copy of a physical object. Modern psychology is concerned with studies which show how we get accurate (and inaccurate) information about the nature of external reality. Can you, for example, determine why the son looks taller than his father, in this photograph? (*Taken for Life Magazine by photographer Eric Schaal. Copyright Time Inc.*)

"mental" events were of completely different and independent character, the groundwork was laid for utter confusion. It is only in recent years that psychologists have been disentangling this mix-up and getting the whole man back together again.

The writings of Plato and Aristotle had a profound influence upon the development of psychology, which persists to the present day. The following paragraphs will show how their ideas on the nature of human psychology are still reflected in much popular thinking.

Human Psychology and Animal Psychology

Plato (387 B.C.) approached psychology from a developmental point of view, discussing plants, animals, and man as be-

longing to a series. Plants have only vegetative functions; animals have vegetative and sensitive functions; man has vegetative, sensitive, and rational processes. However, Plato accepted the dualistic position that there was an immaterial world of ideas, which exist in their own right and are not products of experience. Ideas, he thought, exist in adults in their purest form; in children and animals they are "contaminated" with matter. To lessen this contamination of the rational with the physical is man's highest purpose.

Plato introduced another unfortunate confusion into his psychology, which has tended to persist. As was suggested above, he considered the mental world to be "higher" than the physical and felt that man should strive toward the mental, away from the flesh. Since ideas are independent of the body, they survive after death; the soul, which experiences ideas, also survives. Thus Plato established the notion that the body is bad, the mind or soul good. This polarization of mind-body and good-evil in the same direction provided a foundation for the ill-advised asceticism of many medieval thinkers, and indeed, for whole social groups.

Aristotle (335 B.C.) was a student of Plato but differed from his teacher in many respects. Accepting the developmental approach, he treated it much more consistently. He emphasized the similarities of man to animals, and even to plants, and laid the groundwork (neglected for two thousand years) for a systematic approach to the development of the higher mental processes. He shrank the area assigned by Plato to the soul, stating that practical reason was dependent upon the senses and experience, hence basically like that of animals. Only a special variety of thought ("creative reason") carried Plato's distinction of being immortal and qualitatively different from that of animals. Aristotle's psychology is thus consistently biological in almost every detail.

Rationalism vs. empiricism. While Aristotle has often been blamed for the stagnation of science through the Dark Ages, the responsibility should more aptly be placed upon Plato. Plato's assertion of the separate and higher nature of ideas led to an emphasis upon abstract thought and speculation which became known as the philosophy of *rationalism.* This intellectual school held that we can know the real nature of ideas without experience; hence we do not need to study physical events. Eventually these ivory-tower exponents got into such famous blind alleys as the speculation over "how many angels could dance on the point of a needle."

Aristotle actually laid the foundations for *empiricism,* the approach to psychology which asserts the importance of observation and experiment. Modern American psychology is overwhelmingly empiricist in its orientation, some feel even too much so. There is, after all, a place for reflection and abstract theorizing too, in the advance of science. But it was the rejection of observation, the overemphasis upon pure reason unsupported by fact, which delayed the progress of science until about the sixteenth century.

The revolt against rationalism is a part of the whole intellectual ferment which includes the Protestant Reformation (rejection of theological authoritarianism), the decline of feudalism (rejection of a rigid hierarchy in society), and the Industrial Revolution, with its urgent need for operational scientific knowledge. Descartes (1596–1650) initiated great advances by his penetrating skepticism regarding the dogmas of the past. He held that it was all right to respect Plato and Aristotle as great thinkers, but not to accept their words when these did not check with direct observation of reality. Thus he became the philosophical leader of the empiricist trend in psychology.

No doubt Descartes's greatest contribution to modern psychology was the concept of reflex action. He knew about the sensory nerves which entered the brain and from here "animal spirits" traveled through tubes where they activated the muscles. He conceived of the body as a machinelike contrivance, responding automatically to stimulation.

Animals behave like machines. Human bodies are also machines, but Descartes said that humans have a soul which resides in the pineal gland, a small organ tucked away in the brain. Humans can be activated by the soul as well as reflexively; animals have only reflex behavior. There is some evidence that Descartes really held to a thoroughly monistic position, that human and animal behavior alike depended upon the physical

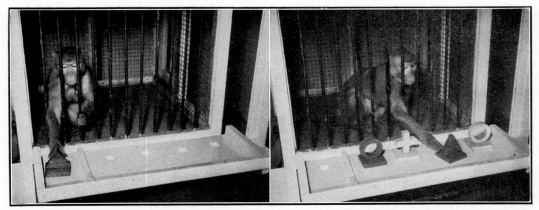

FIG. 1:3. Can animals think? Are there basic differences in psychological functions for man and animals? The great revolution in scientific thinking which made modern psychology possible was the idea that many functions were comparable for humans and animals. The picture on the left shows the monkey studying a stimulus form; in the picture on the right he must pick out this form if he is to get the food reward. This is similar to many tests for child intelligence. (*Courtesy of Dr. H. F. Harlow.*)

stimulus and the physiological structure of the body (Fig. 1:3). It is said that he inserted the notion of the soul, interacting with the body through the pineal gland, to avoid the dire punishments which theological authority was still able to deal out at that time.

While Descartes was ostensibly a dualist, his concept of reflex behavior—that animals do what they must do, given a particular body structure and a particular stimulus—struck many of his readers as offering the best chances of scientific advance. We thus have initiated a period of naturalistic observation of animals, study of the sensory and motor nerves, and comparison of human and animal behavior, which was well under way long before Darwin amassed the evidence for the biological evolution of species.

The Laws of Thinking

While Descartes and his students were beginning one kind of empiricist trend in psychology, the study of behavior, another group—the British empiricists—were studying mental processes as functions of experience. Aristotle, it will be remembered, had accepted the idea that "practical reason" stemmed from experience and was not merely a function of the soul. He had followed through on this with his analysis of memory and association of ideas. He emphasized the notion that the mind works by reproducing the particular sequence of experiences to which a desired idea belongs, or by calling up memories of occurrences which resemble in some way that which we seek (Fig. 1:4). "When we recollect," Aristotle wrote, "we awaken certain antecedent processes and continue this until we call up that particular experience, after which the desired one is wont to appear. That is the reason why we hunt through a series in thought, beginning with an object presented before us, or with something else, or with an object that is *similar*, or *opposite* or *contiguous*." Aristotle expressed the laws of association in terms of motions or processes. Centuries later Locke spoke of "association of ideas," which is less scientific than Aristotle's formulation.

Trends in the History of Psychology

What is the value of surveying the history of psychology? It can serve at least three useful purposes. (1) It can identify for us the persisting problems, the questions which have long concerned men who have reflected long and deeply about psychology. (2) It can make us aware of the diversity of explanations that have been offered for various psychological phenomena. We have avoided quoting too many different interpretations for fear of confusing the student. However, it should be clear that the same facts can be organized into differing theories. (3) It can help us to understand why certain problems were not faced and thus not solved.

We have seen that the persisting problems of psychology through the ages have been on the intellectual, the rational side. Discussion has centered around man's awareness of his external surroundings, his memory for these objects and events, and his thoughts about them. Intelligence, reason, memory, learning—these have been the persistent problems of psychology.

What is lacking here? It is precisely the most important of all—the problem of dynamics. Why does man act as he does? What are the motives, the emotions, the impulses and fears which drive him to action? Plato had proposed that the mind is good, the body bad. The desires of the flesh are clearly, then, something bad. We must seek the life of contemplation and avoid any concern with man's animal desires. Marcus Aurelius, reflecting the true spirit of the ancient philosophers, wrote, "Wipe out imagination; check desire; extinguish appetite; keep the ruling faculty in its own power." Exactly this tradition, the emphasis on man's rational side and the refusal to study the dynamic side.

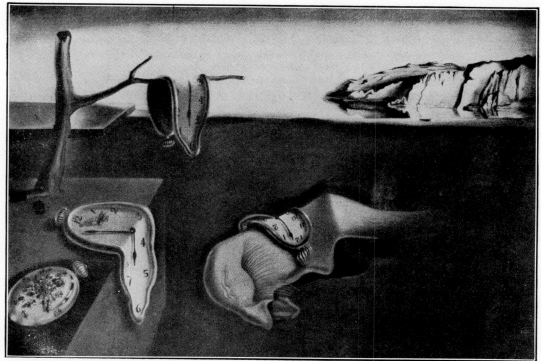

FIG. 1:4. How does memory operate? Aristotle held that memory reproduces past experiences. Modern research indicates that memories become distorted by subsequent experiences, by strong motives, and by the frame of reference of the person remembering. In this picture Salvador Dali visualizes the changing of memory, the distortion of space and time, in an unusually graphic manner. (Courtesy of Museum of Modern Art.)

FIG. 1:5. What is the meaning of dreams? Dreams have long fascinated psychologists. They seem to reproduce real objects which are not present; they relate to strong fears, loves, and hates. Once it was thought that they could foretell the future; now it is known that they reflect the deep emotional problems of the personality. The above picture was painted by a woman to illustrate a dream which was interpreted thus: "In the picture which she painted of this dream she was at the tiller—that is, she was making a conscious effort to go her own way. But the figure which was actually steering the boat was the great archetypal figure of the mother, the image which was really directing from the unconscious. The picture and the dream both showed her that she was still caught in a typical situation. She had not broken from the archetypal mother (that is, from the dependence upon her), and her resentment and bitterness toward the actual mother only blinded her to the fact that she herself was keeping to shallow and muddy waters because she still chose to remain a child. She was in the power of an archetype, that is, of an unconscious force which really ruled her choices." (*From Wickes (1938), Plate 7 and pp. 302–303. Reprinted by permission of the author.*)

prevented great advances in psychological science. It was only with the intellectual revolution of Descartes, and the study of animals, that emphasis upon motivation became widespread. And even Sigmund Freud, writing at the beginning of the twentieth century, was roundly denounced for his concern with man's irrational desires, to the exclusion of his logical capacities.

Naturally we want no one-sided concern with dynamics to the exclusion of knowledge. But the key feature of modern psychology is the notion that motivation comes first; man is primarily a creature of impulse, wanting, demanding, fearing, loving, and hating; he is only secondarily a creature of intelligence and reason.

The great, exciting, and tragic problems of human psychology are not new. The powerful Greek dramatists explored the questions of love and hate, fear and jealousy, just as the Greek philosophers studied the questions of knowledge and thought. It was simply unfortunate that a split developed between the two. Psychology today is just recovering from the unfortunate effects of this divorce, as we see the mental and physical as two sides of the same coin, desire interacting with reason, motives shaped and directed by thought. Man is a single unit; his thinking cannot be separated from his emotions any more than his brain can survive without his digestive system. The recent study of psychosomatic illnesses, for example, shows how constantly bodily conditions and mental states are interacting to determine the sickness or health of the total individual.

The Beginnings of Scientific Psychology

Scientific psychology was impossible until certain other sciences developed first. The lack of scientific method and the ban on vivisection of the human body delayed knowledge of the structure and function of the brain and nerves for centuries. Consequently the Greeks—who rightly guessed that there must be transmitting media in the body—posited an abstraction which they called *pneuma*. The pneuma was a sort of airy substance which connected the mind with the external object. This abstraction is comparable to the physicist's ether, which was invented in order to understand how light is propagated. The lack of the concept of the nerve turned out to be a great obstacle to concrete thinking about mental behavior. It forced thinking onto a highly abstract level of fictitious substitutes. Lacking the know-how of experimentation, philosophical thinking on the nature of man was largely confined to classification of phenomena in terms of similarity and difference. It is remarkable how much was discovered by these primitive means. It suggests that imagination and insight must be valued very highly in any appraisal of the scientific method.

An intelligent answer to the Greek philosopher's question, how does the object "get into" the mind, could not be obtained until the physics of light, sound, and other energy transmissions had been developed. Democritus may have believed in a mate-

rialistic psychology, but lacking knowledge of this kind, he could not give a plausible explanation of sensation. Information was also needed on the side of the organism. What processes go on in the eye, the ear, the nose, and skin which report the characteristics of the external object? Progress was necessary in the field of physiology, before answers could be got to such questions of psychological importance. It is thus not surprising that, as the nineteenth century led to great strides in physics and physiology, the earliest scientific developments in psychology took the form of psychophysics and psychophysiology.

The beginnings of scientific psychology were also dependent upon the new respect for facts which came with the intellectual revolution of the eighteenth century. Sometimes students complain that modern textbooks are too factual; but our respect for facts is a distinguishing feature of our civilization. A fact is an antibody to bias and prejudice. The ability to accept facts dispassionately is not easily attained. The medieval church denounced anyone who was concerned with facts to the extent of questioning the authorities; today in communist countries we see the same imposition of ideas as dominant over facts.

True scientific culture, of course, demands an adequate respect for both the rationalistic and the empiricist approach to knowledge. The quest for fact which ignores theory quickly reduces to counting grains of sand. But the obsession with a theory which ignores fact quickly transforms into a blind belief.

A. N. Whitehead asserts that the twentieth century is unique in that we are passionately concerned with both facts and abstract principles. This new mentality, he writes,

is more important than the new science and the new technology. It has altered the metaphysical presuppositions and the imaginative contents of our minds; so that now the old stimuli provoke new response. . . . This new tinge to modern minds is a vehement and passionate interest in the relation of general principles to irreducible and stubborn facts. All the world over and at all times there have been practical men absorbed in irreducible and stubborn facts; all the world over and at all times there have been men of philosophic temperament who have been absorbed in weaving of general principles. It is this union of passionate interest in the detailed facts with equal devotion to abstract generalizations which forms the novelty of our present society. Previously it had occurred sporadically and as if by chance. The balance of mind has now become part of the tradition which infects cultivated thought. It is the salt which keeps life sweet. . . .[1]

Psychology of sensory processes. This alternation between abstract principles and stubborn facts has been a feature of scientific psychology from the beginning. A researcher sees a relationship among facts and develops a theory; this theory suggests that certain observations should be made; the theory then is confirmed or rejected on the basis of further facts. We shall cite numerous instances of this throughout the present volume. Let us just mention here, as part of our introduction to scientific psychology, the early study of sensory psychology.

By the middle of the last century physicists and physiologists had determined significant facts about the stimulus on the one hand and about the nature of the receptors on the other. The physical properties of light and sound were known. The nature of nerve conduction was not yet discovered, but an important generalization about the sensory nerve was enunciated in the form of the law of *specific nerve energies.* According to this law the different

[1] Whitehead (1925), pp. 3–4. Reprinted by permission of the Macmillan Company, publishers. A name, either in the text or in a footnote, followed by a date means a reference to a research paper or other publication. These references will be found in the Bibliography at the end of this book.

nerves have a specific function—the visual nerve, literally, to see and the auditory nerve, to hear. If the optic nerve or receptor is stimulated mechanically, chemically, or electrically, a light sensation is produced. The visual receptors cannot yield any other sensation—such as sound, for instance. This all sounds commonplace today, but it was a dynamic idea in its time. The physiologists also noted that receptors were highly structured with nerve endings, and this suggested the notion that specific nerves in the receptor complex may have specific functions. The next step was to vary the stimulus and try to relate the locale of the sensory response to specific dimensions of the stimulus. This approach was extended to all the receptors.

Thus by a constant interplay of a theory, some facts, a new theory, and some more facts, a body of knowledge about sensory psychology has been developed and integrated.

The first laboratory of psychology. In 1879, Wundt established the first psychological laboratory at the University of Leipzig. He was himself originally a physiologist. The fact of experimental psychology was so imminent and so ripe that William James is said to have anticipated Wundt with a laboratory at Harvard. The same fact explains the success of Leipzig in attracting students from all over the world. With a dynamic director and an impatience to explore psychology with the methods of science on the part of bright young men, psychology was weaned from its dependence on armchair reasoning. Within a score of years, many psychological laboratories sprang up, not only on the Continent, but in England and America.

What was the job of scientific psychology, and what was its method? Obviously the tradition of centuries of speculation decreed that the central topic of psychology was "the mind." So Wundt proceeded to analyze the mind. His method was *intro-*

spection, and the basic procedure was *psychophysical*. A stimulus was presented under controlled conditions to a subject. Immediately afterward, the subject reported exactly what he had experienced, without benefit of interpretation of the meaning of the stimulus. The attempt was to describe the stimulus in terms as purely sensory as possible, in order to arrive at the "basic mental elements" or structural details of consciousness.

Thus, if the subject saw an apple, he was required to report that he had a visual experience of a reddish patch, having a definite size, and varying in color and brightness. This may seem ridiculous today, but Wundt was concerned with developing a technique for scientific observation in psychology, and he felt that it was important to get behind one's knowledge of the object—to eliminate the details each of us adds to his observations—and describe the pure mental experience itself. As we shall note in Chaps. 5 and 6, this kind of experimentation has led to an understanding of how we get information about our world, which would never have been uncovered without it.

Wundt's students got various things from him. Some of them got ideas, but mostly they received a rigorous training in experimental technique. When they went away from Leipzig, they diverged in various directions in their attempts to develop a scientific psychology. Thus James McKeen Cattell returned to America after studying reaction time in Leipzig. He was far more impressed with the fact of individual differences in reaction time than was his master. In America Cattell started the interest in individual differences in ability and performance, thus unintentionally laying the groundwork for testing of school children, applicants for jobs, and military personnel.

Titchener, another student of Wundt, came to Cornell. He survived as the purest exponent of introspectionism, or structural psychology, which came to be known as a school by that name. Titchener enforced upon his students the technique of introspecting mental contents, and he believed that the mind was composed of elements, just as matter consisted of material elements. This point of view was consistent with the physical science of the day. Just as chemists were analyzing matter into its atomic components, so Titchener was analyzing experience into psychic contents such as sensations, images, and feelings. These elements were further analyzed into their attributes such as quality, intensity, duration, and extensity. These will be examined further in Chap. 5. This careful correlation of sensory attributes with various dimensions of the stimulus yielded exact knowledge of the correspondence of the stimulus and experience which had practical utility in applications such as the development of telephonic communication, technicolor, motion pictures, and methods of measuring and classifying sensory phenomena. Of course, these accomplishments are attributable not only to Titchener, but also to the earlier psychophysiologists and their offspring. It is the accomplishment of, or perhaps the by-product of the *structural school* of psychology, whose exponents were primarily interested to discover the structure of consciousness. A typical example of their work on complex mental problems is Titchener's analysis of attention to the irreducible attribute of sensory clearness. As will be noted in Chap. 6, this is still accepted as the definitive description of attention.

The rise of Gestalt psychology. The structural school came in for criticism within its own ranks. It was branded as a "bundle hypothesis," treating the mind as a bundle of sensations, which ignored much of the mind's functioning and was based on an outmoded atomistic physics. These critics turned the tables on structuralism by saying that the whole is not determined by its parts, but rather the whole determines the parts. They pointed out that modern physics conceives of matter as a field of force in which the pattern of forces is more important than the elements. (Ultimately the elements are reducible to force.) Their interest in psychology centered around perception. Rather than appealing to Aristotle's *sensis communis* or Wundt's apperception as the integrating factor, they stressed the notion that the brain and nervous system is in a sense a field of force; entering impressions set up strains and tensions in this field until an equilibrium is reached, and then what we perceive is the resultant of the innate force properties of the nervous system. Experience does not organize perception, but rather experience comes to us already organized in patterns, or *Gestalten*. Because of this emphasis upon the whole configuration, or Gestalt, they became known as the Gestalt school of psychology.

How the whole determines the parts can be illustrated by a simple demonstration. Read the following list of words and see what kind of picture you build up:

Alcohol
Glass
Noise
Men in white coats

At this point you are likely to have a picture of a bar, with the men in white coats as waiters, the alcohol drinkable, the noise that of conversation, and so on. Now take the next word:

Cat

You can fit the cat into the picture, perhaps wandering around the legs of the customers. But now add three more items:

Bunsen burner
Microscope
Dissecting set

What happens? The whole picture changes. It is now likely to be a scientific laboratory, the men in white coats physicians or research scientists, the alcohol used for preserving specimens, the glass used for beakers and test tubes, and so on. With a change in the whole picture, the specific elements are transformed. That is, in a very simple way, what the Gestalt psychologists mean by saying that the whole determines the parts.

The criticisms of the Gestalt group shook the foundations of the structural school, but they did not demolish the very real contributions to psychology which had been made by the structuralists. In their patient, systematic analysis of the variations in the stimulus and concomitant variations in sensation, the structuralists did much to put scientific psychology on a sound basis. It is true, furthermore, that the structural approach calls attention to certain facts which the Gestalt school tends to ignore: for example, the importance of learning and memory in organizing sensory experiences into meaningful patterns. Significant progress in psychology has occurred, not as one school has overthrown another, but as various groups have studied and developed theories about differing parts of our enormously complex field of study.

Functionalism. The Gestalt protest against structuralism is generally dated as of 1912. Actually, protests started with the very inception of the Wundt laboratory at Leipzig. One of the first American students, James McKeen Cattell, was assigned a laboratory project which concerned a report of what went on in consciousness when a person responded to a sudden light stimulus. Cattell did not relish his problem. Boldly he suggested to Professor Wundt that he study the problem from a different slant, to wit, by measuring the differences among people in their speed of reaction to the stimulus. Here was a problem that appealed to common sense and had practical appeal. To Wundt the proposal was *ganz amerikanisch.* Cattell was forced to pursue his idea in his private room. This story points up the nature of the rise of the *functional school* in America, in part engineered by Cattell and others of Wundt's returning students.

The functionalists got their scientific technique from Germany, but their orientation from Darwin's theory of evolution. It is a doctrine unlike the tight system of structuralism, which they did not so much reject as they incorporated it to their larger purposes. They doubted that the structuralist's method of introspection really got at pure sensory stuff. They would admit that the bare sensation was approximated, but really what you got from circumscribed introspection were little perceptions or small meanings. Anyway, meanings are functionally related to the organism's adjustment to the environment, and so introspection is most valuable when it gets at meaning. Introspection is now generally accepted as a tool in psychology, in both the structuralist's narrow and the functionalist's broad interpretation. In psychoanalysis, introspection is used to uncover unconscious meanings of neurotic symptoms. The organism and all its parts have a purpose and function to perform; the mind (or the brain) has its own function, just as any other organ. The function of the mind is to aid the organism to adjust to new and novel conditions. Evolutionarily, those organisms that developed minds survived; and thus, by natural selection, the special kinds of response called "the mind" came into being.

Functionalists were especially interested in capacities for adjustment; so mental tests and studies of individual differences in abilities flourished in America. Adjustment to environment is a broad concept, indeed, but the functionalists accepted the challenge and promoted psychological studies in special fields such as education, business, law, and medicine. Functionalism is more of an attitude than a neat school of doctrine. Its followers are catholic in their temperament and interests. Indeed, many of them simply consider themselves psychologists, absorbing whatever is useful in promoting the understanding of man from whatever intellectual group is engaged on such problems. The very looseness of functionalist doctrine seems to give it its vitality. In a rapidly expanding field like psychology, groups of men intrigued by special aspects of the psychology of life arise with a special message, but their contributions seem to become sifted out and incorporated in the broad framework of functional psychology.

The strifes and bickerings among psychologists are more apparent than real. Students reading of the various "schools" of psychology are sometimes alarmed; actually, the main body of psychological knowledge is independent of any school. Physicists have different theories about light; neurologists disagree about the nature of the nerve impulse. These differences are not important, and the same is true for most of the differences among psychologists. There are at present about fifteen divisions within the American Psychological Association, representing special interests in clinical psychology; military, industrial, school, or other problems; experimental or social psychology; and so on. Each of these divisions is likely to have within it people of various schools, cooperating, debating, and exchanging knowledge without difficulty.

The development of behaviorism. Structuralism had employed the technique of experimentation to study consciousness; functionalism fostered experiments on adjustment to the environment, either in consciousness or in behavior. A logical further step came with the rise of *behaviorism,* a movement led by John B. Watson,

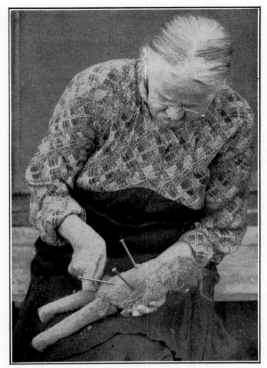

FIG. 1:6. Modern psychology rejects animism. Watson held that a belief in the power of "the mind" to affect the course of human behavior was on the same level with the superstition accepted by this Ozark Mountain woman, who drives nails into a doll to harm the person represented. Watson insisted that we must abandon animistic thinking and study behavior in terms of observed antecedent conditions and subsequent actions. (*By permission of Vance Randolph and David Fox Studio.*)

which would limit psychology to the study of behavior and ignore consciousness altogether. This led some wit to remark that among the Greeks, psychology was the study of the soul, but modern psychology had lost its soul; then it was the study of the mind, but the structuralists analyzed mind into elements, so psychology lost its mind; and finally with behaviorism, psychology lost consciousness.

Actually, behaviorism is an offshoot of functionalism, with close ties to most of modern American psychology. Watson started as an animal psychologist, doing

some interesting experiments on white rats, which will be described in Chap. 9. He was also one of the first psychologists to observe babies (see Chap. 3). Neither group of subjects could introspect and tell him the elements of their experiences, and yet he could get meaningful data about them by observing their behavior. Thus he denied the importance of consciousness to psychology.

Furthermore, Watson believed that scientific psychology had been blocked by this concern with immaterial, intangible considerations. He suggested that all the quarreling about the mind through the centuries was due to our not having got rid of primitive animism. The empiricists got rid of the soul as a spiritual entity; Watson proposed to get rid of the idea of consciousness, which he believed to be only a new label of the structuralist for the metaphysical soul of religion. His bold effort to rid science of "the man within the man" had an appeal but not enough to convince common sense that the feeling of awareness or consciousness is not a reality. However, since performance and awareness are correlated, an exact study of performance should lead to laws predicting behavior. This is where Watson had his greatest success.

Behaviorism also encouraged the extension of our knowledge of peripheral factors such as muscles and the viscera, in considering acts which were traditionally regarded as purely mental. These peripheral factors had been largely neglected historically; so Watson's rejection of the mind in preference to the body was a necessary corrective, although he overdid it. When Watson said we think with our whole body, not merely with our brains, he exaggerated; but he did point up the integration of the whole organism even in behavior as subtle as thinking. When Watson said that physiologists study the special organs separately, whereas psychologists study the behavior of whole organisms, he pointed up the person as a whole as the proper study of psychology. With corrections for Watson's exaggerations, it seems that behaviorism is not too far out of line with the main trend of modern psychology.

Psychoanalysis. Another serious objection to structuralism, or the "science of consciousness," is that mental events are not always conscious. Although Freud, the father of psychoanalysis, did not protest against the original formulations of the first school of scientific psychology (since he paid no attention to psychologists), his contributions show the serious limitations of a science based on conscious states. Freud's line of descent is from Mesmer, the father of hypnosis, and the medical men in France who were studying abnormal behavior. In fact, Freud was a student of Charcot, who noticed resemblances between hysteria and the hypnotic state. Under hypnosis the subject often remembers things of which he is not aware in his normal state. This fact impressed Freud. One day Charcot in lecturing about a young woman who developed neurotic troubles as a consequence of her husband's sexual inability said, according to Freud, "in such cases sex is always the most important thing—always, always, always." His focus on the unconscious manifestations of the sex impulse seems to have stemmed from these early experiences.

Freud was a medical man, and as such his method of gathering data was mostly clinical observation, rather than laboratory experimentation. Many of his ideas, indeed, have proved most difficult to test in the laboratory—which does not necessarily prove them wrong, of course. In dealing with his neurotic patients, Freud was impressed with the extent to which a forgotten memory could apparently determine a pathological symptom. To explain this, he developed the conception of an "unconscious mind" in which activity went on,

quite without awareness of the person. For example, he showed that we often forget names of people whom we dislike, and even forget words or names which are associated with very unpleasant experiences.

While Freud developed a very elaborate, almost fantastic, terminology which most American psychologists avoid, his basic ideas have been incorporated into general psychology. Specifically, his constant emphasis upon motivation has been accepted; and his observations about the impact of motives upon thinking and reasoning are given a very important place. We shall use many of his ideas in this book, particularly in Chap. 3, dealing with emotions, and again in the concluding chapters on personality.

Schools of psychology and the problem of reality. This survey of the different schools of psychology should be understood in relation to the basic problem of psychology as first clearly defined by Plato and Aristotle: what is the nature of reality? It will be recalled that these great thinkers pointed out the difference between the physical object and the psychological object—the fact that "things are not what they seem." In a very real sense, the theories which characterize our various schools of psychology are grounded on this problem. The structuralists staked their claim on reality in the sensory elements of experience; the Gestalters, in the organizing tendencies of the nervous system, which account for the fact that reality appears to us in experience in an organized fashion. The structuralists, by contrast, ascribed organization to the associations based on learning. The functionalists looked at reality from the point of view of the utility of the stimuli to the organism; they emphasized the variety of ways in which the organism adjusts to and transforms reality in meeting its needs. Behaviorism modified functionalism in stressing the role of response, rather than experience, as the major factor in the process of adapting to reality. The psycho-analysts have pointed out the major role of unconscious desires and anxieties in determining how reality appears to us. Each school thus stresses an important determinant of reality; and, because of the validity of their arguments, we now understand that psychological reality is determined in various degrees by all of these factors—or in other words, by the organism as a whole.

If we grasp this point clearly, then we understand that each of the schools of psychology is concerned with the same basic phenomenon; all of them study man as a whole, and his adjustment to his environment. They have, however, used different modes of approach, different descriptive concepts, and different explanatory principles. In the following chapters of this book, we shall be presenting a view of scientific psychology which emphasizes the agreements among these various points of view. Occasionally we shall offer a summary of the special interpretation developed by a particular group; but we will introduce materials from all of the various modern schools as they become relevant. As we have already noted, it is incorrect to think of any one "school" as false or as true. The various groups emphasize different facts and different principles, but they disagree much less than they agree. It is thus possible to present a picture of modern psychology which will be acceptable to most of these groups. That is the kind of picture presented in this book.

A Definition of Psychology

Psychology is what its history has made it. Developing through the various stages, approaches, and schools of thought we have sketched so briefly in the preceding pages, psychology has become a body of knowledge dealing with human behavior and experience. Functionalism, as the broadest and least doctrinaire view of psychology, represents the easiest basis to use for a textbook. It must be conceded that functionalism does not represent a tightly organized group of fundamental principles, and for that reason it is not satisfying to some psychologists who want a highly precise formulation. As long as we have such psychologists (and they are vital to the welfare of the science), there will always be groups or schools in psychology. But functionalism is sufficiently elastic that it can be used as a framework for an introductory textbook, while we bring in the useful points from the other schools as well.

The key principle of functionalism has long been "adaptation to environment." Unfortunately, this one explains so much that it has no explanatory value. It is easy enough to point to the situation on one side, and to the organism on the other, and show that adjustment has taken place; but it is difficult to put a finger on the process of adjusting. What we need is a conception of process which will be specific and observable, which can serve as the basis for a scientific psychology.

Homeostasis. The key concept which is used in this volume to tie the various aspects of psychology together is homeostasis. This term identifies a general biological principle: the tendency of the body to maintain certain normal constant conditions. Homeostasis can readily be observed in certain simple situations: for example, if the body temperature rises substantially, one begins to perspire, and this cools him off. If he is accumulating too much carbon dioxide, his rate of respiration goes up automatically. These are simple homeostatic processes. They keep the bodily conditions at a certain favorable level.

Homeostasis appears to be a useful concept for understanding human behavior on a much more complex level than the illustrations cited. For example, Walter Cannon, a noted physiologist, proposed the "emergency theory of emotions" as a homeostatic explanation of emotional response. In the case of fear, Cannon noted, the organism is faced with a threat to survival or at least to some basic satisfaction. The body meets this threat by mobilizing energy for vigorous action. The adrenal gland pours adrenalin into the blood stream, which in turn releases glycogen from the liver for fuel. Adrenalin also speeds blood-coagulation time, an obvious aid in case of bleeding. The heart rate and blood pressure go up, respiration is speeded, digestion is sidetracked. All these responses fit into a pattern: the mobilization of energy to ward off the danger and protect the organism. This is clearly homeostatic in the same sense that perspiration protects one against heatstroke.

Why is homeostasis a more useful concept than adjustment? Because it is a process which can be observed, taking place in a specific situation. Adjustment is the end result, a by-product of efforts at maintaining essential equilibrium. Homeostasis identifies the general principle of maintaining these constant states, and it is now widely accepted as a general biological law.[1] Individuals adjust to unfavorable environmental conditions by making such changes as will restore their normal condition. The process goes on within the organism; it is merely initiated by external conditions. If a drop of acid is placed on a frog's skin, the foot will come up and scratch it off. This is homeostatic action to restore the prior skin condition. The energy is mobilized inside the organism; the stimulus merely triggers the activity; when the stimulus is removed, the organism lapses back into its previous relaxed state.

The use of homeostasis as a guiding

[1] It should be noted that it is not correct to speak of the organism as trying to maintain homeostasis, any more than a falling body is trying to maintain gravitation. Falling bodies illustrate the law of gravitation, and specific bodily activities illustrate the principle of homeostasis.

concept in psychology helps us with some knotty problems. How about purpose? We can say that activity is purposive, but we do not imply any consciousness of future goals. If I bend a spring, a "purpose" is set up in the spring—to return to its original state. If my muscles accumulate too much lactic acid and other fatigue products, a "purpose" is established—to rest and clear away these disturbing substances. The purpose is within the organism, in the operation of this general principle of removing disturbing stimuli and restoring normal equilibrium. One may be disturbed by many factors other than physical. An insult upsets my equilibrium; my body mobilizes energy for action to wipe out the insult, although it may be used for other actions than fighting. For instance, I may do something to prove the insult unjustified, or I may work up an elaborate rationalization to show that the insult did not apply to me. Various homeostatic devices may be applied in any given situation.

Consider also the body-mind problem, which so concerned the Greeks and many modern psychologists. Perhaps the ancients created a problem by magnifying the mind out of its proper proportion as an aspect of the functioning organism. So it became reified as a "soul" which dominated the entire person. Let us remember the iceberg, which is nine-tenths under water and one-tenth visible. Many homeostatic processes are going on at a given moment, most of which are unconscious and unnoticed. The "mind" as envisioned by the classical philosophers includes only that small proportion which is focal in consciousness. Homeostatic processes may involve "mental" or "physical" mechanisms indiscriminately. Suppose Mary has an unpleasant engagement—one which threatens humiliation or at least embarrassment. She may avoid this disturbance by inventing a good excuse—or by developing a pain in her stomach. In either case equilibrium is restored, but in the one case the process is "mental," in the other, "physical." We shall get farther scientifically if we regard these devices as alternative homeostatic mechanisms, different ways in which a unified organism deals with a threat to normal equilibrium.

The concept of the self. The term *homeostasis* may suggest that we are concerned only with essential biological equilibria, such as the temperature norm, the acid-base balance in the blood, the oxygen–carbon dioxide equilibrium, and so on. Actually, the homeostatic principle extends to include a wide variety of other constant states. The most important of these is the individual's concept of self.

The study of the mind seems clearly too limited a field for psychology, if we use mind in its popular sense. I do not think of myself as merely a mind; when I use the pronoun "I" or "me," much more is included than thinking and reasoning. Thus terms such as *ego* and *self* play a role in modern psychology once occupied by the mind.

The term *self* has been defined as the sum total of one's experiences. This is a purely empirical definition. However, not all experiences contribute equally to one's notion of himself. It is the typical, recurring experiences which are most significant. The fact that I see parts of my body at regular intervals, for example, causes them to become an important part of my self-concept. A little girl, upon having her locks of hair cut off by a barber, looked at herself in the mirror and burst out crying—"But I'm not Sally any more!" These constancies of appearance, clothing, and physique are valued and preserved.

Recurring needs, such as hunger, and need satisfactions contribute to one's developing picture of himself. Habits are acted out often and the child perceives himself as a person who has these kinds of habits. People often struggle to carry out certain habitual acts, even though there is no longer any goal for the habit. Interference with the habit is treated as interference with an important constant state.

One's social status is another significant aspect of the self. I expect to be treated in a certain way by my friends, by strangers, by students, and so on. If a friend seems colder than usual, I am disturbed; if a stranger tries to be excessively familiar, I may also find this annoying. People in positions of authority demand certain forms of behavior as assurance of their status; deviations from these prescribed acts may be seen as threats to status and punished accordingly. Thus the principle of homeostasis appears to function on the social as well as the biological level.

The self can therefore be thought of as an elaborate pattern of desired constant states, which are protected if anything threatens them. Some of these are judged by the person as more important than others; to one man, physical comfort is paramount; another man may be concerned mostly about his professional prestige; and another may be motivated chiefly to maintain his record as a Don Juan. The study of psychology includes the study of how the self develops, how these equilibria are established, and how they are defended.

Determinism and the self concept. This concept of the self can help us with another common problem in thinking about psychology. Many people assert that it is inconceivable that we could build a science of psychology, because science demands predictable, lawful events and man is essentially unpredictable. Some have inferred from man's failure to conform to predictions that he was endowed with free will—that he could, by an act of volition, go contrary to the various pressures upon him in choosing a course of action. If this were true, of course, no scientific psychology would be possible. But these eccentricities are more apparent than real. The error arises because the basis for prediction was unsound.

If I try to predict John's behavior, I shall most likely reason thus: "here is what I would do in that situation; John will probably do the same." The prediction, then, is based on the environment as it looks to me. But it may look quite different to John; and *his* behavior is determined by the field *as he perceives it*, not as I see it. As we learn what John likes and dislikes, what he fears, whom he loves, we get an awareness of the environment as he sees it, and we can predict with a high degree of precision just how he will behave. If John's picture of himself is that of a physically weak, homely man with no sex appeal, our predictions of his behavior at a dance must take this into consideration.

Modern psychology takes the position that behavior is determined. Man is today the product of his experiences up to today. I cannot start speaking Chinese by an act of will, although I can speak French (badly) by an act of will. "Free will," then, is subject to determinism. I cannot hate someone I love, any more than I can fly without mechanical aids. But if we wish to verify the fact that behavior is determined and predictable, we must take into consideration the self of the individual for whom we are predicting. *Behavior is always determined by the situation as this person perceives it*, not by the "objectively real" situation.

The concept of determinism implies that we can predict a person's actions. Generally speaking, this is true. As a matter of fact, if we could not predict with real accuracy, our whole complex civilization would long since have collapsed. We predict the actions of other drivers on the highway, of customers in our store, of students in our colleges, of workers in our factories. Failures of prediction are the exception rather than the rule. When prediction proves inaccurate, we assume this to be a result of insufficient knowledge, not of inherently unpredictable human nature.

The emphasis here is to be placed on the rejection of animism—of mystical forces influencing human conduct. A child's misbehavior annoys his parents. They may explain it as proving that he has inherited a grandfather's malice and obstinacy. A more realistic approach may indicate that the child is frustrated, punished too severely, and denied any open affection by his parents; he is then seen as reacting in a perfectly natural way to the situation as he experiences it. No mysterious inherited influences are necessary to explain his acts. We shall, in later discussions, identify many forms of human behavior which have been considered to illustrate these mysterious forces, and show how they may better be understood on a deterministic basis.

It cannot be emphasized too much that determinism applies to the field as perceived, not to the physical field. Many errors in applied psychology are the result of ignoring this point. A child does not necessarily appreciate a gorgeous new doll, nor does a factory worker necessarily feel grateful for a fine, new employee recreation building. People do not always want what is "good for them" or what they "should" want. If a child decides that his parents do not love him, their shows of affection will be discarded as mere pretense; necessary discipline, on the other hand, will be seized upon as proof of dislike. A "fact" is real only when it is so perceived by a human being. Thought and behavior are determined by perceived reality, not by "physical reality."

In the light of these considerations, we might define psychology as the study of those homeostatic processes which involve the whole organism (as opposed to physiology, which deals with part processes such as digestion and respiration). However, a simpler definition is available. The study of any science involves the operation of observing significant phenomena. In psychology we observe and measure external behavior and through self-inspection observe our own experiences. Operationally, therefore, we can define psychology as *the study of human behavior and experience.*

Why human? This expresses the authors' preference. While animals have many interesting psychological features, the study of human beings seems more significant. We shall therefore confine this volume primarily to the human level.

Why behavior? Obviously man's acts make up a major portion of the field. We shall be concerned to describe and interpret habits such as walking and talking, artistic activities such as painting and singing, purposeful patterns such as running a business or organizing a labor union. The *prediction* and *control* of behavior of others is a major aim of professional psychologists.

Why experience? It is important that the study of experience be accepted as a significant portion of scientific psychology. Behavior often cannot be understood without a knowledge of the thought processes which preceded action. John and Don both refuse invitations to a dance; but we learn that John declined because he is afraid of women, whereas Don's behavior resulted from a prior date to take his girl friend to the theater. Experience and behavior interpenetrate to such an extent that it is both impractical and unscientific to separate them. A scientific psychology must embrace both.

In a negative way, we may point out that the definition excludes the physical, chemical, and biological aspects of man's structure and function. We shall not be concerned, except incidentally, with blood pressure, digestion, electrical reactions, and similar phenomena. Basically the distinction is this: *psychology is concerned with the whole man.* The medical and physical sciences generally are focused upon inde-

pendent functions of specific organ systems. Thus, endocrinology is concerned with the thyroid gland and its hormone; psychology is interested only when an imbalance of the hormone affects the thinking or emotions or activities of the man as a unit.

The Ultimate Basis of Psychological Processes

It may be argued, of course, that psychology is merely another science concerned with a specific system, namely, the brain. It is conceivable that this is correct. We know that the nerve structures of the cerebral cortex are inextricably involved in the processes commonly called *mental.* We know that damage to brain areas produces specific and often catastrophic changes in experience and behavior.

On the other hand, the psychologist usually works with direct studies of behavior and not with the brain as such. We know, in truth, considerably more about experience and behavior than is known about the brain functions which are presumably essential aspects of these psychological phenomena.

Our attitude toward brain patterns is considerably like that of the physicist toward the electron. Nobody has ever seen an electron, but it is a convenient assumption to explain certain experimental effects which can be seen or recorded. In the same way, we find it expedient to assume that certain brain phenomena exist, because they provide a much-needed link between series of observations.

It is plain that memory, for example, depends on some brain change. My remembrances of early childhood, of persons I have known, and of books I have read, are somehow related to changes in my cerebral cortex. Virtually nothing is known as to the nature of this change. Similarly, when I size up a situation and decide upon a course of action, brain patterns form essential elements in the series of events, but these brain events are very poorly known. At best we can assume that the external environment (physical field) affects the dynamic structure of energies in the brain, giving rise to *brain fields* which are the immediate correlates of the *behavioral field* or psychological environment—the facts as they are seen by this particular person. The brain is thus seen as a kind of synthesizing organ, taking various stimuli from the outer world and various needs, memory traces, attitudes, etc., from within the organism, and structuring these in some way so as to provide a guide for thought and action. Something like this must be true, but the facts to bolster the assumption are rather scanty.

Scientific psychologists, consequently, are prone to study behavior and experience; to understand and interpret their findings they use chiefly theories about behavior and experience. A kind of silent assumption is often detected, to the effect that something happens in the brain which underlies the externally observable sequence of events; in the absence of better neurological data, it is often just as well to leave the assumption silent.

Frames of Reference

Human behavior and experience can be studied with different purposes in mind. The salesman and the politician are interested in controlling human behavior, in selling their commodities or their parties. The scientific psychologist has as his purpose mainly the *understanding* of behavior and experience; the knowledge so gained can be used for purposes of control, but that is not inherent in the scientists' activities. The difference in observations and methods of procedure depends upon a difference in ways of thinking about the problem, or, more precisely, a difference in *frames of reference*.

When my radio repairman tinkers with tubes and circuits, he has one purpose in mind: to produce the most satisfactory sounds through the loud-speaker. We may say that his frame of reference is purely *practical*. A "good" result is one which improves the speaker output; a "bad" one is recognized by reduced quality of the audible tones.

The electronic physicist, on the other hand, is working within a *theoretical* frame of reference. His aim is to achieve the clearest comprehension of what goes on inside the radio circuit. He may thus be satisfied with squawks and wails which would cause the radio repairman grievous pain; he demands only that these sounds occur in accordance with a mental picture or theory he is developing. For him a "good" result is one which advances his knowledge, although it may be annoying to other listeners.

Scientific psychology may be distinguished from practical psychology in this same manner. The frame of reference of the scientific psychologist is primarily *theoretical;* he wants to *understand* human behavior. Momentarily, if not over a long period of time, he is profoundly unconcerned about the practical implications of his work. If asked about it, he is likely to reply that pure theory has always proved quite practical in the long run. He may point out, for example, that some of the significant advances in industrial psychology since 1940 stemmed from experiments which seemed purely theoretical when first performed.

This difference between the theoretical and the practical frames of reference means that a person may be a deft practitioner in the art of human relations with little training in the science and, conversely, that many excellent theoreticians in psychology mangle their human relations in practice every day. On the whole, as we make progress in both spheres of activity, it seems that a goodly knowledge of theory is becoming more important in connection with practice. Just as an engineer, who could once acquire a practical knowledge of his art without studying physics, now must needs acquire some background, so the fields of advertising, personnel work, politics, and human persuasion generally are requiring a better backing in the theory of psychology. Even the person with a talent for human relations can improve with such training; and an individual who is decidedly inept may come to be a passable practitioner with proper guidance and supervision.

The Psychological Frame of Reference

The psychological frame of reference can be further identified by contrasting it with those of other scientific disciplines. Human beings, after all, are objects of interest at different levels to many different specialists.

A physicist may well look upon a human organism as an aggregate of electrons, protons, and neutrons in rapid vibration. At the level of molar mechanics he may concern himself with the rate of flow of blood through tubes, the mechanical efficiency of our muscles and joints, or the electrical characteristics of nerve fiber and brain tissue.

A chemist is likely to show special interest in the acid-alkali balance in the blood stream, in the chemical processes of digestion, or in the assimilation of organic substances. A specialist in biochemistry would investigate the hormones produced by the endocrine glands, chemical end products of nervous activity, and the effects of various dietary deficiencies.

The scientific psychologist does not ignore the findings of experts working on these other levels. That is one reason why students planning to make psychology their lifework are urged to get a sound background in the natural sciences, especially in the biological field. The psychologist,

however, is interested in these problems at a different level and within a different frame of reference.

Psychology is concerned with the whole man. One basic feature of the psychological frame of reference is its focus upon man as a unit. When John flies into a rage, certain organ systems may be particularly affected; but we must refer to the whole individual to understand his activities. A study of his blood pressure, his glands, or his muscles might show that *something* was happening; the essential fact of anger is not tied to any one of these specific inner changes but is a function of the entire organism. Similarly, when Tom decides that his vocational ambition is that of becoming a lawyer, specific nerve and muscle changes take place, but they can be comprehended only in terms of the whole person.

A businessman may work industriously for years, saving money, investing shrewdly, and building up his annual income beyond the six-figure level. Then suddenly he gives up his business activities to become ambassador to a foreign country at a salary which does not even cover his expenses. At first glance this seems to represent a complete reversal of a major behavior tendency; from a vigorously acquisitive pattern he has changed to a different course of action entirely. A closer study of his personality, however, indicates that there is a general principle which has not been violated. The man's early acquisitiveness indicated a desire for *recognition* by others, and accumulating money was a means to this goal. When a different course of action offers more recognition, the acquisitive pattern is quickly abandoned. Thus, the understanding of behavior may require a study of man's relationships with his social environment, not merely of his biological functioning.

Psychology seeks general principles of behavior. Suppose you meet Mary S, a new girl on campus. She has flaming red hair, and an equally flaming temper. From this striking instance you may conclude that all redheads have violent dispositions. This seems to be an illustration of a general principle of behavior; unfortunately, it is false. Careful study will reveal that many red-haired persons are meek; and conversely, that many of violent temper are blonds or brunets.

Psychology seeks, through the patient study of one individual in many situations, and through the study of many individuals in the same environment, to determine dependable generalizations about behavior. We want general principles for the individual, as in the case of the businessman turned ambassador, and we want general principles for all humans, or for all animals, insofar as these can be established. Thus, if all college students reacted with increased effort when given a failing grade on an examination, this would be an important generalization. Some, of course, react by becoming quite depressed and exerting even less effort in subsequent studying.

The different fields of specialization in psychology are chiefly matters of the kind of organism studied or the kind of general principle sought. *Comparative psychology* seeks general principles for all living organisms, or for all members of a species. *Genetic psychology* attempts to evolve generalizations which will satisfactorily explain the development of behavior from infancy to maturity. *Social psychology* investigates and generalizes about man's actions as a member of political, economic, religious, and other social groups. *Industrial* psychology deals with the selection and placement of workers on jobs, fitting the machine to the worker, building good morale, understanding union-management problems, and so on. *Clinical psychology* is the branch of the science which deals most directly with persons having mental difficulties. Clinical psychologists have made their greatest contributions in the field of diagnosis of mental

problems, but much research is now focused on the improvement of methods of psychotherapy—treatment of the mentally maladjusted. Since we are concerned in this volume with giving a general view of scientific psychology, we shall draw freely upon the researches and conclusions of all these and other psychological specialists.

Psychology is concerned with individual differences. The general principles evolved by study of particular human groups are often valid only in a statistical sense. Thus it may be correct on the average to say that women express emotion more freely than do men; but this statement must not be interpreted as meaning that every woman will be more emotionally expressive than any man. Within each group there are wide *individual differences*, and it is not at all difficult to find some men who express their emotions more vigorously than some women (cf. Chap. 15).

All organisms are capable of learning, but some learn *faster* than others; some achieve a higher level of complexity than others; some are especially adept at one type of material, but not at others. In every psychological function, individual humans differ from each other in many ways which are important to both the theory and the practice of psychology.

Schoolteachers, factory foremen, and army sergeants become acutely aware of the practical significance of individual differences. One child is poor in arithmetic, another in spelling. One raw recruit seems almost a born soldier; another, equally intelligent, makes every mistake known to man. When we study these differences among children, soldiers, husbands, or citizens of a nation, we find that the differences themselves obey certain rules. Thus we have general laws of behavior and general principles covering specific variations in the way these laws operate in practice.

It is important to study individual differences as well as general tendencies. A factory manager praised one of his foremen and handed him a 5-dollar bill to express his appreciation of getting out a rush job. The foreman was pleased. The manager tried the same method on a second foreman and evoked bitter resentment. This man accepted praise, but was irritated by the offer of money, which he considered patronizing.

The scientific study of any specific problem usually progresses by first proving certain general principles, then analyzing the factors associated with individual differences. Thus early studies on the relation of emotion to memory led to the generalization that pleasant material is retained longer than unpleasant material. Later studies showed that some individuals violated this rule; and that these persons (who could aptly be called pessimists) had a mental make-up such that unpleasant items might fit with their expectancies from life, in the same way that pleasant memories conform to the hopes and expectations of the optimist.

Scientific Method in Psychology

Because each of us grows up in constant association with other people, he necessarily learns something about human psychology. This, however, is not equivalent to the scientific study of psychology, any more than an experienced cook is a scientifically trained chemist. Let us enumerate the respects in which the scientist follows an approach differing from the layman's observation of his companions.

1. *Controlled conditions.* The chemist who would study the properties of a new element or compound knows that he must control temperature, pressure, and other conditions if he is to get accurate results. In the same way, scientific psychologists make use of elaborate experimental controls to eliminate errors in their studies. A simple illustration comes from the famous "talking

horse," Clever Hans, a European wonder of the late nineteenth century. Hans demonstrated to scientists that he could add, subtract, multiply, divide, and answer a wide variety of problems by pawing the number of the correct answer. Even when the problem was presented by a man other than his trainer, Hans was successful. Finally a psychologist had the hunch that the horse was getting cues from small movements of the head and shoulders of the person holding the card carrying the problem. He tried presenting a problem without looking at it, so that he did not know the correct answer, and the horse failed completely. Here the conditions to be controlled included the experimenter himself.

In the study of sensory processes, all kinds of external cues have to be controlled. In one study on smell, the person being tested had to take a shower, dress in special plastic clothing, and sit in an airtight booth in a specially prepared laboratory room in order to eliminate all extraneous conditions. In research on learning, careful controls of motivation, sensory cues, ability, and previous experience are introduced. This exacting approach is necessary if we are to get at fundamental facts of human behavior. Only if relevant conditions are under the control of the observer (or are at least clearly defined and balanced) can we be sure about the validity of our conclusions (Fig. 1:7).

2. *Systematic variation of conditions.* An obvious corollary of the preceding point is the scientific method of varying systematically the factors believed significant, to see if behavior actually changes to correspond. Gates (1917), for example, believed that reading a text was less efficient (as a study technique) than attempts at recitation with book closed. To test this theory, he set up a systematic experiment in which some students read material for 100 per cent of the study time; others spent 80 per cent of their time in reading, 20 per cent attempt-

FIG. 1:7. How do psychologists study mental processes? Because man's psychological activity is so complex, steps must be taken to control irrelevant variables. This picture shows one type of apparatus used to control dependent and independent variables. To ensure that the independent variable (a stimulus word or picture) is presented in the same way to all subjects, it is projected onto a screen. Projecting for only a small fraction of a second prevents careful study of the stimulus and forces a quick judgment. To get a precise measure of the dependent variable (speed of response), the subject speaks his response into a microphone. This stops a high-speed clock (*lower right*) which was started by the projector (*lower left*). (*Courtesy of J. J. DeLucia.*)

ing recall; a third group divided its time 60–40, a fourth, 40–60, and a fifth, 20–80. The results are shown in Table 1:1. Here it appears that there is a consistent, if not proportional improvement in memory score as more time is expended in recitation. Thus

the systematic variation of conditions characterizes scientific studies in psychology.

3. *Control groups.* Sometimes it is important to have a group which does not take part in the experiment at all. The mere fact of being in a laboratory situation may alter

TABLE 1:1. Relative Efficiency of Recall of Nonsense Material under Different Study Schedules
(*Based on Gates, 1917*)

	Percentage recalled immediately
100% reading	35
80% reading, 20% recitation	50
60% reading, 40% recitation	54
40% reading, 60% recitation	57
20% reading, 80% recitation	74

a person's behavior. Stagner and Britton (1949) were interested in the effect of unpleasant experiences on public-opinion questions. They first obtained student judgments about some South American countries. Two groups were brought into the laboratory and, in the guise of a learning experiment, received electric shocks whenever the name of Bolivia (Group I) or Colombia (Group II) appeared. When they were retested on the opinion instrument, it seemed that the shock had made them *more friendly* to these countries. However, a control group which had not been near the laboratory had shifted much more to the friendly side. (This was during the "good neighbor" days of early 1942.) Thus, comparison with the control group showed that the unpleasant experiences had *slowed up* this change. Without a control group, the experiment would have been incomprehensible.

4. *Dependent and independent variables.* It is important, in describing and explaining psychological phenomena, to distinguish between two classes of events, which we call dependent and independent variables. An independent variable is one which is not modified by some other part of the experiment; for instance, in Gates's study of reading and recitation, the percentage of time spent in recitation was an independent variable. In his study, the de-

pendent variable was amount of material remembered. It is obviously affected by the other conditions of the experiment.

Some psychological experimentation uses a complex pattern of independent variables. A recent study used five different groups of subjects (classified according to their personality difficulties in a veterans' hospital), three different kinds of tasks, and two sets of work conditions, as independent variables. However, it is advisable to limit the number of dependent variables or it may be difficult to figure out what the results mean. In that study the dependent variable was the relative loss of efficiency as a result of enforced failure on the task. Experimental design involves manipulating the independent variables and then watching to see what changes occur in the dependent variable. Since some independent variables could not be manipulated for humans (*e.g.*, cutting out part of the brain), it is sometimes necessary to use animals as subjects. The precise analysis of just what is the independent and what the dependent variable in complex social situations will often contribute greatly to understanding (Fig. 1:8).

The differences between the various schools of psychology can now be described as differences in emphasis upon certain dependent variables. As Fig. 1:8 suggests, the psychologist has a wide range of possible changes in behavior and experience which he can observe. The *structural* school was particularly interested in sensations. Students were trained in introspection so that they could report certain essential changes in experience following stimulation, without mixing in memories, judgments, and interpretations. The *Gestalt* group were also interested in experiential changes as the main dependent variable, but their units were much larger than those of the structuralist. They wanted to observe experiences of form and meaning, complex patterns which the structuralists broke up into "conscious elements."

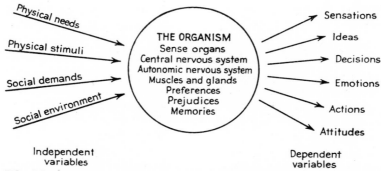

FIG. 1:8. A scheme for understanding the scientific study of psychology. On the left are shown the principal classes of independent variables which affect human behavior and experience. These are shown as having an impact on the organism, its sense organs, nervous and glandular system, plus its memories, prejudices, and preferences resulting from prior stimulation. From this interaction certain dependent variables emerge: sensations, percepts, ideas, decisions, emotions, and actions. The whole of scientific psychology is the study of the interplay of these various factors.

The *functionalist* psychologists worked with a wider range of both independent and dependent variables than their predecessors. Where Wundt had studied sensations of color and pitch, derived from simple light and sound stimuli, the functionalists manipulated a whole physical or social situation and observed the complex process of adjustment. This led to research on learning, thinking, and problem solving. The *psychoanalysts* went even farther in taking the whole life history as the independent variable, and certain symptoms (dreams, neurotic manifestations, etc.) as the dependent variables. The *behaviorists* resembled the functionalists but threw out changes in experience (consciousness) as a dependent variable. Only actions, they held, were worthy of study.

5. *Trained observers.* The layman makes errors in his judgment of various phenomena because he does not have the special training which is necessary. Anyone can listen to heart sounds through a stethoscope, but only the trained physician can diagnose valvular disorders by observing variations in these noises. Similarly, the untrained person, listening to an account of a disorderly child's unruly behavior, is likely not to locate the significant cues for understanding and correction of the problem.

The training of psychologists to observe and interpret correctly has reached its maximum in the clinical field, where the study of emotional disorders calls for sensitive perception of minute indications of trouble. However, such training is important in all fields. An industrial psychologist, for example, who goes into a factory will note little signs of good and poor labor relations which are missed or misinterpreted by laymen.

During the recent war, aircraft observers were subjected to lengthy training to induce quick, accurate identification of approaching planes. How much more important it is to train observers in identifying correctly the significant aspects of complex human behavior patterns!

6. *Repeated observations.* In the lexicon of science, no event is an exception to scientific law. However, apparent exceptions occur, because we do not grasp the essential nature of the event, or try to apply an inappropriate or incomplete law, or make up a new law for this special case. The corrective for such unsound thinking

is repetition of the observation. Often it appears that the first observation was inaccurate or was influenced by uncontrolled factors. Thus, several years ago, considerable excitement among psychologists was created by an announcement that intelligence had been found closely related to speed of nerve conduction along certain reflex pathways. Repetition of the experiment proved that, when all relevant conditions were controlled, these nerve-conduction measures gave no indication whatever of relative intelligence.

Control of conditions and repetition of observations on human beings are inherently more difficult than similar measures in physics and chemistry. Inanimate objects can be subjected to any possible conditions, at the wish of the scientist. Psychologists operate under considerable limitations as to conditions they can apply to humans. Also, memory of prior experiments does not seem to be a significant variable in chemicals, whereas the repetition of an experiment on a human subject often fails because he remembers what happened the first time. Some progress is being made in overcoming these technical obstacles; for example, picture and sound recordings of an experiment make possible repeated observations of the same human responses.

The differences between popular and scientific psychology are in considerable degree dependent upon these matters of technique and method. Much of the student's training, therefore, will consist in acquiring an understanding of scientific method in psychology. Oftentimes this requires a real revolution in the student's way of thinking about human nature.

The Student's Frame of Reference

When an individual has developed a clearcut frame of reference with respect to any set of material, it becomes extraordinarily difficult for him to adopt another. He will ignore facts which do not fit into his established mental pattern; he will distort observations to confirm his views; he will forget as rapidly as possible those unacceptable items which are forced upon his attention. All this, of course, happens as a result of unconscious processes.

This resistance to new frames of reference is a psychological matter of greatest importance to the beginning student in psychology. Unconsciously, each of us acquires a set of generalizations about human nature in general, and about specific kinds of people, early in life. Afterward it becomes quite difficult to replace these by a more accurate set of principles. Human relations do not provide the simple, automatic corrections for error that exist in the world of physics. If you incorrectly assume a "live" wire to be free of electricity, and touch it, you will quickly learn of your error. You may, however, use improper tactics in dealing with an employee, and get the recoil months later in the form of a strike or other trouble. Thus you may never become aware of your mistake.

Charles Darwin once remarked that, if he came across evidence which seemed to contradict his theory of evolution, he wrote it down at once; otherwise he was sure to forget it. Many students have theories about people and psychology; they remember facts which fit their beliefs and ignore or forget contradictory data. This is likely to happen often in an introductory course in psychology. The student should therefore pay special attention to those facts and principles which do not conform to his present beliefs; he should learn to identify the sources of error in his own psychology; and he should take special steps to counteract this tendency toward forgetting ideas which contradict his own.[1]

[1] In this connection the student should read carefully the Preface to this book.

Another problem may arise for the student because the subject matter of psychology is, in the very nature of the case, intensely emotional. When we concern ourselves with parent-child relationships, with anxiety, with personality formation, or with racial prejudices, we necessarily deal with topics heavily charged with personal feeling. One of the tasks facing the student of psychology is that of learning to study and discuss these problems in a cool, dispassionate manner. A chemist who became very angry if his litmus turned red, and was elated if it became blue, would have a hard time in his work. He has to deal with all kinds of chemical reactions equally. In the same way, students of psychology have to learn to discuss criminal behavior, immoral behavior, and peculiar behavior as simply "more about human beings." We cannot become indignant, disgusted, or depressed by these observations, if we are to achieve deep understanding.

The Scope of This Book

The first few chapters of this volume will particularly call for a calm and thoughtful approach. Our first steps toward insight into psychology are in the field of dynamics. We must look for an answer to the question, why? What desires, fears, ambitions, and aspirations motivate man's behavior? This is an area about which there is a good deal of misconception in popular thinking about psychology; scientific analysis leads to rejection of many of these common beliefs.

In the second portion of this book we shall deal with material which is less disturbing. The question asked is: how does man go about satisfying his desires? The answers delve into the field of sensory psychology (how we get information about the world), learning to respond appropriately to this information, remembering, thinking, and intelligence. This area corresponds to the "rational psychology" of the ancient Greeks.

The concluding series of chapters again may get into some emotionally toned topics. There we shall deal with personality formation, how the individual learns to handle conflicts of motives, how psychologists study, describe, and measure personality. Since personality depends upon all psychological processes—motivation, perceiving, learning, thinking—these chapters will try to unify all the facts and theories presented in the earlier sections.

The study of psychology is a little more difficult than the study of the other natural sciences, for reasons such as those we have mentioned. Nevertheless, it is a fascinating and richly rewarding intellectual venture. With reasonable effort it can lead to broader understanding and deeper insight into oneself and one's fellows.

SUMMARY

Man has always found himself an intriguing object of study. From the medicine man of primitive tribes to the philosophical speculations of the ancient Greeks and the well-equipped laboratories of the twentieth century, constant inquiries and investigations into human behavior have sought better comprehension of man and his nature.

A brief sketch of the history of psychology shows some of the persisting problems which have been uncovered and a few of the possible solutions. Closely linked in their developments are the problems of body and mind, of evil and good, and of objects and our knowledge of them. Since it is clear that, when we acquire knowledge of an object, it is not physically incorporated within the knower, the Greeks speculated that there was a different universe, the universe of mind and ideas, separate from but parallel to the physical. This dualism creates so many problems for science that most psychologists prefer to assume a monistic position. They hold that the mind and the body are simply labels for different functions of a single unified organism. This also puts an end to the misleading association of mind with good, body with evil.

Scientific psychology could not develop until certain aspects of physics and physiology were clarified. In the late nineteenth century enough basic knowledge had been accumulated that psychological laboratories were founded, first in Germany, later in the United States and elsewhere. Active, alert, questioning scholars began uncovering facts and developing theories about human behavior and experience. Structuralism, Gestalt, functionalism, behaviorism, and psychoanalysis grew up as schools of psychology, emphasizing different facts and making different assumptions as to underlying principles. These schools, however, are not incompatible with each other; the facts are accepted by all, but differing interpretations are often made. This situation has actually speeded up the growth of scientific psychology in many respects; competition among ideas often leads to progress.

A key principle in psychology, one which is compatible with the thinking of all schools, is homeostasis. This principle asserts that organisms tend to maintain, and to restore, certain essential constant states. This may mean a temperature con-stant, the oxygen–carbon dioxide equilibrium in the blood, the blood sugar level; or it may mean a secure environment, a defined status in society, or a relationship to religious and social ideals. This emphasis upon human behavior as a homeostatic process is an attempt to get away from the primitive animism which explains psychological activities in terms of spirits and mystical forces.

In studying homeostasis in man, we may make use of field observation or of laboratory experimentation. We attempt to pick out an independent variable—something which disturbs the person's equilibrium, perhaps—and then study the dependent variable, the person's efforts to solve the problem and restore his preferred situation. To get precise answers to these questions, we must control all irrelevant conditions carefully, make use of control groups and trained observers, and repeat our observations at least once.

The training of psychological observers could be said, in a very small way, to be an object of this course. The student should become more adept at analyzing and understanding human behavior, both his own and that of others. To achieve this, he may have to forgo some of his own cherished beliefs and emotional prejudices; the study of psychology is thus more disturbing to some young people than is the study of physics or chemistry. The rewards, however, are comparably great.

Recommended Readings

BORING, E. G.: *History of Experimental Psychology.* New York: Appleton-Century-Crofts, 1929.

BRETT, G. S.: *Psychology: Ancient and Modern.* New York: Longmans, 1928. Chaps. 1, 4, and 5.

BUGELSKI, B. R.: *A First Course in Experimental Psychology.* New York: Holt, 1951. Chaps. 3, 4, 5, and 6.

CRAFTS, L. W., T. C. SCHNEIRLA, E. E. ROBINSON, and R. W. GILBERT: *Recent Experiments in Psychology.*[1] (2d ed.) New York: McGraw-Hill, 1950.

DENNIS, WAYNE: *Readings in General Psychology.*[1] New York: Prentice-Hall, 1949.

[1] See p. 547 for a recommended schedule of readings in any of the marked volumes, which are prepared to supplement the introductory psychology course.

GARRETT, H. E.: *Great Experiments in Psychology.*[1] (3d ed.) New York: Appleton-Century-Crofts, 1949.

HARROWER, M. R.: *The Psychologist at Work.* New York: Harper, 1937.

HARTLEY, E. L., H. G. BIRCH, and RUTH E. HARTLEY: *Outside Readings in Psychology.*[1] New York: Crowell, 1950.

HULIN, W. S.: *A Short History of Psychology.* New York: Holt, 1934. Chaps. 1, 2, 3, and 4.

KELLER, F. S.: *Definition of Psychology.* New York: Appleton-Century-Crofts, 1937.

PRATT, C. C.: *The Logic of Modern Psychology.* New York: Macmillan, 1937. (Especially Chaps. 3 and 4.)

SARGENT, S. S.: *Basic Teachings of the Great Psychologists.* Philadelphia: Blakiston, 1944.

TITCHENER, E. B.: *A Beginner's Psychology.* New York: Macmillan, 1917. Chaps. 1–5.

VALENTINE, W. L., and D. D. WICKENS: *Experimental Foundations of General Psychology.*[1] (rev. ed.) New York: Farrar & Rinehart, 1949.

WOODWORTH, R. S.: *Contemporary Schools of Psychology.* (rev. ed.) New York: Ronald, 1948. (Chapters on the various schools of psychology.)

PART ONE

Dynamics

The most important problem of modern psychology is one which was ignored by the ancient philosophers because of their bias toward matters of intellect. This problem is that of psychodynamics. What are the basic sources of power behind human behavior? What drives impel man to act as he does?

When someone asks the question, why? as regards human behavior, he is looking for a dynamic answer. He expects an explanation in terms of hunger, love, anxiety, ambition, or some similar powerful human motive. It is this area of psychology which we must first explore. Later we can investigate the mechanisms by which motives achieve satisfaction.

The simplest dynamic factors are those which arise directly from the nature of man's biological structure. There are certain constant states—the supply of foodstuffs as represented by the blood-sugar level, the water balance, the temperature constant, and so on—which must be kept uniform if the person is to survive. In an evolutionary sense we can say that organisms which mobilized energy and put forth vigorous effort to maintain these constances were those which survived. The others were eliminated.

Man, however, shows much evidence of strong motivation which is only indirectly related to biological survival; indeed, he often follows impulses, apparently blind to his own self-destructive actions. After we have examined the facts regarding basic biological drives, therefore, we shall extend our analysis to consider emotions and social motives.

CHAPTER 2

Biological Drives

Human behavior is dynamic in character. Our acts result from pressing needs and impulses. The quest for food, the search for security, and the pursuit of high aspirations exemplify the motivated nature of all significant human activity.

Human experience is also dynamic. Motives influence what we see, how we feel about it, the ideas we develop, and the opinions we endorse. Problem solving, dreams, and creative imagination are responsive to inner needs. A thorough understanding of human motivation is indispensable to a clear picture of our own mental processes, and those of persons around us.

The process of energy mobilization is chemical, metabolic, physiological in character. It cannot be directly observed. But when a man makes a terrific effort to escape from a burning building, or drives himself past the brink of exhaustion in dangerous battle, he is exemplifying the mobilization of energy to achieve a goal. On a less dramatic scale we recognize the same phenomenon in the striving of a college student for success in his studies, or in the driving ambition of a businessman toward some peak of prestige, wealth, and power.

Characteristics of motivated behavior. Since drives cannot be directly observed but must be recognized in terms of their effects, it is important at the outset that we state clearly the criteria of motivated behavior. We look for three characteristics of any activity in deciding to what extent[1] it is motivated:

1. *Energy.* Motivation is operative proportionately to the amount of energy output for a given situation. A man who has been without food for 24 hours will struggle more vigorously for food than one who ate an hour ago. Rats will run faster, dig through more resistant material, and in various ways put forth more energy as the insistence of the inner need increases. We therefore feel justified in reversing this relationship and inferring that, if Dick works more energetically than Tom, his motivation is stronger.

2. *Persistence.* The motivated individual does not easily give up. A child who has seen some candy hidden in the room may open drawers, pull out books, look under the furniture, and keep trying for a considerable time to locate the sweets. If failure is accepted promptly and effort abandoned, we infer the absence of any strong motivation.

3. *Variability.* Related to persistence is the phenomenon of variability. While the person persists in his effort to achieve some satisfaction, he does not simply repeat the same act

[1] Note that we imply a continuum from behavior with very low energy level (little motivation) to a very high energy level (intense motivation).

again and again. He will try different paths to the goal. A boy who wants prestige in school may try studying; failing to get good marks, he may try athletics; failing in that, he may become a bully, still seeking the same goal, but constantly varying the technique.

Characteristics of motivated experience. The experience of others cannot be directly observed, but another individual may describe his inner experiences to you. Or you may observe your own thought processes. In either event, it becomes possible to identify the phenomena of energy, persistence, and variability, by self-observation, just as on the level of overt behavior. At times you are tense, alert, keyed to react vigorously; at other times you are lazy, relaxed, daydreaming in an idle manner.

When a strong motive is operating, our mental processes are characterized by *intensity*, or high energy level. A young man in love experiences images, thoughts, and feelings about his beloved which have a compelling, controlling quality. They can be ignored or brushed aside with the greatest difficulty, if at all. The thoughts relating to a goal object tend to *persist; i.e.*, they are not readily forgotten; they recur to the mind whenever opportunity presents itself. They are, in general, *variable*, in the sense that they take a variety of forms and may adapt themselves to many different contexts. Thus, a person who is very hungry may think about many kinds of food, about various methods of obtaining food, about ways of preparing it, and so on. The Freudian work on dreams illustrates strikingly how the same motive, the same desired goal, may be disguised in a variety of ways during successive dreams by the same individual.

Varieties of Motivation

While the unifying phenomenon in all forms of motivation is *energy mobilization*, it will be advantageous for us to keep our focus on the motivating factors, not on the mobilization process. After all, our human energy is of one single variety: the chemical transformation of food into energy. The basic physiology is the same whether the energy release is based on the need for food, the quest for a mate, fear of a hungry lion, ambition to become President, or some other goal-seeking tendency. We shall thus find it most valuable, in studying motivation, to concentrate our attention on *the wide variety of conditions* and circumstances which set off this vigorous response of the individual.

It seems correct to say that there are three significant varieties of motivating factors. (The exact number is a matter of disagreement; some psychologists prefer only two, or one, while others argue for a great number.) Whether the correct number is three or six is not especially important. It will be quite helpful to the student, however, to organize these motives into a systematic scheme, such as is outlined below.

1. *Biological drives.* The most elementary forms of energy mobilization arise from definite biological needs of the organism. Hunger, thirst, oxygen lack, fatigue, excretion, escape from pain—these readily suggest some of the conditions which give rise to motivated action.

2. *Emotions.* Such words as fear, anger, joy, love, hate, disgust, and curiosity imply the presence of inner states leading to more or less vigorous activity. They differ from the biological drives in that they are less closely tied to physical needs and tissue conditions; they are more directly related to external situations. They are thus more flexible and variable than the drives.

3. *Values and interests.* At a still more complex, subtle level we recognize the energizing effect of broad nonphysiological tendencies which may be called *values*. An easy illustration is that of a deep religious conviction. The person who feels his religion keenly, personally, will work hard to further his church, will think often and persistently of its welfare, and so on.

In this and the succeeding chapters, we shall summarize the major principles known to apply to these three levels of motivation. The following pages will expand the discussion of the biological or biogenic drives, as the simplest and earliest forms of human motivation.

Homeostasis: a Basic Principle

We have stated that the problem of psychological dynamics is the problem of energy mobilization. Under what circumstances is energy channeled into specific activities? The individual is not equally active and vigorous at all times. Why is he sometimes striving very keenly for some objective, and at other times relaxed and lazy? It will help if we start with some very simple situations of energy mobilization and apply the principles discernible there to more complex adult conditions.

In the simplest kind of dynamic activation of behavior, we have such situations as that of temperature control. When the body temperature falls more than a slight amount below that required for optimum functioning, a reflex center in the mid-brain goes into action. A higher metabolic rate, faster circulation of blood, and increased muscular tension serve to release and distribute heat more rapidly. If the decline in temperature continues, shivering and vigorous muscular action will help to restore the normal temperature. The body is equipped with a number of such systems, which *preserve the desirable equilibrium* of oxygen and carbon dioxide, temperature, and similar physiological necessities.

At a somewhat more complex level, we observe a different kind of return to equilibrium. If the rat's body temperature drops, and the metabolic adjustment fails to restore equilibrium, he will build a nest of paper or other available materials (Fig. 2:1). Or, consider the case of the hungry infant. After a certain number of hours

without food, the baby becomes restless. He squirms, frets, waves his arms and legs. If food is not forthcoming, he cries loudly and threshes about. As soon as he obtains food, this activity diminishes and in a short time, with satiation, he relapses in satisfied quiescence.

The principle of *homeostasis* is well illustrated by these behavior sequences. According to this principle, *energy mobilization begins when an inner equilibrium is disturbed, and continues until this equilibrium is restored*. The physiological balance of food intake and utilization is gradually destroyed by continued metabolism. At a certain point, this disturbance sets off certain muscular tensions. The tensions, in turn, trigger the responses of crying, squirming, etc. Feeding relieves the tension, and the child returns to a state of equilibrium.

This energy mobilization is functional; it has survival value. The organism becomes highly motivated when an inner condition develops which threatens its well-being. Clearly, no conscious *purpose* need be involved; even in adult behavior, many goals are vigorously pursued under conditions of limited conscious awareness, and among children much motivation is plainly unconscious.

Two levels of homeostasis. It appears, as the above examples suggest, that human beings are endowed by inheritance with a tendency toward the maintenance of certain optimum biological conditions: food supply, temperature, oxygen, water, and so on. This homeostatic function is a universal feature of human (as well as animal) behavior.

We must note, however, that homeostasis functions differently in the two examples cited, which correspond to two differing levels of organization. At the simple, reflex level, we observe automatic restoration of equilibrium in a rather precise manner and with virtually no modification due to

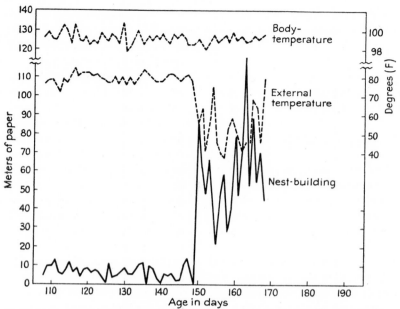

FIG. 2:1. An example of dynamic homeostasis. The rat will build nests of strips of paper, cloth, or other materials. In this experiment a roll of paper was made available on a reel so that the amount used by the rats was automatically measured. While the room temperature was around 80°F., little nest building took place. When the room temperature was lowered to 50°F. (at age 150 days), the rats immediately used large quantities of paper to build nests, thus preserving their essential constant temperature. (Modified from Richter, 1937.)

experience. One does not become better at metabolizing or shivering as a consequence of learning how to deal with the situation of declining temperature. This elemental kind of equilibrium maintenance is called *static homeostasis*.

In contrast to this kind of behavior is the process which occurs in connection with more complex situations. Any disturbance of homeostasis, as in a chill or in hunger, affects not only the reflex centers of the lower brain but also the higher centers which are involved in learning, remembering, thinking, and planning. Thus, through experience one learns to look at a thermometer and don a coat before going outside; to lay up supplies of food against possible future famine; to carry water when crossing an arid waste, and so on. These behavioral patterns are homeostatic, just as deep breathing to eliminate excess carbon dioxide

is homeostatic. But in these complex instances we are dealing with *dynamic* adjustments, modified by experience, often including a planned change of the environment. In contrast to the simple, automatic physiological changes of static homeostasis, these forms of adaptation involve *an active effort of the entire organism* (not just a limited system) to deal with the problem. We shall therefore designate such tendencies toward equilibrium as *dynamic homeostasis*.

The organism as a unit. It would not be particularly misleading to say that psychology is the science of the integrated organism. The study of static homeostasis, as in respiration, circulation, metabolism, and so on, has become an accepted function of the physiologists. Psychology has become organized around those problems associated with dynamic homeostasis, that is, instances in which the whole organism is energized to achieve a restoration of equilibrium.

Actually, the organism is always functioning as a unit. What happens on the level of learning, thinking, remembering, and imagining is modified by the body's blood chemistry, physical status, and physiological condition. As a practical matter, however, some boundary lines between the sciences are necessary; and we shall take it for granted that psychology is only rarely concerned with the simple, reflex adjustments of static homeostasis. Energy mobilization is a significant phenomenon for psychologists primarily as it provides the dynamic forces involved in such major activies as seeking a mate, acquiring an occupation, forming social groups, and developing personality. The principles of motivation are fundamental to an understanding of all these phases of human behavior and experience.

The homeostatic mechanism operates throughout the entire behavioral resources of the individual. It can be shown, for example, that there is a qualitative change in the kinds of stimuli to which the organism responds. Stimuli which previously had been ignored (*e.g.*, salt, water) are now observed, and those which previously had been effective are now ignored. Sensory thresholds—sight, hearing, smell—are lowered. The increase in activity also can be considered as providing a mechanism for survival, in that the organism moves about and therefore quantitatively increases its contacts with the environment. This increase in the number of environmental stimuli encountered tends to offer a much greater probability of finding that which is needed to restore the inner equilibrium. Thus, both the *selective changes* in sensory thresholds and the *quantitative increase* in the total number of contacts with external stimuli can be considered as adaptive mechanisms.

The change in selective response to stimuli can well be illustrated by such experiments as those reported by Richter (1942), in which the adrenal glands were removed from a group of rats. The immediate result of adrenalectomy is the disturbance of sodium metabolism and a tremendous increase in the need for sodium chloride. When these rats were given access to two water bottles, one containing ordinary water and the other a 3 per cent solution of sodium chloride, the rats immediately showed a decided preference for the salted water and increased their intake of sodium chloride by several hundred per cent. The efficacy of the homeostatic mechanism here, in maintaining the inner organic equilibrium, can be demonstrated by the fact that 100 per cent of a group of rats whose adrenals had been removed, and who were not given access to salt-water solution, died, whereas 100 per cent of those similarly operated, and given access to a sufficient supply of salt water, survived.

These experiments illustrate what the physiologist Walter Cannon meant by his phrase: "the wisdom of the body." They suggest that the organism is endowed with an automatic equilibrium-maintaining tendency which helps to preserve existence in the face of many kinds of environmental obstacles and difficulties. It also suggests that *motivation cannot be ascribed to a specific set of inborn needs* or drives. Motivation is a function of the total organism. When an individual becomes motivated, he is motivated as a totality. The motive is not restricted to a specific part of the personality. This means that, whenever homeostatic equilibrium is disturbed, *the energies of the entire organism tend to be mobilized in active effort to restore the balance.*

Focusing of experience. Energy mobilization involves the focusing of both behavior and experience in certain ways. The hungry rat shows a selective response to food; the thirsty rat, to water. While we

FIG. 2:2. Focusing of experience. Under the influence of a strong motive, the field of experience narrows to focus sharply on objects which offer a prospect of satisfying this desire. Here an ingenious photographer suggests how the baby may view life when he is hungry. Only the bottle is in clear focus; everything else is blurred. Under the stress of other motives, the focus would be elsewhere. (*From Life Magazine. Copyright Time, Inc.*)

cannot theorize about the animal's experiences, we know that in human beings this focusing of behavior upon a specific goal object is accompanied by certain conscious processes. Certain objects "stand out" in the environment. Explorers on short rations dream of food; lonely soldiers on islands in the South Pacific dream of women. We become keenly aware of those places and activities which will enable us to satisfy our desires. Figure 2:2 shows an ingenious photographer's interpretation of the hungry child's view—the bottle clear and sharply focused, the rest of the background fuzzy and poorly formed. All major phases of human behavior and experience seem to be thus shaped by our inner drives.

Nonhomeostatic behavior. It must ap-

pear to the student that, while most of human activity can be organized under the rubric of homeostasis, there are many exceptions to this rule. While most people are inclined to seek for equilibrium, others seem deliberately to upset equilibrium. Thus there are men who go hunting for dangerous wild animals, who deliberately expose themselves to hardships in exploring and mountain climbing, and who gamble with their lives as test pilots, racing drivers, etc. On a smaller scale we find children apparently seeking disequilibrium through hazardous play, and adults who gamble for modest sums of money.

It is, in fact, fairly easy to show that these behaviors do not violate the principle of homeostasis, although they seem on the surface to do so. We must recognize that people have many different desires (they are attempting to maintain equilibrium in several different respects) and sometimes they must choose one at the cost of another. It may be necessary to work (disturb one equilibrium) in order to get food (restore another equilibrium). The *principle of dominance* (see below) takes cognizance of the fact that some needs will dominate behavior to the exclusion of other needs. Thus the child who is afraid to go down the slide (avoid disequilibrium) may also be reluctant to accept the razzing of his playmates (another, more complex equilibrium). The mountain climber might be more upset by the accusation that he was a coward than by the hardships he faced in his sport.

The child's readiness to go into a threatening, disturbing situation for a thrill, of course, is related to his confidence in ultimate safety. The child who is intensely disturbed by a threat will be unable to engage in such behavior. But if a boy has successfully mastered dangers of one kind, he approaches another situation with very little fear of failure. The amount of disequilibrium induced by a given stimulus, in other words, is a function of past experience and the person's confidence that he can restore equilibrium by his own efforts.

It is also worth while to note that the principle of dynamic homeostasis implies the possibility of delay in getting equilibrium, in order to do a better job. Primitive man, to develop agriculture, had to forego eating some of his grain and save it for seed. (This is the "reality principle" in action—one mark of a mature personality.) There is even some reason to suppose that it is *more satisfying* to restore equilibrium than simply to maintain it (this is true primarily at the adult human level). For example, most of us would prefer to build up a moderately strong hunger tension before attending an excellent banquet, so that we would enjoy the feast. In general,

therefore, behavior which appears to disturb equilibrium is only a short-run, not a long-range, violation of the homeostatic principle.

Tension and Valence

In the foregoing discussion we have suggested that the organism reacts homeostatically to any disturbance, whether aroused internally or externally. If we consider the specific case of internal disturbances, we find that a need for a particular substance, such as food, water, oxygen, vitamins, or minerals, may underlie seeking behavior and may ultimately be responsible for the release of energy in active behavior of different kinds. This behavior pattern in general tends to locate stimuli which will restore the equilibrium to its original condition of optimum values for survival. It must be noted, however, that not all needs operate in this fashion. It may happen that the individual suffers a deficiency of calcium without this need motivating any particular activity, and he may suffer from decayed teeth, softening bones, and other unfortunate conditions without being aware of his deficiency or without making any search for a diet which would supply the missing substance. It is necessary, therefore, that we introduce an additional concept into the sequence of behavior before we can fully understand this homeostatic process.

It appears that the immediate consequence of the disturbance of organismic equilibrium *in those cases which lead to motivated activity* is the setting up of *tension.* Easiest of these instances to observe and describe is the tension which is associated with hunger. In that case the tension is an actual muscular contraction of the walls of the stomach. Another easily observable muscular tension involved in a motivation sequence is the muscular tension which is associated with the attempt to escape from physical pain. In everyday behavior one commonly notes that his body becomes rather tense when he is trying very hard in any field of endeavor: for example, the solution of a mathematical problem which is quite difficult may be associated with the development of widespread muscular tension.

Whether this tension underlying motivated acts is necessarily muscular in all cases is a question which cannot be answered finally with the information now at our disposal. There is certainly a great deal of evidence to indicate that most forms of motivated behavior are accompanied by muscular tension. In other instances, however, it has been pointed out that motivational tendencies may operate over a period of months or even years; as, for example, the ambition to achieve a certain kind of professional education, or a certain status in the community. In these instances it is hard to believe that a simple muscular state could continue over such a period of time. We therefore resort to the concept that muscular tension may set up a parallel tense state or "representation of tension" in the cerebral cortex. This cortical state may be rearoused whenever any appropriate stimulus is present in the environment. In that case it is not necessary to assume the actual persistence of the physical tension over this period of time.

The state of *anxiety* may be considered to be the anticipation of some disturbing situation which is not yet physically present. Anxiety is certainly accompanied by a great deal of muscular tension in most individuals. If we are troubled, for example, by anticipation of hunger, economic disaster, loss of a loved one, or any other potential threat, we are likely to become very tense and emotionally disturbed. We shall refer later to the widespread role which anxiety tension plays in motivating many forms of complex human activity. It is necessary at this point only to note that anxiety, like its predecessor drives of hunger, pain, and

the like, is actually accompanied by muscular tension.

The state of *elation* and optimism likewise can be defined as anticipation of goal achievement. Elation is experienced when the individual finds that he can surely achieve his goal; the intensity of this feeling depends on how strong his drive was, and how much danger of failure seemed imminent. Elation, like anxiety, involves some muscle tension; obviously, then, we cannot identify tension with unpleasantness. Some tensions are painful but others are associated with pleasure.

Motor set and energy mobilization. An analysis of the energetics of human behavior must take into consideration two dimensions of variation: *goal direction* and *intensity*. As we have noted, disturbance of homeostasis leads to tension, and this in turn is related to an increase in intensity of response. The activity level goes up; more energy is available. The organism can run faster, fight harder, overcome obstacles in its path.

This homeostatic conception, however, pays little attention to the matter of *goal direction*. Actually, tensions do not merely raise the total energy level; the energy tends to be *channeled* into definite acts. Once a baby has learned that sucking on a nipple reduces hunger tension, while sucking on a blanket does not, his tension becomes focalized as a definite motor set. He searches for the nipple. The older child goes to a source of food. Adults get "set" for very complex activities which lead to goal satisfaction and release of tension.

The phenomenon of motor set is most important. It is characteristic of man that he has few goal-seeking acts determined by heredity. Flexibility in tension reduction is the rule. Thus, in one culture, one gets "set" for individual effort, to obtain food, whereas another culture fosters a set for cooperative endeavor. The kind of set established is highly significant because it domi-

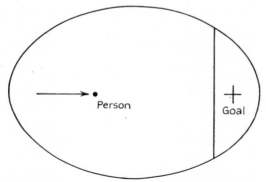

FIG. 2:3. Positive valence. The arrow represents the force pressing the person toward a goal. The symbol $+$ will be employed to identify goal objects which exert a positive attraction upon the person; minus $(-)$ is used to indicate goal objects which repel the person (danger, discomfort, deprivation).

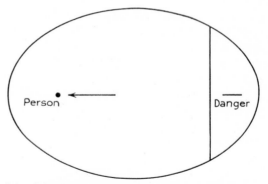

FIG. 2:4. Negative valence. A goal object which threatens pain or discomfort will set off energy mobilization designed to remove the person from this threat. The strength of the negative valence is suggested by the length of the arrow pressing the individual away from the subject.

nates the person's behavior; tension-reducing reactions employed by one man may be ignored, their possible value unknown, by another. As we progress from the study of simple, biologically determined energy mobilization to that which is affected chiefly by external, social situations, this point will become more important.

Valence. Not all motivation is purely internal in origin. In many cases we find that external stimuli are capable of arousing tension and initiating sequences of motivated behavior. A child who is not particularly hungry, for example, may become quite tense, excited, and positively motivated by the presence of an ice-cream cone. In this case we recognize the fact that an external stimulus has been immediately responsible for the development of tension. We shall refer to such an external stimulus by the term *valence.*

The term valence refers (in psychology) to external stimuli which have either a positive or a negative demand value for the organism. Thus stimuli which suggest the satisfaction of needs are likely to have positive valences (Fig. 2:3), and those which threaten injury and discomfort are likely to have negative valences (Fig. 2:4).

Whether any valences are innately determined is a matter of debate. Certainly there cannot be many such; exceptions might be sweet tastes, optimal temperatures, and a few very simple cases of this type. In other instances, stimuli showing the quality of valence are products of a learning sequence. It thus appears that the ultimate determinants of valence will be either the value of the environmental stimulus in meeting homeostatic needs now present, or the value of the stimulus as a *sign* indicating future sources of satisfaction for these needs.

Measuring Motivated Behavior

We have noted that a disturbance of some bodily equilibrium (such as food, water, or oxygen) creates tension. This tension leads to energetic, persistent, variable activity. Approaches to the measurement of motivation necessarily involve the study of activity; the drive itself is never accessible to direct observation. These techniques involve, therefore, the three basic characteristics of motivated behavior: intensity, persistence, and variability. In some cases goal direction is also measured.

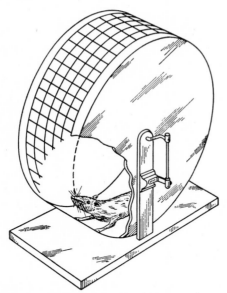

FIG 2:5. Activity wheel. Small animals, such as rats and squirrels, will reveal the intensity of a drive by the amount of running. The wheel has a counter on the axle which records the number of rotations in either direction. (*Drawing by Dr. H. F. Harlow, in Young, 1943.*)

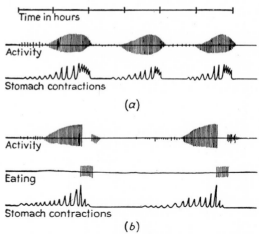

FIG. 2:6. Hunger-induced activity. Curve *a* shows the schematic relation of stomach contractions to bursts of activity in the rat. Note the close correspondence in time. No food was available during this interval, but the contractions die out and then start again. Curve *b* shows the sudden cessation of both contractions and activity when food is made available, thus indicating that the activity was truly dependent upon the food deprivation. The relation to stomach contractions is inferred. (*From Richter, 1927.*)

We shall begin with some methods for studying motives of animals, which are exclusively "biogenic" in the sense in which we have been using the term, *i.e.*, determined by tissue needs. When we consider human motivation, we must deal with more complex issues. Thus there is an advantage in taking up simpler problems first.

The activity wheel. An extremely simple approach to motivation in animals involves placing them in a movable cage connected to an automatic recording mechanism. The kind of rotating wheel-shaped cage often used for pet squirrels (Fig. 2:5) is one of these devices. Another is a triangular cage mounted on inflated rubber supports, so that any motion of the animal is recorded. As the principle is the same, only the activity wheel will be discussed.

When an inner equilibrium is disturbed, the animal becomes restless. Internal ten-sion mounts, and this sets off muscular activity. In small animals, such as the rat or squirrel, the normal activity pattern includes a great deal of running; thus, the activity wheel probably gives us a fairly accurate index of the total increase in action with rising motivation.

It is possible to study relationships experimentally and thus to validate the assertion that activity is related to motivation. For example, we can deprive the animal of food for varying intervals of time. As Fig. 2:6 shows, the amount of activity steadily increases as the inferred need for food becomes more intense. Similarly, Fig. 2:7*a* shows an increase in activity related to the sexual rhythm of the female rat. That this is a genuine sex drive and not mere restlessness is demonstrated by Fig. 2:7*b*. When the female rat is placed in a special cage where she can approach a male when she is in heat, the peaks of activity disappear.

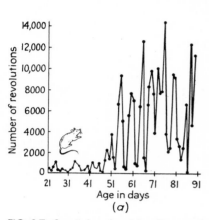

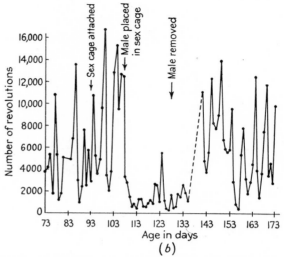

FIG. 2:7. Sex-induced activity. Curve *a* shows running activity of a female rat. Food was available in the cage. Note the 4-day cycle which begins at the age of 51 days, the onset of puberty. That this is a genuine manifestation of the sex drive is shown by curve *b*. The female was placed in half of a double cage, with a male in the other half. The opening between was large enough for the female to pass through, but not for the male. Note the disappearance of the excess running activity when sexual deprivation was removed by giving access to the male. (*From Wang, 1923, and Richter, 1927.*)

Adaptation to infants. Gross muscular activity is no doubt a poor measure of drive in adults, because we have learned not to reveal our inner tensions in many situations. For infants, this factor is not operative. Irwin (1930) devised a crib to record restless motions of babies; Fig. 2:8 shows how hunger drive sets off excess activity at this age level. Movements increase steadily toward feeding time, then fall off. The extreme peak at 6 A.M. is a consequence of an 8-hour food deprivation, as compared with the other feeding intervals of 4 hours.

Preference tests. Relative strength of demand for varied goal objects can be tested by a simple preference setup in which the animal has his choice of two or more items. Thus, an animal with a need for vitamin B will choose a dietary mixture containing this substance, in preference to one lacking in the vitamin (Fig. 2:16, page 56). If the foods are placed at the end of a Y-shaped runway, it will be found that the speed of running down the arm

leading to preferred objects is faster than that to nonpreferred goals.

A few studies of human infants have utilized a form of preference technique. Davis (1928) has reported a "cafeteria" method of feeding babies after they reach the solid-food stage. She found that the babies would, over a period of time, take in larger quantities of needed substances until a deficiency had been met, then taper off and show preference for other foods. Thus it appeared that homeostatic disturbances (needs for calcium, vitamins, proteins, etc.) controlled the behavior of the child and led to increased choice of needed foods.

Learning speed. Increased motivation leads to increased activity. And satisfaction of a motive by a given kind of action leads to learning. (The complexities of this relationship cannot be developed here; they will be treated in Chap. 9.) Thus it seems plausible to suggest that satisfaction of a stronger motive will lead to faster learning.

In general, experimental data confirm

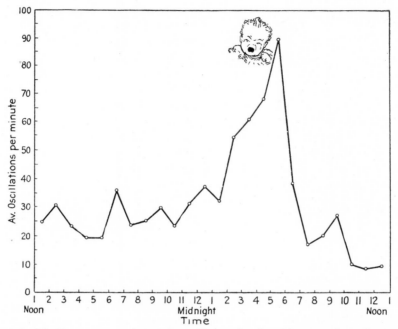

FIG. 2:8. The activity cycle in infants. The peaks of activity occur just prior to feeding time. Note the exaggerated peak just before 6 A.M. after the long night break in feeding. (*From Irwin, 1930.*)

this expectation. As Fig. 2:9 shows, rats learning a maze do better for a preferred food than for nonpreferred foods. A task

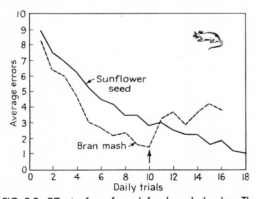

FIG 2:9. Effect of preferred food on behavior. The animals rewarded with bran mash (a preferred food) learn faster than those rewarded with sunflower seed. When both groups received sunflower seed at the end of the run (tenth day of the experiment), the group formerly receiving bran mash actually did worse than the animals which were accustomed to receiving sunflower seed. (*Modified from Elliott, 1928.*)

learned under 48-hour hunger drive is acquired faster and remembered longer than with a 12-hour or 24-hour drive (Fig. 2:10). Heron and Peake (1949) found that, in a discrimination problem, the nature of the food determined whether or not learning would occur. The experimental group was fed a protein-free diet for 30 days; then they and a control group learned to jump to a white card for food. Both were fed shortly before being placed in the learning situation. When casein and the protein-free diet were used as rewards, the experimental rats learned to jump to casein; the control group learned virtually nothing. Thus it appeared that the strong inner need for protein motivated successful learning in the experimental group.

At the human level, it often appears that stronger motivation leads to faster learning. Thus college students may be grouped by intelligence and compared on grades. Some make higher marks than expected;

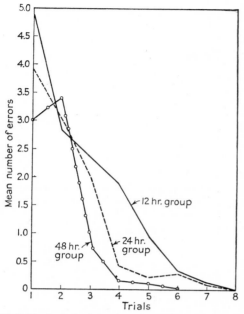

FIG. 2:10. Period of deprivation affects learning and retention. The curves show speed of relearning a maze, which had originally been learned under different periods of food deprivation. Those with 48-hour deprivation show fastest relearning, those with 12-hour deprivation, slowest. Relearning tests were made with all groups under the same degree of deprivation, 24 hours. (*From MacDuff, 1946.*)

others less than expected. The former group is generally found to have a definite purpose in attending college, clear goals they are trying to reach, a desire for education or a professional career; the latter group may be motivated by considerations having no relation to college as such: companionship, athletics, social prestige. Thus we infer that the motivation of the two groups toward educational goals differs in intensity, and this in turn determines the amount of effort expended on educational activities.

Physical work. Animals vary in the amount of physical work they will do to achieve a goal—as do humans. Thus chimpanzees can be trained to pull in a cart loaded with bricks, to receive a piece of banana or other food. More work will be done to obtain two pieces of food than for

one, and more effort will be exerted to obtain preferred than nonpreferred foods (Tinklepaugh, 1928). The speed of running in a straight alley to the food box is also increased if the food reward is greater (Fig. 2:11).

It is commonly believed that humans work harder in proportion to the intensity of motivation. While this statement is true in general, false applications are often made from it. Thus, if a man is receiving $2,000 a year, he will not work twice as hard for $4,000 a year. Many industrial executives err seriously in assuming that kind of equation. There is a rate of pay which is so low that no work is done; and there is a point above which increased pay produces diminishing amounts of work. However, utilization of other human motives may multiply many times the amount of energy mobilized for a given task—as in war, flood, fire, and other disasters.

Obstruction method. A different method of testing the strength of one drive is to pit it against another which can be quantified with some accuracy. In the apparatus developed by C. J. Warden (1931), rats were tested by requiring them to cross an electrified grid to reach the goal object. Thus, a current (painful but not excessively so) could be used as a kind of unit of comparison for various other inner needs.

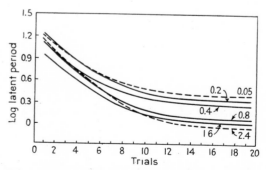

FIG. 2:11. Size of food reward and speed of running. As the size of the food reward is increased, rats run faster to get to it. Period of food deprivation was the same for all groups. (*From Zeaman, 1949.*)

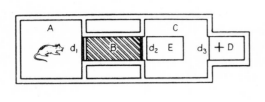

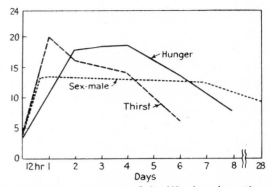

FIG. 2:12. The obstruction method and its results. At the left is shown a sketch of the Warden obstruction apparatus. The starting box is at A. The grid (B) delivers a shock, slightly painful; the question is, how many such shocks will the animal take in order to satisfy a given drive? On the right is a composite curve for several animals showing the number of shocks accepted in a 20-minute period, to satisfy a drive after a given period of deprivation. (*Modified from Warden, 1931.*)

The results for a study of hunger are summarized in Fig. 2:12. As this chart shows, the number of times the animal will take a given shock to get small bits of food increases steadily up to 48 hours, then more slowly to 96 hours. After this time there is a decline in the number of crossings of the grid, which may be a function of bodily weakness, not of decreased drive.

The principle of *dominance* calls attention to the fact that some drives, when activated, will dominate the animal's behavior and force delay of attempts to satisfy other, less potent needs. It is difficult to set up experiments which will pair some kinds of drive to see which is relatively dominant, but the Warden obstruction box makes it possible to pair almost

TABLE 2:1. Relative Potencies of Various Biogenic Drives at Maximum Strength

Drive tested	Average number crossings of grid
Maternal	22.4
Thirst	20.4
Hunger	18.2
Sex	13.8
Exploratory	6.0
No incentive	3.5

any drive with escape from pain (the electrified grid). Table 2:1 shows the results of a study on female rats, clearly revealing wide differences in the potency of different drives. The testing conditions were so arranged that each of the comparison drives was *at its maximum* as far as the experimenter could determine.

Verbal reports on motivation. Psychologists in general are dubious about the value to be got from direct reports as to the motive operating in a given activity. In daily life people are always asking, "Why did you do that?" They usually expect some statement relating to motive as an answer. "I wanted the money," "I stole because I was hungry," are illustrative.

Unfortunately, it appears that these answers often are low in validity; *i.e.*, they do not give an accurate picture of what is really happening. There are at least three reasons why such verbal reports on motivation are undependable: (1) the person may wish to conceal his motives from the questioner; (2) the person may refuse to recognize his own motives, because they are socially disapproved; (3) the person may not know the motive because it arises from obscure metabolic processes of which he is not conscious.

There are, furthermore, wide differences in what people mean by a given verbal report. We do not know exactly how to equate one man's description of a "very strong drive" with that given by someone else. As will be noted later, some men say they are "very hungry" 4 hours after eating, while others say they are "not very hungry" after 16 hours of food deprivation. Thus we do not have complete confidence in verbal report as a measure of intensity of motivation, although it is sometimes our only available method.

Verbal behavior. Instead of asking people directly about their motives, we may simply listen to what they talk about, and how much intensity seems manifest. In the hunger experiments to be described later, verbal behavior tended to focus on food to the exclusion of every other goal object. Strong feeling was apparent in the men's conversations dealing with food. Psychoanalysts concentrate on the recurrent goals brought up by their patients in the interview situation, and the amount of intensity associated with these topics. Certain psychological tests, now widely used, involve handing the person an ambiguous picture and noting what kinds of motivations are talked about—presumably, those dominating the motor system at the moment. If certain motives are repeatedly expressed, the psychologist infers that these are the dominant motivations of this personality.

Variations in Drive Strength

Between individuals and within the same person at different times, behavior is related to drive strength. Pierpont channels all his energy into getting more comforts for himself, while Juan is busy chasing members of the opposite sex. When Oscar is only mildly hungry, he prefers to go for a walk with Mary; but when the demand for food is very strong, her charms cannot compete with those of a hamburger. As drive strength increases, more energy is mobilized; interference is resisted; action toward the goal is more vigorous.

The three main factors affecting drive strength within the individual are *deprivation, satiation,* and *habit.* Each of these merits careful examination.

Deprivation. When we say that a man *needs* some goal object or satisfaction, our meaning is not always clear. In this context, *need* may refer to (1) a true physiological deficit, as a vitamin deficiency; (2) a restless search for the object without knowledge, as in a newborn baby sucking without awareness of the food source; and (3) a conscious feeling of demand for the object (need of friends). Because this concept of need is ambiguous, many psychologists have preferred to shift their emphasis in studies of specific goal-seeking behavior, and to speak in terms of *deprivation.* Thus, we do not know for sure that Oscar needs food, but we do know that he has not eaten for 12 hours. We can therefore speak with confidence of a 12-hour deprivation, whereas the resulting drive, impulse, or demand for food is not so easy to define.

In the experimental control of behavior, deprivation appears to be directly related to drive strength within certain limits. Thus, longer food deprivation will impel more work, faster maze running, etc., where food is the reward. The limit is reached when lack of food leads to physical weakness; from this point on further deprivation leads to less vigorous behavior. (Whether the hypothetical "drive" is weaker cannot be stated; we never study drives directly, but only their effects.)

This solution has considerable merit in studies of animals. It is also useful in some work with humans. We emphasize, however, that deprivations do not affect all persons equally. Much will depend on how one looks at the situation. Loss of one meal may seem a serious deprivation to one

TABLE 2:2. Relation between Food Deprivation and Experienced Hunger

Time without food	Number of men rating themselves				
	Very hungry			Not very hungry	
	1	2	3	4	5
1 hour..........	0	11	17	7	9
4 hours..........	7	12	3	2	0
16 hours.........	16	13	10	1	0

boy, and a minor discomfort to another. McClelland and Atkinson (1948) tested men at various periods of time after their last meal, the time intervals ranging from 1 hour to 16 hours. The men were asked on each occasion to rate themselves on a scale from 1 (very hungry) to 5 (not very hungry). The results are shown in Table 2:2.

This investigation indicates an important caution to be observed in interpreting studies on deprivation in humans, and perhaps on animals too. This is that two persons, deprived for the same time interval, do not necessarily experience the same degree of drive. Even after 1 hour 25 per cent of these men rated themselves "2"— approximating "very hungry"; and on the other hand, after 16 hours without food, 25 per cent rated themselves less hungry than step 2 on the scale. Obviously, hunger as subjectively experienced does not depend exactly on the length of deprivation. Thus, while deprivation may be suitable for laboratory experimentation where one is concerned with measured quantities, the real-life situation may involve intensities of motivation which do not correspond very closely to length of deprivation.[1]

[1] There are numerous factors which may account for the McClelland findings. Perhaps some men really burned up food at a faster rate, hence were more in need of food. More probably, some men feel discomfort more readily, or exaggerate their feelings in marking the report sheet. Infantile depriva-

Satiation. The motivating value (valence) of an external object or goal is dependent upon inner states (tensions), which are in turn functions of disturbed physiological equilibrium. This becomes especially apparent in the condition known as *satiation.* The organism tends to become satiated with respect to any food object or other satisfaction, as the consummatory response is repeated. Thus, Young (1940) found that rats normally prefer sugar to casein; but this preference can be reversed by giving the animals all the sugar they will eat just before the preference test. *Satiation tends to weaken a valence by reducing the corresponding tension.*

The phenomenon of satiation and consequent loss of preference has survival value. If we continued to eat the same foods, enjoy the same pleasures, and in general carry on the same activities, we should miss many opportunities for higher level adjustment. The homeostatic mechanism can select optimum foods only if a variety are tasted. Home environments, clothing, recreations, and the like are modified as new plans are tried. Selection depends on variability. If we are to choose the best diet, the best courses in college, the best physical activities, we must sample and consider the various possible alternatives.

The immediate effect of satiation of a drive is a decrease in its strength. Since other needs may have been undergoing deprivation while this one was satisfied, a new drive now becomes dominant. Exercise follows after rest; sex play follows satisfaction of hunger. Thus, the alternation of deprivation and satiation governs the variation in vigor of activities from hour to hour and from day to day.

Habit. When we say that habit intensifies drive strength, it may seem that we are denying the principle of satiation. The two principles, however, are supplemen-

tion might have led some men to overestimate the need for food.

tary. When the organism has become accustomed to certain ways of satisfying needs, these valences are strengthened. Thus an American boy will react positively to a tenderloin steak but negatively to dragonflies fried in palm oil, whereas a Balinese boy will reverse this preference.

Habit accounts for much of motivated behavior, and indeed it sometimes appears that a habit, once established, becomes a motive in itself. A retired factory worker says, "When I put on my shoes, they just naturally take me down to the shop." Going to the job has been a means to satisfying other needs for many years; now that this function has been eliminated, the habit still tends to direct and motivate action (Chap. 4).

This means that the person comes to value the habits and situations in which drives have been satisfied. A rat who has been fed in a white box seems to desire to get into the box—it has positive valence for him. It can even be used as a reward for learning (see secondary reinforcement, page 64). Children who are disturbed and anxious can be quieted and their tensions reduced by giving them familiar toys; a dish and spoon associated with food may be quite effective. Sucking is a habit associated with satisfaction; so sucking the thumb, a blanket, or other object may be a device for reducing anxiety.

Classification of Drives and Motives

An earlier paragraph suggested that motivating states can be classified into three levels: the *biogenic* or biological drives, emotions, and values. The present chapter deals with the first of these groups.

Biogenic drives can be identified in terms of two criteria: determination by heredity and close association with tissue needs. It is necessary to call attention to these criteria because, within a short time after birth, the human being begins to develop more complex motives resembling but not identical with the biological drives.

Heredity. All animals, including man, are characterized by certain goal-seeking behavior patterns. The demands for food, for water, for escape from pain, and so on, are not products of learning and experience. Deprivation of the appropriate substances produces tension and demand behavior, without learning or thought.

Man has hereditarily determined drives which are less numerous and less organized than those of the lower animals. Humans do not inherit a nest-building drive, and there is grave doubt that they have any maternal drive. Rats have a sex drive and an inherited pattern of behavior for satisfying the drive; humans have the drive but must learn modes of behavior for its satisfaction. Since we are concerned with human psychology, this chapter deals primarily with inherited drives in man.

Tissue needs. Biological drives are characterized by a close association with specific requirements of protoplasm. We can demonstrate, for example, that craving for salt is correlated with a need for sodium in the tissues. On the other hand, a craving for dill pickles may resemble inborn drives but be purely a product of experience, with no relation to tissue requirements.

Appetites and preferences develop as the person learns how many different substances fulfill the same tissue needs. One individual gets his daily calories from rice, another from spaghetti. Protein is supplied by fish or by roast beef. Differences in preference for such items result from learning and are not dependent on any specific tissue conditions.

From the practical viewpoint, it may seem that the biological drives are not too important. Adult human beings do not seem to be acting in terms of immediate demands for food, water, escape from pain, and so forth; but it must be remembered that threat of deprivation in these areas

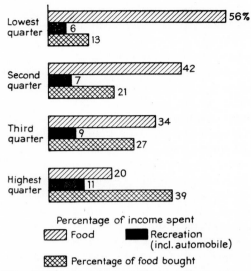

Lowest quarter: 56% | 6 | 13
Second quarter: 42 | 7 | 21
Third quarter: 34 | 9 | 27
Highest quarter: 20 | 11 | 39

Percentage of income spent
▨ Food   ■ Recreation (incl. automobile)
▨ Percentage of food bought

FIG. 2:13. Consumer statistics reveal strength of drives. When the amount of money available for various drive satisfactions is large, only a moderate proportion is spent for food; but when the money available is quite limited, a large part is spent for food. This confirms the finding that the hunger drive is quite potent. (*Based on Federal Reserve Board figures.*)

looms large in the eyes of millions of persons. As we show in Fig. 2:13, poor families spend only one-third as much money for food as well-to-do families; this probably indicates some biological frustration in persons of low income.

From the theoretical side, great stress must be placed on the biological drives. They provide the raw material out of which our more complex motives are developed. Even if adult human beings do not spend much of their time directly gratifying their needs for food, water, or escape from pain, the activities for which they do mobilize energy have often been determined by such need satisfactions in earlier years.

The biogenic drives are closely related to those of other animals; they are sometimes referred to as "man's animal nature." In the following pages we shall consider some of these tissue needs and show how they contribute to an understanding of "human nature."

Specific Drives: Hungers

Deprivation of food leads to a disturbance of homeostasis which we recognize as hunger. Popular speech treats this noun as singular, and assumes that only one kind of hunger exists, although preferences in food are recognized. Recent experimental work indicates that this view is too simple. Human protoplasm requires not only calories, but also vitamins, amino acids, and various minerals, for efficient functioning. Deprivation of any of these may apparently lead to tension and restless seeking. Thus it seems appropriate to speak of "hungers" and to recognize the variety of needs involved.

Since it would be unethical to deprive humans of any substance known to be important in the diet, for the sake of research, studies on the motivating value of hunger for calories, for specific vitamins, and for other foods have been confined to animals. In terms of the various kinds of measures we have described (amount of energy, speed of learning, preference tests, and so on), all these have been shown to have motivational strength. The exact number of hungers is not known; conceivably, there may be a "hunger" for every chemical substance needed by protoplasm for efficient functioning.

"Abnormal" hungers. One of the ways in which these homeostatic needs came to the attention of scientists was through the study of "abnormal" cravings. Cattle in a certain area were found to seek out and chew on the bones of their dead fellows. Children were reported drinking ink, eating dirt, and ingesting other substances of dubious quality. Research, stimulated by these observations, led to deeper understanding of the way in which our bodily needs control our actions.

A tragic and spectacular case which illustrates the "wisdom of the body" in seeking needed substances for the maintenance of bodily homeostasis was reported by Wilkins and Richter (1940). In this case a child of three developed an abnormal craving for salt. He had early shown a strong craving for salty crackers and similar foods and, as soon as he was able to do so, began sprinkling salt on his food as others might use sugar. When he was placed in a hospital for observation and unable to obtain these (relatively) enormous supplies of salt, he died of sodium insufficiency. An autopsy revealed that he was suffering from a disorder of the adrenal gland which caused his body to need a heavy sodium intake (cf. Richter's adrenalectomized rats, page 39); his unusual appetite was clearly a homeostatic adjustment to this physiological need.

We know little about the mechanism by which this kind of motivation is accomplished. It would appear that the deficiency of a given substance in the blood stream brings about a selective sensitivity to foods containing that substance, and that ingesting these foods relieves tension which is not relieved by other foodstuffs. This process, however, is imperfect, and people often fail to eat needed foods which are freely available; as, for example, the Chinese preference for polished rice in the face of vitamin B deficiencies, or American preference for white bread as opposed to more nutritious varieties.

Stomach tensions. Hunger is a particularly useful drive from the point of view of the teacher of psychology, because the relation between need and tension can so easily be demonstrated. One of the classic experiments in this field is that of the stomach balloon devised by A. J. Carlson (1937). Carlson believed that the conscious experience of hunger (hunger "pangs") resulted from sharp contractions of the muscles lining the wall of the stomach. To investigate this relationship, he devised a simple apparatus of a small balloon, a rubber tube, and an outside recording device. The balloon was swallowed, then inflated to fill the stomach cavity. Thus any muscular contraction would be recorded as changes in air pressure in the system (see Fig. 2:14).

When the subject is asked to press a lever when he feels a "hunger pang," it is found that there is a close coincidence of these reported experiences with actual stomach contractions (Fig. 2:15). Thus, when we speak of "tension" as the immediate basis of motivated behavior, pushing the individual toward vigorous action to solve an inner need, we can use this stomach tension as an excellent illustration. The discomfort associated with the stomach contractions is characteristic of the discomfort usually set off by the biological drives.

Several of the important studies on drive phenomena have used this technique. The fact that we are more alert, stronger, and more accurate on mental tests during hunger was demonstrated by Wada (1922) in this manner. Balloon records of stomach activity were related to tests of strength of grip, speed of solving arithmetic problems, etc. When the subject squeezed a dynamometer during these periods of stomach contractions, he exerted more pressure than at other times. He made higher scores on mental tests during these periods, and so on. (The subject could not see the kymograph record and did not know just what was being studied.)

The evidence against the view that stomach contractions are *essential* to the hunger drive, strangely enough, is conclusive. Most emphatic is the study by Tsang (1938) in which the stomachs of rats were completely removed (esophagus attached directly to duodenum). These rats showed just as much evidence of hunger drive as matched controls. Another striking investigation is that of Morgan and Morgan

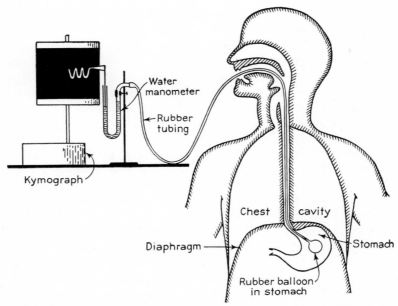

FIG. 2:14. The stomach-balloon technique for studying hunger. This device provides direct evidence of the relationship between stomach contractions and the experience of hunger. The balloon is swallowed, then inflated until it just fills the stomach cavity. Any contraction of the muscular walls will then be recorded on the smoked drum of the kymograph. (*Modified from Carlson and Johnson, 1937. By permission of Univ. of Chicago Press.*)

(1940), who cut all nerves from the stomach back to the brain. Under these conditions the animals could not possibly feel hunger pangs (no "feedback"), yet they showed the usual hunger drive.

These experiments, of course, involved abnormal conditions. For normal animals, it seems safe to say that hunger sets off stomach contractions (*i.e.*, the contractions are a *sign* of the inner need) and also seeking behavior. When the stomach is removed, seeking behavior continues. This may be a function of practice. What would an animal do if deprived of these inner cues to action before he had learned to seek food? The experiment would be difficult; it might prove that, for the formation of food-getting habits, stomach tensions are an essential cue.

Basis of specific hungers. Even though stomach cramps are a necessary element of the normal hunger drive, it would be in-

conceivable that there could be special muscle contractions signaling need for vitamin B, calcium, or amino acids. How does the organism exercise this "wisdom of the body" in choosing food? What basis underlies these specific hungers?

The evidence indicates that the physical need operates through a change in sensory mechanisms: food containing the needed substance becomes *more palatable:* it "tastes better." It is important, however, that a new situation be presented so that new food habits must be learned. When rats are presented with a familiar feeding situation, they tend to take the familiar food, even though it is nutritionally inadequate (habit factor). So we cannot trust little Oscar to forego candy in favor of cod-liver oil, especially after he has learned to appreciate candy. (Prior to establishment of varied food preferences, the child takes cod-liver oil with no apparent distaste.)

The extent to which the taste mechanism is vital in these homeostatic food-seeking activities has been dramatically illustrated by Richter (1942). Adrenalectomized rats will keep themselves alive by drinking salty water if it is available, in preference to pure water (page 39). When the nerves essential to tasting were cut, the animals no longer chose the salt solution, and all died. It seems clear, therefore, that two independent mechanisms are involved: *need* and *palatability*. We may have a dietary deficiency and so need calcium; but the increase in intake of calcium depends on some obscure process by which calcium-containing foods come to taste better. The presence of conflicting food habits, or lack of certain sensory cues, may cause a failure of the homeostatic adjustment. Specific hungers have their physiological basis in some process by which the sensory apparatus becomes selectively sensitive to the needed food (Fig. 2:16).

Infantile deprivation. People develop an especially strong desire for some specific substance, or for food in general, on the basis of past experience as well as on the basis of immediate chemical need. Some individuals become gluttons or misers, hoarding food (and its equivalent, money) or consuming vastly greater amounts than are needed. Their early experiences seem to have made them oversensitive to threats of food deprivation.

Experimentation on this point is obviously impossible with humans. Hence we turn to the animal world for concrete data. Hunt (1941) divided a group of infant white rats into matched pairs. One member of each pair was subjected to rather severe and prolonged hunger within the first month of life. The matched animal got plenty of food at all times. After the first month, both groups were well fed until maturity (age six months). At this age all rats normally hoard some few food pellets, especially if they are given access to food

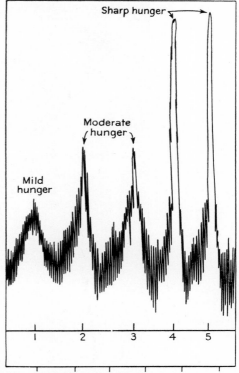

FIG. 2:15. Stomach contractions and hunger pangs. The subject, with balloon in stomach, presses a key each time he feels a hunger "pang." He also rates the intensity of hunger on a scale from mild to severe. Larger contractions are associated with more intense feeling of hunger. (*Modified from Carlson and Johnson, 1937. By permission of University of Chicago Press.*)

after having been hungry for a day. Hunt found that there was a very great difference in hoarding by his two groups. Those deprived in infancy hoarded an average of 37.7 pellets, while those well fed in this early period hoarded only an average of 14.0 pellets of food. Thus hoarding behavior was almost tripled in strength by this early frustration.

One's outlook on life, his approach to everyday problems depends on his past experience. An early childhood deprivation may set up a way of looking at things which could be described by saying, "I expect this to happen to me." An expectation, or

FIG. 2:16. Cafeteria for studying self-selection of food by rats. The array of tubes along the bottom of the apparatus contains various food substances which automatically fill little feeding dishes accessible to the rats. When the mineral, vitamin, etc., content of the diet is varied, the rats generally—not invariably—choose a balanced diet. (*Courtesy of Dr. P. T. Young.*)

anticipation, that severe hunger may be one's lot would naturally lead to hoarding of food. This is a simple homeostatic response to the threat of food deprivation in the future.

Effects of long-continued hunger. Deprivation of food may magnify the importance of food, and it may also cause food to become a kind of symbol of security and protection against hardship. This seems to be particularly true of children. A report given at the International Congress on

Mental Health in London in 1948 throws some light on the intensity and magnitude of the latter problem.

First and foremost . . . were the emotional effects of starvation, well illustrated by an incident . . . at an UNRRA International Children's Center in Bavaria shortly after V-E Day.

Food was actually plentiful at this center for the 250 homeless "unattached" Allied children there, all of whom had been rescued from concentration camps and forced labor under the Germans. The children were permitted to eat as much as they wanted and were so well satisfied with three large meals and a tea-time daily that they showed little enthusiasm for an additional offer of an evening snack. *Yet they persisted in taking pieces of bread from the dining hall and hiding them under their pillows or among their possessions.* It was invariably bread that was being saved, not cake, not candy, but bread. . . . "We understand why it should not be done," volunteered a fifteen-year-old boy to the center's director. "But, whatever we do, we can't stop it entirely. You see, when bread has meant too much to you, you just can't do without it. It isn't a question of being hungry. It's just that you've got to have it."[1]

Experiments on prolonged hunger. There have been a few experimental studies on prolonged fasting by volunteer subjects. These have usually been psychologists interested in the problem, and consequently only one or two individuals have been tested at a given time. These studies have led to such observations as: that physical and mental efficiency tend to increase for a few days (this may have survival value, in helping the organism locate and capture food); that the conscious experience of hunger tends to weaken with time (the organism usually adapts to any continued stimulus by refusing to respond to it); and that physical weakness does not set in until considerably later. There is usually a diminution of sex drive and other motives, and a concentration on the hunger drive. The sense of smell becomes keener, and perhaps other senses as well. Most of these changes fit well with the homeostatic interpretation of energy mobilization.

The most extensive observations on a considerable group of subjects were made by Keys, Brozek, and coworkers (1950). Young men who were conscientious objectors in World War II volunteered as subjects for a lengthy research on effects of

undernutrition. They were kept on a rigidly controlled diet of about 1500 calories, considerably below what is essential to good nutrition, and even more below customary intake in the United States, for a period of 24 weeks. The severity of the diet is indicated by the fact that the average weight loss was over 30 pounds.

The most significant results of the study, from our point of view, fall into three categories: effect on behavior, effect on experience, and effect on other drives. The changes in behavior included collecting recipes, "toying" with the food to make it last longer, licking plates clean, and so on. An outstanding modification of mental activity was observed; there was an intense and persistent preoccupation with thoughts of food to the exclusion of mental tasks. As in the case of explorers on short rations, these young men became mentally obsessed by food—in short, found great difficulty in responding to any other stimuli.

As starvation progressed they became more and more silent, apathetic and immobile. Movements were slow and restricted; stairs were mounted one at a time and the men sat or stood leaning against a wall while waiting. In discussion there was no evidence of confusion of thought or difficulty of expression but the attitude was frequently irritable and morose. Trivial incidents were productive of exaggerated annoyance and complaint. Favorite topics of conversation were food, farming and rural life . . . . [1]

The intensive preoccupation with food made it difficult for the men to concentrate upon the tasks they had intellectually decided they would work on. If a man tried to study, he soon found himself day-dreaming about food. He would think about foods he had eaten in the past; he would muse about opportunities he had missed to eat a certain food when he was at this or that place. Often he would daydream

---

[1] *Nation.* Aug. 6, 1949, pp. 130–131, reprinted by permission. (Italics ours.)

[1] From *Experimental Starvation in Man*, by Ancel Keys, J. Brozek, A. Henschel, O. Mickelsen, and H. L. Taylor, Laboratory of Physiological Hygiene, University of Minnesota, Oct. 15, 1945.

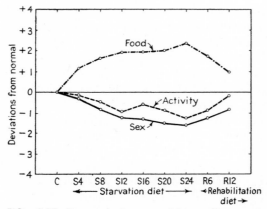

FIG. 2:17. Decrease in sex drive under semi-starvation. There was a steady decrease in the rated strength of the sex drive as the starvation period continued. This may have been due to physical weakness, but in large part it seems due to complete dominance of the hunger drive. (*From Biology of Human Starvation, by Ancel Keys et al., University of Minnesota Press, 1950.*)

by the hour about the next meal, which was not very far away.

Because of physical debility, or this complete obsession with food, their sexual urge gradually decreased (see Fig. 2:17), and it was the rare individual who continued courtship at the end of the starvation period . . . . One fellow's girl friend visited him from a distant city during the low days of starvation, and she found his ostensible affection disappointingly shallow. His reservoir of affectional responses was drying up.[1]

Related to this observation is the study by an anthropologist (Holmberg, 1950) on the Siriono, a South American Indian tribe. Living on a very low food-intake level, with long periods of semistarvation, these Indians had organized their whole culture around the food need. Values were scaled in terms of food, sex was clearly subordinate to food as a goal object, virtually all quarrels were about food. From these and similar studies, it seems safe to conclude that, *when a drive is subject to repeated*

[1] Guetzkow and Bowman (1946), pp. 24, 32. Reprinted by permission of Brethren Publishing House.

deprivation, it is likely to come to dominate the behavior and experience of the individual. This observation will be found significant in many phases of human psychology.

Social Facilitation of Feeding Behavior. We have noted that deprivation intensifies and satiation weakens the strength of motivated behavior toward any given goal. Complete satiation is defined by refusal to accept any more of the goal object. Beyond infancy, however, even this kind of complete elimination of a need is relative to environmental circumstances. The learning process leads to modification of tensions in a variety of ways; at present we want to examine the strengthening of tensions by external stimuli.

The phenomenon of *social facilitation* of feeding behavior is a case in point. Harlow (1932) fed rats to satiation, then introduced into the cage with the satiated animal another which was hungry. Under this situation the first rat, who had refused to eat more, invariably began to eat again. Ross and Ross (1949) fed puppies alternately in isolation and in groups. They found a marked increase in the amount of food ingested in group feeding situations. This checks with the common observation in nursery schools, that children who are "finicky" eaters at home often eat larger quantities in school and tend to accept foods which would have been rejected at home. It seems safe to conclude that *the presence of an animal of the same species, engaged in a given goal activity, tends to reinstate the goal activity of the satiated animal.*

Whether this is proof of an "instinct of competition" is debatable (see Chap. 4). Certainly it indicates that we are biologically so constructed that competitive behavior is easily set off. It may be easier, however, to explain social facilitation without assuming a specific instinctive desire for competition. It may be that the animal fed in isolation does not eat to a point of maximum satiation, but only to the point at which the hunger tension is weaker than alternative tensions such as the tendency to explore the environment. Sight of another animal eating may draw the first rat's attention back to food, so that more is ingested.[1]

Regardless of this point, the social-facilitation experiment serves well to remind us of a basic principle: *the unity of the organism.* The hunger drive does not exist in isolation, any more than thirst, sex, or fatigue will function irrespective of other needs, stimuli, and acts-in-process. The formula, hunger → eating, is too simple to cover the facts. Hunger is a major determinant, but not the sole determinant, of eating behavior. Hunger affects the entire person, and his actions depend not only on his food need but also on a variety of other factors. The conscientious objectors who volunteered for the semistarvation experiment demonstrated that other tensions can overrule the hunger tension. The impoverished aristocrat who starves rather than beg, like the pathological miser who refuses to spend his money even for food, offers a similar illustration.

It must always be understood, consequently, that deprivation and satiation do not have automatic, absolutely predictable effects.[2] Deprivation of sex gratification may mean quite different things to different men. Satiation is relative to the situation in which a person finds himself. A person with a strong "hunger for affection" may show a curious reaction of this type: shortly after eating a large meal, he

[1] Thus it is noteworthy that children when first placed together in a group may eat less rather than more; the excitement and curiosity set off by the unaccustomed group situation may actually inhibit the hunger tension.

[2] If we know a given individual quite well, we can usually predict with high accuracy how he will react to deprivation and satiation. Similarly, we can predict for large groups. Prediction for a single person is hazardous unless we know his pattern of motivations and modes of satisfaction.

finds himself ignored by someone he likes. Immediately he experiences pangs of hunger and feels a compulsive need to go and eat. In this case the strengthening of the hunger tension results from deprivation in another area, which is symbolically equated with food seeking in his mind.

We must therefore recognize that human motivation quickly gets far away from physiological tensions as such. Satisfying the hunger drive is profoundly affected by the kind of foods we have learned to value, the linen and silver we expect, the presence of other people and their behavior, and similar items. Satisfying the sex drive is even more embedded in various incidental or accessory needs. For civilized man the raw satisfaction of his biological needs as such frequently becomes less important than these associated factors—at least, the attainment of the goal may be unappetizing or even repulsive in their absence. Because these problems lead directly into a consideration of "higher" personal and social values, they will be given further extended examination in Chap. 4.

Thirst

Just as the human organism cannot survive without various foodstuffs, so it cannot live without constant replenishment of its water supply. Deprivation of water for any substantial length of time leads to vigorous energy mobilization and energetic activity directed toward this goal. As compared with food hunger in general, a given degree of water deficit represents a more serious threat to survival; and bodily damage will result more quickly. Thus it is not surprising that the obstruction method shows thirst drive reaching its peak more quickly and being more intense at its maximum when compared with the hunger drive (Fig. 2:12).

The physiological basis of thirst appears to be in dryness of the mouth and throat

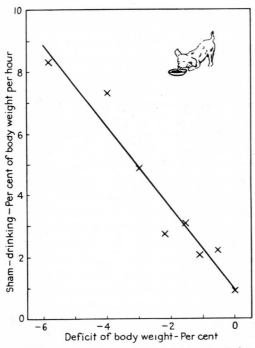

FIG. 2:18. Sham drinking as related to water deficit. The estimated water deficit is based on the known needs of dogs under varying conditions of water deprivation. These dogs did not actually get the water into the stomach, and yet they stopped drinking at a point closely approximating that which would have just replaced the water deficit. (*From Adolph, 1941.*)

membranes. Thus the conscious experience of thirst can be induced by water deficit and also by other factors; breathing hot, dry air; eating salty foods; injections of atropine which stop salivary secretion. This view seems to be confirmed by the fact that the thirst experience can be temporarily alleviated by chewing gum (stimulating more saliva) or by anesthetizing the mouth and throat membranes with cocain.

It appears from further study, however, that throat dryness is only a *sign* of thirst, just as stomach cramps were a sign of hunger. Montgomery (1931) removed the salivary glands from dogs completely. Necessarily this will increase throat and mouth dessication and might be expected

to lead to a marked increase in water intake. Actually, the dogs drank just as much as their normal controls.

Even more convincing is the study of the "fistulated" dog, whose esophagus has been disconnected from the stomach so that water drunk does not reach the digestive tract at all. When these dogs were subjected to increasing periods of water deprivation, and then allowed to drink, they took in almost exactly the amount of water taken by normal controls (Fig. 2:18). Since the first few swallows moistened the throat, and since they could get no feedback cues from filling the stomach, it seems plain that some nervous mechanism controls the amount of intake in such manner as to replace the deficit. Conversely, when water was placed directly into the stomach of such an animal, he would go for days without drinking—he never developed a water deficit. The best evidence suggests that a *relative water deficit* operates upon receptors sensitive to changes in osmotic pressure or perhaps directly upon a brain center, which sensitizes the dog to water and impels him to drink. Dryness of the mouth and throat is a cue for the organism to seek water but is not the true basis for the thirst drive.

Oxygen Deficit

Each of us, in growing up, encounters many experiences in which he suffers some degree of hunger or thirst. He learns to recognize the cues which signal these deficiencies, and acquires habits for restoring equilibrium. The need for oxygen, while in a physiological sense even more urgent than that for food or water, is unique in that no such learning ordinarily occurs. Many people go through a whole lifetime without ever experiencing an oxygen deficit.

This may account for the fact that, in recent studies on high-altitude flying and related problems, it has been found that men may suffer from acute anoxia (oxygen lack) without recognizing their danger. A kind of drunkenness and confusion, with loss of emotional control, is reported. It may well be that, if young children underwent appropriate training in experiencing and labeling mild oxygen deficit, they would be able to react more adaptively as adults.

Physical interference with air intake will, of course, mobilize great energy in child or adult. The mechanism involved here may be merely obstruction of an established habit mechanism, since neither a lowered oxygen intake nor an increased carbon dioxide level sets off this violent behavior. Increase in carbon dioxide will, of course, release unconscious homeostatic processes: deeper breathing, relaxation of pulmonary bronchi—but the reactions which would be appropriate to high-altitude anoxia and similar states do not seem to be set off in the same way as food-seeking and water-seeking behavior.

Maternal Behavior

Some interest may have attached to the fact, indicated in Table 2:1, that the maternal drive in rats was stronger, as measured by the obstruction method, than any other single drive. This was for tests made very shortly after the birth of the litter. The strength of this drive seems to decline rather rapidly.

Maternal behavior in the rat differs from food-seeking and similar goal-directed behavior in that there is a rather specific sequence of activities laid down by heredity. Nest building, cleaning of the young, returning them to the nest when removed, suckling, etc., are unlearned. They seem, in fact, to be largely controlled by endocrine-gland secretions: the hormone *prolactin*, secreted by the pituitary gland, will cause a virgin female rat to begin secreting milk, to retrieve and suckle young, and to build nests.

Similar phenomena have not been observed in human mothers. In fact, as we go up the phylogenetic scale from rat to man, we find a steadily decreasing precision in maternal care of offspring, with increasing variation between individuals. There is no very convincing evidence that human mothers have either an innate drive to care for their children or an innately determined pattern of behavior for so doing. Clinical evidence, on the contrary, suggests that many women have a decided aversion to maternity and come to love their children only after having pleasant experiences with them, or not at all.

Sex

Like maternal drive, the sex drive in rats and other animals of comparable complexity has a definite hormonal basis and a definite behavior pattern of expression. Male rats reared in complete isolation, when sexually mature and placed with a female in heat, show a complete pattern of copulatory behavior. The same is true of females. On the other hand, chimpanzees placed in a similar position show practically no signs of hereditary patterning; copulation is achieved only after considerable trial and error, and variation between individuals is marked.

When tested in the obstruction box, male rats showed a strength of sex drive considerably below hunger and thirst. Unlike these drives, the sex impulse stayed at peak strength for about a week (reaching the peak in one day of deprivation) before beginning to taper off. The males showed no periodic rhythm of sex drive. Females, on the other hand, had very little drive except when in heat (4.6-day cycle). At its maximum, the female drive is apparently about equal in strength to that of the male at maximum.

The potency of the sex drive in affecting human behavior is attested by an enormous variety of evidence. It is significant, for example, that Kinsey (1948) reports masturbation as a means of release of sex tension in 85 to 90 per cent of young single males—even though social disapproval of this act is strong. Marriage is a means to other goals than sexual satisfaction, of course, but sex is a major component of this complex of goals. Even after a man is married, he may crave additional sexual objects; 25 to 35 per cent of Kinsey's married subjects reported some extramarital intercourse, and many men undoubtedly concealed this information.

Hormonal control. As in the rat, the sex drive in humans seems definitely to have its physiological basis in glandular secretions: from the testes in males, from the ovaries in females, and from the pituitary in both. Masculinity of interests has been shown to be related to maturation of the male sex glands and to injection of male hormones.

In females, the cyclical phenomenon of menstruation complicates the picture but makes the endocrine influence even more apparent. Benedek and Rubenstein (1939) studied the glandular status of women undergoing psychoanalysis. Around the time of ovulation, when the hormone known as estrogen is being produced in substantial quantities, the typical female showed, in her emotional life, an interest in men and in heterosexual relationships. In the second phase (balance of estrogen and progestin), conflict, irritability, and flightiness were manifest. The third phase showed a dominance of progestin in the endocrine field; psychologically, her interests were more related to bodily comfort and egocentric values, as opposed to sexual motivation.

Recognition of cues. In the rat, cues from the body for hunger, thirst, and sex all set off seeking activities and can be related to definite consummatory responses (eating, drinking, copulating). In humans, the same sensory cues are no doubt present, but in the case of sex, practice in recognizing and naming the state is prevented. Thus we characteristically find adolescent boys and girls restless, unsatisfied, and seeking, but unable to identify the underlying drive. Even in adults it appears that much sexually motivated behavior is not recognized as such, and such a label, if suggested, will be vigorously denied. That there is no instinctive pattern of response for satisfying the human sex drive is also apparent. Most young people learn something about intercourse at a fairly early age, but the wide variation in sexual behavior in different societies, as well as among individuals in our own culture, indicates the major role played by learning.

Sex, therefore, is not primarily a physiological drive in Western civilization. It becomes intricately enmeshed in all sorts of social and emotional entanglements. In this composite form it has great importance for an understanding of human psychology, and we shall therefore return to it in various connections.

Excretory Needs

Finally, we may mention the needs for defecation and micturition, the emptying of the lower colon and bladder when they are full. These are clearly physiological and necessary for survival. The cue involved is a feeling of pressure from the organ involved.

In some societies, the psychologist would be more correct in classifying these as reflexes rather than drives; the pressure simply sets off evacuation as soon as convenient. In Western civilization, the problem becomes considerably more complex because of the elaborate taboos and social controls placed upon excretory functions of children. Toilet training becomes a major crisis in the lives of many infants; as a general phenomenon, it has sufficiently broad effects to justify the Freudians in paying considerable attention to it.

Perhaps because of the anatomical nearness of the sex and excretory organs, but more probably because of a cultural attitude which links them, the psychoanalysts find a fusion of excretory behavior and sex phenomena. In Chap. 13 we shall summarize the interrelations of the various impulses which psychoanalysis lumps together under the term *sex*.

Pain

Escape from pain is clearly a powerful organic drive. Its homeostatic value is beyond question. Most of the painful stimuli encountered by primitive man are threats to survival.

It must be noted, however, that pain does not operate in precisely the same way as the other biogenic needs. Specifically, the principles of deprivation and of satiation seem to have very little applicability here. It will therefore be more convenient, in terms of getting a systematic classification for motives, to treat pain and its associates—fear, anger, anxiety, etc.—under the heading of emotions instead of biological drives. The following chapter will discuss these emotional tensions as forms of motivation.

Exploratory Drives

Many authors have proposed that curiosity, the quest for knowledge, or a drive to explore and understand one's environment, is biologically determined. The trend in modern psychology is to accept the notion that most human beings develop such a dynamic trend, but question that it has any hereditary, organic basis.

The biological factor underlying this impulse may be identified as follows: Every stimulus, every physical change in the environment, is of potential significance to the organism. It is literally a matter of life and death to primitive man that he detect the approach of a dangerous animal. Every sight, sound, or smell thus tends

automatically to evoke attention (see Chap. 6). The small baby explores objects, is attracted by lights, hunts for sources of sound. If the stimulus merely continues unchanged, the baby loses interest.

This primitive reaction evolves into a curiosity "drive" or need to understand, as the individual matures and has a variety of experiences. He may learn, for example, that thorough exploration of a situation leads to avoidance of pain. In primitive societies, the relief of thirst and hunger tensions may reward the careful student of the environment; under modern conditions, reward is largely a matter of actions by parents and other adults. Thus, the child may learn that he gets praise for acting aggressively in situation A but is punished for aggressive behavior in situation B. It then becomes urgent that he learn to differentiate A from B. Careful study leads to greater reward and less punishment.

In the same way, of course, the school system teaches the child to explore, study, and understand (or, depending on the teacher, to memorize and to bow before authority). The specific influences may vary widely. Outcomes also are quite different. Some children grow into alert, questing explorers with a strong need to know and to understand; others develop a need to accept unquestioningly the words of an authority.

It is most improbable that a need for understanding, or a curiosity drive, exists independent of experience. The conditions are, however, favorable to the universal development of such an impulse, since it serves such basic drives as hunger and thirst, and such emotional needs as for love and for avoidance of pain.

Basic Principles of Motivation

From this quick survey of the facts regarding biogenic drives, we can infer certain general principles of human motivation. These principles will be valuable in organiz-

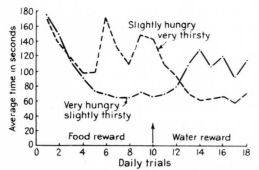

FIG. 2:19. Dominance of drives changed by deprivation. Deprivation of food causes this drive to become
potent, and efficient learning is achieved for a food
reward. Thirsty animals, offered a food reward,
show no learning. However, when water was offered
as a reward, this group suddenly began to learn.
Conversely, the hungry animals no longer behaved
efficiently when the food reward was removed. Rewards are effective only when related to the drive
which is dominant at the moment. (*After Elliott,
1929.*)

ing our knowledge of more complex energy-
mobilization processes to be examined in
subsequent chapters.

1. *Principle of equilibrium.* Energy is
mobilized, behavior becomes vigorous and
persistent, when a favorable equilibrium
is disturbed. Such equilibria include food,
water, oxygen, and other essentials of
survival. The equilibrium principle, however, will be found useful far beyond these
limited needs.

2. *Principle of dominance.* The organism
often has conflicting needs. If both hunger
and thirst are operating as drives, one must
dominate the motor mechanism. The more
potent drive will determine the course of
action. At the purely biological level, this
seems to work out so that the more serious
threat to survival is met first. We shall find
in considering more complex human motives that the latter generalization often
breaks down. Other principles operate at
these "higher" levels.

The principle of dominance should not
be interpreted as meaning that only one
drive can be satisfied through a given

activity. Actually, the typical human
pattern is to attempt to satisfy several
motives through any behavior. A job, for
example, may be related to economic,
social, and even sexual motivation. Dominance refers simply to the fact that, if two
drives are incompatible, the person does
not collapse in a state of helplessness; one
drive dominates until it is satisfied; then
it weakens and the other guides behavior.

3. *Principle of goal perception.* An understanding of motivation is most easily
achieved by emphasizing valence rather
than tension. Only in infancy are we likely
to get behavior determined mainly by inner
tensions. As we mature and learn, our actions are guided by perceived goals. Man
comes to seek one type of food and reject
others. Social facilitation modifies valences
—the goal looks more attractive when
others want it. Parents and other adults
define certain valences as positive and
others as negative. Since these social judgments can be backed up by food, pain, and
other rewards and punishments, most
children learn to accept them.

4. *Principle of secondary reinforcement.*
The organism learns not only to perceive
actual goal objects as positive valences; the
surrounding environment may also come
to have reward value, presumably in
reducing tension. Thus the associated
stimuli also acquire a positive valence (see
Chap. 4) as secondary rewards.

The evaluation of goal objects. Objects
which reduce tension are not all equally
effective as rewards. Preferred foods will
have higher valences than nonpreferred
foods. As soon as the organism learns that
a variety of substances can still his inner
disquiet, a process of evaluation of goal
objects is under way.

The infant, for example, is fed exclusively on milk for some time. Ultimately
he is introduced to solid food. Usually the
first results are distressing. He spits it out,
rejects it as a potential satisfier of hunger

drive. With some coaxing, however, he learns that solids are hunger satisfiers, and soon he may even prefer them to milk (because of their superior qualities in reducing homeostatic disturbances, since they contain many chemicals needed by the organism).

About this time we observe that the child is beginning to study, judge, and choose among objects relevant to a given need. He prefers this, dislikes that. Before long he gives evidence of a "standard of values" and a scale from good to bad, for any particular class of objects.

What is the basis upon which the child develops this scale for judging the value of objects? Several factors appear as determiners. (1) The *homeostatic* value of the object is important. Children with a dietary deficiency will display a stubborn preference for food which to adults seems distasteful or disgusting. (2) But *evaluation by adults* is also highly effective. Parents who like roast beef are likely to transmit the same preference to their children (via imitation, not heredity). Thus, the *cultural norms* affect the child's values. (A Hindu boy learns that cows are sacred, beef inedible.) These cultural standards often become so potent as to overrule the inner homeostatic needs. Then we have the spectacle of people slowly starving in the presence of food. (3) *Unpleasant experiences* may cause a preferred object to lose its status, and pleasant incidents may raise a nonpreferred item. Thus parents who scold and nag at mealtimes may adversely affect, not only the child's present nutrition, but also his preferences and values for food objects.

The development of a scale of values has profound significance for human psychology. Consider: in the field of sex, men come to prefer women of a certain physique, coloring, manner, etc. (usually resembling the man's mother); and women develop similar evaluations of preferred males. Our tastes in food, drink, housing, clothing, and similar items depend upon such value scales. Even more significantly, as will be set forth later, we establish deep unconscious preferences for certain social customs and institutions (such as capitalism, democracy, monogamy). These social values may become the basis for profound cleavages and conflicts, so dynamic that they seem at present to threaten the destruction of our entire civilization.

Substitute gratifications. The principles of secondary reinforcement and of goal perception lead to another principle of great importance in human psychology: the principle of substitute gratification. According to this principle, *the tension aroused by one drive can to some extent be reduced by satisfiers normally related to another drive.*

Tensions for the different biogenic drives are not clearly separated and distinct. Both animals and humans seem to show restless, vigorous behavior to a wide variety of deprivations; and both seem to go through a process of *learning* what is needed to reduce tension. It is probable, therefore, that there is a common tension which is elevated by any biological need.

If this is true, then goal objects which are tension reducing in relation to one need may for a short time be tension reducing as related to another. We referred earlier to the man who, when snubbed by a friend, became very hungry and ate increased quantities of food. In this case food (which is tension reducing for hunger) is being used to satisfy a different tension based on the desire for affection. Rats often show a temporary rise in drinking or copulating when hungry. This seems to be a form of substitute gratification. At the human level such devices for substitute satisfactions become important features of personality.

The mechanism, of course, is the same as for secondary reinforcement; that is, food has been associated with tension reduction; the denial of friendship arouses tension, so

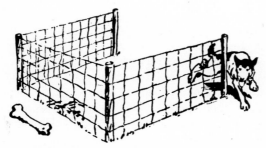

FIG. 2:20. Detour situation. In many circumstances, the person must go away from a goal in order to reach it. Some of the lower animals, such as the chicken, seem unable to do this; they remain close to the food and so cannot reach it. Dogs and higher animals solve the detour problem readily; they can establish the appropriate "set" for dealing with the situation. (*From Natural History, 1947.*)

food is accepted as a substitute goal. Money, power, prestige, and other human goals are often desired for reasons of this kind, *i.e.*, because the person has been deprived of something else.

Control and Direction of Behavior

When a rat runs through a maze for food, or a child solves a puzzle to get candy, it is not necessary for the stomach contractions or other visceral tensions to be constantly pressing the organism toward the goal. What seems to happen is that one develops an orientation, an *intention* to do something, which then persists and controls the specific sequence of acts necessary. This orientation appears to be primarily in the nature of getting "set" to act in a certain way, as the runner gets set for a sprint, or the batter gets set for the pitcher's delivery.

The interpolation of these muscular sets between drive and goal satisfaction is most important. If behavior were directly controlled by the goal object, some problem solutions would become impossible. Suppose we have the detour situation represented in Fig. 2:20, where the animal must go away from the food in order to achieve it. If the reaction were directly to the goal,

the animal would remain glued to the spot nearest the food.

In fact, the organism gets "set" to achieve a certain goal, but this set provides for a certain flexibility. Thus the animal in the detour situation can go away from the food far enough to go around the barrier, but he does not now simply wander off; he is set to turn toward the food as soon as possible.

The persistence of this *intention* to go somewhere and do something is an important aspect of motivated behavior in general. If the underlying drive is powerful (hunger, thirst, sex) the intention may become an *obsession;* the individual is unable to carry on his daily work because of his intense preoccupation with the intended act. The Minnesota studies of semistarvation reported that the men concentrated on thoughts of food and the ritual of eating their scanty fare to such a degree that mental work became impossible.

Motivational set in adult life. In much adult behavior the ultimate "drive" is hard to ascertain. Multiple motivation is very common. When Joe decides that he will go out for the football team, he may be impelled by a desire for prestige, for feminine attention, for money (as a professional, later on—surely not in college!) or to please his father. Regardless of the ultimate motivation, the decision to follow this course of action seems to set up a tension in that direction, and this tension will persist, keeping Joe headed toward his goal despite all the detours he may be required to traverse.

Not all intentions, of course, are carried out. But this is true also of the basic drives, if not essential to life; one may desire sexual gratification, but no drastic harm results from failure to carry out the sex act. But, by the same analogy, intentions will persist to annoy and disturb us until they are executed. The students of Kurt Lewin have performed numerous experiments on the persistence of these task tensions, some of which will be cited in later chapters. In all cases it is found that such task sets will support persistent action, mobilize reserve energy to overcome obstacles, and generally show the characteristics of the drives upon which they are based.

Let us relate the muscular set phenomenon to our basic principle of homeostasis. While sets are products of learning and may be triggered by an external stimulus in the absence of any impelling inner need, they are generally so organized that they will restore or maintain inner balance. Some sets are protective in character. Their function appears to be the *prevention* of disequilibrium. Working, acquiring money, etc., have protective functions; they are not necessarily set off by immediate hunger or pain. On the other hand, some sets persist after the inner need has vanished; many adults show vigorous sexual activity after they have passed the reproductive phase of the life cycle. Males, castrated as adults, cannot have the glandular basis for sex motivation, but they often show persistent striving toward sexual goals just the same. Sets and intentions, therefore, are more flexible than the homeostatic disturbances from which they arise; they make possible anticipation of need, protective action, with the vigor which may be required. They may also determine the occurrence of energetic quests for goal objects, the homeostatic need for which has ceased. In this respect they sometimes motivate abnormal or socially undesirable actions.

Quantitative control. The muscular set is not only specific to a certain goal (food, water) and a given direction to the goal, but is also quantitative. That is, one seems to develop a pretty specific notion of just how much of the goal object he needs to satisfy his inner requirements. An excellent study by Adolph (1941) will clarify this principle. Dogs were operated on in such a manner as to produce an esophageal fistula,

so that food or water ingested would drop out into a container. When such a dog was deprived of water for a definite period of time, he would drink *just the amount needed to restore his water deficit*. This is highly significant because the water was not reaching the stomach; hence the drinking could have been guided only by some inner conception of how much was needed. This seems to have taken the form of a set to continue drinking for a certain length of time. As Fig. 2:18 shows, the actual amount taken in corresponds very closely to the deficit as computed on the basis of normal body needs. The organism thus is provided with some kind of remarkable calculating machine which determines how much is required, and sets the muscular mechanism to take in about that amount, of a goal object.

The feed-back principle. How does the organism direct or control these homeostatic adjustments? How do we know when we have ingested just enough, not too much or too little, of a needed substance? To understand this phase of the dynamics of behavior, psychologists make use of the "feed-back" principle.[1]

Whenever a disturbance of homeostasis occurs, certain sense organs are affected. Nerve impulses travel to the brain and establish patterns there. The brain is sensitized to stimuli indicative of a goal object which will restore equilibrium. When the goal (food, water, etc.) is contacted, muscular mechanisms go into action to take it in. When should they stop? We assume that the infant reacts largely on the basis of cues from the stomach walls. Thus, he may stop sucking too quickly, because the immediate tension has vanished. Later, he may try to ingest too much (anticipation of

[1] While psychologists and physiologists have employed related concepts for many years, the implications of this type of control function would seem just recently to have received a really thorough treatment in Norbert Wiener's (1948) interesting volume on *Cybernetics*.

hunger?) and he will "overflow," a phenomenon experienced parents will immediately recognize. Ultimately, he learns to stop when he has taken in about enough. The control mechanism, therefore, must utilize sensory cues from the muscles involved in sucking, and perhaps from the muscles of the stomach (distention as capacity is reached).

By "feed-back," therefore, we mean the flow of nerve impulses back to the brain reporting the consequences of actions. Feed-back controls are poorly developed in children; they have poor judgment as to probable results of an act. Stomach-aches and other experiences help them to develop better perspective; they can see the situation more clearly and control the goal-seeking activity more wisely.

Sigmund Freud coined the phrase "reality principle" to identify the fact that we learn to accept reality, with its long-range pleasures and punishments, and act accordingly. He contrasted it with the "pleasure principle," the tendency of the infant to grasp immediate pleasure without regard to consequences. Mature adults live by the reality principle; children and infantile adults cling to the pleasure principle, refusing to be guided by consequences. It may well be that some error in the feed-back mechanism is involved in the failure of these adults to foresee the troubles they are storing up for themselves by this behavior. If the consequences were more clearly reported to the brain, if the picture were more accurately perceived by the person, perhaps he could make the shift to reality behavior more adequately.

Complex Homeostatic Functions

We opened this chapter with a discussion of simple homeostasis: the development of a bodily need, disturbance of equilibrium, search for the goal object, and a return to comfortable relaxation. Removal of excess carbon dioxide from the blood stream, control of bodily temperature, correction of water deficit, ingestion of food—all these are simple mechanisms for the restoration of an equilibrium favorable for organic survival.

Homeostasis cannot, however, be limited in its application to this very simple, automatic kind of reaction. Drives affect not only the blood stream, the glands, the reflex centers of the brain. What happens when an organism seeks food? On the first occasion, pure trial and error, perhaps; but on the second and later instances, memory and anticipation begin to operate. One may recall where food can be located; he may prepare in advance against future hungers. We grow crops, build warehouses, domesticate animals, so that we shall not be hungry later on. We build houses and make clothing to maintain optimum temperatures. Elaborate reservoirs and tunnels are constructed to guarantee plenty of pure water. The excretory needs give rise to sanitary engineering. Sex is the dynamic basis for the institutions of marriage and the family.

Looked at from this point of view, homeostasis becomes a basic principle underlying much of human economic, political, and social behavior. That whole confusing abstraction which we call an economic system is an outgrowth of man's need to maintain optimum conditions for survival and growth. As we go on to consider some of the more complex inner motivating states in human psychology, we shall observe that homeostasis can help us to understand a wide variety of phenomena.

SUMMARY

Biogenic drives arise whenever essential bodily equilibria are disturbed. Energy is mobilized in an effort to restore these conditions which are necessary to life.

Dynamic homeostasis is the process of controlling the environment, developing skills, and otherwise adapting to threats of disequilibrium before they arise. Thus learning, thinking, reasoning, and imagining are tools by which essential equilibria are preserved.

We learn to value the objects and activities which lead to need satisfaction. We become set for goal objects which will meet our biological needs, and for tools by which such goals can be attained.

In the last analysis, all human motivation goes back to these biogenic drives. But, as the child develops, he comes to desire and demand many other satisfactions. If we are to understand human behavior and experience, we must start with biological requirements, but we cannot stop there. Secondary goals and activities leading to goals play an enormous part in the dynamics of human psychology.

Since every child's development takes place within a culture, his desires and goals will be modified by cultural conditions. Some kinds of food are rejected because of taboos. Food is most acceptable if eaten under certain conditions. Sexual gratification is subject to extensive cultural controls. The infant may start with man's "animal nature" in the form of biogenic drives, but within a few months he has become a cultural product and is an example of "human nature."

There are many other dynamic processes of great significance. In the following chapters we shall summarize some more complex aspects of human motivation.

Recommended Readings[1]

CANNON, W. B.: *Wisdom of the Body.* New York: Norton, 1939.

DEMPSEY, E. W.: Homeostasis. In Stevens, S. S. (Ed.), *Handbook of Experimental Psychology.* New York: Wiley, 1951.

MORGAN, C. T., and E. STELLAR: *Physiological Psychology.* (2d ed.) New York: McGraw-Hill, 1950.

MOSS, F. A. (Ed.): *Comparative Psychology.* New York: Prentice-Hall, 1934.

YOUNG, P. T.: *Motivation of Behavior.* New York: Wiley, 1936.

[1] In addition to these books, see p. 547 for volumes by Crafts, Dennis, Garrett, Hartley, and Valentine containing supplementary readings for introductory psychology.

CHAPTER 3

Emotions

The organism shows energetic, effortful behavior in behalf of certain bodily needs. Food, oxygen, water, and other substances must be procured or the individual dies. A deficit of these needed materials, therefore, results in the mobilization of increased energy, and the resultant behavior is said to be *motivated*. Motivated behavior has been shown to have the characteristics of goal direction, intensity, persistence, and variability.

The cases of motivation examined in the preceding chapter were those which related to fairly specific organ systems and to identifiable substances which were to be approached or avoided. We now turn to a consideration of dynamic, energy-mobilizing processes which are much less closely related to specific bodily organs, or to particular needed substances. Biological drives, after all, do not determine a large percentage of man's day-to-day behavior, except indirectly. Much of our activity is directed to goals other than the restoration of specific tissue equilibria.

What are some of these other dynamic factors? We can enumerate several: emotions, such as fear, anger, love, hate, surprise, joy, and the like; personal motives (ambition, prestige, financial gain, power, self-expression, creativity); social values (religion, humanitarianism, esthetic enjoyment, the search for knowledge); and interests in a tremendous variety of specific fields. The present chapter will concentrate on *emotions* as motives. It will summarize systematically what we know about human emotions and their dynamic significance.

Motivating power of emotions. Under the stress of an intense fear, men are capable of feats of strength and endurance they would not even attempt under normal circumstances. Rage mobilizes a great deal of energy for combat against the enemy. Love leads us to prodigies of performance.

Emotions show all the characteristics of motivated behavior. *Goal direction* is clearly present in such phenomena as love, in which the lover seeks to possess a particular person of the opposite sex; but it is just as realistically effective in the case of fear, where the energy is mobilized to escape rather than to approach the goal object. The same is true of hate, and in this case the energy is directed toward the destruction of the other person.

The *intensity* of emotions needs no documentation, at least with regard to the more potent instances such as those just mentioned. There is actually a scale of intensity from those emotions which dominate the entire organism and mobilize every last fraction of energy—as in panic—and shut out every competing idea or impulse, down to very mild states of liking and disliking which have minute motivational value. As in the case of the biogenic drives, emotions vary in intensity in accordance with relevant conditions; part of our task is to examine these determinants of emotional intensity.

Emotional behavior also shows *persistence* and *variability*. Whether we think of specific emotions such as love and fear, or more generalized phenomena such as anxiety, we at once realize that the tension persists and pushes the individual toward action; further, if one act fails to reduce the tension, there will be variation of tactics in a continued effort to attain the goal.

In certain basic respects, therefore, we note the same features in the biological drives and in the emotions. Furthermore, the strong emotions are clearly tied closely to our physiological make-up. The visceral phases of emotional behavior are very important. The pounding heart, the heavy stomach, the flushed face are suggestive of the extensive biological basis of vigorous emotion.

By contrast, we need to note that emotions are *not* set off principally by internal metabolic changes, as was true of the various hungers, thirst, sex, excretory needs, and so forth. Normally, an emotion is set off by some external situation. This fact makes the emotions far more flexible and variable from person to person, as compared with the biological drives, which cannot be deflected too far from their metabolic origins. Emotions differ from time to time in the same person in accordance with the nature of the situation, and they differ from person to person as regards the kind of situations which will cause emotional responses.

Do emotions have survival value? Since emotions are biologically founded, they may be presumed to have survival value in either the individual or the racial sense. Indeed, all dynamic human traits may plausibly be expected to contribute to the continuation of the species, though in our consideration of complex motives we shall find that in some instances they have self-destructive implications as well.

The utility of emotions as features aiding the survival of the human species can readily be demonstrated. Consider the case of fear. An organism which did not anticipate pain and injury, which did not run before the saber-toothed tiger took a bite, would not adapt successfully in primitive conditions. Love—as distinct from the sex drive—has survival value in holding the male and female together—thus giving children better food, more protection, and so forth. Anger, whether directed against objects or people blocking us, serves to mobilize additional strength and endurance to overcome the difficulty. It appears, in fact, that most—not necessarily all—emotion is a part of our behavioral and conscious equipment which functions to aid either the individual or the race in a struggle for survival.

Variability of emotions. In later pages we shall consider the question of emotions in infancy and their development to the adult stage. In analyzing the relation of emotion to drive, however, we wish to bring one point into focus: *emotions are not fixed by heredity in the same way as drives.*

By inheritance we are so constituted that we get hungry at periodic intervals. Thirst, fatigue, excretion, and other biological drives are similarly fixed by heredity. The objects which will seem satisfying, and the timing of satisfaction, may vary with environment, but the occurrence of the drive state does not.

Emotion seems basically different in this respect. Fear is not a necessary part of a child's behavior or experience. Many children reach a fairly advanced age before encountering any situations setting off fear or anger. Love is likely to be manifest toward adults, but this is, in large part, a function of care, feeding, cuddling, and so forth, and is certainly not determined by heredity. If a nurse cares for the child, it is she who is loved and not the biological mother. Thus it appears that emotional states are decidedly more variable and flexible, more subject to environmental determination, than the drives.

Is emotion an outgrowth of drive? Many psychologists are now inclined to doubt that emotion should be considered a primary category of human behavior at all. While emotions are dynamic, they have this quality in common with other energy-mobilizing patterns. While they are related to objects, this is true of many nonemotional reactions. Even the qualities of pleasantness and unpleasantness are found in many experiences that can hardly be called emotional.

What, then, is an emotion? It seems most accurate to say that emotion is a subordinate category of behavior—that emotions are secondary manifestations of drive. Let us note briefly why this seems true.

1. *Emotion is generally a reaction to either drive frustration or drive satisfaction.* Anger, for example, is characteristically a response to a blocking of some need-satisfying activity. Fear is usually associated with anticipation of frustration or injury. Joy is experienced when one has achieved a major goal. Love is intimately bound up with sex, a focusing of the sex drive on a particular person. The same analysis will cover most of the types of experience commonly designated as emotions.

2. *Emotions are generally serviceable to drive needs.* Suppose, for example, that one is blocked by a physical obstacle from getting food. The hunger drive sets off behavior toward the goal. Anger is aroused by blocking. This mobilizes additional energy, the obstacle is forced aside, and food is obtained. The serviceability of fear is obvious in case of physical pain. In addition, anxiety about future food supplies, future sex objects, and so forth may motivate anticipatory behavior which prevents the future deprivation from materializing.

3. *Emotion has a sign relationship to need satisfaction.* The distinction between pleasant and unpleasant emotions is a distinction between emotions which signal frustration and increasing tension, on the one hand, and those which signal need satisfaction and tension reduction, on the other. When we experience fear, we anticipate physical pain, hunger, or some other threatening situation. Anger is related to similar threats, with the difference that the person is set to deal with the threat by fighting, not by running away. On the other hand, love, joy, and delight are signals of success. Motives have been satisfied, tension is being reduced. The dynamic value of the pleasant emotions can best be understood if we think of them as representing situations which the person tries to keep, or to restore if lost; the unpleasant emotions have a negative goal direction—the person tries to get away from the situation evoking the unpleasant emotion.

Principle of symbolic gratification. We can draw these different ideas about emotion together in this manner. The biogenic drives were set off by needs for physically real objects, and the tension was reduced when this physically real object was attained (eating of food, drinking of water, etc.). *The needs involved in emotional drives are largely symbolic in character; and tension is reduced by establishing contact with the desired symbol.*

Let us see how this principle helps to organize our material.

1. In the case of love, we note that the young child loves adults who provide him with his physical needs. The mother (for example) becomes a symbol of gratification. Her presence is desired as a sign of equilibrium, an assurance that food and other substances will be available.

2. Fear is evoked when the person anticipates loss of needed gratifications, including

symbols such as the loved adult. It seems plausible to argue that the basic disturbance is due to anxiety about physical deprivation when the mother disappears, since she has become a symbol of such protection.

3. Anger is aroused when an obstacle is interposed between the person and his goal. Physical blockage or the behavior of some other person, as in denying permission, can set off rage and attack.

In the case of love, then, equilibrium is restored when the desired person is again contacted. With fear and other negative emotions, equilibrium is achieved by getting *away* from the symbol of danger or blockage.

The term *emotion*, therefore, is simply a term taken over by psychology from popular speech. It refers to a group of actions and experiences based chiefly upon the biological drives and having an anticipatory or symbolic relationship to these drives. In the adult personality, of course, these emotional patterns may get very far indeed from their biological origins.

The Intensity Factor

In the preceding paragraphs we have pointed out the basic principles of goal direction in the emotions. Like the biological drives, every emotional experience has an element of valence, a positive or negative direction with reference to a goal.

The other major aspect of energy mobilization is the intensity factor. People move toward or away from objects; and these actions vary in vigor. Some situations evoke desperate struggle and violence; others produce only a slight increase in tension and effort. Let us now examine some significant features of this intensity variable.

The "all-or-none" principle. In infancy, emotion follows what has been called the "all-or-none" principle. According to this principle, *any emotion which is aroused tends to function at maximum intensity.* There are

no degrees. Thus the baby cries just as loudly for a minor hurt as for a severe pain; becomes just as angry over trivial as over major frustrations of his drives; and, if he "loves" an adult, does so in a full, unreserved manner.

This childish pattern of all-or-none emotional reaction persists for varying lengths of time. With increasing maturity the average human gets away from all-or-none behavior and responds with *degrees of intensity*, from slight to great excitement, in accord with the severity of the frustration or the importance of the goal. "Infantile" personalities are characterized by their adherence to the all-or-none pattern after most of us have progressed to a more differentiated variety of emotional behavior.

Progress away from all-or-none to discriminating emotional response may be a function of two processes: maturation and learning. *Maturation* involves the modification of sense organs, muscles, glands, and nervous system; *learning* suggests an increasing recognition of one situation as less important, less threatening or rewarding, than another. We shall analyze these factors in later pages of this chapter.

Experienced Emotions. Emotion has its aspects in behavior and experience. Consciously, emotion has the features already mentioned—intensity, direction, goal relatedness. Ideas which are embedded in strong emotions have a high level of vividness, duration, and controlling power. A theory or a plan which acquires an emotional coloring will be adhered to longer and prosecuted more vigorously than others lacking this quality. The young man dreaming of his sweetheart, like the miser thinking of his hoarded wealth, has a conscious experience which is intensely vivid.

Focusing. As we observed in the preceding chapter, a strong drive leads to extreme concentration of the organism upon potential goal objects to the exclusion of other stimuli (principle of dominance). This leads

FIG. 3:1. A dramatic study in the expression of emotion. An alert photographer catches the reunion of Mr. and Mrs. Robert Vogeler after Vogeler's release from a prison behind the Iron Curtain. How would you interpret these facial expressions? Do they suggest anything as to the dynamic power of emotion? Relate this picture to the discussion of frustration given in the text. (*Photograph by Y. R. Okamoto from Black Star.*)

to a single-minded pursuit of a needed object and to the inhibition of any possible competing activities, thus ensuring the most efficient possible action toward the necessary goal.

Emotion shows this same characteristic in even more spectacular form. When we say that love is blind, we refer to the lover's inability to "see" his duties and obligations—as well as his sweetheart's imperfections. A man obsessed by hatred may concentrate so intensely that he fails to observe approaching danger, and destroys himself. A child frightened by a dog ignores his toys and runs for safety. Focusing, then, is a process of *narrowing the field* of behavior and experience. Only the emotional stimulus is clearly recognized; only thoughts and behavior relating to this emotion can continue.

The "free-association" experiment. Psychologists have, of course, known for a long time that a person experiencing a strong emotion will continue to think of the goal and means to achieve it. The psychoanalytic method for diagnosing personality problems relies upon this fact. If a person has an intense and unsatisfied sex drive, he will reveal this by the repetition and intensity of free remarks related to that goal, as the half-starved men in the Minnesota experiment constantly talked of food.

Carl Jung, a well-known analyst, standardized this technique by preparing a set list of stimulus words for presentation to his patients. He found that the characteristic emotional problem of each person was revealed by the kind of answers he gave to these stimulus words, as also by the *length of time* required to respond, stammering, blocking (no response), changes of facial expression, and other cues easily observed by the psychologist. Thus one of his patients who was deeply depressed and considering suicide by drowning gave clear evidence of this in her reactions to words such as lake, death, water, and swim.

An experimental method for demonstrating this involves the use of hypnosis. M. H. Erickson[1] hypnotized subjects and told them they had committed some act for which they would normally feel guilt. Thus one man was told that he had carelessly burned with his cigarette an expensive brown silk dress worn by a poor girl who had bought it in the hope that it would help her get a job for which she was to be interviewed. In the free-association test later, he showed emotionally toned responses to stimulus words taken from the story. These were compared with his responses prior to hypnosis: *e.g.*, to the word "brown" before hypnosis he associated "eyes" and "color"; after this story was implanted, his responses to "brown" were "silk" and "burn." Such experiments show that, if we can induce a strong emotion, the person's ideas become focused around it. Conversely, in clinical work, when free association reveals a focusing of thoughts on some goal, we infer that some intense emotion is present.

Other thoughts and activities are sidetracked by emotion. The person may seem disorganized, confused. His thinking becomes less rational; his skilled acts may become inefficient. From such observations many psychologists have drawn the conclusion that emotion should be described as a disturbed state and even have suggested that the criterion of an emotional response is disruption of competing activity. It is obvious, however, as we have set forth the parallels here, that emotion is by no means the only dynamic phenomenon which disrupts other activities in progress, since

[1] See Huston, Shakow, and Erickson (1934).

strong motives do the same; nor is emotion automatically disturbing. Archibald may be at work at a reasonably interesting project when news comes that he has just been elected to Phi Beta Kappa. His response is one of exuberant joy. The project is forgotten—but one can hardly say that he is disturbed. The outstanding feature of the situation is release of a sudden burst of energy, and basically this is a function of the achievement of a desired goal.

Emotion therefore shares with other dynamic states the quality of sidetracking other activities in progress, but emotions are not necessarily disruptive nor can they be characterized in all cases as disturbing. In some cases it would seem more accurate to speak of the emotion as facilitating or reinforcing an activity in progress. Here is a quotation from a letter written by a middle-aged woman schoolteacher, a former student of one of the authors:

In South Dakota, by my own folly, I angered a large hog insufficiently fenced, and he and seven others took after me. I had about ten feet start and probably beat all sprinting records to date for about an eighth of a mile over uneven ground, coming to rest on the top of a seven-bar gate *without mentionable fatigue*. I had some mechanical difficulties getting down after the hogs left. So the bodily changes brought about by fear are practical.

In speaking of a focusing effect, thus, we identify two aspects of the emotion: (1) a tendency to narrow the field in such a way that other stimuli simply are not observed; and (2) a reinforcement of behavior harmonizing with the direction of the emotion, but disruption of behavior directed toward a goal in a contrary direction.

Emotional control. Can the individual develop techniques for handling this disruptive effect when it appears? Psychology does not offer any simple formula, but several suggestions can be made.

1. More complete knowledge of the stimulus helps to reduce the intensity of the emotion and consequent disturbance of unrelated but important activities. Thus a child who fears electrical appliances (perhaps because of a shock) is helped by learning more about electricity—points of danger, safety devices, etc. The soldier needs to know weapon characteristics, his chances of survival, and other relevant facts. The *unknown* stimulus may evoke almost any emotion in a more intense form than clearly defined factors. It appears, for example, that even the atomic bomb now produces less panicky fear than when its existence was first known.

2. Automatized habits are less disrupted than novel patterns requiring attention. Hence soldiers are given much repetitive drill in habits which may save their lives under fear-inducing conditions.

3. Physical work reduces tension, apparently draining off some of the excess energy mobilized by the emotion; perhaps merely replacing the emotional drive by fatigue and the need for rest. Fear, anger, and love alike may call for this technique in some instances.

Physical Aspects of Intensity

The intensity of emotions can also be studied by examining the visceral responses which are a part of the emotion. It has long been known that emotion was associated with flushing, paling, pounding of the heart, and so on; indeed, the ancient theory that the heart was "the seat of the emotions" derived from such observations. We also know, today, of changes in blood pressure, skin electrical conductance, intestinal contractions, glandular secretions, and blood chemistry. Love, fear, anger, hate, disgust, and similar states arouse such changes, and numerous researches have found that the intensity of such bodily changes agrees very well with the felt intensity as reported by the subject.

The previous chapter has indicated that we can increase our comprehension of the various biological drives by relating them to their respective physiological structures. Hunger is related to stomach contractions, thirst to dryness of mucous membranes, and so on. It is not, of course, true that we have "explained" hunger by relating it to stomach cramps, but we have described it on a different level and so perhaps made the function easier to understand.

The same logic applies to the emotions. While we cannot relate specific emotional demands to specific tissues, we can sketch the general mechanism involved and show how this structural basis determines some of our emotional characteristics.

Energy-release mechanisms. The emotions, particularly those driving states called fear, anger, love, and hate, mobilize organic energy for vigorous action, in the same manner as drives. (1) *Tension* is a feature of all strong emotions, and much of this is muscular in character. During these emotional experiences we may tremble, shake, clench fists, grind our teeth; visceral musculature reacts to produce raised blood pressure, pressure on bladder and colon, etc. Tension makes for more vigorous response to any stimulus; it may also have the effect of increasing our sensitivity to stimulation. (2) Glandular changes, in particular the secretion of adrenin, raise the energy level. Adrenin stimulates the liver to release glycogen into the blood stream; this is then available for muscle tissues needing fuel. Fatigue products are neutralized more rapidly under the influence of adrenin.

The homeostatic value of these changes should be obvious. If fear (for example) is a reaction to danger, the increased energy available and the heightened activity level improve one's chances for successful escape. If anger is the organism's way of responding to blockage of some drive, the higher energy level and vigor of action increase the likelihood of breaking down the obstacle and achieving the basic goal.

Neural basis of emotion. Not much is known about nervous mechanisms in relationship to drives such as hunger and thirst. As we have already pointed out, much of the control for these states seems to be chemical in nature. The emotions, on the other hand, are pretty definitely tied to the autonomic nervous system and the thalamic area of the central nervous system. (The biological drives are also involved with these structures to some extent.)

Figure 3:2 illustrates the relationship between the central nervous system (CNS) and the autonomic nervous system (ANS). The CNS, comprising the brain and spinal cord, is concerned with the behavior of the organism in relationship to the external world, to what we have called dynamic homeostasis—the complex activities which satisfy bodily needs and protect against future deprivations. The ANS is in a sense dominant over the CNS in that autonomic activities may impel and coerce central nervous action. Thus the reaction of pain, fear, or rage starts as an ANS pattern, set off by a driving external stimulus. These nerve patterns are able to (and do) dominate whatever patterns are active in the CNS at the moment (focusing). The musculature and skilled habit patterns are then at the service of the ANS to remove the organism from the threatening object, or to destroy the object.

The ANS is divided into two systems, known as the *sympathetic* and the *parasympathetic*. The sympathetic (inappropriately named) is concerned with such emotional responses as fear and rage. The parasympathetic system is concerned with vegetative activities, such as hunger and sex. The sympathetic is composed of nerve ganglia in the chest and abdomen, outside the spinal cord, known as the *thoracic* and *lumbar* segments of the autonomic system (Fig. 3:2). The parasympathetic includes some nerve nuclei physically within the brain (the cranial system) and some in the pelvic girdle (the sacral system).

With few exceptions, the sympathetic and parasympathetic systems function antagonistically. The sympathetic speeds up the heart, the parasympathetic slows it down. The sympathetic interferes with digestion, the parasympathetic accelerates digestion. The sympathetic raises blood pressure, while the parasympathetic lowers it. The adrenal glands, however, are stimulated only by the sympathetic, there being no antagonistic innervation from the parasympathetic; and in at least one type of response, that of sexual orgasm, there seems to be a simultaneous kind of overflow of nervous activity involving both the sympathetic and parasympathetic systems. Generally speaking, however, it is easy to keep in mind the functions of these two parts of the autonomic by remembering that the sympathetic controls the *emergency* pattern and the parasympathetic the *vegetative*, peaceful type of behavior.

Methods of study. The study of visceral changes in emotion is complex and highly technical, although we find ingenious devices even among primitive peoples. The "rice test" of a criminal (India) involved the requirement that the accused hold grains of rice in his mouth while being questioned. If they were dry when removed (inhibition of salivary secretion), he was presumed guilty.

Questionnaires and interviews have been used to study visceral changes felt by men under acute stress. Table 3:1 shows the frequency with which certain bodily changes were reported by airmen in combat. Novelists and other sensitive persons have given graphic introspective descriptions of these inner responses.

The use of appropriate instruments permits us to observe and record these visceral changes in emotions of less intensity. The *sphygmomanometer* is employed to determine changes in blood pressure and pulse pressure. The *psychogalvanometer* records minute changes in electrical resistance in the skin, related to sweat gland activity.

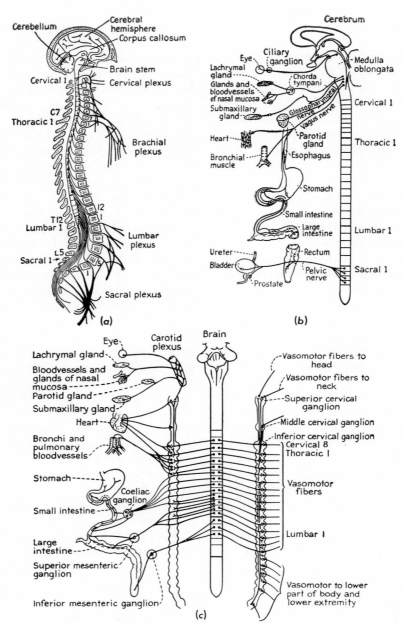

FIG. 3:2. The central and autonomic nervous systems. (a) Schematic layout of central nervous system: the brain, including cerebrum, cerebellum, and other coordinating centers; and the spinal cord, which relays impulses to and from the brain. The cervical, brachial, lumbar, and sacral plexuses shown are mostly autonomic in function. The spinal cord proper ends at the level of the second lumbar vertebra. (b) Schematic layout of parasympathetic or craniosacral division of autonomic system. Some of the cranial section actually arises within the brain. Note that the cranial section innervates organs all the way to the colon. (c) Schematic layout of the sympathetic or thoracolumbar division of the autonomic nervous system. Note that virtually every visceral organ has connections from both sympathetic and parasympathetic. See text for antagonistic functioning of the two divisions of ANS. (a, from Gardner, 1947, by permission of W. B. Saunders Co.; b and c, from Larsell, 1942, by permission of Appleton-Century-Crofts, Inc.)

TABLE 3:1. Signs of Fear during Aerial Combat (*From Shaffer, 1947*)

During combat did you feel	*Percentage reported "often" or "sometimes"*
A pounding heart and rapid pulse...	86
Feeling that your muscles are very tense...	83
Being easily irritated, angry, or "sore"*...	80
Dryness of the throat or mouth....	80
"Nervous perspiration" or "cold sweat"...	79
"Butterflies" in the stomach...	76
Feeling of unreality, that this couldn't be happening to you...	69
Having to urinate (pass water) very frequently...	65
Trembling...	64
Feeling confused or "rattled"...	53
Feeling weak or faint...	41
Right after a mission, not being able to remember details of what happened...	39
Feeling sick to the stomach...	38
Not being able to concentrate...	35
Wetting or soiling your pants...	5

* Since the visceral reactions in anger and fear are very similar, and since both are frustrating situations, alternation between the two is relatively easy.

The *thermocouple* verifies the common observation that we grow "hot" or "cold" in emotional states, with changes in skin temperature. Through these instrumental methods, psychologists have learned that some visceral changes seem to be associated with even relatively mild emotions, such as enjoyment of music, or listening to words which suggest fear or anger. It is this phenomenon which underlies the use of the "lie detector."

The "lie detector" is, of course, an "emotion detector" in function. Most of us have been so firmly trained to answer questions truthfully that we experience a little twinge of guilt, perhaps fear of punishment carried over from childhood, even when lying as part of an experiment. Skilled users of the machine—which records blood pressure, heart rate, breathing, and electrical conductance of the skin—can detect even a little falsehood such as "I did not look at that card."

In criminological use, of course, far more emotion is involved. A person guilty of a crime will tend to react emotionally to all stimuli associated with his act; to the innocent these stimuli may have no emotional meaning; hence no visceral reactions occur. Thus the technique has been especially useful in situations where *only* the guilty person has certain information. It is reported, for example, that the device is very valuable in embezzlement cases. A bank teller may "borrow" $17,300 in the process of gambling on the horses. He keeps careful records, hoping to win and restore the money before discovery. On a lie-detector test of the various tellers, only one knows the significance of the figure "17,300"; his viscera give away his secret and he usually confesses. Needless to say, this technique is not infallible and its results should always be checked against other evidence.

Clinical studies. The extensive changes in bodily functions which go along with strong emotions have attracted attention in medical circles. We shall have more to say in later chapters about *psychosomatic illness*, in which psychological states are actually significant antecedents of physical disorder. At this point we wish only to note the type of observation which confirms, in the real-life situation, our laboratory studies of strong emotion.

One aspect of anger is innervation of the sympathetic nervous system and a consequent increase in blood pressure and heart rate. Different areas of the body surface seem to behave differently under these conditions; some show relaxation of blood vessels, with flushing; others show constriction of blood vessels, with loss of color. In an interesting study of the nose, it has been shown (Holmes *et al.*, 1950) that the mucous membranes become flushed, swol-

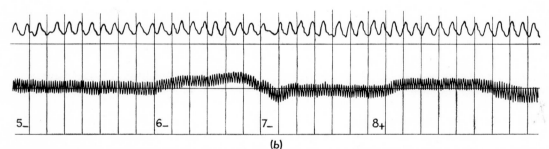

(a)

(b)

FIG. 3:3. Emotional responses used for lie detection. (a) A prison guard suspected of complicity in the Touhy prison break is questioned with the lie-detector apparatus. (b) A record obtained by a typical lie-detector setup. Respiration, pulse, and blood pressure are regularly employed; some experts like also to record the GSR. The value of the record is in identifying strong emotional responses to significant questions, as compared with irrelevant questions (the truth or falsity of the answer being immaterial). In the above chart, the questions asked at 5 and 7 were trivial; questions at 6 and 8 pertained to the killing of the subject's family by setting off a charge of dynamite in the basement of his home. Observe the marked rise in blood pressure after both 6 and 8. (This man later confessed his guilt.) (a, *Chicago Daily News* photograph; b, from Inbau, 1942.)

len, and covered with secretion in persisting anger. One subject studied was a young man, an M.D., who was observed systematically for months. Figure 3:4 shows his response to a situation involving frustration, irritation, and an emotional explosion. His wife had just been delivered of her first baby about 10 days prior to this record. The mother-in-law came to stay with the couple; she was quite domineering, ignored the wishes of the young husband, rejected his advice on medical care for the infant, and thus aroused in him considerable anger. He suppressed this until Aug. 20, when he "blew up" and told her what he thought of her actions. Fortunately, she accepted his reaction without too much hostility and changed her behavior to cause him less frustration. Improvement in the nasal condition followed promptly.

Fear can also cause an exaggerated reaction of the visceral tissues. The following interesting report of an investigator who studied himself will illustrate the point. Hoelzel (1942) has described an unusual experience where the intensity of the emotion can hardly be doubted. It should first be noted that he had been studying his own gastric-acidity variations for years; "the morning gastric aspiration was as regular as washing the hands or face."

On 24th January 1928 there was an attempted robbery at his house in Chicago (emphasis must be placed on the locality) and his landlady was shot dead. Hoelzel was responsible for the arrest of the culprits, and for the succeeding ten days he was in a state of acute anxiety lest he might be shot by the revengeful accomplices of the gangsters. Normally his fasting morning free gastric acidity was between 0 and 0.13 percent of hydrochloric acid; on the morning of the shooting episode it was 0.26 percent, and it remained above 0.17 percent during the period of anxiety. He then moved to what he believed was a safe place and his free gastric acidity fell to within the normal range.[1]

[1] Harris (1948), pp. 24–25. Reprinted by permission of Butterworth & Co., Ltd., and Paul B. Hoeber, Inc.

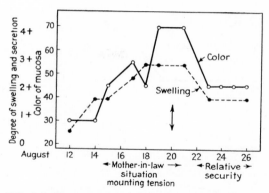

FIG. 3:4. Changes in nasal mucosa under strong resentment. The subject, a young physician, was studied for months as to changes in color of nasal membranes, swelling, secretion, etc. Shortly after Aug. 1 his wife had given birth to her first baby, and the wife's mother had come to help during the first few weeks. The mother-in-law was very officious, rejected the young man's advice even on medical matters, and attempted to dominate both husband and wife. Matters reached a climax on Aug. 20 with his anger becoming acute; on Aug. 21 he exploded and poured out his annoyance; fortunately, the mother-in-law accepted the situation, stopped some of her dominative practices, and restored peace. The swelling and redness of the nasal mucosa parallel these events closely. (*From Holmes et al., 1950.*)

Other emotions give differing results, however; depression seems to have the effect chiefly of interfering with the normal flow of acid as well as with the normal circulatory changes (indicated by change in color of the mucous membranes of the stomach). Figure 3:5 shows the reduction in acidity and in color change in a patient first normal, then depressed (Wolf and Wolff, 1943).

Autonomic and cortical nervous function. We have emphasized the role of the ANS in relation to both biogenic drives and emotions. This is necessary because the energy mobilization and preparation of the body for vigorous actions depend on autonomic mechanisms.

We do not, however, ignore the importance of higher nervous centers in these conditions. Static homeostasis can be mediated through subcortical nerve nuclei,

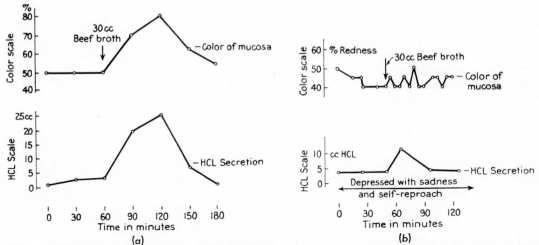

FIG. 3:5. Effect of depression on gastric reactions. (a) Normal reaction of subject to beef broth. Acid secretion and color of stomach membranes change markedly (this subject had a stomach perforation which made possible direct observation of color changes). (b) Reaction to beef broth when undergoing strong feelings of depression. Note the marked decrease in reactivity. (*From Wolf and Wolff, 1943.*)

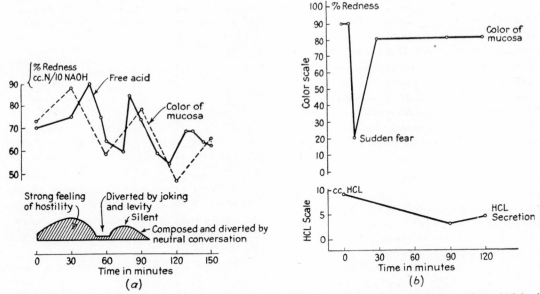

FIG. 3:6. Effects of anger and of fear on gastric mucosa. (a) The patient was angry about an incident which had occurred, and the doctor behaved in such a way as to increase his hostility. Then the conversation was switched to humorous discussion of unrelated topics; note the drop in gastric acidity and in redness of the mucous membranes. There followed a period of silence during which (as was later ascertained) the patient again began brooding over the wrong he felt had been done him. (b) The patient (who was also an employee) was made very anxious and afraid by a doctor on the staff. The patient feared he had mislaid a document for which the doctor was angrily searching. Note paling of membranes, drop in acid secretion. (*From Wolf and Wolff, 1943.*)

but dynamic homeostasis—in man, at least—requires the function of learning, which depends on the cortex of the cerebrum.

How does one know when to be afraid, or angry? He must recognize the situation as a threat. How does one deal with situations evoking such emotions? Usually he relies upon memory and thinking. Thus the higher nerve centers play an important role in determining *when*, and *how intensely*, we become emotional, as well as how we direct the emotional energy toward our goal.

Determinants of Emotional Intensity

Emotions have the quality of drives in that they are imperative, demanding; but they call for *certain kinds* of satisfaction. Love calls for a *particular person* of the opposite sex (as opposed to the sex urge per se, which is indiscriminate as to individuals desired). Anger calls for an attack on a specific individual, group, or object; fear demands escape from the stimulus. Enthusiasms, annoyances, and aversions follow similar patterns. The organism is pressed by the emotion into vigorous action toward a goal. Thus we treat emotion as being a form of motivation differing from the biogenic drives in that it focuses more specifically upon some identified object. Generally speaking, the emotion brings additional intensity and vigor to a motive pattern which had a biological origin.

There are, however, other differences which are even more important. We noted in the preceding chapter that biogenic drives grow stronger with deprivation and weaker with satiation. How do these principles apply to emotions?

Deprivation. In attempting to assess the role of deprivation we must be careful not to become confused. Deprivation of physically needed material strengthens the organic drive. If the deprivation seems due

to a barrier, anger may mobilize additional energy to break down the barrier. This, however, is deprivation related to a biogenic drive, not to the emotion.

Similarly, a soldier who is in love with a woman in his own country may be sent overseas. His sexual deprivation tends to intensify his sex drive, but not necessarily his love. Indeed, he may begin to see local women as possible sex objects and "fall in love" with one of them, thus weakening or eliminating the prior love. The significant deprivation here is related to sex, not love.

The periodic deprivation of food may strengthen the hunger drive (person eats more when food is available), but it also initiates the emotion of fear. Because we remember past famines, we feel anxious about our future food supply. The more often we are hungry, the more acute this fear will be. Again, we note that it is deprivation of a bodily need which intensifies the emotion.

The evidence goes *completely contrary* to the idea that *deprivation* of any occasion to feel angry or afraid will strengthen such emotions. Quite the opposite holds: if John is rarely angered, he will be likely to react with less intensity when a frustration arises. The same holds for fear.

The case as regards love is a little more confused, for this reason: love reflects the care, caressing, helpfulness, and comfort given the child by an adult. Having once learned this emotion, deprivation of a chance to love someone may intensify it. Children rejected early in life, however, often show no need to love others (although some show a strong need to *be loved*).

To summarize, then: deprivation of basic needs may intensify emotions. Anger is proportional to the intensity of the frustrated drive. Fear is intensified by the frequency and severity of biological deprivations. Love is intensified by deprivation of sexual satisfaction, care, caressing, and

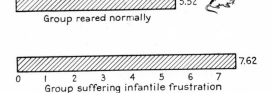

5.52

Group reared normally

7.62

0   1   2   3   4   5   6   7

Group suffering infantile frustration

FIG. 3:7. Effect of infantile frustration upon adult fear reactions in mice. Subjection to painful auditory stimulation over an extended period of time in infancy increases the number of fear responses shown at maturity. (*Data from Hall and Whiteman, 1951.*)

the like, once these have been associated with a specific person.

Infantile deprivation. The same generalizations hold for deprivation during early childhood. What matters is the occurrence of frustration or deprivation of some physical need; and such painful experiences *do* have a significant relation to adult emotional responses. Hall and Whiteman (1951) subjected mice to an unpleasant auditory stimulation with a very loud, piercing sound (the assumption of discomfort or pain seems quite safe). This experience was imposed repeatedly during the first week of life. At maturity, this group and a control group were tested on a standard situation for measuring emotional behavior, and it was found that there was a wide difference between the two groups (see Fig. 3:7). The experimental group showed much more fear behavior than their litter mate controls, and they persisted in fear behavior, whereas the control group rapidly lost their timidity in the test situation.

The view that infantile frustrations and anxieties, loves and hatreds, determine the adult personality has been presented by Sigmund Freud and backed by a tremendous mass of clinical data. He has been able to show relationships between adult loves and infantile loves, adult hostility and infantile anger. The study of phobias and other personality manifestations by clinical methods tends to confirm the theory that adult emotions are in no small degree a product of these infantile experiences.

As in the case of the biological drives, this phenomenon seems to be simply a matter of becoming selectively sensitive to a certain goal object (or class of objects). The rat deprived of food may develop a kind of anticipation of severe hunger and so will value food pellets highly, hoard them, and so on. Hall's mice developed an "expectancy of danger"; all stimuli seemed more threatening to them than to their controls. The human child may develop an anticipation of insecurity, of loss of affection and protection by adults; he may thus value affection highly (and may demand it so aggressively as to scare off potential friends). Children often frightened in early life grow up to be timid and fearful, even if they have no specific phobias. There is a *sensitivity* to objects which threaten injury or loss.

Satiation. All emotions are relatively insatiable. The principle of satiation applies well to biological gratifications, but not to the symbolic goals of the emotions. Thus sex drive can be satiated and disappear, but since love is merely a demand for the presence of the loved one, it does not weaken correspondingly. Similarly, fear is a demand to get away from the danger; if one gets away and then the threat reappears, fear is at once full-blown —indeed, perhaps stronger than before. Anger and fear do weaken with physical exhaustion, but this is not satiation.

As a prominent merchant recently said, "There are goods enough to satisfy our needs, but there can never be goods enough to satisfy our fears." Fear is not weakened with attainment of a goal; if the future still *looks* threatening, fear persists in full strength.

If the basic drive is satiated, some weakening of the emotion follows, but not so much. Sexual satiation *may* reduce slightly the intensity of love, but this is not always true. If anger was evoked in breaking down a barrier to a goal, achievement of the goal weakens the anger. It is, however, easily reinstated if another goal is blocked.

This is the key to an understanding of emotional intensity. The emotions are in service to the basic drives. Hence they are always, in a sense, ready to "go off" when needed. They are *reactions to symbols*, not to real goals—*i.e.*, the threat of hunger, not real food; the threat of pain, not physical pain; the promise of sexual pleasure, not the pleasure itself, and so on. Our demands for symbols are unlimited. Tom's food capacity is limited, but his demand for money (perceived as a source of food) is not. Symbols of need satisfaction can never be too abundant; hence satiation practically does not weaken the emotions.

Habit. The factor which most directly affects emotional intensity is habit. Persons often afraid become more and more afraid; those often angered become more and more angry. This is also true of love. The boy who loved his mother (and perhaps his schoolteacher) can love his sweetheart more deeply than one who felt little love for anyone but himself.

Basic personality patterns are determined by the intensity of emotions and the symbols to which they become attached. The timid, fearful, anxious person has, as a result of his infancy and childhood, developed potent fear reactions. The irascible, explosive man has strong anger patterns. The affectionate individual loves readily and deeply, and so on. Because these habits are so crucial to an understanding of personality, we shall revert to them after our examination of the learning process.

Heredity and Environment

One of the crucial problems facing the psychologist with respect to any pattern of behavior or experience is the role of heredity. To what extent is this particular function determined by "human nature" in the sense of characteristics universal in the race? To what extent is it a product of environment, training, culture?

Studies of emotional behavior have been especially prolific in producing controversies, if not understanding, in this area. We have not only the perennial argument over the inheritance of an instinct of pugnacity, which so often enters into discussions of war, industrial conflict, race prejudice, and such phenomena; but also we find much concern over the inheritance of fears, loves, disgusts, aversions, and the like.

As in so many instances, we shall find that the best answer is not: heredity *or* environment; but rather, an interaction of heredity *and* environment. Let us first consider some of the ways in which the question can be approached.

Inheritance of structures. The visceral expression of emotions depends upon the ANS and the endocrine glands. We shall therefore make substantial progress if we can show that these basic structures are inherited by animals and that such structures are paralleled by variations in the emotional behavior.

Such data have actually been accumulated over thousands of years for certain types of animals. We refer, of course, to the selective breeding of domestic animals such as the horse, cow, and dog. As Stockard (1941) has convincingly shown, different breeds of dogs have temperamental patterns, body build, and endocrine structures which go together. These physical and emotional characteristics are inherited together; they show that heredity is at least one major determinant of the intensity and frequency of energy mobilization in response to emotion-arousing stimuli.

Pavlov's studies of dogs. The famous Russian physiologist, Ivan Pavlov, noted

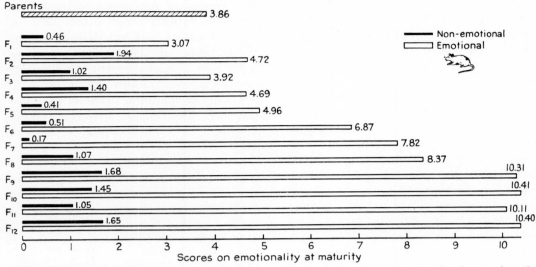

FIG. 3:8. Inheritance of emotionality in rats. Only very emotional males and females were bred to produce the emotional strain, and only those low in number of emotional responses were bred for the other strain. (*Data from Hall, 1941.*)

that his dogs responded differently according to their inherent body build. Some were highly excitable, while others could best be described as inhibited or phlegmatic. Under stress situations which created an "experimental neurosis" (see Chap. 14) these dogs behaved differently; the tall, thin, narrow-chested dogs tended toward uncontrollable excitement, while the stocky, short-legged animals became sleepy or stuporous. (These were simply exaggerations of their normal emotional patterns.)

Hall's work on rats. Perhaps more convincing, because carried out with laboratory controls, is Calvin Hall's study of selective breeding in rats. Hall applied simple tests of fearfulness to white rats in his laboratory; for example, he placed the rat in a brightly lighted, circular open field and found that timid rats showed intense fear by defecation and urination. Repeating this test several times, he was able to select rats (male and female) which were consistently timid, and those consistently bold. By breeding only timid rats he created a strain of animals far more timid than the original parents; and by similar breeding of "bold" animals he obtained a strain notably less fearful than his starting group (see Fig. 3:8).

Yeakel and Rhoades (1941) have done intensive anatomical studies of Hall's timid strain. They found a significant difference in size of endocrines; the adrenals, pituitaries, and thyroid glands were decidedly larger than for normal controls.

Inbreeding studies of humans are not feasible. It is clear, however, that some people inherit types of endocrine glands, autonomic nervous system, and other reactive structures which are excessively disturbed by emotional stimuli. Generally these individuals show parallel emotional patterns of behavior. On the conscious level they also report parallel intensity of experiences. When we speak of *temperament*, we are referring to the emotional aspect of personality. It seems certain from the animal studies and from clinical work on humans that such temperamental features as timidity, aggressiveness, excessive activity, and excitability are substantially determined by heredity.[1]

Inheritance of specific emotions. It is easy to get general agreement among psychologists as to the hereditary determination of structures underlying emotion. The facts are clear: some organisms (human and nonhuman) inherit structures which react more often, more vigorously, and for a longer time to emotion-arousing stimuli than do their fellows.

It is much more difficult to get any substantial consensus as to what stimuli innately determine fear, anger, etc. This is the point at which the theories of specific innate emotions encounter difficulties. Darwin, for example, proposed the theory that we inherit tendencies to respond with fairly specific emotions to situations common in primitive life—*i.e.*, that these emotions are now part of human heredity because of their survival value. Unfortunately, human beings seem to be so flexible, as regards what stimuli will set off fear, rage, and other emotional states, that any conception of the inheritance of specific emotions is difficult to accept. Let us consider some of the research studies bearing on this problem.

Emotional behavior in infancy. The basic difficulty in the study of emotion in newborn children (the obvious way to approach the problem of inheritance) derives from our tendency to read adult patterns and significance into the child's activities. Thus Watson found that babies usually react violently to being dropped 20 to 30 inches through the air, even though caught on a pillow. Reasoning by knowledge of adult experience, he concluded that the child felt "fear" in this situation. Actually, of course, we shall never know just what the newborn child really experiences, nor for that matter shall we ever know what another adult experiences in falling. It is

[1] The psychology of temperament and personality is treated extensively in Chap. 13.

simply not in the nature of human experience that it should be directly communicated to others.

When we come to the study of responses instead of experiences, we find ourselves on somewhat firmer ground. We can observe, record, and photograph the child's movements, cries, and facial expressions. We can also ascertain by experimentation his blood-pressure changes, heart rate, breathing, and other visceral behavior patterns. Let us examine some of these careful studies of emotional behavior in infants.

Watson's pioneer research. The founder of behaviorism, John B. Watson, did the first and most widely quoted systematic study of infant emotional behavior. Watson (1924) hoped to ascertain just what emotions were inherited and which were acquired through learning. He presented to his subjects, infants in a maternity hospital, many stimuli widely believed to be such as would set off emotions: fire, snakes, strange animals, falling, restraint, and so on. From his observations of the infants' responses, he concluded that *there were only three recognizable emotional patterns*, and that a very limited range of stimuli would elicit each of these.

1. *Fear.* Watson reported that his subjects showed a pattern involving catching of breath, convulsive clutching of the hands, trembling, crying, and puckering of the face. This response he found associated with two stimuli: falling through space and a loud sound. For obvious reasons he concluded that this should be called fear.

2. *Anger.* Another response pattern was described as including screaming, holding the breath, flushing of the face, and uncoordinated slashing of arms and legs. This was set off by holding firmly the child's head, arms, or legs to prevent free movement; hence Watson considered it to be a primitive type of anger.

3. *Love.* Completely different from the two preceding patterns was the response of cooing, gurgling, laughter, mild squirming, and arm

TABLE 3:2. Judgment of Infant Emotions without Knowledge of the Stimulus*
(*Modified from Sherman, 1927*)

Judged emotion	Stimuli calling out reactions				Total
	Delayed feeding	Dropping	Restraint	Prick of needle	
Hunger	7	6	2	2	17
Anger	11	14	13	8	46
Fear	7	5	5	9	26
Pain	3	3	4	2	12
Grief	1	1	0	1	3
Hurt	0	0	0	1	1
Rage	2	1	3	1	7
Discomfort	0	0	1	0	1
Sleepy	0	0	1	0	1
None	0	0	0	1	1
Consternation	1	1	0	0	2
Nausea	0	1	0	0	1
Physical discomfort	0	0	1	0	1
Total†	32	32	30	25	119

* The subjects were graduate students in psychology. They saw motion pictures of the infants' reaction but did not see the film portion indicating the stimulus initiating the reaction.

† Not all observers made judgments to every reaction shown.

movements. As this was in response to stroking the lips, nipples, sex organs, and other sensitive skin areas, he concluded that this was a sexual or "love" response.

Sherman's critical study. Many investigators have attempted to repeat Watson's investigation, and it is now clear that he was much too positive in his conclusions. Valentine (1930) has cast doubt on his study of fear, and Pratt, Nelson, and Sun (1930) report little consistency in the "rage" behavior of their group of infants. Some of the babies simply went to sleep when their movements were blocked. The best single study which reveals the complexity of the problem and also gives some hints as to its solution is that of Sherman (1927).

Sherman applied the Watson stimuli for fear and anger to a series of infants and took motion-picture records of their responses. In addition, responses to pain and hunger were photographed. Pain was produced by needle pricks. Hunger was assumed to be involved when the child began to cry when his feeding was delayed beyond its usual time.

These motion pictures were shown to various groups: nurses in a maternity ward, graduate psychology students, and medical students. In one series, only the response pattern was shown, with no inkling as to the stimulus situation. Under these conditions (Table 3:2) the observers reported all sorts of judgments as to what might be going on. As the figures indicate, sudden dropping ("fear") was more often thought to be anger, as was delayed feeding (hunger). The pinprick response was judged to be fear or anger much oftener than pain.

When the film was shown complete, so that the stimuli were known to the judges, they agreed more closely (Table 3:3). Twenty-seven of thirty-three graduate students in psychology now labeled the response to the dropping situation as fear,

TABLE 3:3. Judgments of Infant Emotions When the Stimulus Is Known*
(*Modified from Sherman, 1927*)

Judged emotion	Stimuli calling out reactions				Total
	Delayed feeding	Dropping	Restraint	Prick of needle	
Fear............................	0	27	4	7	38
Mad............................	0	0	1	0	1
Discontented....................	2	0	1	0	3
Rage...........................	0	0	1	0	1
Pain...........................	2	2	1	13	18
Negative emotion..............	1	1	1	1	4
Hunger........................	7	0	0	0	7
Anger..........................	14	4	24	13	55
Discomfort....................	6	0	0	0	6
Irritation......................	1	0	1	0	2
Excitement....................	0	1	0	0	1
Anger or pain..................	1	0	1	3	5
Disgusted or weary............	1	0	0	0	1
Pain with fear.................	0	1	0	0	1
Anger with fear...............	0	4	1	1	6
Rage...........................	1	1	3	0	5
Surprise.......................	0	1	0	0	1
Resistance to restraint........	0	0	1	0	1
Anxiety.......................	1	0	0	0	1
Hate..........................	0	0	0	1	1
Restiveness....................	1	0	0	0	1
Repulsion......................	0	0	0	1	1
Suffocating....................	0	0	1	0	1
No emotion....................	2	0	0	0	2
Emotion doubtful..............	0	1	1	1	3
Total†....................	40	43	42	41	166

* Judges were graduate students, as in Table 3:2, but this group was allowed to see the complete incident and the infants' response.

† Not all observers made judgments to every reaction shown.

whereas only five so designated this response when they were ignorant of its cause. Twenty-four out of twenty-nine called the reaction to restraint, anger, when the restraint was actually shown in the picture.

The complete confusion of pain, hunger, fear, and rage in these and similar experiments suggests two important conclusions: (1) *all four of these stimulus situations release a single, relatively uniform response pattern*, not four distinct patterns; and (2) *the differences observed by adults in the child's behavior are often due to the knowledge of the situation* and to the unconscious judgment, "If I were in that situation, this is the emotion I would have."

Infant emotions and homeostasis. It will be noted that, in the investigations reported, the judges confused such hypothetical emotional states as anger and fear and the somewhat similar conditions of hunger and pain. In other words, the confusion existed among states which were primarily unpleasant in character. No investigators report any confusion of pleasant states, such as Watson's "love" pattern, with these unpleasant conditions.

From this kind of basis Bridges (1932) has inferred that we can identify two fundamental emotional patterns appearing in the very earliest stages of the child's development: delight and distress. Whether it is worth while to present two new terms for these conditions or whether we should simply call them *pleasant* and *unpleasant* patterns is not a matter of great importance. At least, it is clear that in a broad sense we have two fundamental patterns of emotional reactivity inherited. These are the responses to pleasant types of stimulation and those to stimuli which are unpleasant.

If, now, we relate these back to our consideration of biological drives and homeostatic activities of the organism, as set forth in the preceding chapter, we see that the reactions to unpleasant stimuli all have in common the feature of disturbance of equilibrium, or a threat of injury to the organism. Thus hunger obviously reflects a failure of homeostatic processes. Pain reflects a direct threat to the integrity of the organism. Anger may be considered to be a frustration of tendencies toward normal goal-seeking activity, at least, in the situation devised by Watson; and fear may be thought of as a response to sudden and startling stimulation which certainly would disturb an existing equilibrium. That children differ so widely among themselves with regard to these last two patterns would suggest, either that some individuals inherit a tendency to respond to these stimuli and others do not, or that some individuals learn at a surprisingly rapid rate during the early period of life. We are not in a position to draw any inferences at the present time as to which of these is correct.

Conversely, it seems clear that the stimulus situations which give rise to Watson's "love" behavior, *i.e.*, cooing, relaxation, and smooth visceral functioning, are situations in which homeostasis is being restored. The crying child is appeased by food, but he may also be quieted by soft noises and caressing, as in the Watson study. It may be suggested, therefore, that the two broad groups of emotional responses now identified are simply patterns related to the disturbance of or restoration of physiological equilibrium.

Maturation and learning. We are, of course, justified in assuming that *there must be some fundamental similarity* between the behavior and experiences of the child and those of the adult. It is not, however, necessarily legitimate to assume that there must be *exactly* the same recognizable patterns in the earlier as in the later stages. Many influences may bring about an increasing complexity of emotional responses as the child grows older. One of these is *maturation*. The muscles, nerves, and glandular structures mature and may bring about possibilities of response patterns which were not present in the earlier stages. An obvious illustration of this would be sex, which is present in a limited form in the earlier stages of childhood but which reaches its adult characteristic only at puberty.

A second factor which is clearly involved in the increasing complexity and differentiation of the adult emotional pattern is that of *learning*. In later pages we shall consider some of the classical experiments on learning of emotional responses and show how these contribute to an understanding of the wide variety of emotional behavior patterns in adult life as compared with the marked simplicity and uniformity of infants.

Some studies of specific emotional responses. We can clarify the issues in this problem of maturation vs. learning by considering some studies of the modification of specific emotional behavior over a period of time. These studies are in many cases not conclusive as to the effects of these two factors, but they will help

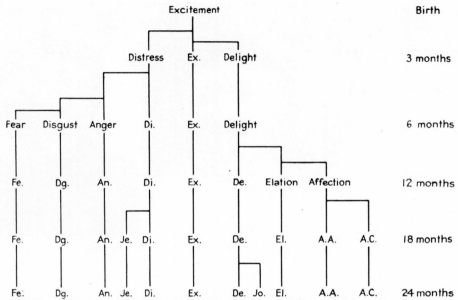

FIG. 3:9. Scheme for the differentiation of emotions in early childhood. According to Bridges, only excitement is discernible in the first week or two. Soon distress, and by three months, delight are observed. Further differentiation goes on with increasing maturity and experience. (A.A., affection for adults; A.C., affection for children; Je., jealousy; Jo., joy.) (*From Bridges, 1932.*)

the student grasp some of the problems involved.

1. *Bridges's study of emotional differentiation.* We have already referred to the suggestion by Bridges that infants show two basic patterns, delight and distress, or pleasant and unpleasant responses. Actually, Bridges's observations of infants as they developed led her to the conclusion that emotional complexity develops as a process of differentiating simple responses, as well as responding to new stimuli. A summary of her observations is given in Fig. 3:9. She began by rejecting Watson's view that fear, rage, and love were manifest at birth; like Sherman, she found only excitement at this early age. However, at three months she found excitement breaking apart into distress and delight; by six months distress had differentiated into fear, disgust, and anger, whereas delight only later separated into elation and affection.

Bridges suggested that *both* maturation and learning were involved here. Maturation might bring on better muscle action, nerve-muscle integration, glandular functioning, and the like. Learning might result as the child experienced success in coping with situations in one way—or simply as responses were associated with specific stimuli.

2. *Studies of smiling.* Let us examine some studies which pin-point more precisely the response to be observed. Jones (1926) carried out a careful study of smiling, a response pattern commonly believed to go along with positive emotions. According to her observations, smiling is not present within the first month of life but has usually appeared by the end of the third month. To induce smiling she presented the following standard situation to all infants studied: The experimenter put the child on a table, bent over so that her face was above the child's and about 12

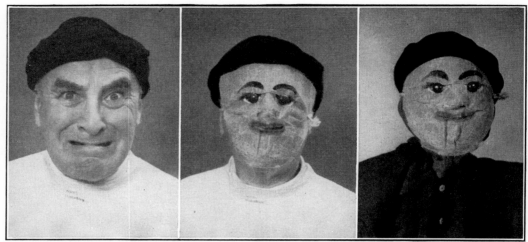

FIG. 3:10. Facial patterns which elicit smiling. Before the age of two months, smiling is virtually nonexistent. After that age, patterns such as these evoke smiles from most children, up to six months. The mask must be moved to induce smiling. (*Courtesy of Dr. R. A. Spitz.*)

inches away; then the experimenter smiled and made a clucking sound. If the child did not smile in response to this stimulus, the child's own mother repeated this performance.

Jones found that none of the 186 infants whom she studied smiled as early as 15 days of age but approximately 100 per cent were smiling in response to this approach by the age of 95 days (3 months) in response to the test situation. Now, obviously this change in behavior could either be due to maturation of the nerve-muscle patterns needed for smiling, or it could be due to learning that an adult face bending over the child is a fairly dependable sign of pleasant stimulation, need satisfaction, and tension reduction.

The latter view is favored by the interesting research of Dennis (1941). Dennis and his wife cared for twin girls over a period from about 1 month after birth until the age of 15 months. During the first part of this period the experimenters carefully avoided talking to the girls when feeding them, changing their diapers, or doing anything else having any direct relationship to the child. (The purpose of this precau-

tion was to attempt to investigate the age at which spontaneous vocalization on the part of the children took place. Obviously, any application of verbal stimuli by the adults during this early period would have been a vitiating factor in that part of the experiment.) As soon as the children began spontaneously to vocalize, the precaution of avoiding speech during the period of feeding and caring for the children was abandoned. *As soon as the adults began to talk to the children at this time, and only then,* smiling became a response to the sound of adult voices.

Spitz[1] conducted an ingenious study of smiling with infants at various ages from birth to one year of age. He interpreted his observations as indicating the importance of maturation rather than learning. However, if we examine the masks he used to induce smiling (Fig. 3:10), there seems no reason to assume that these are not simply treated by the child as stimulus equivalents for the mother's face. If, as is suggested in the preceding paragraph, the child learns to identify the mother as a sign of tension reduction, then any such stimulus might

[1] See Spitz and Wolfe (1946).

be perceived by the infant as such a sign. It may be, of course, that the muscular movements of smiling are impossible before the age of two months, because of incomplete maturation; but the stimulus which elicits the smile must still be a function of learning.

3. *Fear of strange surroundings.* A study of a group of 61 infants during the first year of life by Bayley (1932) included special note of crying in response to strange surroundings. She found that such crying was absent during the first 2 months of life but was relatively common by the age of 10 months. This suggested that maturation may have made the child more conscious of his environment and hence aware that something unusual was occurring, perhaps thus setting off the emotion of fear.

On the other hand, it could be argued that the child has learned that mother, familiar surroundings, and the accustomed stimuli are associated with food, care, and security. Then the intrusion of an unfamiliar stimulus or a change to a new location might be perceived as a threat to the child's safety. This explanation assumes that every baby necessarily encounters a few unpleasant experiences; that these are associated with some change in the environment, and thus the baby learns to be disturbed by unfamiliar situations. On the whole, we are forced to the conclusion that *none of these studies are decisive in indicating the importance of maturation* in the modification of the child's emotional behavior.

The Role of Learning

It has been difficult to show convincingly the exact role of heredity, either at birth or after maturation, in determining specific emotional behavior. No such limitation exists with regard to learning. Masses of experimental and clinical data can be piled up to show the great importance of specific

incidents, exposure to danger, need satisfactions, etc., in determining the direction and intensity of emotional responses.

We can easily observe the rapid process of learning to recognize and respond to emotionally significant stimuli in any young child. If little Oscar is toddling down the street and a big black dog, dashing along, knocks him down, Oscar will quickly develop a dislike or fear of dogs. Children have been known to acquire fears of storms, of people having different skin color, of running water, and so forth, as a result of a single painful or frightening episode.

The most widely cited research on emotional acquisition is that of Watson (1924). After he had tested babies on fear of snakes, fire, etc., he concluded that only loud sound and loss of support would set off fear. The question then arose: where do we get our wide variety of fears in later life?

Using a simple method of paired stimuli, Watson was able to manufacture fears to order. We shall cite only a single study. Albert, an eleven-month-old boy, played readily with a laboratory white rat. Watson then set up a situation in which, every time the rat was placed near Albert, the child was frightened (Watson struck a steel bar with a hammer, nearby but out of sight). After only three repetitions of this, the baby cried and crawled away from the rat as soon as it appeared.

This conditioning process could account for some of our emotions. But we often feel fear, anger, love, etc., when the stimulus seems entirely new. Watson found that the fear learned to one stimulus may spread to others of a similar nature. Thus, he tested Albert with a white fur muff, a Santa Claus mask, and other objects. The two mentioned, which obviously have elements in common with the white rat, also evoked the fear response. Thus it seems that learning accounts for many emotional responses. We learn to fear one

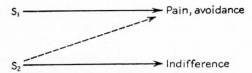

FIG. 3:11. Acquisition of fear. If any neutral stimulus (such as a white rat, a doctor's white coat, the buzzing of an induction coil) is followed by a painful stimulus (needle prick, shock), the neutral stimulus will come to evoke a fear reaction.

object by direct contact, but this fear transfers to similar items which may be encountered years later.

We shall be concerned with detailed analysis of the process of conditioning in Chap. 8. Here we call attention only to the diagram shown in Fig. 3:11 which may help to organize the ideas about to be presented. The diagram represents the acquisition of a specific fear as a response to some definite experience. S_1 represents any stimulus such as a pinprick, an electric shock, a loud sound, or a fall, which will set off in this person an unpleasant feeling or a response of running away. S_2 is a neutral stimulus, having no emotional value for the subject. The combined presentation of these two stimuli makes for a learning procedure by virtue of which S_2 comes to set off the fear reaction. We may generalize from this diagram by saying that the person now *expects* S_2 to be followed by some painful, tension-increasing occurrence; that is, we could say that the individual now perceives S_2 as different from what it was before.

Transfer and generalization of emotion. Psychoanalysts have emphasized the importance of the child's emotional response to his parents as a determinant of his whole future personality, his relationships to employers, the government, his wife, and so on. Experimental psychologists are in general agreement as to the importance of early childhood experiences in this respect, even though there may be some question about some of the specific instances adduced by the Freudians.

The basic mechanism conceived to be involved in this process is that of *transfer*. We can define this concept by saying that, whenever a particular stimulus causes a disturbance, upsets equilibrium, the individual comes to react not only to that stimulus but also to *similar* stimuli. Thus the child fears not only the dog that bit him but also most other dogs. He may even *generalize* to cats, horses, and all quadrupeds. Referring back to Watson's study on conditioned fear of white rats, we note that the child's aversion transferred to a white fur muff, a Santa Claus mask, and similar objects.

Functionally, some degree of generalization is necessary for survival. Man could not accomplish much if he had to learn anew to fear every wild animal, every threatening enemy. Considerable harm, on the other hand, results from overgeneralization and the inclusion of too many cases. The child who fears his pet puppy because of an accident with a large dog, like the young man who fears all women because of one heartbreaking episode, suffers from too extensive transfer. This is particularly true because—a point we shall develop at some length later—emotional responses tend not to be susceptible to rational control. Thus, even though one recognizes that his fear or infatuation is not intelligent, he may not succeed in doing much about it unaided.

Transfer seems to account for a large proportion of our adult emotions. It can be effectively demonstrated in many instances, for example, that the individual has never physically encountered the stimuli of which he is afraid. He has, however, had some fright or pain with some similar stimulus and has generalized his emotions to include this new object as well.

Specific Emotional Impulses: Anger and Aggression

If we wish to clarify the role of the emotions as energy mobilizers, driving man to vigorous action, we may well turn to a consideration of anger. Here we find an excellent example of an "emotion" which functions to release additional energy in the pursuit of a desired goal.

Traditional psychology has explained anger as a phase of the "instinct of pugnacity"—a conception of an innate, hereditary impulse to fight, attack, and destroy. Freudian psychoanalysts have revised this notion in the form of a "death instinct" or "destructive instinct."

Most of the evidence available appears to deny the necessity of assuming an instinct to fight. The term *instinct* implies a need developing within the organism, unrelated to external stimuli. Thus one gets hungry and thirsty at regular intervals. Sex desires develop spontaneously as the appropriate body structures mature. Do we have any such basis for referring to a fighting instinct? The answer, clearly, is in the negative. Very few people develop a need for brawling at regular intervals; and as for the quaint view that wars occur periodically because of the aggressive instinct of the average citizen, this naïvely overlooks conflicts of power and economic interest which determine the decision by national leaders to resort to war as an instrument of policy.

The frustration-aggression hypothesis. The weight of available evidence favors this view of anger and aggression: that the emotion of anger (and the desire to attack) is a consequence of the frustration of some goal-seeking activity. Thus, if you are hungry, and food is available behind a locked door, anger mobilizes additional energy to assist in breaking down the barrier and reaching the goal (see Fig. 3:12).

That anger is a consequence of frustration can be checked by daily observation. A child will react with rage if his candy is snatched away; a college man becomes furious if his roommate dates his girl friend; a salesman flies into a fury if a big sale is lost to a competitor.

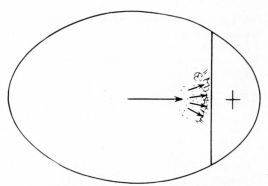

FIG. 3:12. Frustration-aggression relationship. When movement toward a goal is interfered with, additional energy is mobilized to break down the interference and achieve the goal. This is likely to be classed as anger or aggression if, as so often happens, the blockage is due to the presence of some other person.

It is difficult to evoke real anger in humans by laboratory experiments. The frustrations are likely to be too weak (because of ethical considerations), and the subjects know that "this is just an experiment." Useful data on human subjects have, however, been collected by the use of diaries. Meltzer (1933) had his students record each instance of anger, with the situation setting it off, over a period of a week. His data support the frustration-aggression hypothesis; about 86 per cent of the situations listed as causing anger were clearly frustrations of some other motive. In some cases the anger was potentially an aid in dealing with the problem (physical blockage) but more often was no help or even a handicap (as in cases of social frustration). As Table 3:4 shows, only a very small proportion of the frustrations were of organic needs. Frustration by inanimate objects set off almost half of the male responses; two-thirds of the frustrations reported by women were due to persons.

Murder is an extreme manifestation of aggression. But when we seek to *explain* the crime, we do not refer to the emotion of anger, but to the basic frustration. Thus F. T. Jesse (1924), in her popular book on

TABLE 3:4. Frustrations and Anger in Men and Women College Students
(*From Meltzer, 1933*)

	Men, per cent	Women, per cent
Thwarting of self-assertion:		
Defense reaction to persons...	29	45
Aggressive reaction to persons.	7	19
Defensive reaction to things...	47	26
Thwarting of organic needs.....	6	5
Complex situational thwarting...	12	5

Murder and Its Motives, lists six types of murder: for gain, for revenge, for elimination, from jealousy, from lust of killing, and from conviction. All these except "lust of killing," which she concedes to be most rare, imply frustration of a more basic impulse: the desire for money, sex, power, or security. You may kill to "eliminate" someone, but only if that person blocks your path to a desired goal. Similarly, revenge implies a hurt or deprivation, and killing from conviction implies a strong motive such as political fanaticism which is blocked by the victim. Thus it seems fair to conclude that such extreme instances of anger, in virtually every case, are set off by frustration of powerful motives. These are not all biogenic; but money, power, and prestige have a status in psychology much the same as these basic biological drives.

Expression of anger. As the experiments on children indicated, it is doubtful that there is any inherited action pattern or facial pattern for anger. Living as we do in Western culture, we learn early in life how to *communicate* anger, that is, what to do to show others we are angry. But it would be a mistake to assume that these ways of responding are universal. Porteus, during a field study of Australian natives, asked them to do a certain dance for him. The volley of replies was couched in such tones that he was sure they were vehemently angry at his request; he was not even going to wait for the interpreter to tell him. Nevertheless the interpreter assured him that they were saying they would willingly perform—as they did.

Thus the clenched fist, the tightened mouth, and narrowed eyes which are symbols of anger to us, do not necessarily have the same meaning in other parts of the world. It is likely that these are simply parts of the primitive excitement pattern which have become standardized through experience.

Physiological changes. In the same way, it seems that most of the physiological changes in the body are the same for anger, fear, disgust, and pain. All these emotions are unpleasant, all of them involve threats to bodily equilibrium; and all of them set off activity of the sympathetic nervous system. Thus we find higher pulse rate, blood pressure, and respiration in all of them; digestion is interfered with, and so on.

It is possible that some parts of this pattern are more likely to become tied up with anger-arousing stimuli than other parts. For instance, many studies have shown chronic high blood pressure to be associated with persistent anger, especially inhibited anger (cf. Fig. 3:2). This has not been found in persons with persistent fears. Psychologists assume that learning somehow brings about this linkage of anger and blood pressure, although it has not proved easy to demonstrate in the laboratory.

In a primitive context, all the physiological changes listed above would aid survival. If one must fight for his life, his food, or his mate, it is an advantage to sidetrack digestion and speed up circulation. More energy is mobilized and available. The frustration is attacked and destroyed.

In a civilized context, anger and hostility are not necessarily adaptive; they may even be hindrances. Suppose, for example, that my predominant motive is the *desire to be liked;* if someone manifests a dislike for me, and I react with anger, I do not solve the problem, but make it worse. Reacting to frustration by becoming aggressive, then, is likely to increase one's difficulties in social adjustment. Parents spend a great deal of time trying to teach the child that aggression must be concealed in his dealings with other people. Social taboos forbid a resort to violence; thus aggressive behavior may bring about new frustrations—punishments of various kinds. A second reason for inhibiting the expression of aggression is that we may also love the frustrating person and desire affection from him. So, the child is angered by mother's "no"; but he loves her and wants her future good will; hence, he must not give vent to his hostility. Anger consequently may have great positive value in *physical* frustration situations; but in *social* frustrations, the additional energy mobilized may only boil and bubble, with no response outlet. This seems to provide a basis for emotionally determined cases of high blood pressures and cardiac disorders.

Persistent aggression. The frustration-aggression theory suggests that anger is built up anew by each frustrating blockage of a primary drive. But social conditions may prevent the release of this energy. The law of homeostasis seems to be that the energy must go somewhere, be vented in some action. What happens to it?

Displacement. We speak of *displaced* hostility in instances where anger is vented against a more or less irrelevant object instead of the original frustration. So, a man unjustly scolded by his boss and afraid to protest may come home and bedevil his wife; she spanks the little boy; and he kicks the dog. Some people vent their hostilities by slamming doors and banging the furniture. Indulgence in alcohol causes many a man to start brooding over his frustrations, begin feeling aggressive, and fight a perfectly innocent bystander.

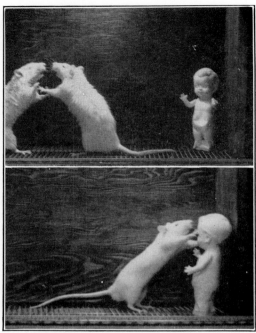

FIG. 3:13. Displacement of aggression. Two rats were placed together in a Mowrer-type box (upper figure) and electricity was turned on in the floor grid. The animals learned that the electricity was turned off when they attacked each other. Soon they would fight as soon as placed in the box. Then one rat was placed in the box with the doll (lower figure). He then attacked the doll, presumably an equivalent stimulus for the other rat. (*Courtesy of Dr. N. E. Miller.*)

Generally speaking, displacement occurs when we fear, do not know, or cannot reach the frustration. Then we "take it out" on someone handy—especially, someone who cannot fight back. Thus the Jews under Nazism, Negroes in the South, and Mexicans in the Southwest are used as scapegoats for displaced aggression. More precisely, we can say that displacement is facilitated by three factors: (1) *threat* to expression of anger against the original frustration (*i.e.,* the result of aggressive behavior will be more frustration); (2) presence of a stimulus object reasonably similar in kind (*e.g.,* another person); and (3) inability of the substitute objects to

FIG. 3:14. A device used in studying aggression. The subject is asked to write in the first reply that comes to his mind. In doing so, he tends to reveal his own patterns of aggression toward others. (*Suggested by the Picture-association Test of Dr. Saul Rosenzweig.*)

retaliate (*e.g.*, Negroes, Jews). Clearly, displacement involves the *transfer* of aggression to a similar stimulus (Fig. 3:13).

Unconscious manifestations. Pent-up aggression may affect a person's behavior in many ways. It may motivate discriminatory behavior, attacking minority groups, labor unions, or some foreign country. It may affect his way of seeing situations—he will find evidence that others "plan to attack us" (his nation, church, or race) or to attack him as an individual.

Why should these be called "unconscious manifestations of emotions"? This label is applied because the individual is unaware of the fact that his own inner state is involved. He believes that he is reacting to the *real actions of real people.*

How can we have unconscious manifestations of any emotion? We get the quickest answer to this by looking at the physical bases of emotions. The autonomic nervous system and the visceral responses (digestion, blood pressure, electrical skin activity, etc.) which it sets off are not subject to conscious control. Often one does not even know that his blood pressure (or other visceral state) has changed.

All emotions, then, are likely to have some unconscious components. If a person often becomes angry, he will associate many external stimuli with the visceral responses involved in anger. *Conditioning* takes place. *Transfer* of the emotion to a new stimulus can occur. So the man may irrationally become angry at the British and in reality be reacting to a series of experiences which did not involve Britons in any way.

Direction of aggression. Since anger can be displaced from the original frustration, we have an interesting problem: in what direction will it be focused? Rosenzweig has proposed that people respond to frustration in three ways: *extrapunitive* (attacking others); *intropunitive* (attacking oneself); and *impunitive* (denying that there was a frustration).

Figure 3:14 illustrates a way of studying direction of aggression. The subject is asked to supply an answer for the worker represented. Extrapunitive replies attack the manager; intropunitive replies accept the blame ("I'll try to speed up"); impunitive replies deny that the situation is significant. It is important—in understanding yourself and others—to remember that anger can be directed against the self. This may take the form of self-criticism, of depression and guilt feelings—and in extreme cases, of suicide. The expressions of extrapunitive aggression are more obvious—verbal attacks, fighting, and murder.

Anger as a motive. It should be clear from these facts that anger (aggression, hostility) functions as a motive. It mobilizes energy; it supports vigorous, persistent activity. It intensifies thought and action regarding certain subjects.

It is also clear that anger need not be considered a *primary* drive. Anger is usually found to *serve* other needs, although persistent hostility becomes an impulse demanding an outlet even after the primary need has been satisfied or forgotten.

Fear

Watson proposed fear as one of his primary emotions; McDougall and other "instinct psychologists" held that there was an "instinct of flight," of which fear was a component. Such views assume the *hereditary* determination of fear.

The evidence for such views seems no better than for the "instinct of pugnacity." Fears vary widely from person to person and from culture to culture; fear is set off by external stimulation, not by spontaneous inner need.

When the organism encounters a painful stimulus, withdrawing responses occur. Later, the mere approach of the painful stimulus may cause withdrawal, and the person says he feels afraid. This suggests that fear is a *learned* response, depending on past experience.

Various studies of children have shown wide variability in their fears. Some babies are remarkably free from fear; others are very fearful. Such differences usually agree with the child's history; *i.e.*, if he has met few painful occurrences, he has little fear, and vice versa. Watson showed that babies do not have an inborn fear of snakes, fire, and other stimuli often believed to carry universal fears. These emotions depend upon learning.

Realistic fears. Every child must learn to walk, and in the process he is likely to have some painful bumps. Thus he may develop a realistic fear of loss of balance, lack of bodily support, and so on. The common fear of high places no doubt reflects these experiences of early childhood. Similarly, getting hurt in the dark can lead to a fear of darkness; and getting lost, alone and far from home and parents, leads to realistic fear of hunger and pain.

Symbolic fears. On the other hand, as the child matures, he normally learns that he is capable of dealing with these threats, and the fear disappears. If it reappears at maturity, the psychologist infers at once that the childish fear is being used to symbolize an adult problem.

Alexander (1948) describes the case of a married woman of forty who developed a "street phobia." She was unable to go on the street alone, especially on those streets where night clubs, theaters, etc., were located. Analytic treatment disclosed that she was unhappy in her marriage and longed to have "one last romantic fling" before accepting middle age. The streets she feared symbolized gay affairs, meetings with handsome men, and the sexual pleasures which had, she felt, eluded her. Thus a childish fear is used to deal with an adult problem. We can understand the symbolic fear, of going out in the street, as a protective device for avoiding the basic fear situation, the fear of being tempted by her own impulses to do something which she considered immoral. The *transfer* of the fear from the original stimulus to the symbol may have been facilitated by thoughts of "acting like a streetwalker" or by some other idea which associated the two situations. Watson, in his studies of children, found that fear transferred only to objects having physical similarity—the fear of the white rat transferred to the Santa Claus mask, white fur muff, etc. Adults, however, can think of so many kinds of similarity that they have almost unlimited transfer possibilities.

Does the symbolic fear have homeostatic value? Apparently it does. Just as a realistic fear helps to prevent the person from risking physical injury, the phobia protects this woman from temptation to behave in a manner which she considers wrong. The phobia thus helps to protect a certain inner equilibrium, although it is a painful kind of defensive mechanism.

We shall have more to say regarding symbolism in later chapters. It is especially important to note here that symbolic fears make up a large proportion of child and adult emotions; and also that it is usually impossible to remove the symbolic fear without first discovering the underlying basic fear. In Watson's experiment, it would have been quite futile to try to cure the fear by establishing pleasant associations to a fur muff if the fundamental fear was directed to the rat. Thus much of clinical psychology is a patient search for the hidden experiences underlying emotional disturbance, since this is essential to the task of correcting these maladjustments. In the case cited above, trying to teach the woman not to fear streets would have been a waste of time unless her marital problems were cleared up.

Anxiety. We differentiate between fear, worry, and anxiety in terms of specificity. Fear is commonly applied to fairly precise stimuli; thus one is afraid of dogs. Worry is more vague; some people worry about economic problems, about their acceptance by other people, about future difficulties. Anxiety is likely to be extremely ambiguous; clinical patients often feel acute anxiety without being able to identify any specific fear or worry related to it. Anxiety, however, is not limited to clinical cases; every person is likely to experience anxiety from time to time. It may have all the intense inner disturbance, physiological upset, conscious torture, and muscular tension of an acute fear; yet it seems to have no specific cause.

Much anxiety is probably based upon specific experiences occurring so early in life that they were preverbal and hence impossible to recall; thus a child left alone by his mother may experience intense anxiety because he is so completely helpless and dependent upon adults for care and protection. Because of the all-or-nothing character of infantile emotion, any fear may be acute enough to set off severe anxiety. In later life any occurrence which resembles one of these infantile fears will reinstate the anxiety.

Adult experiences also provide a basis for anxiety. Let us suppose that Mr. Smith feels very hostile toward his superior executive, Mr. Jones. Obviously, if Jones knew about this, Smith's career would be endangered. This means that Smith must be on guard; he fears that he will make a slip that reveals his feeling. Also he has guilt feelings over his hostility, as Jones has treated him well. He may then *repress* any knowledge of the hostility, but the fear will persist as a vague anxiety. This is due in large part to the persistence of the visceral changes which are a part of the fear response—heart rate, blood pressure, stoppage of digestion, etc. These will be felt as a chronic anxiety without apparent cause.

Anxiety as drive. Much social learning is motivated by anxiety. The child learns to obey his parents and to accept ideas they accept, because of anxiety. Loss of food, of protection, of love—not to mention actual punishment—may seem imminent to the child if he does not conform. If he develops these approved patterns of behavior, he continues to be loved and protected. If threatening situations outside the home set off anxiety, the child rushes home for protection. Particular persons and places become symbols of security. The child will then exert vigorous efforts to reach these goals when anxiety threatens.

Anxiety sets off the same muscular tensions as does fear. The mere presence of these tensions is painful and presses the individual to do something. If no adaptive response is possible (as when the individual does not know the real source of his anxiety), techniques for reducing tension may be learned and may serve as safety valves. Thumb sucking in children is a tension- and anxiety-reducing mechanism. Violent laughing and crying are ways of letting off tensions, as is vigorous physical activity. Tics, nervous mannerisms, and other personal peculiarities seem to fall in this same category.

If anxiety motivates learning of adaptive behavior, it serves a biologically and psychologically useful purpose. If, however, it leads only to the learning of futile and maladaptive acts, it is destructive of personal integrity. Because anxiety is so pervasive in human life, particularly in our social situations, we can hardly hope to abolish it. It is important, at least, to harness this powerful motive for constructive rather than destructive purposes.

Bodily expressions of fear and anxiety. In general, the physiological effects of fear and anxiety are parallel to those of anger. Typical laboratory results from induced fears include an increased heart rate, increased blood pressure, dilation of the pupils of the eyes, general tension of striped muscles, interference with digestion, and an increase in adrenal-gland activity (secretion of adrenin). These all conform to the pattern of sympathetic nervous system innervation.

We do not need to rely on laboratory studies, however, since man is adept at contriving terrifying experiences on a large scale in real life. Airmen during World War II were studied to ascertain the typical symptoms experienced while they were undergoing enemy attack. The frequency of various symptoms was reported in Table 3:1.

As one experienced noncom said, "Anybody who isn't afraid under fire is just a damfool." These physical changes are homeostatic in character; they represent the body's adjustment to a threat situation. Unless additional energy is mobilized, the very survival of the organism is in danger.

These changes, of course, are appropriate to a cave-man mode of existence. They may be maladaptive in modern war. For emergency situations requiring extra strength, freedom from fatigue, and unusual speed, this reaction pattern is appropriate. For the skill and delicate coordination required in handling a jet plane, it is not so good.

We must also note that under modern conditions we have a high proportion of symbolic fears and anxieties. To such stimuli the emergency pattern is not adaptive. A student who is afraid of flunking will not be helped by these bodily changes; on the contrary, they will probably be a handicap. He may focus on the threat and be unable to focus on his studies.

Anxiety sets off a great deal of visceral and muscular tension. It appears that this can also provide a base for psychosomatic illness (stomach ulcers, for example). We shall resume our consideration of such emotional products when we take up the psychology of personality.

Reconditioning fears. Fears are primarily energy mobilizations related to danger of physical pain. This response pattern, however, can be attached to harmless stimuli as signals. Thus Watson developed a *conditioned* fear in little Albert by showing the white rat whenever a loud sound frightened the child. The white rat is now seen as a sign of danger (negative valence) and feared accordingly.

It is obvious that one can also recondition the stimulus so that it no longer is seen as a sign of threat. To do this, we must make it a sign of some positive valence.

The most dependable positive valence for a child is food. Jones (1924*b*) therefore set out to recondition a fear by establishing a new signal function. Little Peter (age two) was afraid of a white rabbit. She proposed to eliminate the fear by making the white rabbit a sign of food.

The child was first placed in his high chair, happily eating. Then the rabbit, in a wire cage, was brought into the room. Peter stopped eating and the rabbit was removed. On the next day he ate with the rabbit in the room—about 20 feet from his chair. On successive days the rabbit was brought closer and closer, until at last Peter ate calmly with the bunny sitting on his tray. (Note, however, that this took about

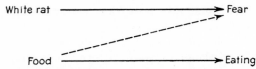

FIG. 3:15. Possible undesirable results of a reconditioning experiment. If the feared stimulus is introduced too suddenly or brought too close, there is a danger that the food may become a signal for fear, rather than the feared object becoming a signal of food.

thirty trials; Watson needed only three to develop a conditioned fear).

Eating is homeostatic and tension reducing. It sets off parasympathetic responses: slow heart rate, low blood pressure, muscular relaxation. Fear is the exact opposite. If the eating response is dominant, the "rabbit" stimulus ceases to be a sign of danger and instead is a sign of food. If Jones had pushed the experiment too fast, food might have become a sign of danger (see Fig. 3:15) and eating would have stopped. This is actually the case where mealtimes involve too much nagging, threats, and discipline.

Love

Our considerations of anger and fear have stressed the thought that both emotions are responses to *frustrations* of basic drives; in the case of anger, extra energy is focused on escape from the imminent danger situation. Both are therefore homeostatic, protective of the biological welfare of the organism; because of modern conditions of life, each can become harmful and inimical to the individual's welfare.

Love is in a somewhat different category. It appears to involve chiefly a focusing of strong positive feelings upon a particular person. It is likely to have sexual desire as an important component, although many people consciously claim to feel love which has no sexual element. Whether this is true, we need not inquire too closely; according to psychoanalytic studies, even the most ethereal love is likely to have a sexual base.

In Watson's study, the sexual element in infantile "love" responses was obvious. The most dependable stimuli for evoking this pattern were stroking of the lips, nipples, and genitals. According to psychoanalytic studies of adults, and to some extent in clinical studies of children with play materials, it appears that the infant develops specific sexual desires much earlier than popular opinion holds. The love of the boy for his mother, can, of course, be based upon her function as a source of food, of comfort, of protection; and indeed, mothers who do not provide these are not loved. But it is common to find a sexual element even in the first two or three years of life in this relationship: it is not at all rare to hear a little boy say to his mother, "Maybe papa will die; then you can marry me and keep house for me." This need not mean that the child understands such concepts as death and marriage; it does suggest that he wants undisputed possession of the mother by disposing of the father (the "Oedipus" complex). Little girls show less uniformity in this respect; as the mother is the source of food and protection, she is loved; as a competitor for attention from the father, she may be disliked. The love life of the female in our culture may therefore be somewhat more stormy and ambivalent than that of the typical male.[1]

Transfer and displacement. Like anger and fear, love can be displaced from its original object and transferred to substitute or symbolic objects. Young men characteristically fall in love with girls who resemble their mothers; young women with men who resemble "dad." (With women, mental resemblance to the father is usually more important, whereas men are most concerned with physical resemblances; this is a com-

[1] For further discussion of these problems see Chap. 13.

mentary on our cultural standards for selecting mates!)

We noted that hostility of the boy to his father is common at about the age of two to five. This hostility arises because the father blocks the son from full possession of the mother. At this stage, the boy may show violent anger responses, negativism, stubbornness, etc. Eventually, however, he recognizes the futility of this struggle. He tends to repress his hostility and to remember only his fondness for his father (as a source of protection, fun, assistance). The hostility of course is not destroyed; it goes underground and may reappear as hatred of foreign countries (who threaten our "motherland"), radical agitators, minorities ("bad" power figures). The affection for the father transfers to "good" power figures (the head of the government, the employer, religious figures, etc.).

Because of the extreme suppression of sex in our culture, it is especially likely to provide material for symbolism. Nobody needs to express food hunger symbolically, because it is perfectly all right if he says, "I'm hungry." But love and desire for a specified member of the opposite sex often cannot be stated openly; thus we find the field of symbolism rich in sexual images. Sigmund Freud was often attacked (because he read sex meanings so generally into everything he studied); his reply was simply that society, not the psychologist, put sex into these forms.

Physiological aspects of love. Love is correlated with the activity of the parasympathetic division of the ANS, whereas fear and anger are related to activation of the sympathetic system. This means that, when love is the dominant emotion, physiological conditions are relatively peaceful.

We can observe this especially with the frightened child. When he runs to mother, and is held, caressed, and reassured, the emergency fear responses are neutralized and harmony is restored. Many wives have discovered that an angry or distressed husband can best be restored to normal by caressing him and assuring him that he is loved. Husbands note that the same treatment soothes a distraught wife.

The antagonism between sympathetic and parasympathetic means that, when one is dominant, the other is suppressed. Thus fear and anger sidetrack digestion. The young husband who is fearful and anxious becomes impotent when in bed with his wife; the fear responses prevent sexual activity. This is one of the reasons why sexual difficulties are so commonly found in cases of emotional maladjustment. Sex may not be a primary cause, but it becomes involved because of the way the nervous system functions.

Emotion and Tension Reduction

In the previous chapter emphasis was laid on the fact that all motivated behavior tends toward tension reduction. The hungry animal seeks food; when fed, he becomes sleepy. Sexual arousal sets off restless activity which is quieted by copulation. The biological drives all seem to have as a common base a physical tension, a visceral discomfort, which impels organismic search for relief. The emotions show the same pattern of action.

Approach to the goal (in the case of love) and movement away from it (in fear) definitely appear to relieve the discomfort of tension, although the muscular effects may persist for some time. When a man wipes his brow and says "Whew! I'm glad to be out of that jam!" we are aware of his relief from tension. In the case of anger, tension reduction seems best accomplished by a violent attack on the object, and if this is impossible, by vigorous physical action—slamming doors, chopping wood, etc. (Indeed, the uncomfortable tensions of fear and love can also temporarily be relieved in this way.)

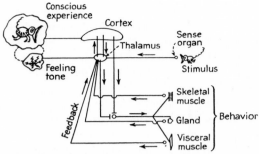

FIG. 3:16. Visceral and cortical tension. Tensions which are set up in the viscera by an emotion-arousing stimulus send back sensory impulses to the brain ("feed-back"). These impulses are presumed to establish a pattern in the cortex of the cerebrum which can then be rearoused on other occasions and reinstate the visceral tension as a motivating force. (*Modified from Harlow and Stagner, 1933.*)

It must be noted, however, that emotional tensions can persist for much longer than physical tensions could be expected to endure. One can hate another person for years. Many fears endure for a lifetime; after 10 years the escape reaction may be as vigorous as if the fright had occurred only yesterday. Even love sometimes endures for considerable time intervals without sight of the loved person.

To understand such phenomena we have recourse to the concept of *cortical representation of tension*. When a real, physical tension occurs in the viscera, nerve impulses go to the brain (Fig. 3:16). Sensations from stomach, lungs, heart, etc., make up a pattern corresponding to tension. If this cortical pattern becomes associated with an object, any later sight or reminder of this object reinstates the cortical tension. If strong enough, this will restore the physical discomfort; but we can assume that the cortical tension itself motivates restless activity to escape the stimulus situations.

It will be easiest to state this in terms of the way the person perceives the object of his emotion. In our discussion of hunger, we noted that the organism quickly graduates from the simple homeostatic stage where

actual hunger precedes the search for food. Very soon we learn to anticipate hunger—to maintain biological constancy by keeping food on hand. When food objects are seen, they are recognized as ways of relieving tension, even before that tension has recurred. Vigorous effort to obtain the food may then follow (perhaps less vigorous than if the person is very hungry).

The object of an emotion is perceived as having valence. The loved person has a strong attraction for the lover. Frightening and annoying objects have negative valence. Whenever I encounter such an object, I experience tension. This tension can be relieved only by getting away from the emotional stimulus which sets off this inner pattern.

Reducing emotional tension is the dynamic force in much of man's daily behavior. Love, gratitude, fondness, appetite, and simple liking are positive states which determine many of our acts. We try to approach and remain close to persons and situations evoking these emotions. Similarly, we expend a great deal of energy getting away from people and objects evoking the emotions of fear, anger, hostility, anxiety, and annoyance. These tensions must be understood if we are to develop insight into ordinary human behavior and experience.

Emotional and Rational Behavior

It has long been asserted that there is a certain opposition between emotion and intelligence as to the control of man's actions. We speak of "blind anger" and "mindless panic." Young people in love are blind to each other's faults and, more important, to the consequences of their own actions. Devotion to a political creed, a religious faith, or any other ideal may lead to irrational behavior.

This opposition can be understood most readily if we refer back to the physical basis of emotion. The major factors in emotional response seem to be the ANS, the viscera, and the endocrine glands. These organs are not subject to voluntary control. Because of the homeostatic principle upon which we are biologically organized, the CNS is subordinate and subservient to this emotional system.

The CNS and the striped muscles are, of course, the agencies of all major adaptive behavior. But, as we have already emphasized, it is the autonomic-visceral system which determines goals; the central system is then pressed into behavior to achieve those goals. The autonomic system has a certain primacy over the central or "rational" system—but this need not mean that the two are opposed. The intellect works toward goals, and these goals are determined by drives and emotions. Emotion disrupts rational action only if too much energy is mobilized, so that control breaks down. Under mild emotion, intelligence seems stimulated and action is more efficient. Further, the positive goals of emotional attachment induce man to strive for valuable ends—the creation of a new equilibrium at a higher social and ethical level.

Frustration tolerance. It will help us to comprehend these facts if we think in terms of the "value of moderation." If there is no motivation, no drive, no emotional impulse, the person does nothing. He simply vegetates. If, on the other hand, the emotional or motivational pressure is too great, he cracks up. Control disintegrates; reality is ignored; there is a blind grasping of the desired goal, or an equally irrational flight, depending on the kind of impulse present. The cortical, intellectual, adaptive system is overwhelmed by the autonomic, vegetative, emotional system. Intelligent behavior, then, is favored by a *moderate* amount of energy mobilization. Either too little or too much motivation is detrimental.

As far as we know, everyone has a break-ing point at which overload occurs. Because it was first studied in relation to frustration (blocking some drive) and the consequent disruption of efficiency, it has become known as frustration tolerance; however, it refers to the person's inability to withstand any high level of tension. This breaking point, or frustration tolerance, varies widely from person to person. If the ANS has a low threshold (reacts quickly and violently), the tolerance level may be

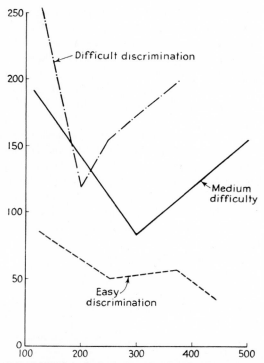

FIG. 3:17. Strength of punishment and learning. If escape from pain is used to motivate learning, results are satisfactory as long as the pain is mild. When more severe punishment is employed, the progress of learning is interfered with and discrimination breaks down. This breaking point occurs earlier if the discrimination task is more difficult. With very strong energy mobilizations, it becomes impossible to control and direct behavior; a "blind" struggle to escape from the punishment results. The vertical axis represents errors made in learning a task; the horizontal axis, intensity of shock. (*From the original of Fig. 5, by R. M. Yerkes and J. D. Dodson, J. Comp. Neurol., 18, 479.*)

low. Also, unfortunate experiences in child-hood predispose the personality to break-down. So, both heredity and environment may play a part in determining the frustration tolerance for any individual.

SUMMARY

The emotions are forms of energy mobilization which play a major role in adult human behavior. They are determined in infancy by the biogenic drives. Anger, fear, and other negative emotions are associated with the frustration of basic needs—loss of food, loss of a sex object, blockage of any goal-seeking activity. Anger is manifest when the frustration is perceived as something one can attack; fear occurs when the frustration is too dangerous, so that flight is the only recourse.

Love, on the other hand, is associated with gratification of biogenic drives. In the infant, love grows out of the relationship to the parent. The parent is a sign of food, of relief from pain, of safety and protection. Later (it seems) the parent can also become an object of sexual desire. Adult love shows elements of both sexual motivation and the desire for the intimate, secure relationship between child and parent.

The negative emotions activate the sympathetic section of the ANS; the positive emotions are associated with para-sympathetic action. These nervous mechanisms are antagonistic; thus fear and anger drive out love—or love can be used, with caution, to eliminate angers and fears.

Many of our fears and angers are today symbolic in character; they do not represent physical dangers. Thus the adaptive value of the "emergency" pattern disappears. Persons with chronic anxiety, fear, or aggression may develop psychosomatic illnesses because the tension is not reduced through physical action. Effective work on this problem depends on a study of man's symbolic processes.

Not all of us develop psychosomatic illness, but everyone has his breaking point. Emotional collapse occurs if the body mobilizes energy sufficiently in excess of what can be handled. Both heredity and environment play a part in determining where this breaking point is located.

Recommended Readings[1]

CANNON, W. B.: *Bodily Changes in Hunger, Pain, Fear and Rage.* (2d ed.) New York: Appleton-Century-Crofts, 1929.

DOLLARD, JOHN, *et al.*: *Frustration and Aggression.* New Haven: Yale University Press, 1939.

LUND, F. H.: *Emotions.* New York: Ronald, 1939.

REYMERT, M. L. (Ed.): *Feelings and Emotions: The Mooseheart Symposium.* New York: McGraw-Hill, 1950.

YOUNG, P. T.: *Emotion in Man and Animal.* New York: Wiley, 1943.

[1] See also p. 547.

CHAPTER 4

Social Motives

We have defined our first problem in human psychology as the understanding of dynamics. In the preceding chapters we have examined some of the facts and theories relating to biogenic drives and to emotions. The present chapter will round out the discussion with a consideration of the more complex dynamics of social motivation.

The biogenic drives were characterized by the fact that energy was mobilized to maintain homeostatic equilibria. Deprivation of food, water, oxygen, etc., leads to the development of tension, and energetic activity follows to restore the necessary constancy. It was noted, however, that static homeostasis, or the automatic return to the former condition, was relatively rare in human behavior. Dynamic homeostasis includes steps to prevent the disturbance from occurring in the future, or to speed up the process of recovery. By learning to identify goal objects and signals of deprivation, we move to successively higher levels of equilibrium and adjustment.

The emotions are related to the biogenic drives in various ways, but they differ in that they are relatively *nonsatiating*. When one eats food, his hunger drive disappears for the time being. If he is in love, contact with the loved person may strengthen rather than weaken his emotion. Emotions also differ from drives in that the goal ob-

ject is primarily *symbolic* rather than physically necessary; *i.e.*, the mother is loved because she has been a symbol of food and care, the black dog is feared because he is a symbol of pain, and so on.

The *social motives* can also be related to the biogenic drives and to the emotions. Basically—as modern psychologists see the problem—all energy mobilization derives from the need to protect the biological welfare of the organism. After these more complex motives have been formed, however, they may lead the individual to perform actions which are biologically harmful to himself, because he values some other goal more highly than his own physical satisfactions. In a sense, this is the key problem of the present chapter.

Social motives resemble the emotions in that the goal objects are symbols. A man values prestige, even though it does not fill his belly. But, as a realistic observation of our society will indicate, prestige is likely to be associated with a surplus of creature comforts. The acquisition of property has symbolic value as protection against hunger, cold, and other deprivations. Thus the social motives will have many features in common with what has already been presented for the emotions.

There seem to be two differences worth noting. One is that in the case of emotion we are largely looking at the inside, at the experience of the individual; whereas in the case of motives like prestige and security, attention is directed more to the outer goal. This, however, is merely a matter of emphasis; ambition may be thought of as directed to a particular goal, or it may be simply a burning inner restlessness pushing the individual toward some achievement.

The second difference, likewise only a matter of emphasis, is the fact that social motives always involve interaction with some other person or group. Thus prestige is a matter of relative standing as compared with other people; gregariousness is a matter of acceptance into a group, and so on. If we look back at the discussion of emotion, we note that most emotions also involve social interaction. However, one can be angry at a physical obstruction, fear animals or storms, etc. Emotions, then, cover both nonhuman and human interactions; social motives involve only human interactions.

What are the major social motives? We have used various illustrations in the preceding paragraphs, arbitrarily assuming that they should be considered social motives. Any listing that is prepared must also be arbitrary; popular language includes many overlapping terms in this area, and we can only simplify and systematize usage here.[1] We therefore propose to discuss five classes of major social motives, as follows:

1. *Security.* This includes the need to feel that the social environment is friendly, that others respect one as an individual, that one is *accepted into the group.*

2. *Dominance.* This includes the need to *achieve high status in a group,* to impose one's

[1] A good argument can be made for throwing out all the popular terms and inventing a new, scientifically precise vocabulary. This would undoubtedly lead to progress in the long run, but it would be exceedingly confusing for the student right now. We have decided to compromise and use popular terms with somewhat more careful definitions than are common.

own demands on others, to obtain power, to throw off control by others.

3. *Acquisitiveness.* This identifies the desire to accumulate physical property, symbols of wealth, and the like.

4. *Group identifications.* In this category we have such impulses as patriotism, religious motives, political idealism (as separated from purely selfish power impulses), and other desires to *strengthen and expand groups* of which one is a member.

5. *Values.* In addition to the desires for fairly specific kinds of social relationships and symbolic rewards enumerated above, we find men striving energetically for certain kinds of socially determined goals which are called *values.* Standards of right and wrong set up values for the individual. The scientist comes to value knowledge and truth without much regard for practicality. Humanitarians value the welfare of other persons, and measures which are perceived as fostering human welfare. Obviously values are often the product of group identifications—especially religious and political values. Similarly, the other motives listed combine in various ways to produce specific patterns of human behavior.

Principles for classifying motives. Before beginning an analysis of specific examples of social motivation, let us explore further this question of classifying the biological and social motives. Otto Klineberg (1940) has proposed that we consider both the physiological base and the degree of predictability of energy mobilization, in working up a classification of motives. Using these two principles, he offers a fourfold scheme for arranging various motives into a system:

1. Motives which have a definite physiological basis and are absolutely predictable. Hunger, for example, has a definite organ system for its expression, and it is universal—timing and type of food, of course, varying from group to group.

2. Motives which have a definite physiological base, are found in all societies, but have individual exceptions. Sex is the obvious example here. Social conditions may operate to

suppress any sexual behavior completely for certain individuals, or for all group members for limited periods of time; neither of these is possible for motives in Group 1.

3. Motives which have a vaguely defined physiological base, are very common, but have many exceptions. The emotions particularly belong here: fear and anger, for example, have ANS and endocrine processes as a basis, but they are not nearly so predictable in operation as the entries in Groups 1 and 2.

4. Motives which have no known physiological basis, but which occur with relative frequency and are related to certain life experiences of the individual. The social motives which we have listed above fall into this category. In terms of the entire human race, they are not at all predictable; some social groups show little dominance behavior, some lack acquisitiveness, and so on. Even within our own culture they are predictable for individuals only with a large margin of error. Obviously, then, our treatment of the social motives will have to emphasize flexibility and variability, whereas the biogenic drives illustrate fixed, uniform elements of human nature.

Relations of ends to means. Physiological homeostasis is the basic law of the organism. But, in trying to maintain biological constancies, the person may learn the value of parents, the usefulness of property, the advantages of being in a group, and so on. In the first instance it would seem that these other individuals and socially valued symbols are seen simply as means to a goal, the goal being physical comfort. With experience, however, most people come to value the means—that is, just being with people, just owning property, etc., can reduce tension and induce a feeling of satisfaction.

Cultural definition. Another important point in Klineberg's principles is the significance of culture. Since the social motives do not correspond to needs without which the organism will die, flexibility is possible. Different cultures manifest differing definitions of what things one must strive for, what desires are forbidden, and so on. Cul-

ture can modify the kind of food one craves, but it cannot eliminate hunger. Social motives apparently can be created and destroyed by cultural influences. It will be worth while, therefore, to examine the role of culture at this point.

The importance of culture. Man is unique among all the animals in that he has a culture. When we try to identify the difference between "human nature" and "animal nature," we focus on these aspects of behavior which are related to human culture. This can be illustrated by referring again to the biological drives.

While man is obviously motivated by hunger, he does not, in general, snatch the first item of edible stuff he sees. He may go through a devious and time-consuming routine of purchasing the material, preparing it according to certain religious or cultural rules, and consuming it in certain surroundings. He is motivated by certain social needs which can oppose and delay gratification of the biological drives. In the same way, few humans, when assailed by a strong sex impulse, will approach the first member of the opposite sex they encounter. Whether in a "primitive" or a "civilized" community, the person feels the requirement to conform to certain cultural standards.

We are not concerned, as psychologists, with the content of these cultural patterns. Professional anthropologists deal with the marriage, child-rearing, food-getting, and other culture patterns of the world's peoples; and amazing indeed is the diversity they report as to ways of satisfying biological drives. Our interest as psychologists is in the relation of this cultural variation to general laws of behavior. The first relationship we note (and the only one we shall be concerned with at this point) is this: man, growing up within a culture, acquires strong needs relating to his social environment. These social motives may become so powerful that they overrule even the very potent biological drives of hunger, thirst, and sex.

FIG. 4:1. Chimpanzee exchanging token for food. In an experiment similar to that by Cowles, this chimpanzee has learned that tokens are valuable because they can be used to obtain food. Here we see an animal putting a token in the machine to get a bit of fruit. (*Courtesy of Dr. Henry W. Nissen.*)

The study of culture demonstrates that the social motives are not hereditary. Primitive communistic societies indicate that we need not assume an instinct of acquisitiveness. There are social groups in which both individual fighting and group conflict are very rare; the Eskimos have no word in their language for war, and several American Indian tribes show virtually no individual competitiveness; such observations cast doubt on such "instincts" as pugnacity and competition.[1] But, since we know that competition, fighting, and amassing property are powerful impulses in some groups, we immediately look for an understanding of how these social motives are *learned*.

[1] For some excellent examples of cultural variability in motivation, see Benedict (1934), or Mead (1935).

Symbolic Rewards

The key to this problem of learning social motives is found in the phenomenon of symbolic reward. To point this up with a fairly complex example first, let us consider the case of working for money. A 10-dollar bill has absolutely no value in itself for satisfying human needs. However, in our culture it can be exchanged for objects and services which will satisfy hunger, thirst, etc. To obtain money, then, the person will work energetically, endure physical discomfort, and by-pass other pleasures which might attract him. How does he come to value money, a pure symbol, to this extent? Obviously, as a result of experience in which he finds that the possession of money is a necessary prerequisite to obtaining these other, highly desired goals.

Now let us examine a simplified experimental version of this process and see how it throws light on the development of social motives. In this experiment, Cowles (1937) taught chimpanzees to pull in a loaded wagon and obtain a poker chip, which could then be exchanged for food. After the poker chip–food equivalence was thoroughly learned, it was possible to use the chips as rewards in learning tasks and to get learning which was almost as efficient as that motivated directly by food reward. The animals also learned to distinguish chips of a different color, which could not be exchanged for food, and refused to work to obtain these chips. The food tokens retained their power to motivate activity over a considerable period of time.

This experiment can be diagramed as in Fig. 4:2. If a person (or in this case, a chimpanzee) is impelled by inner tension toward a goal—food, for example—he may find one or more courses of action open to him. What he encounters, as he acts in a given way, will determine his later responses. The chimpanzees found that the token was necessary to obtaining food, which was the major goal. Soon they looked upon the token as a symbol of food, and valued it accordingly. They would then work almost as hard to collect tokens as they would to obtain real food. Cowles found that his animals had to exchange the poker chips for food fairly often, or this association would weaken; however, they did not have anything like the long training that human children are likely to receive with money.

What is the significance of Cowles's experiment, as a way of helping us to understand social motivation? The first important point is that even the lower animals can learn to value objects which are not in themselves need satisfiers, because they can be exchanged for (equated with) biological need satisfiers. The animals never learned to value poker chips quite so highly as actual food, but we do not know what might have been possible had training continued for years, as with human infants. Even so, many humans never learn to value money quite so much as goods in hand (for example, people who spend today, on things they do not need, the money they know they should save for important needs next month).

Secondly, we want to emphasize the point that the poker chips could function in situations completely different from that in which the original learning took place. The chips were used in a different room, as rewards for visual size and color discriminations, delayed responses, and other tasks. Thus a symbolic reward is not tied to the place, task, or situation in which it is acquired; the animal values this symbol wherever he encounters it.

Social motives show both these characteristics. Human beings learn to value money and other symbolic objects which are not themselves of value. They also learn to value the presence of other people, friendly facial expressions and tones of voice, positions of prestige and power, and

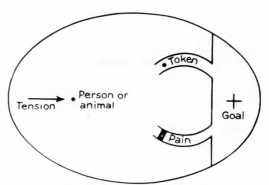

FIG. 4:2. Valence and pathway. The positive valence represents any goal object toward which the organism is striving. The pathways represent different courses of action by which the goal may be achieved. In the token experiment, the animal was impelled toward the goal (food) by inner tension (hunger). Finding that the token is a necessary step in obtaining food, the animal comes to value the token as a symbol of satisfaction.

so on. These stimuli can serve as symbolic rewards, displacing for greater or less periods of time the demands for basic biological gratifications. It is on these bases that men forgo immediate pleasure for future gain, food for higher education, immediate sex release in favor of a socially approved marriage, escape from pain in favor of patriotic acclaim.

Figure 4:2 is arranged to illustrate this last point. If the person (or animal) takes pathway B, he encounters pain. Getting a medical degree, for example, means a lot of discomfort. If alternative ways of reaching a desired goal are available, painful pathways will be avoided. If, however, no alternatives are open, and the person has learned to take the pain in order to get to the goal, he will come to value pain just as the chimpanzees valued the poker chips.

We shall have occasion to refer often to this question of learning to value stimuli which are somewhat painful in nature. The process of *socialization* is a process of learning to forgo immediate pleasure in favor of long-term satisfactions, and to accept immediate discomfort in the interest

FIG. 4:3. Learning of time-reward relationships. Often we must learn that accepting a small pain or discomfort now is necessary to obtaining a greater reward in the future or avoiding a greater discomfort. Similarly, forgoing a small reward now may mean avoiding a severe punishment later on. Maturity is achieved as the person learns to evaluate rewards and punishments over a span of time.

of great future rewards. Figure 4:3 illustrates the problem. The socialized individual has learned to accept the pain of conformity in order to get the rewards society can offer. He must also learn to give up infantile gratifications, for which society might punish him severely in the future.

Symbol, need, and preference. A second line of evidence which will help us to understand the development of social motives comes from the study of preferences for different goals. "Human nature" (as contrasted to "animal nature") is largely defined by the goal objects we *prefer* as sources of need satisfaction. Hunger, for example, can be satiated by raw fish, by chicken à la king, by grasshoppers fried in palm oil, or by garlic salami. What determines the fact that persons accustomed to enjoying one of these may starve to death within the range of another food source? Further consideration of this problem will help us with the broad problem of social motivation.

In the preceding chapters, we have dealt with the concept of *need* primarily in biological terms, as a substance required for adequate homeostasis. Needs, in general, set off tensions, and tension impels seeking after objects until one is contacted which meets the need and reduced the tension. In these discussions little has been said about *preference* for different objects as need satisfiers, and even less about the *enjoyment* of need satisfiers.

It is easy to see that, for any given need,

there may exist a wide range of need satisfiers. Some of these may be more efficient satisfiers than others. They differ also in sensory qualities. For example, a rat with a protein deficiency may relieve it by eating casein or by eating ground whole wheat. P. T. Young[1] has shown that in such cases the rats are not equally ready to accept casein and wheat. They show a marked preference for wheat (Fig. 4:4).

Under certain circumstances rats (and humans) show decided preferences for substances having no homeostatic value. Protein-starved rats will continue to prefer sugar over casein, even though the sugar is not "needed" and casein is. Rats sometimes prefer saccharin, which meets no metabolic need, over foods which do. Young suggests that the rats *enjoy* saccharin and prefer it for that reason. Now, such facts present the psychologist with a very important problem. In the majority of instances need reduction *must* go with preference and enjoyment. Otherwise we could not explain the survival of the human or any other species of animal. Any type of animal which consistently preferred poisonous or even useless substances to need reducers would soon die out.

We may suggest, therefore, that animals are inherently so made up, biologically, as to enjoy and prefer need satisfiers. Some of this may be a matter of hereditary sensitivity. Human babies soon after birth show preferences for sweet over salt, salt over bitter, etc. Foods at body temperature are preferred to those much hotter or colder. Both these preferences make sense in terms of homeostasis. The infant has an urgent need for calories, and mother's milk, the source available under primitive conditions, is sweet. We can assume that by heredity we are selectively responsive to the biologically provided stimuli such as milk; or that, during the first few days, we learn that "sweet" is a *signal* for tension reduction.

[1] See Young and Chaplin (1945).

FIG. 4:4. Young's preference-testing apparatus. The animal is placed in the starting box at A. Foods to be tested for preference are placed in the two cups at B. As soon as the animal has chosen one food, the cups are lowered to prevent his eating both samples. (*Courtesy of Dr. P. T. Young.*)

By either line of reasoning, we conclude that other sweet substances (*e.g.*, saccharin) will be equated to milk, will have an advantage on preference tests, and may be "enjoyed" even when nonhomeostatic.

Sensory qualities and signal function. Let us explore more carefully the problem of signaling. The individual must inspect objects and decide whether they are probable tension reducers. After a few experiences he comes to expect need satisfaction when a certain object is encountered. The emotion of love, for example, traces in large part to the need satisfaction (food, comfort, etc.) associated with mother's presence.

Preferences for specific foods (or for sex objects, thirst quenchers, comfort devices)

will thus develop out of need satisfaction. But a stimulus object may be preferred because it has *in the past* satisfied needs, which are *not now* present, or because it *resembles* an object which is a need satisfier.[1] Preferences can also be established for social situations, for eating in a group rather than in isolation, and for receiving certain signs of deference from others. In short, we can learn to desire and enjoy those goals defined by our society as good.

At the human level we can say that *in general* objects are *pleasant* which satisfy needs and reduce tensions. Objects are *unpleasant* which block satisfactions and

[1] For a discussion of the learning process involved here, see Chap. 8.

increase tension. Agreement is not perfect because the signaling system is imperfect. Pleasant but nonsatisfying objects resemble pleasant need satisfiers. We fear many harmless stimuli because they resemble noxious objects. (Note the *transfer* of fear from a truly dangerous situation, such as pain, to a harmless but associated stimulus such as the doctor's white coat.) Facial expressions, tones of voice, and gestures are seen as pleasant or unpleasant, accordingly as they signal satisfaction or deprivation. A seat on the platform, a gay uniform, listing in the Social Register, may be pleasant because of prior associations. There is nothing inherent about any of these preferences. In America we are inclined to look down upon a woman who marries a man purely for his money. But in Kaffir country, a wife acquired without a bride price is an object of contempt.

Enjoyment. We are leading up to the point that, as one matures, he may be motivated toward certain situations simply because he *enjoys* them. This possibility was pointedly ignored in Chap. 2. At that point we emphasized tension reduction. Enjoyment becomes a basis for energy mobilization after some learning has occurred. An object can be enjoyed even if it is useless or harmful, provided only that it resembles— seems to be a sign of—some need-satisfying substance.

This does not rule out the possibility that we by heredity enjoy certain stimuli (tastes and smells, colors, tones, etc.). But if these perferences are hereditary, it may well be because, in primitive circumstances, animals so constituted as to prefer these had a better chance of survival—*i.e.*, that these sensory qualities signaled common need satisfiers. How long would the human race have lasted if babies were revolted by sweet tastes?

Once we have set up this idea of enjoyable stimuli as signs of need satisfaction, we can easily understand why one may ap-

proach objects having no immediate significance for homeostasis. We like to be with people because people have in the past been signs of food, comfort, and protection. We *love* a person who helps us achieve tension reduction, but we *like* others who resemble him or her.

In human psychology we feel no hesitation about saying that "John did this because he likes Jim." In other words, we recognize that motivation for activity may come just from preference or enjoyment, not from actual physical need. Here let us suggest that such likes and dislikes function to mobilize energy because of past association with need satisfaction. And, if "helping Jim" does not in general lead to some kind of need satisfaction, it will not continue very long!

Symbolic threat; anxiety. The focus of these pages has been on the concept of symbolic reward as a key concept in the understanding of social motives. Let us, in closing, note the importance of symbolic threat. The concept of anxiety was developed briefly in the preceding chapter as an important element in interpersonal relations. It plays an equally important role in social motivation.

Once an individual has acquired a preference for a certain social situation, objects and persons blocking his path to that goal are perceived as threats. If it seems likely that the goal will not be achieved, anxiety will probably arise. This mobilizes additional energy and effort toward the goal. Thus Mr. Jones may desire election as mayor of his town. If a rival candidate appears on the scene but has little chance of election, Jones is undisturbed; but if the rival looks as if he may succeed, Jones becomes anxious. He will then try harder to achieve his goal.

Parental disfavor is associated with punishment. Reproof by the teacher, rejection by playmates, will connote loss of certain pleasures. Such phenomena will stir

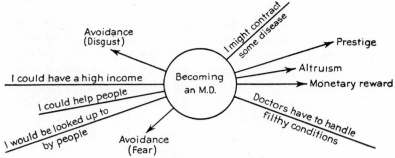

FIG. 4:5. Multiple motivational pressures. The decision to follow any particular pathway or course of action is likely to be a summation of many pressures, both positive and negative. Not all of these are conscious. If judgments are to be made rationally, it is important to know consciously as many of these pressures as possible. (*Adapted from R. B. Cattell, 1950.*)

up anxiety in the child. As an adult, similar facial expressions and words will likewise cause anxiety. These are the tools by which society enforces conformity. Real physical punishment is very rarely necessary. Usually, less than 1 per cent of the American population is in jail at a given time. Symbolic punishments suffice to keep 99 per cent of us in reasonable conformity to social demands.

Signs of social disapproval lead to anxiety and, of course, to tension. When a tension arises, the person does things which in the past have reduced tensions. If he is clear about what started his anxiety, he can probably choose a good course of action. In many cases he does not know; hence he may simply engage in some past tension-reducing act. Thus some people eat all the time, as a way of reducing chronic anxieties which they do not understand. Others amass fortunes, or have a series of sexual affairs, or take to liquor or drugs. Whenever a person indulges his taste for a certain activity to an extreme degree, we can infer safely that it is his method of reducing anxiety.

Multiple determination. Both positive and negative goals (rewards and escape from anxiety) contribute to the potency of social motives. If Cowles could have made

his poker chips also symbols for escaping from an electric shock, the chimpanzees might have worked as hard for the chips as they did for bananas; and they might have continued to work even when the hunger drive was completely satiated, because anxiety can always be aroused.

When a boy does something to win his mother's praise, his behavior also serves to avoid criticism and punishment. This multiple determination of social motives is very common and probably accounts in no small degree for their effectiveness. Figure 4:5 illustrates the interaction of multiple pressures with a specific goal (becoming an M.D.). After the person has once made up his mind and started on his way, the desire to obtain the degree will itself become a motive which can influence other choices.

The signs and symbols of reward and anxiety in our culture lead to the establishment of a variety of such social motives. Indeed, it is plausible to suggest that no two persons have exactly identical social motives, since they are subject to different learning situations. However, everyone growing up within a given culture is exposed to certain common pressures and tends to develop similar desires and fears. All these concern the person's relation to his group. *Security* involves the person's acceptance into a group; *dominance*, his relative status within the group; *acquisitiveness*, his collection of objects valued by the group; *group identification* refers to his efforts to expand or strengthen the group; and *values* are the various specific goals toward which he becomes oriented, chiefly under group pressure. Let us examine each of these social motives briefly.

Security

The desire for security finds its origin in the helplessness of the human infant. The child must be cared for by an adult, or he cannot survive. Thus acceptance by at least one other person becomes a sign of essential satisfactions. The presence of his mother (or her equivalent) may thus become most important to him. As was suggested above, the maintenance of his inner tissue constancies (blood sugar, water balance, and so on) depends on the maintenance of an outer social constancy. The desire for, and dynamic struggle toward, this social constancy is known as the desire for security.

Consider the wide variety of tension reductions which serve as a basis for developing the security motive. The mother is a source of food—relief from hunger and thirst. She removes cold, wet and irritating clothes, thus ending tensions based on these stimuli. She is a source of caressing, warm, and tender bodily stimulation which seems innately capable of reducing some tension (cf. Watson's studies of "love"). She may protect the child from painful and frightening situations, thus reducing anxiety. Under these circumstances, it is not surprising that the sight of mother and the sound of her voice acquire powerful positive valences. Furthermore, her departure will be experienced as a frustration (threat of loss of these valued objects) and will result in crying or other forms of aggressive behavior.

Because some of these functions may be taken over, at times, by father or by other adults, the infant transfers this desire from the mother as a specific goal object to familiar adults as a generalized object. "Mother is best but someone else will do." At this point we begin to identify a desire for security as a specific social motive in this child.

The secure child is one who gets food when he is hungry, is protected against pain, cuddled, caressed, and comforted. He develops a view of his environment as safe and interesting. From his experiences with his parents the child generalizes that people are essentially good, and life is worth living.

The insecure child, on the other hand, is one who is fed at the whim of the parent, ignored, allowed to experience pain and discomfort for considerable intervals of time, and given a minimum of protection. He tends to see his environment as full of dangers and hazards. One must grasp whatever is at hand; the future is too uncertain. (In some instances the child even becomes afraid to seize present pleasures; he anticipates punishment if he does so.) People are essentially bad; no one is to be trusted.

This does not mean that the insecure child necessarily ignores other people; on the contrary, he may be aggressive in demanding affection from others. The insecure adult may be an employee always asking the boss for praise, a student asking his professor for signs of approval, a wife demanding constant demonstrations of love from her husband. The need for security is determined by childhood learning, but it is not always easy to predict just how the learning will operate.

The desire for security is present in both the secure and the insecure individual—and of course most of us who are in between the extremes described. By virtue of this early dependence, all of us seem to need group acceptance, warmth and friendship from others, manifestations of affection, and so on. But the secure individual takes it for granted that he will get these, and if not now, a little later. The insecure pattern involves fear that these goals will not be forthcoming, and any little slight, any lack of recognition, is seen as a serious threat.

Role of infantile deprivation. To help understand such variations in the security motive, it will be useful to refer once more to Hunt's experiment on the effect of infantile deprivation of food. In that case, it will be remembered, the adult rats hoarded food (valued food pellets) more than rats not deprived in infancy. A similar lesson can be learned from Hall's study on mice. The mice, subjected to a traumatic stimulus in infancy, were more timid than their litter mate controls in maturity. They placed a high *negative* value on strange stimuli which perhaps threatened a re-arousal of the early fear.

A more illuminating type of evidence on the importance of infantile deprivation in the realm of security comes from studies of human infants and adolescents. Ribble (1944) has shown that the infant actually needs (in the physical sense) cuddling, caressing, stroking, and handling. Infants deprived of these stimuli, even if adequately fed, often became ill, diarrheic, apathetic; they lost weight, developed circulatory and skin troubles, and so on. This condition tended to clear up with the introduction of a foster mother who provided such infants with the physical contacts indicated. Obviously, then, a neglected child may be undergoing biological frustrations over and above those suggested by irregular feeding, diaper changing, and the like; and a secure, loved infant gets many rewards besides food and comfort.

What would we find if we took two groups of human infants and deprived one group of this attention, while providing it for the others? No one is likely to try this experiment, because we respond to the very strong social motivation to conform to ethical standards. The experiment, however, has been conducted for us by our society, which is much less moral than the individuals who compose it. Goldfarb (1944) obtained his two groups by studying adolescents who had been orphaned within the first year of life. One group was composed of those placed immediately in foster homes, so that they continued to have the individual attention and affection of at least an average family. The second group were children who had spent a substantial part of the first 3 years of life in an orphanage, where the amount of such affectionate care was severely limited. His results indicate that early deprivation and insecurity lead to an exaggeration of cravings for security in adolescence. The youngsters who had been institutionalized showed chronic demands for affection, apprehension in their relations with others, and varied emotional disturbances. Like Hall's mice, they seemed perpetually afraid of a repetition of their infantile trauma. The value of security was overestimated because of their early deprivation.

Effect of early gratification. If an infant has an extremely high degree of security, extending to the point that he gets everything he asks for, and never experiences loss or punishment, this does not mean that he fails to develop any desire for security. It may, however, lead to a passive dependence upon others ("somebody will take care of me") with no apparent energizing of behavior. That is, the individual has a desire for security, but it is incapable of motivating effective action. He is so sure he will be secure that he feels no tension.

No great degree of psychological acuity is needed to conclude, from these observations, that the optimum in child training calls for a small amount of insecurity, at least enough so that situations signaling security will be valued and energy can be mobilized to attain them.

Variations in security goals. We have developed the idea of security particularly as a function of the child's relation to adults: his feeling that he will be cared for, loved, and accepted. Obviously, this provides a basis for the developing need to be accepted and liked by playmates, persons of his own age group. Out of this develops *gregariousness*, the need to be with others, fear of aloneness. Early observers of society noted that men everywhere came together and lived in groups; from this they inferred the presence of a "gregarious instinct." When we recognize the urgent importance to the baby of being with adults, we quickly see that no instinct need be assumed. Security can be had only through being related intimately to others. As we mature, we learn that this relationship does not have to be so close as the child-parent bond; nevertheless, a craving to reestablish such an intimate tie with some individual seems important in many marriages.

The goal of security also spreads, or transfers, from personal to impersonal situations. When factory workers say they want security, they are likely to be referring to security against arbitrary discharge by the employer; to security against hazards of sickness, accident, and old age; or to similar protection for their children in case of the father's death. That is, we may think of physical security (protection against injury), economic security, security as a member of a group of friends, security in relation to one's employer. All these can be analyzed as outgrowths of the child-parent relationship; the specific goal sought is a symbol of that early state of satisfaction.

Dominance

The typical reaction of an American who comes into a new group is to strive for security, *i.e.*, to seek acceptance as a member of the group. To this end he will wear odd bits of clothing, allow himself to be hazed in initiations, repeat verbal rituals, and persecute persons not members of the group. However, as soon as he has become assured of his acceptance in the group, he is likely to manifest a desire for status, a desire to stand out above the other group members. He may attempt to become a leader, to give orders to others, to move the organization in the direction of his own personal motives. Or he may wish only to have others look up to him as a particularly attractive, talented, or wealthy member of the group. This desire for preferred status within the group we have designated as one phase of the *dominance motive*.

Several psychologists have argued that the desire to dominate was hereditary in character. Studies of the *pecking order* in chickens, and of similar dominance orders in other animals, are cited to support this view. Poultry raisers know that, if several young cocks are penned together, they will fight until a definite pecking order, or dominance-submission hierarchy, is established. Bird A pecks all the others; B pecks all but A, and so on. Access to food, females, roost location, and the like will vary with dominance status. The same kind of dominance motive seems to operate in goats, dogs, monkeys, and probably many other species.

The pecking order becomes stabilized as a kind of equilibrium in the group. If a new animal is added, fighting starts all over again until the newcomer has been placed in the hierarchy. According to some observers, the animal fairly low in the scale is more vicious in its despotism over those lower down than are the individuals nearer the top. This has been explained as the result of frustration. A bird pecked by those higher up, and unable to better his status, displaces aggression by pecking more furiously at those below him.

The will to power. Alfred Adler, a famous Viennese psychoanalyst, built an entire theory of personality around the notion that man is born with a desire for power: that ambition, personal striving, aggressiveness, and other characteristics were simply expressions of this basic will to power. We are inclined to doubt the necessity of the explanation in terms of heredity; but there is no question that Adler pointed out some very significant forms of motivated action.

Adler was impressed by the fact of organ compensation. If one kidney is damaged, the other grows larger to try to carry the load. If a heart valve leaks, the heart muscle grows thicker and beats more strongly, again a compensation. A man who is quite short is likely to become loud-spoken and aggressive, as if to make himself seem bigger than he is. A person who feels inferior because of lack of education may compensate by attacking "impractical intellectuals." Napoleon and Hitler seem to be unusually clear examples of men striving for power and dominance because of small size and other felt inferiorities.

Women, Adler noted, are especially prone to problems in this area. Not only they are smaller and weaker, physically, than men, but our culture denies them many positions of power and prestige. Some women react to this by becoming skilled at manipulating men to get their own desires satisfied; others develop what has been called the "masculine protest," in which they may affect mannish clothes, haircuts, gestures, etc., along with a rather aggressive personality pattern.

Prestige. Not everyone expresses the desire for dominance by seeking a position of power over others. Some are oriented more toward prestige; they seek a position where they will be looked up to by others. This is socially a somewhat more desirable manifestation of the motive. Scientists, artists, writers, and other professional people are often found to be motivated by strong desires for prestige.

Role of childhood experiences. Like the desire for security, the desire for power and prestige can be traced to rewards and punishments, goal satisfactions and tensions in childhood. Almost from the day he

is born, the typical American boy (or girl) is subject to pressure from his parents to compete with and surpass others. Mothers vie with each other about "how much Johnny has gained," "how well Tommy eats his spinach," and so on. Early walking, early speech, and early toilet training are matters of great importance. As soon as the child can navigate, he is urged to run faster, make better grades, or, in some neighborhoods, fight harder than anyone his size.

The rewards and punishments related to this competition are derived largely from the security need, i.e., from parental approval and disapproval. Some parents actually use candy and other bribes, and occasionally we encounter parents who resort to physical punishment, to reinforce the competitive tendency. But, on the whole, children seem to learn to compete for the "first place" because of the desire for parental approval.

This appears in early years particularly in the form of *sibling rivalry*. Competition between siblings (brothers and sisters) offers an early situation within which power needs may develop. In the course of attaining desired goal satisfactions, the older or stronger child may manipulate his siblings for his own advantage. Learning what a useful technique this is, he may continue it and get more and more gratification by dominating others. Eventually the technique of domination becomes a need in itself; that is, the exercise of power is satisfying even when no other biological or social tensions remain to be reduced. Power, of course, is self-reinforcing once achieved; the person who attains power in our culture gets economic, physical, sexual, and social rewards as a concomitant. It is not surprising, therefore, that few individuals are willing to relinquish power after having wielded it; as Lord Acton pithily remarked: "All power corrupts, and absolute power corrupts absolutely."

Let us emphasize here, once more, that

this is not an instinct, that it is a product of our culture. Among various cultures it is considered rude, if not somewhat indecent, to surpass others in tasks requiring skill or knowledge. Among the Zuñi, a young man who wins a foot race more than once or twice is disqualified from further competition. Among the Ojibwa, anthropologists found that it was futile to ask a question after one member of the tribe had failed on it, because no one wanted to make his brother seem stupid. Porteus tried to give his maze test to Australian aborigines and found that they had no conception of one man trying to do better than another; all their problems were solved cooperatively, and it was virtually impossible to get them to try to outdo one another on the task.

Apparently man is born with the potentialities for either cooperation or competition. If the culture is such that competitive, prestige-striving behavior is rewarded and encouraged, then we find people manifesting a strong motive in this direction. If the culture fosters cooperation, then the prestige motive seems to develop only slightly or not at all.

Acquisitiveness

The "instinct of acquisition" is another popular misconception about human psychology. According to this notion, man is born with a desire to acquire and hold property. The error of this view can readily be demonstrated, even with reference to American culture; certainly large numbers of our citizens show little concern with, and exert little energy toward, the acquisition of wealth. The case is more convincing, however, if we consider other cultures in which acquisitiveness simply does not exist. Among many South Sea groups, all property is held in common; the fish catch, for example, is divided up not according to each man's efforts, but according to the size of his family. Land is owned by the

village; this may also be true of houses, canoes, and other large items. Community ownership of land was common in Europe up to the time of the Industrial Revolution.

Even in those societies where people seem strongly acquisitive, closer study throws doubt on the belief that accumulation of property is the major goal. Among the Kwakiutl Indians of British Columbia, property in the form of sheep, blankets, canoes, etc., may be amassed with great industry, only to be destroyed in a great "potlatch," or ceremonial festival held for the humiliation of one's rivals. Thorstein Veblen acidly pointed out the similarity of some American behavior, such as that of the businessman who toils feverishly to accumulate money and then squanders it on an elaborate debut for his daughter and other forms of "conspicuous waste."

The desire to accumulate property and symbols of wealth (money, stocks, and bonds) may thus be an expression of *dominance* and prestige seeking. It may, on the other hand, be a manifestation of the *security* motive. Hunt's rats hoarded food pellets in adult life because they had been very hungry in infancy. The data on food hoarding among war-deprived children (page 56) indicate that food can become a highly valued symbol of security.

Miserliness. The accumulation of food supplies and other property is readily understood as a form of dynamic homeostasis—a precautionary measure against deprivation. But such behavior often goes far beyond any protective needs. The industrialist who has a fortune of 10 million dollars can hardly fear further frustration; but he may, for prestige or power considerations, or to relieve anxiety, continue busily to pile up wealth.

Acquisitiveness in its purest form gives rise to the personality we call "the miser," the individual who irrationally hoards wealth without regard to his own physiological needs. A check of the *New York*

FIG. 4:6. The Collyer household. After the death of Homer and Langley Collyer, police found the old mansion completely cluttered with junk of every description, much of which had been saved for over 50 years, most of it quite valueless. (*From The New York Times.*)

Times indicates that each year several persons in that city die in surroundings of dire poverty and are found to have very substantial resources. The most spectacular case, no doubt, is that of the Collyer brothers, Homer and Langley,[1] whose house proved to be stuffed with assorted junk of every description which had been saved for approximately fifty years (Fig. 4:6). The two men were sons of a successful physician, and Homer had been an admiralty lawyer until blindness and later paralysis forced him to retire to the big brownstone home in midtown New York. Langley, also said to be a talented man, took care of his older brother. Neighbors often saw Langley rummaging in garbage cans, salvaging items from rubbish heaps. The two men appar-

[1] *The New York Times*, Mar. 22, 1947, to June 21, 1947; *Life*, Apr. 7, 1947.

ently lived chiefly on peanut butter, rolls, and oranges. They owned property of substantial value in the city but forfeited it rather than pay taxes. At their deaths in March, 1947, their estate was estimated at several hundred thousand dollars.

The miser undoubtedly must be understood in terms of his childhood experiences. In most instances he has undergone at least some period of severe emotional deprivation. His anxiety about property becomes so strong, and so independent of rational evaluation, that it dominates his behavior. The overvaluation of any goal in adult life is usually related to deprivation of that goal or its equivalent in infancy.

Deprivation and satiation. We should note, in the case of all social motives, that the effects of deprivation and satiation are dependent chiefly upon the individual's perception of what is satisfactory. Society defines the value of status or property and may set either on a high or a low level. Within the range so defined by the culture, the person *expects* a certain amount of goal attainment, and this indicates his *level of aspiration*. Failure to achieve up to this level may be exceedingly frustrating; a common wisecrack after the Wall Street crash of 1929 was "No one is so aggressive as a millionaire who is down to his last yacht." One man feels poor at a level where others would feel rich. Chronic failure to accumulate any wealth prevents acquisitiveness from developing at all. For example, minority group workers (Negroes, Mexicans, etc.) find that they are paid low wages, laid off when business slows down, etc. Such a man gradually lowers his level of aspiration approximately to zero—that is, he gives up any hope of accumulating wealth and lives for the immediate physical gratifications only.

Similarly, what constitutes *satiation* will depend upon the person's level of aspiration. Observers have commented that, during the nineteenth century, the pearl divers of the South Sea islands could have amassed great wealth, as the whites were offering them all kinds of bribes to bring up the precious jewels. But the Melanesian would work long enough to get what he needed, then quit. In our own culture we find many individuals who are content with a very modest income.

The satiation point varies so widely for different people because the goal is symbolic. Acquisitiveness, as we have noted, often goes far beyond the realistic level of preparation for emergencies. If property is accumulated to relieve anxiety, the process can go on indefinitely.

Group Identifications

The problem of social motives cannot be covered adequately without examining many phenomena to which it is difficult to give a name. One class of such phenomena includes those cases in which a person strives energetically to foster the welfare of a group rather than of himself as an individual. We can think of these as cases of group identification; the individual thinks of the group as an extension of himself and feels benefited by whatever benefits the group.

The most obvious of such identifications is *patriotism*. We feel secure as our nation becomes more secure; we feel power and prestige in the strength and status of the nation. However, there are many other such instances: the church member may work hard for the welfare of his church, giving up his own desires even to the point of martyrdom; the labor unionist may devote a great deal of energy to aiding the cause of unionism outside his own local (*i.e.*, where no immediate benefit to himself is probable). Members of political organizations in Nazi Germany suffered imprisonment and torture rather than abandon their groups.

Nineteenth century psychology tended to explain all such observations in terms of a "herd instinct" of some kind. Specifically, it was often held that patriotism was instinctive. Hitler used the myth of "German blood" for his own propagandistic purposes, but many social scientists seriously believed that heredity determined one's national allegiance.

Belief in an instinct of patriotism has waned as more social scientists have become conscious of the switching of allegiances from one nation or society to another. The multitude of new Americans, escaping from totalitarianism of one or another variety, who hold their new citizenship with great emotional zeal, illustrate well the fact that patriotism is a learned motive. The error was easy to make in earlier times, especially in Europe, where population mobility was low and it might seem that Frenchmen and Germans were born, not trained.

The dynamic power of patriotism is not the less important on this account. Certainly we see great willingness to exert energy and endure hardship on behalf of the nation among most citizens of all major countries. The Germans under Hitler, for example, endured a great deal of personal regimentation and arbitrary restriction of consumption, on the basis that by this policy a Greater Germany could be built. And certainly in America we have seen ample evidence that patriotism is a strong force activating the individual along lines of group effort and cooperation. Like other strong motives, such as hunger, love, and fear, patriotism often also has the effect of blinding us to reality.

Parents and patriotism. The evidence is now convincing that this strong social motive is a product of experience. It appears that patriotism actually develops along with, and parallel to, what we have called the *feeling of security* and, like security, is tied closely to the child's relations with his parents. ("Fatherland" and "mother country" are significant idioms in almost every known tongue.) Children apparently love first themselves, in pure narcissistic egocentrism; later they learn to love their parents, who minister to bodily needs and provide affection and protection. The same process can extend to the neighborhood, the community, and the nation. Frequently the child is assured, in school, that his "mother country" feeds him, protects him, provides him unequaled opportunities, and makes it possible for him to feel prestige and superiority as a member of a very great culture.

If this interpretation is correct, we could predict that children who felt unloved by their parents would be less patriotic than those who felt secure in their relations with their parents. This has been verified in statistical studies (Stagner, 1944) and also in clinical investigations. Studies by psychoanalysts at the time of the death of King George V of England and of President Franklin D. Roosevelt showed clearly that the head of the government was a father substitute for large numbers of his citizens.

Patriotism can also function as a satisfaction for other motives. There is a good deal of evidence, for example, that repressed aggression can be vented in this way. Living in society, we cannot resort to physical violence against our neighbors as we might occasionally desire to do when we are frustrated in some impulse. This aggressive tension apparently can pile up and be discharged later (displacement). So we find people who are (by their own account) highly patriotic being considerably higher than average on hostility to foreigners and to internal minorities commonly called alien, such as radicals.

Other group identifications. We have analyzed patriotism at such length because more facts are available and also because it makes such an excellent pattern with which to compare other such motives. To take the labor-union member: he gets security from the protection the union gives him on the job; he gets a feeling of power from the strength of the union; he vents repressed aggression against management. Because the goal he is seeking is symbolic, there is no end to it; so we get increasing demands for power, security, and so forth. Church membership in the United States has perhaps become too much of a perfunctory matter to serve as a good illustration, but members of some of the small evangelical denominations show these phenomena of obtaining security, a feeling of power, and release for hostilities in their church roles. Members of college fraternities develop strong loyalties which may motivate a lot of vigorous effort; the more fundamental satisfactions here are security and status.

The generalization on which we can close this discussion is as follows: a person can become identified with any group. Once so identified, he can obtain security, power, release of aggression, and perhaps other rewards, through building up this group. These satisfactions may be particularly important if the individual has failed to achieve these goals through personal achievements. Thus the existence of widespread personal insecurity, suffering, and frustration may lead to group formation and drastic social conflicts such as are associated with fascism and communism.

Values

Finally, it is important to note that social motivation includes the striving of the individual for various values which have special significance for him. In many respects, values overlap with group identifications. Religious, political, nationalistic, and other values may be highly esteemed by a particular person because of his identification with the group espousing these. On the other hand, it must be noted that one may come to value a particular ideal without regard to its group support.

Conscience. One of the obvious approaches to social value as a form of motivation is in terms of conscience. Why does a person reject an opportunity to steal a large sum of money, even when he would not be in danger of punishment? Why do some people forgo sexual gratifications because of a moral or ethical code? What does a person mean when he says, "My conscience would bother me if I did that"?[1]

Like most other social motives, conscience has its positive (reward) aspect and its negative (anxiety) aspect. As children, we were rewarded by our parents for certain kinds of behavior, and punished for contrary actions. These behavior patterns carried verbal labels: kindness, selfishness, stealing, lying, generosity, and so on. Be-

[1] The Freudian concept of the Superego (Chap. 13) is an elaboration and perhaps a clarification of this point.

cause they are associated with rewards, they can become symbols of positive value; insofar as they are related to punishment, they can become cues for anxiety. It is the verbal label which the person attaches to his own action, therefore, which is the immediate guide to behavior. If he can say, "But this isn't a lie, it's almost half true," he eases his conscience. Conversely, some people develop such rigid definitions of proper conduct that they use up, in meeting these standards, much energy which might have gone into more constructive activities.

Other values. Men come to direct substantial amounts of energy into the pursuit of many other kinds of values besides the ethical. Scientists are likely to value the pursuit of knowledge; artists value esthetic form, the expression of their own ideas, and so on. Vernon and Allport (1931) developed a pencil-and-paper test for estimating the relative strength of six personal values, which they defined as follows:

1. *Theoretical*—truth and knowledge for its own sake
2. *Economic*—use, practicality, financial, and property goals
3. *Esthetic*—beauty, in art, music, and literature especially
4. *Social*—charity, philanthropy, generosity, helpfulness, humanitarianism
5. *Political*—power and dominance over others, giving orders, self-assertion
6. *Religious*—God, ethical values, and spiritual considerations (a feeling of unity with Nature, not just church membership)

As was true of group identification, it appears likely that man can come to value, and strive for, almost any symbol or activity. So, a person trained in accounting may come to value orderliness, attention to detail, and other aspects of his work. A factory manager may value production, to the extent of ignoring profit, the attitudes of his workers, or other considerations. A man may become interested in world government, and focus a lot of energy on this ideal value, even though he gets little group support. In all such cases, when enough information is gathered, it is found that the particular symbol which is valued highly has this role because of prior experiences associated with security, prestige, reward, or anxiety reduction.

Explaining vs. explaining away. Perhaps this is a good point at which to deal with a common protest against psychological analysis of the major social motives. Many people seem to feel that scientific psychology not only "explains" patriotism, artistic creativity, social idealism, and ethical values, but "explains them away." The complaint suggests that these "higher" aspects of life are somehow demeaned by coming under dispassionate analysis.

To the psychologists, such a complaint seems totally unjustified. If we say that Lord Byron, because of his clubfoot, felt a need to compensate and achieve superiority, and adopted the writing of poetry as a means to this end, we certainly do not change the quality of Byron's lyrics. A painter may sublimate a frustrated love impulse by producing lovely works of art; our psychological analysis of the motivations involved does not detract from the quality of his painting and indeed may add a depth of human emotion to the purely esthetic appreciation we feel. The psychologist is concerned with tracing these dynamic forces back to their origins in heredity or in early environmental influences; such genetic investigation does not bear in any way on the social value of the behavior involved. Almost anyone will admit, for example, that patriotism has been responsible for many noble acts and that it has also caused the needless deaths of many innocent citizens of other nations. Preparing a balance sheet of the good and bad in patriotism is not primarily a psychological problem and is certainly beyond the scope of this book.

The student, therefore, in reading psycho-logical analyses of complex social dynamics, will do well to focus on the problem of understanding, without attempting at the same time to evaluate. At the very least, he should understand that this penetration into early origins of social motives does not imply a denial of their strength or of their significance in modern life.

Self-enhancement

One fact stands out from this consideration of social motives in American culture. This is that the child becomes increasingly aware of himself as an individual and seeks by various means to enhance the importance of that self. Any activity, legal or criminal, any group or symbol can come to be valued if it leads to self-enhancement. Indeed, some psychologists have argued that this is the *only* social motive.

Motives, as the foregoing pages should have made amply clear, are not fixed demands for particular objects (as are the biological drives); they are, on the contrary, highly flexible in seeking states of satisfaction and tension reduction. They are related primarily to symbols of reward and threat.

Self-enhancement means that each man looks at the situation facing him and mobilizes energy for that course of action which will enhance his own status. He seeks to maximize long-run enjoyment, and reduce anxiety. Thus, a businessman may give up an income of $200,000 a year to become a university president at $25,000 a year, because the latter is perceived as a higher status. Workers may suffer considerable hardship during a strike to force recognition of their union, because they feel more important as a consequence. The desires for prestige, for property, for power, and for the strengthening of social groups all come into focus as aspects of this one major motive in our civilization—the individual's desire for self-enhancement.

Some psychologists have used the term "self-actualization" to refer to this tendency for motivation to be channeled in any way advantageous to the self. Maslow (1943) has asserted that

Even if all these needs (biogenic, prestige, etc.) are satisfied, we may still often (if not always) expect that a new discontent and restlessness will soon develop, unless the individual is doing what he is fitted for. A musician must make music, an artist must paint, a poet must write, if he is to be ultimately happy. What a man *can* be, he *must* be. This need we may call "self-actualization."[1]

Now, of course, if this statement is taken at face value, it is ridiculous. Each of us has so many potentialities that he would be in a state of perpetual conflict if he tried to actualize all of them. I could be a chemist, a tightrope walker, a novelist, etc. It is plainly impossible to act out all such possibilities.

What Maslow seems to mean is that, once certain abilities have been developed into skills through the application of the rewards and punishments derived from more basic motivations, self-actualization can impel the person to continue and improve. Thus a boy may practice the violin because his parents bribe, push, scold, and encourage him. As he develops some skill and self-confidence, he may come to enjoy playing the violin and channel a great deal of energy into this activity. Self-actualization, then, may motivate behavior which has been set in motion by other motives; it probably never initiates a totally new pattern.

A hierarchy of human motives. The facts of satiation and deprivation indicate that, as one motive is weakened by attainment of its goal, another takes over and dominates behavior. Within a given class, such as the biogenic drives, it is possible to compare these impulses directly and predict

[1] Reprinted by permission of The American Psychological Association.

TABLE 4:1. A Hierarchy of Human Motives
(*Based on A. H. Maslow, 1943*)

Self-actualization	The need to do those things which develop us as individuals; to use our abilities constructively
Esteem	Including the need for achievement, and the need for recognition by others
Love	Need for affection, for belonging to a group, for a friendly social environment
Safety	Including protection against violence, against economic hazards, against an unpredictable reality
Physiological	Hunger, thirst, sex, fatigue, etc.

which will control behavior. If we attempt to cover the whole range of motivation, this task becomes impossible of precise determination and there will be substantial variation between persons. Maslow proposes the hierarchy shown in Table 4:1 as a generalization about the relative potency of motives. According to the principle of dominance, serious deprivation of one of the motives at the bottom of this scale will monopolize consciousness, dominate behavior, and push aside activity based on one farther up. Conversely, as the impulses at basic levels are gratified, "higher" motives take over and direct behavior. As we have commented many times, such a ranking will vary considerably from individual to individual and must not be thought of as any kind of absolute scale. Nevertheless, it may be useful by providing a framework for thinking about the relative strengths of different motives.

Résumé on Human Motivation

In the preceding three chapters we have summarized some of the major facts with regard to the dynamics of human behavior. It is hardly practical to try to condense further this already shortened account. It may, however, be useful to note once more some of the main principles to which attention has been drawn.

1. *The principle of homeostasis.* The human being is first of all a biological organism. As such, he is governed by biological laws, and homeostasis is one of these. This principle asserts that the organism will exert effort to maintain certain essential constancies. The biogenic drives, hunger, thirst, etc., show the potency of such energy mobilizations. We have further noted that the emotions and the social motives can be understood in terms of homeostasis. Man does not try simply to return to a former state; he attempts to build up a physical environment which will guarantee need satisfactions, and then he tries to erect a constant social milieu which will protect him against insecurity, loss of affection, inferiority, and isolation.

2. *The principle of deprivation.* Since drives and motives cannot be directly observed, their strength is inferred from the amount of effort expended in attempts to reach the goal. Experimental attempts to vary strength of motivation, therefore, start with depriving the person of a specified goal object for varying periods of time, and then observing his behavior. This leads to clearly intensified motivation in the case of biogenic drives, up to a certain point (which may be that of physiological damage to the organism). In the case of emotions, the deprivation was characteristically not directly related to strength. Neither love nor fear is modified by relatively long periods away from the object of the emotion (unless other factors intervene.) In the social motives, deprivation tends to strengthen the desire up to a point, but continued deprivation leads to abandoning the goal. This is possible because the goal is chiefly symbolic; it is not possible with the biogenic drives, since the achievement of the goal is essential to life.

3. *The principle of infantile deprivation.* In almost all cases, we get evidence that infantile deprivation of a certain goal leads to overvaluation of that goal in adult life. This is indicated by experimental evidence in the case of food hoarding, and by clinical material in case of the need for affection and security. It is probably true also for safety (using that as the goal which is deprived in the case of fear and anxiety).

4. *The principle of satiation.* Satiation weakens biogenic drives, but it has no effect on emotions. There is some evidence that satiation weakens social motives, however; people who have been highly secure do not show so much concern over security as others do, and persons who have long occupied a prestige position seem able to forgo such satisfactions better. This is related very closely to infantile deprivation; if the person has lacked security in early life, his security demands later on will be literally insatiable.

5. *The principle of goal evaluation.* Motivation arises originally from tension, but it soon comes under external control. We learn to evaluate perceived goal objects and to prefer those which give a maximum of tension reduction. Cultural factors enter at this point; if a person persists in using methods of tension reduction which are socially disapproved, he encounters punishment. The method or goal will then be perceived as anxiety arousing, and (probably) rejected.

6. *Barrier function.* In connection with evaluation of goal objects, we noted that the presence of a barrier, if not too rigid, may actually enhance a valence. A slight interference with attainment of a specific goal may make it seem more attractive. Thus "distant pastures look greenest," a phenomenon which makes for exploratory behavior and hence for superior adjustment in the long run.

7. *The principle of goal substitution.* If a goal is unattainable (*e.g.*, the barrier is impenetrable), goal substitution takes place. One does not starve to death simply be-

cause tenderloin steaks are unavailable; he can live on hamburger. However, the culture sets limits on substitutions; in America, grasshoppers would not be an acceptable substitute. The medieval robber barons had their own method of obtaining security and prestige; this goal is no longer permissible.

8. *The principle of symbolic reward and punishment.* The emotions and social motives derive their potency from their relation to the biogenic drives. The goals of emotion and social motive are symbols of need satisfaction or threat on the more fundamental level. (After these symbols have been firmly established, new symbolic functions can develop from them; thus one can fear loss of prestige, and this sets off anxiety.)

9. *The principle of multiple determination.* Obviously, man is endowed with a wide variety of motives for action. It is hardly surprising, therefore, that a number of them can be activated simultaneously. The course of behavior seems to be a resultant of these forces. Motives making for approach to the object summate and reinforce each other; motives making for withdrawal set up a conflict. Behavior is a result of this interaction, although it need not be a compromise. (For further discussion of conflicts of motives, see Chap. 14.)

The pleasure-pain paradox. The thoughtful student may be inclined to raise a question at this point with regard to the scientific analysis of motivation. Is this, he asks, anything more than the old notion that man seeks pleasure and avoids pain? The question is important because even a casual observation of human behavior shows that man frequently forgoes pleasures, accepts pain to achieve later pleasure, and may even seem to enjoy pain, as in masochism.

Actually, a careful examination of the foregoing account of motivation will reveal that the pleasure-pain paradox is no paradox at all. Man can learn to value an extraordinary range of symbolic goals, some of which may in the immediate sense be painful, or may carry some discomfort along with them. Animals, too, are capable of such learning to a limited extent. As we have noted elsewhere, the organism must, when faced with alternative goal objects, make a decision; hunger and sex drives cannot be gratified simultaneously, nor can thirst and fear. Thus, even at the biological level, there is frequently a process of evaluating different goals and moving toward that which is most potent at the time.

We can clear up this question, perhaps, with three summary principles: (1) the organism seeks tension reduction and avoids tension increase. This is true of all varieties of human motivation. With experience, pleasure becomes a signal for tension reduction; pain, for tension increase. (2) The organism learns that immediate pleasure can be a signal for future tension increase, and vice versa. This means that it becomes possible to evaluate quantitatively the present pleasure and future discomfort, and make a choice. (3) The principle of multiple determination means that, when various motives are operating, the organism responds to the summation of them all. Thus, to reduce a major tension, it may be necessary to accept increase of minor tensions.

Conscious and unconscious motivation. Little attention has been paid, in the two prior chapters, to the problem of unconscious motives. To simplify the presentation, the discussion has been set up as if all motivation were consciously understood by the experiencing organism. Actually, this is not true even of the biological drives and is much less true of emotions and social motives.

One of the authors has noted that, if circumstances compel him to miss regular meals and eat at odd times while engaged in pressing mental work, he may develop a headache, become quite irritable, and show restless activity for some time before he realizes that he is hungry. The stomach balloon experiment (page 54) indicated that many people have contractions considerably prior to conscious recognition of hunger. Adolescents give good illustrations of unconscious sex motivation. The rowdy tomboyish girl suddenly becomes concerned about her hair, her complexion, her clothes; she studies the art of make-up and subdues her raucous voice; yet, if the suggestion is offered that she has become interested in boys, she rejects the idea violently and with obvious sincerity. The same process, of course, can be noted in adolescent males. Thus, needs may set off restless seeking and even some degree of adaptive behavior without conscious awareness of the tension.

Emotions, of course, are often unconscious. The psychoanalysts have supplied us with numerous proofs of these phenomena: slips of the tongue in which we reveal unconscious hostility toward another person; agitation set off by unrecognized fear; irrational jealousy which is denied with fervor and obvious (conscious) sincerity. Love is often denied, especially if for some reason there is an obvious barrier to its satisfactory expression.

Finally, we should emphasize that a great deal of social motivation is completely unconscious. Here is a person who is constantly arranging occasions to be with his superiors, entertaining them socially, indulging in sly criticisms of men competing with him on an equal level, and arbitrary in his relations with those under his direction. If one suggests to him that his power drive is rather strong, he may indignantly deny this notion.

We do not, of course, find a sharp dichotomy between conscious and unconscious motives. What we do find is a range from tension states which can easily be verbalized and described to others, through states which can be identified with study and effort, to states which resist any but the most prolonged probing under hypnosis or psychoanalysis. We also find that *control* of motivated behavior is increasingly difficult as we go down this scale. If a tension is not available for symbolic representation (as, by words), one has a real problem in trying to evaluate the relative potency of reward and punishment. Hence, under the pressure of unconscious motives, people may repeatedly get themselves into identical scrapes. Unless the tension is somehow symbolized in consciousness, it is highly resistant to modification.

A major contribution which can result from the study of psychology is a clearer awareness of one's own motives, with resulting opportunities to plan intelligently for actions most likely to lead to the desired satisfactions. "Know thyself," said the Greek philosopher; the man or woman who denies the presence of strong motives merely because it seems shameful to admit them is in the situation of trying to navigate a course beset by grave dangers without a chart.

Infantile and Adult Motivation

Sigmund Freud pointed out many years ago that the nature of motivation tends to change from infancy to maturity. While some adults maintain infantile personalities, the general trend is clear.

Infantile motivation is characterized generally by what Freud called "the pleasure principle," or the imperative demand for immediate gratification. With increasing intellectual maturation, with a longer memory span, and with the perception of future pleasure or pain as well as that now offered, the child becomes capable of delay, of sustaining tension, of seeking the maximum long-time reward. Thus his behavior tends to conform to the "reality principle," the principle that actions are directed to the

long-run maximum of pleasure and minimum of pain. Adults may forgo glowingly
attractive rewards now at hand to attain
greater ones or to avoid severe punishment
later.

Frustration tolerance. A generalized
characteristic of personalities which will
identify this change from pleasure principle
to reality principle has been called *frustration tolerance*. In the preceding chapter it
was noted that frustration of any desire
mobilizes additional energy and that people
differ in the "overload" they can tolerate.
Babies characteristically react with overt
aggression to any frustration; interference
with food, with free movement, etc., leads
to an outburst of crying, violent flailing of
the arms and legs, and widespread visceral
changes. At this stage frustration tolerance
is low or nonexistent.

Developing frustration tolerance may be
in part a function of heredity. It may be
that the infant's nervous system simply is
not capable of absorbing and sustaining
tension but must react with overt movement. The major contribution, however,
comes from environment. Nonreward of
aggression, or actual punishment of aggressive actions (including failure to observe
social taboos against seizing desired goal
objects) by adults leads the child to delay
overt action. In some persons this process
remains always incomplete; they show
some infantile, demanding responses even
at maturity. In others it may go too far;
the individual may become cowed, afraid
to want anything, accepting orders from
anyone in the environment. The usual
result, however, is a developing ability to
accept frustrations, to judge situations,
and to delay the demand for satisfaction
until the threat of punishment is absent or
the reward is at its highest attainable level.
In this manner we achieve the maximum of
pleasure and the minimum of pain over a
long period of time.

Frustration tolerance, then, should be
identified as a limitation upon the principle
of homeostasis, the principle of maintaining
equilibrium. With increasing frustration
tolerance, increasing degrees of disequilibrium can be sustained by the organism
without an immediate quest for gratification. Nevertheless, we assume that each
person has a limit beyond which he cannot
go; a sufficient piling up of frustration will
exceed the tolerance of any individual.

Complexity of adult motives. Another
important distinction between infantile and
adult motivation is found in the relative
complexity of the two. It is relatively rare
to find a major activity of an adult human
which is powered by a single motive,
whereas in young children we often observe
behavior which is clearly dominated by a
single, rather specific impulse. This increase
in complexity is not, of course, a function of
motivation alone. Adults have a tremendously wider span of attention; they bring
to bear memories, imagination, probabilities, and possibilities as modifiers of the
immediately present situation. Whatever
the cause, we wish to emphasize that most
adult activities are powered by more than
one motive. Thus the choice of a profession
is likely to involve economic status,
prestige, attractiveness to the opposite
sex, and other goals. A worker going on
strike usually does so not merely because
of the simple controversy over wages,
hours, or other issues which goes down in
the statistics of the Department of Labor.
Often enough he is influenced by resentment at poor supervision, loyalty to a
union leader, fear of future economic
insecurity, and dislike of action against the
choice of a majority of his fellows.

**Adult motivation is primarily not physio-
logical.** It appears reasonably adequate to
conceive of the motivation of the newborn
as exclusively physiological in character.
The needs of hunger, thirst, excretion, and
physical comfort dominate the behavior of
the child. This status does not long con-

tinue. Soon the importance of acquired tensions becomes obvious. The child desires the presence of his mother and manifests extreme anxiety when she disappears. He develops an attachment to physical surroundings and to stimuli which are signals of comfort and physiological satisfaction. With increasing maturity he gives evidence of tension-valence relationships which may be labeled curiosity, gregariousness, family loyalty, gang loyalty, idealism, and so on.

This analysis implies that in adults the complex and elaborate superstructure of hates, fears, loyalties, and other adult motives covers up the hard core of physiological drives. Adults rarely act on a basis of hunger alone, or thirst alone, or sex alone. Always present is an acute awareness of the involvement of this act with other goals. Thus one might suffer considerable hunger and yet refuse to eat food with a detested person. Idealism or devotion to a specific person may be enough to counter a very intense sex drive. The adult is dominated by physiological needs only under the most extreme pressures of deprivation.

Yet we feel it necessary again to emphasize that these ideals, loyalties, and other social motivations arise on a physiological basis. Let us note very briefly four reasons why most psychologists accept this view.

1. *The development of the individual.* As we study the development of the human being from infancy to maturity, we are clearly impressed with the primacy of the physiological drives and with the fact that they serve as a substructure upon which the social motives are evolved.

2. *The evidence from catastrophe.* Another reason for holding the physiological needs to be basic is the dominance they attain under extreme circumstances. If a man is suffering from extreme deprivation of food, emotional security, prestige, and status, it is the need for food which dominates his actions. He does not respond to the social needs. With limited incomes (Fig. 2:13, page 52) people buy food, not football tickets.

3. *The evidence from comparative anthropology.* It is now well known that the social motives vary significantly from one culture to another. The prestige motive, so powerful in America, is almost lacking in some primitive groups. Others, equally primitive, carry it to an extreme most of us would consider insane. Group loyalty can become so strong that, according to one observer, a native of a certain African tribe will not try to escape from crocodiles if he falls into the river. He considers that he has been chosen by the crocodile god, and if he got away, great harm would befall the village. But in all these groups we find the same physiological impulses operating. Hunger, thirst, comfort, and sex are universals.

4. *The phylogenetic argument.* Finally, we may comment on the fact that a theory to explain motivation should explain animal as well as human motivation. Animals clearly are dominated by physiological drives, although the extent to which social influences can function when the environment favors them has surprised many observers.

All biological and psychological science is organized around the conception that man and animal form a continuous series. Thus, if biological motivation is clearly dominant in the lower animals, one presumes that it might be basic also in human beings. This point can hardly be considered crucial by itself, but it reinforces the implication of the preceding three.

SUMMARY

Energy mobilization is the term by which we describe the dynamic aspect of human behavior and experience. We actually observe behavior powered by energy mobilization in man's quest for certain defined goals. Many of these goals are related to the maintenance of essential biological constancies: blood sugar level, temperature, oxygen and water balances, and so on. Any interference with these constant states will result in the mobilization of large amounts of energy; vigorous, persistent effort will be exerted to restore the homeostatic equilibrium.

By the process of dynamic homeostasis, the organism (especially man) attempts to build a constant environment which will protect his biological constancies. Thus he builds houses, plants crops, and stores food, invents air conditioning. He also seeks to develop a constant social environment, in which his parents, friends, and other familiar signs of need satisfaction will be readily at hand. He desires affection, security, power, prestige; he works for group expansion and for attainment of social values. Economic and social motivations thus derive from the biological drives, such as hunger, thirst, and sex, and the emotional drives, such as love, anger, and fear.

Under extreme deprivation, the biological drives are likely to dominate the behavior of human beings. However, as basic tissue needs are gratified, emotional and social motives come to direct activity. Although these motives are considered to arise originally from biological needs, they may become sufficiently powerful to overrule biological impulses. The mature human being is one who can tolerate frustration of needs, evaluate goals, and choose a course of action which will bring the maximum of gratification and minimum of pain over a long period of time. Infantile motivation is characterized by an immediate grasping of pleasure or avoidance of pain, without regard to long-run consequences.

Motivation provides the power which impels adaptive behavior, including learning, understanding the environment, thinking, and reasoning. Thus an understanding of human behavior must first aim at a comprehensive view of motives and emotions. In the following chapters we turn to a consideration of the processes by which man seeks gratification of his motives: perceiving his environment, learning how to deal with it, thinking about it. But we must remember that motivation is basic to these "higher" mental processes.

Recommended Readings[1]

BLACKBURN, J. A.: *Psychology and the Social Pattern.* London: Kegan Paul, Trench, Trubner & Co., 1945.

FREEMAN, ELLIS: *Social Psychology.* New York: Holt, 1936. Chaps. 9–11.

LEWIN, KURT: *Resolving Social Conflicts.* New York: Harper, 1949.

MURPHY, GARDNER (Ed.): *Human Nature and Enduring Peace.* Boston: Houghton Mifflin, 1943.

TOLMAN, E. C.: *Drives toward War.* New York: Appleton-Century-Crofts, 1942.

[1] See also p. 547.

PART TWO

Cognition

So far we have been concerned to present the basic facts of human motivation. It should be clear that man is a dynamic organism, restless, seeking satisfaction, searching for positive goals, and escaping from threatening situations as best he can.

How does he achieve these aims? As the chapters on dynamics presented answers to the question, why? the following pages will focus on the question, how? Man must become aware of his environment; he must identify objects which promise tension reduction, and objects which threaten tension increase.

Furthermore, he must acquire techniques for dealing with these external situations. The principle of dynamic homeostasis asserts that man does not merely restore a previous state of equilibrium; he takes steps to prevent future deprivations, and he devises new living conditions which provide for superior ways of dealing with threats.

In our psychological analysis of these cognitive processes, we again start at the simplest level. What kinds of information does man get from his environment? Here we must consider the sensory processes, vision, hearing, taste, smell, and so on. Then we study the perceptions which are derived from sensations and which are the immediate guides to behavior.

Learning is the most important cognitive function in everyday life. Scientific research indicates that there are several different kinds of learning; we shall deal with association, conditioning, and problem solving.

Finally we must consider thinking, which is the most complex and so, perhaps, the most characteristically human of all cognitive processes. Man is unique in his unparalleled ability to develop symbols for environmental realities and then to solve problems by manipulating these symbols. Unfortunately, it is not uncommon for him, in the process, to create new problems for himself. We shall thus find it worth while to examine briefly ways of improving the accuracy of thinking.

Men differ with regard to their cognitive abilities, at least in a quantitative way. Some acquire knowledge rapidly, some slowly. The most important dimension along which they differ is that which is generally called *intelligence*. In a concluding chapter of this section we treat briefly the nature and measurement of intellectual abilities.

CHAPTER 5

Sensing

Mankind lives in a world of energy. Physics tells us that we are constantly being assailed by cosmic rays, light waves, heat waves, sound waves. For adaptation and survival, we must understand the messages they bring us. There are also bodily processes going on within, based on the conversion of food into energy, and information from these may also be of vital significance. At the surface of the skin we also come into contact with objects, chemicals, and gases which are important to the maintenance of homeostatic equilibrium.

From a subjective point of view this description sounds unrealistic. We never have any direct awareness of these waves, these chemicals. We are conscious of sights, sounds, temperatures, textures, tastes, smells, and the like. Our bodies are so constituted that specialized organs receive physical energies and translate them into sensations; these sensations then become the basis for guiding behavior for the satisfaction of motives.

In Fig. 5:1 is represented, in highly schematic form, the relation of stimulus source to stimulus to sensory process to conscious awareness and behavior. The sun, as light source, sends energy waves to the earth. Bouncing off houses and objects, the light waves become a *stimulus* to the eye (*sense organ*). Nerve impulses set up in the eye travel to various centers of the brain, ultimately arousing *visual sensations*, which can then become the basis for *perception* of meaning. However, *responses* can occur even though no meaning is aroused. While this figure represents the situation as regards vision, a similar diagram could be drawn for any other kind of sensory process.

There are many types of energy to which we are not sensitive. We lack, and often need, built-in detectors for cosmic rays, gamma rays, X rays, ultraviolet and infrared radiation, supersonic vibrations, and so on. We can comprehend this situation in terms of an evolutionary process by suggesting that, under primitive conditions, these energy forms had little significance for survival. It is only recently, for example, that man has contrived situations in which a built-in Geiger counter might be essential to his continued existence.

The study of sensations. This chapter is concerned with the processes by which we become aware of those energy changes to which we are sensitive. We shall, of course, pay minimal attention to the physics of stimuli. Light waves, sound waves, etc., are the proper subject matter of physics. The chemicals which set off tastes and smells belong to chemistry. Detailed analyses of these stimuli would be outside the scope of our work. We shall limit our discussion

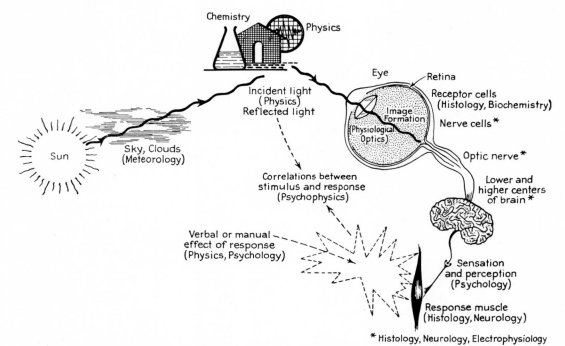

FIG. 5:1. Energy source, stimulus, and sensation. This diagram shows the variety of processes which are involved in a single sensory experience, such as vision, and the number of different sciences which would be involved in a complete description of the occurrence. (*By Sol Ehrlich, from Physics Today.*)

to what goes on in the sense organ, and the resulting experiences, insofar as that is possible.

The phenomenological method. One way to study sensory processes is to examine human experience by careful observation of ordinary occurrences. This method is sometimes called the *naïve* or *phenomenological* method. It involves trying to understand the sensory process as it goes on in everyday life, without introducing any special laboratory controls. The student can use this method himself, by simply observing his own way of sensing the world about him. Thus, when you look at a table, you see a meaningful picture in terms of objects. The surfaces look colored; they feel (and look) hard; the corners are square. Furthermore, you see this object as a table, having certain uses and certain associations in your own life. As you will later learn, most of these characteristics are not

"out there" at all; they are contributions your organism makes to the process of observation.

The analytical method. This approach is naïve in comparison with the highly analytical devices for studying sensation which developed later. For example, the quality of visual experiences is changed if the surrounding field is cut out, *e.g.*, by looking through a pinhole. Or we set up a controlled situation by putting the observer in a dark room, letting in a tiny light, and gradually increasing it in intensity. The observer then reports that the light looks brighter. Or we vary the wave length of the light, and the observer says it changes in color.

This is the essence of the experimental method in psychology. In studying motives we noted that we could vary the length of food deprivation and find that animals (and humans) would exert more effort to obtain food. The *independent* variable was the length of time without food, and the *dependent* variable was the feeling of hunger, or the amount of work done. In studying vision the independent variable is the physical stimulus (wave length of light) and the dependent variable is colored sensation. When we are engaged in studying such variables, we try to keep all other factors constant, so that the results will not be a confused mixture of many variables. Hence the use of the peephole, the dark room, soundproof laboratories, and so forth. These are devices for eliminating stimuli which we do not want, so that we can study the sensations produced by one stimulus at a time. In this way the properties of the sense organs (receptors) have been carefully segregated from the influence of memories, values, and other variables.

It should not be inferred that the analytic method is superior to the phenomenological method. Each has its values and its shortcomings. One complements the other. However, the phenomenological method gets a more complex kind of information, in which meanings, context, and values play a role; the analytic method gets down to the basic process of sensing physical stimuli. We shall therefore deal in this chapter with the reactions of our receptors, specialized nerves, to stimuli, in the form of sensations. In the next chapter we shall move on to a consideration of how we use these sensations to get our complex understandings of objects, persons, and situations.

The Nature of the Stimulus

Although the analytic method of observation is not the best approach for all psychological problems, it is a sophisticated method. Before it could be used successfully, the properties of the stimulus had to be known. Physics has furnished the necessary information on the physical side. In addition, knowledge of the structure of the sense organs and the nature of nerve conduction is necessary. Physiology has contributed in these areas. The term *stimulus* is generally used to identify any objective situation that sets off a response in the organism. Examples are ice on the skin, a thunderclap, or an insulting word. In sensory work a stimulus is defined more rigidly as *some form of physical energy that activates a receptor*. The stimulus for the eye is radiant energy of certain wave lengths; for the ear, mechanical vibrations at certain frequencies; for touch, pressure on the skin: for taste, chemical composition of dissolved substances on the tongue; and for smell, gaseous particles in the nostrils.

The adequate stimulus. For each sense organ there is a particular form of energy which usually stimulates that organ. Thus the *adequate* stimulus for vision is a range of radiation within certain wave lengths; but pressure on the eyeball can also cause visual sensations. In this case we say that pressure is an *inadequate* stimulus. Chemicals in solution on the tongue provide the adequate stimuli for taste, but an electrical current will be "tasted"—an inadequate stimulus.

The interesting point here is that, if *any* stimulus activates the sensitive nerve cells of the retina of the eye, they give rise to visual sensations. They cannot report pressure or electrical current. Similarly, the taste buds can report only tastes, even though the stimulus applied has no connection with taste. The human species has evolved in such a way as to have certain specialized nerves for reporting certain changes in the environment; if anything activates these nerves, they automatically "report" the only kind of message they can send.

Stimulus and receptor are intimately related. It is always possible to define a stimulus in physical terms, but we cannot understand the significance of the stimulus without knowing how the receptor is

TABLE 5:1. Physical-energy Sources Corresponding to Different Sensations

Type of stimulus	Receptor	Sensory experience	Possible perceptions (or meanings)	Sensory modality
Radiant energy of wave length less than 10^{-5} cm. (cosmic rays, X rays)...............	None	None	None	None
Radiant energy of wave length 10^{-4} to 10^{-5} cm. (light waves).	Retina of eye	Hue, brightness	Persons, objects	Visual
Radiant energy of wave length 10^{-2} to 10^{-4} cm.............	Cells in skin	Heat	Stove, weather	Cutaneous
Mechanical vibrations of frequency 20 to 20,000 per second	Cochlea of ear	Pitch, loudness	Voice, music	Auditory
Mechanical pressures..........	Cells in skin	Contact	Fabric, metal	Cutaneous
Mechanical pressures..........	Cells in muscles, tendons, joints	Pressure, weight, movement	Sprained ankle, heavy load	Kinesthetic
Movement of head............	Semicircular canals	Equilibrium	Loss of balance	Vestibular
Chemicals in liquid solution....	Taste buds	Tastes	Pickles, candy	Gustatory
Chemicals in gaseous solution...	Olfactory membrane	Odors	Flowers	Olfactory
Chemical or mechanical action..	Cells in viscera	Pressure, visceral disturbance	Hunger, nausea	Organic
Extreme energy of any class....	Free nerve endings	Pain	Wound, illness	Cutaneous

aroused. In Table 5:1 we have brought together the various kinds of physical stimuli which are adequate for the specified receptors, and the sensations to which they give rise. In subsequent pages we shall discuss each of these various sensory processes in greater detail.

The physics of sensing. In the case of light and sound, our knowledge of the physical stimulus is so complete that we can determine what aspect of the stimulus determines a specific sensory response. Thus, in the case of light, the physical stimulus can be varied independently in wave length, intensity of the waves, or composition of the waves. For each of these variants there is a specific sensory experience. With variations of wave length there is a conscious appreciation of change in hue; with the intensity variable, brightness of the light changes; and with composition of wave lengths we get color mixtures. Such correlated changes in experience with changes in the dimensions of the stimulus constitute the subject matter of the science of *psychophysics*, or the relation of mental processes to physical stimuli. The precise stimuli for some of the other sense organs are less well understood; taste and smell, for example, are known to be initiated by chemicals of some sort, but the exact energy process is not known.

The physiology of sensing. It is relatively easy to determine the psychological correlates for physical dimensions of the stimulus. It is more difficult to explain what happens. For each psychophysical correlation there must be a *specific effect* in the receptor process and its nerve connection to the brain. An explanation of sensory experience requires the discovery of these specific receptor and nervous functions. In other words, we need to know the physiological correlates of sensory dimensions. In this area our knowledge is quite incomplete. The search for physiological bases for sensory data is the science of *psychophysiology*. The study of sensory experience is, therefore, a combination of psychophysics and psychophysiology. We shall mention only a few rudimentary facts about the physiology of sensing in this book.

Sensations

Just as physicists have worked on the problem of classifying energies and determining the physical dimensions of stimuli, so psychologists have been engaged in determining the essential categories which must be used if we are to classify and organize our knowledge of sensations. We shall summarize these concepts very briefly; their meaning will develop as we examine the results of specific investigations.

Sensory modality. Each sense organ gives its own unique kind of report to the brain. It is just as impossible to compare the color of an object with the sound it gives off, as it is to compare its weight with its chemical constitution. The data are simply different in kind. The term *modality* is used to identify this particular classification of sensations. There are far more than the traditional five senses; there are probably fifteen or sixteen separate modalities, some of which are difficult to name: vision, hearing, taste, smell, temperature, light touch, deep pressure, pain, muscle sensitivity, static sensitivity, organic sensitivity, and so on. Some of these, while undoubtedly valuable in terms of survival, have little significance for psychology and will be glossed over or ignored in this volume.

Sensory attributes. Within each sensory modality we get many variations of a qualitative nature. The eye responds to light, but lights can vary in many ways. From these stimuli we get variations in color, in brightness, and in saturation. Sounds are heard as varying in pitch, loudness, and duration. Within each sensory attribute we usually get quantitative differences—how much brighter, how much louder? But of course it is impossible to make comparisons between attributes.

Sensory qualities. When a light stimulus

changes in wave length, the observer reports changes in color: red, blue, green, yellow, etc. These are not quantitative; they are differences in the *kind* of sensation reported. Similarly, tastes differ as bitter, sour, sweet, and salty. These are qualitative differences. Such variations in the sensory process will be called *sensory qualities.*[1]

Usually these qualities can themselves be judged in quantitative terms; *i.e.,* one taste is sweeter than another, one red is more intense than another. Qualities also vary quantitatively as regards *extension* and *duration.* Extension refers to the spatial distribution of the stimulus and duration to its distribution in time.

The continuum principle. Wherever possible, psychologists like to get their sensory data lined up in such a way that a continuum is formed, with degrees of differences. So, for example, we can arrange visual sensations this way:

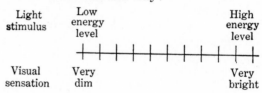

Here we have a true continuum; every gradual change in energy level produces a corresponding small change in visual intensity. However, we have trouble with this on colors; wave lengths form a continuum, but the sensations change in quality from red to orange, from orange to yellow, and so on. Such variations make scientific work difficult. We shall therefore try to arrange our data in continua wherever possible.

Thresholds. As soon as we find a sensory attribute or quality which can be arranged

[1] Sensory qualities are, of course, attributes of sensation. We have emphasized the attribute of quality here because studies of behavior indicate that quality is a more efficient aid to adjustment than other attributes such as intensity, size, or duration.

on a continuum, we want to know things about it. We want to know the low end of the dimension; what is the *least stimulus* which will arouse that sensation? We also want to know, how much of a change in the physical stimulus will cause a change in the experienced sensation? These are problems of thresholds.

The minimal stimulus necessary just barely to stimulate a receptor is called the *absolute threshold*. The absolute thresholds for the eye and ear reveal that these organs are more sensitive than most delicate instruments for measuring the energy of light and sound. The olfactory sense is so keen that a tiny drop of perfume diffused in an ordinary room is obvious. The smell of a dead skunk on the highway is sensed a good distance from the source.

There is also the measure of the upper limit of sensitivity. Thus the limit of man's hearing a tone is about 20,000 vibrations. Hunters know that dogs can hear a Galton whistle which man cannot hear. The bat is known to perceive a sound frequency of 50,000 per second. It is difficult to measure upper *intensity* limits, because very powerful stimuli also arouse pain. The upper threshold is sometimes called the *terminal threshold*.

An important measure of sensitivity is the *difference threshold*. How keen is your ear in discriminating pitch differences? Many accomplished musicians can discriminate a difference between two notes of one-half of a vibration. The Seashore records of musical talent contain a record measuring pitch discrimination. Discrimination of differences between sensations is so important for psychology that something should be said about how the difference threshold is determined.

Early in the history of sensory psychology, the so-called *psychophysical methods* of measuring sensation were developed. There are several basic methods. One, the *method of limits*, is very simple and is widely used in determining the absolute and terminal thresholds. A variation of the method is the way the oculist uses the Snellen chart in testing one's vision. The chart consists of lines of print varying in size. The subject reads the letters in each line until he comes to his limit, or the line which he cannot see well enough to read. From this fact and the distance of the subject from the chart, the oculist can measure the amount of defect in visual acuity. In using the method of limits the value of the stimuli is known. Thus in the Snellen chart the letters vary in size.

A typical way of determining the absolute threshold for light is to present a patch of light in a dark room to a subject who is properly seated before the patch. He observes the light with one eye through a square aperture 2 mm. wide which is placed as close to the cornea of the eye as possible. This aperture or hole serves as an *artificial pupil*, controlling the variable of pupillary dilation. The experiment is started with the light obviously visible and its intensity is gradually reduced until the subject first reports that he cannot see any light. The value of the light is noted at this point. This measure was obtained by the *descending series*. On the next trial the *ascending series* is used. The experiment is started with the light intensity below the threshold. All that the subject sees is a tiny point of light which indicates the position where the light patch will appear. The experimenter then gradually increases the intensity of the light until a point is reached when the subject reports that he first sees the light patch. The threshold is determined by averaging the values obtained by the descending and ascending series. If the threshold figure is important, many ascending and descending readings are obtained. Ascending and descending series are used because the inertia of the organism tends to delay changing the judgment of "seeing" to "not seeing" the light on the descending series, and from "not seeing" to "seeing" the patch on the ascending series. By taking an average of both series this error is corrected.

The difference threshold. It is important to know the slightest stimulus to which a sense organ will respond, and it is also valuable to learn the smallest change in stimulus which will be sensed as a change. The *method of minimal changes* can be used to obtain the *differential threshold* or the difference limen. In this case a *standard stimulus* must be chosen. For example, in the Seashore measures for musical talent the standard pitch was held at 435 d.v. The *variable* stimulus, or the comparison stimulus, must be capable of being greater or smaller than the standard. In the case of pitch discrimination the comparison stimulus consists of a set of tuning forks which are at fixed frequencies above and below the standard 435 d.v. In this case the stimuli must be presented in succession. Again we use the ascending and descending series. For the ascending series we begin with the comparison stimulus considerably "lower" than the standard and keep increasing it until the observer reports that the pitch he hears is "the same" and finally to higher in pitch than the standard. In the descending series the converse procedure is employed. The difference threshold is determined by finding that difference in pitch which can just be detected; it is computed by averaging the results of the ascending and descending series.

The difference threshold has many practical implications. It enables us to answer such questions as, how many different colors can the eye see? If we treat as a different color any hue which is just noticeably different (just beyond the difference threshold) from its neighbor, the answer is that the normal eye can see 156 different hues in the spectrum. In the yellow region discrimination is very sensitive; at the red and violet ends it is very coarse. The utility of such information in the color and dye industries is obvious. Medical diagnosis, particularly in neurological disorders, is often facilitated by measurements of difference thresholds such as in the sense of touch.

Weber's law. The difference threshold is also important because it is the basis of an important law of psychology. The Weber law states that in the medium ranges of intensity for most sense modalities the difference limen (j.n.d.) divided by the intensity of the stimulus is a constant. It is usually stated mathematically by the formula

$$\frac{\Delta S}{S} = C$$

Δ is the j.n.d. and S is the value of the stimulus in physical energy. The practical application of this law can be illustrated in the field of illuminating engineering. If 1 candle of light added to 100 candles produces a just noticeable difference in brightness, how many candles must be added to 500 candles to produce a noticeable difference in illumination? The answer according to Weber's law is 5. In other words, the Weber fraction is $\frac{1}{100}$, and it is a constant. There are many other situations where Weber fractions are useful.

The Weber fraction differs from one sense modality to another. Therefore, the sensitivity of the different receptor organs can be compared in terms of their respective Weber fractions. Thus the fraction for visual brightness is roughly $\frac{1}{100}$, and for auditory loudness, $\frac{1}{5}$. The following order of sensory sensitivity from most to least sensitive is taken from data under particular experimental conditions. Most sensitive is deep pressure, then come visual brightness, lifted weights, tone, smell, light cutaneous pressure, and taste. This order is fairly representative, though the fraction varies with the particular conditions of experimentation even in the same sense modality.

The fact of the Weber fraction indicates that the sense organ is subject to some kind of inertia, because the differential threshold does not reflect the extraordinary sensitivity of receptors as measured by the absolute threshold. However, if we look at this phenomenon from the point of view of need satisfaction, it does not seem undesirable. It is important for us to know that a stimulus is present (light, sound, smell, etc.). In general it is less important to know whether the stimulus is changing. At any rate, the fact is this: the difference threshold for all senses is much larger than the absolute threshold, so that just barely detecting a stimulus is much easier than detecting a change in a stimulus already noticed.

Frame of reference. Whenever we measure a difference threshold to obtain the j.n.d. or to compute a Weber fraction, we must ask the person to judge his own sensations. He must say, "This weight is heavier" or "That line is longer" or "That sound is louder." This implies that the individual has some kind of inner yardstick which he applies to the sensations for comparative purposes. (This is true even if they are presented simultaneously.)

The inner measuring device which we use for evaluating differences in sensations is called a *frame of reference.*[1] We refer a new sensation to it for comparison. By the time we reach maturity, most of us have long since developed fairly precise frames of reference for length, weight, sound, etc. Even those can be greatly improved by a few minutes' practice in the laboratory.

[1] It will be noted that this is a phenomenon we have already encountered. In Chap. 2 we discussed the evaluation of goal objects and showed how the child builds up a set of standards for judging "good" or "bad" objects in terms of their homeostatic value, the judgments expressed by parents, and so on. The development of a sensory frame of reference is a very similar process; we acquire standards, "mental pictures" in a manner of speaking, with which a new sensation can be compared.

If, on the other hand, a novel problem is presented, the development of a frame of reference can be observed. Suppose I am asked to judge odors as stronger or weaker. Never having done this, I am at first confused and judge at random. After a time, however, I begin to detect differences which I first failed to notice; and with a few hours of training, I become quite sure of my judgments and they agree rather closely with the physical measurements of the stimulus.

Changes in thresholds. Man has, we can see, a marvelous built-in detector system. Like most such sensitive systems, it runs some danger of overloading. As we noted above, stimuli near the terminal threshold are usually painful; this can serve to arouse anxiety so that the person gets away from the stimulus. The sensory mechanism, however, has its own inherited device for reducing overload. This is a process of changing thresholds.

If you step from a lighted room into the dark, you can see only the brighter stars. After 10 minutes in the dark, you see thousands of dimmer stars as well. The absolute threshold has dropped to adapt to this situation. Conversely, if you keep looking at a bright light, it begins to seem dimmer; loud sounds lose some of their intensity, and so on. By these changes in threshold the sense organs apparently can compensate or rather protect themselves from the danger of overloading. Most sense organs cease to respond to a given stimulus after a certain time. This is known as the phenomenon of *sensory adaptation.* Adaptation to odor is very rapid and often complete. Taste is altered by adaptation; that is why we eat dessert at the end of the meal. We become used to the touch and pressure of our clothes on our bodies and do not notice the constantly changing pressures with bodily movement. Sensory adaptation is partly due to *fatigue* of the sensitive cells. More complicated forms of adaptation, such as negative adaptation in learning, and *satiation*, a concept we have used frequently in connection with motives, have a function similar to that of sensory adaptation—to protect us from overstimulation. It should be remembered that the organism tends to maintain the *status quo*. When the stimulus has been noticed, its signal value has been furnished and its main utility served. From there on it no longer adds much to adjustment. We know about it; for all practical purposes it is unnecessary for further signaling. Therefore, its sensory compellingness can be reduced.

Subliminal stimuli. It is obvious, from the foregoing, that we do not sense all the stimuli even in the adequate categories. A stimulus which is not consciously sensed because of its low intensity is described as *subliminal* (below the threshold). There seem to be three classes of subliminal stimuli: (1) A stimulus may be so weak that it is below the absolute threshold. It simply is not capable of activating a sensory neurone. (2) A stimulus may be above the absolute but below the physiological threshold. This can be demonstrated most easily with vision; the light-adapted eye cannot sense weak lights, but when the eye is dark-adapted, they are clearly visible. (3) A stimulus may be above the physiological but below the conscious threshold. The ticking of a clock, for example, does not lower the physiological reactivity of the auditory sense organ, but it drops out of consciousness. These three types of thresholds are diagramed in Fig. 5:2.

The "five senses." When most people think of the human sensory mechanism, they remember the phrase "five senses." Scientific psychology has identified many more than five; between 15 and 20 sensory modalities are reported by different investigators. In the following pages we shall sketch only some essential facts about the modalities most important in human adjustment.

Somesthesis, or the Body Sensations

From what has been said already, it should be apparent that the study of sensation is the province of several professions. The physicist is concerned with the stimulating energy (Fig. 5:1). The physiologist and neurologist study the nature of the receptor and its nervous connections. The psychologist is faced with the problem of estimating the role played by particular aspects of the stimulus and the sense organ in producing the experience of sensory attributes. It is important that the student have some knowledge of the nervous system at critical points in psychology. In the chapter on emotions we presented some basic facts regarding the ANS. In sensation and perception some knowledge of sensory physiology and the central or peripheral nervous system is essential. The following order of presenting the special sense organs was selected because, by proceeding from the simplest sense organs to the more complex, we can also introduce a discussion of the nervous system on a continuum from simple to complex. Thus in this section on the body senses it is easy to introduce the concept of the specialized nerve cell which is sensitive to a particular form of energy, the nerve impulse which goes from the sense organ to spinal cord and brain, and the muscular response which customarily

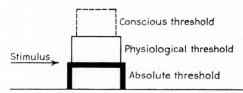

FIG. 5:2. Different types of thresholds. A stimulus below the absolute threshold cannot be sensed at all; it cannot activate the sensory cell. Somewhat higher stimuli may be blocked out by physiological states, such as fatigue or light adaptation. Still more stimuli are blocked out by the attention mechanism (if attention is focused on one stimulus source, other stimuli are shut out).

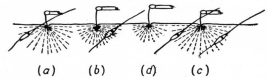

(a)   (b)   (d)   (c)

FIG. 5:3. Skin tester. Sensitivity of the skin is mapped by pressing down with horsehairs. The short coarse hair (a) exerts more pressure than the long thin hair (d). Considerable pressure is likely to stimulate two sensitive spots (c). The bulb-shaped structure is at the root of a hair. (From Boring, Langfeld, and Weld, 1935, by permission of John Wiley & Sons, Inc.)

follows. Let us first consider the sensory side of this process.

Somesthesis means *bodily feeling*. The ancients regarded feeling as one of the traditional five senses. Modern research indicates that bodily feeling is made up of several different sensations, each having special receptors and nerve pathways to the brain. Somesthesis is generally classified into three main departments: (1) the skin senses; (2) the internal sense, or *organic* sensations, in the alimentary canal, the viscera, and the vital organs; and (3) the kinesthetic sensations which are aroused by the action of muscles, joints, and tendons.

Skin senses. The skin surface is a multiform sense organ. The skin responds to contacts on its surface from the external environment. The contacts may be *mechanically* administered by contact with another object, *chemical* such as an acid on the skin, *radiations* from a light source or the temperature of the surrounding media. The sensory experience is always located on the body surface. In this respect the skin senses are distinguished from the distance receptors, such as the eye, ear, and nose, which locate the stimulus in objects at some distance from the body. All the somesthetic senses are characterized by reference to some part of the body.

The skin offers a variety of experiences: cold, warm, hot, tickly, itch, softness, roughness, wetness, dryness, for example.

The classical opinion is that there are only four primary skin sensations: pressure, pain, warm, and cold. All other skin experiences are regarded as patterns or fusions of these four. Thus wetness has been synthetically produced by a mixture of touch (pressure) and cold sensations. A thin dry rubber bag, full of water and cracked ice, feels wet.

Skin sensitivity varies on different parts of the body. This can be easily demonstrated by moving a blunt pencil point along the inner surface of the forearm. As the point moves, there will be areas which are more sensitive to touch than others, patches of cold sensation are passed, occasionally warm spots, and here and there relatively dead places. A more systematic exploration requires marking off a definite area on the skin by stamping a millimeter grid on it and stimulating definite points on the skin marked by the grid. The stimulator is usually a pointed instrument of simple design. The classical work in this field was done by exploring the skin for pressure sensations with horsehair, for pain with needles, and for warm and cold with small metal cylinders. (These cylinders were cooled or warmed by being placed in water of appropriate temperature and then the pointed end of the cylinder was applied to a point on the skin.) In Fig. 5:3 is an illustration showing how horsehair can be used to control the intensity of the touch stimulus. The short coarse hair in *a* presses harder than the long thin hair in *d*.

Such explorations show that the sense organs in the skin are distributed in punctiform manner. That is, over a given area some points respond to touch, others to cold and warmth. In Fig. 5:4 are examples of maps of pressure spots on a hairy region of the skin. The pressure receptors are closely associated with the hairs on the skin. If the intensity of pressure is great enough, practically every point on the skin is sensitive. However, this is apparently due

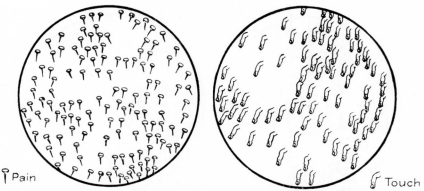

FIG. 5:4. Maps of pressure- and pain-sensitive spots. Pain spots are very numerous, but there are spots on the skin which are not sensitive to pain unless enough pressure is applied to stimulate an adjoining spot as in Fig. 5:3c. Light touch or pressure is also sensed at many spots on a given skin area, especially at the base of and on the "windward" side of a hair. The two maps are of the same skin area. (Modified from Gerard, 1941, Fig. 29, p. 64, by permission of John Wiley & Sons, Inc.)

to the fact that, if more pressure is exerted, the deformation on the skin may extend to a neighboring sense organ (c, Fig. 5:3). The real stimulus to pressure is thus the stretch or tension on the skin.

Pain. Pain spots are quite numerous per unit area and they are widely distributed over the skin surface. Originally it was thought that pain was an intensive attribute of all the other skin receptors, that is, of overstimulation of these receptors. Since the free nerve endings are most common of the nerve structures in the skin, pain has been attributed to them. The fact that the mucous lining of the cheek has no free nerve endings and is insensitive to pain, is corroborative evidence; so is the fact that, in the regions of the body most sensitive to pain, such as the cornea of the eye and the inner parts of the ear canal, only free nerve endings are found. Fig. 5:4 shows the pain map for a small skin area.

To the person who is tortured by a headache or the pain following an injury, it may seem that the sense of pain is one he would prefer to eliminate from his psychological make-up. This would be a serious mistake. Pain is one of our most important sources of information in our never-ending quest for survival. Mowrer (1950) has described a young woman who seems to have been born lacking this particular form of sensitivity.

As an infant, this individual almost chewed her tongue off. Enjoying the pleasure of biting on this meaty object in her mouth and perhaps liking the taste of its juices, she had all but destroyed this important part of her own body. Later, at the age of about three, she had pretty thoroughly cooked a portion of, and thus seriously injured, one of her thighs by standing overlong against a hot radiator. . . . At the seashore she is likely to find her feet seriously cut and bleeding because of having unheedingly walked over sharp stones or glass.[1]

Temperature. The reception of temperature sensations has been attributed to two separate receptors—the cold and warm spots. Cold spots are more common than warm spots, and they are more quickly aroused than warm spots. Warm and cold spots can be found and verified by repeated examination. Yet, when the skin in such areas is cut out and examined microscopically, no specialized nerve endings other than free nerve endings have been found.

[1] Mowrer (1950), p. 33. Reprinted by permission of Grune and Stratton, Inc.

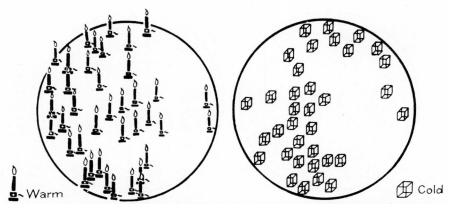

FIG. 5:5. Maps of warm and cold spots. Generally cold spots are more numerous than warm spots, but neither compares with the touch and pain distribution (Fig. 5:4). These maps are for the same skin area as in that figure. (*Modified from Gerard, 1941, Fig. 29, p. 64.*)

There are two kinds of temperature experiences which support the idea that cold and warmth are mediated by separate receptors. One is called *paradoxical cold*. A cold spot may be excited by a warm stimulus. A stimulus temperature in the neighborhood of 113°F. will excite some cold spots, although warmth is generally an inadequate stimulus for cold. Many people report paradoxical cold upon first getting into a warm bath. The other experience is the sensation of "hot." It has been shown that, if cold and warm spots are aroused simultaneously, heat is experienced. An easy way to demonstrate the above fact is by the use of a heat grill which consists of parallel metal tubes. Cold water is passed through half the tubes and warm water through the alternate tubes. If this grill is placed on the volar surface of the forearm, the grill feels hot.

On the other hand, the facts about relativity of temperature experience suggest that the temperature receptor may be a single nervous mechanism. The skin temperature varies with different parts of the body. This temperature is known as the *physiological zero*. On the average, skin temperature is around 87°F. Whenever a given skin area is in the process of having its temperature raised above its physio-

logical zero, one feels warmth, and vice versa. The more it is raised or lowered, and the more quickly the temperature is changed, the more intense is the feeling. Suppose, for example, that the back of the hand has a temperature of 87°F. and a metal object with a temperature of 89°F. is applied. Since this object is warmer than the skin, and since the metal is a good heat conductor, one will feel warmth. But if the physiological zero at that moment were 91°F., then the object would feel cold. These facts can be easily demonstrated with three buckets of water: hot, cold, and lukewarm. Place the right hand in hot water, the left in cold, and leave for 2 minutes. Now place both hands in the lukewarm water: it feels warm to the left, cool to the right. When one goes swimming, the water at first feels cool; as the physiological zero shifts, it seems warm. Temperature adaptation is a good illustration of the process discussed in Chap. 2: the organism building up an equilibrium with the environment.

The nervous basis of skin senses. We have sketched a few facts about the skin senses. There are at least four modalities: pressure, pain, warm, and cold—unless we decide that warm and cold are different qualities of a single sensory mode, in which case there are three. These sensations are tied to particular points on the surface of the skin. It ought, therefore, to be easy to locate the specialized nerve endings just beneath these points; but, as noted above, we are disappointed in this hope. Nevertheless, it is certain that the various sensations are mediated through sensory cells in the skin. Let us take a quick look at some elementary but important facts about this nervous mechanism.

The sensory-motor arc. If you touch a hot stove, you will snatch your hand away *before* you are conscious of the pain. If a frog without his brain has acid placed on his skin, a foot will come up and scratch at that point. These simple skin-sense behavior units can serve as a model for the basic unit of the nervous system—the sensory-motor arc. The arc consists of a chain of neurones which together form the functional unit of the nervous system. The individual neurones that make up the arc may be conceived of as anatomical units. The function of the arc is a response to a stimulus. Such things as hand withdrawal, winking, coughing, knee jerk, etc., are typical reflex arcs. To produce these responses a certain concatenation of characteristic nerve structures is necessary. A *receptor* must be stimulated. The impulse set up in the receptor must be transmitted along a nerve fiber which is called the *sensory neurone.* The sensory impulse must be relayed to a *motor neurone* which is in contact with a muscle or gland at the end of the arc. Muscles and glands are called *effectors* because they result in action. The relays between sensory and motor nerves are known as *connectors.* Connectors are usually located in some center in the spinal cord or the brain.

In Fig. 5:6 a reflex arc at the spinal-cord level is illustrated. This simple hookup is more common in connection with the skin senses than with most of the other receptors. The sensitive cell is activated by

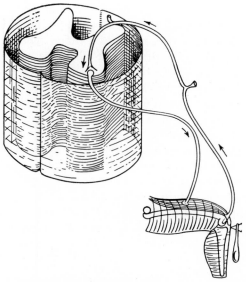

FIG. 5:6. Sensory-motor arc. This diagram represents the ordinary knee-jerk reflex. A tap with the rubber hammer stimulates a sensory cell in the tendon; an impulse goes up the sensory fiber to the spinal cord, across a synapse, and out a motor fiber to a muscle cell, which contracts, causing the leg to kick in the direction of the stimulus. (*From Krieg, 1942. Reprinted by permission of The Blakiston Company.*)

some physical change, *e.g.,* contact with an insect on the skin. An impulse travels along the sensory fiber, across the gap which is called a *synapse,* along a connecting neurone, and out over a motor neurone to a muscle (and we brush off the fly).

In such a simple sensory-motor arc the brain may or may not be involved. Consciousness of the sensation seems clearly dependent on an impulse getting to the brain; the muscle response does not. At the spinal level responses are aroused without the necessity of a brain. Thus the scratch reflex can be elicited from a dog whose spinal cord is severed below the brain. Such simple spinal reflexes are neat for showing the arc or loop character of a simple reflex. But one should not take the loop analogy too literally, because at synaptic centers, even at the spinal-cord level, the sensory nerve impulse may be shifted to any part of the nervous system, and its activity may be facilitated or inhibited by impulses reaching it from the brain. Since synapses are loci of facilitation or blockage of the nerve impulse in the reflex arcs, the concept of *synaptic resistance* has been used in theories of learning.

Neurones in a reflex arc transmit impulses always in one direction. They enter the dendrites and pass out at the axone,[1] whose terminations are sometimes called *end brushes*. The receptor can be envisaged as an elaborate dendrite which picks up the appropriate energy, then funnels it through its own axone to the dendrite of the sensory nerve, which in turn transmits the impulse to its own axone and thence to the dendrite of the motor neurone.

The sensory nerves. Each spot sensitive to pressure, warmth, cold, or pain is a receptor, a specialized neurone. The axones of these fibers join together (outside or inside the spinal cord) and go up to the brain as a unit. The curious feature of this, inside the cord, is that all the pressure pathways get into a single bundle or tract, all the pain fibers in another, and so on. In the condition known as *locomotor ataxia*, certain tracts in the cord are destroyed, while others are not. Thus the person still gets contact sensations from his feet and can walk by shuffling along. But his normal muscular sensitivity is lost—the connection to the brain destroyed.

Brain representation of the skin. Even more interesting, perhaps, is the fact that there is a special portion of the cortex of the cerebrum on which the skin senses are represented. The brain makes a kind of map of the body (see Fig. 5:13), and a nerve impulse from any skin receptor is reported to the proper place in the brain. We shall have more to say on this later.

[1] Generally speaking, the term *dendrite* simply means the receiving end of the neurone, and the *axone* is the transmitting end. There are some structural differences, but they need not concern us here.

Organic sensations. The skin is not all exposed to the external world. Much skin lines the esophagus and the alimentary canal. The vital organs, such as the lungs, heart, etc., have skin surfaces. Ordinarily the internal organs are not very sensitive. It is known that the brain can be cut without producing pain. This seems to be the case with visceral organs. However, the viscera are sensitive to pain produced by pressure. Balloons and tubes injected into the stomach and colon have proved that the viscera react to pain, pressure, and temperature.

Typical organic experiences not due to outside interference are hunger, thirst, nausea, fatigue, gas pains, and cramps, to mention but a few. The traditional view is that all of these are complexes of pressure and pain. Their importance in connection with motivation has already been discussed (Chap. 2).

As might be anticipated from the comments on the role of the autonomic nervous system (ANS) in motivation (Chap. 3), the organic sense receptors are linked more closely to the ANS than to the cerebrospinal system. The central nervous system (CNS), which includes the cerebrum, cerebellum, and spinal cord (Fig. 5:11), is concerned mostly with adaptation to the external world. The ANS is related primarily to inner homeostasis, including sensory reports of organic conditions ("All's well" or "Something is wrong"). Thus the sensory-motor arcs starting with organic receptors go mostly to the ANS, while those starting with skin receptors go mostly to the CNS.

Kinesthesis. Kinesthesis derives from the Greek words meaning "the sense of movement." The receptors are located in the muscles, joints, and tendons. The physical stimuli are stretching of the muscles and tendons, and movements of the joints. These movements send impulses to the somesthetic area in the brain where

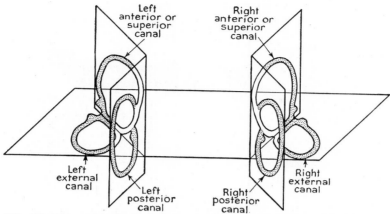

FIG. 5:7. The semicircular canals. As this diagram shows, the canals are so arranged that there are two in each of the three planes of space. This provides us with an excellent device for sensing movement of the head in any direction. (*From Warren and Carmichael, 1930, by permission of Houghton Mifflin Co.*)

information seems to be correlated as to the position of our limbs. From here the impulses are shunted to the motor area of the brain, and back to the muscles, tendons, and joints to induce further activity. Because the muscles, joints, and tendons are self-stimulating, they have sometimes been called *proprioceptors*. It is because of the capacity for self-regulation by the muscles that motor habits acquire the high degree of automaticity that they do.

Few people, prior to studying psychology, think of muscle sensitivity as important. Actually, it underlies all kinds of skilled activities, such as speech, dancing, typewriting—anything in which a complex series of movements must be run off with split-second timing. While the kinesthetic impulses go up the spinal cord in a tract separate from the skin senses (as illustrated by locomotor ataxia), the two sets of impulses are reunited in the cortex. This is functionally necessary because touch and muscle sense cooperate so closely in guiding motor adjustments of the body.

The equilibrium sense. Another sensory system of the greatest importance for walking, swimming, and other movements is the sense of equilibrium or balance. The

special organ of this sensory system is found in the inner ear. The inner ear has two essential parts—the vestibular and the cochlear mechanisms. The former is characterized by three semicircular canals which act like levels in indicating the inclination the head (Fig. 5:7). The latter looks like a snail shell and contains the essential organs of hearing. It will therefore be discussed later (pages 162–164).

The vestibular mechanism consists of two functionally different parts—the semicircular canals and the vestibule. The canals

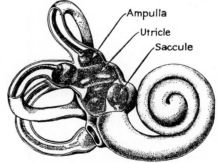

FIG. 5:8. Relation of semicircular canals to vestibule and cochlea. In addition to the canals (left), the ampulla, utricle, and saccule also play a part in our sense of equilibrium (see text). The cochlea (right) is concerned only with hearing. (*From Scientific American.*)

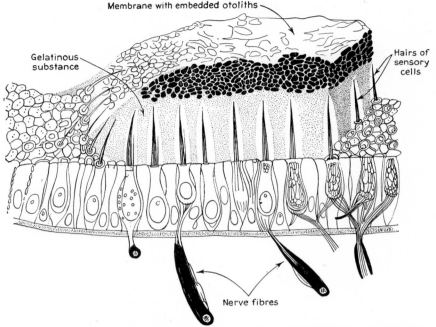

Membrane with embedded otoliths

Gelatinous substance

Hairs of sensory cells

Nerve fibres

FIG. 5:9. Sensory cells involved in equilibrium sense. A highly magnified cross section of a membrane in the vestibule. The mechanical action of the otoliths is explained in the text and illustrated in Fig. 5:10. (*From Scientific American.*)

are concerned with rotation; the vestibule with movements of the body forward, backward, up, and down. In Fig. 5:8 the canals are shown where the outer bone has been cut away. The canals contain a saline solution known as *endolymph*. At the end of each canal is a bulblike elaboration called the *ampulla*. In each ampulla is a gelatinous mass containing hair tufts which are called the *cristae*. When the head is tilted, the fluid in the canals presses against the hairs in a direction depending upon the inclination. Stimulation of the hairs sends impulses to the brain centers which interpret the head position. The canals are arranged in a special manner. If the head is inclined about 25 degrees one canal is virtually parallel with the ground. The other two are perpendicular to the base canal and are slanted so that one canal, anterior, leans forward 45 degrees from the median plane of the head, and the

posterior canal 45 degrees backward. Figure 5:7 shows the plane relations of all six canals of the two ears. In Fig. 5:10 the mechanical action of the canals is depicted under typical phases of head rotation.

Each canal is connected with the vestibule as a common base. The same fluid activates the receptors in the canals and in the vestibule. The vestibule contains two saclike structures which are coterminous with each other and are called the *utricle* and the *saccule*. The nerve endings in these sacs consist of hairs which have at their ends tiny stonelike particles called *otoliths* (Fig. 5:9). It is the weight of these otoliths and their response to gravity, their momentum and inertia, which bend the hairs and thus stimulate the sensory receptors at their bases. It is thought that the sacs are responsive to starts and stops of the body in straight directions, and to gravity. The canals seem to be limited to rotation or change in direction. The combined function of all the canals and the sacs is regarded as adequate to indicate any bodily movement.

Localization of stimuli. If a large grid is stamped on the volar surface of the left arm, and a particular point on this grid is touched, the subject with eyes closed is able to touch the same point with a pencil in his right hand. The error is remarkably small. Now, if the experimenter should touch a point on the left arm and ask the subject to locate the touched spot on his *right* arm, the subject makes a larger error but still does very well. In fact, if, instead of touching the stimulated point on the arm, he is asked to locate the point on a *picture* of his arm, he does almost as well as he would reproducing the touch on the real arm. This kind of evidence means that the subject carries a *body image* or *schema* in his mind, in terms of which he is able to locate one part of the body with reference to another. It also proves that he knows what muscle or joint in the body is in action. Besides aiding in adjustment, such a body schema is important to the development of the concept of the self (see Chap. 13). This is generally true of the somesthetic experiences. They are all localized somewhere in the body. Distance receptors tend to project localization to external bodies and so do not give a feeling of intimacy or self-reference as do the contact senses. Consequently somesthetic sensations are extremely important not only for their value in adjustment but for their vital contribution to our feeling of selfhood. (Traditionally the distance receptors were emphasized, a trend which culminated in the philosophy of rationalism. It was only later in the development of psychology that bodily feelings began to be emphasized in relation to the psychology of personality. Gerard nicely indicates this transition in our conception of psychology by noting that Descartes would have been more nearly right if he had said, "I feel, therefore, I am" instead of "I think, therefore I am.")

Two-point threshold. The sense of touch yields a measure of sensory acuity known as the *two-point limen*. If the areas of the skin are stimulated with fine points, these points must be separated by a definite distance to be sensed as two. The smallest distance that can be reliably perceived is

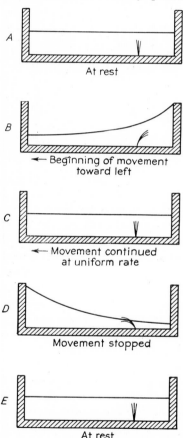

FIG. 5:10. Mechanical action of the semicircular canals. Effect on hair cells of movement of the body. Movement in one direction causes hairs to move in the liquid in the opposite direction (*B*); with continued rotation, an equilibrium is established and the hairs again come upright (*C*); when movement is stopped, the otoliths lean in the direction of movement, giving rise to after sensations of movement. (*From Boring, Langfeld, and Weld, 1935, by permission of John Wiley & Sons, Inc.*)

TABLE 5:2. Average Values for Two-point Limen in Different Skin Areas
(From Geldard, 1948)

	Least distance in millimeters sensed as two points
Tip of the tongue..............	1
Palmar side of the last phalanx of the finger...................	2
Red part of the lips...........	5
White of the lips, and metacarpus (base) of the thumb.........	9
Dorsal side (back) of first phalanx of finger...............	16
Skin on forehead and back of cheekbone.................	23
Back of the hand.............	31
Forearm, lower leg............	40
Back of foot, neck, chest.......	54
Middle of the back, and of the upper arm and leg..........	68

the measure of the limen, or threshold. The limen varies with different parts of the body. It is smallest on those parts which are manipulable, such as the hands and lips, and largest in those areas, like the back, which are less likely to be used in making contact with the outside world. Table 5:2 gives a summary of the two-point limens from different areas of the body.

These data are intriguing because of the further light they throw on the notion that one develops an image of his own body. What are the active, exploring parts of the body? The hands, lips, and tongue. A baby discovering a new object handles it and mouths it. These are the most sensitive areas; hence maximum information is obtained in this way. It seems likely, therefore, that in the body image these active, manipulating surfaces will make up a relatively large part and the passive, unused skin (as on the back) will be a small part of the picture. The data on brain function confirm this expectation.

Somesthesis and the central nervous system. We have shown that skin sensa-

tions are aroused when a specialized nerve cell is activated by external energy. We elaborated on the neurological events here to the extent of considering the simple sensory-motor arc, by which quick, automatic adjustments can be made to remove the skin from danger, and so on. However, we have not really considered the question of the conscious sensation. What neurological mechanism is involved in the awareness of contact, temperature, and the like?

Consciousness of sensations is a function of the highest levels of the CNS, in the cortex of the cerebrum. To appreciate what happens there, we must give a quick glimpse of the path by which the nerve impulse gets from the skin receptor to the cortex.

Figure 5:11 gives an over-all view of the brain and spinal cord, so that you can get a general orientation.[1] However, the sensory impulse goes through different mechanisms on its journey up to the brain, to which we must give attention.

In Fig. 5:6 was shown a cross section of the spinal cord. The sensory fiber comes in at the dorsal root of the nerve shown; the motor fibers come out from the cord by way of the ventral root and take their way to muscles and glands. When a hot object touches the skin, an impulse goes into the cord by way of the dorsal root, travels over a connecting neurone, and goes out the ventral root to a muscle which snatches the skin away. This is the simple reflex response described earlier. The impulse, however, also goes up the sensory tract in the cord, to the brain. Here it hits a nucleus or clump of connecting neurones in the thalamus, where it is switched into a bundle of fibers going up to the somesthetic area of the cortex, arousing a contact sensation.

The cerebrum. What we ordinarily call the brain, since it makes up such a large portion of the total, is the cerebrum. This organ is composed of two hemispheres,

[1] See also Fig. 3:2.

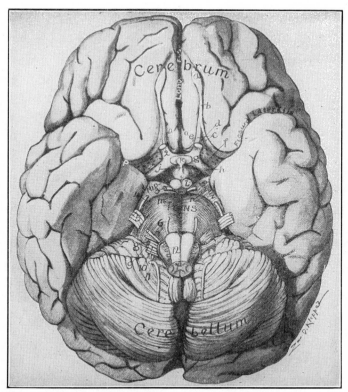

FIG. 5:11. The brain from below. Compare this with Fig. 3:2A, p. 78, to get the normal spatial relationship. The great light gray mass is the cerebrum. At the bottom of the picture, closely striated, is the cerebellum. In the lower center (12) is the spinal cord, emerging and starting downward. The medulla oblongata is the bulge at the upper end of the cord; just above is the pons, an important reflex-coordinating center. The thalamus and hypothalamus, so important in emotion and motivation, are above the pons, but concealed within the folds of the cerebrum. (*From Santee, 1907. Reprinted by permission of The Blakiston Company.*)

with a wrinkled or convoluted surface. On this surface, a layer of about ⅛ inch constitutes the cortex; and it is this thin layer of nerve cells which provides the physiological basis for civilization. In man the cerebrum is greatly enlarged as compared with other animals (Fig. 5:12).

The thalamus. A very important part of the cerebrum, with the cortex over it like an umbrella, is the thalamus. This major nerve nucleus has already been mentioned (pages 76–83) as playing an important

role in motivated behavior. We are now interested in it as a sensory switching station. At this point impulses from the skin are directed to one cortical area, from the ear, to another, from the eye, to another. There is some evidence that a kind of polarized good-bad consciousness resides in thalamic functions; when the thalamus is removed from cortical control, stroking of the skin may give rise to rapturous reports of pleasure (out of all proportion to the stimulus); similarly, a pinch may

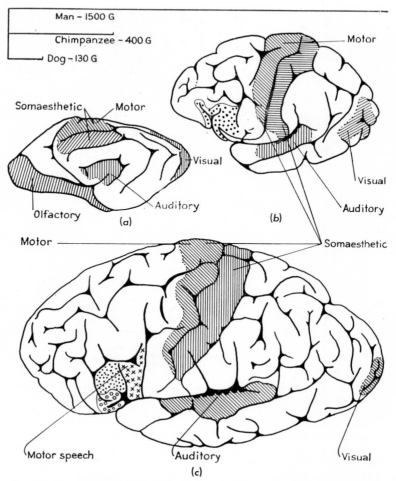

FIG. 5:12. The cerebral cortex in (a) dog, (b) chimpanzee, and (c) man. This shows the relative size and complexity of development of the cortex. The chimpanzee's cerebrum (400 grams) is three times that of the dog; man's cerebrum (1,500 grams) is almost four times the size of the chimpanzee's. Note the large olfactory area in the dog, which is lacking (actually, a small concealed area) in ape and man. The proportion of the cortex assigned to *specific* sensory and motor functions (shaded areas) decreases steadily as we go up the genetic scale; the white areas, presumed to function as association areas, may indicate the basis for man's superior symbolic functioning. *(From G. W. Bartelmez, in Newman, 1926, by permission of University of Chicago Press.)*

be reported as a horrible pain. Under normal conditions, however, sensory consciousness seems limited to the cortex.

The projection areas. The cortical area which receives impulses from the eyes is called the *visual projection area;* that receiving skin-initiated messages is called the

somesthetic projection area, and so on. We shall confine ourselves for the moment to the somesthetic area. This is located just to the rear of the great central fissure (look at Fig. 5:12 to identify these locations). On this area, the various nerve fibers are sorted out in such a way that sensory

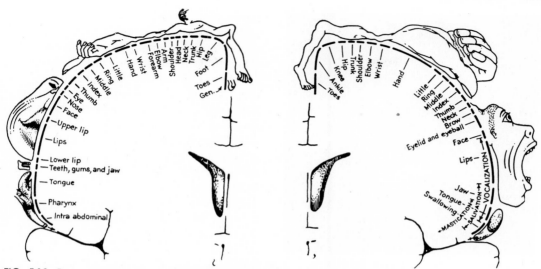

FIG. 5:13. Projection of body image onto somesthetic and motor areas. The figure on the left represents the localization of somesthetic (contact, pressure, movement) sensory impulses on the cortex. The diagram must be thought of as a cross section through the cerebrum, so that the feet send impulses to the top of the brain; the hand, face, and tongue, progressively down the side of the brain. Note that the amount of cortex devoted to a part of the body is roughly proportional to the two-point limen, or to the functional importance of getting sensations from that area.

On the right figure the corresponding arrangement is shown for the motor area. Again the control of foot and leg movements is at the top of the brain control of hand, face, and speech mechanism, lower on the side. While it is customary, as in Fig. 5:12, to show the motor cortex in front of the central groove and the somesthetic area behind it, there actually are some sensory fibers in the motor area. There is an extremely intimate connection between sensation and action for any given part of the body. Again, note that the cortical space allotted to an organ is proportional to its adaptive significance. (*From Penfield and Rasmussen, 1950, by permission of The Macmillan Company.*)

impulses from the feet go to the very top of the cortex, and the trunk, arms, and head follow in order down the side. This arrangement is shown in cross section in Fig. 5:13. If you will examine this closely, you will notice that the amount of cortex devoted to a particular part of the body is roughly proportional to the two-point limen, as suggested above, and to the functional importance of this part in manipulation and exploration. Note the amount of space for thumb and index finger, for example, as opposed to the entire trunk.

Motor projection area. Just forward of the central fissure is the motor projection area. Unlike the somesthetic area, this is a center from which impulses go out to the body. As its name implies, this center initiates voluntary motor impulses for movements of the parts of the body.

It is surely no accident that the somesthetic and motor areas parallel each other so closely. As Fig. 5:13 shows, the foot-leg-trunk-arm-head arrangement is duplicated. This is appropriate because a skin sensation from a given place is most likely to demand adjustive action from a nearby muscle group. Again we note that the amount of space corresponds closely to the amount of functional activity customary in that part of the body.

The cortex apparently contains no projection area for pain. Direct electrical stimulation of other projection areas gives rise to flashes of light, noises, skin tingling,

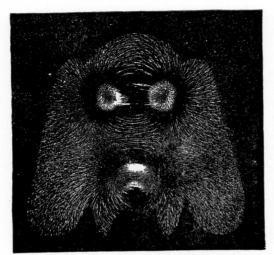

FIG. 5:14. Picture formed by magnetic field. This picture is produced by photographing the distribution of iron filings as they are arranged in a magnetic field. By changing the location of the poles, different shapes can be formed. Some neurologists have speculated that stimuli build up brain fields in the sensory cortex in some manner analogous to this. (*From Science Illustrated, February, 1948, p. 9.*)

etc., according as we stimulate visual, auditory, or somesthetic areas. But no area on the cortex gives rise to pain sensations, and it is possible to cut on the cortex without the patient's feeling anything.

Direct electrical stimulation of the motor area causes movement of the part of the body represented at this point. Such movements are not the jerky twitch of direct muscle innervation, but smooth, coordinated actions. Furthermore, the person reports that *he made the movement himself:* in other words, activity in the motor area seems to be the basis for a consciousness of intentional movement.

Association areas. The proportion of the cortex for which we have found definite functions is fairly small. There are great "silent areas" where brain tumors and operations cause no apparent loss of function, where electrical stimulation causes no report from the subject, and where no definite connections to the body can be located. They do have great networks of

nerve fibers connecting them with the sensory and motor areas and with each other, and we therefore conjecture that their function is to mediate *associations* of stimuli, ideas, or movements; as, for example, when you learn that the dinner bell means food, or that a red glow from the stove means that it is too hot to touch.

An injury to one of the specialized areas labeled in Fig. 5:12 will cause damage to the corresponding function; thus a wound in the occipital area will reduce or destroy vision. When the association areas are injured, there is no specific loss, but a general decline in mental efficiency. When rats learn a maze, for example (cf. Chap. 9), no brain operation to cut out a small area will destroy the habit. Memory and relearning are less efficient, however, and the decline is *proportional* to the percentage of brain destroyed. From this fact Lashley (1929) has derived his theory of equipotentiality, or the notion that all the association areas have equal value in complex processes. While this is a very important point for understanding the physical basis of psychological processes, the problems which arise are beyond the scope of an introductory textbook.

The facts of the body schema (representation of parts of body on the cortex, Fig. 5:13), of mass action or equipotentiality[1] in learning, etc., suggest the interesting thought that the cortex reproduces in some manner the relationships among external stimuli. One speculation about this process assumes that the brain develops electrical fields just as magnets will establish a field of force which may take a complex form (cf. Fig. 5:14).

The cerebellum. We should not leave this subject without a brief mention of the cerebellum (Fig. 5:11). This small knot of nerve tissue at the back of the head, almost completely overlaid by the cerebrum, has many connections from the kinesthetic

[1] See page 294.

receptors. Its function appears to be that of coordinating muscle movements; complex acts like balancing, dancing, swimming, etc., are especially disturbed by any injury to it. The evidence is that it is a motor, not a sensory, center; however, it must have a continuous inflow of information from the muscles, tendons, and joints if delicate coordinations are to be maintained.

Brain and adjustment. Static homeostasis could undoubtedly go on without a brain, or at least with a minimum of nerve tissue; reflex changes in breathing, heart rate, glandular function, and so on, occur without activity of the higher brain levels. Dynamic homeostasis, on the other hand, is a cortical function. We must explore the stimulus object, decide whether it is satisfying or threatening, and plan a course of action with regard to it. Most of the information used for this comes, not from the body senses, but from the distance receptors—smell, hearing, and sight. However, it has been convenient to introduce brain function in connection with the somesthetic impulses because of their greater simplicity and the neat localization they show. From this point on, localization becomes less clear, and the higher mental processes, such as thinking and reasoning, cannot be related to any particular portion of the brain.

The Chemical Senses

Taste and smell are the senses by which we detect our chemical environment. In the case of taste, the chemicals must be in solution. Dry substances placed on the tongue will not elicit a taste sensation until the fluids in the mouth have dissolved them. On a dry tongue a cube of sugar is tasteless until the saliva begins to dissolve it. The smell receptors in the nasal cavities are sensitive only to chemical substances in a gaseous state. The exact chemical struc-

tures of the stimuli for both taste and smell are not known as yet. The stimuli are therefore denoted by object or substance names, such as salt and sugar in taste, and smoky or flowery in smell.

Taste and smell are obviously of considerable homeostatic significance. We have noted particularly the role of taste in adjusting to dietary deficiencies. Smell seems to play an important part in sexual arousal and perhaps in other emotions. It has been shown (Laird, 1932) that a pleasant odor, even though unnoticed, biases a person's judgment decidedly. Unfortunately, we do not know enough about the operation of taste and smell to discuss them at any length.

The Distance Receptors

The ear and the eye, like all specialized sense organs, developed from the primitive skin senses of lowly organisms. As we go up the evolutionary scale, we get more distance sensitivity, and more refinement in analysis of the nature of the stimulus. Protozoa respond with the same mechanism to all stimuli, mechanical, chemical, thermal, and optical. Later organisms show differentiation of sensitive spots, which eventually become receptors for taste, smell, hearing, vision, etc.

The ear is actually stimulated mechanically, just like the contact receptors in the skin. However, an elaborate mechanism has grown up around the sensitive nerve endings in this case, making it possible for the vibrations to be analyzed with far greater precision than a skin receptor could ever manage. Similarly, the retina of the eye is an evolutionary improvement over the sensitive spot on the skin of low-level amphibia. Instead of reacting simply to changes in light intensity, man can analyze fine details of visually presented stimuli. This is possible because of the cornea, lens, and other accessory structures which

TABLE 5:3. Comparison of Visual and Auditory Senses

Dimension of physical stimulus	Corresponding dimension of auditory sensation	Corresponding dimension of visual sensation
Wave length, or frequency of wave	Pitch of sound	Hue or color of light
Intensity, or amplitude of waves, amount of energy	Loudness of sound	Brightness of light
Composition of wave lengths, purity of stimulus	Timbre	Saturation

have developed around the sensitive cells themselves.

The adjustment value of the distance receptors is obvious. Dynamic homeostasis is possible only if we have advance warning of dangers or of possible goal objects. In lower animals, smell is a major distance receptor, but with man's assumption of upright posture, smell lost some of its utility. This has been more than replaced by the finer analysis of objects possible through audition and vision.

Both sound and light travel in waves. However, the sound waves are counted in hundreds and thousands per second, while light waves must be figured in trillions per second. Sound waves are fairly long; middle C has a wave length of 4.34 feet. Light waves are infinitesimal; yellow light has a wave length of 580 millimicrons, one millimicron (mμ) being equal to 0.000001 millimeter. The adequate stimulus for sound is a mechanical vibration in the liquid in the inner ear, whereas for light it is some kind of chemical action (bleaching) on sensitive cells in the retina. Despite these seemingly extreme differences, we shall find some intriguing parallels in their functions.

The most striking similarity is found in stimulus analysis. Since the physical energy arrives in the form of waves, in both cases, this analysis produces parallel results.

Table 5:3 shows this parallel. If we measure the amplitude of the stimuli (as in Fig. 5:15), we get a stimulus dimension corresponding to loudness or brightness. If we measure the length of the waves (distance from peak to peak), we get a variable corresponding to pitch or color. If we separate waves as to purity of composition, we get timbre or saturation. Thus there is a psychological dimension, a variation in sensory result, for each physical dimension.

This correlation is not perfect. For instance, in vision, brightness is affected not only by intensity but also by wave length. The eye is more sensitive to yellow than to red or violet. A similar variation is found in the ear, wave lengths low in frequency being less easily heard.

Another difference is in keenness of analysis. The ear is a keen analyzer; most people can, with training, recognize the harmonics of a sound. On the other hand, a red book obstinately continues to look red, even though a spectroscope tells us that the book is reflecting all wave lengths to the eye, the red band just slightly stronger than the others. What the eye sees is only the *dominant wave*. A related fact is that auditory stimuli, presented at intervals of 0.1 second, will be heard as separate; visual stimuli at that speed will fuse. These differences in analytical precision are functions of the sensory mechanism: mechanical in the ear, chemical in the eye.

Hearing

Sound waves are produced by vibrations of an elastic body, which means almost any solid object. A taut string or a tuning fork set into vibration carries sound to the ears in the form of particles of air which strike the eardrum. (Sound waves will not travel through a vacuum.) Since air is an elastic medium, it is easily displaced by the vibrations set up by the fork. As the

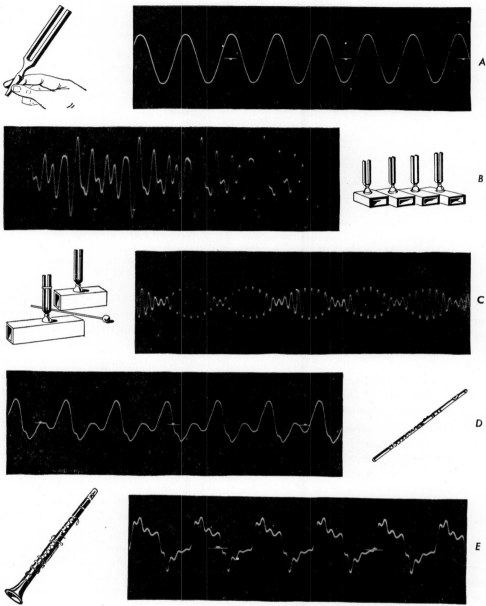

FIG. 5:15. Sound waves. When a single tuning fork is struck, a smooth sound wave is produced, giving a record like curve A. If several forks are struck simultaneously, the curve produced is a complex one, as the various waves summate to reinforce or interfere to weaken one another (curve B). This type of complex wave can always be reduced to its component simple waves if the pattern is symmetrical. Curves D and E show such complex curves; the same note, played by a flute and by a clarinet, gives a different pattern. The fundamental tone is the same, but the overtones are different. This gives each instrument its characteristic timbre. Curve C shows the phenomenon of beats, the rising and falling sound produced by two tones very close together in wave length. On all such curves, the vertical dimension (peak to valley) gives the amplitude of the wave (loudness), and the horizontal dimension (peak to peak) gives wave length (pitch). (From Miller, 1937, by permission of The Macmillan Company.)

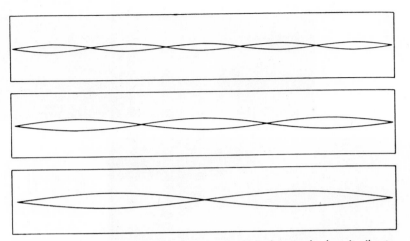

FIG. 5:16. Partial vibrations. When a string is plucked, not only does it vibrate as a whole, producing its fundamental tone, but also each half, each third, fourth, and so on, will vibrate. These partial vibrations sum with the fundamental, producing the timbre of the instrument (cf. Fig. 5:15). (From Miller, 1916.)

prong of the fork swings to the right, it compresses the adjacent air. When the prong swings to the left, it suddenly stops compressing and the adjacent air is rarefied, causing a partial vacuum. Meanwhile the compressed column has gone on. Now a second swing of the fork to the right starts another compression which follows the first. This wave of compression and rarefaction can be represented by a line record which represents compression as the peak of a wave, and the rarefaction as a low

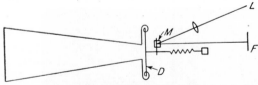

FIG. 5:17. The phonodeik. This is an instrument for recording the pattern of sound waves on a moving-picture film. The megaphone collects the sound waves and concentrates their energy on diaphragm (D). Attached to the diaphragm is a delicate thread which is looped around a tiny pulley and thence is attached to a small coil spring. On the pulley is a tiny mirror (M). From a light source (L) a beam of light is focused on the mirror and reflected from it into a camera containing a moving film (F). The sound waves shown in Fig. 5:15 were recorded by this device. (From Miller, 1937, by permission of The Macmillan Company.)

point in the line (Fig. 5:15). From such a record the wave length and the amplitude of the wave can be determined.

If the fork is struck softly and loudly, the frequency (wave length) will be the same, but the peaks will be higher for the stronger blow. We have already stated that amplitude is related to loudness, and frequency to pitch. However, the human ear can pick up only a limited spectrum of frequencies: the limits are roughly 20 and 20,000 cycles per second.

There is another characteristic in the sound waves which is significant to experience—*wave composition*. Every object vibrates with its main or natural frequency and also with other frequencies (Fig. 5:15). If there is no clearly audible main tone, but rather a mixture of a wide range of frequencies, we speak of "white" *noise*—by analogy with white light, which is a mixture of all common wave lengths.

There is no such thing as a *pure tone*, though the tuning fork approximates it. When a violin string is plucked or bowed, or when the piano wire is struck, this sets it to pulsate at a rate which varies with the size, length, and tension of the vibrator.

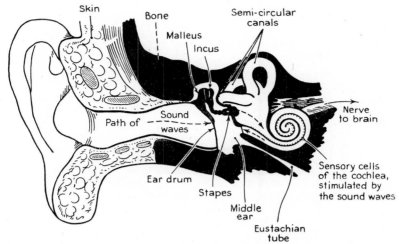

FIG. 5:18. The ear. The external ear (pinna) serves little or no function in hearing. In this drawing it is much smaller than it should be, in proportion to the middle and inner ear. Sound waves pass down the auditory canal and strike the eardrum. This sets in vibration the bones of the middle ear (malleus, incus, and stapes), which magnify the vibration and transmit it to the oval window. The fluid within the cochlea is compressed and a wave travels up the cochlea (upper dotted arrow) and so back to the round window (at the end of the lower dotted arrow). (*From Morgan and Stellar, 1950, adapted from Hearing and Deafness, edited by Hallowell Davis, Murray Hill Books, Inc.*)

The composition and size of the material being constant, we say that the frequency will vary with the tension and length. The shorter the string and the greater its tension, the more rapid is the rate. The string shakes as a whole, with the greatest movement in the center of the string. But the string also vibrates in parts; it shakes in halves, in thirds, in quarters and fifths, and in every possible fraction of the total length. The vibrations of the string as a whole give the loudest note; it is called the *fundamental tone*. At the same time the partial vibrations are heard. As the string vibrates in halves its frequency is twice the fundamental; in thirds it is three times the fundamental, etc. These partials are experienced as *overtones*. The first partial vibration, of course, is when the string vibrates in halves, and this is called the first *overtone*. In Fig. 5:16 the partial vibrations sounding the first, second, and fourth overtones are illustrated. Note that

the amplitude of vibration decreases as the string vibrates in smaller parts. This explains why the fundamental is the most intense sound and why the higher partial vibrations are difficult to hear.

A single note played on a musical instrument results in a complex sound wave. When the wave reaches our ears it is heard as a single note. The pitch of the note is not altered by the addition of these overtones, but the quality or timbre is. Figure 5:15 shows the same note as played by a flute (*D*) and by a clarinet (*E*). For comparison, the relatively pure tone of a tuning fork (*A*) is included. The difference in auditory quality is due to the difference in overtones. The fundamental is the same in all three cases, but the partials are different. The unanalyzed complex wave is a summation of the wave motions of its components.

Physicists, in the study of sound waves, prefer to make them visible to the eye. This

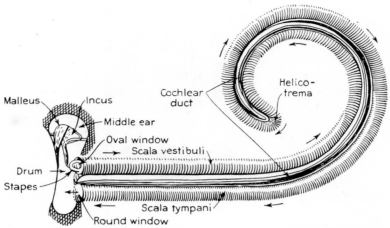

FIG. 5:19. The cochlea uncoiled. The arrows show more clearly than Fig. 5:18 the path of transmission of sound vibrations. *(From Krieg, 1942. Reprinted by permission of The Blakiston Company.)*

is done neatly by an instrument called the *phonodeik* (Fig. 5:17). The wave patterns shown in Fig. 5:15 were recorded by this device.

The auditory receptors. The essential organ for hearing is located in the cochlea, a part of the inner ear which looks like a snail shell of two and three-fourths turns. The ear has, however, an elaborate accessory mechanism. These accessory organs act as collectors and transmitters of the sound waves. The funnel-shaped *pinna*, commonly called the ear, is movable in animals and points toward the source of sound. The opening penetrating the head is the external meatus, or *auditory canal*, which ends at the tympanic membrane, or eardrum. All this constitutes the outer ear. On the inner side of the eardrum is the middle ear. It contains a transmission belt of bones known as the hammer, the anvil, and the stirrup. The air compression on the eardrum is transmitted to these bones; the stirrup is attached to the *oval window* in the wall opposite the eardrum in the middle ear. The middle ear also has an opening to the outside air through the Eustachian tube which leads to the pharynx behind the nose (Fig. 5:18).

The eardrum is connected with the inner ear by means of these bones and the oval window. This window is a membrane which is in direct contact with the *cochlea* at its base. Within the coiling configuration of the cochlea is a spiral passage, like a winding staircase, and the passage grows wider as it mounts. The staircase divides the snail-shell cavity into two sections which are filled with liquid. This staircase or ribbon dividing the canal as it coils to the apex is a membranous structure known as the *basilar membrane*. This membrane is attached to a bony shelf which coils around the core, and to the outer wall, by muscles known as the *suspensory ligament*.

Figure 5:19 depicts the cochlea partly extended to show the double canal, the upper one being the vestibular canal and the lower the tympanic canal. Separating the two canals is the basilar membrane; and this membrane itself forms the base of a smaller, triangular-shaped inner canal, known as the *cochlear canal*. In effect, then, the cochlea is divided into three canals, the innermost of which contains the receptors.

Figure 5:20 presents a detailed diagrammatic cross section through the cochlea showing the superstructure on the basilar

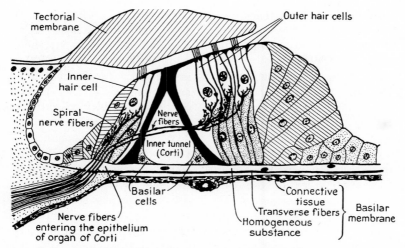

FIG. 5:20. The organ of Corti. This is the essential mechanism for hearing. The auditory nerve enters at left and branches to the hair cells which are the sensory receptors. It is assumed that distortion of the basilar membrane, the layer upon which this mechanism rests, exerts pressure upon the hair cells, and these transmit impulses to the brain which are interpreted as sound. (*From Rasmussen, 1943, by permission of the Wm. C. Brown Co.*)

membrane. The most important structure is the *organ of Corti* which contains the vibration-sensitive hair cells, divided by a tunnel into one row of inner cells and three rows of outer cells. These hair cells and their nerve endings form the primary receptor mechanism. Over the hair cells, unlabeled in the diagram, is the *tectorial membrane* against which the hair cells are said to press when the basilar membrane is activated. The basilar membrane consists of transverse fibers, analogous to a coiled pathway formed by ropes or strings laid across the path. All these structures are very small. The cochlear canal is only about 2 mm. in diameter.

How does the ear work? We know quite well what is transmitted to the inner ear; but precisely how the receptor cells are activated is still in the realm of speculation. The vibrations of air which strike the eardrum are transmitted and *amplified* by the bony transmission system of the middle ear. These bones are arranged to act as a lever. The amount of amplification is roughly correlated with the ratio of the area of the effective eardrum to the area of the stirrup. Amplification as high as 30 to 1 has been estimated by some authorities. (These bones are said to serve another important function. They are so arranged geometrically that the amount of extraneous sound that could be picked up through bone conduction in the head is at a minimum.) As the eardrum vibrates, it pushes the stirrup against the oval window. The piston action on the oval membrane agitates the liquid in the vestibular canal. The liquid flows along this canal to its apex where there is an opening, and then down the tympanic canal to the round window which is an elastic membrane similar to that in the oval window. When the oval window is pushed in, the round window is forced out. Thus the agitation at the oval window is conversely reflected at the round window. This agitation or pressure on the liquid selectively affects the basilar membrane and its receptor cells; a sensory process is set up which is communicated over the auditory nerve to the higher centers of the brain. Just how the attributes of the sound wave are selected out must be postponed until later.

The Eustachian tube plays little part in essential stimulation. It is simply an air tube joining the middle ear with the throat. The lower end of the tube is normally closed. However, it opens during the act of swallowing, thus serving to equalize any difference in air pressure that might happen to occur on the two sides of the eardrum, and so preventing damage to this membrane.

What do we hear? We hear tones and noises. Tones are due to *periodic* vibrations; noises to *aperiodic* or unsystematic mixtures of sound waves. We usually hear the dominant frequency or the fundamental, which gives us the *pitch* of the sound. Overtones do not affect the pitch but give us a change in the quality of the sound which we call *timbre*. We also hear sounds varying in loudness. Under certain conditions (when the frequencies of the sound waves are close together) we hear *beats*. The piano tuner detects the off key by comparing it with a standard fork. If the key is off by one vibration, there is a rise and fall in the sensation once in a second. If the key is badly out of tune, say 10 vibrations, there will be a ripple in the sound at the rate of 10 per second, etc. After a difference of about 50 vibrations per second, the beat smooths out.

We sometimes hear sounds which are not in the external environment. Under favorable conditions two sounds set off simultaneously produce, in addition to the fused mixture, a soft sound whose frequency is the sum of the two sounds. These are called *summation tones*. Sometimes *difference tones* are heard. A good demonstration of difference tones consists of a series of steel bars of 3,000; 3,100; 3,200; 3,300; 3,400; 3,500 vibrations per second. The difference between the steps is 100 vibra-

tions. If any two bars are struck in succession, a low hum is heard. If all the bars are sounded in succession, the hum is more audible. This hum is at 100 vibrations and is called the difference tone. Difference and summation tones are believed to be due to secondary vibrations in the bony transmission system.

We also hear consonance and dissonance. *Consonance* is the amount of fusion of two sounds. Fusion is based on the ratio of the frequencies of the two waves. If the frequencies are the same, we get unison. The ratio of 2 to 1 is the octave relation which also gives a fused unitary note. The statement has been made that, when tones are sounded together, the ratio of whose frequencies can be expressed only in large numbers, an unpleasant effect is produced. But culture and training are important in judgments of consonance and dissonance.

What we don't hear. We do not hear sounds below about 20 vibrations per second, nor those much more than 20,000 per second. Ordinarily we do not hear the overtones specifically, but we do hear them if we are set to detect them. Many tones are not heard because they are *masked* by other tones. Thus a loud tone will mask a soft one, and, in general, low-frequency sounds mask high frequencies. The fact of masking has led to a way of measuring the loudness of sounds. Suppose that we wish to state objectively the loudness of a riveting hammer. The measuring rod is a sound source which approximates the pitch level of the riveter. This source is calibrated in decibels. It is set at a loudness which masks the riveting noise, then gradually reduced until the riveting sound is just unmasked. At this point the rivet is as loud as the standard. Figure 5:21 is a chart depicting the loudness and pitch characteristics of various sounds.

The Weber law for loudness. The derivation of the acoustical engineer's unit of loudness, the decibel, is psychologically

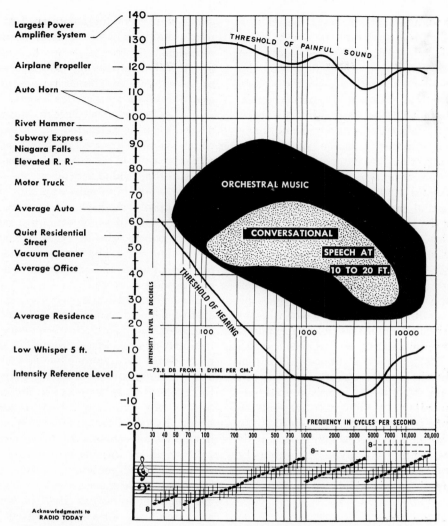

FIG. 5:21. Summary of the facts of human hearing. The horizontal scale shows the relation of musical pitch to frequency of sound waves. The vertical scale is calibrated in decibels. Some typical sound sources are listed on the left margin. The irregular curve starting near 60 decibels, curving downward and then up slightly, shows the absolute threshold for sounds of a given frequency. The "threshold of painful sound" is the terminal threshold. The central area indicates the pitch-loudness characteristics of normal conversations and music. (*Courtesy of the Maico Co., Inc.*)

interesting because it is based on a psychological measurement of sensation. Thus, if two tuning forks of the same pitch are compared for intensity, it will be found that a just noticeable difference requires that one stimulus to be 26 per cent more than its mate, over a certain range of intensities. It has been shown that, from 36 decibels on, the Weber fraction is practically constant (see page 141). The fraction here is about 9 per cent. However, this value was obtained under the best laboratory conditions. Under ordinary conditions, a 26 per cent change in intensity is the smallest change in energy level that can be heard. This change of 26 per cent alters the level of intensity 1 decibel. Since the average increase in power detected by the ear is 26 per cent, 10 intermediate steps between two stimuli would mount roughly in this fashion: if the lesser stimulus had a value of 100, then the next step would have an absolute-intensity value of approximately 126, then 26 per cent of that, or roughly 155, then 195, 245, 325, 400, 500, 625, 800, and 1,000. In 10 just noticeable steps, we find that the power has increased 10 times the starting point. The increase is geometrical. Ten such steps are defined as a *bel*. Each separate step therefore represents a decibel, or a tenth of a bel. In Fig. 5:21 the chart shows that the various typical noises are so many decibels above the faintest audible sound. Thus a low whisper is 10 decibels above this reference point, and a vacuum cleaner, 50 decibels.

The Weber law is approximated in pitch discrimination above 1,000 cycles per second. Man is very sensitive to differences in pitch. A difference of only 3 per cent is discriminated successfully over most of the frequency range. It is estimated that, at favorable intensity levels, 1,500 steps of pitch, 1,500 separate tones, are distinguishable.

Theories of Audition

While we have a tremendous variety of facts regarding the auditory sensations, we know relatively little about the precise process which converts vibration in the inner ear to nerve impulses along the auditory nerve. For that reason, our discussion of the auditory process must be conducted in terms of theories, with some occasional facts to support them.

For a long time men have speculated about the process of hearing. Some of the early conceptions have considerable merit, but in the last few decades our knowledge about nerve conduction has advanced so much that the older conceptions must be remodeled to fit the new facts of nerve propagation. Therefore, it is necessary to to introduce the discussion on auditory theories with a look at these facts.

The nerve impulse. The resting sensory neurone can be activated by any stimulus which reaches its *absolute threshold*. (This varies, of course, for different senses.) Once this threshold value is reached, the neurone fires, or sends an impulse along its axone to the synapse. The discharge is of maximum strength regardless of stimulus strength; that is to say, the neurone works on an all-or-none basis. The *all-or-none law* will be found significant in our analysis of auditory and visual processes.

The nature of the nerve discharge is electrochemical. No energy is derived from the stimulus itself; all the energy comes from food substances stored in the cell body. With a galvanometer we can detect a wave of negative ionization passing along the axone; this is the nerve impulse, to the best of our knowledge. Heat is also produced by the discharge—in microscopic quantities, of course. The maximum speed with which the impulse moves along a fiber seems to be 120 meters per second (a little less than 400 feet per second).

After a neurone has fired, it cannot be activated again for a short interval of time, no matter how strong the stimulus. This is called the *absolute refractory period;* it may run to as much as 0.001 second. After the absolute refractory period comes a period during which the neurone can be set off by an excessively strong stimulus; this is the *relative refractory period*. It may last as long as 0.002 second.

The all-or-none law means that strength of stimulus does not affect the strength of the nerve impulse. However, the relative refractory period operates to let a strong stimulus send through *more frequent impulses* as compared with a weak stimulus.

(A strong stimulus will reexcite the neurone earlier in the relative refractory period.) The absolute period, of course, sets a ceiling on the number of impulses that can travel over a fiber per unit of time.

If we are exciting a neurone electrically, the time during which the current flows is important. Even a very strong stimulus may not set off the impulse if the time is too short. The minimum excitation time of a neurone is known as its *chronaxie.* Very high frequency currents may not affect us by virtue of the fact that the current is on for less than the chronaxie period.

What has all this to do with the problem of hearing? Just this: these facts set some very drastic hurdles for theories which attempt to explain how sound vibrations get converted into impulses giving rise to auditory sensations. These problems did not arise in connection with somesthesis and the chemical senses because the question of high-speed vibrations did not enter. While the skin is sensitive to vibrations, it cannot detect anywhere near the number of vibratory rates which can be distinguished in audition. Thus the facts on nerve conduction set up a major road block for sensory theory only when we get up to the complexity of audition and vision.

Resonance theory of hearing. Near the end of the last century two men made significant syntheses of previous knowledge of the auditory mechanism, and first stated what turned out to be the opposed conceptions of auditory theory. Helmholtz likened the basilar membrane to a piano keyboard and came out with a *resonance theory* in which the individual fibers in the membrane were excited sympathetically by the sound wave. Thus each fiber has a specific energy of its own, corresponding to a definite musical pitch. (Sympathetic vibration is easily demonstrated by sounding a tuning fork over the strings of a piano. The string having the same frequency as the fork will sound with the fork.) On the other hand,

Rutherford supposed that the ear works like a telephone receiver. He assumed that the hair cells of the organ of Corti faithfully reproduce every pattern of sound. Theoretically, a single hair cell could mediate all the auditory sensations if it could pick up a vibratory pattern, duplicate it, and transmit it along the auditory nerve. This would assume that the hair cell could vibrate at all different sound frequencies, and hence is known as the *frequency theory.*

The resonance-place theory. Helmholtz's conception failed to stand up on two counts. He explained frequency as a correlate of the position of a fiber on the basilar membrane. Since the fibers were short at one end and long at the other, he attributed low frequencies to the latter and high frequencies to the former. The cochlear duct is such a tiny thing that the differences in length were not sufficient to account for the pitch range. However, by assuming that the fibers were under different tension at the appropriate ends, this matter of fiber size was somewhat overcome. Recent work indicates, unfortunately, that the

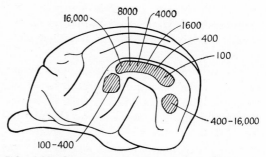

FIG. 5:22. Cortical localization of pitch. The resonance-place theory seems to be supported somewhat by the fact that different sound frequencies set off activity in different cortical areas, suggesting a similarity to body representation on the cortex (Fig. 5:13). In the dog, electrical recordings show that different parts of the basilar membrane are connected to cortical areas as shown here, giving a spatial representation of the pitch scale. The dog also shows the two areas for "low" and "high" sounds which are separate from the more finely differentiated upper area. (*From Adrian, after Tunturi, 1944.*)

basilar membrane and the whole cochlear duct, which contains a viscous fluid, is relatively elastic and so is not under the degree of tension necessary for the theory. The basilar membrane is stiffer at the base than at the apical end, but it is characterized by elasticity rather than tension. This fact creates difficulty for a resonance theory. Furthermore, Helmholtz explained loudness as being due to the intensity of vibration of the fiber. We now know that, because of the all-or-none law of nerve conduction, intensity of the stimulus does *not* incite a more intense response in the neurone.

Interestingly enough, although Helmholtz erred in details, he was essentially correct in asserting that pitch determination depended on the *place* in the basilar membrane where vibration was picked up. There is considerable evidence that different parts of the membrane give rise to differing pitch sensations. For instance, guinea pigs exposed continuously to loud low tones show degeneration at the broad end of the membrane on post-mortem examination. In men who have worked in a boiler factory, similar areas of injury have been reported. Hence the original resonance theory has given way to the so-called *place theory*.

The most acceptable place theory today conceives the basilar membrane, in effect, like a tongue sticking into a tube of water. When the liquid is agitated by the piston-like action of the stirrup on the oval window, a traveling wave is set up in the membrane of a peculiar kind. This wave arrives at a maximum in a particular region of the membrane, depending on the frequency of the sound. In this region the membrane bulges to its maximum and stimulates the hair cells on it, which in turn pass the impulse along to the auditory nerve. This conception involves the hydrodynamics of water pressure on the membrane, in producing a *traveling bulge*. According to the theory low frequencies set up the maximal bulge near the top of the cochlea and high frequencies near the base. This conforms with Helmholtz's gradient, but the bulges stimulate areas and not specific fibers.

The frequency theory. The frequency theory seems automatically eliminated by the fact that the refractory period limits the number of impulses passing through a nerve. It is claimed that individual fibers cannot respond more than 500 to 800 times a second. Therefore, how would it be possible for a nerve to register frequencies in terms of thousands of vibrations a second? Wever and Bray tackled this problem, and they have demonstrated that somehow the auditory nerve transmits frequencies at least as high as 5,000 per second. They placed electrodes on the auditory nerve of a cat and then led the wires into another room where they were connected with a radio amplifying system. Speech, directed to the cat's ear, was clearly reproduced by the amplifying system in the other room. This experiment lent support for the frequency theory at least up to 5,000 vibrations. In order to explain this phenomenon without contradicting the law of the refractory period in nerve propagation they proposed what is now known as the *volley theory*.

This theory invokes the use of the *number of fibers firing* to explain both pitch and loudness. Intense stimuli stimulate many fibers; so, in general, the number of fibers stimulated has been accepted as the neurological correlate for the intensity attribute of the stimulus. Loudness therefore is a function of the *number* of active fibers. How about quality or frequency, then? Suppose that we beat a drum with one hand at a definite rate per second. Now the frequency of impulses can be doubled by beating with both hands at the same rate, but alternately. If we had four hands, we could double the rate again, with each hand still at constant speed. Now, if we imagine a sound of fairly high frequency to affect several nerve fibers, but these fibers start firing at different times, because of different chronaxies, the end result on the target would be a *summation* of the impulses reaching it at the same time. In this manner a charge of 5,000 per second could be attained if the firing squad is adequate. The particular formulation of such a synchronous firing by nerves, as developed by Wever and Bray, is the *volley theory*.

The volley theory explains pitch by assuming that groups of neurones, firing in a synchronized alternation like that illustrated, can transmit high-frequency patterns to the brain. Intensity is also explained by increasing numbers of fibers, but in this case they would fire simultaneously. Four neurons, for example, might give a weak tone of a stated pitch. Another squad of four would give more intensity, three squads still more, and so on.

The volley theory, as sketched here, can deal with pitch and intensity within limits. The facts available seem to limit the pitch ceiling to 5,000 vibrations per second, however, and we know that normal hearing goes up to about 20,000 vibrations. At this point it seems essential that we bring in the place theory and assume that there are differences in pitch sensitivity of different parts of the basilar membrane. Although it is probably more complicated than this, we could sketch a solution by saying that the volley theory can handle a range of 5,000 vibrations; so all we need to do is divide the basilar membrane into four parts, handling successive steps of 5,000, and we would cover the entire range of 20,000 vibrations. At least, the facts of nerve conduction seem to force us to the conclusion that both volley and place theories are necessary to a complete account of the hearing process.

Hearing and Speech Reception

On Fig. 5:21 was charted the normal range for pitch and intensity of human speech.

TABLE 5:4. Approximate Frequency Characteristics for a Few Vocal Sounds
(*Based on Woodworth, 1938*)

Spoken sound	Normal frequency in vibrations per second
m, n, g	250
u (as in true)	325
oo (as in book)	420
o (as in roll)	450
aw (as in jaw)	730
a (as in father)	950
a (as in bat)	1,800
e (as in ten)	1,900
i (as in tin)	2,200
i (as in machine)	2,500–3,000
s	5,000–9,000

This gives us some guide as to the practical significance of a wide range of clear reception. Even more interesting, perhaps, is Table 5:4, which shows the characteristic vibration frequencies for different speech sounds (these will differ, of course, for individuals, but the ranking shown remains rather constant).

The clearness with which speech can be received, *e.g.*, over the phone system in an airplane, depends on the signal-to-noise ratio. That is, the speech must be more intense than the background noise by at least 1 j.n.d. In studies on this problem, it has been found that the high-frequency sounds contribute more to comprehension of the message than the low-frequency sounds. Thus communication systems which must function with a high background noise level often amplify the high frequencies more than the low ones. Similarly, hearing aids for persons with impaired hearing are usually devised to amplify the high frequencies; this is especially true for older people, who suffer a selective loss of sensitivity in the upper ranges.

Vision

Most people value vision more than any other sense. It is a source of enjoyment, as well as a guide for the most precise kinds of adjustments. It is unexcelled as a distance receptor for identifying objects which may satisfy motives or threaten injury, although both hearing and smell make important contributions in these respects. Because of its importance and complexity, psychologists have found it a particularly fascinating field for research; unfortunately, we can sketch only a few basic facts about it in this introductory approach.

The structure of the eye. The eye has been compared with a camera (Fig. 5:23). The outer covering is the hard, protective *sclerotic membrane*. Inside this is the *choroid* coat which provides the dark lining for the eye. At the front the sclerotic coat bulges forward and, becoming transparent, forms the *cornea*. The cornea receives light rays into the eye and helps to focus the image, for it has a curved surface. And the choroid coat gives place at its front to the *iris*

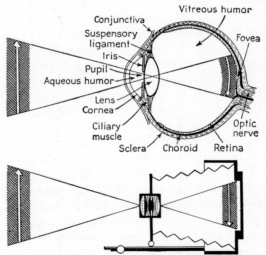

FIG. 5:23. The eye as a camera. The diagram shows the essential parts of the eye structure (upper figure). Light rays from an object (arrow) pass through cornea, pupil, lens, and so to a focus on the retina. Note that the image will be upside down and reversed as to left and right. The fovea is the area of clearest vision; the blind spot is at the point where the optic nerve leaves the retina. The lower figure shows the comparable functioning of a camera. (*From Scientific American.*)

muscle, the pigment of which colors the eye. A round hole in its center, called the *pupil*, is the adjustable diaphragm of this camera, its size being regulated by iris muscle fibers. Back of the pupil is the *lens*, which serves the same function as the lens of the camera. The lens of the eye, however, may bulge and become thicker by the action of the ciliary muscle to which it is attached, or it may be pulled thin. The action of the ciliary muscle in flattening the lens, or in causing it to thicken, thereby adjusts the eye for far and near vision. The space in front and in back of the lens is filled with a transparent jellylike fluid which keeps the eye in its normal spherical shape.

All these are accessory structures, just as the eardrum, middle ear bones, etc., were accessory to the basilar membrane, the essential organ of hearing. The sensitive cells for vision are also located in a membrane, lining the back of the eyeball, the *retina*. Here the visual neurones are acted upon by light waves and impulses are transmitted to the brain. The cornea, the pupil, the lens, the intervening watery fluid, and the six muscles attached to the sclerotic coat which move the eye make up the accessory appendages. The muscles move the eye in the direction of the light, which is then transmitted and focused on the retina by the accessory mechanisms. The retina is the sensitive photographic plate of the eye. The image formed on this plate is the effective stimulus for vision. An understanding of the retinal structure is essential to theories of vision.

The retina. The retina is a complicated nervous structure about as thin as a sheet of paper. It lines the back half of the eye, next to the dark pigment surface of the choroid layer, but it is not attached to the choroid layer. It is suspended in a fluid. Actually, the retina is an extension of the brain into the eye. The membrane is formed of layers of nerve cells perpendicular to the

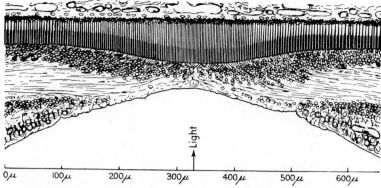

FIG. 5:24. Microscopic structure of retina at the fovea. The cones are densely packed here (heavy black figures). Rods are rare here, thicker as we move from the fovea to the edge of the retina. Note that light enters from below and must pass through the various structures (capillaries, neurones, etc.) to reach the rods and cones. The back of the eyeball is at the top of the diagram. (*From Polyak, 1941, by permission of University of Chicago Press.*)

choroid coat. The innermost cells are next to the choroid layer and because of their shape are called *rods* and *cones*. These rods and cones are the photoreceptors of the eye. For us to see light, these cells must be stimulated. The cells toward the front of the eye connect with nerve fibers which run on the surface of the retina, then out to the optic nerve and the brain. Thus light entering the eye through the pupil must, unfortunately, traverse the retina to reach the sensitive layer of rods and cones. The retina has therefore been likened to a transparent carpet, lying upside down on the floor, the pile of the carpet corresponding to the rods and cones.

The rods and cones are intermixed except at the *fovea*, a little depression in the retina, straight back from the pupil, where only cones are present. The rod-free fovea is about 1 mm. in diameter. It is the area of clearest vision. Figure 5:24 is a section of the human retina at the foveal area. In the edges of the figure a few rods are seen as straight lines. The cones in the foveal pit are not so bulky as they are away from it. In Fig. 5:25 are samples of typical rod and cone cells and their connecting neurones.

The retinal image. Several interesting psychological problems derive from the nature of the retinal image, although most of them belong to the treatment of perception rather than sensation. However, let us note these points: (1) The retinal image is upside down. As you can readily see from Fig. 5:23, the light rays from the lower part of an object must strike the upper half of the retina, and vice versa; similarly, left and right are reversed. (2) It is impossible to have a straight-line image on the retina, because its surface is curved over the inside of a sphere. (3) It is impossible to have three-dimensional images, since the retina is a thin film. (4) The size of the retinal image of an object is constantly changing as we move nearer to it or farther from it; shape will also change as we change visual angles. The intricate complexity of the sensory and brain processes is suggested by the fact that none of these conditions seem to hamper our effective use of vision to any extent.

The visual stimulus. The adequate stimulus to the rods and cones is light. Pressure and electricity are inadequate stimuli; if applied, they result in reports of light flashes. Like sound vibrations, light waves differ in wave length or *frequency*, ampli-

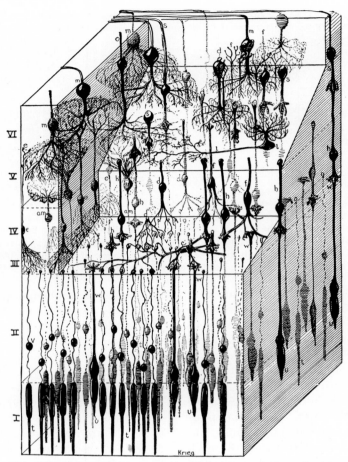

FIG. 5:25. Rods and cones, the essential sensory elements in vision. Layer I includes the rods and cones; II, nuclei and axones of rod and cone cells; III, IV, interconnecting neurones within the retina (note that several rods join a single neurone, while the cones usually have individual continuation neurones); V, VI, beginnings of fibers which go to optic nerve and brain. Light rays enter at top, go down through this tangled mass to reach the sensitive cells. Back of the eyeball is at bottom. *(From Krieg, 1942. Reproduced by permission of The Blakiston Company.)*

tude or *intensity*, and composition or *purity*. Variations in frequency give rise to sensations of *hue;* variations in intensity are experienced as *brightness;* and variations in purity of wave composition are seen as changes in *saturation*.

Ordinary daylight is a mixture of most wave lengths from 400 to 750 mμ in length.

It can be separated by passing a narrow beam of light through a prism. The correspondence of hue to wave length is indicated by Fig. 5:26, in which the spectrum is shown from violet, the hue corresponding to the shortest visible waves, to red, stimulated by the longest visible waves. Within the limits of modern printing, this shows

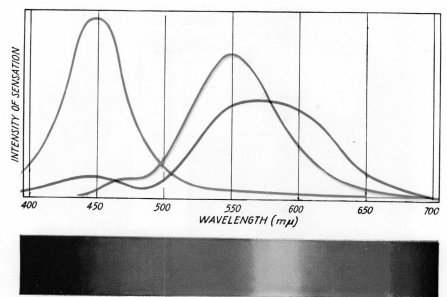

FIG. 5:26. Hue and wave length. When Newton passed light through a prism, he bent different wave lengths by different amounts. This gives us the familiar rainbow or spectrum from violet to red. Above the spectrum are shown the sensitivity curves of the normal eye to blue, green, and red, based on the assumption that there are three sensitive elements in the retina which respond maximally to one or another of these colors. (*From College Physics, by Weber, White, and Manning, McGraw-Hill Book Company, Inc., 1952.*)

how, as wave length changes, there is a gradual shift in the sensed quality of the light.[1]

It is apparent that such studies require elaborate apparatus for providing the closest possible approximation to a pure wave-length stimulus. Probably there is no such, just as there is no pure sound wave, but successive approaches are being developed. One of the more successful of such devices is that developed by J. B. Cohen and shown in Fig. 5:27. This apparatus starts with light filtered through a gelatin filter, so that it looks monochromatic to the naked eye. This is passed through a prism, behind which is a narrow slit, so that only a few wave lengths can

[1] Note that there is no true purple in the spectrum. However, if the band of Fig. 5:26 were coiled around to make a circle, we should leave a little space between the red and the violet, and treat purple as a mixture of these hues.

get through. This beam is then reflected from a spherical mirror and along a lucite tube to the objective at which the subject is looking. By an ingenious arrangement of templates, Cohen can produce visual stimuli which are combinations of wave lengths which could never occur in nature.

Attributes of visual sensation. The three attributes of visual sensation, then, are hue, brightness, and saturation. These are related within each category and between categories, in a systematic way. Figure 5:28 shows the *color cone* which summarizes these relationships concisely.

The vertical axis depicts the range of brightness from black to white (or, from zero brightness, black, to maximum brightness, white). White is depicted at the cone apex because all colored lights, if sufficiently bright, look white. Likewise with decreasing intensities colors look darker and approach a black.

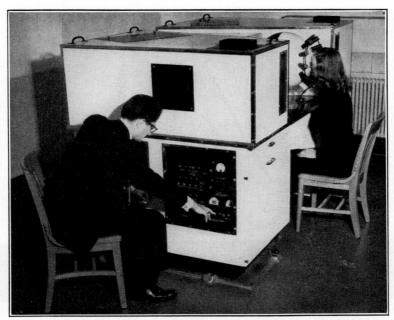

FIG. 5:27. Colorimeter. Dr. J. B. Cohen at the controls of the apparatus he developed for presenting light of carefully defined wave composition to the subject (observing at eyepiece). Colors of any predetermined wave composition can be presented, or any color can be analyzed into its wave pattern, by the device. *(Courtesy of Dr. J. B. Cohen.)*

The circle in the middle of the system is the *hue circle*. Along this circle the hues are arranged in spectral order, with the purples between red and violet. The colors on the circle are as pure as they can be, that is, there is less admixture of other wave lengths. That is why the cone circle is maximum at this point.

From the circumference of the circle a line can be drawn to the vertical axis from any point on the circumference. In the diagram one line is drawn from red. This line identifies the dimension of saturation. The red on the circumference is pure. This red becomes *less saturated* as it approaches the brightness axis. What happens is that red loses its purity and looks more gray as the gray point (the vertical axis) is approached. When the axis is reached the red is completely desaturated and becomes a medium gray. Loss of hue, or desaturation, also takes place on all the cone circles

below and above the largest circumference. Above it the colors are brighter as they progress toward the apex of the cone, but brightness is attained at the expense of purity of the color. Below the great circumference, purity of the hue is lost with increasing darkening or shading of the hues. This solid depicts the fact that any color can be specified in terms of hue, brightness, and saturation. The system is quantitative in terms of all three variables.

The total number of separate visual experiences (distinct sensations) possible is very great. Since we have not only variations in brightness and hue, but their *fusion* in the various tints and shades (pink, maroon, etc.) which vary in saturation, a conservative estimate puts the total at more than 300,000. This is roughly comparable with the number of auditory sensations possible, with this difference: the ear can analyze complex mixtures,

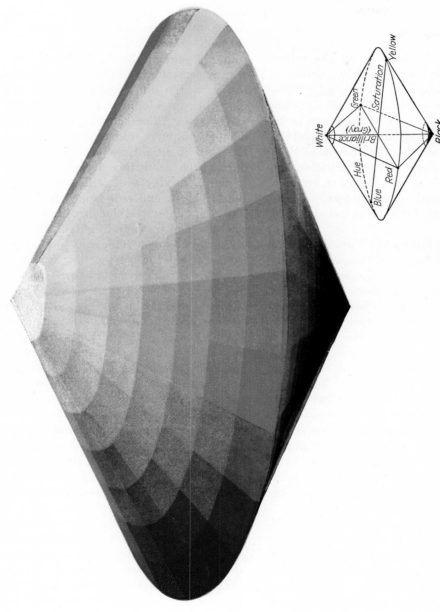

FIG. 5:28. The color cone. If the spectrum is bent into a circle, and cones extended upward to white and downward to black, we produce a double cone which covers all possible visual sensations. Because of problems of printing, the cone shows abrupt changes from one tint to another; there is actually a series of continuous gradations. The circumference of the circle gives differences in hue; the vertical axis, white to black, gives us degrees of brightness; and the horizontal diameter gives differences in saturation (see the diagram at lower right). (*Reproduced by permission from More Business, copyright 1937 by the American Photo-engravers Association.*)

whereas the eye cannot. Thus each visual sensation has a certain *unique* quality, which is not so true in hearing.

The Visual Receptors

We have already noted that the retina contains two kinds of sensitive neurones, the rods and cones. It would be most satisfying, from the point of view of scientific psychology, if the rods would prove to be sensitive to variations in amplitude, and the cones to variations in wave length of light stimulus. Unfortunately, the situation has some elements of this solution, plus a variety of complicating factors. Let us examine some of the facts on rod and cone function.

The duplicity theory of vision. The retina in effect is a duplex visual system. The rods function in night vision; the cones in daylight. Under night conditions the fovea is practically a blind area. That is why some stars cannot be seen when looked at directly but become visible if one focuses his eyes a little to one side, thus allowing the light from the star to fall on areas off the fovea. In such areas rods predominate. Nocturnal animals such as bats and owls have only rods in their retinas. Such animals are relatively blind in daylight but see extraordinarily well in twilight and at night. Although humans and diurnal animals have both rods and cones, under certain conditions the rod and cone functions can be separated.

The visual field. One way to separate rod and cone vision is to move a colored stimulus slowly into the visual field, keeping the eyes focused straight ahead. Small buttons of various colors are used for this purpose. At the extreme edge of the field, the button will first be sensed as a blurry, colorless patch. At this point it is reflecting light to a retinal area with few cones and many rods. (It is blurred because of a number of physiological factors operating at the periphery.) As the colored button slides in toward the center, it will first become more clearly defined as to shape, and then will take on color. The point at which hue is first sensed corresponds fairly well with the outer distribution of cones in the retina. A normal visual field, as plotted by perimeter, is shown in Fig. 5:29. The significance of the difference in range for the four primary colors will be discussed later.

Shifts in illumination. A spectacular demonstration of rod and cone vision is the shift in brightness of colored objects during the transition from daylight to twilight. In daylight, yellow flowers are the brightest, and reds look brighter than blue. In twilight, the blues are brighter than the reds, and the high brightness of yellow gives way to green. This shift in brightness from the red toward the blue end of the spectrum with decreasing light is known as the Purkinje phenomenon, from the physiologist, Purkinje, who observed this shift of color brightnesses over a hundred years ago. In terms of the duplicity theory this shift in brightness is explained by the dominant role of cones in daytime vision and of rods in night vision, with both rods and cones functioning at twilight.

If patches of colored light are observed in a dark room over a period of time, the patches looked at directly (foveally) tend to be seen as colored. The patches off the fovea tend to bleach out and are seen as dazzling white blurred spots. The blues and greens bleach out very rapidly; yellow and orange persist longer, and red hardly bleaches at all. This is explained on the ground that the rods are least sensitive to red and most sensitive to green and blue.

The differential sensitivity of the rods and cones to spectral lights has been studied quantitatively. The sensitivity for the fovea, or cones, shows the greatest sensitivity for a greenish-yellow hue, or 554 mμ. From this maximal point the sensitivity declines rapidly and approaches

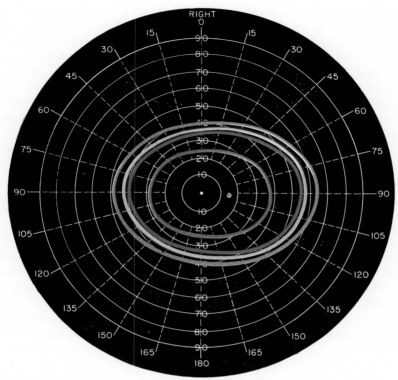

FIG. 5:29. Color zones in the retina. This figure shows the distribution of color sensitivity in the normal eye. Blue is visible over the widest range; then yellow, red, and green in successively narrower limits. (*From Abney, 1913.*)

zero at the ends of the spectrum. Since the rods respond only when the light striking the retina is very weak, a sensitivity curve for the rods can be obtained by the same method as for the cones, only using a much weaker light standard, and one which is large enough to fall on the rods surrounding the fovea. The rod-sensitivity curve has the same shape as the cone curve, but its maximal sensitivity is displaced toward the blue end of the spectrum. The maximum is at 511 mμ, or yellowish-green. The entire curve is shifted 43 mμ so that in relative darkness the blue end of the spectrum can be seen only by the rods. It will look colorless, however. Conversely, the far red end of the spectrum can be seen only by the cones. In Fig. 5:30 the sensitivity curves for rods and cones are shown. These curves constitute the quantitative data for the duplicity theory.

Adaptation. Because the eye contains two kinds of receptors, there are two kinds of adaptation. Usually sensory adaptation

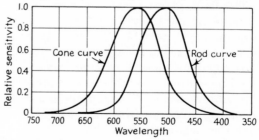

FIG. 5:30. Sensitivity curves for rods and cones. Dark adaptation involves a shift from cone to rod vision. The differences in the two curves indicate that the duplicity theory of rod and cone function must be substantially correct. (*From Butler and Karwoski, 1936.*)

shows a decrement in sensitivity, as though the receptor suffered from fatigue. This is true for cone vision, since there is a noticeable decrease in sensitivity to lights on prolonged exposure. It is also true for the rods, but the process is so rapid in them (if the light is fairly bright) that in effect the rods are not functioning at all. This kind of adaptation is called *light adaptation*. The best way to prove the existence of light adaptation in the rods is to go from the dark movie house into broad daylight. For a few seconds we feel an annoying glare. The rods are too sensitive for daylight conditions. However, this sensitivity quickly diminishes and the cones take over.

The other form of adaptation is called *dark adaptation*. It refers to the increase of sensitivity of the retina when light is reduced to a low level such as that prevailing at night. Both rods and cones dark-adapt, but the rods are much slower than the cones. After about 5 minutes in a dark room the cones are completely adapted whereas the rods continue to adapt for several hours; but they approach full adaptation in 40 minutes. Actually, the cones do undergo an increase in sensitivity, but they still maintain such a high absolute threshold that faint illumination induces no response at all. The cones undergo an increase in sensitivity of the order of 100 to 1; the rods, 10,000 to 1.

The light-adapted eye is almost useless in darkness. For this reason, air-crew members on night duty during the war were required to remain dark-adapted for at least 40 minutes before going on duty. This could have become quite a morale problem if it simply meant sitting quietly in a dark room. However, use was made of the fact that the rods are hardly sensitive to red. Tight-fitting red goggles were worn to maintain dark adaptation while reading, chatting, or doing work which did not require fine visual discrimination. If a person had to study charts while wearing the goggles, it was important that they be printed in blue or green; red figures would of course be invisible through the goggles.[1]

The structure and neural connections of rods and cones fit the theory of double functioning in the retina. The rods have blunt ends which are favorable for picking up small amounts of light. They are usually connected along "party lines" to a single nerve fiber—that is, each rod does not report separately to the brain, but a whole group may activate the same fiber (Fig. 5:25). This maximizes the chance of picking up a stray wisp of light (sensory summation) but reduces the possibility of getting fine detail. Conversely, the cones typically end in points and, at least in the fovea, have private lines direct to the brain. They are very tightly packed in the fovea also.

The fact that the fovea only contains cones looks like a break for science, since the rods are not there to complicate the retinal function. But, since the cones in the fovea are as structurally alike as peas in a pod, the advantage of cone segregation fades out. In all theories of sensory function the big problem is to explain the quality attribute. How are different sense qualities to be explained physiologically? In the case of vision, how do we see hues: red, green, blue, yellow, etc.? Over the ages, hundreds of theories have been proposed, and new theories are continually coming out. As far as the histology of the cones is concerned, there are no differences in the foveal cones which could account for differences in quality. Theories of color vision, therefore, have resorted to using circumstantial evidence from certain classes of color facts

[1] Considerable publicity also attached to the fact that these flyers received extra vitamin A. This treatment was based on the observation that vitamin A deficiency leads to night blindness, a failure of dark adaptation. There is no reason to assume that a person who is night blind will improve with vitamin A unless his deficiency is due to a lack of this vitamin.

RED BEAM

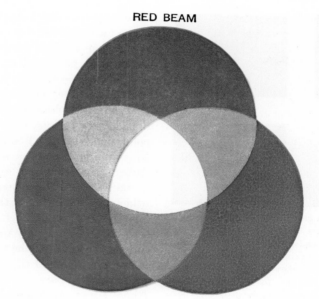

GREEN BEAM   BLUE BEAM

FIG. 5:31. Additive color mixture. Ordinary color mixture by mixing pigments is really subtractive color mixture, in that each additional color tends to prevent the reflection of more wave lengths. Additive mixture is achieved by projecting beams of colored light onto a reflecting surface, or directly into the eye. In this case we get the mixing effects shown here; red, blue, and green in proper proportions give white light. Note that red and green give a yellowish light. For a different additive mixture, cortical rather than retinal, see Fig. 5:32. (*From College Physics, by Weber, White, and Manning, McGraw-Hill Book Company, Inc., 1952.*)

which the particular theorist has considered to be especially significant. We shall proceed by describing certain areas of color vision which have led to the most acceptable conceptions of color vision.

Color mixture. When Newton passed light through a prism and broke it up into a spectrum (Fig. 5:26), the stimulus for color became known. Soon the laws of color mixture were determined. Colored lights could be mixed in definite measurable quantities, directly on the eye, and the individual colors could be specified physically in terms of wave lengths of light. This is *additive mixture* (in contrast to subtractive, or pigment, mixture, with which the artist is familiar). In subtractive mixture

what the eye gets is the residual waves that are not absorbed by the pigment, and so are reflected to the eye. Such a complicated mixing process is not suitable for quantitative scientific work. In additive mixture the wave lengths of light are mixed directly on the eye without any problem of absorbing media being involved.

Three laws of color mixture are usually stated. The most important is that, with three spectral lights, selected from the middle and end regions of the spectrum, all the colors of nature can be reproduced. These colors are the "primary colors" of additive mixture. The three usually chosen are a red of a certain wave length, a green, and a blue or violet (Fig. 5:31). The *second*

FIG. 5:32. Color fusion and afterimages. To produce afterimages, simply stare intently at the center of the figure for about 45 seconds, then look at a white surface. The afterimages are complementary: green will seem red, blue will seem yellow.

To demonstrate cortical color fusion, place a sheet of stiff paper or cardboard along the gray line. Look at the two top colors, green and red, by placing the nose along the edge of the cardboard. The left eye will see green, the right eye, red. Relax the eyes as if looking at a distant object. Where the two squares overlap, the segment will look yellowish. Now move the book upward, so that the blue and yellow squares are before your eyes. The overlapping segment will appear gray.

Because the colors are not equally bright, there may be a tendency to see the brighter color drowning out the other, even in the binocular fusion. To counteract this factor, place your book so that a window or light is on your left.

This demonstration shows that color mixture can take place in the brain. If you continue to stare at the colors, you will notice an alternation, with one color predominant and then the other. This illustrates the phenomenon of retinal rivalry.

law of mixture is that certain hues, when mixed with another particular hue, cancel each other to produce a gray. These colors are called *complementary* and are usually arranged on the color circle charts so that they are opposite to each other (see Fig. 5:28). Thus blue is complementary to yellow, and a bluish green is complementary to red. The *third* law states that certain colors, when mixed with other single colors (of a definite wave length), produce blends which are the resultants of the two colors conceived as forces. These are called *blends*.

Blends never cancel out to gray. All three laws can easily be demonstrated in a psychology or physics laboratory and are illustrated in part by Figs. 5:31 and 5:32.

The first two laws have played prominent roles in theories of color vision. The fact that all the colors in nature can be produced from fusions of only three primary colors led Thomas Young as early as 1807 to assume that there are three kinds of "fibers" in the retina, each responsible for a characteristic sensation, one for red, another for green, and a third for blue (violet). Each type of fiber is assumed to be sensitive to practically the entire spectrum, but for the red fiber the *maximal* sensitivity is in the red part of the spectrum, for green in the green part, and similarly for blue (these curves are shown in Fig. 5:26). The various color sensations are said to be the result of the relative strengths with which the three different fibers are stimulated by the objective light. Young's idea was overlooked for 50 years. After Johannes Müller enunciated the doctrine of "specific energies of nerves" (the idea that each nerve or sensory neurone, however stimulated, gives rise to but one type of sensory process or specific quality of sensation), and this became a basic concept in sensory research, Young's idea fitted in with the prevailing trend. Helmholtz elaborated Young's theory in more modern terms, treating Young's three fibers as three species of cones. The theory is now known as the Young-Helmholtz theory of color vision. However, since all cones in the fovea are exactly alike, and nerve impulses in all nerve fibers are essentially similar, just where color specificity resides is in question. (If it is not in the specific nerve fibers, then another possibility is that the specificity is in the brain.)

The quantitative basis for the Young-Helmholtz theory is furnished by color predictions of sensation curves. In Fig. 5:26 the three sensation curves are plotted in terms of the effectiveness of spectral light in arousing a red, green, or blue sensation. Effectiveness is indicated by the height of the curves, or sensed intensity, for each part of the spectrum. The curves may be thought of as derived from red, green, and blue cones. At the ends of the spectrum, the theory assumes that the blue and the red cones are primarily stimulated, as is shown by the height of the blue curve at one end and the height of the red curve at the other end. Consequently we see saturated blue and red at the ends of the spectrum. Saturation (or purity) of hue, then, is a function of dominance of one of the cones over the others. In the yellow region of the spectrum, saturation is low. This is accounted for by the great overlap of the red and green curves. At 480 mμ all three curves overlap considerably. At this point the blue-green is quite pale. According to the Young-Helmholtz theory, if the red, green, and blue cones are stimulated in equal amounts, the sensation of white or gray is produced (as in the center of Fig. 5:31).

So far everything is straightforward. The mixtures at various points along the spectrum look like the dominant sensation curves at these points. There is, however, an important exception. At about 580 mμ we get a yellow which does not look like a red or green or a blend of red and green. Yellow looks unique, and does not resemble either red or green. This happens because the red and green cones at the point of intersection of the red and green curves are stimulated equally (see Fig. 5:26).

The sensation curves were actually obtained quantitatively by matching each part of the spectrum with a standard red, green, and blue light. The curves are valid measures of the amounts of the three components necessary to get any specific color sensation. These curves state the facts of three-color mixture. (Purples are outside of the spectral series; they are obtained by mixing red and blue, or two-color mixture.)

Few experts regard the Young-Helmholtz theory as a complete theory of color vision. The theory, however, has elicited much research. Its basis, on the facts of three-color mixture, is tied up with important practical consequences, such as the development of technicolor and its great utility in the control and specification of dyes and color fabrics.

The question of primary colors. What are regarded as primary colors is rather arbitrary. There are various kinds of primary colors. The Young-Helmholtz primaries are the *minimal specific colors* from which all other colors can be obtained by additive mixture. These primaries are "stimulus mixture primaries." On the other hand, psychologists and artists hold to four colors, red, green, yellow, and blue, as the four *psychologically simple colors*, and, therefore, they are regarded as being the psychologically primary colors. All other colors seem to be blends of various pairs of these four colors. Physiologists have isolated four colors which can be said to be *physiologically primary*, because they are the only four specific colors which, when moved from the periphery to the center of the visual field, do not change in hue. These physiological or invariable colors approximate the psychological primaries.

Opponents of the Young-Helmholtz theory feel that it does not do justice to the traditional recognition of four rather than three primary qualities of vision. This argument has been countered by saying that yellow (which is no doubt a unique color, bearing no sensed resemblance to any other color in the spectrum) is in fact a primary which is contributed by the brain. This gets startling support from Hecht's observation that, if a green light is focused in one eye and a red light in the other (so, *e.g.*, the right eye sees only green and the left eye only red), the lights mix in the brain and one sees a yellow. The fact of *cortical fusion* can be easily demonstrated by standing a

FIG. 5:33. Brightness contrast effects. The apparent brightness of any object is markedly affected by the background against which it is observed. Which of the above lamps seems most brightly illuminated? Actually, all are of equal brightness. (This can be demonstrated by laying a sheet of paper over them and punching holes so that only the gray of the lamps is visible, without the background.) Does this raise any problems regarding the kind of visual sensation produced by a stimulus to a specific retinal cell? (*From Johnson, 1948.*)

cardboard on edge between the red and green squares in Fig. 5:32, then placing the nose against the edge of the cardboard and looking at the colors.

Afterimages and contrast phenomena. If the eye is exposed to a bright light for a fraction of a second, one experiences a short dark interval, followed by a sensation which resembles the stimulus in hue but is less bright. This is called the *positive afterimage* and seems to be a form of persistence of stimulation. This image is short-lived. If the stimulus is looked at for longer periods of time, the following afterimage is complementary in color and lasts quite a while. If one fixates the point between the four colors in Fig. 5:32 for 20 or 30 seconds, and then looks at a white sheet of paper, the afterimage of green will look reddish; of red, greenish; of blue, yellow; and of yellow, blue. These afterimages are called *negative afterimages.* It will be remembered that complementary colors are two colors which, when mixed, produce a gray. Obviously the negative afterimage of a color is also its complementary color.

Color contrast, like negative afterimages, follows the law of complementary colors. If a small gray patch of paper is placed on a larger sheet of yellow, and both are covered with tissue paper, the gray patch looks

bluish. If the gray is placed on green paper, the patch looks reddish. (The tissue paper merely enhances contrast by weakening the contour between the gray and the colored papers.)

There is also a *brightness contrast.* Thus, if a gray patch of paper is placed on black, it looks whiter than it normally does; and if it is placed on a white background, it looks darker. Color contrast is most effective if the contrasting colors are of the same brightness, because then brightness contrast is at a minimum and the color-contrast effect is more obvious. An ingenious illustration of brightness contrast is shown in Fig. 5:33.

Negative afterimages and contrast support the idea that black is a sensation rather than merely the absence of light. In fact, on entering a dark room, the excessive darkness at first is due to contrast with daylight. After ½ hour in the room, it no longer looks black, but gray. If black is a sensation, it is the complement to white, and thus white has its complementary color. This is recognized in the color cone (Fig. 5:28); all points opposite each other in the figure are complementaries.

The Hering theory. Now Hering, a physiologist, was impressed with the facts of negative afterimages and contrast. He was also influenced by the fact that the psychological primaries are four and that they are paired as complementary colors. Thus blue and yellow are complementary pairs, and he regarded red and green as complements. Moreover, black and white are complementary achromatic sensations. Hering, therefore, assumed (like Young-Helmholtz) that there are three elementary cones which form the basis of color vision. However, unlike the Young-Helmholtz primary cones, Hering's were double-acting cones. Thus, one cone responds to both red and green, the other to yellow and blue, and the third to white and black. The three cones are, in effect, three different substances each of which can be excited in two different ways. One way is to initiate *catabolism*, or destruction of the substance, the other way is toward *anabolism*, or building up of the substance. Catabolic excitation gives red, yellow, and white; anabolic, green, blue, and black. This is the essence of the *Hering theory* of color vision.

The complementation in afterimages is simply explained as due to the automatic tendency for the color substance to regain metabolic balance. If the red-green is continually stimulated catabolically, we see red; but if the stimulus is removed, anabolism automatically sets in, and we see green. (The Young-Helmholtz theory also explains afterimages as a recovery process, but in different terms. Suppose the eye is stimulated by a blue of 470 mμ. It will be seen from the sensation curves that the stimulus, at this point, also stimulates red and green in equal amounts, but less than for blue. The blue cones become more fatigued than the red and green cones. When the stimulus is removed the red and green cones recover faster than blue, so we see their mixture, or yellow.) Color contrast is simply explained by Hering by assuming that the metabolic processes aroused in a given area induce the antagonistic process in the surrounding area.

(Helmholtz tried to explain contrast as an "unconscious inference.")

Color blindness is difficult for the Helmholtz theory but fits in readily with Hering's. Most so-called "color-blind" individuals tend to see the world as blue and yellow, which could be explained as an impairment of the red-green cone. But, if Helmholtz's red and green cones are malfunctioning, it is difficult to see how the color blind can see so much yellow.

Color zones. As we noted earlier (page 176), the normal eye is completely color blind in the far periphery of vision. It will be recalled that peripheral vision differs from central or foveal vision in being less clear. For some distance around the foveal area the eye sees hues, but chromatic vision is not so highly developed as it is in the fovea. The cone vision of the peripheral retina may be regarded as more primitive in evolution than cone vision in the central area.

We have already mentioned the test for peripheral vision. If a colored button is brought into the margin of the visual field, it is sensed as a blurry gray patch, no matter what color is used. As the colors are moved farther along toward the fixation point, the blue and yellow are recognized; then red and green. Indeed, red and green pass a zone in which they may not look red and green at all. Any yellow or blue that the red or green may have will be enhanced in this intermediate area; red may look orange or yellow before the real red is recognized. The results of visual field tests support the idea of three color zones in the retina: the colorless zone, in the far periphery, a yellow-blue zone extending from the fovea to the middle area, and a red-green zone only in the central area (see Fig. 5:29). The color zones of the normal eye offer a rough analogy with types of color blindness. The far periphery is totally color blind, the intermediate zone is red-green blind, but the central zone is not color blind at all.

FIG. 5:34. Demonstrating the blind spot. Close the left eye and look at the cross. As you move the book slowly closer to or farther from the eye, the black circle, or the white square, or both, will disappear. The blind spot is the point at which the fibers come together to form the optic nerve and go back to the brain. Obviously there can be no rods or cones at this point (cf. Fig. 5:25).

This method can also be used to map out the blind spot. About 15 degrees to the right of the fixation point for the right eye, color patches are not seen at all, but they are seen again after they pass through the blind area. The blind spot is due to the fact that the rods and cones point the wrong way. The light-sensitive tips are against the back of the eyeball; the nerve fibers come out toward the lens. Obviously they must get back through the retina somewhere, to go to the brain. They converge on one point and leave there as the optic nerve. Since there can be no rods or cones at this point, it is literally blind. This cannot be noticed in ordinary seeing, because the optic nerves blank out different parts of the visual field in the right and left eyes. Hence what is not seen by one eye is usually visible to the other. Figure 5:34 shows you how to test for your own blind spot. In the map of the visual field (Fig. 5:29), the blind spot is shown by the gray circle just to the right of the fovea (the center of the field).

Color blindness. Color blindness, as the phrase is commonly used, is really a form of partial color blindness. Most color-blind persons confuse reds and greens. Red-green blindness is usually inherited, though it may be acquired as a result of injury or disease of the nerve structures concerned with vision. Excessive use of tobacco may temporarily cause color blindness.

The phenomenon of color blindness can be best understood when compared with normal vision. Normal color vision is *trichromatic* because at least three wave lengths are required to match all the hues in the spectrum as seen by these persons. *Monochromats* see the spectrum in terms of one color, or rather, a colorless band whose parts differ only in intensity (black to white). Such cases are relatively rare and are commonly referred as total color blindness. *Dichromats* see the spectrum in hues which can be matched by two wave lengths of light. Since only a few cases of blue-yellow blindness have been reported, dichromats consist mostly of the common red-green type of color blindness. Sometimes confused with red-green blindness are certain cases of *color weakness.* Certain individuals, although not color blind, are unequally sensitive to red and green. They are called *anomalous trichromats.*

The red-green dichromats have been differentiated into two kinds, deuteranopes and protanopes. As *deuteranopes* are classified those who seem to experience only color sensations blue and yellow, but whose spectrum is of normal length. As *protanopes* are designated those whose color systems again consist of blue and yellow, but who, in addition, have the spectrum shortened at the red end. Yellow-green forms the point of maximal brightness in the former, but green in the case of the latter. Anomalous trichromats are related to these two groups of dichromats: deuteranomalous trichromats, whose sensitiveness to green is below normal, and protanomalous trichromats, whose sensitivity to red is below normal.

The color blind may be detected by well-known tests. The most reliable tests consist of a series of charts made up of colored spots in which a number is discernible to the normal eye. The number is outlined in dots which are alike in hue but vary in intensity (Fig. 5:35). Since the color-blind person makes much greater use of intensity differences to compensate for lack of hue, he cannot see any pattern at all. Some of the most ingenious tests have one number outlined by hue and another by intensity, so that the color-blind person reports seeing a number—but the wrong one. Figure 5:36 shows how the test figure may appear to a color-blind person as compared with the normal.

These tests have now been widely applied in most countries. It appears that a conservative estimate of the persons having defective color vision is of the order of 10 per cent of the total population. About 4 per cent are male dichromats; less than 1 per cent are female dichromats; and 6 per cent are anomalous male trichromats. For many practical considerations color blindness is so slight a handicap that it is entirely possible for a color-blind person to go through life without ever becoming aware of his defect. However, in many occupations color blindness is a serious handicap: medicine, painting, the trade of the weaver, tailor, upholsterer, milliner, or florist, the armed services, the railway, post office, and so on.[1]

The Ladd-Franklin theory of color vision. The facts of color zones and color blindness serve to introduce us to a third major theory of color vision. Christine Ladd-Franklin was a student of Helmholtz and probably studied with Hering also. In addition she was a logician in her own right. She was quite aware of the logical shortcomings of both Young-Helmholtz and Hering theories. Her main complaint against the Young-Helmholtz theory was that it was not based on the four psychologically primary colors. On the other hand, the Hering theory did not recognize that red and green are noncomplementary and

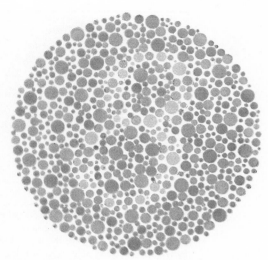

FIG. 5:35. A test plate for color blindness. This is plate 2 from the Ishihara test for color blindness. The dots of varying hue and brightness make different patterns. A normal person groups the dots by hue and sees the figure 8. A color-blind person groups the dots by brightness and sees no figure. Some test plates will reveal one figure to the normal eye and a different one to the color-blind individual. This type of test is sometimes ineffectual because of illumination which enables the color blind to see the figure. The Freeman Illuminant-Stable Test avoids this complication. (By permission of the C. H. Stoelting Co., Chicago, distributors of the Ishihara test in the United States, Canada, and Mexico.)

that their mixture produces a unique yellow. Ladd-Franklin devised a conceptual theory which ironed out these discrepancies. She chose the data on color zones as a starting point for her theory. For this reason her theory is known as the *evolutionary theory* of color vision, because she used hypotheses regarding primitive vision.

Ladd-Franklin assumed the presence of a single photochemical substance in both rods and cones. The rods, she suggested, are the original primitive undifferentiated receptors which respond to all light by giving a sensation of gray. Primitive vision is present in the outermost zone of the retina where the rods predominate. The cones of the intermediate zone underwent differentiation into two components, one

---

[1] Some well-meaning and no doubt patriotic young men have attempted to memorize the normal answers to the standard color-blindness test, so that they can gain admission to the Navy or Air Force. It is only proper to point out that such a person would be a menace to himself and his comrades. Naturally no reputable psychologist will allow test answers to be misused in this way.

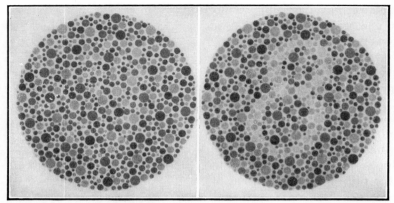

FIG. 5:36. Apparent effect of color blindness. The photograph on the right shows the figure 8 of Fig. 5:35 as it seems to be outlined to the normal eye. The photograph on the left suggests the probable appearance of Fig. 5:35 to a color-blind individual—a mass of dots of varying brightnesses, without pattern. (*Suggested by Cruze, 1951.*)

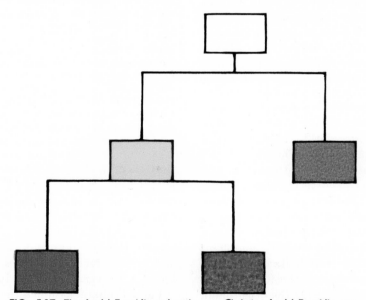

FIG. 5:37. The Ladd-Franklin color theory. Christine Ladd-Franklin proposed that the primitive eye had a sensitive cell which responded to degrees of white light. Later this evolved into two types of cells, one sensitive to blue, one to yellow. Still later, the yellow evolved into red and green. Note that this would fit the facts on color zones in the retina (Fig. 5:29) and on the frequency of red-green blindness (whereas blue-yellow blindness is extremely rare). (*From Varnum, 1942.*)

of which reacts to the short waves of the spectrum with the sensation of blue, and to the long waves with yellow. In the central zone, the yellow component was still further broken up into two new components, a red-sensitive and a green-sensitive component. This theory is difficult to understand in terms of these stages of differentiation of the same molecule during the course of time. Put in modern dress, it amounts to saying that besides rods the retina, in effect, has four different cones. The hypothetical evolution of the Ladd-Franklin molecule is shown in Fig. 5:37.

The theory is somewhat plausible because it gives a coherent explanation for three sets of facts:

1. If red-green receptors were the latest to evolve this would account for the commonness of red-green color blindness, since the most recent acquisitions would presumably be most frequently affected.

2. The smaller area of the red-green color zones as compared with blue and yellow would also be explained by the more recent acquisition of the red and green receptors.

3. It takes into account that red and green give a yellow instead of white, whereas blue and yellow give white when mixed. The answer is in terms of evolution as sketched above.

General appraisal of theories of color vision. We have covered the data of color vision in terms of the three prominent theories because each theory developed out of an important class of facts. In this way the facts could be presented and held together by the theory which each area of fact elicited historically. Of the three theories, the Ladd-Franklin theory, though logically consistent, has produced least research. The theory is physiologically difficult, because its conception of molecules splitting off from an original molecule and then the new derivatives splitting off into other molecules is very speculative, even if "molecules" is translated to mean "rods and cones." There is not sufficient evidence of evolution

from rods to the various types of cones. Some species even seem to have developed rods from cones.

The Hering theory also suffers from speculative concepts. The modern physiology of nerve conduction does not give any support to a notion of two kinds of processes in the same neurone. As we noted earlier (page 166), when a neurone is activated, it fires, and this discharge is an all-or-nothing process. We have not found neurones with two types of discharge. Moreover, how stimulation could "build up" a sensory response anabolically is unknown. The external stimulus always breaks down, does not build up the receptor molecules. Recovery usually takes place in the absence of stimulation. The Young-Helmholtz theory is the most acceptable of all three in that its physiology comes nearest to a fit with modern conceptions[1] of nervous and sensory function.

[1] We advise the student at this point to remember that "a modern conception" is not the same thing as a final and satisfactory answer. Modern conceptions of nerve physiology are in a state of flux and may very well be quite different a few years hence. In writing this chapter on human sensory processes, we have tied the facts together to conform to the law of specific nerve energies— the doctrine that sensory qualities are correlated with specific structures in the receptors or in the CNS. This neurological theory has led to important discoveries and certainly fits many of the observed facts. Data are accumulating, however, which indicate that the theory is an oversimplification. We cannot, for example, locate either sensory structures or CNS areas determining the sensed qualities of warm and cold; and indeed, there is some evidence (Nafe) that the same skin spot gives rise to different qualities on continued stimulation. This, if verified, deals a heavy blow to the doctrine of specific nerve energies.

In connection with audition we noted that the volley theory had to be introduced because "specific nerve energies" could not account for the psychological facts. Likewise we have trouble with vision. The clean-cut differences between cone function and rod function are being thrown into doubt by new experiments. It is perfectly conceivable, therefore, that the single-cone conception of vision, advanced by Ladd-Franklin, or the double-cone function proposed by Hering, will become more "modern" than the neat specificity advocated by Helmholtz.

Receptors and Homeostasis

Our study of receptor functions has brought out certain processes which are of great utility to the organism. Receptors are the means by which the various stimuli, for good or bad, in the external and internal environment are noticed and analyzed. Receptors do not, of course, respond to all changes; they are *selective*.

For adequate recognition of the stimulus under varying circumstances, the model stimulus is broken down into gradients of *quality* and *intensity*. The organism responds not merely to light or sound, but to discrete parts of the light or sound. Thus we see red, green, blue, yellow, etc. The fragmentation of the sense modalities is extensive. Consider that we see and hear 300,000 different lights and sounds. This is a measure of the organism's capacity for discrimination. By the same token it is a measure of the organism's ability to detect significant things in the environment. This remarkable detector system owes much of its refinement to the principle of *fusion* of sensations, which is a very economical device. Obviously we cannot have a receptor for every sensation; so we have fusion of qualities and intensities. The organism can use qualitative distinctions more readily than intensive ones. That is why we tend to regard any sensed difference as a difference in quality. These variations can be used as cues for variation in the external object (see Chap. 6).

Sensory experience tends to become patterned. Sensations which occur together again and again—such as stimulation of various parts of the skin, kinesthetic sensations, and the responses of the semicircular canals—become organized as systems. In this way we obtain a conceptual schema of our body, of our position in space, and of our muscles. Here pure sensation begins to disappear as it grades into perceiving (Chap. 6). These schemata seem to be represented in the brain in a form something like a map. We shall have occasion to refer to this conception many times in later chapters. The concept of frame of reference is another one which develops from sensory phenomena and which we shall find widely useful in relation to more complex psychological processes.

Adaptation is also significant for adjustment. We have seen that the sense organ automatically protects itself from overstimulation. The receptors illustrate the homeostatic principle most clearly in adaptation. The differences in rate and kind of adaptation in the various receptors need to be better understood. Usually adaptation is merely a reduction of sensitivity. In smell, however, it tends toward temporary annihilation of the stimulus. In audition there is very little adaptation. In vision, adaptation is most highly developed. Not only is protection served by reduction of sensitivity but the eye automatically adjusts itself or adapts to two kinds of world—the daylight, and the dark world.

When reception is considered from the brain level, similar homeostatic processes are discerned. These will be noted in the chapter on perception and in all the remaining chapters of this book. However, at this time it is appropriate to point out, as an indication of what is to come, that homeostasis on the brain level is not so simple as on the sensory level and that in some respects it seems to be entirely different. There are two reasons for this.

1. The brain is very *complex*. It is the integrating center for all the senses. It would hardly be expected that essential homeostatic principles would be as easily discernible as in a receptor or gland. Unfortunately we know little about the mechanism of the brain. However, we do know that it is a very complicated organ; and because of its complexity, it has a greater measure of freedom than a simpler one. A machine is a simple thing. A pulley

is activated by force applied in one direction so it seems to be obviously a mechanical business. However, a complicated system of pulleys is another matter. Thus, the modern "brain machines" or calculators, though they are mechanical, have a capacity for variability so great that they seem to be almost human. The more possibilities for variable action an organism or machine possesses, the more freedom it manifests.

2. There is another important fact about the brain. The receptors are able to respond at a distance, but the brain responds to *both distance and time*. Events long past and those yet to take place are effective factors in what the brain does at the moment. These associative processes pointing to the past and the future, which are performed by the brain, often make it difficult to detect the underlying homeostatic nature; yet the essence of dynamic homestasis is the use of past experience to prevent future deprivations.

The goals of brain action are symbolic. A symbolic need is not time- and space-bound, as is a visceral one, for instance. Therefore, on the mental level

we are not merely trying to adapt ourselves in order to stay alive, but are trying even more energetically to live. . . . life interflows with reality in full circles. We do things not only because we have a sensation, but also in order to make a sensation. Any rubber ball can react, but it requires life to act. And life does act. It seeks experience.[1]

SUMMARY

Man's efforts to obtain satisfaction for his inner needs would speedily come to naught if he had no method of obtaining information about the external environment. Actually, the human organism has a complex, built-in detector system, sensitive to a wide variety of external energies and

[1] Eastman (1917).

capable of reporting relatively minute stimuli.

The skin senses include many different qualities of experience, but most authorities hold that there are only four primary sensations: pressure, pain, warm, and cold. Closely joined with them (grouped under the general term *somesthesis*) are sensations from the organs within the body, and sensations from muscles, tendons, and joints. This group of sensory experiences is highly important in connection with the control of skilled movements; it also plays a major role in the child's developing awareness of self. The "body image" has a significant role in the formation of personality.

The chemical senses, taste and smell, provide guides for the organism in relation to foodstuffs particularly but seem also to be intimately related to other motives, such as sex. Odors particularly seem capable of exerting an effect outside of conscious awareness upon one's judgment of "good" or "bad" qualities.

Hearing is a response to mechanical vibrations of air particles. Both as to absolute threshold and as to analysis of vibratory pattern it is an amazingly sensitive function. Auditory stimuli seem to have special significance as warning signals; while many observers disagree with Watson as to loud sounds being an innate stimulus for fear, there is a consensus that sounds very readily become fear stimuli. Since it is non-directional under ordinary conditions, it serves as an excellent supplement to vision, which operates only toward the front of the human organism.

Sound waves vary as to frequency, amplitude, and composition. Corresponding to these three dimensions we have three variables in auditory sensations: pitch, loudness, and timbre. The question of how the very high speed vibrations can be handled by the auditory nerve leads into an interesting neurological problem. Since the range of audible frequencies is from roughly 20 to

20,000 per second, some form of the volley-place combination of theories seems necessary.

In terms of stimulus energy required to set it off, vision may well be the most sensitive of all our receptors. It goes almost to the theoretical limit indicated by quantum theory. Like sound vibrations, light waves vary along three dimensions: frequency, amplitude, and composition. The visual experiences correlated to these are hue, brightness, and saturation. The combinations of these give us approximately 300,000 differentiable visual sensations—about the same as for the sense of hearing, incidentally.

The chief problem in connection with vision is to explain our sensitivity to color. The Young-Helmholtz, Hering, and Ladd-Franklin theories of color vision were sketched briefly; each tends to focus on certain facts to the exclusion of others, and none can be said to be fully acceptable, although the trend seems to be toward preference for some adaptation of the Young-Helmholtz view.

Recommended Readings[1]

ADRIAN, E. D.: *Physical Background of Perception*. New York: Oxford, 1947.

BARTLEY, S. H.: *Vision*. New York: Van Nostrand, 1941.

————: *Beginning Experimental Psychology*. New York: McGraw-Hill, 1950. Chaps. 5–8.

BEKESY, G. VON, and W. A. ROSENBLITH: The Mechanical Properties of the Ear. Chap. 27. In Stevens, S. S. (Ed.), *Handbook of Experimental Psychology*. New York: Wiley, 1951.

BORING, E. G.: *Sensation and Perception in the History of Experimental Psychology*. New York: Appleton-Century-Crofts, 1942. (Especially Chaps. 1 and 3.)

————, H. S. LANGFELD, and H. P. WELD: *Foundations of Psychology*. New York: Wiley, 1948. Chaps. 11, 12, 14–16.

BUTLER, R. J., and T. F. KARWOSKI: *Human Psychology*. New York: Pitman, 1936. Chap. 7.

DAVIS, H.: *The Psychophysiology of Hearing and Deafness*. Chap. 28. In: S. S. Stevens (Ed.), *Handbook of Experimental Psychology*. New York: Wiley, 1951.

EVANS, R. M.: *An Introduction to Color*. New York: Wiley, 1948. Chaps. 8–12.

KATZ, D.: *The World of Color*. (Tr. by R. B. MacLeod and C. W. Fox.) London: Kegan Paul, Trench, Trubner & Co., 1935. Parts I and II.

KOUWER, B. J.: *Colors and Their Character*. The Hague: Martinus Nyhoff, 1949.

MORGAN, C. T., and E. STELLAR: *Physiological Psychology*. New York: McGraw-Hill, 1950.

PARSONS, J. H.: *An Introduction to the Study of Color Vision*. London: Cambridge, 1924. Part 3.

PIRENNE, M. H.: *Vision and the Eye*. London: Chapman & Hall, 1948.

SEASHORE, C. L.: *Psychology of Music*. New York: McGraw-Hill, 1938.

STEVENS, S. S.: *Hearing*. New York: Wiley, 1938. Chaps. 10, 11, and 12.

WEVER, E. G.: *Theory of Hearing*. New York: Wiley, 1949.

[1] See also p. 547.

CHAPTER 6

Perceiving

Picture to yourself a man who is surrounded by thousands of flashing signals, sounds of all descriptions, smells, contact stimuli, tastes, and so on. Each of these sensory impressions may signal life or death to him. Most of them, at any given moment, are innocuous; but he does not know which can be disregarded. How shall he deal with this complex and confusing situation?

It is clear that he cannot be equally responsive to all these stimuli. To attempt to do so would be to wreck the organism. There must, consequently, be a *selective mechanism* by which certain cues are brought into focus, inspected, and either dealt with or disregarded for a time while others come into focus; and there must be an *integrating mechanism* which organizes this almost infinite diversity of stimuli into a reasonable number of units which can be handled by the organism. The first of these is the process of *attending:* one attends to certain elements in the environment and ignores others. The second process is that of *perceiving:* one learns that a large group of visual, auditory, tactual, and other cues "go together" as indicators of the presence of some specific object: "kitty," "auto," "daddy," and so on.

In the previous chapter we noted the extraordinary sensitivity of the sense organs. The human eye and ear, particularly, are amazingly effective at bringing us information about the outer world. This sensitivity can, at times, be an embarrassment of riches. Young children are likely to have great difficulty in accomplishing any task because they are so readily distracted. Even adults have their troubles with concentration when changing visual and auditory stimuli are present. The ability to shut out these irrelevant elements tends to increase steadily from birth to maturity, and perhaps into the twenties; it declines in later life, as older people complain of distractions they once ignored.

Perhaps the preceding chapter gave the impression that knowing the external world is just a question of how the sense organs work. This is far from the truth. The organism puts together the cues from the various sensory modalities, weighting some heavily, ignoring others, and even distorting some. This process goes on automatically and unconsciously in the adult; the brain is a kind of lightning calculator, summing up all these cues to reach an interpretation: what kind of an object is out there; will it satisfy my needs; does it threaten danger?

Consider for a moment the perception of your table top. The exact wave frequency of light reaching your eye from this surface varies with the kind of illumination. As you change your position, the size of the image on your retina varies. Only rarely is the shape rectangular; most of the time it is an irregular trapezoid. And, of course, *never* is the retinal image composed of straight lines, for the retinal surface is curved. Despite all these facts, the table top blandly continues to *look* the same color, the same size, and the same shape. Obviously what is "out there" in the external world is not identical with our sensations.

Take a look at Figs. 6:1a and 6:1b. These were produced by placing a camera lens at a peephole and photographing what is seen by the human eye in one of the ingenious perceptual demonstrations devised by Adelbert Ames. In each instance you see a little chair; chair b actually looks a little better constructed than chair a. Now look at Fig. 6:2. This shows what was behind the peepholes. String pattern A corresponds to chair a, and string pattern B to chair b. As can readily be seen, chair b was "put together" inside the organism from diverse cues reaching the eye. This is not to suggest that everyday chairs have such an unsubstantial construction. Rather, it shows what goes on in the process of perceiving; in everyday life these cues are interpreted as showing that a chair is "out there." For most of our physical perceptions, these cues are sufficiently dependable that our behavior is adaptive. People driving cars at high speed under unfavorable conditions frequently misinterpret their cues; the resulting behavior is often fatal.

This, then, is the problem: the organism must satisfy its needs, maintain homeostasis, avoid disturbance and injury. To accomplish these ends one must know, not that there is a red stimulus out there, but that there is a red apple, a red-haired woman, a fire, or a splotch of blood. To get from the world of stimuli and sensations to the world of objects, we must have (1) attention, selection, and elimination; and (2) perception of objects by organizing the remaining cues into meaningful patterns. Let us first turn to the analysis of the attention function.

Attending

The process of attending to the external world includes both physical set and mental set. Physically the world is all around us; visually, the eye spans about 180 rather than 360 degrees, and only a small part of the visual field is clear at any moment. We have maximum clarity in the fovea, the central 2-degree arc; blurring increases toward the edges of the field (see Fig. 6:3). Although the world seems continuous, we actually see it as a series of part pictures as the eyes shift position. It can be shown that the eye is virtually blind while moving; but we fill in the gaps and "see" a continuous landscape. If you look at one of the windows of a house, the other windows—and the whole house, in fact—are "seen" rather clearly; but *close inspection* reveals that only the window fixated is clear, the others being quite vague. Our first impression is clear because a house is a familiar object; the cues, though vague, give us clear meanings; our confidence in these meanings gives clarity to the total picture. This illustration will serve to illustrate the role of *preperception*, of being mentally set to see something and consequently "seeing" it on the basis of inadequate cues.

Both physical set (orientation of body) and mental set (expectancy) are thus involved in attention and perception. Basic to both is motivation. We have referred to the phenomenon of focusing in connection with drives and emotions. Objects related to satisfying a drive and reducing tension are focused upon, while others are relatively ignored. We are by heredity so constituted that certain kinds of cues (loud sounds, visual movement) dominate the perceptual field automatically. By learning, many other cues acquire dominance value. Ordinarily we ignore minor skin sensations; but if I suspect that I have acquired some fleas from a stray dog, these vague experiences

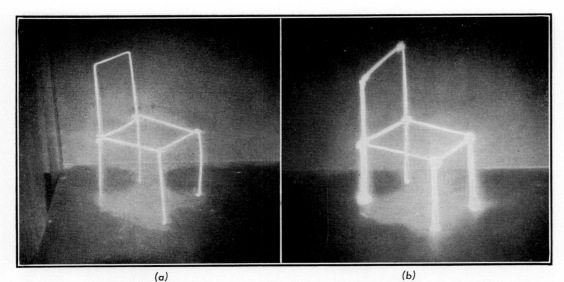

(a)   (b)

FIG. 6:1. Chairs as seen in the Ames demonstration. The person looks through peephole *a* and sees the figure on the left. He then looks through peephole *b* and sees the figure on the right. (These photographs were made by placing the camera lens at the peephole.) Would you say that the chairs are very much the same size, the same distance away, etc.?

may dominate the conscious field to the exclusion of other stimuli. As was noted in Chap. 2, any drive tension seems capable of lowering sensory thresholds and making us selectively sensitive to possible goal objects. *Drives, therefore, determine the direction of attention.*

Bodily adjustment and attention. We must avoid the trap of treating attention as " a little man inside of me " who can focus my sensory searchlights wherever he wishes. Obviously, attention must be considered to be a function of the entire organism. I move my whole body as I explore a novel situation. Man's head swivels on the neck, so that without moving the body he can still scan the environment nearby. The main distance receptor, the eye, is equipped with three sets of muscles which make it an ideal motile organ. By these arrangements the organism exposes itself to wide areas of the stimulating environment in a short time.

Because the visual field is so important in the behavior of the normal human, we shall use it as a model here. Photographs of

eye movements show that we cannot fixate upon a specific stimulus for any but very short time intervals. Even if I am inspecting a small object such as a diamond, my eyes will be found to shift frequently. Careful studies have revealed that these movements are actually part of a constant *shifting of attention.* For example, in the ambiguous pictures (Fig. 6:4) most people get a regular shifting back and forth between the two perceptions.

The basis for this shifting seems to lie in the fatiguing of the sensory cells in the retina. We cannot focus clearly on a single figure for more than a few seconds or it will begin to blur. Apparently, then, shifting of attention is a device to relieve those end organs being fatigued, and bring others into play. Consciously we seem to try to maintain the stimulus clearly at all times, and we achieve this by shifting attention to new aspects of the object. Sporadic movements of the eyelid also block out the stimulus momentarily and rest the retinal cells. It is probable that similar muscular mechanisms for shifting operate in hearing,

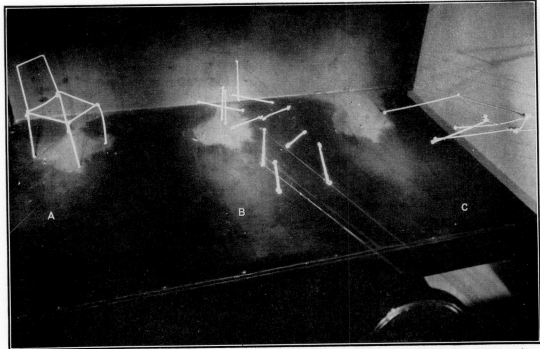

FIG. 6:2. The setup of the Ames demonstration. After the person has looked through the peepholes (Fig. 6:1), he is invited to look behind the screen, and this is what he sees. Do both A and B now look the same? (C is also seen as a chair, when viewed through the peephole.) How can string pattern B give rise to the perception of a chair? Does this show that the organism contributes something to the nature of what is perceived "out there"?

smell, and taste, although they are difficult to observe in action.

The process of shifting is clearly homeostatic in character. If one concentrated on a particular stimulus to the point of fatiguing the sensory cells, important changes might occur, endangering the life of the individual. Fatigue in the retinal cell sets up a tension; this tension is reduced by shift.

This principle even carries over to more complex behavior. Change and variation of response seems to be natural and pleasant; lack of variety leads to boredom and feelings of fatigue.[1] Even a white rat shows a tendency to alternate between right and left turns when he is in a novel learning

[1] This rule is limited by extreme cases in which too much change is overstimulating; constant excitation due to the need for alertness may also be fatiguing, in a different way.

situation. We can relate this back to our principle of *satiation* (page 50). When one is hungry, he takes in food; this satiates the hunger drive, and activity directed toward this stimulus disappears. Similarly, a loud sound may arouse tension (attract your attention); you investigate it and then, satiated, you drop it and are ready for some new stimulus to dominate. Sleep is a response pattern adapted to remove the organism from external stimulation; one goes to sleep when bored by unchanging stimuli or when fatigued by too many changing stimuli.

External factors in attention shift. Shift due to sensory fatigue and boredom does not occur entirely at random. The nature of the external stimulus influences the direction as well as frequency of shift. The organism is so constructed that certain

FIG. 6:3. A child's world. The imaginative photographer has here given a representation of the young child's perception of his world which psychologists believe to be rather accurate. Actually, much adult perception may also have this quality of clarity at the center, blurring at the edges, but we unconsciously "fill in" the objects in the periphery and "see" them on the basis of memory. (*From Life Magazine. Copyright Time, Inc.*)

stimuli are dominant over others. Especially noticeable is the potency of a loud sound to attract attention. This is very probably a matter of hereditary determination by its value as a danger signal—cf. Watson's experiment on fear. Visual movement is another extremely compelling stimulus. This also could be thought of as possibly hereditary; in a primitive environment, any moving animal is a potential threat.

Whether you are trying to get the attention of a friend who is engrossed in his work, or you are preparing advertising material to attract the attention of millions, there are certain simple points about the physical aspects of stimuli to keep in mind. The following is a very sketchy account of the

major variations in physical stimuli which are effective in attracting attention:[1]

1. *Intensity.* Other things being equal, strong stimuli are more compelling than weak ones. An increase in the brilliance of lighting, or in the loudness of sound, will cause the stimulus to stand out against the background of other stimuli.

1a. *Contrast.* It follows from the preceding statement that any stimulus which contrasts strongly with its background will be perceived readily. A diamond is most effective on black velvet. Complementary colors create effective contrast where they can be employed. A small

[1] Any of the standard textbooks on the psychology of advertising will give an elaboration of these principles in terms of the techniques used by modern advertisers. Cf., for example, Lucas and Britt (1950).

FIG. 6:4. An ambiguous figure. Look carefully at the black band in the foreground. Does it look like a circular wedge cut out of the gray block? Or does it appear as a pie-shaped wedge glued onto the corner of the block, projecting out and up from it? If you watch closely, it will shift between these two percepts. (*By Adeline Cross. From The Language of Vision, by G. Kepes, 1944. By permission of Paul Theobald, publisher.*)

printed message, centered in white space, is often better than filling the advertisement to the edges with printed material.

1*b. Novelty* is a variation of contrast. Occasionally an advertiser will print his material upside down; distorted pictures, challenging headlines, the use of color in a medium normally black and white, and other devices fit in this category. Novelty is due to the contrast with surrounding material; in a magazine filled with colored advertisements, one in black and white might have attention value. Talking animals and similar devices are noticed because of their rarity. We should always remember that for survival the organism *must* notice and inspect new objects as they appear. This mechanism is so thoroughly established by the time we reach maturity that it operates even in completely irrelevant contexts.

2. *Movement and change.* As noted above, moving stimuli are especially potent at getting attention. A change in cue is also readily noted. The ticking of the clock gets boring and drops out of consciousness; when it stops, we notice the change. A relatively small variation in the pitch of a given sound has attention value, although the interpretation depends on special training; *e.g.*, an airplane mechanic may get a lot of information from such variations.

3. *Size.* This factor is probably a variation of intensity and contrast. Large stimuli tend to be noticed, but this may be because they are competing with smaller objects for attention. When several billboards are together, each loses rapidly in potency. Either a tall man or a midget may attract our eyes. Greater size, of course, also gives more opportunity for other cues to operate.

4. *Repetition.* Very weak stimuli may attract attention if they are repeated. This is based on the principle described in the preceding chapter, of *summation of stimuli*. Water dripping from a faucet may become extremely irritating with repetition. In general, however, this phase passes and the monotonous stimulus is ignored. Thus advertisers employ repetition with variation. Like repetition, *duration* is sometimes effective; but a long-drawn-out stimulus may

also become boring and, so to speak, be blocked out of consciousness.

Kinds of attention. It will be appropriate for us to consider the determinants of attention *within the organism,* as a parallel to the preceding pages on external determinants. Before we can do this effectively, it is desirable that we consider the fact that acts of attending to stimuli take different forms.

The external determinants of attention operate largely without regard to man's motives and sets. Indeed, we identify such factors particularly by their ability to *compel* attention even when the person is oriented in a different direction. This form of attending is known as *involuntary attention.* The response is dominated by the external stimuli.

At the opposite extreme from this we can designate a form of attending which is controlled mainly by *internal conditions.* Motivation is the major variable here. If I am strongly interested in finding food, distracting stimuli will be of little effect (unless threatening, in which case motivation changes). If I am strongly motivated to solve a mathematics problem, an unusual sound outside my window may go unnoticed. This persistent orientation to a task is called *voluntary attention.* Teachers and parents utilize rewards and punishments to foster voluntary attention in children; *i.e.,* extrinsic motives are used to induce attending to a selected stimulus.

If voluntary attention is practiced over a considerable period of time, it can become *habitual.* In this case, certain kinds of stimuli may be so firmly associated to the response of attending that they function in the same manner as the external influences cited above for involuntary attention. Figure 6:5 shows the eye movements made while examining the picture of a group of men. Note the concentration in the face and head area. We have learned to attend

to faces and facial expressions—they have important consequences for us. Architects automatically notice details of building design, a printer observes details of printing format, and so on. Such forms of attending to stimuli were in their origin voluntary, but practice has made them unconscious. The untrained observer finds it difficult to distinguish involuntary from habitual attention, as neither requires conscious effort. The easiest way to separate them is to note that habitual attending was once voluntary and is still determined mainly by internal conditions of motivation, past learning, and the like.

It may be helpful at this point to introduce the following diagram:

Attention

Dominated by external stimuli		Dominated by internal conditions	
Involuntary	Habitual	Voluntary	Anticipatory

Involuntary attention is almost purely a function of the outer situation. In habitual attention, we are oriented to the outer stimuli, but the real basis for attention is in our motives, mental sets, habits, etc. Voluntary attention is dominated by inner states but must of course focus on the outer world to satisfy these impulses. *Anticipatory* attention represents the relatively complete dominance of inner needs; the person becomes aware of what he wants and then searches the environment for that object. When the object is located, the difference between anticipatory and voluntary attention vanishes.

Role of muscle tension. In all these kinds of attention, we notice the mobilization of energy. Attending, in other words, is just one segment of that total pattern which we called *motivation.* Involuntary attention shows the development of muscle tension

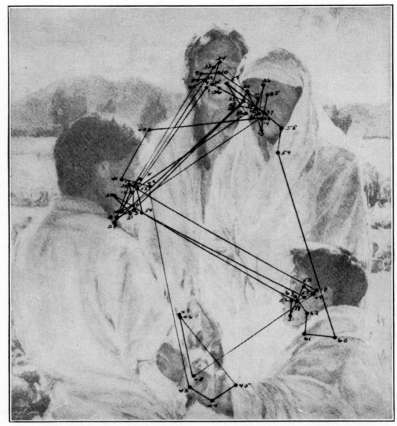

FIG. 6:5. How people look at a picture. Eye movements were photographed as people looked at different pictures. Here is a typical record. Note the concentration of attention on the faces of the people, with a few fixations on the hands, none on details of the figures or background. While it is more difficult to demonstrate, this is also what one does when observing a real person. (*From Buswell, 1935, by permission of University of Chicago Press.*)

very clearly. However, voluntary attention is likely to involve even more tension, because of the problem of maintaining a given orientation against the distractions of other enticing stimuli. Self-observation will indicate that when you are attending closely you become tense in eyebrows, jaws, shoulders, back, and other areas. Notice the quiet concentration of a symphony or drama audience during a performance, and the sudden squirming, sighing, and coughing at an intermission. This is the same phenomenon which we discussed earlier as

focusing. Attending is the device by which we exclude irrelevant stimuli, the more effectively to deal with those of importance to the motives of the moment.

Shifting also occurs on the conscious level. Close your eyes and try to think intently about a specific problem, such as the relation of the light waves to visual sensations (page 171). Your thought does not remain static; there is a steady shift from one aspect of the problem to another. Trained observers of thinking report that "the same idea does not persist for many seconds, and its constituent parts do not remain unchanged for more than a fraction of a second." It may be that all such shifting, whether based on sensory processes, muscle tensions, or cortical activities, is really the same. Satiation seems to be involved in every case. First there is a need to inspect a certain stimulus (or examine a certain idea); this is satisfied, and a new need immediately takes its place.

Internal factors in shift of attention. It is easiest to describe and analyze attention in terms of the dominance of a particular outer stimulus. However, this is by no means the whole story. As soon as we consider the process of concentrating to shut out these external stimuli, we realize that inner influences also determine the selection of dominant stimuli. When we note the existence of voluntary, habitual, and anticipatory attention, we are saying that, in very many cases, these internal factors are more influential than the external cues.

In our discussion of attention we have emphasized that attention is constantly shifting. The world around us is constantly changing; sense organs get fatigued; a different sight, sound, or smell is dominant almost every second. Inner conditions can also cause shifting, as when one suddenly notices that he is hungry; but far oftener, the contributions of internal conditions are in the direction of *reducing* the speed of shifting. Motivation and mental set direct the organism to pursue some goal object (or to escape some dangerous stimulus). Obviously, in such cases, attention shifting must be kept within very narrow limits, or the goal may be lost.

Interest in a stimulus helps to keep it in focus. Years ago Breese (1899) devised a simple demonstration of this type. He had his subjects look through a stereoscope so that one eye saw a red square, the other a green square. The subjects reported a rhythmic oscillation of red and green as one eye was dominant, then the other. Now he placed a small cross mark on one square. Immediately that color tended to stay in focus much longer than its rival. By making that square more interesting, he made it the center of attention.

This fact is of importance to the public speaker or the advertiser. We have mentioned some of the devices by which the advertiser captures attention. But this is not the same as *holding* attention. An advertisement which, through size, movement, or intensity, attracts my attention, may be displaced a moment later before I even note the name of the company. Hence the problem of holding the focus for some time is also very important. The picture of a beautiful woman has interest value; it appeals to persistent motives of both men and women. Prestige, economic gain, and interest in children are other inner conditions to which advertisers regularly appeal in their attempt to hold attention on their product. After all, the arousal of some need is the most effective device for making an advertisement interesting.

Most of the tensions so aroused are fairly short-lived. We may curiously inspect the filling station with a cardboard tiger curled round the gas pump, but this attention value wanes rapidly. Advertisers distinguish between short-term and long-term appeals with consideration for this variable. Short-term appeals work satisfactorily for inexpensive or often-needed commodities (food, etc.). Long-term appeals are necessary for infrequent, expensive purchases such as automobiles and radiophonographs.

A persisting mental set interferes, obviously, with attention to objects outside its scope. Thus a college teacher finds it difficult to deal with a class whose members have an important examination the next hour. The last class before a vacation is also inattentive to the lecture. Long-term mental sets tend to persist when there may be a need to shift; thus the teacher who desires also to write a book may find it difficult to go from the classroom directly into the writing activity. It is hard to focus on the latter without some delay. This period of reduced efficiency on the new task is often called a *warming-up* period (getting started and developing clear focus with other matters excluded from consciousness), but it could sometimes be called a *cooling-off* period (getting rid of some prior mental set which is interfering).

Definition of attention. Because attention is a rather tricky concept to define, we have deliberately discussed first some of the obvious facts of common knowledge regarding this function. This gives us a starting point from which we can derive a definition.

The significant fact about attention is the phenomenon of stimulus selection. Certain stimuli are dominant in experience at any given moment, to the exclusion of others. The kinds of stimuli which seem naturally to dominate attention can be understood in terms of heredity and natural selection; *i.e.*, if we think of living under primitive conditions, we can infer that organisms so constructed by heredity that they attended to these stimuli had a better chance to survive. Those who were not selectively attentive to loud sounds, movement, etc., probably were liquidated. Thus we assume that hereditary structure explains the dominance quality of these external stimuli.

But this is only part of the story. We know that we can override many potent external variations by mental set. Does this conflict with the analysis of attention already given? No conflict is really necessary. People trained in introspection tell us that, when external stimuli are reduced to a minimum, the process of shifting and scanning goes on. It is simply switched to the realm of memories and internal changes. At any moment some need, drive, or memory is dominant. Strong needs can remain dominant and exclude other thoughts, just as

strong external stimuli can shut out competitors.

In infancy, the structure is already organized for dominance of external stimuli. However, it is also organized for certain inner changes. Hunger and pain, for example, will dominate over most other factors. It is worth noting that even an infant crying from hunger can be induced to stop momentarily, by a shiny moving object in his line of vision. Briefly, this stimulus is dominant, but quickly a shift occurs and he is yelling again.

As one grows, he learns that certain objects lead to satisfaction of drives, others lead to pain. The high attention value of such objects is thus based on their motivational significance. When I am hungry, a piece of food has attention dominance even though I was not specifically looking for it.

A story is told of some American soldiers in an enemy prison camp during World War II. The men had been talking incessantly of food because of their hunger. Finally the ranking officer present decided this was bad for morale and forbade any further mention of food for a time. One of the men started speculating on what the postwar automobiles would look like. "I wish I had one of those cars right now," said the sergeant, "smothered in potatoes and gravy." Exclusion of high-dominance stimuli is virtually impossible.

Attention, then, can be defined as the process by which stimuli attain clarity. It is impossible to study attention directly; we can study it only in terms of its effects— *i.e.*, some stimuli achieve clarity and others do not. The factors determining selections are those which we have described—internal and external.

Attention is not the muscular process of moving the head or focusing the eyes. Usually these motor adjustments occur after a stimulus has become dominant. I hear a loud sound, then turn to look for its source. I note a moving object, then focus for better inspection. The process of attending seems to occur primarily, if not exclusively, in the sensory mechanisms and the brain.

Attention, then, is defined as stimulus selection (reinforcement) or stimulus dominance. Clearness of perception, and muscular adjustment are consequences of attention. The basic fact is that, at a given moment, the organism is related to a particular stimulus and excludes other stimuli from consideration.

Attention is unitary. Can we attend to more than one object or activity simultaneously? While it is difficult to prove conclusively, most psychologists doubt that we can really do so. The great rapidity of fluctuation of attention, however, makes it possible to oscillate between two foci of attention so rapidly that for practical purposes both are in focus. This is feasible only when at least one activity is highly practiced and semiautomatic. For example, the novice on a bicycle must keep his attention focused on his balance and thus neglects his steering, or vice versa; with some practice he can handle both functions by rapid oscillation between them; and soon he can ride, converse, and enjoy the scenery, attending to his riding only for minute fractions of each second. Reading gives another illustration of attending to more than one stimulus. The printed words are so laid out that, while focus is on one word, both that immediately preceding and that following are near the focus. Thus we see one word clearly but *reinforce* earlier or later perceptions of the adjacent words. Each fixation occurs within a context of past and future reference.

Figure and ground in attention. Psychologists describe the pattern of attention in experience in terms of focus and margin, or figure and ground. The focus (or figure) is characterized by vivid clearness, with plenty of detail. The margin or ground is less clear and poorly differentiated, the outer margin being virtually unconscious. Figure 6:3 gives an ingenious photographic interpretation of a child's field of attention.

The phenomenal field. We have already had occasion to point out (page 19) that man's behavior is not necessarily determined by his physical environment. A given physical object may have positive valence for John, negative valence for Bill. It is obvious, in terms of our discussion of attention, that the object will guide behavior if it is in focus but will have less effect if it is in the margin.

It will simplify matters in the long run if we now introduce the concept of the *phenomenal field.* This is the field or environment as perceived by the individual. The external world has a multiplicity of objects and stimuli; the phenomenal field has as figure the object which is clearly in focus, the other items present being blurred and in the background. It is obvious, therefore, that *behavior is controlled by the phenomenal field.* In general there will be correspondence between the physical field and the phenomenal field. As physical organisms, we obey the law of gravitation, Newton's laws of motion, and so on. Anyone who ignores the laws of physics does so at his peril; he will learn to perceive objects realistically or he will not survive. But it is still true that it is the perception, not the physical world, which guides behavior. The pedestrian who sees the beautiful blonde across the street, and not the approaching car, behaves in accordance with his phenomenal field—perhaps with fatal results. At all times, the focus of attention determines the figure in the perceptual field, the marginal objects providing the ground.

The phenomenal field can include imagination as well as direct perception of reality. The normal person can shift attention back and forth between physical perception and imaginal perception. The "figure" may at this moment be a real object, but in the next instant it is an imaginary picture of what that object might be if manufactured differently or composed of different raw material. This type of process makes possible learning, improved adjustment, better satisfaction of motives. However, it is important to keep a proper balance between attention to the imaginal and to the physical present. When people lose the ability to distinguish the imaginal from the perceptual field, they are insane.

Because man is a symbol-manipulating animal, it is possible for one man to instruct or propagandize another. If I say to a friend, "See the plane in the sky," the word can arouse an image of the object in his mind, and then he scans the sky in search of it. His attention was set to perceive the real plane by a preliminary symbolic plane. (And he is thus likely to misperceive a bird or a small cloud as a plane.) Similarly, my need for a typewriter eraser may cause me to image the eraser, and all objects of that general size and shape suddenly have high attention value. Changes on the symbolic level can thus guide attention on the perceptual level.

The importance of distinguishing between the physical field and the phenomenal field should be apparent. In scientific psychology we are frequently troubled by the fact that an identical object is perceived differently (the phenomenal object is different) by different persons. Mental set and expectancy operate to affect the perception derived from a sensory cue. So, if we attempt to create a panic by blowing smoke into a room and shouting "Fire!" our subjects remain calm, feeling sure it is just an experiment. A given electric shock is perceived as severely punishing by one person, a mild annoyance by another. Likewise in everyday life, we must know how a person perceives a situation. An overhanging crane may be seen by the workmen as a threatening safety hazard, while the plant engineer sees it only as a necessary piece of machinery. Behavior toward the crane is determined by its phenomenal character (perception), not its physical character. The attention of various individuals will be directed toward different aspects of a situation by their needs, by their past experiences, and by suggestions from other people. Some of these factors we shall consider in later portions of this book.

Methods of Studying Attention

Much of the foregoing is based simply on introspection, self-observation under conditions of attention. There is also an extensive body of literature on experimental studies of attention. The reaction-time experiment will serve as an example of many of these kinds of investigation.

Reaction time. The speed with which a person responds to a stimulus can be accurately measured by means of a chronoscope, a very accurate clock which is started by the stimulus and stopped by the response. The unit of measurement is usually 0.001 second. (See Fig. 1:7, page 25.)

The reaction-time experiment typically involves at least two aspects of the attending process. The first is mental set. The subject is instructed to respond as rapidly as possible when the stimulus is presented. The second phase is muscular, adjusting the sense organs and the response organ (the finger, if the response is pressing a button). These two phases represent preparation for the stimulus; together they comprise the "foreperiod" in the experiment. Introspection reveals that awareness of the situation is concentrated in this foreperiod. The response itself goes off virtually automatically.

During the foreperiod, the expected stimulus becomes the figure in the phenomenal field, and everything else is ground. Under these circumstances the speed of response to the stimulus measures the efficiency of the feed-back mechanism; it is obviously a matter of considerable adaptive significance. In a few parts of the country a decidedly subnormal reaction time is grounds for denial of a driver's license.

Reactions to different stimuli. Since man's life seems so much dominated by vision, it might be expected that attention to visual stimuli (and thus reaction time to such stimuli) would rate highest of all the senses. This happens not to be true. As Fig. 6:6 shows, vision runs a poor third in terms of speed in setting off a predetermined response; both hearing and touch are faster. There may be some connection between the extremely rapid response to auditory stimuli and the fact that loud sounds easily come to set off fear responses in young children. Perhaps the cave man who ran quickly from unexpected sounds survived and passed his auditory sensitivity on to later generations. There may also be an advantage for hearing in the fact that the ear responds to a mechanical vibration (see page 158) whereas the retinal cells must respond chemically.

The slow response to pain has raised questions as to its biological value. This, we think, is an error. For survival value, the organism should respond to a signal, not wait for pain itself to set in. Hence it seems plausible that attention to other stimuli is more rapid than to pain as such.

Intensity of stimuli. We have stated above that attention is determined by the intensity of the stimulus. Within the limits of normal functioning, increasing intensity of the stimulus leads to increasing rapidity of response.

Foreperiod. Speed of reaction time also varies with the length of the foreperiod. If a subject is instructed to "get set" for the stimulus, he tenses his muscles and focuses the relevant sense organs. This kind of set can be maintained only for a short time. A foreperiod longer than 5

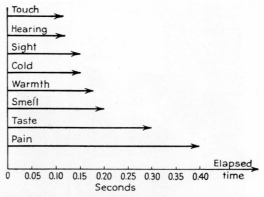

FIG. 6:6. Speed of reaction to various stimuli. Reaction to touch is fastest, with hearing a close second. Taste and pain are relatively slow to set off reactions. The figures are for precise measurements under laboratory conditions; in everyday life they would be slower. Averages for several subjects.

seconds causes a loss of efficiency. When crews are synchronizing actions, as on a large airplane, the act of counting builds up to a peak of attention; the foreperiod is not actually as long as the total count.

Sensory and motor set. The kind of instructions the experimenter gives the subject (or the way the person gets himself set) will affect speed. Instructions which emphasize the *response* speed up reaction, while an emphasis on the *stimulus* slows it down. That is, if the subject is told to be sure he hears the bell before pressing the key, he will delay by a measurable fraction of a second longer than if he is told to press the key just as quickly as possible when he hears the bell. Sensory set gives somewhat greater accuracy, of course; with a motor set the individual often responds to a false stimulus.

Complex reaction time. The types of experimentation noted above are classified together as *simple-reaction-time* studies because the subject is not required to make a choice. He simply attends to a single, predetermined stimulus. Suppose now that we require him to respond to a bell but not to a buzzer. This situation calls for

FIG. 6:7. An Air Force reaction-time test. The vertical panels carry signal lights which are controlled by the tester (man at left foreground). The circular dial sets off a light stimulus to which each man must make a choice reaction. Standing on the test (high-speed response) has fair predictive value for passing or failing pilot training. (*From Melton, 1944.*)

discrimination, and slows down the speed of response. More organismic activity must intervene between stimulus and reaction. Such studies deal with *complex* reaction time.

Discrimination reaction time is only one form of complex reaction. Another type of experiment requires that the subject respond with his right hand to stimulus A, with his left to stimulus B. This is usually called *choice* reaction time, to indicate that it involves a selection of responses as well as stimuli. Obviously every choice reaction must also be discriminative; there must first be selection of the correct stimulus, then of the response. Naturally choice reactions require more time than discriminations calling for response or no response.

Physical condition. How well we can pay attention is a function of the physical condition of the organism. Old people and young children have very slow reactions. Early maturity is associated with fastest response and most efficient attention. Aviators at high altitudes (low oxygen supply) or under acceleration pressures are slowed down. This is obviously important under modern conditions of high-speed flight, where a plane may travel a mile during the period between stimulus and reaction. It explains the use of attention tests by the Air Force in selecting crew members; complex reaction-time tests are standard parts of the selection battery (Fig. 6:7). The ordinary intelligence tests are in a sense measures of speed of reaction, as most of them operate with a time limit.

Certain commonly used drugs affect one's efficiency of energy mobilization. Contrary to popular notions, the caffeine in coffee will slow you down, not speed you

FIG. 6:8. Device for testing effects of increased gravity. High-speed airplanes may impose pressures several times gravity, especially in dives and turns. How does this affect reaction time? Warren tested visual and auditory reaction time of men subject to pressure by rapid rotation in this centrifuge; he found all reaction times slowed by increased gravity. (*Operated under contract with the Office of Naval Research; contract N6ori77 Task Order III, Neil D. Warren, responsible investigator.*)

up. Alcohol in very small amounts may have a slight facilitating effect, but in larger doses it quickly interferes with efficiency. Aspirin also slows reaction.

Individual differences. It may also be that the physiological make-up of the individual predisposes him to rapid or slow attending. Simple reaction time is somewhat variable from one trial to the next for a given individual, perhaps reflecting the constant shifting of attention; but, as soon as we take the average of a sample of reactions, the person's relative standing in his group is pretty well fixed. The reliability coefficient of a simple reaction time measure is about .90, which means that a given person will persistently be fast, average, or slow in speed of responding.

This is not to say that individuals do not improve with practice. Even on simple reactions there is a definite speeding up, although a limit is soon reached. Much

of this may come as the person switches from a sensory set to a motor set (see above) and can operate with reduced cues from the stimulus. Workers on routine jobs tend to develop motor sets, so that they give their habitual motion even to inappropriate stimuli—like the absent-minded professor who lifted his hat to the department-store mannequin.

Energy expenditure and attention. Another way to study attention experimentally is by way of the amount of energy expenditure. The most direct technique is to measure oxygen consumption during a task. An ordinary basal-metabolism test can be utilized. Another method is to have the subjects expire into a rubber balloon; from the carbon dioxide content, it is possible to compute the energy expenditure. The amount of finger pressure on a key, hand pressure on a rubber bulb, or biceps muscle contraction, gives a rough index of energy mobilization. Measures of electrical action currents in the muscle are also used.

Consciously, we are aware that studying in the midst of noise demands more effort. Does this correspond to the physiological facts? Early studies showed that people could work in the presence of noise distraction without loss of efficiency; in fact, some subjects even improved under these conditions. Freeman (1939) demonstrated that these performances were achieved at increased physiological cost; the persons who did not drop off in efficiency were found to be burning up more fuel, using more energy to compensate for the distraction. His subjects solved problems under quiet and noisy conditions. Oxygen use was measured, and electrical recordings made from muscles in all four limbs. He found that work performance decreased when distraction was introduced, but compensation soon canceled this out, for both number of solutions and accuracy. Paralleling the work curve was an increased, widespread bodily tension, and an increase in oxygen consumption. As the distraction period continued, the muscle tensions began to be localized in the parts of the body used in the problem solving. As the diffuse muscle tensions dropped out, oxygen use also declined. Freeman's experiment indicates that you can adapt to working with the radio on, but such habits are wasteful of energy.

Jacobson (1932) has demonstrated that, when one imagines moving his right arm, electrical activities occur in that arm and not in the left (Fig. 11:7). These observations suggest that merely attending to one part of the body may change the level of physiological activity there. Attending is a process of energy mobilization to get need satisfaction. When faced with an unfamiliar or difficult problem, the whole body mobilizes; when one knows just what muscles to use, he mobilizes specifically in that area. Obviously this makes for less total energy cost, and greater efficiency.

Attention and mental set. It is obvious that attention is in part a matter of physical set. This can just as well be called mental set; functionally there is no distinction between the two. Short-term mental sets can easily be related to muscle tensions, as in the above experiments. However, it becomes difficult to conceive of physical sets in the musculature which endure for days, as when one gets ready for a particular assignment and then drops it from consciousness until the appropriate occasion arrives. We have already proposed the solution to this problem (page 104) with the concept of "cortical tension." Each muscular set sends certain sensory impulses to the cortex. A pattern is organized there which corresponds to the muscular pattern. Later, when the appropriate stimulus is received, the muscle tensions are rearoused.

Considerable interest has been manifested by psychologists in the theoretical question: is attention primarily peripheral (muscular), or is it primarily central (cortical)? The evidence at this time is ambiguous. At present it seems most accurate to say that attending is a function of the whole organism, depending chiefly upon widespread muscular set in difficult or novel situations, upon very specific muscles in the case of familiar habits, and upon cortical set under conditions of delay.

Primitive Perception of Objects

The process of attending, of course, is important because it is an essential part of getting information about man's environment. Without a selective mechanism, one would be overwhelmed by this multitude of stimuli which surrounds him. But the major task is that of learning the kind, characteristics, and location of objects "out there" in the external world. To satisfy needs and avoid dangers, here are the kinds of things I must know: that there is (1) an object (2) in a given direction (3) and at a given distance (4) having certain characteristics which are important to me. Attention focuses the sense organs upon cues (light, sound, etc.), but this is only a part of the total process of perceiving objects.

Why are these questions important? Let us consider briefly the role of vision as a major source of information. Vision does not tell us that an object exists; it reports brightness, color, etc., which must be integrated into a percept of an object. That this organizing is done inside our bodies was demonstrated earlier in this chapter (Fig. 6:2); under certain conditions we put cues together to perceive objects which do not exist. Furthermore, vision does not tell us much about the direction of objects; the pattern on the retina is upside down, left and right are reversed, and the exact cells stimulated depend on the direction of regard. We have to learn to identify directions, distances, and characteristics of objects. These examples may help to show why the perception of objects is far more complicated than would appear at first thought.

Definition of perception. Perception is the process of obtaining knowledge of external objects and events, by means of the senses. William James put it well when he wrote, "Perception is of definite and probable things." In other words, man takes his sensations (about which he is sure) and reaches conclusions about real objects (about which, actually, he is less sure if questioned). He may, however, reach a very high level of probability in dealing with nearby physical objects; he is aware of the chances of error when dealing with distant or unfamiliar objects.

A first approximation to this process can be made hypothetically. Suppose that you had been born blind, but now were suddenly able to see. Suppose further that you now see the world as other adults do—a most unlikely supposition. Even under such conditions you would not know what you were looking at. There would be various shapes, colors, contours, brightnesses before you, but what they meant would be a puzzle.

The experiment suggested above has actually been performed. Senden (1932) collected reports on 66 instances of persons who had undergone cataract operations permitting vision at a delayed age. Most were adults who had been blind from birth. It was hoped that these reports would enable a determination of what a person can see when presented with a visual environment for the first time. One conclusion stands out clearly from these observations; the patient is aware of being visually stimulated, but he does not identify objects as such. Even though these people knew objects from tactual experience, and had the use of language, they could not answer questions because the words simply did not relate to vision. "Do you see objects projected in space?" was a meaningless question to them.

Such a man could distinguish visually between a ball and a block, but he did not know which was which *until allowed to handle them*. A girl sees a patch of color moving toward her, but only when she touches it does she exclaim, "Why, that's kitty!" Two strips of cardboard, 10 cm. and 20 cm. in length, were perceived as different, but the individual could not say which was shorter—although he knew the meaning of this word in terms of touch. The perceived object, as we said above, is a totality involving vision, touch, smell, etc. But there is no inherent connection between these cues; the relationship must be learned.

Senden's data may be of some help in understanding the development of perception. Different visual factors were learned at different speeds. *Naming colors* was

FIG. 6:9. Reversible figure and ground. This is an ambiguous figure, but, unlike Fig. 6:4, the entire figure and ground switch places instead of merely the figure changing. This can be seen as a white goblet on a black background, or as two profiles in black against a white ground. *(Redrawn from E. Rubin.)*

apparently easiest. *Motion, size,* and *distance* were acquired fairly soon. But *it took months to identify common shapes.* Long ago William James suggested that the infant's world is a "big blooming, buzzing confusion." One of Senden's patients is reported thus: "so many different things, and the rapid movement of the mass, confused his sight to such an extent that finally he could no longer see anything." Yet, eventually, these patients developed visual functioning which was essentially normal in every respect.

Riesen's study of chimpanzees. There might be some questioning of these observations on humans, in that the eyes obviously were somewhat defective. But they have been confirmed in all significant respects by Riesen (1947), who reared two chimpanzees in complete darkness for 16 months, or until they were substantially mature. He found that his animals did not for a considerable period of time learn to use visual cues in any manner, although it was clear from their behavior that they could see "something" in the environment. The apes showed a strong desire to cling to the keeper when brought into the light, and yet, once separated from him, they could not return to him and groped blindly around until a familiar touch indicated his presence. They showed no eyeblink to an object approaching the eye, and were incapable of forming a fear response to a visual stimulus (a distinctive visual pattern paired with electric shock). Normal animals formed this connection in one trial; the darkness animals did not learn in eight repetitions.

Heredity vs. learning in object perception. These observations call for some drastic overhauling of popular ideas about our knowledge of the external world. It is easy to assume that man is born with a perceptual system which provides him with accurate information about the objects around him. This assumption is not easy to check with normal humans because we go through a long helpless period in infancy, during which incredible quantities of learning can go on without detection. It is, of course, an axiom of modern psychology that much of personality is determined during these early months; but only within the last 10 years have psychologists begun to realize that our means of knowing the physical world also depends substantially on these early experiences. The data collected by Senden and Riesen seem to prove conclusively that learning plays an important part in our ability to identify objects and their characteristics.

Heredity, of course, provides the structural basis for perception—the sense organs and nerve connections. These structures are probably so arranged that certain kinds of cues are learned very quickly—color, for example, and size. Survival value would demand very rapid learning of some kinds of distance perceptions, for escape from natural enemies. The trend in psychology today, therefore, is not to ask: Is perception inherited or learned? Rather, the question is: In what respects are hereditary influences more important, and in what areas does learning play a decisive role? How do heredity and environment combine to produce our knowledge of the world about us? The remainder of this chapter will examine some of these problems.

Differentiation of figure and ground. Both Riesen's chimpanzees and Senden's cataract patients showed evidence in their first visual experiences of perceiving a figure as distinct from its ground—awareness that "something" was present and separate from everything else. This suggests that a very important part of object perception is hereditarily determined. While the visual world was confusing and poorly structured, it was not totally lacking in form.

Differentiation of a figure from its ground depends on the experience of *contour*. As Fig. 6:9 illustrates, figure and ground may be interchangeable; under some circumstances, the white area is the figure (a vase on black background); under others, the black surface outlines two faces on a white ground. In either instance, there is an edge between the black and white, marking the boundary of the figure. The retinal stimulation on one side of the edge is clearly different from that on the other side. A contour thus corresponds to a definite difference in sensation.

There is, however, little evidence to indicate that other aspects of perception are completely determined by heredity. When we come to study depth, distance, direction, etc., we find that considerable weight must be given to experience and learning.

Perception of Direction

The eye is a highly motile organ, and the same retinal cell may now be stimulated by an object up and to the left, later by one down and to the right. Hence directional cues cannot be assumed to depend upon local signs from specific cells.

Nevertheless, accurate direction based on vision develops fairly quickly. The cases studied by Senden soon began to localize directions from which stimuli came. There may be innate tendencies for the eyes to focus on an intense stimulus in the field, and then for the body to orient parallel to the eyes. This, if true, would "point" the body in the direction of the object with relatively little learning.

An experiment by Lashley and Russell (1934) seems to confirm this. They reared 13 rats in strict darkness to maturity. During this time the animals did not even see

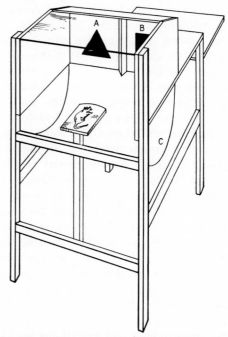

FIG. 6:10. Jumping stand for studying perception of figures by rats. The rat is placed on the platform. Before him are two cards, A and B. Behind one of them is food; if he jumps to it, it slips aside and he gets the food. If he jumps to the wrong card, it is locked in place and he falls to the net (C) below. By varying the design on the cards, the limits of the rat's perceptual ability can be tested. (*Adapted from Lashley, 1938.*)

the cage walls except for a few seconds every other day when food was introduced. At 100 days (maturity), each rat was brought into a lighted room and tested on a jumping platform (Fig. 6:10). They were first required to step across a 5-cm. gap, and then to jump a 20-cm. gap. Twelve of the 13 rats succeeded in doing this on the first trial. This indicates that a sense of visual direction is quickly acquired.

The visual frame of reference. The purpose of localizing objects, of course, is to direct behavior toward or away from them. Adults show a highly efficient system of localizing directions in visual space under normal conditions, but it can easily be disturbed. Students of aviation psychology are particularly interested in this problem because of the survival value of accurate localization in rapid flight, landing, etc.

The precise direction of a visual object is apparently determined by the frame of reference within which it is perceived. When the eye is focused on a point, the visual field has reference points such as the center, up, down, right, and left. If the subject is placed in a dark room so that only such a simple frame of reference is available to him, his directional sense is disturbed. However, if several objects are visible, his accuracy is much improved.

Another important element of the visual framework is the perception of one's own body. The body has a special mechanism for sensing the vertical position (the semi-circular canals). No man was ever drowned because he swam to the bottom when he meant to rise to the top of the water.[1] A paratrooper may somersault in midair, but he manages to land feet first. Thus, as long as the body remains in a normal, erect position, we have an important cue to support the visual framework and to increase our accuracy of localization. If

this cue is made useless by preventing vision of the body and hands, localization is less accurate (Loemaker, 1930).

Directionality is no doubt fostered by the nature of the physical world. Trees grow vertically, and man-made objects tend to have clearly aligned vertical and horizontal dimensions. Thus, even if I tip my head, I can keep my directions clear because I assume that these vertical and horizontal lines have maintained their same physical location.

Witkin's studies on localization. The importance of visual and postural cues in our sense of visual direction has recently been demonstrated by some ingenious experiments by Witkin and Asch (1948). In one experiment, subjects were individually tested in a dark room on their ability to set a luminous rod to the true horizontal or the true vertical. Judgments were very accurate as long as the body remained vertical; but if either head or body was tilted at an angle (in a reclining chair), errors began, and they were greater as the angle of tilt was greater.

In other studies only the visual frame of reference was changed. For instance, subjects in the dark room could see a luminous line within (but not touching) a luminous square. The square might be tilted, but the subject was ordered to set the line at true horizontal or vertical. Almost all people tested made errors because they adjusted the line somewhat in the direction of tilt of the visual frame. An ingenious variation on this required the subject to look through a peephole into a lighted room containing a table and a picture on the wall. On the back wall was a rod, to be set at the horizontal or vertical. When this room was tilted, the errors of direction were even greater than with the simple luminous frame. The room offered a better structured visual framework, and it exerted a more compelling influence on the observer in causing errors in direction.

[1] This would not, of course, be true if the semi-circular canals were damaged, as in some cases of deafness.

FIG. 6:11. Tilting room and chair. The subject sits in the small chair (A) which can be tilted at will by experimenter, as can the small room built around the chair. In this way a highly realistic distortion of the visual framework can be combined with upright or tilted body posture. When the subject sets the lever to indicate what he considers to be the true horizontal, he makes errors which can be related to the visual or somesthetic framework. The value of such tests for submarine or airplane personnel is obvious. (*Courtesy of Dr. H. A. Witkin.*)

With an elaborate new setup, Witkin (1949) has been able to test the effect of vision and posture when in conjunction or in opposition. He uses both a tilting room and a tilting chair (Fig. 6:11). It is thus possible to show which factor is more effective. When posture is tilted, but the visual framework is held vertical, few errors occurred; whereas, when posture was upright but the visual frame tilted, many errors were made.[1] When both the visual frame and the bodily position were changed from the normal, errors were maximized.

This problem is particularly important for high-speed aircraft pilots and gunners. It seems likely that the pilot's task is made simpler by the fact that, for most people,

visual cues have more effect than posture. The earth and the horizon give him a visual frame which is highly dependable. Even so, some fatal errors probably are made. The gunner, with both visual frame and postural location constantly changing, has a most difficult task; it is not surprising that he has far more errors than successes.

Recent experiments for the Air Force indicate that a landing device which gives the pilot a visual picture of the relationship between his plane and his destination reduces errors. Best results were obtained when the field shows the airport in a fixed position and the plane moving. Such an arrangement presumably makes use of our years of experience in which the person moves while the environment stays fixed.

Learning a visual framework. It is impossible to study the learning of the up-down-right-left frame from the beginning

[1] People differ with regard to their use of visual or somesthetic cues in this situation. Passey (1949) reports that his subjects were not especially disturbed by a change in the visual framework.

FIG. 6:12. Effect of reinverted vision upon adjustment. The image of objects on the retina is upside down. What would happen if it were turned right side up? Here a man is repeating Stratton's experiment of wearing lenses which reinvert the visual field. For the first few days, even such a simple activity as shaking hands was impossible. By the end of 30 days, however, he was riding a bicycle. (Taken for Life Magazine by photographer Carl Iwasaki. Copyright Time, Inc.)

of life because we have no techniques for ascertaining what goes on inside the infant. It is possible, however, to contrive an abnormal visual situation for an adult and watch the process of adaptation.

Stratton (1896) was the first to devise this technique. As you know, the retinal image has objects upside down as compared with their "real" spatial localization. Stratton put on lenses which reinverted the image, so that the bottom of the object was now at the bottom of the visual field, and so on. The first few days of this were very upsetting. Nausea and discomfort were acute. Muscular adjustment was very difficult; the act of opening a door might require extensive trial and error (Fig.

6:12). However, most behavioral adjustments had been achieved in about a week.

What happened here was primarily a readjustment of the postural and kinesthetic cues to parallel the visual framework. Even though Stratton wore the glasses during all waking moments for 3 weeks, the visual world never looked right side up. What did occur was a readjustment of muscular actions to conform with this new appearance of things.

The same phenomenon can be demonstrated more quickly in the Ames distorted room (page 230). The subject looks at this room and sees it as a trapezoidal space. However, when he sits in the required spot, using one eye, and adapts to the room, it looks square. If now he tries to touch objects in the room, his localization is quite inaccurate; but within a few trials he improves very noticeably. The room still looks square, but he has unconsciously changed his manipulation of the pointer to conform to the tilt of the floor and walls.[1] These experiments indicate that muscular and postural cues are relatively less effective than vision in determining our perceptions of up, down, level, tilted, and similar directional relations.

The auditory framework. While vision dominates our spatial localization, auditory cues are used for many adjustments. P. T. Young (1928) repeated the Stratton experiment, using a device called a *pseudophone* which reversed the sounds to the two ears. His experiences wearing this were similar to those of Stratton; at first there was confusion, but soon the correct directions were perceived despite the reversal.

Stratton commented that the visual experience seemed to dominate over others. After he had worn his glasses for several days, he found that sounds seemed to come from the visual location of the object; for instance, the "sputter" of a fire in the fire-

[1] Some people report that the room shifts back somewhat to the trapezoid as this happens.

place was heard in its appropriate place in the inverted visual field. Wooster (1923) developed a simple experiment to illustrate this: the subject fixates a beating metronome and of course, the sound is heard where the object is seen. Now a prism is placed before the eye, so that the apparent visual location of the metronome changes; *the sound is now heard as coming from the new spot.*

Auditory localization of direction is surprisingly accurate, when vision is not in conflict with it. The average person can localize a sound coming from the right or left within 3 degrees when visual cues are excluded. However, localization in the up-down plane is quite poor; in fact, under laboratory conditions, a sound which is "up" will be judged to be "down" about one-third of the time. Since our normal dealings with objects are on the ground, this defect does not seem important; as man begins to move more in three dimensions, the problem could become significant except that our present flying machines make too much noise to permit of hearing any sounds from other sources.

Localization of sounds is mostly binaural; if one ear is plugged, localizing is poor. There are four kinds of binaural effects, any one of which can give rise to a perception of direction: (1) Differences in *intensity* in the two ears. If telephone receivers are strapped over the ears, and a slightly louder click led to one than to the other, the sound will be "heard" in the direction of the louder stimulus. (2) Difference in *time* of stimulation. If sound waves are led to the two ears through rubber tubes, and one tube is a little longer, sound will get to that ear a little later. The object will be localized as in the direction of the ear stimulated first. A time difference as small as 0.0003 second will produce such a localization. (3) Differences in *phase*. A sound wave is a succession of crests and troughs. If the waves striking the two ears

are thrown slightly out of phase, the sound will be heard as coming from one side or the other. (4) Differences in *timbre*. Every complex sound includes overtones and harmonics. When the sound reaching the

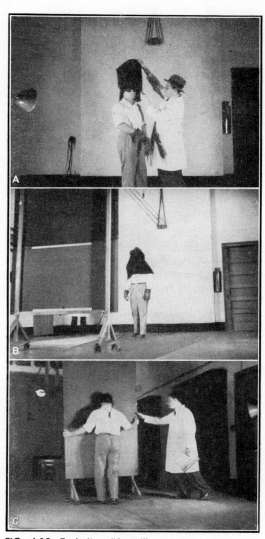

FIG. 6:13. Excluding "facial" cues. It was formerly believed that the blind developed "facial vision," a keen sensitivity of the skin, by which they detected their approach to walls and objects. In this test, wearing a felt hood (A) did not interfere with the subject's ability to avoid obstacles (B), but effective sound screens cause him to bump into the partition (C). (*Courtesy of Dr. K. M. Dallenbach.*)

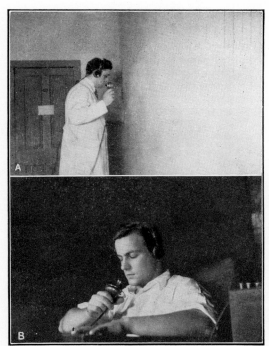

FIG. 6:14. Proving the effectiveness of auditory cues. To test the hypothesis that the blind person really avoids objects by hearing sounds reflected from them, the subject sat quietly in a room, wearing earphones. These were connected to a microphone in the hand of the experimenter (A), who held it shoulder-high and walked toward a movable partition. With very little error, the subject (B) told the experimenter when to stop to avoid bumping into the obstacle. (*Courtesy of Dr. K. M. Dallenbach.*)

two ears differs in timbre, in these over-tones, a directional effect is obtained.

Auditory perception in the blind. Before leaving this intriguing question of determining location by sound, let us consider a particularly interesting application of it. It was long believed that the blind locate obstacles by facial vision (more precisely, perception of air currents on the skin of the face). Conclusive experiments have recently proved that this ability to avoid obstacles is auditory rather than skin sensitivity. A blind subject's face was completely covered with felt, and yet he was able to announce when he came close to a movable partition used in the experi-

ment (Fig. 6:13). This indicated that he was getting slight reflections of sound from the walls and objects around him.

As a control, a microphone was carried by the experimenter, and the blind subject wore headphones connected to the microphone (Fig. 6:14). While he remained stationary, the experimenter walked closer to the walls of the room. Each time he signaled the experimenter to stop just before the wall was touched. (Subjects with intact vision, but blindfolded, could learn to do this after some practice.)

Apparently there are three kinds of sound cues used by the blind person. (1) The object itself is a source of sound. We know a blind student who shoots pheasants on the wing. He judges direction and distance by the sound. (2) Sound "shadows" are reflected from objects. There is usually some random noise in the air about us; the presence of an object is indicated if some of this is shut off. (3) "Echolocation" is the term used when the subject's own sounds are reflected back to him from objects; *e.g.*, the blind man tapping his cane gets a good deal of information from the echoes bouncing off of walls, fences, etc.

Echolocation is also used in sonar, the technique by which sound waves are bounced off submarines, the ocean bottom, etc. An increased interest in the psychology of audition quickly followed the development of this technique during World War II.

Perception of Movement

Movement is another kind of perception which seems almost exclusively determined by heredity. The essential cue is a gradient of excitation moving across a sensory surface. Thus, if an object slides across the surface of the hand, there is a continuous change in the stimulation of adjacent nerve endings. Similarly, a visual stimulus moving across adjacent retinal cells would give rise to perceived motion. This apparently requires little or no learning.

The phi phenomenon. Psychologists have been particularly intrigued by studies of apparent movement—*i.e.*, stimuli which give rise to a perception of motion without a moving stimulus. It follows from the preceding paragraph that, if we can stimulate successive sensory cells in proper sequence, we ought to get perceived movement. This is quite easy to do. Figure 6:15 shows the arrangement for a demonstration of this sort. If the lights go on and off at intervals of 0.06 second, the light will appear to move from the center to each end of the bank simultaneously. Such devices are used in electric signs to make use of the high potency of movement in attracting attention.

Motion pictures depend on this same mechanism, plus the inertia of the retinal cells. The projector shows still photographs at the rate of 24 per second, about 0.04 second each, with a very short dark interval between. If an object is placed slightly farther to the right in each successive photograph, the viewer will perceive it as moving, the speed being a function of the distance it has been displaced.

A simple demonstration of apparent motion is to hold the forefinger before the eyes and focus on a distant point. Now, if you rapidly close each eye in turn, the finger will seem to jump back and forth.

Wertheimer (1912), who has studied this phenomenon extensively, called it the *phi phenomenon*. It occurs in many forms: if two lights (close together) go on and off at intervals of about 0.06 second, they will be seen as one light swinging back and forth. Too great a distance or too long a time will break up the misperception.

The phi phenomenon probably occurs because it duplicates normal perception of movement. In scanning the environment, one's attention shifts rapidly. Vision fixates

FIG. 6:15. The phi phenomenon. If the center light is first turned on, then the end lights, in proper timing, the light will seem to move outward in both directions. Similarly, the two outer lights can be made to seem to converge and fuse into the center light. This arrangement proves that the perception is not due to eye movements.

here, then there, in short, quick jumps. A moving object thus is seen as being in different locations in these successive "snapshots" of the environment. As the alternating lights give the same kind of cue, they are perceived as a single light in motion.

Perception of Distance

It is important for us to know, not only in what direction is an object, but how far away. This is a particularly vexatious problem in vision, because the visual field is necessarily two-dimensional. In a photograph, distance objects are not farther from the eye than near items; both are in a flat plane. Nevertheless, we perceive distance in photographs as we do in daily life. How do we manage?

Types of distance cues. There are a variety of cues from which perceptions of differing distance are derived. First we may mention the *muscular* cues from the visual mechanism. At short distances, we get differential signs from the *accommodation* of the lens (contraction of the ciliary muscle to produce the optimum focus of light rays on the retina). However, this is useful only at short distances and even then is quite unreliable when other cues are ruled out. *Convergence* refers to the sensations from the muscles controlling movements of the eyeballs; as an object moves closer, the two eyes point toward the nose in order to keep it in focus. Convergence likewise is usable only to about 30 feet and is not very accurate within that range.

FIG. 6:16. Stereoscopic photographs. This pair of photographs was made to be viewed through that entertainment device of pretelevision days, the stereoscope. By placing two cameras about 4 feet apart, these views were obtained. When viewed so that the left picture falls only on the left eye, and the right picture only on the right eye, a remarkable depth effect is experienced. Note the difference in location of the small table, the footstool, etc. These differences are somewhat exaggerated as compared with the images on the two eyes, but they are of the same kind.

A second group of cues is visual in character but derives from the fact that the two eyes do not see objects identically. These are called *binocular* cues. Binocular disparity and double images are the important phenomena here.

Finally, we shall consider some *monocular* cues, so called because they are effective if only one eye is used. They include the relative brightness of different objects, location in the visual field, interposition of one object between the observer and another object, changes in perceived color, and changes in apparent size. These are the cues used by painters, or the cues we can identify by studying a photograph to decide why one object is seen as farther than another.

All these cues vary by degrees. There is a gradual change in the muscular sensation as the eye shifts from near to distant focus; there is a gradual change in the apparent size, color, etc., of objects at increasing distances. The organism (human or animal)

becomes astoundingly sensitive to slight variations in these gradients.

Binocular cues. Muscular cues, as noted above, are not very effective in space discrimination. The distance of an object is perceived directly from its phenomenal characteristics, *i.e.*, its appearance. The maximum precision in visual perception of depth comes from binocular disparity—the difference in the retinal image on the two eyes.

The nature of binocular disparity is detectable from Fig. 6:16, which shows photographs of the same object by two cameras, placed so that the lenses were in positions like the two eyes. With some care it can be noted that there are distinct differences in the aspects projected onto the two eyes. The illusion of depth created by viewing these two pictures simultaneously, the left eye seeing only the left picture and the right eye only the right picture, is startling. A common item of entertainment some fifty years ago was the *stereoscope*, a picture holder with a partition down the median plane so that each of the two pictures was seen only by the appropriate eye. Recently, military uses of the stereoscope have been important. Reconnaissance planes take successive photographs at intervals of ½ to 1 mile; stereoscopic inspection of successive pairs of photographs helps penetrate camouflage, estimate bomb damage, etc. X-ray photographs are now customarily made with stereoscopic focusing, to give three-dimensional effects of bony structures.

Double images. Binocular vision not only gives different views of the object fixated; it also results in double images nearer or farther than the fixation point. Hold your forefingers in front of your eyes, one behind the other, pointing upward. If you fixate on the far finger, the near one is seen as two blurred images; if you fixate on the near one, the farther image is doubled. By closing one eye and then the other, the finger not in focus is made to jump back and forth.

In ordinary vision, of course, one does not see double images; he sees objects at different distances. The brain apparently takes this cue and translates it, automatically and almost instantaneously, into awareness of the object's location. Double images provide a nice example of the use of *gradients* in perception, referred to above. We get a neatly graded series of images from no doubling at all (at the point where the eyes are focused) to marked doubling at distant locations. This gradient thus provides a picture of objects successively farther away in space.

How does it happen that we do not observe these double images and other cues for distance? The answer apparently is in terms of survival value. It is not important, in satisfying motives, to see double images; it is very important to judge distances accurately. Thus the brain uses the information without its becoming conscious.

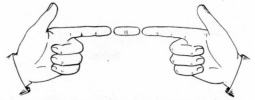

FIG. 6:17. Floating-finger illusion. Hold the hands about 10 inches before the eyes, finger tips touching. Gaze beyond them to a distant object. Now draw the finger tips slightly apart, slowly, and a piece of finger will be seen floating in mid-air.

To some extent this nonrecognition of the effective cues for a perception is simply a matter of not noticing them; the light stimulus functions as a *reduced cue* for something which originally included other elements. Thus you may as a child have seen objects some distance away and walked to them; the visual cue now sets off the total knowledge got from distant and close observation. Nonrecognition of cues can also be a function of *suppression.* Try this little experiment: hold your fingers pointing to each other, as in Fig. 6:17, about 10 inches before your eyes. Fixate on a point farther away, and slowly draw the fingers apart. You will see a piece of finger floating in mid-air with no visible means of support. What happens in this case is that the brain accepts the portions of the retinal image which correspond in the two eyes but rejects that which is in conflict (so that no clear expectancy exists regarding the stimulus). Thus the anchorage for the tip of the finger gets lost. Figure 6:18 gives another dramatic example of suppression. Suppression of conflicting cues is fairly common in all sensory fields; however, when there is a substantial degree of conflict, the whole field is likely to become blurred or confused. The brain adds up cues to get a "probability" that a certain object is out there; conflict of probabilities leads to a blurred visual field.

Monocular perception of distance. Persons having only one eye are commonly believed to be deficient in depth perception,

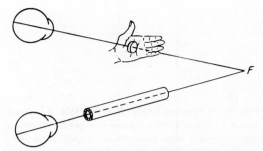

FIG. 6:18. Hole-in-palm illusion. Hold a cardboard or other tube in front of the right eye, and the open palm before the left eye. Now focus on a distant object (F) and you will "see" your hand with a hole through the palm. Point the tube somewhat to the left, as shown in the diagram.

and yet some stunt aviators have to rely on monocular perception. They seem to do quite well. Photographs appear quite flat under ordinary conditions, but when suggestions of flatness are minimized by creating special viewing conditions, such as keeping the visual field inside the margins, they may have striking depth qualities. This is why artists often view paintings with one eye through a tunnel formed by the hand or a sheet of paper. The one-eyed person, being forced to rely upon monocular cues, can apparently become quite skillful at compensating for the loss of the binocular cues.

Space does not permit an extensive consideration of the various monocular cues which are effective in creating a perception of depth. We shall merely list and define them. *Interposition* refers to the fact that an object physically nearer will cut off part of an object farther away. Thus I cannot see all of a student in the second row of the class and infer that he is farther away than the front-row student, all of whom is visible. *Perspective* refers to the gradual change in size of objects of known physical size (railroad tracks converging, telephone poles getting smaller, etc.). *Aerial perspective* identifies the blurring and mistiness of distant objects—due mainly to dust in the air. Easterners who visit the Rocky Moun-

tain areas are amazed to learn that the mountain which seems 4 or 5 miles away is actually nearer 50. *Color perspective* is the change in color values with distance; remote objects look bluish or purplish, because of selective absorption of long-wave light by the air and dust.

Light and shadow are differently distributed for objects at varying distances. An interesting phenomenon in this connection is illustrated by Fig. 6:19. If it is examined with the book upside down, the crater becomes a mound of earth. We learn to expect certain patterns of light and shadow at given distances from us. *Height in the visual field* is an interesting kind of cue. If you look across a landscape, you will observe that, from your feet to the horizon, objects higher in the visual field are more distant. Above the horizon, however, the higher an object, the nearer it is. Size, blurring, height in the visual field, and other depth cues are *gradients*. As we see objects at increasing distances, we observe minute degrees of difference in these cues and judge the distance accordingly.

Distance perception and learning. Psychologists formerly accepted the binocular cues for distance as innate and considered the monocular cues to be products of learning. It is plausible that an awareness of the significance of mistiness and color change would have to be learned, and in fact, modern psychology is in agreement with this latter point. The main change has been that today majority support seems to favor the view that all visual cues for distance are somewhat dependent upon learning.

As we noted earlier (page 208), the only visual perception which we feel reasonably sure to be innate is that of contour—the perception of a bounded object against a background. All the other cues we have examined—binocular disparity, double images, muscular cues, monocular cues—have an innate, structural basis but become

FIG. 6:19. Effect of shadows in depth perception. This is a photograph of the famous meteorite crater in Arizona, at Canyon Diablo. Seen in normal position, this picture clearly represents a depression; but if you turn the book upside down, the crater takes on the appearance of a mound of earth. This is effective because we have had many years of experience in interpreting such light-and-shadow patterns. (*From Scientific Monthly and Studio Grand.*)

effective as guides to distance after some minimum amount of learning. Each individual has to learn to perceive the distance of objects. The fascinating feature of this process is the amazing accuracy most of us develop in using this very limited instrument, the retina, for such a complex function.

Perception of Form and Shape

The individual who has just gained vision through a cataract operation perceives figure-ground relations. He can say that there is *something* here which is somehow different from something there. The person may not know that he is perceiving a table, a ball, or a triangle, but he does see a complete figure, surrounded by a different stimulating surface which serves as ground.

These figures are perceived as being in a certain direction and at a certain distance from the observer. We have not, as yet, said anything about the perception of the nature of the object. Yet, in the normal course of behavior, we are always responding in terms of what the object is, not just to its location.

There are several intricate problems in connection with the perception of identity. First, of course, is the perception of shape: circle, triangle, square, and so on. This is complicated by the fact that, as a person moves about, the shape of the retinal image is constantly changing; a circle looks like an ellipse, a square looks like a trapezoid. Developing a stable identity for shapes is thus no simple problem. Then we have the problems of size and color. The retinal image of an object varies with its distance

FIG. 6:20. Role of nearness in visual organization. While you could theoretically perceive these dots in clusters of five or ten, you will actually find yourself impelled to see groups of six and four. Nearness of elements to one another is a determinant of perception.

from the eye; yet we must learn to identify it as being of a constant size. Color varies with differences in illumination, yet the average adult perceives the color as constant under a wide range of light values. Finally, there is the problem of the use value of objects, or their *meaning* in terms of actions that can be performed upon them, their qualities as need satisfiers, and so forth.

The determinants of form. Each retinal cell is discrete and separate from the others. A triangle is a pattern of light projected upon the retina, but it is a series of activated cells as far as the brain is concerned. Why does this pattern of dots (stimulated cells) come to be perceived as an organized form? The following are some of the factors enumerated by psychologists who have specialized in this area of research.

Nearness. Elements of a stimulus pattern which are nearer to each other tend to be organized into forms. Look at Fig. 6:20, for example. You will see groups of dots; and

these groups are composed of dots close together. You do not spontaneously organize a group which includes those separated by wide spaces; indeed, it is difficult to do so voluntarily.

Similarity. Elements which are similar in kind tend to cohere together. (To some extent this presumes prior learning; the simpler forms must be recognized as similar before this factor can operate.) Figure 6:21 gives two illustrations of pattern formation based on similarity; in both cases nearness is held constant and yet groups do organize and form definite shapes. (For another example see the colored figure for testing color blindness, Fig. 5:35. The dots of similar color are seen as a figure.)

Continuity. A continuous line tends to hold together, even though it is broken up on the retina into discrete points. In Fig. 6:22 some of the individual points in *B* are closer to individual points in *A* or *C* than points in *A* and *C* are to each other. Yet we see a vertical line over a horizontal line (*B/AC*), not *AB/C* or *BC/A*. Points forming a continuous line will stay organized. In Fig. 6:23, similarity and continuity are both involved in forming the picture of the eye.

Closure. The Gestalt psychologists have laid a good deal of emphasis on the principle of closure, or the tendency for incomplete figures to complete themselves. In Fig. 6:24 the average person sees an incomplete triangle (*a*) and a broken diamond (*b*),

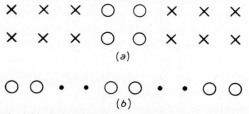

(a)

(b)

FIG. 6:21. Role of similarity in visual organization. It might be possible to make up clusters using both × and ○ in the upper figure, or both circles and dots in the lower. But, in fact, one perceives the similar elements as a group, leaving out the dissimilar items.

FIG. 6:22. Role of continuity in visual organization. Some of the dots going up toward *B* are closer to the line *AC* than to other dots in the line toward *B*. Yet we see a vertical line over a horizontal line. Continuity holds the dots in a definite organization.

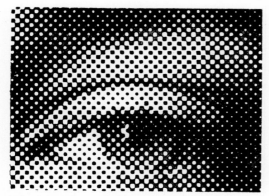

FIG. 6:23. How the eye puts elements together to form a picture. If an ordinary halftone engraving (such as those used in reproducing photographs in this book) is enlarged considerably, it breaks up into a series of dots. However, if you hold the book away from the eye, so that they are visually close together again, the picture of an eye becomes recognizable. Similarity and continuity are especially involved here, although nearness is a factor in part of the figure. (*From Kepes, 1944.*)

although he could just as well see open angles in both these drawings. Cartoonists make use of the closure principle to caricature a famous person by drawing only part of the face. How do you decide what is pictured in Fig. 6:24c?

Contour. In the earliest perceptions of shape, the principle of intensity differences which form contours is basic. Let us describe a simple experiment to illustrate contour formation. If, in a dark room, a triangle of light is projected very dimly onto a screen, the subject observes a blur of light without form. As the intensity of illumination is increased, a contour suddenly emerges; the patch of light has a sharply defined edge, and its triangular form is apparent. Contour, then, is a function of a sharp difference in stimulation along an edge. In the situation just described, the intensity of stimulus to give a perceived shape is about twenty-five times as great as at the threshold for the light patch. However, much smaller differences in brightness give contours under full illumination.[1]

[1] Helson and Fehrer (1932).

When we use colored stimuli, any just noticeable difference in the color of adjacent patches will give an edge. If colored dots of varying intensities are used to form shapes, as in the Ishihara test (see page 185), the dots of similar color will be organized into a familiar shape. The color-blind person cannot find the shape because he discriminates mainly by brightness, not hue. In fact, it seems safe to generalize that any sudden change in the visual gradients will set up a contour. Figure 6:25 illustrates two forms of contour based on pattern stimulation, rather than color or brightness.

Awareness of identity. For efficient perception of objects, one must be able not only to perceive contours, but to recognize

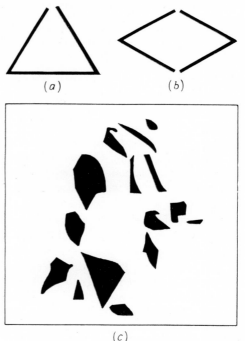

FIG. 6:24. Role of closure in visual organization. In the preceding illustration (Fig. 6:23), you fill in gaps unconsciously to complete the picture. In the present instance, you will tend to see a broken triangle (a) and a broken diamond (b), although it would be just as plausible to see two open angles in each case. Similarly, you probably will have no trouble in identifying the picture presented at (c), as a result of the operation of closure. (*From Street, 1931.*)

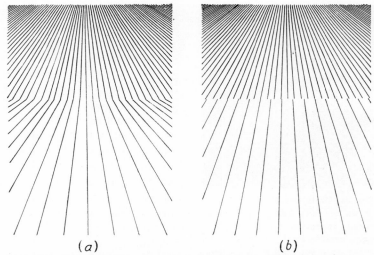

(a)   (b)

FIG. 6:25. Illustrations of contour without continuity. Under normal circumstances a contour involves a continuous line or edge (as in Fig. 6:9). It is possible, however, to have a clearly defined contour without continuity. In (a) we see a change in the patterning of the visual field which is perceived as a corner; in (b), the kind of change corresponding to an edge. (From Gibson, 1950, by permission of Houghton Mifflin Company.)

a duplication of one already seen. The child who learns to recognize a ball is one who can get the circular contour which is characteristic of the ball and also identify it as the same contour he experienced yesterday. All object perception, therefore, depends upon learning and memory in some degree.

In earlier chapters we commented on the perception of goal objects and noted that the individual must show some generalization from one shape to highly similar shapes. No two bananas are exactly identical, but man must be capable of carrying over responses of eating based upon a single successful experience to later occasions. The term *equivalent stimuli* was employed to cover cases in which the person gives identical responses to nonidentical stimuli perceived as being the same.

The mechanism for perception of identity seems to be something like this: the organism has a memory trace of a contour previously observed. Now another contour is directly seen. The present shape is compared with the remembered observation, and if they match sufficiently well, a perception of identity results. All this, of course, is swift and unconscious, like the other summative processes described earlier in this chapter.

As the child develops breadth of experience, he comes to recognize more and more shapes of familiar objects. He also learns to differentiate, *i.e.*, to identify significant differences and thus to break up equivalences. The earliest stage, however, seems to be one of overgeneralization. Thus many small boys have embarrassed their mothers by shouting "Daddy!" to every strange man who comes along; all adult males are perceived as equivalent. Later the boy comes to observe differences in height, weight, coloring, tone of voice, and other cues by which he can distinguish daddy from other men.

Ambiguous figures. Since no one ever reaches perfection in identifying every possible shape and contour, it is possible to draw ambiguous figures which set off more than one perception. Thus Fig. 6:9 shows a figure which can be perceived alternately as a vase or as two human faces. The contour remains unchanged, but it is matched mentally with different contours remembered from past experiences.

If you look at the picture steadily, you will get spontaneous, involuntary changes from one percept to the other. This shift can be slowed or speeded up to some extent, but it cannot be completely inhibited. There is no generally accepted explanation for the involuntary fluctuation, but it may well be an example of the need for change due to satiation of one group of cells and dominance of a different group.

Misperceptions. If the same contour can give rise to more than one perception, we immediately recognize the occurrence of misperceptions. We shall employ this term to refer to cases in which the individual "perceives" one object, but upon acting in terms of his perception he finds that the physical object was something else. If we took the traditional position that perception gave us a copy of the real object, errors in perceiving would be hard to explain. When we concentrate on the fact that all we get from the environment is cues, and the perception is built up inside the organism, such errors immediately become perfectly comprehensible.

It is interesting to reflect that, at the moment, there is no difference between a perception and a misperception. It is only in the light of subsequent action that new perceptions lead us to correct our mistakes. In Fig. 6:1b we showed you what seemed to be a chair, but "really" was just a random string pattern. A person looking through the peephole and then leaving the laboratory would have perceived a chair and this percept would have, for him, all the quality of reality.

The Qualities of Objects

A perceived object is more than a contour. It has size, color, and texture as well as shape. Since nature stimulates us with a multitude of similar forms, these perceived qualities play an important role in the perceptions of identity and difference. Like most of the other aspects of perception we have considered, this is by no means a simple matter.

We have already examined (Chap. 5) the relations between physical stimuli and sensory processes. Light waves strike the eye, sound waves the ear. The color red is not in the light wave but in the cortical reaction to impulses originating in the retina. Physical contours are continuous and often have straight edges; the retinal pattern is always a series of dots, and the edges are never straight. Nevertheless, we learn to identify shapes—after many, many trials, as any mother can testify, and as illustrated by Senden's patients.

These are only a few of the paradoxes of perception. Consider, for a moment, the question of size. The physical size of an object is presumably constant. But its retinal projection varies from time to time. As your eye moves away, the image grows smaller. Generally, we do not perceive this. *We perceive the object as being of constant size.*

The same is true of brightness. Take a look at a pile of coal which is partly in shadow. The variations in brightness, as measured by light reflected to the eye, are very great. Nevertheless, you perceive the coal as uniformly black. A yellow surface under red illumination tends to look orange. Yet you unconsciously correct for the red of the ground, and keep the figure constant as yellow.

These *perceptual constancies* are of great significance in psychology. In Chap. 2 we pointed out that a basic principle in psychology is the principle of homeostasis. The organism must have dealings with objects to satisfy needs and avoid dangers. Clearly, these perceptual constancies are vital to such a process. The sabre-toothed tiger at a

FIG. 6:26. The test for size constancy. The subject sitting in the chair is asked to designate which of the cards on the table is the same size as that in his hand. Usually the task is accomplished easily and accurately, although the retinal image of the card in the hand is at least 36 times as large as the image of its match on the table. (*From Newman, in Boring, Langfeld, and Weld, 1948, by permission of John Wiley & Sons.*)

distance would look like a harmless kitten if it were not for size constancy. Ripe apples would look green under some conditions. Aiming an arrow, building a house—almost any activity one can imagine requires that we continually make decisions based on physical size and characteristics of objects, not the varying retinal image.

Size constancy. An object of constant size, at increasing distances, projects a decreasing image on the retina (Fig. 6:26). However, if a known object, such as a man, moves away from us, there is at first no perceived change in size. The retinal image may have decreased by 50 per cent before any perceptual difference is noted.

Here is a simple experiment which may sharpen the nature of the problem for you. Look intently at some sharply defined object (*e.g.*, Fig. 6:9) for about 45 seconds, or until you get a good afterimage. Project this image onto your notebook on your lap; then shift your eyes to the ceiling. The small figure now looks enormous. Yet the retinal process is identical. The perceived size of an object is determined in part by the ground against which it is observed. Edgar Allan Poe once wrote a terrifying little story about a man looking out of his window at a mountainside and seeing a huge, frightening monster. As he backed away, he realized that it was a little spider hanging by a thread from the window frame. When the ground changed from mountain to window, the perceived size changed abruptly. Movie close-ups do not seem grotesquely enormous, because we relate size of picture to background.

Under normal conditions of observation, the object is seen against a background which includes familiar objects. Thus various size constancies reinforce each other. When the observation is made in a dark room with no visible ground, size constancy tends to disappear. Size judgments then are made on the basis of the retinal image. The various cues which we have enumerated in distance perception also reinforce size constancy. As long as one knows the approximate size of the "real" object, *and can judge its apparent distance*, he is inclined to report constant size perception rather than shrinkage proportional to the distance.[1] Figure 6:27 illustrates how a change in the suggested nature of the white ball leads to a change in your perception of its size and distance.

[1] Hastorf and Way (1952).

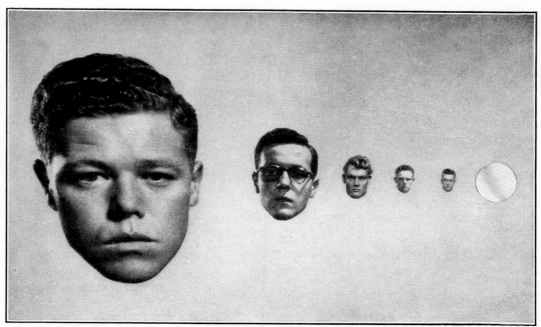

FIG. 6:27. How far away is the ping-pong ball? If you think of the white circle as a ping-pong ball, it seems to be right up close, in line with the first of the faces. But if you change your mind and decide that it is, after all, a tennis ball, it recedes to a point in line with the (perceived) location of the third or fourth face. (*Taken for Life Magazine by Photographer Eve Schaal. Copyright Time, Inc.*)

Perceived size is also affected by use value or motivation. We apparently overestimate the sizes of valued objects. Bruner and Goodman (1947) reported that children estimate coins to be larger than cardboard disks of the same physical size (Fig. 6:41). This obviously depends upon a learning process.

Constancy of shape. The dilemma in the case of shape constancy arises from the fact that the shape of the retinal image changes with every movement of the observer. A square table top will project a square (with curved edges) onto the retina only under very rare conditions. Most of the time the figure is more of a trapezoid. Most circles are actually projected on the retina as ovals. Yet we must learn to perceive object identities in this kaleidoscopic visual world. This is achieved, apparently, by an unconscious process of correcting automatically for the angle of vision.

If the eye is kept in a fixed position, we can draw geometrically the projection of any figure onto the retina. Thouless (1931) investigated the phenomenon of shape constancy by presenting his subjects with figures in fixed positions, so that he knew what the retinal image would be. In Fig. 6:28 the essential elements of the experiment and its results are shown. The broken lines give the "real" physical stimuli presented to the observers. The black figures show the retinal stimulus or perspective shape (the outline which would be projected onto the retina). The continuous lines show the perceived or phenomenal shape as sketched by the subjects. In all cases the percept is something of a compromise, but it tends toward the "real" object rather than toward the retinal image.

To some extent shape constancy is maintained by ignoring minor changes in the

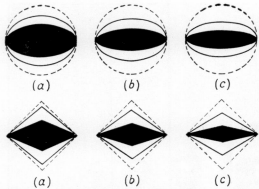

(a)   (b)   (c)

(a)   (b)   (c)

FIG. 6:28. Results of experiment on shape constancy. If you take a half dollar and hold it perpendicular to the line of sight, the retinal image is a circle; but as it leans over, it projects an ellipse. But does the average person see it as an ellipse? No; he tends to cling to the "known" shape. In this figure Thouless summarizes his work on this problem. The broken line shows the "real" physical shape of the object; the solid black figure is the figure cast on the retina; and the continuous line is the subject's drawing to indicate what he saw. Plainly this is a compromise between the retinal image and the "real" object. (*From Thouless, 1931.*)

physically received stimulus pattern. It is possible to learn to notice some aspects of a situation and suppress others. Schafer and Murphy (1943) presented the two designs shown in Fig. 6:29(*a, b*) separately to children. For a given child one was always rewarded (money was given when it appeared); the other was made frustrating by taking away money when it was shown. After a training series of this kind,

they were shown Fig. 6:29*c*. In 54 of 67 cases, the child reported seeing only that shape which had been rewarded. The other design apparently was unnoticed. Such experiments indicate that we observe and perhaps exaggerate those cues associated with the satisfaction of motives—a point which will prove of great importance when we take up the general problem of learning.

Brightness and Color Constancy

If you take a white sheet of paper, illuminate it with a red light, and look at the center of the sheet through a tube, you will see a luminous red film. However, if you look at it without the limitations of the tube—seeing the edges of the sheet, and the background in the room—the sheet of paper will be seen as white. When the tube is used to eliminate cues about background and source of illumination, your perception is based directly on the stimulus to the retina. When the sheet is viewed in a total context, the white remains constant despite the red illumination. This, then, is another example of the organism's ability to deal with the "real" object despite misleading cues from the visual mechanism.

Like size constancy and shape constancy, the phenomena of brightness and color constancy are adaptive in character. We have shown that organisms are constantly operating according to homeostasis—that is,

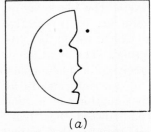   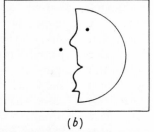   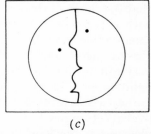

(a)   (b)   (c)

FIG. 6:29. Drawings used by Schafer and Murphy. In the training series, one group of children was rewarded when (a) appeared (won 4 cents) and punished when (b) appeared, losing 2 or 4 cents. The other group was rewarded with (b), punished with (a). In the test series, (c) was presented; a substantial majority reported seeing only the face which had been rewarded. (*From Schafer and Murphy, 1943.*)

they are trying to maintain a constant environment. But the brightness and color of an object will vary according to the kind of lighting, the background colors, and so on. The task of avoiding dangers and obtaining goals would be infinitely complicated if we did not learn to perceive the real object, discounting its continuously changing appearance. We accomplish this by our memory of what the object looked like under other circumstances; and by relating it to other objects in the immediate surrounding area. As the experiment with the tube proves, cutting out these two influences will destroy the color constancy.

The perception of distance and brightness constancy are tangled together, because light obeys the inverse-square law—*i.e.*, the amount of light reaching the eye from an object drops off in proportion to the square of the distance. Thus we make judgments about distance based on decreasing brightness, and judgments about brightness based on estimated distance. Because such observations are made with illumination diffused over the entire scene, and with an easily visible gradient of objects decreasing in apparent size and clarity, they seem not to offer much difficulty. (This is true at maturity. Children have trouble because they lack the frame of reference, the remembered standards for comparison, which the experienced adult employs.)

In all these constancy situations—size, shape, brightness, and color—the organism shows a marvelous talent for integrating cues. On the one hand certain physical influences come to us from the environment. On the other hand we possess certain images derived from past experience. There seems to be some kind of automatic summation of probabilities; and, if this leads to a perception of identity ("this is the same one I saw before"), then the law of constancy operates to keep the perceived object as close as possible to the remembered object. Again we emphasize that this proc-

ess is entirely unconscious; not only is it unobserved, but its speed is far greater than would be possible on the basis of conscious judgment.

All this leads to the following interesting conclusion: to a very marked extent, each of us constructs the world he lives in. The world which controls and guides behavior is the perceived world; and this perceived world is determined to a major degree by factors inside, not outside, the organism. This does not lead to any particular problems of adjustment—on the contrary, it facilitates adjustment—in dealing with physical objects. The maintenance of a constant environment helps a great deal in the external task of survival. But we also tend to develop perceptual constancies in the social realm, and these can cause more trouble.

Illusion and Camouflage

The facts on perception of distance, location, shape, and size indicate that man is equipped with a most amazing set of sensory mechanisms. The constancies which we have just reviewed confirm the opinion that cues are utilized to perceive objects quite accurately, even though the physical stimuli presented to the senses are in constant variation. To balance this impression we must refer to the fact that misperceptions frequently occur; most people learn fairly early that seeing is *not* believing.

Illusion and camouflage are topics relating to misperceptions. We can learn just as much about the psychology of perceiving by studying these problems as we can by studying accurate percepts—more, sometimes, because the error can often be traced to a specific cue.

Illusions are often simply effects based on size, shape, and other constancies. It is difficult to find a precise way of stating the relationships between realistic perception, illusion, and misperceptions, because, to the

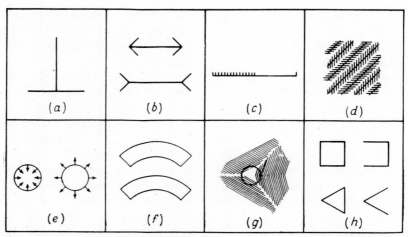

FIG. 6:30. Illusions. In the upper row are a series of illusions which distort length or direction of lines. (a) The vertical-horizontal illusion: although the lines are of equal length, the vertical seems longer. (b) The Muller-Lyer illusion: the lines are equal in length, but the arrowheads give an appearance of inequality. (c) The filled-empty space effect: the left half of the line seems longer than the right. (d) The effect of context: the long lines are really parallel, but the context makes them seem to lead off in different directions. In the lower row are distortions of size or shape. (e) The circles are of equal size, but the arrows create a perception of increased size on the right. (f) The two sectors are equal in size, but the lower one looks smaller. (g) The angular lines distort the shape of the circle. (h) The closed figures on the left are actually the same size as their corresponding open figures.

perceiver, whatever he perceives is real. When we discussed size constancy, we pointed out that a distant object looks bigger than it "really" is, *i.e.*, bigger than it should look, based on the size of the retinal image. It is seen as being approximately its physical size (Hastorf and Way, 1952). Now what is the error? Shall we say that all constancies are errors, since they fail to agree with the light waves reaching the eye? The solution most psychologists prefer is to say that *every perception is real* but that *some agree with other perceptions* and some do not. Thus, when I see a bent stick in water, I can run my finger along it and find that touch reports a straight stick. Or we rely on the perceptions of others; if one person says there are little babies cuddling on the branches of the tree, and everyone else disagrees, we accept the verdict of the majority.

The problem of illusions and hallucina-

tions is thus a problem of the interaction of outer and inner determinants of perception. A "realistic" percept is one which agrees with the physical stimulus. An "autistic" percept is one determined by the individual's memories, or what he desires to see. Hallucination is the extreme form in which a person sees or hears something which is not perceived at all by others around him; in such cases we usually diagnose a complete mental breakdown or psychosis.

All the sense organs are subject to illusion, because in every case the physical stimulus will be related to these inner factors: memory, motive, and so on. Thus we observe misperceptions based on auditory, olfactory, tactual, and other cues. However, optical illusions are easiest to demonstrate, particularly within the pages of a book, and so this treatment will rely primarily on them.

FIG. 6:31. The tangled-cord illusion. The black lines are arranged so that they form broken parts of perfect circles; but, slanting inward, they produce an irresistible impression of a spiral. (*Adapted from Fraser, 1908.*)

These visual misperceptions are not unique to man; they can also be demonstrated in animals. Hens show size-constancy effects, and they also show size illusions, such as the "sector illusion" (Fig. 6:30). This, of course, does not prove that such phenomena are determined by heredity, although it does suggest that the nervous system of most animals is so structured that these misperceptions are inevitable. It would appear that illusions, like constancies, are natural products of a certain kind of nervous structure functioning in a given physical environment.

Constancies have great survival value. Illusions apparently are the price we have to pay for this mechanism. As we have pointed out in preceding pages, the constancies require that the brain make various changes in the retinal image; some parts

are ignored, some are distorted, some are exaggerated. These are exactly the kinds of errors we make in illusions. Look at the opposite page. In the upper portion of Fig. 6:30 we show some figures which give rise to exaggerations of length and distortion of direction. The lower row shows various distortions of shape due to contrast of circles (*e*), contrast of adjacent curves (*f*), and the operation of closure upon size (*h*).

In our discussion of the perceptual constancies (size, shape, color) we noted that these constancies are maintained by relating them to background stimuli. In the visual illusions shown, there is likewise a context calculated to induce a perceptual distortion. For example, in the Müller-Lyer illusion the presence of the additional short lines makes a difference in one's perception of the long lines. Because of the

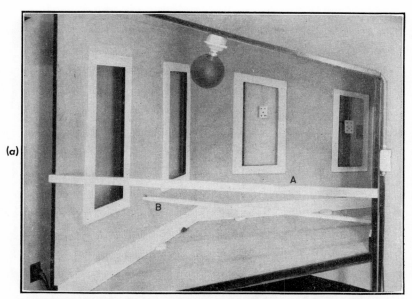

FIG. 6:32. (a) The Ames distorted room. The room is built with trapezoidal floors and walls, the right wall being much smaller than the left. This actually fits the retinal image of a rectangular room if the viewer were standing at the left wall. If, however, we have the person put his chin on the chin rest at A, close his left eye, and stare at the room, it begins to look like a normal, rectangular room. The right wall now creates a retinal image about the size of that for the more distant left wall, the windows begin to look the same size, and so on. At this time the trough, B, which actually slopes slightly downward from right to left, seems tilted upward at the left end, and when a marble rolls from right to left, it is seen as rolling uphill.

(b) When the camera lens is placed at the chin rest (A in the photograph a), the room looks much more like a normal room. The two back windows seem almost the same size; note what happens to the playing cards.

(a)

(b)

FIG. 6:33. Misperceptions induced by the Ames room. (a) When the camera lens is placed in eye position (Fig. 6:32), the light rays reflected from the left wall and the right wall project equal images on the film. Under these circumstances, our past experiences indicate a probability that the two walls are equal in size. But if the walls are equal, then the two women must be of quite unequal height (physically they are both 5 feet 8 inches tall). Once we perceive the room as rectangular, we are literally forced to make an error regarding their height.

(b) Similarly, we assume that the two windows in the back wall are rectangular and of equal size. Under these circumstances, the face at the right is perceived as decidedly inflated, since it fills up the entire window. When the trapezoidal nature of the room is perceived, the windows appear unequal and no size distortion of objects occurs (see the playing cards in the windows in Fig. 6:32a). (*Courtesy of Institute for Associated Research.*)

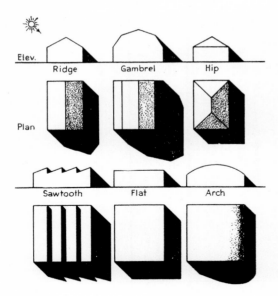

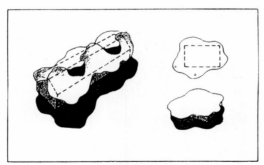

FIG. 6:34. Application of principles of perception to camouflage. A major principle in camouflaging buildings and other large installations is to break up contours. Note how sharp and distinct the buildings appear in the upper picture, and how roof netting can break contours and cause the building to disappear (below). (*From Civilian Defense, U.S. Army Engineers, 1942.*)

simplified situation, it is easy to measure the line and prove that a distortion has occurred; but these same distortions, in daily life, are adaptive rather than sources of error in behavior. Under certain circumstances they could, of course, cause trouble, but the difficulties resulting from their absence would be much greater.

Most of the simple illusions can be "unlearned"—*i.e.*, with a little effort and practice one can learn to make accurate judgments of the lengths, sizes, etc. This apparently operates by removing the context; one develops skill in responding only to the cue of the specific line, ignoring those around it. (It is also possible for people to learn a critical attitude which reduces both constancy and illusion; artists cling close to the stimulus and are less affected by both.) It would follow that one probably could not unlearn an illusion in which the specific cue could not be disentangled from its context. Such an illusion is shown in Fig. 6:31; so far as we know, this illusion cannot be corrected by concentrated study and practice.

The Ames demonstrations. We have already had occasion to refer to the very ingenious demonstrations of visual perception developed by Adelbert Ames, Jr., at the Dartmouth Eye Institute. While these could be called *illusions*, they utilize such large stimuli and produce such striking effects that they are commonly referred to as *demonstrations*. Perhaps the best known is one mentioned earlier in this chapter, the "distorted room." This room is so constructed that it duplicates the proportions of the retinal image for a truly rectangular room, if the eye is in a fixed position.[1] Figure 6:32a shows the distorted room as viewed from some distance away; its deviation from a rectangular shape is apparent. But if one closes his left eye and puts his chin on the chin rest (A), the room begins to square up. The right wall looks equal to the left, the two rear windows are equal in size, and so on (Fig. 6:33). Now, if we insert into this context some object of known size, the size constancy of the object (figure) will be overcome by the structure of the perceived room (ground). Figure 6:33 shows what happens to the size of a man's face in this case.

[1] A little reflection will indicate that, if you stand in the corner of a room, the retinal image of the room is trapezoidal in structure; the near wall is much larger than the far wall, and so on.

FIG. 6:35. Puzzle medallion. "Napoleon and Tomb at St. Helena." Can you find the figure of Napoleon, in characteristic pose? The figure tends to disappear because its contours are also the contours of familiar objects in the picture. (*From Fernberger, 1950.*)

In this same room one sees marbles roll uphill. The trough (*B*) in Fig. 6:32*a* physically has a slight down slope from right to left. However, as we expand the right wall and lower the right side of the floor, in constructing a rectilinear perception, the right end of this trough moves lower. A marble rolling across is thus clearly perceived as rolling uphill. This is very disturbing to some observers.

The Ames demonstrations reaffirm the statement that the organism creates its phenomenal world. The objects and persons that I see are not necessarily the same as those you see; indeed, it is relatively improbable that they correspond perfectly. However, our perceptual processes operate with sufficient uniformity that we have relatively little disagreement as to the nature of physical objects. When we come to consider perceptions of people, social groups, and social institutions, the amount of variation between percepts of different persons may be relatively enormous and can play a major role in such social conse-

quences as group prejudice, industrial conflict, and international war.

Camouflage. Objects are perceived as figure upon ground. To destroy a perception of an object, it would be helpful for the figure to merge with the ground. Wild animals do this very effectively. Protective coloration, shape, and texture make it possible for insects to look like the twigs on which they sit, for birds to merge with the nest, and so on.

The principles of effective camouflage, then, are simply reversals of the principles of object perception. (1) *Contours* should be eliminated by reducing intensity and color differences of adjacent surfaces. Contours should also be broken by irregular contours cutting across them and by more continuous contours which cause the important object to disappear. (2) *Isolation* is to be avoided. A single oil tank or building stands out; when it is in the midst of many, it loses its identity. (3) *Novelty* and movement must be avoided. The perfect circle or square is a novelty in nature; hence a perfect geometrical figure is easily spotted. Movements must be slow. (4) *Light and shade* are particularly troublesome in camouflage work. A gasoline-tank farm will cast a revealing pattern of shadows in early morning or late afternoon—which explains the frequency of reconnaissance flights at those hours. Photographs made at noon are

 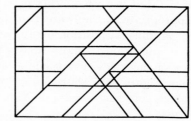

FIG. 6:36. A simple figure embedded in a complex one. See how long it takes you to locate the double triangle at the left in the complex figure at the right. This is the type of task used by Gottschaldt in his studies of perception. The problem is somewhat like that of locating a goal object embedded in its background.

(a)

(b)

FIG. 6:37. Ambiguous figure. Does this look like a pirate? Or is it more like a rabbit? (*From Leeper, 1935.*)

FIG. 6:38. Figures used to establish mental set. If students are shown only the pirate (a), then they see only the pirate in the ambiguous drawing (Fig. 6:37). Conversely, if they first see the rabbit (b), then they see only the rabbit in the ambiguous figure. (*From Leeper, 1935.*)

less useful. (5) *Misperceptions* are particularly valuable as protective camouflage. If the object to be concealed can be made to resemble something which normally would be in the area, it will "disappear" much more readily (Fig. 6:34).

Puzzle pictures. The principles of camouflage are well illustrated by the puzzle pictures with which most of us have played as children. The form disappears because its contours continue on into the outlines of other objects, because slight distortions make it fit in with another perception more appropriate to the context, or because it is in an unusual position for the object's normal appearance. Many artists have made use of these devices for one or another reason. Figure 6:35 shows an early medallion which conceals a figure of Napoleon in full dress.

The German psychologist Gottschaldt (1929) studied the effect of practice upon ability to perceive a simple form concealed in a more complex design. Figure 6:36 resembles one of his simple designs and the complex pattern within which it is em-

bedded. Familiarity with the simpler form did not improve ability to locate it in the complex design; some subjects studied the simple figures for as many as 520 repetitions and still did not spontaneously see it in the complex figure. This experiment shows the great potency of ground or context in determining whether a figure will or will not be perceptible.

If the second figure is ambiguous, however, prior experience can be quite effective in influencing perception. Leeper (1935) performed an experiment using the ambiguous drawing of pirate and rabbit (Fig. 6:37). When it was presented without prior preparation, the number of students seeing each figure was about the same, and all of them succeeded in seeing the alternate view rather easily. With new groups he showed altered drawings; one group saw only the pirate (Fig. 6:38a) and another saw the rabbit (Fig. 6:38b). When these groups saw the ambiguous drawing a substantial majority saw only the figure they had been "set" to see; and many of them were completely incapable of perceiving the alternative figure. Thus what we perceive can readily be influenced by what we expect to see (preperception).

Perception of Persons

The primary problem of perception is, of course, the perception of objects. To the extent that a human being is simply a physical object, the same principles enunciated above are adequate. We recognize people in terms of contour, skin color, hair color and texture, and so on. Once we know a person, we tend to keep his attributes constant, even to the extent of "seeing" his mustache after he has shaved it off.

The human being is, of course, much more than a physical object—especially in terms of his value for need satisfaction and frustration of our motives. To the child, the adult is actually far more important than the physical objects as such. If we keep clearly in mind that perception is a tool for satisfying motives, we shall realize that learning to perceive people may well go on at a faster rate than learning to identify objects, differentiate their characteristics, and so on. In one respect, of course, objects present a simpler problem. Physical objects obey simple laws of physics. A chair which is too hard to kick in comfort today will be the same tomorrow. Humans are more perplexing, because they will reward you today and punish you tomorrow for the same act. Thus there is more confusion and less certainty in our perceptions of persons.

Especially important to the young child is the awareness of the emotional state of the adult. When we say that babies are extraordinarily sensitive to adult emotions, we need not impute any special talents to them. The child's comfort or discomfort, satisfaction or frustration depends on the emotion of the mother particularly. There is a great deal of evidence that babies respond to muscle tensions which build up unconsciously in adults as motivational intensity rises. Thus the mother who is frightened, angry, or anxious may communicate such states to the infant without knowing it. She handles him more roughly, her motions are jerky, her voice changes timbre. Since these cues have great significance to the child, perception is speedy and accurate.

The recognition of facial expressions is also important to the child. The evidence so far (see page 89) leans to the view that we do not inherit many specific patterns of emotional response. However, we learn to make grimaces which convey our feelings to others; most adults have certain facial patterns, partly determined by the culture and partly unique to the individual, which reflect their inner states. The child must learn to perceive these and behave accordingly. In later years he may be perturbed by some one of his acquaintances, without knowing why; the reason may be that he perceived a facial expression as resembling one which was always associated with punishment by his father during his childhood.

The voice seems to be particularly expressive of inner tensions. In experiments designed to test which cues most adequately conveyed an emotion to observers, it was found that the voice was judged far more accurately than facial patterns. [Could this be involved in the suggested relationship (page 87) between auditory sensitivity and emotions of fear and anxiety?] Frieda Fromm-Reichmann (1950) recounts this incident from a patient undergoing psychotherapy. This patient, a young woman, told her psychiatrist that she had decided to attend a party the next evening (this was a great step forward, as she had a real dread of meeting people in groups). Dr. Fromm-Reichmann said, "Fine!" A week later the patient confessed that she had not gone. Under questioning she explained that the psychiatrist had said "fine" in exactly the same tone as the patient's mother when the latter pretended to approve but actually disapproved of a proposed act. If we acquire such habits of perceiving—and apparently we cannot avoid doing so—they will color and distort our perceptions of people throughout life.

Father image and mother image. The two adults whose roles have the most far-reaching significance for the child are of course the father and the mother. The child's perception of these two persons has broad implications for his whole life.

The mother is likely to be perceived as a source of food, as protector, as an object of affection, and so on. The father is perceived as having characteristics of strength and power, money, wisdom; he is also a source of punishment and control. (The specific percepts developed by a child will vary according to the role of each parent in the family constellation.) There is a great deal of evidence to indicate that little girls find the father far more attractive, while little boys perceive the mother as more desirable. This leads to certain kinds of personality complications which we shall consider later.

If the boy comes to perceive his father as stern, forbidding, dictatorial, and arbitrary, he develops a perceptual constancy along these lines, just as he develops constancies for the size and color of objects. Once this pattern is organized, almost anything the father does is likely to be interpreted as proving that the percept was correct. If the father comes too close, he is trying to dominate; if he remains distant, he is showing lack of affection. Thus perceptual distortion operates with people just as with objects.

It is worth while repeating here that what is important is the phenomenal field, not the physical field; or, in other words, that the boy's behavior is guided by the way he perceives his father, which may not correspond to the objective behavior of the father. Furthermore, this perceptual constancy may persist throughout life; and

this young man tends to perceive his employer as arbitrary and dictatorial, his military officer as having these same traits, and so on. In other words, wherever he encounters an older man who has a role of authority over him, this man is perceived as having the attributes of this father image.

Similarly, the young man is likely to look for and marry a woman who resembles his mother (as she looked in his early childhood). He is likely to expect her to behave as his mother did, to demand from her the same services he got from mother, etc. This persistence of the mother image is a major psychological problem in marriage— as is the wife's father image.

Stereotypes. We develop fixed pictures of objects, of persons in our immediate family, and also of people as representatives of social groups. The term *stereotype* is used to refer to a fixed, arbitrary picture of some national, religious, racial, or other category of persons. Psychologists have been keenly interested in the study of stereotypes because it appears that much of our social behavior is guided by such perceptions.

Photographs have often been used in such investigations. Rice (1926) presented his subjects with pictures of various individuals: a member of the United States Senate, a prominent member of the Communist Party, an alleged gambler, and so on. The task was to indicate for each photograph the person represented. The operation of stereotypes was shown by the fact that some pictures were chosen by almost everyone as representing the Senator, the gambler, and the communist because they fitted the popular conception of these groups. (Most of the choices were wrong, however.)

Stereotypes may arise from one's own personal experience; thus he associates a certain complexion, hair color, facial pattern, etc., with need satisfaction or threat and later acts accordingly. Much oftener he simply accepts a stereotype from other people. Southern children get unfavorable stereotypes of the Negro from parents and older children in the absence of or in contradiction to their own personal experience. Blake and Dennis (1943) found that young Southern children did not have any Negro stereotype until about the age of four or five. Then they got an extremely unfavorable picture, which included no favorable traits. By the age of ten or eleven, the children had adopted the routine adult stereotype, which includes a few complimentary characteristics (musical, good-humored, etc.).

As we have noted in the case of size constancy, social stereotypes operate so powerfully that the individual ignores the immediate stimulus. Persons who are prejudiced against Jews apparently cannot see the behavior of the real, physically present Jew because they are looking at their mental picture. During the war a large manufacturing concern was trying to break down the hostility of the foremen to women workers. The training director asked a group of foremen to pick their best workers, and several of them named women. But a few minutes later these same men were protesting that women workers were no good!

The judgment of personality. It is just as vital for the child to get some standard for judging personalities as for judging objects. He must know the characteristics of hot radiators, sharp knives, unstable chairs, bouncing balls. In the same way, if he is to adapt and get need satisfactions, he must develop perceptions of people. To some extent these will merely be transfers from the father image, mother image, etc., or from group stereotypes. However, the child does also learn to differentiate between individuals he meets and to recognize their unique characteristics. He observes smiles and frowns, voices, gestures, and language. Thus he works out a frame of reference within which he can evaluate perceptions

of people, just as he develops such frames for judging visual, auditory, and other stimuli.

The concept of *empathy* is particularly useful in this connection. Dymond (1949) has studied people's ability to judge the personality traits of themselves and of others. She found a significant tendency for those who perceived themselves most accurately also to be superior judges of other people. This suggests that they may have been more empathic.

Even more convincing is the work of Estes (1938). He got reports from persons who had been found to do excellently at judging personality in others, and also from persons who had done poorly. He reports that the procedure of the poor judges of personality was self-consciously analytical and logical. The judgment process was typically one of inference from specific objective actions of the person being judged. The best judges, on the other hand, reported that they did not make a deliberate analysis of their reading and observation, but rather tried to "feel" the other personality. "I let myself go" was a typical comment. Estes concluded that the superior judges were those who made use of empathy, rather than of logic and analysis. People can best be understood by trying to feel as they do and perceive the world as they perceive it.

It is important to note that the personality of the judge determines what he will perceive in other people. Clinical psychologists have found that a person with a strong sex drive will exaggerate the sexual misdeeds of others. Students who cheat on examinations report that they have seen a lot of cheating going on, while noncheaters report that they have seen much less. The old proverb says, "To the pure all things are pure." Such observations indicate that great deal of empathy works in reverse; *i.e.*, we *project* our own characteristics onto others. Actually, this is very much like our reading certain qualities into objects. The colors of objects do not exist "out there"; the observer projects them onto the external reality. A color-blind observer constructs a perceptual object which is unlike that of the observer with normal color receptors. So—the characteristics of the judge influence the perception he gets of an object—or of the personality of some other individual.[1]

The Determinants of Perception

Each of us lives in his own private world. The chair which I see is not identical with the chair as you see it, even though there may be a common physical object which triggers both our perceptions. The college is not perceived the same by an honor student and by one who is on probation for poor grades. The General Electric Company is not perceived in the same way by a banker as by a communist. The United Nations intervention in Korea was not perceived identically by people in the United States and the U.S.S.R.

It does not follow from this divergence of private worlds that we cannot cooperate and interact effectively. As far as physical objects are concerned, we can reach a high degree of unanimity and we can chart courses of action which do not clash. Our troubles are much greater when human beings are objects of perception, but even here, if backgrounds of experience and culture are not too divergent, a moderate amount of success is obtained. Children will presumably never be quite capable of seeing the world as parents see it, and men will always differ from women in many perceptions. Despite these difficulties, most marriages do not end in divorce, and most children get along reasonably well with their parents, barring minor explosions.

The psychologist is then pressed to answer the question: what are the determinants of the perceptual process? To what

[1] Bender and Hastorf (1950).

extent is it a function of purely physical stimuli? To what extent is it an outcome of the dynamic character of the human organism?

Structural and behavioral determinants. If we look back over the numerous kinds of perceptions which have been examined in this chapter, we see that two kinds of determinants have constantly appeared. These can be labeled, respectively, structural and behavioral. Structural determinants include (1) the nature of the physical stimuli, light waves, sound waves, physical surfaces, sizes, and shapes; and (2) the nature of the sense organs—retinal and cochlear structures, skin nerve endings, and so on. In certain phases of perceiving, such as contour, location, and direction, the structural factors are very important. However, much of these perceptions remains unexplained on a purely structural basis; we must turn to other factors to round out the picture.

The behavioral determinants are completely internal in nature; as the term suggests, they can be detected only in behavior. They include such factors as the following: (1) *past experience;* the child does not perceive a dog in the same way after he has been bitten; (2) *unconscious assumptions* about the object (as in the experiments to follow, which show change in percept with change in assumption as to the nature of the object); and (3) *needs, attitudes, and values* of the perceiver. These behavioral determinants are in continuous interaction with the structural factors to produce the phenomenal field as perceived by the individual at any moment in time.

Structural factors necessarily receive a certain priority in understanding perception. The kind of stimuli present, and the nature of the sense organs, determine whether we shall perceive anything. The preceding chapter was therefore devoted to an examination of these physical and neurological factors. Unless we can first see, hear, smell, taste, and touch, we cannot perceive objects or people.

In recent years, however, psychologists have uncovered more and more evidence showing that the structural factors are not enough to explain perception. Even in the laboratory, under precision conditions, it was found that what the person observed depended on his attitudes and sometimes on his emotions. Thus the study of behavioral factors in perception has expanded rapidly. Let us take a look at some of these investigations and their results.

Perceptual assumptions. When a pattern of light waves strikes the retina, the person reports that he sees an object "out there." It would be more precise, in many cases, to say that he *assumes* an object out there. We have noted, for example, how people will "fill in" the gaps in an incomplete figure, will report seeing a man carry out routine actions because they expect him to do so, and will ascribe the correct shape, size, and color to objects in contradiction to the physical cues available. In early years we check our assumptions by getting other perceptions—*e.g.*, we feel as well as see the object. Babies explore objects by touch and taste. Adults get away from this realistic way of studying the environment and frequently trust to symbols rather than getting down to reality, with unfortunate consequences (cf. Chap. 11).

It can be shown that assumptions about the nature of the object will result in distortions of the cues to fit in with the assumption. Such assumptions take the form of "hypotheses" that "an object having certain characteristics is out there" and then perceiving in accordance with the hypothesis.

Many assumptions arise because of *past experience* with the stimulus. Adams (1923) describes an amusing experiment with artificial flowers. Three flowers were used, a pink rose, a red rose, and a bunch of violets. The pink rose was perfumed with violet,

the red rose with lily, and the violets with lily. Ten of twelve subjects tested reported that the perfume was the characteristic odor of that flower. One subject said: "I saw the violets in the vase on the table, and thinking they were real, leaned over to smell them. As I got very close I noticed the clothy texture of the petals and realized they were artificial. I sniffed at them just the same and for the first instant they smelled just like freshly plucked violets; then their odor changed to lily." Many of the other subjects clung to their misperceptions of the odors, although when tested with eyes closed they identified the scents correctly.

Once an assumption has been established, it can block the arrival of the correct perception. Galloway (1946) presented his subjects with blurred pictures to be identified. Eight degrees of blurring (corresponding to fixed positions of a slide projector lens) were used, position 1 being clear focus and position 8 being a vague pattern of lights and shadows. Different groups of subjects started at different degrees of blurring and received successively clearer views until correct identification occurred. The striking phenomenon was this: an object might be identified by almost everyone when seen for the first time in position 4; but this same object, when seen in positions 8, 7, 6, etc., was not identified until it got down to 3 or 2. What happened was that the subject, being forced to guess as to the nature of the object, got a wrong hypothesis, and this clung until the clarity of the picture forced its rejection. When first exposure was clearer, the correct identification was made more promptly.

Assumptions based on instructions. Instead of allowing the subject to evolve his own assumptions, the experimenter can supply one. It is possible to show that such instructions have a significant effect upon perception. Hastorf (1950) gave his subjects the task of adjusting a circle of light so that it looked to be the same distance away as a target. When they were told that this circle was a ping-pong ball, they made different size settings than when told it was a billiard ball. At an assumed constant distance, the billiard-ball disk was set larger. Similarly, if they were simply shown a disk and asked to judge its distance, the same size was seen farther away as "billiard ball" than as "ping-pong" ball. These results fit perfectly, of course, with the size-constancy data cited earlier.

Suggestions about personality. In three sections of a course in psychology, the students were introduced to a new instructor who was to take over the class. In two sections the same man acted as the new instructor; in the third section, a different man with quite different personality traits took over. In all three sections the students were given a written statement about the importance of finding out how they reacted to different teachers. Appended to this was a short "personality sketch" of the new instructor, allegedly obtained from a person who knew him well. The sketches were identical in all three sections, except that on half the sheets he was described as "rather cold" while in the other half the phrase "very warm" was substituted.[1]

After the class meeting, the students were asked to write a free description of the instructor and to rate him on 15 rating scales. The results showed that the assumption of a "warm" or "cold" personality had a decided effect upon all ratings, both for the same instructor and for the two different men who served as instructors. When the teacher had been described as "warm," he got more favorable ratings than when "cold." He was judged to be more considerate of others, more informal, more sociable, more popular, more humorous, and more humane. However, the two men who were judged differed so sharply in some traits that the "warm-cold" in-

[1] See H. H. Kelley (1949).

structions were not effective. The stimulus resists distortion if it is obviously incompatible with the assumption. We might get a subject to perceive a circle of light as an orange, but hardly as the silhouette of the Empire State Building.

Assumptions based on social suggestion. Suggestions may come from the actions or words of others in an indirect manner. One's past experience leads him to assume that, when others attend to an object, it may have importance for him. We also accept the interpretation as to size, value, etc., held by others. Sherif (1935) devised an experiment to measure this social effect. He first had his subjects tested individually on the autokinetic phenomenon (in a dark room, one watches a point of light, actually fixed, and it seems to move). Each person developed his own characteristic estimate of the number of inches the light moved. Then three people would work together. Under these conditions, the judgments moved together; a person who had made high movement estimates would lower them, while a person who had made low estimates would increase his judgments (Fig. 6:39). Basically, this means that we will modify our own perceptions of size, movement, and value to conform with the judgments expressed by people around us. This is the way in which cultural standards are transmitted from parent to child, and from old to new members of an adult group.

Assumptions based on motives. Our discussion of biogenic drives (Chap. 2) included the fact that, when a drive state is operative, objects which are potential satisfiers get special attention. This effect probably spreads to drive-related objects, symbols, etc., as well as to the final goal object. A psychologist friend reports the following self-observation: "I drive a car which carries the fanciful label, 'Silver Streak.' On several occasions, when I was quite hungry, I glanced at this and read it as 'Silver Steak.' " McClelland and Atkinson

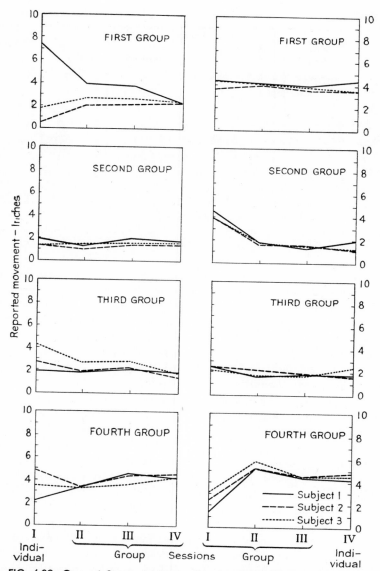

FIG. 6:39. Group influence on perception. In the four groups on the left, each person started working by himself, observing the autokinetic phenomenon and establishing his own "norm" of estimated movement. Then groups of three worked together; note how the estimates converge toward a common standard. In contrast to this, the people who started in groups and worked their final session as individuals follow pretty much a common standard throughout. In ambiguous situations, we tend to accept the standards of other people. (*From Sherif, 1935.*)

FAN FARE

By Walt Ditzen

FIG. 6:40. Motivation and perception. When the need to accomplish and the fear of failure are both strong, perception may become disorganized; obstacles seem much larger than they "really" are. (*By Walt Ditzen, copyright 1951 by John F. Dille Co., courtesy of the Champaign-Urbana Courier.*)

(1948) showed blurred pictures to their subjects at 1 to 16 hours after eating. As the amount of presumed food need increased, the perceptions reported showed a decided increase in the number of food-related objects. One can infer from various lines of evidence that a woman who is plain or even ugly may look quite beautiful to a sex-starved man. Clinical psychologists find that a person with a strong sex drive will perceive sexual objects or sexual implications in stimuli which are not so perceived by persons not highly motivated by sex. In Fig. 6:40 a cartoonist presents an amusing example of how object size seems grossly exaggerated when strong motivation is involved.

Values and perception. The dynamic strength of symbols of value will presumably depend upon the underlying needs which they serve. Bruner and Goodman (1947) asked children to adjust the size of a circle of light to match the size of coins: nickel, dime, quarter, etc. In another series they adjusted the circle of light to match simple gray cardboard disks, the sizes being the same as for the coins. Figure 6:41 shows their results. All the children overestimated the size of coins.

Postman, Bruner, and McGinnies (1948)

used a standard test to identify people who had high religious values, high economic values, and so on (page 124). To these people words were presented in a tachistoscope (a device somewhat analogous to a camera shutter) at very short exposures (0.01 up to 1 second). In the majority of cases, words which related to the person's high value were perceived at much shorter times (faster perception) than when the word related to a value on which the subject made a low score. Thus religious individuals on the average perceived "sacred" at much faster speeds than nonreligious persons. The experimenters claim that two processes are involved: *perceptual selectivity* (more efficient use of cues which fit in with motives or values) and *perceptual defense* (active resistance to certain perceptions which were contrary to the person's values). It may well be, in the light of what we have said about focusing (pages 39, 73), that both are simply aspects of one process. The organism is searching for objects and cues which lead to satisfaction and is excluding irrelevant or threatening objects and cues.

Subception. These experiments seem to prove that some kind of vague recognition of the word actually precedes conscious identification. The same phenomenon is more clearly demonstrated by McCleary and Lazarus (1949), who had subjects study a list of nonsense syllables, thus avoiding differences in familiarity of words. Certain syllables always were accompanied by shock. Such syllables, when seen later, gave rise to the GSR (electrical skin response). Now McCleary and Lazarus presented the syllables in a tachistoscope, at very short times. *Before the syllable was recognized*, the GSR measures showed a sizable difference between shock and non-shock syllables.

These studies suggest that some kind of basic recognition of a stimulus as "good" or "bad," rewarding or threatening, occurs faster, at a more primitive level, than conscious identification of the stimulus. Neurologically it may be that subception (unconscious perception) is based upon an emotional response mediated through the thalamus, to which sensory impulses go before they reach the cerebral cortex (see Fig. 5:11, page 153). Much experimentation is now being done along these lines, and in a few years psychologists expect to be much better informed about this aspect of perception.

We always have subception, of course, as a phase of normal perception in some situations. Note the role of double images in distance vision. Nobody notices these double images unless he is specifically instructed to do so, and even then he requires some practice to acquire skill at it. Under ordinary conditions the brain swiftly and unconsciously translates the double images into an awareness of the distance of objects, just as in the experiments reported above some slight cue was translated into an awareness of threat.

Realistic and autistic percepts. We can sum up this discussion of structural and behavioral determinants of perception as follows: When structural factors are predominant, as in the perception of physical objects, where the nature of the stimulus and of the sense organs is primary, we get

realistic perceptions. These can be checked by other people and by the techniques of the physical sciences. When the behavioral factors are uppermost, we get *autistic* perceptions—percepts based mostly on conditions within the self. Thus, if the stimulus is vague, the response of the sense organs poorly defined, and the surrounding context hazy, structural influences are at a minimum. In this case, the desires of the individual, his attitudes and expectancies, will determine what he sees. Normal perceptions will mostly be somewhere between completely realistic and completely autistic —a compromise between the structural and behavioral factors.

Illusion and hallucination are extreme forms of autistic perception. In the field of social relations, however, most of us do a good deal of autistic perceiving all the time. A young man is likely grossly to overestimate the beauty of his sweetheart; an artist perceives his paintings as revealing extraordinary talent; and the salesman may

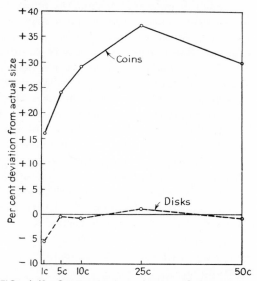

FIG. 6:41. Overestimation of coins. Children were asked to set a circle of light equal in size to a coin and, on a different occasion, equal to a gray disk of the same physical size as the coin. Note how much they overestimate the coins as compared with the valueless disks. (*From Bruner and Goodman, 1947.*)

even (sometimes) see his commodity in the glowing way he describes it to the customer. Citizens of a nation perceive other countries primarily in autistic terms; when we were fighting the Nazis, they were seen as very, very bad, but today, when they have less threat value, many people seem to have changed their perceptions of German storm troops and concentration camps.

Perception and personality. Since behavioral factors influence so profoundly many of our everyday percepts, it is clear that the individual's personality is one of the determinants of perception. In fact, it is possible to define personality as one's characteristic way of perceiving himself in relation to his environment. We shall elaborate on this point in Chap. 13. At this point we wish only to emphasize two ideas which have been noted earlier in this discussion.

1. The relative use of different kinds of cues in the process of building up a picture of the external world is clearly different in one person from another. Take the question of brightness constancy. Some people who look at disks of varying brightness under different illumination stick closely to constancy—they perceive the disk "as it really is." Other subjects judge the disks according to the retinal illumination—they react to the light waves, not to the inferred object. We may call the former "object-bound" and the latter "stimulus-bound." Artists have to be in the latter group; they must paint a picture as it appears to the eye, or they will not get their effects across to the observer. Henneman (1935) has shown that some people consistently obey the stimulus, while others cling to object-constancy, although both can be influenced by training.

2. Another personality difference which affects perception is that revealed by Witkin's studies on visual cues vs. postural cues in space perception. Some people were consistently guided by the visual frame, while others were influenced more by the tilting of the body. Women, for example, were more affected by the visual frame, men by the postural conditions. There were other general personality differences, which suggested that perhaps outward or inward orientation might be reflected in these ways of responding to perceptual cues.

Homeostasis and Perception

In our analysis of motivation we pointed out that the organism is constantly trying to achieve an optimum equilibrium. Size constancy, color constancy, and other perceptual facts fit in with this principle. It is more likely that man can satisfy his needs if he can maintain a constant physical environment, one which is not so slippery that it changes even as he is responding to it. Object constancy, therefore, is an extension of the homeostatic principle.

Furthermore, the experiments confirm the earlier inference that adjustment will be facilitated if needed objects "stand out" in the environment. It appears from the studies of perception that the existence of a need may bring awareness of certain objects close to the focus of attention. A relatively slight cue, a mere flash of exposure, thus brings a clear perception and a quick response. Obviously this kind of mechanism aids in satisfying needs.

In social life, manners, customs, and traditions provide us with constant external situations. As we become familiar with these, and satisfy our motives by responding to them, we also develop perceptual constancies which maintain them apparently unchanged. Furthermore, it appears that a deviation from such a constancy is quite disturbing to many people, just as it would be disturbing to see physical objects defying gravitation and doing other unpredictable things. In our interpersonal relations, we expect our friends to behave in a constant, predictable way, and will see them as behaving thus unless there is a really substantial deviation from the norm. Young men develop expectancies about the behavior of a wife, and women about a husband, which provide certain assumptions for marriage. If the mate fails to conform to these, difficulty in adjustment follows.

The utility of ambiguous stimuli. Perception is normally a compromise between structural and behavioral determinants if there is any divergence. Structural factors, however, can be very compelling. If we wish to study the role of behavioral influences with any precision, it is necessary to provide structural conditions which are not too coercive. The ambiguous figure provides such a situation. Several psychologists are now working with tests composed entirely of ambiguous drawings, in their study of perception. Some of the most important and widely used tests of personality, the Rorschach and the Thematic Apperception Test (see pages 535–537), for example, present the subject with ambiguous figures. Thus what he sees will be a function of his inner personality, not of the test situation.

Nowadays we think of abnormal personalities as having normal traits carried to an extreme. Thus, for example, the abnormal person will distort perception much more than the normal individual. One woman, an inmate of a mental hospital, looks out the window and points to the cute babies on the branches of the tree. She thus reflects her own desire for marriage and children, but she distorts reality beyond the realm we consider normal. However, presumably normal people will misperceive objects when strongly motivated; a book is seen as a box of candy, a woman's kindness is misperceived as evidence of love and passion.

The validity of experimental studies of misperception in explaining daily-life phenomena has been questioned. It must be conceded that, in normal environmental situations, objects are likely to be structured with considerable clarity as compared with ambiguous drawings. On the other hand, the intensity of motives operating is vastly greater than anything we can manipulate in the laboratory. It seems likely that these factors cancel out and that the experimental studies really do reflect day-to-day phenomena. Clinical psychologists particularly find their observations agreeing with these results on distortion. Sigmund Freud, in his *Psychopathology of Everyday Life*, has collected an impressive variety of illustrations of distortion resulting from strong motivation.

Limits on constancies. The forces making for perceptual, social, and personal constancies are very strong. People try to build constant environments to avoid the pressures of hunger, temperature extremes, thirst, and the like. Yet we should not press this point too far. If constancy maintenance is too successful, we come out with a rigid world, rigid society, and rigid personalities. This has happened in some primitive and tradition-encrusted societies. They approximate the condition of static homeostasis.

But only plants, in the world of organic life, really maintain static homeostasis. Moving organisms are dynamic. We have related the motivation of human behavior to a disturbance in the balance within the body. To correct this disturbance, man makes a corresponding disturbance in the external world—obtaining food, building a house, killing wild animals. He must select certain features and accent certain parts; after all, it is only a particular part of the environment, not the whole, which can satisfy need and reduce tension. Thus perception must disrupt this static external world, break it up into parts, to find the objects which are needed for restoration of inner equilibrium. Sometimes the motivational state will require a restructuring of the environment—putting things together in a new way. We call this *thinking* or *inventing;* clearly, a rigid way of perceiving would prevent efficient thinking.

The process of human adjustment, then, is a constant flux of equilibrium, disturbance, action, and restoration of equilibrium. While the perceptual constancies can be of assistance in this process, they can also be detrimental to chances of progressing to a higher level equilibrium based on a new organization of the environment. Man progresses by trying out changes. Neither rigidity of technology nor rigidity of social institutions will make for the optimum in human adjustment. A nice compromise between constancy and variability is required for this achievement.

SUMMARY

The organism finds itself faced with a tremendous variety of stimuli which may mean danger or may mean goal achievement. To deal with these stimuli the organism must have a selection mechanism and an organization mechanism. The former is the function of attending, the latter, of perceiving.

Both attending and perceiving are affected by both structural and behavioral factors. Attention is dominated in some instances by external factors of size, intensity, duration, and change; but it is also profoundly affected by motivation and mental set. These variations can be measured by changes in reaction time and in expenditure of energy.

Perception has been analyzed with respect to primitive awareness of "things," their direction, distance, movement, and qualities (size, shape, color, and brightness). Recognition of "something" as a unified percept bounded and different from its background is primitive and probably determined structurally, *i.e.,* by heredity. Most of the other phases of perception are profoundly modified by past experience, by expectancy as to the kind of object, by reward and punishment, by desire, and by mental set.

Persons are perceived according to the same principles which govern object perception. All the information we get about a person comes through sensory mechanisms, and all these cues are subject to distortion by the processes listed above. Like objects, we develop "constancies" for people and perceive them as the same even when they have changed. We also project our own notions onto them, even though their behavior gives little support for such interpretations.

Perception is an integral part of the process of adjustment. Needs arise as a result of disturbances of inner equilibrium. To restore this equilibrium one must identify relevant objects in the environment. Size constancy, color constancy, and other perceptual processes aid in the speedy location of needed goals. On the other hand, excessive rigidity of perception may prevent man from seeing possible better levels of equilibrium which can be achieved by changing his physical or social habits. Optimum adjustment thus calls for perception which is not too rigid and also not too variable.

Recommended Readings[1]

BILLS, A. G.: *General Experimental Psychology.* New York: Longmans, 1934. Chaps. 6, 7, and 8.

BLAKE, R. R., and G. V. RAMSEY: *Perception: An Approach to Personality.* New York: Ronald, 1951. Chaps. 1, 2, and 4.

CANTRIL, H.: *The "Why" of Man's Experience.* New York: Macmillan, 1951. Chaps. 4 and 5.

[1] See also p. 547.

CARR, H. A.: *An Introduction to Space Perception*. New York: Longmans, 1935. (Especially Chaps. 2, 3, 6, and 7.)

GARDNER, E.: *Fundamentals of Neurology*. Philadelphia: Saunders, 1947.

GERARD, R. W.: *The Body Functions*. New York: Wiley, 1941.

GIBSON, J. J.: *The Perception of the Visual World*. Boston: Houghton Mifflin, 1950.

HARTMANN, G. W.: *Gestalt Psychology*. New York: Ronald, 1935. Chaps. 6–9.

HEBB, D. O.: *Organization of Behavior*. New York: Wiley, 1949. Chaps. 1–3.

KATZ, D.: *Gestalt Psychology*. (Tr. by R. Tyson.) New York: Ronald, 1950. Chaps. 1–12.

KÖHLER, W.: *Gestalt Psychology*. New York: Liveright, 1947. Chaps. 4–6.

LUCKIESH, M.: *Visual Illusions and Their Applications*. New York: Van Nostrand, 1922.

PILLSBURY, W. B.: *Attention*. London: Sonnenschein, 1908.

POSTMAN, L., and J. P. EGAN: *Experimental Psychology*. Harper, 1949. Chaps. 7, 8, 9, and 10.

SCHOEN, MAX: *Psychology of Music*. New York: Ronald, 1940.

VERNON, M. D.: *Visual Perception*. New York: Macmillan, 1937. Chaps. 6–9.

WIENER, N.: *Cybernetics*. New York: Wiley, 1948. Chaps. 1–4.

WOODWORTH, R. S.: *Experimental Psychology*. New York: Holt, 1938. Chap. 27.

CHAPTER 7

Association

The human being is constantly in active quest of satisfactions for his inner needs, be they biological drives, emotional impulses, or values. In this process he perceives environmental objects, manipulates them, finds out about their satisfying or threatening qualities.

On the second and later contacts with a given object or situation, the person does not perceive it in exactly the same way as at first, nor does he act toward it in the same manner. Objects are seen as inviting or alarming, in accordance with happenings at the first occurrence; and behavior conforms to this perception. We may say, then, that *perception and behavior are modified by experience;* and this process of modification is labeled *learning.*[1]

Organism-environment contacts may be relatively active or passive. Typical of passive relationships are those of viewing a landscape, hearing the sounds of birds and insects, and smelling the odor of flowers. Modification occurs even in this kind of situation; at a later time I can recall the landscape and describe it, the accuracy of the description being taken as a measure of the extent to which modification has taken place.

Frequently the learning process involves a more active relationship of the organism to its environment. A man may become hungry. This drive requires discovery of food objects, and the inner tension sets off seeking activity. The goal object is, so to speak, embedded in the environment, and must be distinguished so that it can be eaten and equilibrium reestablished. Thus the man singles out particular places to look for food, and specific objects which might serve as food. Eventually a satisfactory substance is located. The next time the hunger drive recurs in this situation, the food will be located more rapidly, because the place where success was experienced is now perceived differently, and movements not leading to success are now made less often. There has been a *modification* of perception and behavior.

What is the ultimate nature of the learning process? To this question most people expect an answer in nonpsychological terms, *e.g.*, in terms of the nervous system. Studies of brain disease, brain injury, and brain operations make it clear that learning —a psychological process—goes along with some modification in the central nervous system. These modifications are sometimes

---

[1] There are other ways in which perception and behavior are changed; *e.g.*, by maturation. As the organism matures, hereditary potentialities unfold; these changes do not depend upon experience. Learning is the process of modification as a function of contacts between the organism and its environment.

called *traces*, even though we do not know much about the nature of these changes. The analogy of feet walking across grass, marking a trail, is certainly wrong; but the correct answer still eludes neurological research.

This lack of a sound neurology of learning is not too serious. Let us treat the brain modification as a hypothetical *construct* to refer to the fact that some neurological change has occurred, without defining the construct more precisely. Not so long ago physicists set up the *ether* as a construct to explain the observed behavior of light, although they knew nothing of its properties; and many of the concepts now so freely bandied about regarding the processes of atomic fission relate to constructs. This does not prevent them from being useful; so likewise we can use a construct of brain trace without worrying over its specific physiological correlate at this moment.

Learning implies *selection*. The external environment assails the organism with a tremendous variety of colors, shapes, sounds, and smells. We cannot comprehend this milieu in its totality in a single glimpse. Learning involves the *differentiation* of objects as having recognizable characteristics—some move, some squeal, some bite, some taste good. Hence learning depends upon motivation and attention, which select from this complex totality. When William James pictured the world of the infant as a "big blooming, buzzing confusion," he employed a phrase which has not yet been improved upon. Intelligent, adaptive behavior becomes possible as we organize this confusion. We learn to perceive objects, relate them to one another, and anticipate what they will do to us, what we can do to them.

Learning as association. The simplest form of learning may be defined as the process of combining or associating at least two experiences which occur in close proximity in space and time. Even the protozoa, one-celled organisms, can make such associations. A Russian investigator reports that he induced contractions in a colony of Infusoria by tactile stimulation with a fine glass rod. A light, which did not at first cause contraction, was presented simultaneously with the rod. Later on, contraction was caused by the light alone. Learning here has taken the form of an association between the visual stimulus and the jarring by the glass rod. The two experiences have been combined. We may say that the light is now perceived differently; it functions as a *signal* of disturbance.[1]

Associative learning makes up a large part of human education and training. The child associates the presence of his mother with food and with other desirable situations. He associates clouds with rain, snow with cold, money with candy. In school he acquires verbal associations: Columbus with 1492, numbers in series, names of chemicals with their properties. Employees learn signals in connection with their work. Research work becomes necessary when associations prove difficult to form; thus, without Pasteur the control of disease would have been most improbable, because bacteria cannot be perceived without special equipment; hence their presence could not become associated with the occurrence of illness. In the same way, any consequence of an event which is delayed for a considerable period of time offers difficulties for learning the right association. Some primitive tribes have not associated intercourse with pregnancy because of the 9-month delay between its occurrence and childbirth. Human-relations problems are similar. A factory manager may do something which irritates

[1] As noted in the preceding chapter, differing qualities of the same object become associated; so, the taste of an orange now "stands for" the whole pattern of sensations which an orange can stimulate.

his workers, and months later he has a strike; it is not easy for him to associate this with his own action.

Complex learning. Simple association, however, is not an adequate concept for picturing the whole of human learning. Learning takes place through trial and error, and through problem solving. Another form of learning is that which is called *insight*, in which previous associations are *rearranged* to give a new pattern, not before experienced. Reasoning and thinking thus are often forms of learning. The development of complex motor skills is rather different from learning ideas.

When we attempt to devise experiments for measuring, in a precise scientific manner, the progress of learning, we are led to the conclusion that there may be several kinds of learning. Perhaps learning by association, by trial and error, and by insight are fundamentally different from each other. Perhaps the nature of the situation determines which of man's numerous abilities can be brought into play. This has become an important research problem, because so much of our experimental work has to be done with animals. Can we set up studies on animals which really give us a dependable basis for inferences about human learning?

Lloyd Morgan's canon. Prior to the development of scientific psychology the usual tendency was to explain animal behavior by analogy with humans. Thus pets were credited with the ability to understand spoken words, rather than with association of pleasure or pain to a particular tone of voice. Some of these human interpretations of anecdotes about animal learning became so fantastic that a decided counterreaction set in. Lloyd Morgan (1894) attacked "anthropomorphism" (interpreting animal behavior in human terms) with his famous canon: "In no case may we interpret an action as the outcome of a higher psychical faculty, if it can be inter-

preted as the outcome of the exercise of one which stands lower in the psychological scale." This commandment to use the simplest possible explanation provided a healthy corrective to the earlier, imaginative discussions of animal learning.

Like many logical canons, however, that of Lloyd Morgan can easily be overextended. Specifically, the so-called "behavioristic psychologists" tended to reverse the principle; they sought to explain human learning only by principles which could be verified in animal experimentation. Further, these principles were largely couched in terms of simple association and trial and error, ignoring even the possibility that animals might have potentialities for "higher" forms of learning. Some of the resulting "explanations" of human learning became so devious and involved that we may doubt if they really obeyed Morgan's principle of the simplest possible explanation.

The use of animals for experimental purposes has been necessary for several reasons. (1) It is not permissible to deprive human infants of certain experiences (*e.g.*, rearing them in darkness) in order to verify hypotheses. (2) It is likewise not permissible to interfere surgically or medically with a human child to determine the role of specific mechanisms. (3) Because man has more complex abilities, it is sometimes impossible to get pure evidence as to his simpler levels of performance. Measures of the simple activities are contaminated, so to speak, by the higher level aptitudes. For these and other reasons, such as convenience, experiments on human learning are often checked by resort to animal subjects. Our emphasis throughout this book will be on human psychology. Nevertheless, we shall find it necessary in many instances to refer to studies of animals as the definitive proof of many points in psychological theory.

Human and animal learning alike seem

to take different forms according to the nature of the task presented and the response required. To take account of this variation, this and the following chapters will describe results from a variety of distinctive learning situations.

Association

The importance of associative learning in human life has been indicated above. Much of our everyday adaptation (as well as that of animals) takes the form of associating one stimulus with another, so that when the first is presented, the organism behaves in a manner appropriate to the second. While keeping in mind that more complex forms of learning are important, let us, in this chapter, focus our attention on this relatively simple process of learning by association. We need to consider some of the methods used by psychologists in research on association, after which we can examine the general conclusions which have been developed.

Learning and remembering. In principle we can separate the formation of an association from its operation on a later occasion. Obviously, learning and remembering must be closely related processes; but, in time, learning must be prior to memory. Learning is a process of *impressing* (forming "traces" in the nervous system); retention is persistence of the impression; and forgetting is its decline. Unless memory can be demonstrated, therefore, we cannot be certain that learning took place. Much of the following discussion consequently centers around methods of measuring memory, although our immediate concern is with the learning process which established the memories.

Methods. We shall deal first with the process of memorizing symbolic material, such as words and numbers. This is a type of learning in which the young child spends a considerable amount of time. It is also instructive in that it provides the raw materials for thinking. Most of man's reasoning and planning goes on by manipulating symbols, and the kinds of associations he utilizes will depend to a marked extent upon the memorization of material in earlier years.

A standard technique for studying this learning process is to present a series of items, which may be words, nonsense syllables, numbers, drawings, etc. The subject is required to learn these items so that he can reproduce them in some manner. *Efficiency* of learning is thus measured by the amount remembered. There are many variations on this standard experiment:

1. *The method of retained members.* The person studies a list for a specified time, or they are presented to him in series for a stated number of repetitions. He then attempts to recall them. The method of *anticipation* demands that he anticipate each word before it is actually shown to him; if he fails, it is presented and he attempts to give the next one. Scores may be based on the number of correct recalls, the time required to reach a perfect reproduction, number of errors, etc.

2. *The method of paired associates.* Pairs of items are presented, and the subject is instructed to learn them in such a way that he can give the second whenever the first appears: *e.g.,* Columbus—1492. To test his performance, the first item is shown and he attempts to reproduce the second.

3. *The method of recognition.* The items of the original list are scrambled with a large number of new items in the same class (words, numbers, syllables), and the subject attempts to identify those he studied in the learning situation. This is much like the task of identifying people from photographs, or of answering true-false questions on an examination.

4. *The method of relearning.* This is simply a repetition of the original learning task. Suppose, for example, that a subject requires 10 minutes to memorize a given list to the point of one perfect performance. A week later he is asked to relearn it to the point of one perfect recall,

FIG. 7:1. Memory drum. This device is simply a rotating cylinder covered by a shield. On the cylinder can be mounted lists of words, pictures, numbers, nonsense syllables, etc. One or two windows in the screen permit exposure of one item at a time, a pair at a time, a pair in succession. The speed of rotation, and hence the time the subject can study each item, is controlled by a small electric motor, usually with adjustable gears.

and achieves that goal in 4 minutes. We would estimate that he had retained some 60 per cent of his prior learning, since he "saved" 6 of the original 10 minutes.

The method of retained members is the crudest of these. It does not measure partial learning. Thus a word may be "on the tip of the tongue" but does not get out to be scored. In the method of recognition such imperfect learning can be demonstrated (compare the difficulty of essay and objective-type examinations, the latter requiring only recognition). The method of relearning is no doubt the most sensitive; even after 40 years it has been possible to show some memory of learned material by this technique. Since animals cannot give verbal indications of recall or recognition, the method of relearning must be employed to test their memories.

Materials. The question of proper learning materials is important. Ebbinghaus (1913) noted that people do not start at the same level when learning words; some

are more familiar with particular words, have pleasant associations with them, and so on. He devised nonsense syllables to try to get all his learning to start from zero. Even nonsense syllables (zat, tep, bim, etc.) are likely to have some meaning, however, and so the learners do not in fact start at a common zero point[1] even when such materials are used.

To present the various items in sequence and at regular intervals, the *memory drum* was devised (Fig. 7:1). This is simply a drum with the list of words, numbers, syllables, or pictures on it, behind a screen. A slot in the screen is so placed that each item appears briefly and then disappears. By changing the speed of rotation the time interval is modified, forcing the subject to work rapidly or allowing him more time.

Serial learning in real life. Much everyday learning is a matter of building up associations. The child needs to learn his multiplication tables and other number combinations. He makes paired associations of dates and events, names and offices, names of elements and their properties. He memorizes lists of laws, events, explanatory principles (often enough, in a purely mechanical fashion; in fact, mechanical or rote memory must to some degree precede understanding).

Adults, too, find it necessary to memorize lists of items or to make purely mechanical associations. A person who moves into a new city is likely to find it helpful to memorize the order of certain streets from some landmark. The employee of a large manufacturing concern must learn a long list of products and brand names. The salesman should memorize key facts about

[1] For example, one young man startled us by memorizing a very difficult list of nonsense syllables in record time. He explained that he had worked on a railroad, and these odd combinations of letters reminded him of the abbreviations for different roads!

his important customers, if he wants to maintain favorable relations with them.

If we are to acquire any psychological insight into this type of learning, we must examine the process of forming associations. Let us consider now the general problem of association of events, and then some experimental studies of how associations are formed.

The principles of association. Before learning was studied experimentally, speculations about learning, memory, imagination, and thinking were based upon the observer's study of his own mental processes (introspection). Such cogitation (often very shrewd) has aptly been called *armchair psychology.* Aristotle pointed out two thousand years ago that all memory followed the pattern of an association of events and that the ideas as recalled tended to reproduce the original occurrence. For example, one remembers a summer vacation. He tends to remember one incident, the scene in which it occurred, what followed after, and so on; the place and time relationships are in general maintained.

If this were strictly true, however, memory should completely duplicate the learning situation. Obviously that is not the case. For example, my vacation memory is followed not by the thought of the train ride home, but by recall of the similarly pleasant visit to the seashore even earlier in time. The sequence of thoughts, then, is not determined by mere space-time connections (contiguity) but also by similarity and other influences. Aristotle proposed three general laws of association: *contiguity* (closeness in space and time), *similarity*, and *contrast.* Later writers multiplied these laws, but it would serve no useful purpose to list them here. Let us say only that much learning and memory takes the form of relating one item or group of items to others by a variety of connections which are called *associations.* How well associations con-

tribute to effective learning can be quickly illustrated by the following three lists:

kev	lake	house
sof	red	window
bim	chair	floor
laz	egg	hall
cor	paper	roof
neg	grass	door
tul	table	bath
zin	rain	ceiling
var	clock	stair
mef	tree	brick

The first list, of nonsense syllables, provides few associations between items. It will require several minutes to memorize. The second list presents familiar words, although with no apparent connection between them. It is much easier than the first. The third list can be memorized in one reading, because of the many associations already established among the words shown.

Schema. This suggests that people become efficient in learning various kinds of materials because they get a general pattern or *schema* into which the specific items fit neatly. Thus a child can go on an excursion and bring back a lengthy report of his observations. A chemist can read a technical article on bromine and days later repeat it in great detail, where a nonchemist would recall little. We hear bits of gossip about friends and remember them for long periods of time as part of our associations to that person's name but forget such items relating to strangers.

Our efficiency at these tasks seems to depend on the development of various schemata. City children do poorly at reporting country details; the savage who can track animals in dense jungle could get lost at Fifth Avenue and 42nd Street. Our language is structured conventionally so that adjectives precede nouns, verbs follow them, meaningful phrases are grouped, and so on. Remembering such material, therefore, fits into a pattern which is extensively

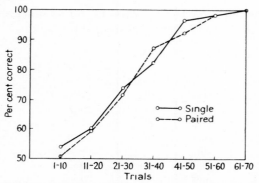

FIG. 7:2. Learning curve for a simple visual discrimination. The animal must choose between a small and a large circle to get food. He starts at approximately 50 per cent correct (chance) choices. He soon begins to improve and after 70 trials makes perfect runs. The close agreement of the two curves shows that he can learn equally well whether he sees the two circles simultaneously or in succession. The important point, however, is that some learning has taken place long before a perfect series of 10 choices is made. (*From Grice, 1949.*)

practiced and offers many close associations. These associations include cause-and-effect relations, general-specific and part-whole relations, learned classifications, similarities, contrasts, etc. In this sense, the laws of association of ideas are descriptive of man's processes of thinking. They also describe how he learns much everyday material.

The experimental approach. The modern psychologist does not object to this conception of how man thinks, as a succession of associations, a series of mental or nervous processes. However, he often raises objections to some of the so-called "laws of association of ideas" because they have limited value for many types of learning, *e.g.*, of skilled movements. Cause and effect, similarity, contrast, and such principles are of no use in this context. Modern psychology seeks general laws which apply to all kinds of responses and to all kinds of materials.

The observation of everyday occurrences is also unsatisfactory because the experi-

mentalist wants precise control of all conditions. Thus he devises nonsense syllables and other novel, unfamiliar tasks, sets up routines in laboratory procedures, eliminates distractions, and systematically varies such other factors as the motivational pressure to learn the task. Within this rigid framework of operating conditions, he is forced to define association with sharp precision. He therefore discards the general principle of association of ideas and instead defines association to mean that a specific situation has acquired the property of setting off an identifiable response. The initial situation is said to be associated with the phenomena that follow it. Since association always means that a response is attached to a stimulus or situation with which it was never before related, we can generalize or extend the concept of association to a definition of learning, as follows: Learning takes place *when a response formerly evoked by one situation is now given to a new situation which previously did not evoke it.* (Thus, in Watson's experiment on conditioning fear of a white rat, the responses of crying, squirming, and crawling away were not at first called forth by the presence of the rat; after learning, the rat evoked these actions. A new association had been set up.)

Strength of associative factors. Given a precise definition like this, we can measure the strength of some factors in associative learning. It is possible to plot a curve to show the regularity with which the desired response is set off by the stimulus presented. Thus Fig. 7:2 shows the progress of a group of 10 rats learning to get food by going to the smaller of two white circles in a choice box (Grice, 1949). In this situation, the rat at first would be expected to make the correct choice just by chance about half the time—the curve actually starts at about 51 per cent correct. As learning continues, the regularity with which the smaller circle is chosen steadily increases, until, after 60 choices, perfect performance is seen. The *association* of "small circle" with "getting food" has now been perfected. But it is important to note that the association was *imperfectly formed* much earlier; the signal value of the circle begins to influence the rat's behavior significantly after about 10 choices. (As we shall see later, some associations are established virtually instantaneously, *i.e.*, on the first choice. The type of learning situation involved here makes it possible for us to analyze the factors influencing speed and strength of association, which would get lost if such rapid learning were involved.)

Frequency. One factor in associative learning is that of frequency. Thus, in Grice's experiment just described, accuracy of association increases with the frequency of successful choices. It is customary to say that the association becomes "stronger" with repetition. Similarly we assume that students know more of a foreign language after two courses than after one, that factory workers are more skilled after 10 years' experience than 5, and so on.

Contiguity. Since Aristotle's basic law of association was that of contiguity in space and time, this has been a matter for much experimental study. It appears (Fig. 8:3) that the optimum for learning is close contiguity of the presented stimulus with the desired response, except that difficulties arise if the response comes first. The bell cannot become a signal for food if it follows the presentation of food (cf. page 281).

Recency. Generally speaking, we remember recent happenings better than those distant in time. An interesting experimental formulation of this principle comes from the study of maze learning in rats and humans. The typical maze (Fig. 7:3) consists of a series of choices of right and wrong paths to a goal (food, for the rat; praise, for the human subject). In rats particularly, the wrong choices nearest the goal are eliminated first; that is, perfect

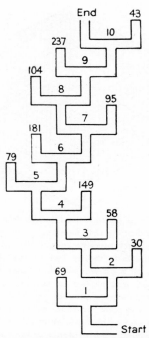

FIG. 7:3. A simple maze pattern. This is a stylus maze, *i.e.*, the blindfolded subject traces through the grooves with a metal stylus. He must learn to make the correct turns at the choice points, numbered from 1 to 10, and avoid the blind alleys. Number of errors made by a typical group of subjects on each alley is given by the figure at the end of the alley. On the average, turns near the goal are learned faster than those at the start, and both are better than the middle. (*Modified from Husband, 1931.*)

choices will be attained first at point 10, then 9, then 8, etc., on the maze shown. As the subject reaches the goal, he associates the most recent choice with the tension reduction.

Another way of saying the same thing is to say that modification of behavior is less as the distance from the goal (in either space or time) increases. This is the *goal-gradient* hypothesis. According to this principle, goals (rewards and punishments) distant from the response will have little effect on the response (cf. Fig. 8:13, page 305). This is especially true of children but appears in much adult behavior as well.[1]

[1] Thus one reason given for the frequent failure of profit-sharing plans to modify the behavior of

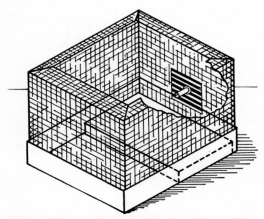

FIG. 7:4. Visual pattern used in one-trial condition-ing. In the end of the rat's living cage an opening was cut, and the black bakelite square striped with white lines was inserted. Shortly before the start of the experiment, all food was removed, and then all the animals. Food was placed on the protruding metal holder. Then rats were placed, one at a time, in the cage; when one took the food, he received a sharp shock to the end of his nose. With this single experi-ence, rats showed clear evidence of learning to avoid the striped pattern. (*From Hudson, 1950.*)

Other variables. Other factors, such as *familiarity* and *intensity*, undoubtedly affect the speed of formation of associations. Our observations on speed of learning nonsense syllables as opposed to words indicated that familiar materials can be organized into a memorized list more rapidly than unfamiliar items. It follows from this that *similarity* will be a factor. If learning task B involves items which resemble those in task A, the learning of B is affected (see the discussion of transfer and interference, below, pages 262–268). Usually, such similarity makes for faster association, but there are exceptions.

Intensity is another variable like simi-

larity, which is important but difficult to measure. It is impossible to set up a numeri-cal scale for the intensity of an experience in the same way that we can count the number of seconds or trials required to memorize a list. However, we do know that, within limits, making lights brighter and sounds louder speeds up animal and human learning.

A good illustration of the role of intensity can be got from Hudson's study of "one-trial learning" in the rat. Most animal learning requires several repetitions, but Hudson felt that an intense experience would set up an association in one trial. He inserted a distinctive pattern (Fig. 7:4) into the rat's cage, baited with food. When the rat nibbled at the food, he received an electric shock on his nose. After this, the appearance of the broadly striped pattern evoked clear avoidance responses (backing away, kicking sawdust over the object, etc.). As Grice's study shows, with only food as a reward, associations build up slowly; but with the intensification of an electric shock, an association can be estab-lished in one trial.

Most learning, among humans and animals, involves contiguity, frequency, recency, similarity, and intensity. How-ever, it is inevitable that psychologists should speculate on the question: which factor is absolutely essential for learning? This seems to be a question to which there is no answer. In another form it becomes: which factor alone can produce learning? Here the best case seems to be made for contiguity. Even here, the association of A with B seems to require repetition; that is, contiguity has to be reinforced by frequency.

Man is such a complex organism with such an enormous memory capacity that it is most difficult to set up simple learning tasks which will be learned in terms of a single factor. Even a simple association such as winking the eyelid when a buzzer

workers is that the bonuses are given only at the end of the year. One very successful plan seems to owe its excellent results to the fact that bonuses are handed out monthly—thus the *goal* is brought nearer to the work behavior it is expected to modify. The desired association is then easier to establish.

sounds is modified by numerous variables operating within the person.

Learning Curves

In a scientific psychology it is important not only to identify the various factors which are involved in the learning process, but also to measure and plot the speed of learning. To obtain a graphic representation of the learning process, and to study the effects of different factors on learning, we plot a *learning curve*.

One type of learning curve has already been shown (Fig. 7:2). In this case groups of 10 trials were lumped together and the number of correct responses in each set was plotted. The curve rises steadily until about trial 40 and then tapers off. It will necessarily become perfectly flat when the animal becomes completely accurate in its choices.

If we are dealing with a complex performance, each trial can be plotted separately. Thus a subject memorizing a list of 20 nonsense syllables can be scored on the number correctly anticipated on each trial. This curve will resemble that of Grice's discrimination problem. On the other hand, a rat learning a maze is scored in terms of the number of blind alleys he enters and other errors made. This curve will slope sharply downward and then level off; that is, the rat will eliminate errors until he finally runs the maze without a mistake. In industrial training, an "error" curve can be plotted in terms of the number of pieces spoiled by the learner (Fig. 7:5).

Another way of plotting a learning curve is to plot trials against time. A common laboratory task is that of having students learn to trace a star pattern while watching it in a mirror. The reversal of right-left and forward-backward movements when seen in mirror image makes this a most confusing task. One can see his pencil and also see where he wants it to go; but the

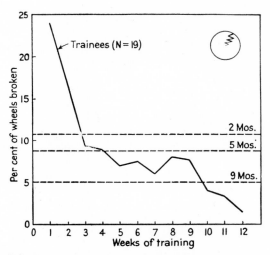

FIG. 7:5. Error curve in learning. The progress of learning can be plotted by decrease in errors, as well as increase in correct responses. This curve shows the gradual reduction in breakage of cutting wheels by industrial trainees. The dotted lines show the number usually broken by employees after 2, 5, and 9 months' experience; these trainees reached the 9-month level after only 10 weeks, indicating that the method is a good one. (*From Lindahl, 1945.*)

muscles move in a different direction. Thus the first trial will take a long time; this is gradually improved, until finally the subject reaches a smooth, rapid performance. This type of curve will drop and flatten out but of course cannot reach zero, as some measurable time is always required to trace the star.

The learning curve is smooth only when several persons or several trials are averaged. For any single subject, animal or human, the curve tends to fluctuate rather wildly. Trial 3 may be good but trial 4 may be very poor. We do not know what causes these variations, although we can often guess—for instance, if the human subject indicates that he is bored, is trying too hard, or is distracted by thinking of the beautiful blonde with whom he has a date for tonight. Individual fluctuations can be ironed out by plotting the averages for a group of subjects (Fig. 7:6). Chance factors cause one subject to improve while

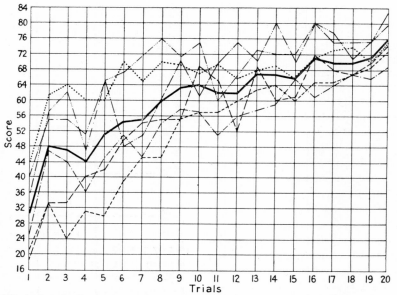

FIG. 7:6. Individual and group curves of learning. Six subjects were given a simple learning task involving substituting numbers for letters. Score is the number of digits written in 1-minute practice periods. Note the marked fluctuation from trial to trial for a specified person, and how these tend to smooth out when the scores are averaged by trials for the six subjects. With a larger group, the curve becomes quite regular. (*From Kingsley, 1946.*)

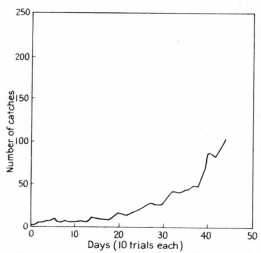

FIG. 7:7. A positively accelerated curve. Sometimes we get a learning task in which the subject makes very little progress for some time but eventually begins to improve and makes increasing progress every day. In this experiment the subject was perfecting a motor skill involving tossing and catching a ball. Note the slow improvement at first, rapid later on. (*From Swift, 1903.*)

another may deteriorate on any specific trial; the group curve thus gives us an estimate of the "true" course of learning without these chance variables.

The shape of the curve. Different studies have led to different-shaped learning curves. In most cases we get a *negatively accelerated* curve; most of the progress is in the early trials, slowing down toward completion of learning (Figs. 7:2, 7:5, and 7:6). A few studies have produced *positively accelerated* curves; progress is slow at first but speeds up toward the end (Fig. 7:7). Obviously this cannot continue indefinitely, although it may seem so if the experiment ends soon enough. A third type of curve is the *S-shaped curve;* all positively accelerated curves become S-shaped if learning continues, as one necessarily hits a ceiling somewhere (Fig. 7:8 shows an S-shaped curve).

The shape of the curve is determined in

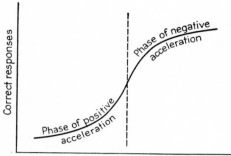

FIG. 7:8. The S-shaped learning curve. Some psychologists hold that the complete learning curve is S-shaped, as drawn here. One can get a positively accelerated curve, as in Fig. 7:7, if he stops at the right point; but the curve could not continue that way indefinitely. It must taper off and hit a ceiling somewhere. On the other hand, if our learning task is one where some prior improvement has taken place, our measures may start where the dotted line is drawn in, and the curve is the negatively accelerated learning curve, as in Fig. 7:2, 7:6, or 7:9.

part by the nature of the learning task. If one is memorizing material which is uneven in difficulty, learning will be negatively accelerated. The easy items will be learned quickly, while the difficult items will be picked up one by one; in this case it is common to speak of *diminishing returns* for equal amounts of practice. If, on the other hand, a task is very difficult at first but becomes easier with practice, the curve will be positively accelerated. Learning motor skills seems often to be of this character; Fig. 7:7 shows the progress of a subject in a ball-tossing study. Until some basic movements are learned, almost no progress is made. Then the process speeds up rapidly. If the experiment stops here, we have a positively accelerated curve. If the subject practices till he reaches his ceiling, the total curve will be S-shaped.

What do learning curves measure? The various kinds of curves we have described are actually plots of *performance*. The subject is presented with some kind of task, and if he is motivated, he will attempt to deal with the task. The psychologist

then records the quality of performance, in terms such as speed or accuracy. The implication is that these measures give an index of learning, but it is not always entirely adequate. Learning may go on for some time with little or no change in performance, as in the early stages of the positively accelerated curve.

Plateaus give another illustration of learning with no change in performance. Sometimes, in complex learning, we find a fairly long period of no improvement, followed by another spurt of progress. Figure 7:9 shows the record of a man learning to receive Morse code by telegraph sounder. In the middle portion of the graph, it will be noted that there is a considerable period of no progress. The explanation offered for this type of plateau runs as follows: in learning telegraphy, one must first learn to perceive and identify the sounds for individual letters. When he is quite familiar with the letters, he may broaden his span of attention and take in words without noting the separate letters. Later he may even take in phrases. It is suggested that, while one phase (letter

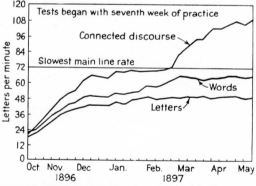

FIG. 7:9. Plateau in learning. Some complex learning tasks show a period of progress, then a flat level of performance, followed by another spurt. The topmost of the three curves shown here illustrates this well. The flat period is called a plateau. It is ended when the person begins to develop higher order habits, for handling Morse code in words and phrases rather than as isolated letters. (*Redrawn from Bryan and Harter, 1899.*)

learning) is being perfected, there may be no measurable improvement. When the person feels sure of his letters, he begins learning words, and the curve of progress starts upward again. This *higher level habit* interpretation of plateaus suggests that learning can be going on when the curve of performance is not climbing. The benefit in terms of performance comes later.

Plateaus are sometimes due to fatigue or boredom—loss of interest in the task. We are not sure, however, that even such plateaus do not mask some improvement in learning. Performance is not quite delicate enough to be a perfect indicator of rate of learning.

Efficiency in Serial Learning

Despite the fact that the performance curve is not a perfect index of learning from the scientific point of view, it is the only device now available. Furthermore, it corresponds with practical demands. If a person cannot perform, most schoolteachers (and employers) are likely to believe that he has not learned and deal with him accordingly. Efficiency in learning is thus characteristically gauged by performance.

Let us now get back to the problem of learning items in series. Because efficient performance in such learning is, in modern life, important for both child and adult, psychologists have conducted many experimental studies on the factors making for efficiency. Particularly important are *quantity* (size of task), *time distribution*, and *interaction effects* (influence of parts of the task upon each other).

Quantity. How large an assignment should teachers give? This is a question about which teacher and pupil opinions differ violently. Those receiving assignments will derive some pleasure from the experimental finding that shorter tasks are learned with relatively greater efficiency. An increase in the length of task requires more than the proportional increase in time and effort. Thus Henmon (1917) had subjects memorize lists of nonsense syllables, with results as follows:

Length of list presented, syllables	Average learning time per list, seconds	Time per syllable, seconds
10	120	12
20	400	20
30	870	29

Thus, for a given amount of associative learning, the 30-syllable task is more than twice as costly, or less than half as efficient, as the 10-syllable presentation.

Intraserial interference. This drop in efficiency for longer assignments seems to be a general characteristic of serial learning. It has been verified for poems, word lists, advertisements, and so on. The best explanation seems to be in terms of the *mutual interference* of responses (*proactive* and *retroactive* inhibition) within the series of associations.

Proactive inhibition is demonstrated by the fact that the first member of a list is learned more easily than the second, the second more easily than the third, and so on (to the middle of the list—see Fig. 7:10). Suppose you are trying to memorize the American Presidents in order. "Washington" will tend to be followed, not only by Adams, but also by Jefferson, Madison, etc. We might say that the first item is seen as a signal not only for item 2, but also for 3, 4, etc. This conflict of responses gets worse to the end of the list. The superiority of these earlier items is identified as a *primacy* factor in serial learning. Perhaps primacy is effective mostly because of the small number of interfering associations. However, as we get past the middle of the series, *recency* comes into the picture; the final items are again learned more rapidly. Compare the maze-learning data (Fig. 7:3).

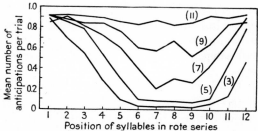

FIG. 7:10. The bow-shaped curve of serial learning. When one memorizes words or syllables in a series, he tends to learn the first members of the series, then the final items, and the middle last of all. These curves show the progress of learning a list of 12 syllables (each point is an average of 12 lists learned by 12 subjects). The curve marked (3) is an average of the results when the subject just recalled 3 of the 12 syllables; (11) is the curve when only a single error was made in recalling the list. Note that the middle syllables are learned much later than the others; this is explained by the operation of proactive and retroactive inhibition. (*From Ward, 1937.*)

Retroactive inhibition may also be a factor in producing the bow-shaped curve for serial memorization shown in Fig. 7:10. This concept will be elaborated below; we note here only that the later items in the list seem to interfere with recall of the preceding items. Thus proactive and retroactive inhibition would reach a peak in the middle of the list; and the longer the list, the greater the damage done by these inhibitory factors.

Distribution of practice. How shall the student most efficiently distribute his time? Is it better to spend 4 hours in 1 day on a difficult assignment, or 1 hour on each of 4 days? A host of studies confirm the view that distributed practice is better than massed practice.

Figure 7:11 shows the progress of learning to copy a design reversed in a mirror. Here improvement is measured by speed; so the learning curve slopes downward as less time is needed. The three groups of subjects were matched for speed on the first trial. Group I had 20 trials with no rest intervals; II, 20 trials with 1-minute rest between trials; III, 20 trials, one on each of

20 successive days (24-hour interval). As the curve shows, there was a decided superiority of both II and III over I. Studies using verbal and other materials have found this also to be true, but the 24-hour interval often gives a much larger advantage than in the study of mirror drawing. In fact, for complex learning tasks, the 24-hour spacing of trials seems to give optimum efficiency.

Materials which are very easy should be learned in one sitting (massed practice). In problem solving, where one needs time to find hidden relations, massed practice may help, but one may also get stuck in a rut; a time interval between trials may be advantageous in such a case. In no case can the time intervals be too long, or forgetting impairs the prior learning.

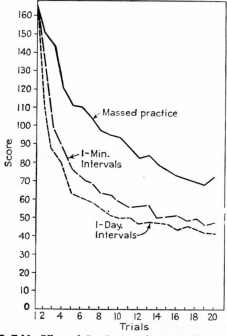

FIG. 7:11. Effect of distribution of practice. The upper curve represents progress (fewer errors) in a mirror drawing experiment, with no delay interval between trials. The middle curve is for a group which rested for 1 minute after each trial; the lowest curve (fastest progress) is for practice distributed one trial every 24 hours. (*From Lorge, 1930, page 16.*)

Considerable speculation plays over the fact that distributed practice is superior. Some authorities have suggested that *rehearsal during the interval* (even unconscious rehearsal) explains the superiority. *Fatigue* and *boredom* resulting from long massed trials may also slow down learning. Some experiments, however, lead us to doubt that fatigue and boredom are decisive, although they may, of course, be experienced in everyday learning. An intriguing theory is that the hypothetical "traces" in the nervous system require time to consolidate and grow. It was William James who suggested the provocative thought that "we learn to skate in summer and to swim in winter." Better than any of these proposals seems to be the idea that the *interferences* (proactive and retroactive inhibition) drop out during the interval of rest, and the pattern becomes clearly organized, thus allowing a more efficient learning and remembering of the correct material.

Transfer and Inhibition

So far we have been talking about the interaction of one part of a learning task with another part of the same task (intraserial). Fundamentally similar, but different in some respects, is the problem of interaction of different learning tasks. What effect does prior learning have upon subsequent learning? And what effect does the subsequent learning have upon memory for the material learned earlier? This is the problem of interserial effects.

It is generally found that learning a given kind of material today does have an effect upon learning similar material tomorrow. Thus, if one spends several hours memorizing poetry this week, he will be more efficient at poetry memorization next week than if he had not done so. This kind of improvement in later learning is referred to as *positive transfer*, or facilitation of the second learning activity. There are, however, instances in which learning of one task interferes with the acquisition of a later task; this, of course, is called *negative transfer*.

If we set up the above experiment a bit differently, we can measure the effect of later learning upon memory for material learned earlier. Thus, we can have people memorize list A, then list B, and then try to recall list A. If list B interferes with recall of A (as it frequently does), we have another variety of negative transfer. This particular experimental finding is often referred to as *retroactive inhibition*—implying that list B works backward in time to interfere with list A. (The users of the term did not, of course, believe in such an impossibility; it was understood that the process is an inhibition of the recall of A, not of the past learning.)

The similarity of this problem to that of interference effects within a learning list (see above) will be noted at once. We found in that instance that *proactive inhibition* operated to hinder learning of new items from the beginning toward the end of the list and that *retroactive inhibition* decreased efficiency of learning, starting at the end of the list and working backward to the beginning. Thus the middle of the list, being subject to both types of interference, was hardest to learn.

If we simply divided one long list into two short lists and memorized the first completely before starting the second—as good judgment dictates in many cases—we might expect that retroaction and proaction would operate in just the same way as they did when one was learning a single list. However, when we divide the list and memorize each half separately, at least three new variables are introduced. (1) There is always some activity between the two lists—the *interpolated activity*. This is the most important factor, as experiments show. (2) Another variable is *order of learning.* In memorizing the first list, we are acquiring methods and attitudes which help efficiency. Thus list B may be learned faster because it came second, and thus benefited from these improved techniques. (3) The third variable is *functional isolation.* As we have seen in our discussions of perception, isolated material stands out; it is perceived more easily and learned more efficiently. When lists A and B are separated, there is more isolation of material and hence better perception. (For example, there are two groups of items which benefit from primacy, and two from recency, instead of only one.) If there is a sizable time interval between A and B, this helps isolation and reduces interference. If A is *overlearned* (practiced beyond one perfect recall), it tends more to be isolated as a perceptual unit, with less chance of being confused with items of list B.[1] These three factors help to explain the results for long and short learning assignments, cited above, the advantage to short assignments arising especially from the second and third of these factors.

The typical experimental model for studies of transfer of training and retroactive inhibition has the following design:

Initial period	Interpolated activity	Final period
Experimental group: Learn list A........	Learn list B	Retest on A
Control group: Learn list A..............	Rest	Retest on A

Let us see how this design is used in the study of positive transfer. We may be interested in the question: does the study of Latin improve one's performance in English? In this case A becomes skill in English, B, skill in Latin. Our subjects will be divided into two groups, which should be equal in skill with English—*i.e.*, they have learned English materials to an equal level of performance. Now the experimental group studies Latin for a year, while the control group does not. Then we test both groups on skill with English. If positive transfer is present, the experimental group will have gained over the control group in English performance.

As a practical aside, we may note that these studies have shown little or no positive transfer from such courses as Latin and mathematics to other academic skills. The common belief that these classical disciplines "train the mind" arose out of the fact that students taking these courses were usually superior in all fields. Thus, before taking Latin, they were already superior in English. This is a type of error which has been very common in experimentation on educational problems, although it is now, fortunately, rare.

To transform the experimental design shown above, so that we get a measure of retroactive inhibition, we may reduce the amount of preliminary practice on A, and also the time intervals between activities. Generally speaking, retroactive inhibition is discovered only when original learning and interpolated learning are close together in time.

[1] The alert student will note that the superiority of functionally isolated materials, for learning purposes, seems to run counter to the common observation as to the superiority of the whole method. It might appear that breaking an assignment up into parts would lead to increased efficiency, based on functional isolation. To some extent this is true; when we are memorizing nonsense material, part learning does offer this advantage. However, meaningful material can more advantageously be studied by the whole method, for in this case one is trying to learn a pattern of connecting ideas, and this pattern is destroyed by the part method. The whole method, on the contrary, gives a kind of functional isolation to this meaningful pattern. Generally, we tend to use both the whole and part methods interchangeably: one studies the assignment as a whole to isolate its logical structure, and then proceeds to segregate difficult parts for special attention. Functional isolation can operate in either kind of learning; and any advantage of one method over the other is attributable to which kind of isolation offers relatively greater returns in the particular situation.

TABLE 7:1. Retroactive Inhibition Produced by Learning Materials Similar to or Dissimilar from the Original Learning
(*Based on McGeoch and McDonald, 1931*)

	Percentage of original list recalled	*Readings required for relearning*
Group learning:		
Synonyms............	12	9.1
Antonyms...........	18	7.0
Unrelated adjectives..	22	6.7
Nonsense syllables....	26	7.2
Numbers............	37	5.1
Group resting (reading *College Humor*).......	45	5.2

An experiment on retroactive inhibition. It will clarify the preceding discussion of method, and the following discussion of principles, if we describe one of these experiments in detail. In a study by McGeoch and McDonald (1931), all subjects memorized a list of common adjectives. This was followed by an interval of 10 minutes during which different groups engaged in differing activities. One group rested; another group learned a second list of adjectives, composed of synonyms of the first list. A third group memorized antonyms for adjectives in the first list, and others learned unrelated adjectives, nonsense syllables, and numbers, respectively. At the end of the 10-minute interpolated period, all groups first tried to recall all the adjectives in the original list, and then relearned the original list.

The results are summarized in Table 7:1. It is clear that there was a great deal of interference (retroactive inhibition) produced by the interpolated learning. The group experiencing maximum interference included those subjects who had to memorize adjectives synonymous with the original items; they lost 88 per cent in 10 minutes, recalling only 12 per cent of the adjectives. Even the interpolated task of memorizing numbers, which certainly would not be confused with the adjectives, caused a loss of 63 per cent. The latter figure seems less impressive when we note that even the group reading *College Humor* forgot 55 per cent of the adjectives. Forgetting of such material as a list of adjectives obviously occurs with great speed; however, the interpolated learning reduced efficiency of recall much below the level for the resting group.

We may generalize from this and similar researches that learning activity, when interpolated in this way, interferes with memory more than does nonlearning activity; and also, that the greater the similarity of initial to interpolated learning, the more forgetting of the original material. This generalization has been verified by other investigators using quite a wide variety of learning material (numbers, geometrical designs, nonsense syllables, etc.).

An experiment on transfer of training. The results obtained in studies of transfer have depended very much on the design of the experiment. It has sometimes seemed that the only improvement carried over from one learning task to another was something in the way of method (how the learner approached his problem), familiarity (getting used to the test situation), and so on. Recent experiments have been more precisely designed and have made it possible to measure more accurately the nature and amount of transfer.

For such a study the method of paired associates happens to be particularly useful. In a typical instance, a subject is shown one word (on the left of a learning apparatus), and, 2 seconds later, a paired word on the right, for example:

WINDOW—GRASS

His task is to learn to speak the second word before it appears. Since we have, in this form of learning, a clearly separate stimulus and response, we can vary each

TABLE 7:2. Effects of Having Identical Stimuli and Identical Responses, in Terms of Transfer to Later Learning
(*Based on Bruce, 1933*)

First list learned		Second list learned		Condition	Percentage of trials saved
Stimulus	Response	Stimulus	Response		
Reg*	Kiv	Reg*	Zam	Stimulus same Response different	−9
Lan	Gip*	Fix	Gip*	Stimulus different Response same	+37
Xal	Pom	Bef	Yor	Stimulus different Response different	+16

* These items are samples to show the identity of stimulus (or response) from one list to the next. Thus *reg* was a stimulus for kiv in list 1, for zam in list 2. Similarly, *gip* was the response for lan in list 1, for fix in list 2.

of them independently. (This is impossible in memorizing poetry, series of dates, etc.) Using this procedure, we can design lists for memorizing which contain identical stimuli, identical responses, or no identity whatever.

In the experiment performed by Bruce (1933), two lists of paired associates were learned by each subject. The problem was to ascertain the effect carried over from learning the first to learning the second list; *i.e.*, did the learning of the first help or hinder in learning the second? One experimental group received a second list containing identical stimuli, but new responses; a second group, new stimuli but the identical responses; a third, new stimuli and new responses; and a fourth or control group learned only the second list. (Three examples are given in Table 7:2 to clarify this experimental plan.) The efficiency, or transfer effect, is shown at the right of the table, in terms of how well the experimental compared with the control group.

We are first struck with the −9 per cent entry where the stimulus is the same, response different. This is interference, not facilitation. *Negative transfer*, then, can be expected when we try to break an old habit and learn a new one of the same kind.

(When S is presented, we must stop giving R₁, and instead give R₂.)

On the other hand, facilitation or *positive transfer* occurs when one is required to give the old response to a new stimulus. Here it is not necessary to break a habit, but only to produce a familiar response in a new situation. (Consider the thrill of the youngster who has painfully learned that $2 \times 3 = 6$, and later discovers that $3 \times 2 = 6$! He has only to attach the response to a new stimulus.) In Bruce's experiment, this condition clearly gave positive transfer, amounting to 37 per cent increase in speed of learning.

When both stimuli and responses are new, no positive transfer would be expected. Actually Bruce finds a saving of 16 per cent, which may be due to the subjects' becoming more familiar with nonsense syllables, with the laboratory situation, etc. Other investigators have reported zero saving for this type of learning assignment.

Principles of interserial effects. These experiments, while they are only a small sample of what has been done in this troublesome area, will illustrate the ways in which psychologists have attacked the problem. To present all the experimental evidence would be tiresome and would be inappropriate in an introductory text. Let us therefore simply pull together some of the general principles about the effect of one learning activity upon another learning activity.

1. *Whenever two learning tasks present the same stimuli but call for different responses, interference occurs, its amount increasing with degree of stimulus similarity.*[1] Some students may have learned this painfully, by taking two beginning language courses at the same time. The stimulus (English word) tends to set off conflicting responses (French, German); and the student's grade suffers. This problem of conflicting responses to the same stimulus is illustrated in the following diagram. It will be useful to keep this picture in mind, as it helps in understanding later discussions of thinking and personality.

This is involved also in McGeoch's study of retroactive inhibition. When the interpolated learning presented similar adjectives, the subject became confused as to which response he should give.

2. *If two learning tasks present different stimuli, to elicit the same responses, facilitation occurs, the amount increasing with the degree of similarity of stimuli.* As diagramed below, this suggests that, as S_1 and S_2 resemble each other more closely, the connection to set off R will be established more rapidly. Thus a dog will learn to do his tricks for a new master more rapidly if his tone of voice and other characteristics are closely similar to those of the dog's trainer. Conditioned fears (see page 99) transfer in this way.

[1] Based on the treatment of this problem by Osgood (1949).

3. *If both stimulus and response are different in the second learning task, interference occurs unless it is masked by such factors as positive transfer of technique and familiarity with the situation.* In this case, when the stimuli become more similar, the interference becomes greater.

The learning of similarity and difference. Let us pause for a moment and relate these experimental studies in the laboratory to everyday learning. A major portion of the task of memorizing serial lists of items is a matter of recognizing similarities and differences. In learning a list of dates, for example, one focuses first on the similarity (all items are of the same classification) and then begins to differentiate them in such a way that each elicits a distinctive response (date of Magna Carta, date of Russian Revolution, etc.).

In the chapter on thinking we shall expand on the importance of this process. In early life, the child takes some time to learn that a given object is the same from one occasion to the next, but when he learns this, he perceives many other objects as being identical. This is the process of *generalization,* or association by similarity. At first it is carried too far; but gradually the child comes to observe the slight differences (to him) between a fork and a spoon, a car and a wagon, a dog and a cat.

The child continues to improve in his perceptions of similarities and differences, but not equally in all directions. Just how accurate he must be in perceiving depends on the task at hand. The difference between sodium chloride and potassium chloride is unimportant to the cook but very significant to the chemist. Most spectators react to identical twins by noting their similarity; the parent must distinguish them. For day-to-day purposes (and all perceiving is purposive), there is considerable economy in making rough classifications of types of houses, breeds of dogs, or kinds of illness. The architect, the dog breeder, or the physician must be more discriminating; their purposes demand clear discrimination of differences.

Similarity associations seem to be made with less effort and in less time than difference judgments. The child who has been frightened by a rabbit will generalize his fear to a white fur muff, and this will occur quickly, with no apparent learning time; for him to differentiate the muff from the animal does require time and effort, *i.e.*, learning. For this simple kind of generalizing we use the phrase *equivalence of stimuli*. This simply means that we often perceive a new situation as being in essence just the same as a prior one; thus one may behave identically to all policemen, all store clerks, and so on. With repeated contact we become aware of differences and modify our behavior to fit these differences (discriminative learning).

This process of perceiving differences seems fundamental to the kind of learning we have been discussing (serial learning). Look at the list of nonsense syllables on page 253. While they are obviously different, when you close the book and try to recall them, each seems very much like all the others. It takes time and concentration to bring the differences into the foreground so that each can be named in its proper position. This difficulty is not nearly so apparent with the lists of common nouns. One has had more experience with these words and knows the differences in meaning for each of them. If you go on a summer vacation and visit only one national park, you have no trouble recalling its name; but if you visit several, you may well have blockages on naming them until you have described your travels several times. If you have a very vivid experience in one park, it will stand out (be perceived differently) and so will be recalled more quickly than the others. Americans in Japan (and Japanese in America) have trouble in associating names with faces at first—they all look alike. Only with familiarity are differences seen.

Stimulus equivalence. In discussing motives and emotions, we pointed out that the organism learns to perceive certain objects as goals to be approached, and others to be avoided. This learning is not highly specific; similar objects tend to be perceived as identical. Little Johnny learns to like roast beef, and this readily transfers to other meats of similar appearance. Sam may repeatedly fall in love, and each of his sweethearts resembles all the others. In such cases we spoke of "equivalent stimuli" producing identical responses.

The experiments on retroactive inhibition and transfer get at the same phenomenon, but emphasizing now the learning process rather than the function of satisfying need. Our concern is to show how confusion and error may make for inefficiency, whereas repetition of similar impressions makes for efficient learning.

In Bruce's experiments on retroactive inhibition and transfer, only one of the three variable patterns clearly brings out the process of stimulus generalization or stimulus equivalence. This is the condition in which the stimuli differ but the response is the same. Here we have a situation much like everyday life. When we change from one car to another, we manage to shift gears correctly, even though the size, shape, and position of the shift lever may vary. The more the structural parts resemble each other, the greater the transfer. This ease of transfer has not always existed; years ago, the stimulus "shift into low" set off a forward lever motion in one car, backward in another. It was necessary for the driver to *differentiate* what would otherwise be equivalent stimuli, if he was to make the correct response. (Here the stimuli tended to be perceived as the same, but the response had to be different—this led to confusion, which we call *negative transfer*, or *interference*.)

Making a different response to a familiar stimulus is always confusing. Even more upsetting, sometimes, is the task of learning both new stimuli and new responses. It is probably fortunate that we memorize our addition combinations, multiplication tables, and language patterns early in life. Perhaps children do not find this repetitive rote learning as monotonous and irritating as do adults.

In practical life similar responses to equivalent stimuli make possible a great deal of efficiency. We press certain kinds of objects (doorbells, switches, buzzers); we pull other objects, twist still others. Most of our routine movements readily transfer to equivalent stimuli, and this seems to be the way in which complex motor skills become possible. Without transfer such learning would offer far greater difficulty.

It is also important to note that transfer of a practical and significant kind occurs when we learn *methods* of aproaching a task. A student who has learned one foreign language may do better with his second, not because of the transfer of specific words (this is likely, if anything, to be negative transfer because of variation in spelling and pronunciation), but because he develops response patterns which make for efficient studying and organization. He may learn to use index cards for memorizing new words; or, in a broader sense, he may learn how to analyze and identify tenses, sentence structures, etc., in a useful manner. If we let R in our diagram represent method of attack, then this kind of positive transfer follows pattern (2) above—new stimulus, old response.

The difference between positive and negative transfer can again be stated and illustrated by reference to this matter of learning a new language. Students invariably find that it is easier to acquire a reading knowledge than spoken fluency in a foreign tongue. Reading permits maximum operation of positive transfer: the new printed stimulus is associated with a well-learned S-R pattern. Thus one learns that the French word "*enfant*" should evoke the meaning response "child." But spoken speech elicits negative transfer, the interference of old with new responses. The student tends to say "infant," whereas he should say "ahnfahn." Thus many people retain severe accents even after many years in a new land; and bilingual children are handicapped by tendencies to stutter, or become educationally retarded because of this negative transfer which prevents the efficient use of either language.

Education, training within industry, and even the ordinary processes of transmitting information by speech and writing are affected by positive and negative transfer. It will be expedient, however, to consider these implications in later chapters where they can be properly related to some other psychological factors. Real human behavior is extraordinarily complex; when we dissect out a specific process such as transfer, we eliminate other variables for teaching purposes. To use such knowledge, the student must develop skill in identifying these simple phenomena in a more complicated context.

Forgetting

Learning is a bidirectional process. We advance and then retreat; we acquire new response patterns, but, unfortunately, they do not always remain with us. The negative phase of this process is known as *forgetting*.

When we become analytical about these phenomena, we find it necessary to identify three aspects rather than two. These three are *acquisition*, *retention*, and *reproduction*. Acquisition has already been discussed, although more varieties of acquisition remain to be treated in subsequent chapters.

Retention concerns the stage intervening between study and the examination, between learning and the use of the learned patterns. Learning, obviously, would be futile without retention. If one had to learn anew each day all his skills, man would live at the level of the amoeba; in fact, the race would long since have become extinct. It is possible, by consideration of brain-injury cases, operations on animals, etc., to show that retention is a function of the neural cells making up the cortex of the cerebrum. Beyond this we do not know much about the nature of retention. When we speak of *memory traces*, we do not refer to any physical, chemical, or electrical changes in the brain which are now known to occur. Perhaps, some day, neurological research will succeed in identifying the cell processes which underlie memory; at present our knowledge of this field is inferred from an analysis of what was learned and is remembered.

Reproduction refers to the testing of memory—to the ability to reproduce responses previously learned, when the appropriate stimulus is presented. The lad who recites "The boy stood on the burning deck" at a school assembly is *reproducing* a response pattern learned earlier. Reproduction is the use function of learning; we learn in order that we can reproduce the material as required. The savage who learns to track game, to use arrow and spear, would die if he could not reproduce the results of his learning. It is well for us to keep constantly in mind the fact that these "higher mental processes," learning, thinking, and the like, are ultimately related to homeostasis and need satisfaction. If the learned response could not be reproduced, it would be impossible to achieve tension reduction and the organism would die.

The measurement of forgetting. It is obvious that we can measure the extent of forgetting by determining what remains, *i.e.*, the amount reproduced. There are several common methods for testing memory; all show that forgetting proceeds at a parallel rate, but they differ in sensitivity.

The application of one might indicate a total loss of the learned material, while others would show some retention. These are, in fact, the same as the methods of measuring progress in learning (page 251): the method of *recall* of "retained members"; the method of *recognition;* the method of *rearrangement* (a variation upon recognition; in this test one may be required to arrange events in chronological order or to match names of authors with books or to place pieces of equipment in their proper relations to each other); and the method of *relearning.*

The method of relearning has been employed to study very long time retention (William James relearned some poems he had memorized 40 years previously and found evidence of some retention even after this time lapse). It can also be utilized in determining memory for events and influences of which the person is not consciously aware. An unusual example of such an investigation is that of Burtt (1932).

Burtt read selected passages of Greek epic poetry (in the original) to his infant son, between the ages of 15 and 36 months. Each passage was 20 lines in length and was repeated 90 times before going on to a new one. Later, at the age of eight years, the boy memorized the Greek poems, including some passages of equal length which had not been read to him. The results indicated a positive saving of 27 to 30 per cent for the passages heard in infancy; apparently there was some memory trace, even though we should doubt that much learning activity went on with passive listening to words in a strange language.

The rate of forgetting. A major purpose in devising measures of memory is that of ascertaining the speed with which we forget. Certainly at times the rate is dismayingly rapid.

This is one of the earliest problems attacked by experimental psychologists. Ebbinghaus, having devised the nonsense

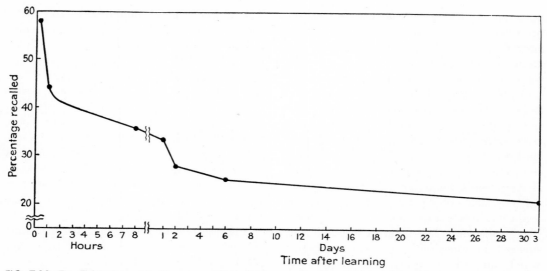

FIG. 7:12. The Ebbinghaus retention curve. Note that as much is lost during the first 20 minutes as during the next month. After one day the rate of decline becomes rather slow, and there is no evidence that the curve ever reaches zero. The loss is less rapid for meaningful material, but the general shape of the curve remains the same. (*Data from Ebbinghaus, 1913.*)

syllable as a learning task, used it in his monumental study on memory. His general procedure was to memorize a list of syllables, then relearn them after a predetermined number of hours. Then he would memorize a new list of presumably equal difficulty, and relearn it after a different time interval. He repeated this with hundreds of different lists. While his technique has been improved upon in later years, the shape of the curve of retention (or forgetting) as he determined it has been confirmed. We therefore reproduce in Fig. 7:12 the original Ebbinghaus curve of retention.

As this figure indicates, forgetting is continuous and is most rapid in its early stages. The amount forgotten in the first 24 hours may be as great as in the succeeding 5 days. After the first few days, the decline is very gradual. Remember that in McGeoch's study of a list of adjectives, 55 per cent was lost in 10 minutes.

It will be noted that the curve is shown as approaching but never reaching the base line. This seems to be correct. Apparently one never completely forgets any experience, although he may encounter great difficulty in recalling it. This conclusion fits in with clinical experience, in which it appears that the memory of a childhood occurrence may determine one's behavior 30 or 40 years later, even though it is consciously forgotten, *i.e.*, not subject to recall. We shall devote more attention to this aspect of forgetting in a later chapter.

The essential nature of forgetting. Since we do not know the neurological character of memory traces, it may seem obvious that we cannot know much about the nature of the process which is operating as forgetting goes on. It is, however, possible to vary certain external conditions and study variations in the forgetting rate. This technique has been applied especially to one very important question: is forgetting merely a passive process of decay, or is it an active function?

Traditionally the view has been adopted that memory traces, once formed, begin to disappear. Their loss has been compared by various theorists to the oxidation of iron as it rusts, to grass growing over an unused path, and so on. While these comparisons undoubtedly have poetic or imaginative value, recent experiments prove them to be misleading if not completely incorrect.

It is not time, but what happens in time, that determines the rate of forgetting. The key to this observation has already been given with the experiments on retroactive inhibition (see page 264). These studies showed that various activities, interpolated immediately after learning or before recall, affected memory for learned material. In one experiment reported, a difference in interpolated activity accounted for a difference of 33 per cent in amount recalled. Maximum forgetting was associated with the interpolated task of memorizing synonyms of the original words; minimum forgetting was associated with resting. A new learning activity tends to inhibit memory of immediately prior learning; and the more similar the tasks, the greater the loss of efficiency.

It can be deduced from this that minimum forgetting should occur when there is minimal activity following learning. The closest approximation to this condition with human subjects is sleep. It is thus crucial to our problem to ascertain, what is the effect of sleep upon the rate of forgetting?

Jenkins and Dallenbach (1924) answered this question by experiment. They had groups of subjects memorize nonsense syllables at different times during the day. Some learning was scheduled late in the evening, and the subjects went to sleep as soon as possible after learning the list. They were awakened at varying time intervals for testing. Some sessions began in the morning; the retention tests were given after the same number of hours as for the sleepers, but in this case these hours were full of normal activities, including classes, conversation, study, etc. As can be seen from Fig. 7:13, there was a decisive differ-

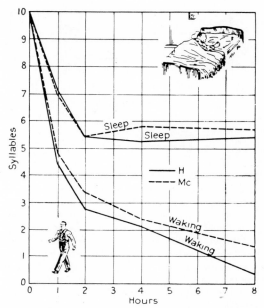

FIG. 7:13. Relation of sleep to retention. The upper curves show the average number of syllables recalled by each subject after various periods of sleep; the lower curves are for the same subjects, after equal intervals awake and active. The advantage of studying just before going to sleep is obvious. (*From Jenkins and Dallenbach, 1924.*)

ence in favor of sleep as leading to better memory. This difference is small at the first hour (the subjects may not have gone to sleep promptly) but is relatively large for 8-hour and longer periods. Forgetting over 24-hour periods is less if learning was followed immediately by sleep, greater if learning was followed by activity.

It may be urged that humans are not completely inactive, even in sleep. Most of us dream; some talk and walk in their sleep. What would be the effect of complete inactivity? Dallenbach turned to animal experiments for a procedure not suitable for humans. He taught cockroaches to run a maze for food. Following learning, some were packed tightly in a dark box where they went to sleep. Others were kept in an active state by walking on a treadmill. The inactive cockroaches showed less forgetting than the active group (Fig. 7:14).

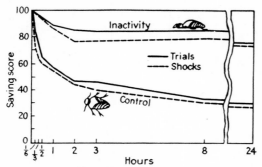

FIG. 7:14. Effect of inactivity on forgetting in the cockroach. Cockroaches were packed in containers which virtually prevented movement and were placed in a quiet, dark closet immediately after learning; their retention scores are shown in the upper curve (inactivity). Another group was normally active (control, lower curve). The saving due to inactivity is clear. A third group was forced to unusual activity by putting them on a treadmill; they lost even more than the control group. (*Modified from Minami and Dallenbach, 1946.*)

Thus it appears that cessation of activity immediately after learning will reduce the amount of interference and thus improve memory performance.

Some facts remain unexplained if we state that *all* forgetting is due to interpolated activity following learning. Both Figs. 7:13 and 7:14 show a certain amount of loss during the first hour or so after learning, regardless of activity status. Also, it will occur to most students that, if forgetting is due to activity, successive days of normal action should eliminate more and more of the learned material, but in fact, it is during the first few days that most of the loss occurs. It seems that there is something especially significant about the period shortly following learning.

This thought is strengthened by the phenomenon of *retrograde amnesia*. Often a blow on the head will cause loss of memory for events over a period of time, extending back for some hours prior to the accident. It is as though certain memory traces had not quite "set"—had not quite got themselves firmly established in the nervous system. The blow causes them to be lost.

Duncan (1949) proved that it is actually the first minute after learning which is crucial in this "setting" process. He had rats learn a simple avoidance problem. Immediately after a correct run the rat was picked up and given an electroconvulsive shock of the kind now used in treating psychotics. His results are summarized in Fig. 7:15, which shows that, if the electroshock is delayed as much as 5 minutes, relatively little loss of memory occurs; but within the first minute the disruptive effect is great.

Because of these facts (the rapidity of loss just after learning, the failure of interference to keep piling up, and the effect of shock), many psychologists hold that there are *two* processes involved in forgetting: the effect of *activity*, which the retroactive inhibition and sleep experiments show so well;

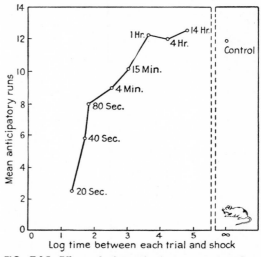

FIG. 7:15. Effect of electroshock on retention. Rats were trained to run from an electrified grid to avoid electric shock, one training trial being given each day. At varying times after completion of the trial, they were given electroconvulsive cerebral shocks of the type used in treating psychotic patients. As the curve shows, electroshocks given 1, 4, or 14 hours after the learning trial had no effect on memory (scores as high as the control group). With intervals of less than 1 hour, however, the loss in retention is great, and if it is less than 1 minute, most of the learning effect is wiped out. (*From Duncan, 1949.*)

and another process, a kind of *solidifying* of impressions, which endures for only a short time.

The first of these processes is easy to understand. We think of the organism, trying to satisfy motives, trying to perceive the environment correctly and deal with it adequately. If one object (*A*) is met, and the organism learns how to respond—then a rather similar object (*B*) must be handled differently, there will be confusion. The sight of either *A* or *B* will tend to set off both actions; the acts will block each other; and it appears to an observer that no learning has taken place. According to this view, it is not time, but the number of new faces and names we have learned, that cause us to forget our college chums; not time, but a mass of new experiences, that causes the fading of particular memories.

As we noted in our analysis of perceiving, the principle of *segregation* is important. An object is better perceived if it is sharply isolated from other objects. Similarly, memories are better maintained if they are clearly set apart from others. An incident on vacation, in Yellowstone Park, perhaps, may be easily recalled years later, while an equally vivid occurrence in the home, much more recent, has faded. The vacation memory is, so to speak, protected against interference by being isolated; other events do not become confused with it. Thus cues for the recall of the incident will always lead straight to it; they do not also evoke a hundred other memories which block out the one for which we are looking.

An awareness of the principle of interference, therefore, leads to practical applications such as this: try to isolate important memories and keep them from getting confused with similar but less important items. In learning names and faces, study each one carefully before going on to the next, and look for distinctive features in each. In studying, avoid having similar activities too close together; thus, do not

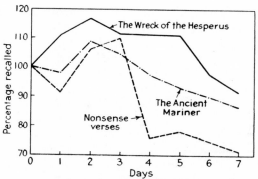

FIG. 7:16. Reminiscence. Obviously reminiscence (higher memory score after a delay than at the final practice trial) can appear only if learning is less than perfect. If one makes a perfect score on the final trial, no higher score is possible. If meaningful material is partly learned, a retest after a day or two may show better performance than at the close of the learning period. The above curves show reminiscence in poetry memorizing. The 100 score is arbitrarily taken as the best performance in the learning series. (*From Ballard, 1913.*)

study two foreign languages in immediate succession. It is a good idea for a young couple to "go away" on a honeymoon; the memories of this pleasant period will be kept apart and can be recalled later when domestic frictions may make it seem that the marriage has always been unhappy.

Reminiscence. Let us now consider some special phenomena in the field of forgetting. One very interesting instance is the phenomenon called *reminiscence*. This term is used in technical psychology to refer to the curious case in which memory is actually *better*, some time after learning, than at the point where learning stopped. Thus, suppose you read a short poem through at this time, and immediately try to recall it. An hour later you attempt another recall and actually give a better performance than before. This improvement (where we would expect forgetting) has been given the name reminiscence. Data from an illustrative experiment are shown in Fig. 7:16 (Ballard, 1913).

It was once suggested that reminiscence was due to rehearsal of the material during the intervening time. Experiments proved that this was not correct; rehearsal can be prevented and yet reminiscence occurs. There are three factors, these experiments show, which favor reminiscence. They are: (1) use of meaningful material (as compared with the nonsense material so often used for laboratory purposes); (2) incomplete learning (stopping the practice before a perfect performance has been achieved); and (3) strong motivation to recall the material.

These three facts lend themselves to the following explanation: there is an active process of organizing material which goes on during learning and may continue after learning, especially if the person is interrupted just before he has grasped all the material. Meaningful tasks can be organized into a sensible pattern, whereas nonsense syllables cannot. And a person with a strong desire to remember will probably continue, perhaps unconsciously, this organizing process.

This looks like the "closure" phenomenon encountered in our discussion of the perception of incomplete drawings (page 221). We noted in that connection that the organism does not just take in perceptual material; the picture observed is subject to changes which will make a "good" pattern. The same process would account for reminiscence. One is trying to complete the learning task, to get a "good" organization of the memory material. Always man is trying to satisfy his needs, grasp his environment, deal effectively with the facts his perceptions bring to him.

The effect of altered environment. Learning tends, on many occasions, to be specific to a particular environment. Children who can recite their numbers in the schoolroom often fail at home; animals trained to do a trick in the laboratory sometimes cannot duplicate it in the home cage. Carr (1925) has given an interesting illustration of this phenomenon in the following quotation:

An individual lived for several years in China and laboriously acquired the ability to speak the Chinese language. Upon his return to this country for a couple of years' vacation, he found to his dismay that his ability to speak and understand this language had practically disappeared by the end of this time. Naturally he expected that a considerable amount of effort and time would be required to relearn the language, but to his surprise he found that he was able to speak the language quite fluently upon his return to China.[1]

Everything one learns is isolated from the total learning situation, but this isolation is rarely complete. We are aware of specific tasks to be learned, but our sense organs are bombarded simultaneously by many other stimuli. These other cues become indirectly or weakly associated with the task on which we are focused; if they are present at the time of recall, we may be helped a great deal. If remembering is attempted in a new environment, the absence of accustomed cues may hinder recall; indeed, stimuli from the new situation may evoke competing responses in sufficient strength to block memory entirely. Dulsky (1935) verified the phenomenon experimentally by presenting paired syllables against one background for learning, and against another background for recall. There was a loss in accuracy as compared with a group which had the same background for both learning and recall. Another study (Abernethy, 1940) showed that students do less well on examinations when moved to a different classroom, or when proctored by a different instructor. The loss in recall was greatest when both room and proctor were changed from the original learning combination.

Incidental learning. If, as suggested in the preceding paragraphs, one learns not only a specific task, but also the task in a complex environmental setting, then it seems

[1] Carr (1925), pp. 251–252. Reprinted by permission of Longmans, Green & Co.

to follow that we learn a great deal without definite motivation. Certainly the students were not intentionally associating their knowledge with their classroom. And to do so would be unadaptive, since skills should be available for use elsewhere besides in the place where they were acquired. Any learning of that kind must have been incidental.

It may be, however, that it would be wrong to stress incidental learning as the explanation for these memory losses. If we set up experiments deliberately to test for incidental learning, we get just about nothing. An excellent illustration comes from the Bell Telephone records, prepared to show the effects on sound of screening out certain wave frequencies. The same speech is played over and over again, with minor changes in wave pattern, and the students are directed to note the effect of these variations in the quality of the sound. After 30 repetitions of the speech, the instructor asked the students to write it from memory. Not a single one, among 30 students, recalled it correctly, but a speech of the same length took only five trials when these same subjects were set to memorize it.

These and similar experiments indicate that incidental learning, to the extent that it exists, is not very important. Then how can we explain the loss in memory efficiency when the students were changed to a different room? A plausible alternative is that any change in the external environment may set off certain conflicting responses, which interfere with those we desire to recall. The man who learned Chinese returned to America, where all kinds of stimuli tended to evoke responses in English. When he returned to China, these interferences disappeared.

All this is a far cry from the old theory that forgetting was just a process of gradual atrophy from disuse. No valid data prove that disuse, the mere lapse of time, causes

any forgetting.[1] In senility, an individual may learn very poorly (cannot recall what happened yesterday) but may remember childhood incidents 70 years past. Perhaps one never really forgets anything. Much, and perhaps all, forgetting is merely the active process of overlaying prior by later learning. This would suggest that, with appropriate techniques, we could uncover these past, "forgotten" memories. Much of the work now being done by clinical psychologists involves just that.

SUMMARY

This chapter has presented an introduction to the problems of learning. Any modification of behavior or perception as a result of experience is defined as learning; the association of one idea with another, or of ideas in series, was taken as an important example in terms of which methods and results could be discussed. This type of modification by experience occurs throughout life but makes up an especially important part of formal schooling.

The environment presents a mass of stimuli to the person. The number of associations he might form is infinite. He must actively select from this mass in terms of his motives and the specific instructions under which he is operating. The speed or accuracy with which he forms the desired associations can be plotted on a learning curve.

When associations must be formed in a series, two kinds of interaction effect develop. Intraserial effects are mostly inhibitory in character; proactive inhibition refers to the fact that the earlier part of the list interferes with learning the latter part; retroactive inhibition refers to the fact that the latter portion interferes with remembering what was learned in the earlier part. Interserial effects occur when two or

[1] This is especially true of emotions. Reconditioning is the only dependable way to eliminate a conditioned fear.

more series are learned; in this case either facilitation (positive transfer) or inhibition (negative transfer) may be obtained, depending upon the similarity of stimuli and responses to be associated.

Learning is an extension of the perceiving process. We define similarity and difference of stimuli in terms of how they are perceived. After learning, the stimulus is perceived in a new way. Furthermore, some of the principles governing perception apply to learning, particularly the principle that material must be isolated and organized into a unit if it is to be recognized and reproduced. Interference apparently causes most forgetting by interposing conflicting responses and preventing the development of an organized pattern of response.

There is some evidence, however, that forgetting depends on a process other than the presence of interference. It is possible that the organizing process in learning takes time, that associations become stabilized or "set" after an experience, and that any interference or shock just at this point is particularly disruptive of learning.

The emphasis in this chapter has been largely on learning and forgetting as determined by the environment, the stimulus conditions presented, and the responses demanded. This would suggest that learning is a passive process of adaptation by the organism to its environment. While associative learning does fit this picture, it is obvious that much learning, especially human learning, is more active in character. The following chapters will therefore extend the scope of this analysis by considering more types of learning and more determinants of learning.

Recommended Readings[1]

GUTHRIE, E. R.: *Psychology of Learning.* New York: Harper, 1935.

KINGSLEY, H. L.: *Nature and Conditions of Learning.* New York: Prentice-Hall, 1946.

McGEOCH, J. A.: *Psychology of Human Learning.* New York: Longmans, 1942.

THORNDIKE, E. L.: *The Fundamentals of Learning.* New York: Teachers College, Columbia University. 1932.

[1] See also p. 547.

CHAPTER 8

Conditioning

In the preceding chapter the problem of learning was examined in terms of a fairly complex type, rote association or serial learning. This is a decidedly common and important kind of learning activity among humans, and a knowledge of its determinants has considerable practical value. Its apparent simplicity was shown to result from a complicated interaction of several factors.

For purely scientific purposes, serial learning is not the best object of investigation. Because it is complex, we cannot always isolate the specific perceptions and responses which are becoming organized into patterns. Furthermore, the role of motivation is obscured in human learning. From earliest childhood humans become accustomed to the necessity for learning new tricks. Even the young child, therefore, may conform to instructions that he memorize words or copy actions, without any obvious motivation being brought into play.

When psychologists attempted to verify some of their learning studies on animals, the paramount importance of motivation immediately came into focus. A well-fed, and otherwise unmotivated rat, placed in a maze or puzzle box, lies down and goes to sleep. He may explore, but he shows no sign of learning. On the other hand, deprive

him of food for 24 hours, put his food dish at the end of the maze, and he quickly learns the shortest path to food.

In the long run, all behavior, either human or animal, is homeostatic in character; it seeks reduction of inner tension. This principle is harder to establish in man, whose tension systems are most intricate; it is easy to demonstrate in animals. Unless the rat is motivated—unless some disturbance of inner equilibrium has occurred—he just does not learn. As he solves the problem, he is modified in various ways; he does not simply restore his previous equilibrium. He perceives objects differently and responds in new ways. This is what was referred to in earlier chapters as dynamic homeostasis; that is, behavior in restoring favorable tissue conditions may result in a new equilibrium on an entirely different level from the old. The point is that animals learn (and, within limits, think and solve problems) only when some inner equilibrium has been disturbed. Learning is an effort to regain the tension-free state.

A variety of inner tensions can be manipulated by the experimenter to induce learning by animals. Hunger and thirst are easily controlled and, to some extent, varied in intensity by varying length of deprivation. Sex has also been used to motivate animal learning. Escape from pain or discomfort

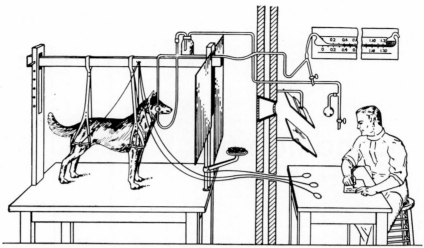

FIG. 8:1. Pavlov's apparatus for salivary conditioned reflex. The dog is held within limits by a harness, and a suction cup is attached to the fistula from the salivary gland. The experimenter can watch through the mirrors, but the dog is effectively shut off from any stimuli other than those to be used in the experiment. Visual, auditory, tactual, and other stimuli can be applied from the experimenter's booth. The salivary measuring device (over experimenter's head) is enlarged in Fig. 8:2. Food is delivered to the dog by the food pan on the shaft (in the picture, out of reach and sight of the animal). (*From Pavlov, 1928, by permission of International Publishers Co.*)

(electric shock, immersion in water) is also widely employed. Any of these states can set up inner tensions which will energize the animal and activity will continue until a solution is evolved and the tension is reduced. Since the experimenter is not free to use such tensions and their reduction in studies of humans, we shall now turn to a series of animal researches to expand our knowledge of the learning process.

Conditioning as a model. The preceding chapter used serial learning, as in memorizing a list of items, as a model. Serial learning was analyzed, in that connection, into *associations* between perceptions, or between perceived stimuli and motor responses. If we now look for an animal experiment which clearly continues this pattern, we find it in the *conditioned-response* experiment.

The most famous conditioning experiments are those of Pavlov (1927), the great Russian physiologist and psychologist. In his work on the digestion of dogs, he found that the animals began to secrete gastric juices and saliva at the sight of the food dish or even when they were brought into the laboratory for experimental feeding. Following this out, he demonstrated that the animals would learn to salivate to a bell, a light, a metronome, back scratching, and virtually any other known stimulus, even a mild electric shock (Fig. 8:1). He considered that secretion of saliva when food was placed in the mouth must be an inherited kind of response, but secretion to a bell depended on the conditions to which the dog had been subjected. Thus he called the first an *unconditioned* response (UR) and the learned reaction a *conditioned* response (CR). Food then is referred to as the *unconditioned* stimulus (US) and the bell as the *conditioned* stimulus (CS).

The course of learning in the typical conditioning experiment, such as Pavlov's, has been considered to follow this pattern:

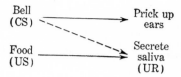

If the bell is rung and is immediately followed by feeding, the animal soon begins to secrete saliva at the sound of the bell. We could generalize this by saying that the bell has become a signal for food (it is perceived in a new way), that food is associated with the bell, or that the salivary response has become conditioned to the bell stimulus. Each of these three statements calls attention to an aspect of the learning process. For the present we want to focus on the idea of establishing a new connection between a stimulus and a response (the dotted line in the above diagram).

Humans show many examples of learning which reduce to the conditioning model. The smell of food causes secretion of saliva, and a picture of a frightening experience readily sets off a heart flutter. Babies will automatically open their mouths when some object is seen approaching, at least when they are hungry. The experienced driver slams on his brakes as the light flashes red, without stopping to think. His reaction is automatic—a conditioned response.

Extinction and recovery. Pavlov quickly became convinced that he had hit upon a most valuable technique for studying the functions of the higher centers of the nervous system. Learning, after all, is basic to all the more complex mental phenomena such as thinking, reasoning, imagining, and inventing. Pavlov therefore embarked upon a lifetime project of research into conditioning phenomena. Supported alike by the Czarist and Soviet governments in Russia, he and his colleagues accumulated enormous quantities of data. For our purposes, it is worth while only to consider some general principles of conditioning—or

learning—which have evolved from these investigations

In a moderately hungry dog (where feeding is followed by some degree of tension reduction) salivary conditioning proceeds fairly rapidly. After a few pairings of the CS with food, the CS begins to elicit a flow of saliva; and the quantity of secretion to a given CS increases, the more often it has been presented with food. (An elaborate apparatus was devised to measure this secretion; see Fig. 8:2.)

What happens if we ring the bell and give no food? The dog has established an expectancy (so it seems) that the bell will be followed by food. If we now ring the bell and do not feed him, he continues to salivate for a number of trials, but the quantity begins to decline, and eventually he secretes no saliva to the sound of the bell. This process of *learning not to respond* is known as *experimental extinction*. The conditioned response is said to be extinguished if it is repeated numerous times without reinforcement by the unconditioned stimulus, so that the CS finally elicits no response.

Experimental extinction, curiously enough, seems less durable than the original conditioning. By repeated stimulation we can extinguish a salivary response right down to zero today; if the animal is tested tomorrow, the conditioned response will be manifested once more. Pavlov called this *spontaneous* recovery of the CR.[1]

Conditioning, extinction, and spontaneous recovery point to the importance of learning as a signaling function. As was noted in the chapter on perception, a given stimulus comes to be perceived as a cue for

[1] The student will immediately note that this "spontaneous recovery" resembles the "reminiscence" phenomenon described in the preceding chapter. Both obviously depend upon some process which goes on in the brain after the learning situation ends—a kind of adding up of experiences to reach a conclusion about the correct way to respond. This is not a reasoning process; it is entirely unconscious.

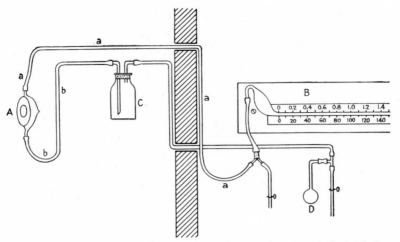

FIG. 8:2. Measuring device for salivary secretion. Many of Pavlov's conclusions depend on precise measurement of the amount of saliva secreted during the seconds preceding and following the application of the conditioned stimulus. The suction cup (A) is fastened over a fistula in the dog's cheek, removing saliva as fast as it is secreted. Number of drops can be determined in the graduated tube (B). (*From Pavlov, 1927, p. 19, by permission of Oxford University Press.*)

the whole complex situation of which it is a key part. In that connection we called attention to the role of probability, based on personal experience. This principle can be helpful in understanding the phenomena of conditioning. As the experimenter arbitrarily pairs the bell with the food, he builds up a succession of probabilities that the CS will be followed by the US. As these accumulate, the animal acts as if he expects food to follow the bell; but, we might say, he hasn't much confidence in this expectancy, as he salivates only slightly. With more stimulation the probabilities increase and his response is strengthened accordingly.

Now, if the experimenter starts an extinction series, he builds up the probability that bell will *not* be followed by food. The dog now expects "no food" and his salivation declines; when he is, so to speak, absolutely certain that no food will appear, secretion hits zero. If the experiment now is adjourned until the next day, the animal seems to behave in terms of probability based **on** both learning and extinction

series; *i.e.,* "maybe" the bell signals food, hence we observe spontaneous recovery of the conditioned response.

Time relations. Most efficient conditioning is attained if the CS precedes the US by a very short time interval, 1 second or less. This fits with an interpretation of conditioning as learning a signal. The signal must precede what it signifies, but not by too great a time. Humans can establish signal functions over long periods, but they make use of mechanical secondary cues such as clocks and calendars. Furthermore, the attention span of the human is much greater than that of any other animal. Thus it is not surprising that CS and US must be near in time for really efficient learning by dogs (cf. Fig. 8:3). Pavlov did report, nonetheless, that with many trials he could establish CRs with a lapse of as much as 30 minutes between CS and US.

In the analysis of serial learning (in the preceding chapter) note was made of the possibility that *backward* associations might be established (associating one item to another which preceded it in the list). Such

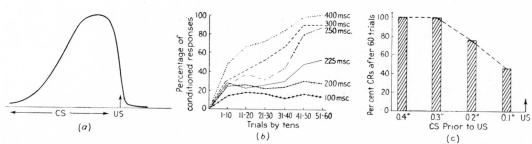

FIG. 8:3. Time relations in conditioning. Conditioning is most effective if the CS is applied about ½ to 1 second before the US. Most animals can form CRs if the CS is applied as much as 5 minutes before the US; dogs can be conditioned to a delay of as long as 30 minutes, but with difficulty. This relationship is shown in (a). There is a slight possibility of backward conditioning (CS occurring after US), but most experiments find that it does not occur. If CS is applied less than ½ second before US, conditioning is not as efficient. In (b) is shown the rate of conditioning when time intervals varying from 0.1 second (100 milliseconds) to 0.4 second (400 milliseconds) are used. Learning obviously proceeds at a slower rate with the very short time intervals. Another way to show this is in (c), which shows the number of animals giving anticipatory CRs after 60 reinforcements, separated according to the time between CS and US. 100 per cent of animals showed CRs in the 0.4-second group, whereas about 45 per cent showed CRs in the 0.1-second group. (*From Kimble, 1947, pp. 8, 9.*)

a possibility, however, is not to be given much weight; if I say "Yankee," many Americans will say "Doodle," but if I say "Doodle," not many will respond with "Yankee." They are more likely to respond with "Pencil" or "Picture."

The possibility of *backward conditioning* has also been explored. This would involve putting food in the animal's mouth just before the bell rang. Under these conditions, most experimenters report, the animal never does learn to salivate when the bell is rung by itself. The sound cannot signal the approach of food if the food got there first. The probability "bell will be followed by food" remains at zero.[1]

So, if we diagram efficiency of conditioning as in Fig. 8:3, we get a curve which peaks sharply and drops even more sharply.

[1] In the experiment by Hudson (1950) mentioned on p. 256, a boldly striped pattern appeared in the rat's cage and delivered a shock when the animal took the food on it. If, instantly, the lights went out and the striped pattern were removed in the dark, the rats often failed to establish a fear CR. This indicated that inspection of the pattern *after* the shock was an element in the conditioning process for some animals. However, the visceral responses to the shock could continue for some time; hence it is not certain that backward conditioning is involved.

Learning is best when CS precedes US, but very slightly; as CS occurs earlier, learning is slowed. But if CS follows US by even a slight amount, learning seems to drop to zero.

Instrumental Conditioning

Because Pavlov was dealing with a glandular response, he had to measure mostly quantity of response and in some cases could measure the time delay in responding. Many other aspects of the learning activity were concealed. Also, since the activity of the animal did not decide whether or not he would get the food, the process was mainly passive (or appeared to be). This kind of conditioning experiment can be repeated with humans, using the reflex response in the iris of the eye and other responses of similar character, and the results resemble those of Pavlov. This is known as the "classical-conditioning" experiment.

In recent years more attention has been paid to a different experimental model, known as *instrumental conditioning*, in which the activity of the animal is more important. This experiment was developed by another Russian, Bekhterev, who used pain as the inner tension instead of hunger, and lifting the foot as the response instead of salivary secretion. Thus, he rang a bell, then administered a mild electric shock to the dog's paw. With repeated pairings of bell (CS) and shock (US), the dog learns to lift his paw automatically when he hears the bell. The sound now functions as a signal of the approach of pain.

The instrumental-conditioning model has been used by many psychologists in their explorations of basic principles in learning. For that reason it is worth while to give a fairly clear and detailed picture of what happens in the process. The following description from Culler (1938) will serve as an illustration of the many varieties of instrumental conditioning experiments.

. . . When a shock is applied to a wholly naive animal, its response will include many of these features: quick gasp or yelp, hasty withdrawal of the foot, adduction of tail, then whining or barking, biting or snapping at nearby objects, twisting or jerking, occasional evacuation. The whole body seems to be vigorously involved, but with little effective result. Now suppose a bell be rung just before the shock. After a few times we witness a display of behavior (as soon as the sound begins) which seems to duplicate the actual UR; indeed, so realistic is the animal's performance that I have sometimes been misled into thinking that shock was being inadvertently applied along with the bell. Never have I seen an actor give a more convincing portrayal than does the conditioned behavior of some dogs in this early stage. Similar observations have appeared elsewhere. Jones reports that, in a human infant, bell plus shock was administered 3 times, directly followed by bell alone 5 times. The reactions during the last five were "indistinguishable from those elicited by the primary stimulus"; indeed the keeper of the protocol, who observed each trial with great care, mistakenly assumed from the infant's behavior that all 8 trials included shock instead of only the first three. In this initial stage, when UR is still tentative and diffuse, the CR may indeed give a photographic reproduction. Thereafter the two

diverge, UR and CR, each in accord with its own function. Let us first be clear that UR itself is not stable and definitive at the start. It alters and accommodates until some "optimal" form has been attained, though it be hard to define just what optimal means, or to tell when the optimal is achieved. But in any case, after a dog is often shocked, the same charge applied in the same place no longer yields this loose and wide-spread activity. It yields rather a quick, effective removal of foot, which is then slowly replaced. The UR thus means at first, readiness for something; the problem being not yet clear, the response not yet defined; and so the animal reacts in a way suitable to a large class of stimuli. But if this improved UR were his only recourse, the animal would still be forced to wait in every case for the stimulus to arrive before beginning to meet it. The veil of the future would hang just before his eyes. Nature began long ago to push back the veil. Foresight proved to possess high survival value, and *conditioning is the means by which foresight was achieved.* Indeed this provision gave the distance-receptors most of their value. Neither sight nor sound of an approaching enemy is intrinsically hurtful; without conditionability, these exteroceptors would have lost their phylogenetic significance.[1]

Culler's analysis indicates that classical conditioning and instrumental conditioning are not two completely separate processes. Indeed, we might say that they form a continuum. The early conditioned responses almost duplicate the UR, as in Pavlov's work. The later phases, however, show modification of the response, a feature of instrumental conditioning.

The difference between "classical conditioning," as used by Pavlov, and "instrumental conditioning" lies in whether or not the activity of the subject is effective. In Culler's experiment just described, the dog avoids shock if he lifts his foot in time. In the classical experiment, the unconditioned

[1] Culler (1938), pp. 135–136. Reprinted by permission of the American Psychological Association.

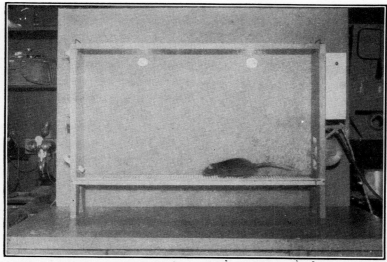

FIG. 8:4. Rat in a Mowrer shuttle box. In this simple device, the two halves of the floor grid are wired separately. The rat must learn that, when the lights go on, he must run to the other end of the box (the grid at this end will be electrified in a moment). Simple avoidance conditioning of this type is very rapid. It is thus convenient to use for the study of other variables. (*Courtesy of Dr. O. H. Mowrer.*)

stimulus (food, in Pavlov's setup) appears regardless of the dog's response. Shock can also be used as the US in a classical conditioning experiment; Liddell (1942) has utilized a wide variety of animals—sheep, pigs, rabbits—in an apparatus which makes impossible the escape from the shock. He is interested in measuring the respiratory, circulatory, and other changes which become conditioned responses in the same way that Pavlov studied salivary secretion.

Mowrer (1940) has devised a simple apparatus for instrumental conditioning (Fig. 8:4) consisting of an electrified grid and a small fence. The CS is given, followed by US (shock). If the rat jumps over the fence, he escapes the painful stimulus. Conditioning occurs rapidly and endures for a long time.

It would appear that, where the situation makes it possible, animals will always attempt to avoid the painful stimulus and thus develop an instrumental CR. Curiously enough, college students do not

always react thus. We have a standard experiment in which the subject learns to lift his finger at the sound of a buzzer, to avoid shock. Some men simply stiffen the shoulder muscles at the sound and absorb the shock rather than lift the finger. Thus what was intended as a demonstration of instrumental conditioning inadvertently turns into an instance of classical conditioning.

Both methods of conditioning are subject to the same laws of reinforcement, extinction, and recovery. Instrumental conditioning, however, reveals more clearly the initial and final stages in the learning process. It will be remembered that Pavlov had to prepare the dog to attend to the food supply. In instrumental conditioning, this preliminary phase is taken care of by the shock itself, thus revealing the development of the preparatory set. The nice precision of leg lifting in the final stages is preceded by more awkward efforts; this calls our attention to the fact that learning involves

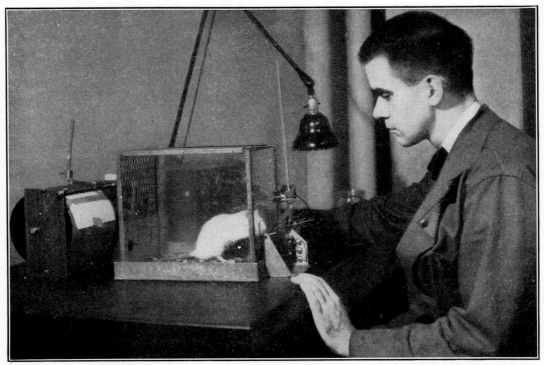

FIG. 8:5. A rat in a Skinner box. The Skinner box differs from the Mowrer box in that the rat must learn to press a lever, turn a wheel, step on a platform, or make some other movement to obtain food. It is used to establish instrumental CRs to a positive goal. In this photograph Dr. Dinsmoor requires the animal to learn a simple bar-pressing response. Drum in back of cage automatically records each time the rat presses the bar. (*Courtesy of Dr. J. A. Dinsmoor.*)

changes in the response, not just attaching the response to a new stimulus. We shall be examining more instances of such response modification when we deal with trial-and-error learning in Chap. 9.

Instrumental conditioning should not be considered as limited only to escape from pain. It is also possible to use positive reward, such as food, in this type of learning study. Skinner (1938) devised a box in which the animal presses a bar to release a pellet of food, which falls into a dish near the bar (see Fig. 8:5). Pigeons can be taught to peck at specified targets, cats to pull strings, etc., by this technique (Fig. 8:6). Instrumental conditioning has been one of the basic experiments through which American psychologists have explored the variations in the learning process.

Flexibility of Conditioning

An examination of Pavlov's salivary experiment, or observation of Culler's dogs after they have been thoroughly conditioned, might lead to the notion that the conditioned response was a highly rigid affair in which a narrow, specific, localized response became attached to a precisely defined stimulus. This view was held by Pavlov, and by many American theorists, for a long time. The notion was particularly tempting to them because it fitted in well with the atomistic tenor of science at the turn of the century. In those days physicists were still thinking in terms of atoms as specific, unchanging units; chemists believed that every molecule of a given substance behaved exactly like every other molecule;

FIG. 8:6. Pigeons trained to "read." These pigeons have learned an instrumental CR which resembles reading. When the blue light goes on, the pigeon pecks at the card labeled Blue and obtains food; similarly for red, green, and yellow. If only four colors are used, the average bird learns in a few days to make the correct responses; but adding another color makes the task very difficult. Training was in a Skinner box similar to Fig. 8:5, of a size suitable for pigeons. (*By Life photographer Yale Joel. Copyright Time, Inc.*)

and biologists held that animals inherited a large number of inflexible, automatic stimulus-response connections, so that a given external change automatically set off certain behavior.

Stimulus generalization. In the early stages of conditioning, the animal responds not only to the specific stimulus being used in training, but to a whole range of similar stimuli. If a musical tone is being used at 440 cycles, the animal may respond to everything from 110 to 1,760 cycles. If a buzzer is employed, a bell, a metronome, and other intermittent sounds may also evoke the response. It might be said, in human terms, that the animal has a "vague notion" that some kind of sound is the signal for him to lift his leg or to reach for food or to jump out of the box. More precisely, we say that the specific stimulus has been *generalized* so that other stimuli of the same class tend to evoke the conditioned response.

The generalization gradient. If the animal is reacting to stimulus similarity, then we would expect that he would respond with decreasing frequency as the test stimulus differed more and more from the learning stimulus. This has been verified experimentally. Hovland (1937), working with humans, conditioned the galvanic skin reflex to a specific musical tone. Then he

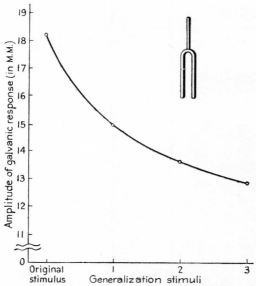

FIG. 8:7. The generalization gradient. When a CR is established to a given stimulus, it will be aroused, in lesser strength, by adjacent stimuli in the same sensory dimension. In the above curve is shown the conditioned GSR to a tone; 1, 2, and 3 represent other tones differing in pitch by increasing amounts from the original stimulus. Note that, as the difference in stimulus value increases, the magnitude of the CR diminishes. If the new stimulus is sensed by the organism as completely different, there would be no generalization (no CR) at all. (*From Hovland, 1937, p. 136.*)

tested with a variety of other tones, differing by defined amounts from the original CS. As Fig. 8:7 shows, he got smaller and smaller responses as the test stimulus became physically less similar to the original stimulus. When we speak of a generalization gradient, we mean that there is a scale of stimulus similarities and that maximum response will occur at the point where the training stimulus falls. As test stimuli move away, in any direction, from this stimulus, the organism responds less vigorously or less frequently.

This is exactly what we reported in the preceding chapter on learning of verbal materials. In that connection it was pointed out that serial learning is characterized by positive and negative transfer. As long as the response required of the sub-

ject remains the same, he will show positive transfer to similar stimuli. But the amount of transfer decreases as the similarity becomes less. This gradient of generalization should be related back to the discussion of "equivalent stimuli" on page 267. At that time the student may have felt that stimulus equivalence was an all-or-nothing affair. Plainly, it is not. All organisms, man included, may perceive *degrees of similarity*, and a conditioned response, established to a specific stimulus, will be evoked in lesser degree by a similar but nonidentical stimulus.

We might draw these sets of experiments together in this manner. Whenever a stimulus affects an organism, a certain expectancy tends to develop. "This red light probably signals food." With repetition, the expectancy becomes stronger. Now, if we show a pink light, the animal has no previous experience but tends to generalize or transfer from the other learning: "this is similar to red, so maybe this signals food too." (We can demonstrate the occurrence of such conscious generalization in humans by asking them; but even much of human generalizing and transferring behavior is unconscious, and of course we make no assumptions that the nonverbal animals go through such a deliberate process of generalizing. It is often easy to demonstrate with humans that the generalization develops first, unconsciously, and then is verbalized as in the example.)

Generalization was shown in Watson's experiments on conditioned fears; when the infant learned to fear the white rat (expected it to be accompanied by a loud noise), this response generalized to a white fur muff, a Santa Claus mask, etc. The process is also characteristic of the higher mental processes; as we shall note in Chap. 11, inductive reasoning consists largely of generalizing from one specific stimulus (Newton's falling apple) to a whole range of similar occurrences (mutual attraction of masses).

Differentiation. How, then, does the animal reach this level of precise, mechanical reproduction of a required response, to one specific stimulus and no other? This depends on rewarding (reinforcing) responses to the specific CS and not reinforcing the other, similar stimuli in the series. When Pavlov wanted to teach his dogs to secrete saliva only to a metronome beat of 50 per minute, he simply gave them food whenever that beat was sounded, but presented beats of 30, 40, 60, and 70 without food. The animals then began to *differentiate* the specific stimulus which signaled food and ignored those which were too fast or too slow.

All animals have limits to their capacity for differentiating stimuli. When the metronome beats got within 2 or 3 per minute of the rewarded stimulus, the dog became, so to speak, confused; he could not choose between an expectancy of reward and an expectancy of nonreward. At this point most animals showed a characteristic kind of "nervous breakdown" or "experimental neurosis." Some became wildly excitable, barking, biting the harness, urinating, and defecating; others went to sleep and ignored the stimuli entirely (cf. Chap. 14). Humans are also likely to become upset by being required to differentiate situations which are beyond their capacity. Thus a child may learn that it is all right to be noisy and boisterous in one house but not in another; if the difference is not clear, he may react to a strange house with sulky sullenness or with violent hostility.

Response generalization. We find evidence of flexibility not only on the stimulus side but also in the conditioned response itself. The organism often makes other responses besides that desired by the experimenter. In Culler's description (page 282) it was noted that the dog, in response to shock, moves his whole body, not just the leg. Even in later stages of learning he may move one of the other limbs instead of that being trained. On the whole, however, we

note in both humans and animals a tendency for responses to be rather specific.

In terms of a functional psychology, this makes very good sense. The world of stimuli is much richer than the world of responses. I am constantly being presented with a terrific variety of sights, sounds, smells, and contacts, many of which may have exactly the same significance in terms of homeostasis—that is, a needed goal object may be seen, heard, smelled, or tasted. Thus, in terms of my basic motivation, it is important for me to connect many stimuli to a particular response, but it is rarely important for me to connect several different responses to the same stimulus. Indeed, to do so would be inefficient, because I would then experience conflict when the stimulus appeared, not knowing just which response to give. If one can write adequately with the right hand, there seems little point in developing skill also in the left. Thus it is not surprising that we have extensive evidence for stimulus generalization and only a small amount for response generalization.

It may be significant, however, to note that certain kinds of response generalization become phases of human personality. It has been found that people who tend toward broad, sweeping gestures with their hands will, when required to use their legs and feet, make similar movements. Persons who smile readily tend also to frown and to use other facial patterns more often than the average. Persons who tend to emphasize small, meticulous details in an ink-blot test seem also to be fussy about details in their work habits.[1]

Response variation. In addition to pure response generalization with a constant stimulus, we have flexibility indicated by

---

[1] Some psychologists, however, have interpreted this kind of observation as evidence of stimulus generalization; *i.e.*, the similarity in behavior derives from "how the person looks at the situation," not just from the response mechanism as such.

minor variations in the response to keep pace with changes in the stimulus. Consider the experiment by Gibson *et al.* (1932), in which the student subject rested his right hand on a pair of electrodes. A buzzer was sounded, followed by shock through the electrodes. The subjects quickly learned to withdraw the hand at the sound of the buzzer. Now the situation was changed so that the left hand rested on the electrodes. At the first sound of the buzzer, 8 of the 13 subjects withdrew the left hand. Here a *new but similar response* is given, appropriate to the modification of the total stimulus situation.

This experiment is interesting particularly because it emphasizes, contrary to common belief, that most habits are not blind and automatic. The habit is usually automatic with respect to some motive (avoiding pain, in the experiment cited) but is not automatic as to form. The person builds up an expectancy of some kind with regard to the stimulus (that it will hurt, that it is good to eat, etc.) and reacts automatically to that anticipation, but not necessarily with the same muscles.

Response specificity. We have already emphasized that, in the instrumental conditioning procedure, a massive response of struggling against the shock becomes sharpened and focalized into a precise paw movement. This, of course, resembles much complex learning; the beginning typist tenses his arms, shoulders, and back, but as his skill increases, he uses only finger and arm movements.

What is often overlooked is that the classical conditioning experiment also shows this. Pavlov spoke of his dogs as giving the same response to CS (bell) as to US (meat). In fact, they did nothing of the sort. They did not engage in chewing and swallowing movements. Salivation is an appropriate response to *anticipation* of food; the other elements of activity drop out. Thus we can say that all conditioning shows this trend toward increasing specificity. The response pattern changes as irrelevant or inappropriate elements drop out.

Sensory conditioning. It should follow from the foregoing remarks that one could, with the conditioning technique, establish the expectancy that one stimulus will be followed by another, even though no muscular response seems to be involved. This theory has been verified. Brogden (1939), for example, presented a light and a bell to dogs for 200 repetitions. Following this "preconditioning," the dog learned a CR of lifting the hind leg whenever the bell was sounded, to avoid shock. When the light was now presented, the dog immediately responded with leg flexion, although *the shock had never been paired with the light.*

This type of experiment can be utilized to give rise to hallucinations. Ellson (1941) presented a light stimulus along with a musical tone which began very faintly, rose somewhat in volume, and then faded away. After several repetitions, he began delaying the onset of the tone for several seconds; the subject characteristically reported that he heard the sound before it actually was produced. Before the end of the experiment every subject reported at least one hallucinatory tone, and some subjects heard them almost every time the light was flashed. As in the case of Brogden's dogs, we have here an illustration of the light functioning as a signal for the sound; the person claimed that he heard the sound when it was not physically present.

We must now extend still further our conceptions of stimulus generalization and positive transfer. A response may be given to a totally new stimulus, not because the stimulus resembles the old one, but because of a learned association between the two stimuli. In this case we speak of *equivalence of meaning.* For signaling purposes, one can replace the other.

Time interval as stimulus. It is easy to think of the CS as a flash of light, the sound

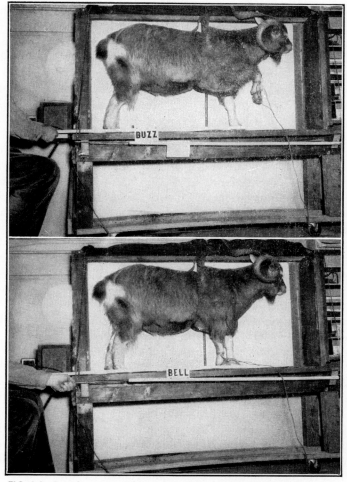

FIG. 8:8. Development of response specificity. At first the goat responds to shock on the leg by thrashing wildly about; later he makes just the minimal movement necessary to avoid the shock. To the bell, which has never been paired with shock, he makes no response at all. (*Courtesy of Dr. H. S. Liddell.*)

of a buzzer, or some such physical change in the environment. Somewhat more difficult may be the idea that a time interval can itself act as a stimulus for a response. Pavlov found that, if he rang a bell and, exactly 10 minutes later, presented food, the dog would learn not to secrete saliva immediately after the bell, but would secrete after 10 minutes (actually, about 9½ minutes, as there seemed to be some anticipation). This indicates the adaptive,

homeostatic functioning of the CNS. If the organism is to obtain food or other goal objects, it must correctly anticipate and be prepared for the object when it appears. The bell sets up a process of excitation which is maintained, probably by intro-organic stimuli such as heartbeat, breathing, or digestive peristalsis, until the appropriate moment for responding.

Higher order conditioning. If a stimulus is directly associated with the drive-stimulus (US), such as food or shock, we form a primary CR. This process is called *first-order conditioning*. Suppose a dog has learned to salivate when a bell is rung. We may now pair light with bell *but never give food with the light*. Nevertheless, as the light becomes associated with the bell, it will evoke saliva. This we call secondary or *second-order conditioning*, because the light was never directly conditioned to the food.

Pavlov and his students also succeeded in developing third-order conditioning; in the above example, this would mean pairing some new stimulus, *e.g.*, scratching the skin, with the light. Eventually it could be expected that the skin stimulus would produce salivation, by the association chain: scratch signals light, light signals bell, bell signals food.

Higher order conditioning is extremely difficult to set up by this method, and it breaks down very readily. The inherent difficulty is this: the experiment requires that the higher order stimulus never be presented with the unconditioned stimulus. Thus the animal is faced with this situation: bell alone always signals food, but light plus bell always equals no food. Any smart dog is thus likely to figure out that the light is a negative signal, and so he inhibits saliva when the light is used.

What is needed, therefore, is some kind of reinforcing agent, to reward the animal for giving the higher order CR, or to punish him if he fails to do so. Finch and Culler (1934) solved this problem by using retraction of the leg as the UR and administering a shock in the thorax if the animal failed to respond to the higher order CS. (Since this kind of shock has no relation to lifting the leg, we are not dealing here with primary conditioning; but we do punish the animal if he fails to learn the higher order connection.) Under this experimental technique Finch and Culler were able to produce conditionings of the fifth order and probably could have gone much higher.

The kind of process which we call *association of ideas* in humans can obviously extend to considerable distances from the original rewarding or punishing experience. In psychoanalytic work, for example, one may uncover a chain of associations beginning with a traumatic (painful, frightening) experience in childhood, associated with the name of the person involved, generalizing to other persons with the same name, and then to some situation associated with this name. For example, a man might trace his hostility to religion to a terrifying experience in childhood when he was hurt by a man named Bishop. Human beings, by virtue of their more complex neurological organization and the variety of social motives which can reinforce learnings, can establish much higher order conditionings than is possible with other animals.

Hudgins' study of pupillary conditioning. A striking illustration of this point is found in a study of developing voluntary control over an involuntary response, the pupillary reflex. Hudgins (1933) first associated a bell with a light flashing into the subject's eye; soon, the sound of the bell caused contraction of the iris. This training required 125 to 225 paired presentations of the two stimuli. The subject was then instructed to squeeze a dynamometer; this caused the bell to ring and the light to turn on. At the instant of exerting pressure, the subject was told to repeat the word "contract." After some repetitions of this procedure, the pupil would contract to hand pressure and verbal response, without the light. After 200 more trials, it was possible to omit the hand response and obtain pupillary constriction to the word. Then in successive steps this was reduced to a whisper and finally the subject could induce the pupillary reflex merely by subvocally forming the word "contract."

In a parallel experiment other subjects developed a CR of pupillary dilation to the word "relax." Obviously the specific words used are unimportant; nonsense syllables could have been just as effective as conditioned stimuli. Of particular interest, however, is the fact that the responses to the verbal stimuli showed *strong resistance to experimental extinction*. As we noted above, animal experimentation with higher order conditioning has been handicapped by the readiness with which extinction occurs. Hudgins reported that the CR to bell and to light underwent extinction fairly readily, but *the responses to verbal stimuli did not extinguish*.

Experimental Extinction: Some Problems

The student may well ask: Is this important? Why be concerned about experimental extinction of CRs anyway? Our answer is twofold: (1) Scientific psychology must be concerned with *all* aspects of behavior; we assume that everything happens in accordance with some harmonizing natural principle, if only we can locate it, and all these principles must fit mutually together. (2) Extinction is important because it relates to the elimination of behavior patterns. This may be very valuable (or very unfortunate) in terms of practical realities. Children, for example, sometimes become conditioned to purely accidental situations and would go on forever responding to these irrelevant stimuli if extinction did not eliminate these nonadaptive CRs.

We can make progress in our analysis of conditioning as a form of human learning by closer study of those cases in which the CR does not extinguish. A survey of the many experiments on conditioning indicates that extinction *fails* more often (1) in adult human than in children, (2) when the CS is verbal rather than sensory, and (3) when the subject is conscious of the nature of the experiment. In animals, extinction fails in the case of instrumental escape from shock. (This is easy to understand; the animal lifts his leg when CS appears, and

consequently he has no way of knowing that the grid was not electrified. His expectancy of shock continues unchanged. If his leg were fastened down, and no shock occurred, it may be assumed that extinction would follow.) This is also true for humans. "The burned child dreads the flame." Once he is conditioned to avoid a given stimulus, he is not likely to test it and find if it has lost its dangerous character. This is the basis for many neurotic symptoms.

Extinction occurs readily to food-reinforced situations of either the classical or the instrumental type. The appearance of CS leads to anticipation of food; if no food is forthcoming, the anticipation changes rapidly. Extinction of a CR to shock occurs in the classical-type situation (where nothing the animal does will suffice to avoid the shock). In this case the expectancy "no shock" soon replaces the anticipation of shock.

Humans differ from animals in several ways. Conditioning of humans is generally not so mechanically precise as in nonhuman forms. Razran (1933) states that children up to about four years of age show CRs along the same lines as animals. After this age, conditioning becomes unstable, appearing and disappearing and varying in amount. Most of the experiments he reported were based on the salivary reflex, using candy or some other attractive food as the US. Such a stimulus may have more reinforcing value for children, thus making for stability in response. More important, probably, is the attitude taken by the adult to the experiment. Adults often verbalize to themselves about the situation; they try to figure out what the experimenter is doing and how they "ought to" respond. Thus, in one series of experiments, Razran failed to get extinction with adult subjects. But when he repeated the study, misinforming his subjects as to his purpose, extinction occurred promptly.

Self-instructions, which may include

verbal CRs based on many years of practice, are very important in such studies. Razran found that he could get better CRs with his adults by asking them to think of eating steak (or some other preferred food) than he could obtain by actually placing food in the mouth. Salivary secretion to the thought of food is obviously a CR, but it has been practiced so much that it serves excellently as a base for new conditioning.[1]

Extinction may affect one part of the CR and not another. Jones (1930) conditioned children to fear a low tone by pairing it with shock. When they were tested, the children showed both overt fear responses and the GSR (electrical change in the skin). Extinction of the overt behavior was induced by repeated presentation of sound without punishment. A month later Jones again presented the sound. No overt reaction occurred, but *the GSR was practically as strong as it was on the first day.*

Conditioning involuntary responses. In the foregoing pages, we have used indiscriminately examples of CR formation with responses which are under voluntary control, such as finger flexion and retraction of a limb, and others which cannot be directly controlled by the subject, such as pupillary change, electrical skin response, and salivation. The experimental data available suggest that "voluntary" and conscious responses are highly flexible; they may condition quickly and extinguish just as rapidly. Involuntary, unconscious reactions may condition more slowly (although such reactions to pain condition very rapidly), but they may resist extinction for long periods of time. Thus Jones's data indicated that the children quickly learned

[1] Menzies (1937) found that many of his subjects showed constriction of blood vessels in the skin upon thinking of ice, wintry scenes, etc. Adult humans are likely to have a wide variety of these CRs without being aware of them; this makes the task of the experimental psychologist more complicated.

not to be consciously alarmed by the sound, but their viscera continued to react to the sound as signal of shock.

Another experiment which may throw light on this point is that of Diven (1937). Using the "free-association" experiment as a concealing device, Diven pronounced stimulus words to his subjects and administered a mild electric shock following certain words. On a memory test the shock words were forgotten by more subjects than forgot neutral words in the list. Five minutes later the words were repeated, this time with no shock, and the galvanic skin response was recorded. To the "shock" words, all subjects gave GSRs, and *those who had forgotten these words* showed a larger GSR than those who remembered. This suggests that the persons whose viscera reacted strongly to the shock tended to "avoid" the stimulus word by forgetting it.[1] This tendency will be discussed again in Chap. 14.

Involuntary conditioning and social motives. This is a good point to look back at the problem of social motives for a moment. In that discussion it was noted that ideational stimuli (thinking of a career as a physician, business success, or political power) might come to evoke tensions mobilizing energy for vigorous action. The experiments we have just summarized show how easily this can happen.

Tensions relating to biological drives involve actual muscular and other responses in the viscera. Stomach walls, blood vessels, the adrenals, and other involuntary mechanisms participate intimately in these inner tensions. These changes can become conditioned to verbal stimuli ("I want . . . ") as well as to actions of parents and other adults. Anxiety

[1] Diven also found that stimulus generalization occurred. If the shock stimulus was "barn," the conditioned GSR appeared for a variety of "rural" words when they were added to the list for test purposes.

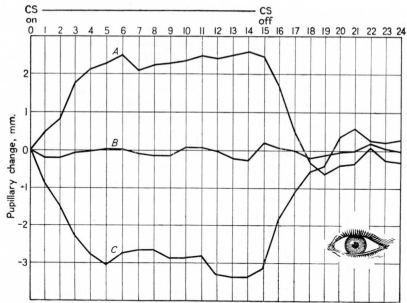

FIG. 8:9. The conditioned pupillary reflex. The upper curve (A) shows average magnitude of the change in size of pupil when conditioned dilation is well established. The lower curve (C) is for conditioned constriction. The line at the top (from "CS on" to "CS off") shows the duration of the conditioned stimulus, which was in this case a subliminal auditory buzz delivered through earphones. The prompt rise and fall of the curves leaves little doubt that this is a genuine CR. The line (B) is the average for control readings, when the experimenter pretended to apply the CS but in fact did not activate the sound stimulus. (*Modified from Baker, 1938, p. 9.*)

and fear of pain become associated with thoughts of failure. And, as these experiments show so clearly, the escape CR does not extinguish readily. It may persist for years. So, an individual who develops the expectation, early in life, that his hope of avoiding anxiety rests on economic success, may show the same energetic behavior as the infant demanding relief from a physical pain. Certainly we know that many emotional disturbing situations set off extreme visceral discomfort.[1]

Subliminal conditioning. Clearly, for conditioning to take place, a person need not be conscious of the response he gives.

[1] Persons discussing, in a therapeutic situation, a condition which arouses their anxiety, have been found to show marked reactions of the digestive system, circulatory system, and other viscera. For a further discussion of these phenomena see p. 471.

Interestingly enough, he can also be conditioned without being aware of the stimulus. Baker (1938) ascertained the auditory threshold for his subjects; he then presented, by earphones, a buzz which was definitely too weak to be consciously reported. Simultaneously with this sound, a bright light was flashed into the eye. A CR of pupillary contraction was quickly established (Fig. 8:9) *and was remarkably resistant to extinction.*

This is the same phenomenon described in Chap. 6 as *subception.* That, it will be recalled, was manifest when the individual's perception was affected by stimuli so weak—or so blocked off by the attending process—that they were not consciously noticed. Thus the presence of certain unobserved cues caused people to perceive an object as near or far away. Similarly, words flashed too rapidly for the person to identify them could still set off conditioned visceral changes. All these experiments show that our brains respond to a multiplicity of stimuli which never become conscious.

Subliminal conditioning probably accounts for many of our "hunches," "intuitions," and other vaguely felt judgments. A boy may become conditioned to fine shadings of tone in his father's voice and react with anxiety to certain vocal inflections. Later, meeting another man, the boy feels anxious without knowing why; he is unaware of the auditory cues which have affected his inner state.

Physiological Basis of Conditioning

The neurology of learning is, as a recent author puts it, "regretfully obscure." While we know little enough, from the viewpoint of professional psychology, about learning as behavior, we know even less about learning as a process in the nervous system.

Conditioning and other forms of learning *normally* depend upon processes in the cortex of the cerebrum. This can be demonstrated by operating to remove specified cortical areas after conditioning has taken place; if the right area is removed, the CR disappears. It is obvious, however, that there is a great deal of plasticity here. For example, Ades and Raab (1946) established an auditory CR in chimpanzees. If they removed the temporal cortex on both cerebral lobes at the same time, the CR was lost. But if they removed the temporal area on one side, tests showed that the CR persisted; and *if they now removed the area on the opposite side, the CR still remained!* That is, the function, whatever it is, can be shifted about from one group of cortical cells to another.

Association of cortical fields. It has been suggested that the essential basis for normal learning is the association of two or more cortical fields, one representing

the CS and one the US. Some evidence for this comes from the experiments on conditioning where a response is impossible. Light and Gantt (1936) proved that instrumental conditioning can occur when the dog cannot move the muscles to be conditioned. They crushed the motor roots of the spinal nerves leading to the dog's hind leg. A buzzer was paired with shock to this leg. The dog, of course, could not withdraw the leg; but, when the damaged nerves had healed, the buzzer alone now produced leg flexion!

Finch (1938) performed the same experiment with the salivary reflex. During the training sessions he prevented any secretion of saliva by giving injections of atropine (which paralyzes the gland). But, when the CS was given after the effects of the atropine wore off, a conditioned salivary reflex was observed.

It has been argued by some psychologists that the animals used in these experiments used other muscles or glands as substitute mechanisms; that some action outside the brain is necessary for learning to take place. Harlow and Stagner (1933) paralyzed *all* the striped musculature in their animals with curare; they then presented light and bell, followed by shock (Fig. 8:10). A conditioned pupillary reaction was formed, but when the curare wore off, no instrumental avoidance response to the light or bell was found. This suggests that the dogs studied by Light and Gantt may have been responding with other muscles, and then transferred the response to the hind leg when the motor nerves regenerated. However, psychologists who have repeated the Harlow-Stagner experiment find that curare depresses cortical activity, so that this study cannot be considered as clear proof that learning occurs only with some motor response.

On the other side of the question, note should be made of the experiment by Loucks (1938), in which direct electrical

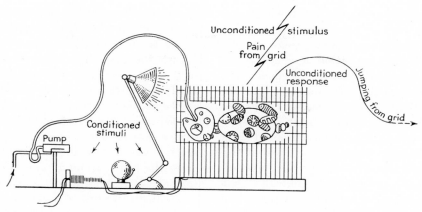

FIG. 8:10. Setup for experiment on learning under complete paralysis. The buzzer, bell, and light went on in that order. This was followed by shock delivered through the iron grid. In normal animals this resulted in prompt conditioning to leap from the grid when the CS went on. Paralyzed animals were kept alive by artificial respiration (tube in mouth). After numerous pairings of CS and US, they were restored to normal; tests showed that no conditioning had occurred. Later studies indicate that some simple conditioning can occur in the paralyzed state. (*From Harlow and Stagner, 1933.*)

stimulation of cortical fields was utilized. An electrical stimulus to a sensory area (visual, auditory, or somesthetic) could become the CS for a response aroused from outside. But it proved impossible to establish a CR simply by a direct stimulus to the sensory area, followed by one to the motor area. The US had to originate elsewhere in the body.

Majority opinion seems to hold today that no response is necessary for conditioning. Mere presentation of the CS in close contiguity with the US is said to be sufficient (cf. sensory conditioning, above). This would mean that only sensory mechanisms and brain are necessary. There is no question, on the other hand, that *making a response speeds up the efficiency* of learning markedly.

Conditioning as total organismic function. Probably any attempt to pin down the formation of a CR to any specific part of the nervous system, or to a specific stimulus-response connection, is doomed to failure. After all, the CR does not constitute a case of a specific stimulus setting off a specific response. In the early stages of learning, as Culler (page 282) and others have shown, it is a massive, diffused response to a whole class of stimuli. Rapid shifts of attention may result in associating many irrelevant stimuli to the response. The earliest CR to shock may look very much like the UR. But as training continues, it becomes different; it has a longer latent time, is less intense, and may be less stereotyped than the UR. In final form it is not a true reflex at all, but a form of adaptive behavior fitting the conditions of the experiment.

Conditioning, especially in human beings, undoubtedly involves functions of the total organism, happening on different levels. Experiments have shown that attitudes and mental sets can influence the course of CR formation. Studies of unconscious conditioning and the differential retention of overt and autonomic CRs indicate that the human can be conditioned on different levels at the same time. It may well be that conditioning is as complex a form of learning as memorizing Greek poetry.

Theoretical Analysis of Conditioning

Let us now see if we can put these various aspects of the conditioning experiment together into a systematic statement. We have found that the three main parameters of conditioning are *contiguity, frequency,* and *reinforcement.* This means: (1) that the CS and the US must be presented close together in time (contiguity); (2) that the presentation usually must be repeated several times (frequency); and (3) that each presentation must be accompanied or followed by the UR (reinforcement). The CR is apparently an integrated act involving all three parameters.[1]

One wonders, however, if all are necessary or of equal importance in the conditioning process. Pavlov, and other early students of conditioning, were impressed by the fact that *repeated presentations* were necessary if a salivary CR was to be established. The fact that the CS seemed to take on the function of US suggested a process of "stimulus switching" or substitution. The fact that the dog was motivated by hunger was not recognized as being a crucial factor, because it could not be directly observed. Moreover, the ideational climate of that period favored emphasis on frequency and stimulus substitution.

Dashiell (1949), writing primarily from Pavlov's research reports, states the principle of conditioning as follows: "If a stimulus that is effectively arousing a given

[1] Actually, experiments make it clear that reinforcement is not needed on every trial. Very efficient conditioning takes place if the animal receives a food reward (or punishment) after a majority of presentations of the CS, so that the *probability* is in favor of reinforcement. (In the case of avoidance CRs, conditioning occurs even if the punishment follows the CS less than half the time.) As was noted in Chap. 6, we perceive situations in terms of their probable implications for tension reduction and homeostasis. Hence, reinforcement need not be present every time, but must occur often enough to build up this expectancy that it will appear.

response is frequently preceded or accompanied by an ineffective neutral stimulus, the latter may itself acquire the power to arouse the given response: it becomes a substitute stimulus to that response." Dashiell notes the inadequacies in the statement and formulates another. These inadequacies have been brought out in our earlier discussions: (1) the response does not necessarily remain the same to the new as to the prior stimulus; and (2) the function of the new stimulus is often not that of a substitute, but of a signal, in relation to the prior stimulus. (3) Furthermore, the definition as stated overemphasizes the role of frequency of pairing the two stimuli.

Stimulus substitution as a key concept in conditioning theory was severely weakened as experiments demonstrated that the CR and UR differ in duration, intensity, and form. The well-established CR appears to be an essentially new response, although it is possible under special conditions to get substantial duplications of the UR. When graphic records of the progress of conditioning are made, as in Fig. 8:11, it becomes apparent that the CR is *not* just the old response hitched to a new stimulus.

The efficiency of frequency as an explanatory concept has also been thrown into question by careful research. Many CRs are established after one or only a few paired presentations. Obviously at least one pairing is the minimum possible, but numerous repetitions are not required if motivation is strong. On the other hand, if motivation is weak, a great number of repetitions may produce no conditioning. A compromise statement may be that frequency offers *more opportunities* for contiguity and reinforcement to establish the CR. In decorticated dogs, and in very simple organisms such as protozoa, many, many presentations are required to establish any conditioning. This might mean that, in damaged or sluggish organisms, the increment per repetition is small; or, that

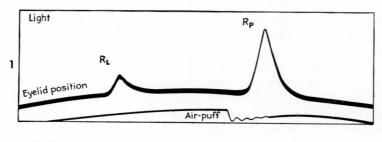

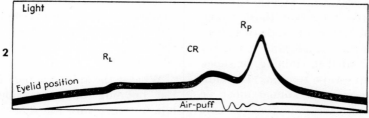

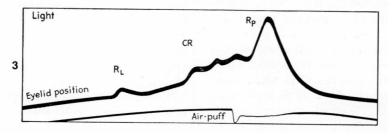

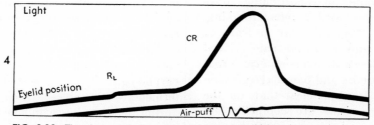

FIG. 8:11. The changes in form of a CR during acquisition. There has been a tendency to treat the CR as if it were identical with the UR, simply hooked onto a new stimulus. These photographic records prove this to be incorrect. Here R_L indicates the flash of the signal light (CS) and R_P is a puff of air to the cornea, causing the eyeblink reflex. Note that there is a small R_L even on trial 1. However, R_P is much larger and clearly different. Record 2 shows that, after some conditioning trials, an anticipatory movement of the lid (CR) occurs after the light, before the puff. Record 3 shows the uneven building up of this conditioned lid reflex, and Record 4 shows that the CR has grown to equal in size the original R_P but occurring before the puff of air. The distance between light and puff is 0.4 second. (*Sketched from Hilgard, 1936.*)

frequency is a low-order or primitive principle which shows up only in physiologically simple types of organisms.

That mere contiguity of CS and US is not enough to explain conditioning has been emphasized by many psychologists, recently by Hull (1943) who has stressed the role of the *consequences* of the conditioning situation to the organism. Typical effective conditioning procedures are those which involve motivational tensions, disturbances of homeostasis; the animal is kept hungry and food is presented in training, or shock is used to set up escape tensions. If conditioning is to occur, the animal must be able to achieve tension reduction; he eats the food or escapes the pain. According to this view, contiguity is actually a matter of bringing both US and CS in close proximity to the reward. The real explanatory concept is reinforcement by the rewarding situation. The animal learns CRs which help restore homeostasis; he fails to learn if no tension reduction is effected.

This concept, that reinforcement is the primary determiner of conditioning, looks very neat. It fits with popular thinking, since everyone "knows" that we learn to seek pleasure and to avoid pain. (Need reduction is a less controversial term; arguments over pleasure and pain have gone on for centuries.) It seems clear that, for the most part, organisms are compelled by tensions to act, and this action must move in the direction of decreased tension. Any external situation which builds tension will be avoided; a situation which reduces tension will be sought.

The concept of tension reduction as the reinforcement for CRs works well with the appetitive drives such as hunger, thirst, and sex. When these tensions are used to motivate learning, the reward occurs at the end of the response and seems to "reinforce" the tendency to do the same thing in the future. But we run into an anomaly when we try to apply this concept

directly to escape conditioning. The dilemma has been clearly stated by Hilgard (1948):

> If an animal runs down an alley, meets a charged grid, and leaps ahead from it to safety, the leap is associated with need reduction (pain alleviation) so that by strict reinforcement theory, the next time the animal should do what it last did, only perhaps more intensely. It should run down the alley faster, touch the grid and take a jump to safety. . . . *Rats do not do this.* They slow up in the alley and try not to approach the grid.[1]

What is the animal doing? He is avoiding the building up of tension, instead of blindly going into the shock situation and then escaping. In avoidance behavior the tension reduction takes place before, or at the onset, rather than at the termination of the situation. So the animal does *not* acquire a CR of stepping on the grid and then leaping to safety.

To salvage the tension-reduction theory, it is necessary to posit what is known as an *intervening variable*. In the conditioning procedure the intervening variable is based on the fact that the CR takes place before the UR, therefore, as it were, anticipating it. This time lag is cited as proof of the anticipatory character of the CR. Different psychologists have suggested different intermediate variables which may occur during this time interval. The most popular one is *expectancy;* the implication is that the organism responds not to the outer situation, but to an expectancy of reward or of nonreward. Another proposal, by Mowrer (1940), is that the intervening variable is fear. In the example cited, he would say that the total situation set up fear tensions; behavior then is determined by courses of action which will minimize or reduce fear.

Weaknesses of reinforcement theory. It seems unquestionable, from what has

[1] Hilgard (1948), p. 108. Reprinted by permission of Appleton-Century-Crofts, Inc.

been presented here, that some form of reinforcement is essential to explain some forms of conditioning. On the other hand, we have such experiments as that of Liddell, in which the animal cannot escape (no tension reduction occurs); the conditioned pupillary reflex, in which no apparent reward or punishment occurs; the sensory preconditioning study by Brogden; and the study by Light and Gantt in which the dog was paralyzed and incapable of making the response which would have reduced tension. Such experiments seem to compel a recognition of CR formation *without reinforcement*. As a consequence of this situation, many psychologists now feel compelled to accept a *two-factor theory* of conditioning, although they would prefer a neat, one-factor explanation.

Two-factor theory of conditioning. To account adequately for the facts, it becomes necessary to separate the conditioned response into two phases, which have most often been referred to as "conditioning proper" and "learning."[1] Conditioning in its pure form is best illustrated by the classical CR, such as the salivary CR, the conditioned pupillary reflex, or Liddell's shock-without-escape technique. When Pavlov's design is followed—that is, a neutral stimulus is paired with an unconditioned stimulus—an association is formed between the two in relation to a common response. Thus, in the bell-food situation, the dog is conditioned to respond to the bell as he would to the *sight of food*. The sound and the sight of food are both related to a common response, the act of eating. Note, however, that the adaptive activity of the animal is not involved. He does not actively change his response (chewing, swallowing, etc., do not get involved in the CR). All that has happened

[1] The presentation here is modeled on that of Maier and Schneirla (1942) and Birch and Bitterman (1949).

is that an auditory stimulus now substitutes for a visual stimulus.

Instrumental conditioning reveals a significantly different state of affairs. Here the activity of the organism is a significant variable. When the animal hears a bell and is shocked on the leg, a vigorous response is obtained. At first the bell produces this same massive, effortful reaction. The animal has established a CR, but it is a CR in which the sound signals the approach of pain, and this leads to tension and attempts to escape. Because the dog can respond actively, he varies the leg response in different ways, until he succeeds in avoiding the shock. This response variation is probably dependent upon shifts of attention. The perfection of this avoiding movement is *subsequent and supplementary to conditioning proper;* it represents variability of behavior and selection of that movement which is reinforced, *i.e.*, which reduces the tension.

We might say that pure conditioning "happens to" an organism; the animal or person is acted upon but plays no active role. If I am so conditioned that my knee jerks to a flash of red light, or that I expect the bell to be followed by shock, this has the quality of something from the outside imposed upon me. Learning, on the other hand, has the form of self-initiated activity to reach a goal. The response changes in form; indeed, the CR may have no resemblance to the UR (cf. Hilgard's comment about the rat which should step on the charged grid and jump but actually does something quite different).

The two-factor approach to conditioning may help clear up any remaining doubts about the difference between "static" and "dynamic" homeostasis. In the classical conditioning experiment, the bell is followed by food. The bell, having acquired a positive valence by association, disturbs the equilibrium of the animal. A dormant hunger tension is activated. Then the reward (food) is presented and the equilibrium is restored. This process is quite mechanical and involves no modification of the environment; it resembles strikingly the precision of the self-regulatory mechanisms such as breathing and temperature control. However, in pain-escape conditioning, the organism is forced to try different variations of the response to attain equilibrium. The method evolved may result in a totally new action pattern or in a modification of the environment (by going away from the pain signal, or by destroying the apparent source of the pain). We may say, then, that in low-level "pure" conditioning (pupillary, salivary, etc.), and in spinal animals, homeostasis is of the static type. When the organism actively varies its behavior ("learning") in quest of a goal, homeostasis is dynamic.

Learning and conditioning in daily life. The separation of pure conditioning from learning clarifies matters which often become confused. In daily living we acquire many CRs by pure happenstance. We note certain uniform stimulus relations, such as bells ringing at noon, fire sirens when a house is burning, prevailing customs and mores of the community, cultural beliefs, and prejudices. These we pick up without effort or active analysis. We are conditioned, so to speak, by the molding forces of our environment, passive victims of external pressures. On the other hand, we regularly encounter tension situations about which we have to deliberate; we consciously consider a variety of responses in order to reduce the tension and regain equilibrium. The housewife matching expense to income, or the businessman solving a production problem, are obvious examples. In such cases active learning, not passive conditioning, is going on.

The principle of dominance in conditioning. Conditioning, we repeat, involves the whole, integrated organism. One may become conditioned on several levels simultaneously. On the sensory level he may form an association of bell and shock as stimuli having a signal relationship. On the response level the CS becomes related to a muscular activity. On the feeling and emotional level changes also go on, but they are often ignored because they are invisible. Various experiments, such as those using the GSR, show that visceral changes condition even more readily than most skeletal responses. Modification of behavior is most easily observable, but conditioning also modifies experience in terms of feeling, perceiving, and desiring.

The strength of these components of conditioning will vary with circumstances and with the organism. In the adult human the dominant effect may be a modification of perception, so that the automatic response is not observed. Or the response may be obvious while the person shows no awareness of any change in his behavior. Some nervous mannerisms and other expressions of personality fall in this category.

Major importance attaches to the emotional component in conditioning. This phase of the total CR becomes established more promptly, endures longer, and exerts a more decisive impact upon other behavioral patterns than the perceptual or voluntary motor phases. As we have noted in the preceding pages, conditioned visceral responses such as the GSR may persist long after the situation has lost its former meaning and become neutral in terms of any conscious feeling. This is undoubtedly the basis for many seemingly irrational human peculiarities, superstitions, and prejudices.

There is another respect in which it is most unfortunate that emotional conditioning is dominant over other CRs. Emotions are polar in function. They tend toward extremes. We have spoken of need satisfaction and need frustration, and their correlated feelings of pleasantness and unpleasantness. Muenzinger has pointed out that most emotions are polarized in pairs, as love-hate, fear-courage, despair-hope, doubt-confidence, and elation-depression. Physiologically we find a basis for this polarity in the polar functions of the ANS, where the sympathetic and parasympathetic segments are antagonistic (page 77). These systems tend to go off on an all-or-nothing basis; it is difficult to grade the response according to the seriousness of the situation.[1] Thus people, especially in childhood but often in later years, tend to over-react to emotionally toned situations. Recognizing the threat from a given direction, they go too far in the opposite.

It may be that in the ANS we have a physical basis for the polarity of good and bad which only too often dominates human thinking. Judgments are too commonly in terms of black or white, rather than in shades of gray. In social situations, "our" side is all good, "their" side is all bad. Such a behavioral mechanism makes for errors in judgment and failures of adaptive behavior. We must learn to differentiate, to accept the fact that reality is not polarized, that individuals and nations are both good and bad. The dominance of conditioned emotions makes this kind of learning extraordinarily difficult and makes us easy victims of distorted propaganda.

Limitations of the Concept of Conditioning

The student, reading the preceding pages perhaps too rapidly, and under pressure, may have come to the conclusion that we propose to explain all forms of learning as conditioning. Let us make it clear that we

[1] The real basis for discriminating as to the importance or degree of danger in a situation is found in our perception of it. These perceptions depend upon cortical processes, whereas the emotional response is largely subcortical, and in fact, the ANS is mostly independent of cortical control. You can readily verify this by attempting voluntarily to slow down your heart rate when you are excited, frightened, or angry.

do not wish to extend the term so far. Many laymen have overgeneralized the concept, and a few psychologists have aided and abetted this confusion. Sometimes it is said that one's ideas on a certain topic are determined by conditioning, when what is really meant is that one recalls certain memories or impressions. The idea of a bull may well be due to conditioning, especially if I suddenly find myself in the presence of one in an open field and take to my heels. But a bull as an idea, in or out of the pen, may serve as a topic suggesting all sorts of ideas, in or out of the pen, or in a china closet. In these examples we have learning both by conditioning and by association. In conditioning we learn to equate one stimulus with another; by association we recognize the stimulus and relate it to the varying contexts in which it has been experienced. Another example: a young man says he has been "conditioned to be studious." This would be true if he meant that certain hours of the day, or a certain room and desk, tend to set off studious behavior; but if he is referring to his long-range goal to become a doctor, then his studying is controlled by a motive or value which can override most specific CRs.

Of course some aspects of complex behavior justify this generalized usage of the term *conditioning*. In the process of becoming socialized, the child passively acquires habits of conformity to social norms. Why does the fork go to the left of the plate? Why can't we eat with our fingers? So much of our social behavior is completely nonrational acceptance of arbitrary standards. Because intelligence cannot be applied to the problem, the child can learn only by conditioning.

Much of language actually must be learned on this level. There is nothing about the word "cat" that resembles the animal. The child learns an arbitrary association of sound and object, just as the dog learned that the bell signaled the approach of food.

"See what I mean? Every time I snap this switch, his feet go up."

FIG. 8:12. Much of our day-to-day learning takes the form of conditioning. (*Courtesy of Burr Shafer and the Curtis Publishing Co.*)

Most foreign equivalents are acquired in a similar mechanical way. Why should "black" become *"noir"* in French? One simply establishes automatic responses by which the two words are interchangeable; or, on the receiving side, they become substitute stimuli for each other.

Much of psychopathology, the realm of abnormal behavior, involves conditioned emotions. Bagby reports a case of a girl with an intense fear of running water—so strong she could not even draw her own bath water. It was traced to a single traumatic experience with a waterfall in her early childhood. People come to psychiatrists and clinical psychologists with phobias for knives, elevators, girls with red hair, men with curly hair, telephones, and a thousand other oddities. In most instances these phobias can be traced to some violently frightening or threatening situation in which that particular element played the part of a conditioning stimulus, although it was a minor, almost irrelevant, factor in a logical sense. Conditioning does,

consequently, play a large role in patterning our day-to-day behavior.

The Principle of Conditioning in Terms of Two-factor Theory

On page 296 we stated the principle of conditioning as stimulus substitution. This statement holds quite well for what we have identified as "pure" or classical conditioning. It is particularly accurate for those instances in which homeostasis is served by the original response, as in the case of the salivary reflex. It is, of course, increasingly inadequate as we go up the scale of complexity of response and of the animal kingdom. A new factor enters; the CS no longer functions as a true substitute for the US, and instead functions as signal. Thus, in rewriting his definition of conditioning, Dashiell developed this formulation:

If an indifferent, neutral stimulus is presented one or more times along with or just before an adequate stimulus to which the organism is responding in an appropriate way, the neutral stimulus may acquire potency to arouse much the same kind of appropriate behavior. It thus becomes a signal standing for the original stimulus.[1]

Now we have to clarify the principle emphasizing the learning, or final, phase of the CR, in which the organism changes the substitute response to adapt more adequately to the situation. Instrumental shock-escape conditioning offers the best example. From it we derive the following formal statement:

When the conditioned response encounters frustration, tension-arousing stimuli or failure of need reduction, the response is modified or replaced by a new conditioned response which leads to tension reduction. Selection and modification tend to continue until

[1] Dashiell (1949), p. 423. Reprinted by permission of Houghton Mifflin Company.

maximum tension reduction has been achieved.

Conditioning and Symbolic Learning in Humans

We have noted that conditioning gives an excellent paradigm for human learning in social situations, where norms of behavior are established in terms of "what is done, or not done" and evaluated in terms of good and bad. Such dichotomized situations fit the CR pattern nicely because, as was noted above, pure conditioning is built around the occurrence or nonoccurrence of a response. The dog either salivates or he does not. The iris either contracts or fails to do so. The baby is either frightened or undisturbed by the white rat.

It is possible to set up human learning experiments in such a way as to duplicate the conditioning technique. Thorndike (1935) has reported extensive studies with humans on this level. The title of his book, *The Psychology of Wants, Interests and Attitudes*, indicates the fact that he was concerned especially with conditioning tensions (or some dynamic inner state) to symbolic stimuli.

The method could be summarized by saying that Thorndike induced the subject to give a random response to a stimulus, and then either "rewarded" this response by saying "right" or "punished" it by saying "wrong." Inasmuch as the subjects were adults on work relief, and they stood to gain or lose money by these rewards and punishments, there seems no question that real visceral tensions were aroused. By an ingenious system of varying the distribution of rewards and punishments, Thorndike was able to demonstrate formation of unconscious associations, the establishment of bias, and similar phenomena.

The experimenter read a word, and the subject responded with a number at random, between 1 and 6, or 1 and 10, for varying experiments. The response was labeled right or wrong according to a prearranged pattern. The pace of the experiment was such that memorizing as we considered it in Chap. 7 was impossible. Thus we have a situation closely resembling classical conditioning, in that the subject's own activity is virtually excluded as a factor.

This description will be made clearer by an example. Here is part of a series of 40 words, to each of which the subject gave a number between 1 and 10. Numbers marked C are those which were called "right."

	Trial 1	Trial 2	Trial 3	Trial 4
Catnip.........	2	4	10	2
Cedar..........	3	3	6	2
Chamber.......	1	2	9	8
Chorus........	8	10	7	6
Dally..........	4	8	5	4
Dazzle.........	C2	6	9	1
Deduce........	9	7	2	5
Early..........	4	C5	C5	C5
Effort.........	3	6	C7	C7

Thorndike's logic is simple. The word "right" is a reward because it signals a money bonus; the word "wrong" is similarly a punishment. If the subject gives increasingly more "right" responses on successive trials, that would mean that reward fixes connections or enhances learning. Since the subject must respond rapidly and goes through many series in a short time, the conditions are not favorable for association learning. Sometimes a correct number will be given by chance; but since the chance probabilities are measurable, the effectiveness of reward can be determined. Thus, in an experiment using six numbers, the chance success ratio is 16.7 per cent. As the preceding table shows, there is a tendency for some right responses to be learned and reproduced. For "early" the correct number is repeated every time after it was hit on the second trial; for

TABLE 8:1. Effect of Verbal Rewards and Punishments in Learning Verbal Connections
(*From Thorndike, 1935*)

	Strengthening in per cent
One rewarded first occurrence.....	26.9
One punished first occurrence.....	5.8
Two consecutive occurrences (rewarded).....................	64.4
Two consecutive occurrences (punished).......................	16.7
Two nonconsecutive occurrences (rewarded)...................	67.4
Two nonconsecutive occurrences (punished)...................	12.3

"effort" the correct number is repeated after being discovered on the third trial.

Thorndike's original formulation of the "law of effect" held that satisfying consequences should strengthen a connection or association, and annoying consequences should weaken it. His experiments do not entirely confirm this. As the following table reveals, both satisfying and annoying consequences may strengthen a connection; however, reward has more reinforcement value than punishment. (The table should be read as follows: if a particular word-number connection occurs once and is rewarded, it will in the future occur 26.9 per cent oftener than would be expected by chance.)

It should be remembered that a wide range of stimulus-response connections are available to the subject. In the experiment described he could associate the word "early" with any number from 1 to 6. There is no reason within himself, or in these numbers, to make him prefer one over another. If his performance, then, shows an increase in use of a particular word-number combination 64.4 per cent above chance, this must be ascribed to some factor in the experiment. The experimental factors are so controlled that *only* reward and punishment vary for these con-

nections. Thorndike holds, consequently, that the effect of a response can influence the strength of the stimulus-response connection. If the consequences are "good" for the organism (reward), we find a marked increase in the probability that this response will occur again.

The data show that *punishment also strengthens bonds.* This is paradoxical, since the organism should avoid punishment and need frustration. Thorndike concludes that reward strengthens connections directly, whereas punishment operates indirectly by informing the learner that "such and such a response, in such and such a situation, brings distress." Punishment thus *emphasizes* the response, and the emphasis may for a time cause it to be repeated.

Does the effect of a reward spread to nearby responses? Thorndike examined his data to see if the occurrence of a reward had any effect upon those responses just before or just after. It immediately became apparent that some spread of reward did occur. The punished response immediately before or immediately following the rewarded R was clearly strengthened somewhat. Those connections two steps removed were strengthened also, but to a lesser degree. The results are shown in Fig. 8:13, in which a punished response five steps away from a rewarded R is taken as showing zero spread or zero facilitation.

It is clear from this figure that we have here a gradient similar to the gradient of positive transfer or stimulus generalization. Perhaps what happens is that the subject recalls having been rewarded "somewhere along here" and therefore repeats his prior choices in that portion of the list. This resembles the behavior of the dog who got food to a tone of 512 cycles and later salivates to a tone of 256 more than to 128. The situation is perceived as somehow similar to that involving reward.

With animals learning a maze it has been noted that the errors first eliminated (correct turns learned) are those nearest the food box. This has a marked similarity to Thorndike's spread of effect; Hull has called it *spread of reinforcement.*

The law of effect or reward, according to Thorndike, is the main principle of learning; and learning is defined as *forming connections between events.* Thorndike's law is similar to Hull's law of reinforcement but is more general. Hull assumes that reinforcement must be a physiological need reduction, or tension reduction in the case of social or acquired motives. Thorndike evades the physiological problem, leaving it for future research. However, he considers the law of effect to be a statement of universal law:

The satisfier acts (upon a neighboring connection) unconsciously and directly, much as sunlight acts upon plants, or an electric current upon a neighboring current, or the earth upon the moon. From a satisfier issues a strengthening force which the connections absorb. Which of them will absorb it depends on the laws of nature, not of logic and teleology.[1]

Thorndike's generalization has not gone unquestioned. In learning such as Pavlov's CR, or Thorndike's arbitrary correct-response series, the situation is so simple that reward or reinforcement can scarcely be separated from the connection-forming phase. However, other factors such as contiguity and recency are also operative in his experiment.

The unraveling of these complexities has not yet been achieved to the general satisfaction of professional psychologists. We shall therefore summarize the problem of forming stimulus-response connections as follows: There seems no question that, when biological drives are involved, the process of need reduction decisively affects learning. In such instances homeostatic adjustment is more significant than mere contiguity of stimulus and response. On the

[1] Thorndike (1933), p. 48. Reprinted by permission.

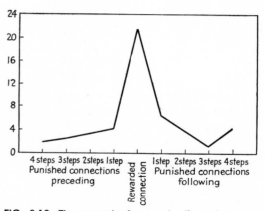

FIG. 8:13. The spread of reward effects from one connection to others. In the Thorndike experiment, it was demonstrated that saying "right" to a given response increases the probability that this same response will occur to this stimulus on the next time through the series. What is the effect on adjacent (wrong) connections? This chart shows that there is a slight spread of reinforcement, such that punished connections 3 or 4 steps away are still strengthened perceptibly by the reward. Such evidence as this leads us to hold that reward, not punishment, is the decisive factor in the acquisition of new responses. (Punishment may sometimes help by inhibiting a wrong response which prevents the correct one from appearing.) (*From Thorndike, 1935, p. 34.*)

other hand, it is also clear that, in most of the CR experiments, stimulus substitution takes place in accordance with the principle of contiguity, and need reduction is not necessarily involved. The two-factor theory, including both these principles, therefore seems required. If a single formula is ever evolved, it must adequately explain both contiguity learning and reward learning.

Some psychologists have held that the CR experiment is not sufficiently comparable with adult learning activities to merit extensive study by psychologists. We cannot accept this position. Conditioning represents an accurate paradigm for much childhood learning of great significance for personality and, indeed, for a considerable amount of adult learning. The child is largely passive in relation to his environment. Especially in infancy, he learns by contiguity and by reward in what must

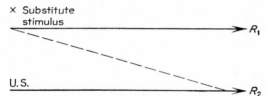

FIG. 8:14. Stimulus substitution or classical conditioning. In this type of experiment, the CS becomes a true substitute stimulus for the US, and elicits R_2 in a form substantially similar to the original response (salivary CR, conditioned GSR, etc.).

necessarily be a highly arbitrary sequence. Cultures are essentially nonrational. No one could ever learn by rational analysis why he should drive on the right side of the street in New York and on the left in London, why he should not go out in the street without clothing, why girls and boys must use different toilet facilities, and so on. Yet the whole foundation of social psychology, and the psychology of personality, rests on just such learning of arbitrary patterns. A child's fear of the dark or of cats, his preference for short, dark women, his timidity in the presence of older people trace to experiences which closely parallel the conditioning experiment. Classical conditioning represents the *constant* environment molding the plastic human. It is from such learning that we get the rigid duplication of parents' personalities by children, blind adherence to cultural ideas, and fear of cultural differences. It is therefore important for us to analyze the type of learning represented by this example.

Classical conditioning may be characterized as learning imposed from without. A considerable amount of adult learning differs notably in that the individual is an active, selective agent, choosing what he will learn. Chapter 9 will deal further with this type of learning.

Diagrammatic representation of conditioning. It may be helpful to the student to represent CR formation diagrammatically. Figures 8:14 to 8:16 have been prepared

to summarize the ideas set forth in the preceding pages. They are arranged in order to show the temporal sequence of changes as conditioning proceeds.

The first diagram is the ordinary stimulus substitution model, corresponding to what we have called *pure conditioning*. In this case the CS becomes to all effects a substitute for the US, evoking a response which differs perhaps in intensity but not in form from the response to the US. The second diagram shows the shift from stimulus substitution to the beginnings of adaptive behavior. The CS now takes on the character of a signal that the US is approaching, and the organism shifts from passive awareness of stimuli to actively doing something about the stimulus. The animal has, in his behavior repertoire, various reactions which *might* meet the situation. Thus, in the escape reaction, he may try lifting his foot, arching his back, shifting the whole body, etc. These possibilities are represented by the array of lines, each line being one trial response. They correspond to trial and errors in maze learning. As selection occurs, we get the situation in the third diagram, where one of these possibilities has been chosen and the others have been eliminated. The line ends at a point prior to US, indicating that the adjustive process involves *anticipation* which actually prevents US from being received.

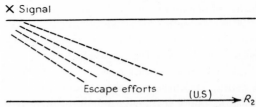

FIG. 8:15. Beginnings of instrumental conditioning. If the experimental setup permits, and US is a noxious stimulus, CS will function as a signal of the approach of US. This will set off a series of new responses which have the nature of efforts to escape the application of US. As long as these efforts are unsuccessful, US will appear and R_2 will follow.

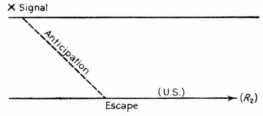

FIG. 8:16. Perfection of instrumental conditioning. If an anticipatory or escape response succeeds in avoiding US, it will be selected and perfected. The CS now functions as a signal, setting off anticipation of US and the escape CR follows, thus avoiding US (indicated by parentheses) and the original R_2 now disappears.

These three diagrams actually do not represent completely separate phases of a process. There is considerable overlap in time of phases 1 and 2, and even of 1 and 3. However, it is convenient to think of them as representing successive stages in a single process.

The three diagrams have another value for the student of psychology. They emphasize a most important point in our understanding of human behavior: that there is a continuum from pure conditioning or passive learning to pure adjustment or active learning. Furthermore, they indicate that learning cannot be sharply distinguished from thinking, since thinking consists of considering various alternatives and making a choice. Our analysis of thinking, in Chap. 11, will show that thinking is a form of learning.

Eliminating Conditioned Responses

It is often a matter of great practical importance to know how we can eliminate a CR once it has been established. The obvious illustrations come from unfortunate childhood experiences which establish undesirable emotional responses to inappropriate stimuli. However, many other examples could be noted.

The two-factor formulation of conditioning suggests that both the "substituted response" and the "adjustive response" may be occurring simultaneously. To eliminate the CR, must we change one, the other, or both of these? Observation of animals indicates that it is easier to modify the adjustive response. Similarly, studies of breaking habits in humans have shown that it is easier to substitute a new movement for the old than simply to break off the habit entirely. Thus chewing gum is substituted for smoking, etc.

What about the visceral CR in an emotional response? We may teach the person how to act, but if he is still upset internally, not much progress has been made. Jones (1924a, b) examined this problem of eliminating conditioned fears and identified several different methods which could be tried: the method of disuse, frequent application of the stimulus, ridicule, social imitation, verbal appeal, and reconditioning.

Most of these are very unsatisfactory. As could be guessed from our comments on forgetting (page 271), keeping the child from contact with the feared stimulus does not weaken the visceral CR. Frequent application does not extinguish such CRs, but instead is likely to increase their strength (principle of habit, page 50). Ridicule simply adds more unpleasant tension and so may actually strengthen the fear instead of weakening it. Social imitation of children without fear is sometimes valuable, but the results apparently are undependable. Verbal appeal has little utility because the visceral responses are involuntary and hence beyond verbal control. Reconditioning is most effective; it involves a laborious process of conditioning the child so that the fear stimulus is now a sign of a positive valence, usually food. The magnitude of the problem is indicated by the fact that it is estimated that a fear established in three repetitions of the CS and US will require

30 combinations of CS with food to eliminate. Furthermore, there is even a little danger in this method if reconditioning is pressed too rapidly; the child may come to fear the food (Fig. 3:15, page 102).

It is pretty obvious that few situations arise, in our normal training of children, analogous to reconditioning. Thus conditionings hostile to animals, to people with some physical appearance, to people with some group label attached, to social situations of specific types may be established in early childhood and persist throughout life. There may be some modification on an intellectual level ("I know that such people are not to be feared") but the fear continues on an unconscious level and may dominate thought and behavior even if unrecognized.

The conditioned fear is a form of substitute stimulus conditioning (red hair is a signal for pain). The intellectual awareness that redheads are just like other people is a form of adaptive learning based on consideration of alternative responses and selection of one which seems justified. Learning by stimulus substitution thus seems tied up with the all-or-nothing, polarized emotions (love-hate, desire-fear, etc). Adaptive or rational learning requires that we get away from these absolutes of good and bad; that we recognize variations in degree, differences within groups, and so on. The polarized, substitute stimulus learning seems simpler, more primitive; in time of disturbance, the complex rational patterns are disrupted and the simple conditioned emotions dominate behavior. This fact is crucial for understanding panic behavior, mob action, and other responses to stress situations.

SUMMARY

The typical experiment in learning by association presented the learner with a series of items to be acquired in that order. To simplify this procedure and to look for basic principles explaining all learning, psychologists turned to the conditioning experiment with only a pair of stimuli and (presumably) a single response.

It has developed that the conditioning experiment does not greatly simplify the psychological analysis of learning. We have found that classical conditioning corresponds to passive learning—molding of the organism by the environment—a close approach to what we have called *static homeostasis*. Instrumental conditioning, by contrast, is an active process by which the organism adjusts to environmental pressures.

In both forms of conditioning we find that the CS acquires a signal function, reporting to the organism that the US is approaching. Conditioning is thus very rapid if US is highly tension arousing; it is quite slow if little tension is involved.

Instrumental conditioning reveals most clearly the progress from a massive, diffuse muscular response to a precise, limited, focal response. However, even classical CRs show dropping out of nonessential elements in the total response pattern.

Classical conditioning undoubtedly is the process by which most of our prejudices and preferences, superstitions and cultural taboos are established. It builds upon visceral elements of emotion and is thus polarized, extreme, and resistant to conscious control. These facts point to far-reaching implications for personality and social psychology.

Recommended Readings[1]

HILGARD, E. R.: *Theories of Learning.* New York: Appleton-Century-Crofts, 1948.

——— and D. G. MARQUIS: *Conditioning and Learning.* New York: Appleton-Century-Crofts, 1940.

[1] See also p. 547.

KELLER, F. S., and W. N. SCHOENFELD: *Principles of Psychology.* New York: Appleton-Century-Crofts, 1950.

MAIER, N. R. F., and T. C. SCHNEIRLA: *Principles of Animal Psychology.* McGraw-Hill, 1935.

MILLER, N., and J. DOLLARD: *Social Learning and Imitation.* New Haven: Yale University Press, 1944.

MOSS, F. A. (ED.): *Comparative Psychology.* New York: Prentice-Hall. Chapters by Liddell and Tolman.

PAVLOV, I. P.: *Conditioned Reflexes.* New York: Oxford, 1927.

THORNDIKE, E. L.: *The Psychology of Wants, Interests and Attitudes.* New York: Appleton-Century-Crofts, 1935.

CHAPTER 9

Problem Solving

We have now considered two relatively simple forms of learning: rote serial learning, in which the person more or less passively memorizes a series of words or ideas presented to him from outside; and conditioning, likewise rather passive, in which the person is presented with arbitrary paired stimuli, the CS and US. The conditions of learning in both such instances severely limit the person's behavior. He has no choice as regards the stimuli to which he shall respond; they are set by the experimenter (or teacher). Except in instrumental conditioning he has little choice as to response, and even here he has only a narrow range of possibilities. Thus in these simpler forms of learning the organism is prevented from using its whole range of abilities.

In the kind of learning to which we now turn (problem solving), the operational conditions allow the subject to select stimuli as well as responses. Consider a hungry dog in a strange environment. He gets all sorts of smells, many of which suggest food. He cannot respond to all of them at once. So selection of stimuli (attention, perception, and discrimination) is essential to problem solving. More than anything else, it is this emphasis on *perceptual analysis of the situation* which distinguishes complex, problem-solving behavior from simple memorizing

and conditioning. The immediately succeeding pages will clarify this process as a background for the experiments on problem solving which are the main concern of this chapter.

Learning as Choice Behavior

In the instrumental conditioning situation, the animal had two tasks: to identify sound as a signal for shock, and to choose among various responses which would minimize the tension. A moment's reflection will indicate that while perfect learning on the first trial may be adaptive as regards signal function (learning that the sound is followed by shock), it would actually be unadaptive to have perfect one-trial learning as regards the second phase. Unless a person tries several paths, he cannot learn which is the "best" for reaching his goal. It is thus an advantage, in a quest for survival, to have variations in response in a painful situation, so that gradual learning can select the most effective method of restoring homeostasis.

Let us use the term *choice point* to identify those places in the learning process where the animal (or human) must choose between alternative ways of getting satisfaction. At a "choice point," all the capacities of the organism become involved. Perception, including vision, hearing, and other senses; awareness of different needs; memory of past experiences, and other inner processes may affect the particular response to be made. Responses may be improvised (chiefly by combinations of of old reactions) to try to meet the situation. In every problem situation there are many responses which could be given, and if it is complex, many probably will occur before a final selection is made. Final selection seems to depend mostly upon success in reducing tension, although other factors are also operating.

To the extent that selections made at these choice points become permanent—so that they are reproduced when the situation reappears—learning has occurred. The organism has been changed or modified and demonstrates it by repeating the correct response with greater ease on future occasions. The selection among responses during early trials, however, involves processes which are ordinarily not called learning. Perceiving, discriminating, and thinking may be involved, depending on the capacities of the animal. *Learning may be defined as the process of making permanent this particular problem solution.*

In the present chapter we shall be concerned with learning activities in which the initiative is, so to speak, in the hands of the learner. The organism is presented with a complex problem. Some freedom is allowed for moving about in order to find significant choice points which lead to a goal. This goal is determined by some need, as to escape from confinement or to obtain food.

A completely free situation, however, would make it difficult for the inquiring psychologist to observe significant changes in behavior. Some environmental limitation is therefore imposed. The animal may be placed in a puzzle box, a maze, or a discrimination apparatus so that he can be more conveniently and precisely observed.

Role of motivation. In these problem-solving types of learning tasks, the predominant role of motivation at once becomes apparent. When we dealt with human rote learning, we could easily ignore motivation, because it was concealed. Much of human activity is motivated by a generalized desire to please others, a desire for approval and security. College students particularly, the standard guinea pigs of psychological experimentation, are motivated to please their professors by participating in such studies. When we deal with animals, or when we get outside the routine memorizing study of humans, we become acutely aware of the basic rule: *no learning without motivation.*

The typical learning problem in this group—at least, the one on which most research studies have concentrated—is the maze. A white rat is placed in a device composed of a series of pathways (Fig. 9:1) and required to learn the correct path from start to end. If this animal is placed in the maze, well fed and comfortable, he does not learn; he goes to sleep. At best, he may wander about the alleys with a sublime disregard for whether they get him closer to the goal. However, if he is quite hungry, and food is placed in the goal box, we observe a different state of affairs. There is an active search of the environment, and the correct turns at choice points are learned rapidly. We shall therefore find it convenient to characterize this kind of learning as *goal-directed.* Tensions, whether internally or externally aroused, press the animal toward a goal. Reaching the goal results in tension reduction. As in the case of instrumental conditioning, the selection process seems to be chiefly one of choosing the particular response pattern which achieves maximum tension reduction with minimum effort.

Two questions become paramount in the study of goal-directed learning. How is the goal attained in the first place? And how does the solution become a permanent

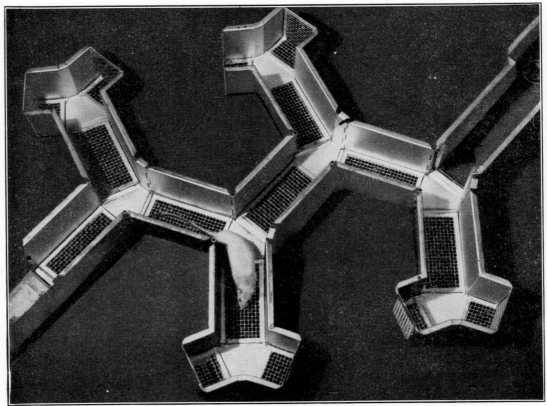

FIG. 9:1. The rat in the maze. For a variety of reasons, the experiment on maze learning by rats has become a standard device in psychological research. It lends itself to studies of sensory function, diet, brain operations, and other independent variables. This photograph will help visualize the experiment, which will be referred to often in this chapter. The starting box is at lower left, food box at upper right. (*Lilo Hess, photographer. From Three Lions, Inc.*)

acquisition? From the point of view of "pure" scientific psychology, these are the only important matters to be studied.

Goal direction. As we have already demonstrated, man's needs and goals are intimately related. The goal is the reward, the need satisfier. It could be called a projection of the need in time and space. It would be easy to say that the goal exerts a selective influence upon learning, but it is much more accurate to say that the motive is the selective factor. This does not make much difference for experimental purposes, since we equate the two; that is, we deprive the animal of food and then interpret his behavior as food seeking. If various goal

objects are present and the animal strives vigorously to obtain one, we say that this stimulus has a *positive valence* or that it is a desired goal.

What we must avoid, in this analysis, is attributing magical qualities to needs and goals. The need does not "find its goal" in any occult fashion. If an animal is hungry, it seeks stimuli which will end this tension (cf. page 39). When the place is familiar and the food location is known from past experience, the organism moves efficiently toward the goal. But consider the same problem in an environment which is completely novel to the animal. The behavior of the hungry rat is directed toward food, but this fact is not revealed until food is obtained and the activity subsides. In searching, the rat moves about at random, crawling here, climbing there. By accident he finds the food. When eating is followed by relaxation, we infer that hunger was the underlying tension.

Goal-directed learning is *purposeful* in that the energy mobilized by some need drives the organism into activity. This does not imply that the rat is conscious of a definite purpose. It only means that he is pushed into activity by an inner discomfort which will not cease until the needed object is contacted. Man behaves in a similar manner, but often—instead of moving about physically—he moves symbolically, that is, by picturing certain acts and their possible consequences. This process will be examined in Chap. 11.

Permanence of solution. When first taking up the problem of learning we offered a rather loose definition of learning as acquisition of knowledge. This was tightened up by stating that learning always involves a *relatively permanent modification* of behavior. The modifications were ascribed to the nervous system and were referred to as *memory traces.*

It must be noted that changes of behavior as such are not necessarily instances of learning. For instance, when a boy fails to impress his girl friend by cave-man tactics, he may change and try the candy-and-flowers approach. The modification here is due to the persistence of tension, but if he achieves success and fixes this as a relatively permanent feature of his behavior (so that it appears in similar future occasions), we can say that learning has taken place. Thus we now redefine learning as a *relatively permanent modification of behavior as a consequence of tension arousal and reduction.*

This definition implies that purpose and proficiency become involved in a determination of learning. The action must be successful in terms of goal achievement. This does

not mean that human beings always learn the optimum method of getting satisfactions; sometimes, after a series of failures, the individual refuses to try for the goal or accepts an inefficient, low-level achievement. But, in general, we must include in our study of human learning the conception that it is related to the attainment of a goal.

The Nature of the Stimulus

The scientific study of goal-oriented learning requires that we examine more closely the problem of the perceived situation. In seeking tension reduction, the animal must study the terrain and the objects present. A college student must correctly perceive the books, the laboratory equipment, the objects which must be manipulated. The significance of this perceptual process can be illustrated by the following example:

The two-rope problem. The student is confronted with two ropes, suspended from the ceiling, and is instructed to tie them together. The ends of the ropes are about 7 feet apart, so that the student, holding one, cannot reach the other (Fig. 9:2). He is told that he can use any of the objects on a nearby table. One of these items is a small clamp; however, its use as a clamp will not be helpful. The efficient solution is to tie the clamp on one rope end and set it swinging like a pendulum, grasp the other rope, and catch the clamp as it swings near. He can then tie the two ropes together. From an examination of the students who succeed and those who fail on this learning task, it is clear that perception is a major factor in the solution. Those who perceive the objects available only in their familiar roles (*e.g.*, as a clamp for holding objects together) are not successful. It is necessary to perceive some object as a pendulum bob in order to reach the goal. (For example, one student used a pair of shears, another a clock, in making the pendulum.) *Flexibil-*

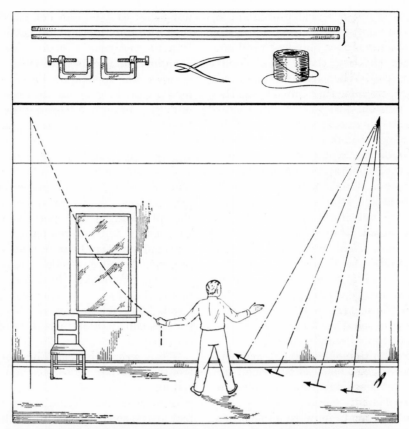

FIG. 9:2. The two-rope problem. This is the kind of complex problem which must be employed if we are to let human subjects use the wide variety of responses at their command. At the top of the figure are the materials available to the subject; at the bottom, the efficient solution. (If others are devised, such as tying more cord onto one of those hanging down, or tying one cord to the chair, the subject is required to keep searching until he develops the pendulum solution.) (*From Crafts et al., 1950, p. 413.*)

ity of perception is a key aspect of learning to solve problems.

We have considered in Chap. 6 the difference between the physically "real" situation and the situation as it is perceived. Again we must emphasize that perception dominates behavior; it is not physical objects, but their perceived qualities, which determine our acts.

Let us examine the application of this principle in an experiment. Suppose a rat has been trained to expect food when he goes to a square, but not when he goes to a circle. Further, the square is larger than the circle. When the rat is going to the square on every trial, we assume that the rat has learned to distinguish the square from the circle. A check experiment, however, using a smaller square, shows that the discrimination was really based on size and not on form. Because the difference in shape was so obvious to us, we assumed that the rat perceived it. Similarly we often assume that children see a situation as adults see it, and we become quite angry when the child fails to distinguish the proper object and respond to it. Such an error in the interpretation of behavior, based on the loose assumption that facts about the stimulus *as we know them* are determining the subject's response, is a kind of *stimulus error*.

To identify and avoid the stimulus error in describing animal behavior, we systematically vary the stimulus situation. Thus, in the foregoing example, when the circle was made distinctly larger than the square, the rat went to the circle. This proved that size, not form, was the perceived guide for the animal; it was the *effective stimulus*.

Plainly, in goal-oriented learning, a stimulus is adequate only in relation to a functioning need. Unless a hunger tension is present, the rat will ignore both square and circle. If we now reflect back upon our studies of conditioning, we realize that the same rule held but was unnoticed. A flash of light causes contraction of the pupil of the eye, because there is a continuing need to protect the retina against overstimulation. A buzzer signaling shock will quickly become an effective stimulus, because the need to escape pain is always present.

Since the effective stimulus must be related to a functioning need, it is clear that we must distinguish two elements in the stimulating situation. They might be called the inner and outer stimuli, although that would not always be precise. We must differentiate: (1) the *drive stimuli*—the inner processes, such as stomach cramps, sex-gland tension, and so on—which initiate activity and persist until equilibrium is restored; and (2) the *guide stimuli*—the influences from the external environment which the organism selects as signposts pointing toward potential need reduction.

In our earlier discussions of motivation, emphasis was placed on the first of these conceptions: the inner tensions. However, it was noted at that time that the actual direction and control of behavior depend on external stimuli. The object which signals need satisfaction comes to possess a positive valence. The *value* of the stimulus is more or less equivalent to its *meaning;* that is, whether it signals gratification or deprivation. However, the term *meaning* carries for most people the idea of logical or intellectual significance. We shall therefore use the term *sign* or *cue* to indicate that an animal can react to a stimulus as pointing toward a goal without any necessary conscious knowledge of its significance.

If new needs are established, valences change. Changes in perception and behavior of a group of men on severe semistarvation for 6 months illustrate this point. Food and food objects obsessed them; strange behavior patterns relating to food became regular habits. A man who has been in isolation for months may perceive the homeliest of women as a beautiful vision, and so on. Freud (1904) collected numerous cases of slips of the tongue, forgetting significant items, accidents of various kinds, as proof of man's tendency to see and act in accordance with the need of the moment, without conscious awareness.

Similarly, once an activity is in progress, the valences and meanings of stimuli tend to fit in with that pattern. If I am "set" to mail a letter, a mailbox stands out in the environment; at other times, it disappears. If I undertake a committee assignment, factors in my surroundings which relate to that task take on new significance.

Choice points. When we attempt to trace the learning process by which man develops this way of perceiving his milieu, we find it convenient to break up an activity into segments. In moving toward a goal (whether it is a physical need or just the completion of a set task), one encounters certain points at which decisions must be made. In the maze, the rat must turn right or left. A college student must select his courses or must decide on studying vs. play. The businessman must choose between a few sales at high prices, or many sales at lower prices (Fig. 9:3).

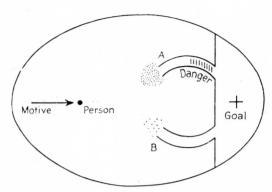

FIG. 9:3. The choice-point situation. In most problem solving, the person faces one or more choice points at which he must decide upon a course of action. In this diagram we have represented the situation in which path A leads to pain, discomfort, or danger, while path B is relatively safe. The individual must learn to perceive the different appearance of the two paths and choose accordingly.

At these choice points, one restructures his environment in terms of experience. This course appears to lead to the goal; that one does not. Or both lead to the goal, but one is more difficult and hazardous. The acquisition of these specific ways of looking at key stimuli is a major phase of learning. Thus *perceiving* and learning are inextricably intertwined in this process by which man tries to satisfy his needs and desires.

It is worth while to note at this point that the learning which goes on is frequently *unconscious*. Consider the case of the blind man who reaches his goal without bumping into the walls and other obstacles. As was noted earlier, psychologists once believed in a kind of skin sensitivity called *facial vision* and even blind psychologists thought they were using such cues. Experiments, however, proved that auditory stimuli were providing the bases for choice. It is quite likely that, in choosing our friends, teachers, husbands, and wives, we react unconsciously to key stimuli without ever knowing their nature.

An easy way of demonstrating the role of these unnoticed stimuli was devised by Laird (1932). He took four identical pairs

of silk stockings. One was placed in a box without perfume; the others had packages perfumed with sachet, a fruity odor, and narcissus. Housewives were asked to look at the stockings and decide which pair was best made, would give best service, and so on. None of the housewives mentioned the perfume, but only 8 per cent chose the unperfumed hose. About 50 per cent thought best service would be given by those carrying the narcissus perfume, although it is most unlikely that any of them—consciously—believed that perfume had any connection with service.

Goal-directed learning and the two-factor theory. We have suggested that "pure" conditioning is completely passive: the organism expects that stimulus A will be followed by stimulus B, regardless of his actions. Goal-directed learning is of course different, in that the organism is actively seeking an object or situation. Nevertheless, conditioning forms an essential part of the process. If the rat goes into a certain pathway, he must expect a shock. If I go out in the rain, I must expect to get wet. Needless to say, if the motivation is strong enough, this unpleasant consequence will be accepted. Muenzinger and his students found that shocking human and animal subjects when they made *correct* choice actually increased learning efficiency, presumably by bringing the choice point more vividly into attention. Thus, in instrumental conditioning, one would predict that stimuli which signal pain would be avoided, but in goal-directed learning, they may function quite differently.

Such a situation obviously means that the individual no longer takes the "path of least resistance." Goal learning requires expenditure of energy in vigorous activity. Old habits and ways of perceiving must be abandoned. Painful and threatening situations must be approached. No one is going to do this unless the inner tension is quite potent. Under ordinary conditions we prefer to be lazy, habit-bound, and routinized. To break up this comfortable equilibrium demands a strong inner need and an external goal perceived as very important (either positive or negative).[1]

This slant on the learning function should help us to understand why people go blandly on using inefficient techniques as citizens in their political behavior, as husbands or wives, as employers and as workers. Passive conditioning, the expectancy that X will be followed by Y, acceptance of our fathers' ideas, habits, and customs—these provide an easy guide to behavior. Until a real crisis arises, the inner tensions are not potent enough to compel a restructuring of the field. Often the choice points are so far from the final punishment (or goal) that it is difficult for us to see the connection. Thus the learning of habits making for efficient progress—material, industrial, or international—is seriously hampered.

Experiments on Choice Behavior

Choice-point behavior is basically a problem in perception. When faced with the necessity for choosing a path to a goal, it is important for the person to know whether this is simply a repetition of a situation already experienced. In real life it is, of

---

[1] The principle of hierarchy of motives (Chap. 2) assures that most of the human race will not lapse into complete inactivity when biological drives are satisfied. Satiation of these needs weakens them, and allows other, socialized or idealized impulses some opportunity for expression. Many people have strong desires for exploration, for prestige, or for achievement which set off problem solving and break up routine ways of behaving.

On the other hand, we should not assume that the entire population resembles the psychologists. Many people do not develop strong motives beyond the biological level; they find themselves caught in a mechanized environment which punishes exploration and curiosity. The reservations made in this footnote do not, therefore, have such wide significance as we might wish.

course, rare for a situation to be duplicated exactly; and, even if it were physically the same, it would not be perceived in exactly the same way because of changes inside the person. Hence the problem becomes one of choosing on the basis of an *approximate identity*. This is the same question discussed in connection with motivation: when is one goal object perceived as equivalent to another? It is thus important for us to consider the question: what stimuli will be perceived as equivalent?

Equivalence of stimuli in rats. Before considering the phenomenon of choice in complex tasks, let us examine an experiment in which only stimulus equivalence is studied. Lashley (1938) required his animals to discriminate between two forms by jumping to a card for food (Fig. 9:4). If the rat jumps to the correct card, it slips aside and he gets food. The wrong card is locked in place and the rat falls into a net (punishment).

Lashley used a great variety of stimulus forms, some of which are illustrated in Fig. 9:5. His first finding, as might be expected from our discussion of figure and ground in perception (see Chap. 6), was that the animal readily discriminates a card bearing a form (triangle, square, or circle) from a black card carrying no design. This was the easiest of all discriminations tried. Next easiest was differentiation of the *direction* of major axis. Thus horizontal lines were easily distinguished from verticals. A circle proved hard to differentiate from a square set level, but if the square was rotated 45 degrees (tipped on one corner), the choice was easily made. The slanting lines evidently have a distinctive quality for the animal. But lines with the same slant, in opposite directions, are reacted to in the same way; if one card has a line angled 45 degrees to the right, and the other a line angled 45 degrees to the left, discrimination is very difficult for the rat.

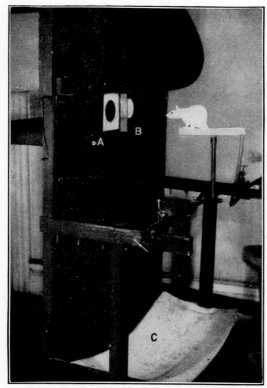

FIG. 9:4. A Lashley-type jumping stand. This stand, used by Dr. N. R. F. Maier in his study of conflict and frustration, is substantially the same as the Lashley apparatus diagramed in Fig. 6:10, page 209. The rat must learn to perceive differences in cards A and B; jumping to the right card means food, jumping to the wrong one means a fall into the net. Behind the rat is a compressed-air jet which can be used to force jumping when he refuses to choose. (*Courtesy of Dr. N. R. F. Maier.*)

Distance is also readily discriminated. Rats readily learn to choose on the basis of the distance of the shape from the dividing partition between the cards. If a complex pattern is presented, the rat is most likely to find some distinctive partial cue and utilize that, rather than taking in the whole form. This can be tested by systematically varying small details within the complex pattern. Some changes make no difference; some disrupt the entire choice process.

If we attempt to understand the rat's preference for discriminations in terms of direction, distance, and partial aspects of shapes, we can find a pretty good explanation in terms of this animal's normal environment. Living largely underground or within human structures, he learns that such factors are likely to have survival value. For getting food or escaping enemies, speedy recognition of such choice cues is vital. Complex forms, on the other hand, have little or no adaptive significance.

Tests for equivalence. Lashley's rats were first trained to jump to a triangle for food, avoiding the cross (which signals punishment). Later they were tested with a variety of figures having progressively less resemblance to the original patterns (Fig. 9:5). If the rat meets the criterion of choosing the correct figure (as defined by the experimenter) 95 per cent of the time, he goes on to another pair. Lashley found that his rats successfully transferred to all the designs reproduced here, except numbers 18, 25, and 26. Of these, 18 involves reversal of brightness, 25 a coarsely striated ground, and 26 a rotation of the figures. We can infer that such changes affect the perception so drastically that no equivalence is seen. Success on the other figures occurs in spite of changes in the surrounding context, or the figure being "masked in a totally different pattern." Incidentally, this experiment proves that the rat can perceive form as such, since form is the only constant in these changing designs.

Comparison of man, rat, and monkey on studies of equivalent stimuli indicates that the processes of perception are basically similar in all three species. The rat's form vision is probably inferior. However, we must not ignore the role of experience and attitude. The rat's small size restricts the kinds of observations he can make. It is unlikely that he will get above the object and look down at it, as ape and child often do. Hence rotation may break up his established patterns without similarly affecting the higher organisms.

TRAINING SERIES

Figure 15

PAIRS TESTED FOR EQUIVALENCE

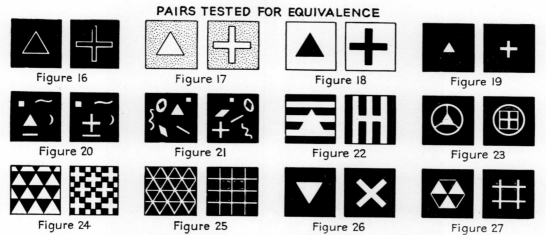

Figure 16   Figure 17   Figure 18   Figure 19

Figure 20   Figure 21   Figure 22   Figure 23

Figure 24   Figure 25   Figure 26   Figure 27

FIG. 9:5. Forms used in Lashley's study of stimulus equivalence. The rats were first trained to choose one of the two figures at the top (either triangle, for some animals, or cross, for others). Then they were tested on the pairs shown below. The animals showed equivalent behavior (transferred successfully) to all pairs except 18, 25, and 26, which presumably involved perceptual changes too great for the animal to accept them as equivalents for the training figures. This experiment provides an animal analogue for equivalence of meaning in human subjects. In a complex situation, one must learn to approach stimuli approximately the same as those experienced earlier and to avoid those perceived as similar to danger signals formerly encountered. (*From Lashley, 1938.*)

Abstract relationships. Much of man's scientific progress has depended upon his ability to perceive similarities of a highly abstract character. But even this ability is present in the lower animals. Köhler (1938) trained hens to peck grain from a light gray card and ignore that on a medium gray (these were glued down, so that pecking was unrewarding). After this habit was well established, he presented a new pair of cards: the light gray (positive) stimulus and a still lighter gray (*transposition* experiment). Does the hen continue to peck at the card which has been a dependable source of calories? No; she now pecks persistently at the new card. How can we explain this change? Obviously it shows that she is responding to *relative brightness*, not to absolute brightness. The "good" card is "lighter than" the other (Fig. 9:6). Children also learn this abstraction in regard to skin color (Horowitz, 1936). The process depends on reward and punishment by adults.

Stimulus equivalence and stimulus generalization. In a preceding chapter we noted that dogs conditioned to salivate to a tone of 500 d.v. would also respond to a tone of 1,000 d.v. However, they would quickly suppress the latter response if the 1,000 d.v. tones were presented several times without food, while the 500 d.v. tone always signaled food. This appears to involve the same basic process as the equivalent-stimuli experiment, even though the latter ordinarily involves pairs of stimuli.

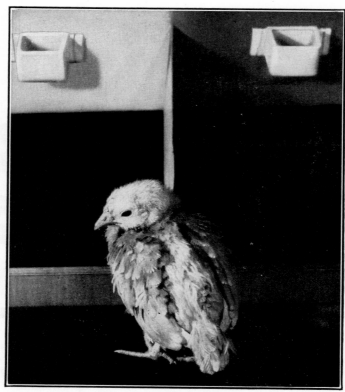

FIG. 9:6. The transposition experiment. In this case the chick has been trained to get food from the cup on a gray background, avoiding the white card. When switched to a new pair of grays, the original medium gray and a darker gray, the chick will go to the darker card, indicating a response to the relative brightness, not to the specific card. (*Lilo Hess, photographer.*)

At first glance we might think that the dog was stupid for responding to the 1,000 d.v. tone, since this is not the exact stimulus for food. This, however, would be another case of the so-called "stimulus error." Because we define the stimulus as a tone of given pitch, we assume that the dog should do so. Actually, the dog is probably responding in terms of "any tone signals food"; hence he is behaving intelligently within the limits of his experience. Either natively or by experience, he is set to respond to the stimulus *type* rather than to stimulus *attributes* (see page 139). By rewarding one tone and not another, we can compel him to attend to attribute (pitch). This is essentially the case with the transposition experiment; the animal first learns to treat one stimulus as positive valence, the other negative. He will then respond to new pairs of stimuli in terms, not just of the positive valence alone, but of the relationship between the two. We then get what is called *stimulus equivalence*.

In goal-directed learning the stimulating conditions are quite complex. This means that the animal will find himself faced with the necessity for making choices at many points. Whether he generalizes from past positive stimuli, or from past negative stimuli, or whether he responds to relationships between pairs of cues, he is making use of the stimulus-equivalence–stimulus-generalization mechanism to guide his actions.

Significance of stimulus equivalence. What is the bearing of all this on everyday, adult human behavior? Many answers can be pointed out readily. Let us first consider the question of goal objects. Suppose an accustomed source of satisfaction has disappeared. The individual must seek a substitute. What determines his choice? In the light of the foregoing discussion, it must be apparent that *stimulus equivalence* is the key.

First, it seems clear that an object will be acceptable which is perceived as *physically similar* to the lost gratification. Foods which are "like mama used to make" are preferred. The young man, in choosing a wife, is also prone to fall in love with young women who resemble his mother (as she appeared during his childhood, of course). People, by and large, evince a preference for houses, automobiles, and other objects which resemble those associated with rewarding experiences. If I have a choice between two men who offer me advice, I am likely to accept that of the man who reminds me of my father (or some other man whose advice has proved trustworthy).

Secondly, man's extensive use of language and symbols makes possible the reaction to stimulus equivalence on a basis of *functional similarity*. Thus a man may not crave to be rocked in his mother's lap, but he may want his wife to "mother" him in other ways. Or, he may wish to have the all-protecting arms of his "mother country" around him. Aggression toward the father may be expressed as aggression toward the employer (a father symbol). In Freudian dream analysis it is found that long, pointed objects frequently symbolize the male sex organ (physical similarity) but that the female sex organ is more often represented by a cave, box, or other receptacle (functional similarity).

Man *must* be guided by his experiences. As someone once remarked: "Good judgment comes from experience, and experience—that comes from bad judgment." As we learn that certain cues signal reward and others threaten punishment, we must be able to transfer these lessons to situations which are not exactly identical. This is the function of stimulus equivalence in guiding behavior.

The Nature of the Response

In the foregoing pages we have considered the role of the stimulus in goal-directed learning. We must now turn our attention to a consideration of the modifications in response pattern which occur during this type of learning.

Again it may be helpful to draw a distinction between this type of learning and conditioning. In classical conditioning only slight response modification was evident. Eyewink, salivary reflex, heart-rate acceleration—these are typical objects of classical conditioning. In those instances the animal was passive; stimuli acted upon him, and he learned to *expect* stimulus B following stimulus A. But the response continued with slight modification.

In instrumental conditioning, on the contrary, a substantial amount of response modification was observed. The animal might develop a totally new pattern (pressing a bar, leaping over a partition, pecking at a colored dot). Since such conditioning is an active process, and since it must be motivated by a definite goal (food, escape from pain), this is in fact a simple case of goal-directed learning. We shall be concerned in this chapter with more complex instances of learning. The discussion will bring out, however, the parallels of instrumental conditioning and the more complicated forms of adaptation to the environment in quest of a goal.

Trial-and-error learning. Psychologists have often spoken of "trial-and-error" learning, though a more correct term would be "trial, error, and success." This process requires that the organism be strongly motivated to attain a goal (food when hungry, water when thirsty, escape from pain or confinement at any time). A second requirement is that the problem be difficult —not one which can be solved by simple perception plus an already established response. Ordinarily, therefore, the learning process is gradual, although it may show sudden acquisition under suitable circumstances.

A simple example of trial-and-error learning is the following incident:

A daughter of mine lost the key to her bank, a small imitation pirate's chest. She asked me to open it. I took a hairpin and poked around in the keyhole. After picking more or less at random I suddenly got it open. The next time this happened sooner. On subsequent occasions all I had to do was poke in the upper right corner, and after a little fumbling I would get results. (Focusing of response.) However, I was not aware of precisely how the lock was snapped. There was improvement of response—a time record would show a typical learning curve.

Even at the beginning of such a sequence, behavior is not entirely haphazard. All the efforts are directed toward the goal. But there is constant *variability* of behavior. One keeps trying slightly different motions, different lines of attack. With a "chance" success, one concentrates on this area and on the kind of movement which was rewarded. Gradually, a fairly efficient way of responding will be worked out, even without any understanding of why it is successful. This is characteristic of many skilled factory workers on their jobs and of most automobile drivers in handling their cars. It is also characteristic of most

of us in our use of speech and writing. Generally we put forth little effort to try to analyze and deliberately improve our habits.

Performance of such actions can be materially improved if a clearer perception of the action-goal relationship is developed. Let us finish off the pirate-chest example:

For a while I was satisfied to open the chest after a few fumblings with the hairpin in the upper right corner. Each occasion seemed to require about the same number of fumblings. Apparently I had reached a *plateau* in the learning process. Since the demand to open the lid was threatening to become a chore, I decided to determine precisely how the lock worked. By holding the chest up at an angle under the light, I was able to locate the hidden trigger and see how it moved. Thereafter, I immediately opened the lid without fumbling. The learning curve dropped to a new low level, following the acquisition of *insight* or knowledge of the principle of the lock.

Ruger's study on puzzles. Years ago Ruger (1910) did a careful laboratory study on solution of mechanical puzzles. Some of his findings give quantitative records of the kind of process sketched above. Most of the puzzles were made of wire and involved removal of some part of the apparatus, such as a ring, star, or heart, from the rest. One subject had apparently mastered the Star and Crescent puzzle, to the extent that after many repeated trials the solution time was about constant. His progress to this level is shown in the first part of Fig. 9:7. At X the subject worked out a newly discovered aspect of the puzzle, using up much time in that trial. Thereafter the solution took much less time, and variability was reduced. Although Ruger had asked his subjects to be alert, so that they could give introspective reports as to how they learned, the first solutions were often completely unexpected.

Figure 9:8 illustrates the Heart and Bow puzzle used by Ruger. Individual differ-

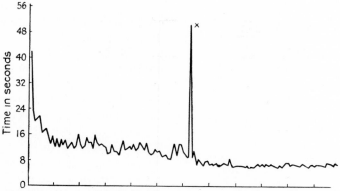

FIG. 9:7. Time curve in puzzle solving. The subject was working on the Star and Crescent puzzle. He had made considerable progress, but at x he noted something about the puzzle, spent a long time studying it, and from then on reached a new, superior level of performance. (*From Ruger, 1910.*)

ences in solution time on this puzzle were great. One of the five subjects took more than 3 hours for his first solution; the fastest time was less than 6 minutes. Second solutions came much sooner; 6 minutes for the slowest, 12 seconds for the fastest. In Fig. 9:9 we have reproduced the learning curve for subject Mt, whose first solution was in less than 6 minutes, and who achieved a speed of 4 to 5 seconds. The laboratory protocol on this subject is typical of puzzle performance. In the beginning there is a chance success after first localizing the pertinent part of the puzzle. Thereafter, sharp improvements are made with improved "hypotheses" or a clearer perception of the twist in the puzzle which separates the parts, or improvement in techniques of manipulating the wires. One of Ruger's findings is that improvement usually follows an innovation in the attack, although sometimes a new variation leads to disturbance. The most time-consuming part of the process involves persistence in wrong solutions. Ruger states that about 70 per cent of variations or shifts in mode of attack, which usually came *without premeditation*, were consciously utilized in later trials. Frequently

his subjects entered a period of no apparent improvement, or a *plateau*. Such plateaus were attributed to persistence in using an inefficient method for the solution.

All Ruger's puzzles were genuine problems. None of the subjects solved an unfamiliar one on sight. The nature of the puzzles was such as to invite immediate motor manipulation. In all cases, random

FIG. 9:8. Heart and Bow puzzle. This is one of the wire puzzles used by Ruger in his classical study of problem solving. Each puzzle requires both perceptual analysis and a definite pattern of movements for its solution. (*From Ruger, 1910.*)

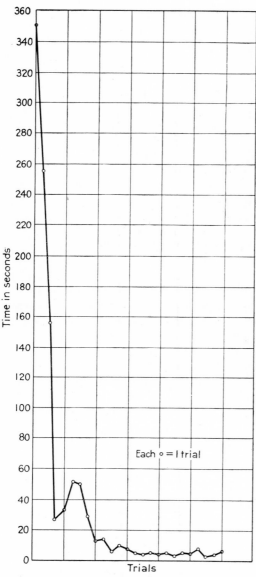

FIG. 9:9. Time curve for solving Heart and Bow puzzle. Note the rapid progress in the first four trials, followed by a slowing up in the immediately following trials while features of the puzzle are analyzed out. Insight here occurs in a series of steps, rather than in a single trial as in Fig. 9:7. (*From Ruger, 1910.*)

twisting and turning of the puzzle played a part—and in some a very considerable part—in gaining success. There was often no improvement in time for several trials.

Acts which made no change in the situation were repeated indefinitely. Such motor irrelevancies were due to the fact that the solution was only partially grasped. On the other hand, many subjects exhibited complex powers of reasoning, with sudden drops in time to new low levels, quick adoption of short cuts, and elimination of errors. The value of the "variation" in puzzle solving varied directly with the precision of analysis. If perception improved, there was an associated improvement in the manipulation of the puzzle. Drops in time curves were coincident with consciously adopted modifications rather than unconscious variations in approach.

Puzzle-box experiments with animals. The nearest duplicate of Ruger's studies, using animal subjects, is the pioneer work by Thorndike (1898). In this research, cats (and dogs) were placed in a puzzle box when hungry. Food was visible outside. The animal had to escape by pulling a loop, pressing a button, or pushing against a bar. Figure 9:10 shows a similar box. Of the animal's activities Thorndike wrote as follows:

When put into the box, the cat would show evident signs of discomfort and of an impulse to escape from confinement. It tries to squeeze through any opening; it claws and bites at the bars or wire; it thrusts its paws out through any opening and claws at everything it reaches; it continues its efforts when it strikes anything loose or shaky; it may claw at things within the box . . . . The vigor with which it struggles is extraordinary. For eight or ten minutes it will claw and bite and squeeze incessantly . . . . The cat that is clawing all over the box in her impulsive struggle will probably claw the string or loop or button so as (accidentally) to open the door. And gradually all the other non-successful impulses will be stamped out and the particular impulse leading to the successful act will be stamped in . . . until, after many trials, the cat will, when put in the box, immediately claw the button or loop in a definite way . . . . Cats would claw at the loop or

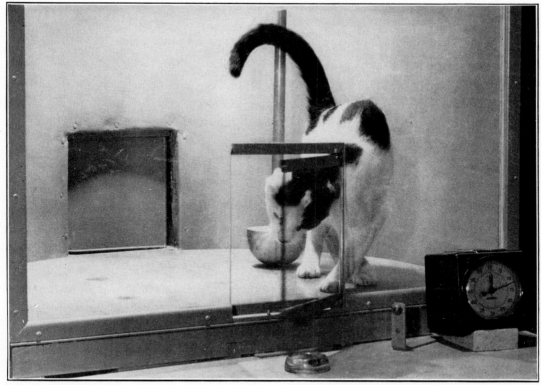

FIG. 9:10. Puzzle box for cats. This puzzle box, used by Dr. M. E. Bunch in a study of the effects of oxygen deficit on the learning ability of cats, is modified from one used in Thorndike's original study. The cat must learn to tip the pole in the center of the cage; the door opens automatically, and the food reward is in the dish, center foreground. The electric timer records automatically the time required for a solution. This cat uses her tail; others use paw, head, or body. As noted in the text, a given animal does not stick to a stereotyped movement pattern; apparently the animal learns a goal relationship, not a mechanical action. (*St. Louis Post-Dispatch, from Black Star.*)

button when the door was open . . . . Cats would claw at the place where the loop had been, though none was there. The reaction was not to a well-discriminated object, but to a vague situation, and any element of the situation may arouse the reaction.[1]

From such observations, and from his learning curves (cf. Fig. 9:11) which showed gradual, irregular improvement, Thorndike argued that animals had little, if any, comprehension of what they were doing. His monkeys (in a somewhat different apparatus) behaved similarly to the cats

[1] Thorndike (1898), pp. 13, 80. Reprinted by permission of the American Psychological Association.

and dogs. To Thorndike, random movements and their selection in terms of consequences were the important features of animal learning. Once selected, these movements persisted "even when the loop was no longer there"—an emphasis upon blind, irrational rote learning, similar to that described in Chap. 7, or to classical conditioning (Chap. 8).

The problem box, like Ruger's puzzles, offers a good device for the study of learning behavior, because everything is visible. Overt action is required of the subject, and the manipulation essential to success can easily be observed when it occurs. However, the interpretation of puzzle and puzzle-box

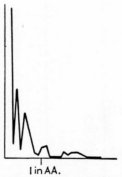

I in AA.

FIG. 9:11. Learning curves for animal puzzle box. This shows the curve of time for a dog to escape from a puzzle box somewhat like that shown in Fig. 9:10. The gradual and irregular character of the animal's progress was used by Thorndike as an argument for pure trial and error, without insight, as the explanation of learning; however, as Figs. 9:7 and 9:9 show, similar irregularities in human problem solving may accompany perceptual analysis of the situation, followed by insight. (*From Thorndike, 1898, p. 33.*)

studies has not been so easy. Ruger's emphasis upon observation of the essential features of the puzzle becomes lost in Thorndike's interpretation which stresses the role of chance. Watson, following closely after Thorndike, published his research on maze learning in rats and interpreted it as reinforcing Thorndike's views. Thus the trial-and-error conception of goal learning became firmly established in American psychology.

Let us restate this view before going into the research data and theoretical considerations which argue *against* its accuracy. The trial-and-error interpretation of learning emphasized the motor side of behavior, or random movements. From this hit-or-miss sequence, those which "panned out" were selected. (Various theories as to how the successful act was "stamped in" and the errors "stamped out" were proposed.) The movements were viewed as being directed blindly to the total situation or stimulus pattern. The responses were elicited by specific aspects of the stimulus situation, as they were encountered, in a more or less stereotyped manner. The work on maze

learning (see below) particularly seemed to support the idea that responses were made to specific elements of the problem in turn and that these responses were then linked together in some way: the "chain-reflex" theory, closely tied to the trial-and-error theory.

Change from trial-and-error view. While there can be no question that response modification as described by trial-and-error theory does sometimes occur, there is general doubt among psychologists today that this theory should be accepted as a general explanation of learning. Let us first consider a repetition of Thorndike's puzzle-box study and see how a different report on animal behavior comes out of it.

Adams (1929) repeated Thorndike's study, using identical escape mechanisms as far as possible. However, his description of the cats' actions differs considerably from the original report. His cats did not all show the vigorous activity emphasized in the Thorndike passage quoted above. Most of his animals were calmer; often they seemed to spend considerable time "looking over" the situation. The first solution was usually accidental, but from that point on, learning could not be correctly described as a "gradual elimination of useless movements." When this kind of slow improvement occurred, Adams found it associated with excitement and inattention. The more deliberate and attentive animals acquired the correct act in fewer repetitions and more *abruptly* than the more excited cats.[1]

[1] One wonders about such questions as: did both groups of cats really show parallel behavior, Thorndike perceiving what he was set to observe, and Adams perceiving what fitted in with his own predilections? That this question is not crucial is indicated by the fact that, if *any* cats show the behavior described by Adams, the universal applicability of Thorndike's trial-and-error conception is opened to serious question. Actually, it appears that Thorndike discarded cats who seemed lazy to him; hence he may have missed the kind of solution Adams found most impressive.

This difference is linked with *focusing of the cat's attention* and activity near the latch. The animal's behavior was not purely random, was not directed by a particular simple stimulus, and was not a mechanical repetition of the same motor act. As Table 9:1 shows, many different movements were used by a single cat in solving the same puzzle. This suggests that the animal is guided by an attempt to attack a particular figure within the perceptual field (and perhaps, in some cases, to modify that perceived figure in a specific direction); but it makes no difference whether paw, teeth, or claw is the instrument used for this purpose.

We are likely to find trial and error in human learning when a clear perception of the field is impossible. Such a situation is present in complex tasks such as typing or piano playing; or where part of the situation is concealed, as in driving a car. Clashing of gears, for example, used to be eliminated only by trial and error because few people could perceive the (hidden) relationship between speed of car and speed of engine. Ruger's puzzles were of such a character that it was difficult to perceive the significant figure; it was "lost" and became part of the ground (cf. page 233, illustrating how a simple figure can disappear into a more complex pattern). Many of these trials must be interpreted as efforts to rearrange the stimulus pattern so that a clear figure can be brought into focus.

It may well be that some kinds of human learning must necessarily be rote, mechanical, trial-and-error activity. But we now have an overwhelming mass of data to indicate the superiority of clear perception of the essential relationships. In factory training, for example, it is now known to be efficient to give the new worker a trip around the factory and a chance to observe how his job fits into the total product. Effective performance on his isolated part

TABLE 9:1. Different Methods of Escape Used by Ace
(*From Adams, 1929*)

Method	Number of times used
By pulling string with teeth.........	8
By pulling string with paw...........	4
By pulling loop with paw............	4
By pulling pulley, or string on pulley, with paw.......................	2
By pulling loop, holding it between chin and paw, and moving back ...	2
By pulling string with teeth and paws.	1
By pulling loop with teeth...........	1
By pulling loop with teeth and paws..	1
By pulling string with teeth, loop with paw..............................	1
By pulling string to mouth with paw, then pulling with teeth............	1
By pulling knob of latch, outside, with paw..............................	1
Not noted........................	1
Failed............................	4
Total........................	31

of the job is greatly enhanced if he knows how his part fits into the work of others. (This is entirely apart from the greater motivation which accrues from his feeling that management respects him as an individual and wants him to know where he fits in the picture.)

In the same way, less emphasis is being placed on rote learning in the schools, more on perceiving relationships. Students acquire more in less time if they can "see" how ideas and facts fit together. The relationship to the student's purposes—motivation—also facilitates this process, of course, since maximum energy is mobilized if his personal motives can be channeled into this activity.

Maze learning. One of the most extensively used experiments for the study of trial-and-error learning is the maze experiment. The apparatus consists of a series of pathways which the organism is required to explore in the attempt to reach a goal

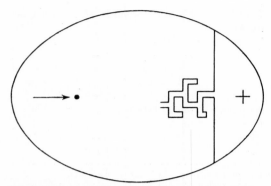

FIG. 9:12. The maze as a pathway to a goal. This diagram is intended to visualize the tension-means-goal relationship described in the text. Compare Fig. 9:1.

(Fig. 9:12). The perceptual situation is so arranged that it is not possible to get a clear picture of the problem or to isolate the significant stimuli at choice points. It thus conforms to the puzzle technique just described in certain basic respects. It is different in that it presents a clean-cut series of choice points; thus the experimenter can study the progress of learning by counting the correct responses—not, as in the puzzle, getting only a single success or failure.

The maze principle goes all the way back to Greek mythology with the tale of Theseus and the Minotaur. Theseus, however, did not learn to avoid the errors and blind alleys of the Cretan labyrinth; Ariadne helped him with a spool of thread. In our modern studies of maze behavior, we take extensive measures to prevent the organism from getting any outside assistance.

The first maze pattern used for experimentation was the Hampton Court pattern (Fig. 9:13). This is a copy of a garden pattern introduced by William III of England as an amusement for his guests at Hampton Court. High hedges prevented the person from seeing which path led to the goal in the center; true trial-and-error behavior thus resulted. This pattern, however, is irregular and the choices are not of equal difficulty. It has long since been replaced, for experimental work, by the T-maze (Fig. 7:3, page 255) or one of its variants (Fig. 9:1). This presents the organism with a series of simple left-right choices. Animals are usually run through a series of tunnels; human subjects may be required to trace a raised wire pattern with the finger (Fig. 9:14), to push a stylus along a series of grooves, or to walk a narrow enclosed path to the goal. Blindfolds or screens are used to prevent use of vision. The problem has some similarity to the task of learning one's way around in a strange city, or operating a machine in which the sequence of movements is more important than the kind of movement.

Mazes for earthworms. If the maze pattern is reduced to a single left-right choice (a single T), even the lowly earthworm can deal successfully with it. Yerkes (1912) used escape from light as the motivation for his worms, this being as potent as escape from electric shock for higher organisms. The animal showed persistent effort, variability, and final selection of the correct response, just as Ruger's subjects had done with the puzzles.

Yerkes also showed that the worm could choose turns on the basis of sensory cues. A strip of sandpaper was placed across the floor of the wrong alley. If the animal crossed this, he received an electric shock. About 100 trials were required for the earthworm to perfect the habit of turning back when it encountered the sandpaper, but success was eventually achieved.

Maze learning in rats. Yerkes studied the sensory control of behavior in the earthworm by adding cues and showing that the organism could profit by them. Watson (1907) reversed this technique in his studies with white rats; he successively removed various sensory cues and showed that his rats could do without them. Rats were blinded, or deafened, and still learned the maze about as well as normals. The vibrissae were removed, and the soles of

FIG. 9:13. The original Hampton Court maze. Constructed of high hedges, this was a source of amusement to guests at the castle. It was adopted for use in some psychological research about 1900 but was later replaced by the more uniformly designed mazes such as are illustrated in Figs. 9:1 and 9:14. (*Courtesy of Dr. J. F. Dashiell.*)

the feet anesthetized. Most of the rats were still capable of learning the correct pathway with little handicap. Even more striking: animals who had presumably used vision in learning performed almost perfectly after loss of vision, according to this report.

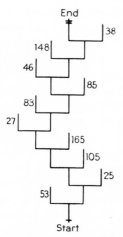

FIG. 9:14. A finger-tracing maze. This maze is made of heavy silver wire fastened to a plywood panel. The blindfolded subject traces the path with the tip of his finger. Numbers at the ends of the blind alleys show the errors made by a typical group of subjects. (*From Husband, 1931.*)

Watson concluded that his animals were learning by using kinesthetic cues from the muscles. Remember that every muscle is both a motor and a sensory organ. As the rat ran the maze, he was constantly feeling the contractions of his muscles. He could gauge distance and avoid bumping into walls by this cue. Watson further theorized that the pattern of correct turns was preserved as a *chain reflex* (more properly, a chain of conditioned reflexes). This concept can be explained as follows: As the rat runs, he perceives movement of his body. When he runs a certain distance, he is forced to turn, and immediately after, bumps into a wall. The kinesthetic sensations just prior to the turn can now function as a cue *not* to make this turn—that is, they can function as a sign for bumping the nose. This can be diagramed as follows:

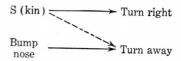

After learning, the "chain reflex" would run off like this:

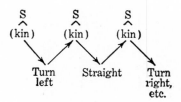

There is a limited amount of truth in this theory. Motor responses do sometimes get chained together in this automatized way. Humans bump into furniture that has been moved from its accustomed position, and many complex habits have to be run off from the beginning—they cannot be started in the middle. Ask a child just learning the alphabet which letter comes after "K" and he will start with "A" and run through the series to "L." Carr and Watson (1908) demonstrated this phenomenon with the rats by changing the length of runs just prior to a turn. The rats would bump the end of a shortened alley or try to turn in the middle of one which had been made longer.

The chain reflex gives a good description of many automatic habits. Knitting requires close visual attention at first, but later the feel of successive motions guides the process without vision. Many factory jobs become so routine that the muscular sensations control the work without conscious attention. This kind of behavior illustrates the process of *stimulus reduction* in extreme form. Where, at first, seeing the knitting needles and thread and identifying the place in the design were essential cues for action, the cue is now reduced to a kinesthetic sensation from muscle action.

This process of stimulus reduction is of great potential value in human adjustment. It makes possible the freedom of the distance receptors for other purposes. We can walk, converse with a friend, and watch for possible dangers, all at one time. The factory worker on a monotonous job can daydream and let his chain reflexes control job performance. A person who is a skilled typist can concentrate his attention on thinking through his ideas, and automatic motor habits transfer the words to the paper. Because the number of essential stimuli has been reduced, attention need be directed to the skilled act only for brief intervals (perhaps 1 second in each minute), leaving much time for other activities to be in focus.

It is also significant to note that, having once acquired such sequences, we can imagine them. It is easy to run off a skilled act "in the mind," to hum a melody, or to repeat a poem. However, if one is interrupted, he frequently has to start all over, or at least return to an earlier point in the sequence. Rats in the maze do this; it is called *backtracking*. If the rat is confused in the middle of the maze, he may return all the way to the starting box or go back several turns. As he heads for the food again, he presumably builds up his pattern of kinesthetic cues again so that he knows "where he is at," just as one may start over on the tune in order to get it straight. Reading shows the same phenomenon. At times we have to "backtrack" in order to place the present sentence in its proper context. Much of our reading is a more or less mechanical series of responses to visual cues plus the kinesthetic sensations from the act of pronouncing the words. If the latter chain is interrupted, "backtracking" may become necessary.

Watson was wrong, nevertheless, in building his whole theory of learning around the chain-reflex concept. In the first place, repetition of his experiments (Honzik, 1936) has shown that kinesthesis does not have the primary role Watson ascribed to it. Vision and other senses do play a significant role in learning (Fig. 9:15). In the second place, various studies of rats, men, and other species have shown that such learning as that of the maze involves directional orientation which cannot be reduced to chain reflexes. Thirdly, our considerations of complex learning indicate that, while human learning can occur on this simple, mechanical level, most of it takes the form of schema and relationship learning which does not conform to the reflex pattern.

It may have seemed that Watson's emphasis on kinesthesis in maze learning could not be absolutely disproved, since the rat must use his muscles to run the maze. However, Lashley and Ball (1929) eliminated kinesthetic senses by cutting the sensory nerves in rats who had learned the maze. The animals now could not feel their legs moving (indeed, they could not coordinate well, as running depends on sensing muscle movements); but they rolled, waddled, and floundered through the maze without entering blind alleys. Thus kinesthetic cues cannot have been essential. MacFarlane (1930) had his rats learn a wading maze, then filled it with water so that they had to swim. The muscle movements were quite different, yet there was no significant disturbance of the habit.

Such researches challenge us to face the question: what is the "over-all" control of skilled movements? The evidence seems to support the theory of E. C. Tolman (1948) that the organism forms a "cognitive map" or inner picture of the situation-action relationship. Thus the rat may have a brain pattern corresponding in some way to the pattern of correct turns in the maze.[1] Normally this cognitive map is geared to kinesthetic sensations; but when they are cut out or arbitrarily changed, the animal can still guide itself through the maze by recalling the correct path. According to this point of view, the data from distance receptors (eye, ear, etc.) are organized in the rat's brain as *cues to goal attainment*. The true unit of behavior, then, is not a single muscle movement, or a single turn in the maze, but an *act leading*

[1] Compare the map of the body in the brain (p. 155).

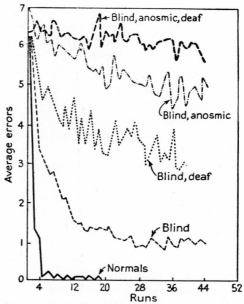

FIG. 9:15. Role of sensory cues in the maze. Watson asserted that most of his animals were unaffected by loss of vision, hearing, and smell. Honzik repeated this study with a much larger number of animals and found results indicating that serious loss of efficiency does follow loss of sensory cues. As the curves above show, loss of vision had least effect; vision and hearing, more; vision and smell, still more; loss of all three sensory avenues almost eliminates learning completely. (*From Honzik, 1936.*)

to a goal. Each part action is thus integrated into a total pattern, and it is the pattern, not the separate movements, which is controlling. In brief, we might say that the rat learns "this is the way to get food in the maze"; he does *not* learn "run twenty steps, turn left, run thirty steps, turn right . . . ." The key concept in learning, then, is the *perceiving of a course of action to a goal.*

It is not possible to ask rats for a verbal report on how they learn. One advantage of human subjects is that they can give such reports. Perrin (1914) had people learn mazes (full-scale, through which they walked blindfolded, and also stylus mazes, such as that pictured in Fig. 9:14). Some people tried to build up a picture of the pathway; others memorized a verbal sequence of turns; others just tried to "feel" their way through. Anticipation of turns was noted, just as in the rats; and "mental backtracking" was common—the subject would verbally rehearse the part of the path he had already traversed. The successful learners developed a visual or verbal plan of the maze, into which the separate turns were fitted.

This is a "higher" form of learning than the mechanical memorizing of movements in a series. Rats apparently do about as well when forced to use the blind, mechanical approach as when allowed a chance to develop a visual plan. As we go up the phylogenetic scale, this is no longer true. The apes and man, particularly, *can* learn passively and mechanically, but on a vastly inferior level. Efficient human learning is based on organizing movements into meaningful patterns. When the experiment prevents this, the human subject is forced to learn in a subhuman manner.

Learning as goal expectancy. The experimental evidence in favor of the view that learning is a form of goal expectancy takes many different forms. We can summarize here only a few of the experiments which support this theory.

A very simple but significant observation is that of Tinklepaugh (1928). He would place food under one of two cups while a monkey watched. Later the animal would be allowed to lift the cup and eat the food (the delayed-reaction experiment). While a screen was down, Tinklepaugh replaced the banana (which the monkey had seen) by lettuce. When the monkey lifted the cup and found the lettuce, he seemed surprised and disturbed; he searched the apparatus carefully (presumably for the banana) before accepting the lettuce. Evidently he had learned to "expect" banana and not the lettuce. Elliot (1928) has shown that rats will learn a maze either for sunflower seed or for bran mash, but they prefer the latter. He switched from the bran mash to sunflower seed in the middle of the learning process and produced an obvious disturbance in his animals (Fig. 2:9). Thus it is clear that the quality of the goal is immediately involved in the learning activity; it cannot be thought of as something outside the learning process.

Place learning. As psychologists have learned more about experimental method, they have relied less on trying to "figure out" how the animal does something (as Watson had) and have placed more emphasis on setting up a situation which forces the animal to provide the answer by his actions. A good illustration is the following experiment on the learning of place or location vs. learning a specific response pattern.

Tolman *et al.* (1946) trained rats to follow a fixed path to the food box (Fig. 9:16).

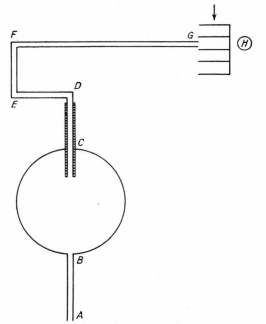

FIG. 9:16. Original path learned by rats in Tolman study. The animal started at A and had to run straight across the table top, out the alley, and make a left turn before getting to the food. (*Tolman et al., 1946.*)

After 4 days of practice, the animals were shifted to another maze (Fig. 9:17) in which the original path C was blocked, but a variety of paths radiated from the table top. Although path C had forced the animals to go to the left before reaching the food, only 14 per cent of choices were on the left side. The largest number of choices of any single path favored number 6, which was closest to the spatial location of the food box in the training period. This seems to indicate that the rat does not learn a specific pattern of movements, or even a specific pathway to the goal, but rather a general orientation as to the direction of food.[1] It is easier to establish a general expectancy ("the food is over there") than to build up a precise pattern of movements. Furthermore, the general orientation is more adaptive; it is less easily broken up by minor changes in the physical situation.

Control of learning by perception. What is the significance of these studies on place learning and goal orientation in animals for human psychology? Largely, the result has been a shift in emphasis from action to perception. The Watson "chain-reflex" idea tended to exaggerate the importance—in education, for example—of having children make the *right pattern of movements*. The focus was on action, on muscle sensations, on responding. Modern psychology emphasizes the role of perception. The distance receptors, especially vision, are given a much larger part in the control of behavior. *What a person does is a function of how he*

---

[1] Years ago John B. Watson, the most vigorous exponent of the theory that one learns responses rather than orientations, reported a casual observation which should have disturbed him. He moved the rat maze from one part of the laboratory to another, and the learning of the animals was interfered with. If they had been learning mechanical-response sequences, this should not have happened, as the maze paths were unchanged. But the relation of the goal to the window and other landmarks had changed.

TABLE 9:2. Performance of Three Groups Learning a Maze by Different Methods
(*From Husband, 1931*)

Method	Number using	Average trials to learn
Verbal.................	29	19.5
Visualization............	14	24.3
Motor.................	10	44.5

looks at the situation. The exact pattern of movements is not so important.

The superiority of the perceptual method is indicated by the work of Husband (1931) in which human subjects were required to learn a maze pattern. One group used muscle sensations alone—*i.e.,* they simply developed a feeling for the correct turns without much awareness. A second group tried to develop a visual picture of the maze pattern in their minds. The third group talked to themselves, counting and labeling the turns. Group 3 was most efficient, Group 2 second, and Group 1 a poor third in performance (Table 9:2).

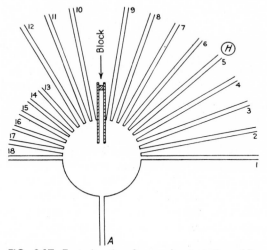

FIG. 9:17. Test situation for goal orientation. After the animals had 12 runs on Fig. 9:16, they were faced with this setup. Very few rats went to the left, although they had been doing so on the preceding runs; the largest number chose path 6, which leads straight to the former goal location. (*From Tolman et al., 1946.*)

Thus, even when blindfolded and restricted to contact and muscle cues, man does better when he makes use of his enormous symbolic and representative capacities.

Learning, according to this view, takes place when the organism perceives the significance of the stimulus as a cue to goal achievement. Anything which facilitates such perception aids learning. Let us consider the "principles" stated on pages 255–256. *Frequency* aids perception because, with repetition, the organism has more opportunities to perceive—to act on misleading cues and reject them—to identify and remember the correct one. *Contiguity* makes it possible to get, in a single perception, the important stimulus relationships. Rats learn a maze with short alleys faster than an identical pattern with longer alleys. Errors near the food box are eliminated faster than those in the middle of the maze. The biological function of learning is tension reduction; those stimuli which *immediately* lead to tension reduction are perceived more vividly and recalled more efficiently.

In Chap. 6 we pointed out the adaptive value of constantly shifting attention. Here we see that idea illustrated. If the learner shifts often and regularly, he will have more chances of getting clearly in focus the critical cues which are necessary to an efficient solution. (Compare Ruger's puzzle solving, where this point is also most important.)

Furthermore, we noted that cues which are related to strong motives quickly dominate in attention. So—if a rat finds that a certain path leads to food—that cue will next time "stand out" in attention and the animal will make the correct choice.

Even painful or unpleasant stimuli can speed up learning if they intensify perception of critical stimuli. When humans are learning a maze pattern, they give a superior performance if mild shock is given when they enter a blind alley (Bunch and Magdsick, 1938) or *when they make the correct turn* (Gurnee, 1938). The latter experiment shows clearly that the function of the electric shock is not to eliminate the wrong response but to enforce vivid perception of the choice points.

Snygg (1935) has shown the importance of perceptual cues in another way. He trained one group of rats on a maze in which all the alleys and true paths were black. Another group learned the same maze, but with the true path painted white, blind alleys black. The all-black maze required an average of 34 trials; the black-white pattern, 7 trials! Thus rats can easily use such cues if permitted to do so.

An industrial observation will perhaps illustrate the importance of this change in emphasis. Motion-picture films have been used for years in training factory workers on complex jobs. Yet in many cases the films did not seem to be of much value. Recently the explanation was discovered; the films were usually made with the camera in front of a skilled worker, photographing his *movements;* whereas, to guide the learner, the film should show the work materials as *he* would be handling them. By pointing the camera over the shoulder of the trainer, a picture was obtained which resembled that which must be seen by the trainee; a marked increase in efficiency has been attributed to this change.

The Acquisition of Skill

Psychologists have often treated the problem of acquisition of skill in connection with experimental studies of complex goal-directed learning because both are to some extent likely to involve gradual, piecemeal improvement. In both cases the goal is known. The problem is how to get there. The novice in golf wishes to land his ball on the green. He must learn to perceive correct and incorrect ways of holding the club, swinging at the ball, allowing for hazards, etc. Learning to play golf is harder than learning the usual maze because, at any given choice point, there are many possibilities as to the correct action. In the typical maze only two choices are presented simultaneously.

There are, of course, important differences between complex motor skills and a simple task such as running a maze. Only persistence is required to guarantee success on a maze; keep going and eventually you reach the goal. First success in a task such as walking a tightrope may elude the beginner a long time; unless the motivation is intense, he may become discouraged and quit. Even in golf the great difficulties at the beginning prevent many aspirants from continuing.

Limits and plateaus. In a complex skill the final criterion of success is also likely to be more elastic. One soon reaches a *physiological limit* of performance on a maze or other simple task. This limit is defined as the speed with which one can perform the task under maximum motivation, and it cannot be exceeded because of inherent limitations in our neuromuscular structure. The rat can run a maze only so fast. Man early reaches his limit in simple handling of objects; but, as the task increases in complexity, the physiological limit quickly becomes unimportant. Consider the case of a man learning to type. He is likely to use the one-finger method. After years of practice he does well enough for his purposes, and stops improving. He has reached a limit. But this is not the true physiological limit. It is known as a *plateau,* which can be exceeded if new motivation enters the picture. Under strong pressure the man decides to learn touch typing. At first he may actually slow up, but soon he is at a new high level of speed. He has adopted a new technique. This suggests that few of our skill limits are physiological limits. Mostly they are due to poor methods

or to inadequate motivation to develop superior techniques. (They are limits *at this level* of motivation.)

The shift in emphasis away from physiological limits is in accordance with modern medical work. It used to be believed that motor paralyses were permanent; *e.g.,* after a cerebral hemorrhage, a man is paralyzed on one side. This was considered a permanent and irremediable handicap. And indeed, direct effort to move the affected limb is almost certain to meet with failure. However, a powerfully motivated effort to carry out some action involving the entire body sometimes results in moving the paralyzed muscles. Starting from this tiny beginning, many paralytics have been reeducated to adequate motor control.

Inadequacy of guidance. It is important to note, in this connection, that guidance or outside movement of the limb is of little value. It does not help the paralytic to watch others, to be advised, or to have his limb moved by someone else. The first success must come with a movement initiated from within.

This fact fits with a variety of other observations. One experiment asked people to learn to wiggle their ears. Since many subjects could not attain even a first success, the experimenter tried to help them by stimulating the muscles electrically. The subjects felt the movement, and observed it in a mirror, but did not improve in making it themselves. Only if the ear muscles became involved in a gross reaction of brow, jaw, and cheek did it become possible to control them voluntarily.

Similar studies have been made on other performances. Rats guided through a maze (*e.g.,* led through on a collar) benefit very little. Educators have experimented with teaching young children handwriting by guidance. Cardboard stencils were grooved so that the pencil would necessarily describe the correct letter shape. Children who practiced for hours on these guided trials

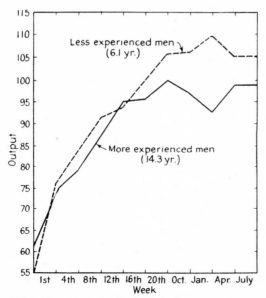

FIG. 9:18. Effect of increased motivation on long-established habits. The men were typesetters of considerable experience (dashed curve is for younger men, averaging 6.1 years at the trade, solid line for older men, averaging 14.3 years experience). Their performance had been almost level for some time prior to the introduction of the bonus. Within 8 weeks they had increased production about 50 per cent. After a year they leveled off at a performance figure almost double the beginning figure. (*From Kitson, 1922, p. 65.*)

did not learn handwriting any faster than an unguided control group.

Such observations confirm the view of learning stated earlier. The learner must *identify cues* for the correct response and develop the capacity to *respond selectively* to these cues. Guidance is therefore futile in many instances because the wrong cues are involved. The successful movement must originate within the learner, so that the kinesthetic cues for motor action are observable. The guided rat learns to respond to a pull on the collar; he does not learn to make choices for himself. The school child learns to trace a groove; he does not learn to shape letters. The paralytic must learn to identify obscure cues within his own body which can be utilized

in producing limb movements. Guidance helps only if it helps focus attention on the right cues.

Role of accidental success. It is also interesting to observe that these experiments supplement the studies of Ruger and others on the role of accidental success. The first success is often unconscious. It is difficult even then to identify what we did correctly, how we held the club, what stance we adopted, etc. Kinesthetic cues are not so sharply defined as visual cues. Once I have learned to spot the significant lever on a machine, much of the problem is solved. The visual apparatus is excellent for analyzing a total perceptual situation, identifying the key stimuli, and relating parts to the whole field. This is not true of kinesthesis. I may make a fine golf shot and wonder afterward just how I did it. I cannot clearly perceive, cannot analyze, the key muscle cue in the total complex of body movement.

Principle of frequency. This is the point at which the principle of frequency is truly important. How can one learn to identify these obscure kinesthetic sensations? How can he detect the minute difference between a correct and an incorrect swing? Repetition is the answer. If I keep repeating this movement, I will gradually identify all the various elements and spot the significant muscular cue. Practice, then, does not make perfect; but it offers an opportunity to approach perfection.

Frequency alone does not produce learning (cf. page 303). Kitson reports a study of typesetters, many of whom had been working at an even pace for 10 years. When a large bonus was offered for faster work, some of these men soon doubled their speed (Fig. 9:18). They had had plenty of practice; but without motivation, they had not searched for and identified the movements which would give high efficiency.

Learning by doing. Guidance, and even pictures of a good performance, thus help little in the acquisition of skill. Purely intellectual skills can be taught with some success through reading books (although even here some action seems greatly to facilitate learning). But motor skills are helped slightly or not at all by symbolic study. Reading a book on tennis has never made a star; many people are worse after reading such books than before. Skills are acquired primarily by practice, by trial and success, under conditions which *help the learner to identify the specific cues* which signaled the onset of the successful movement.

Principle of least action. As efficient skills are developed, unnecessary movements drop out until only the precise, adaptive motion remains. A beginning typist hunches over the machine; not only fingers, but arms, shoulder, and back are involved in the response. As the correct cues for finger movement are perceived, the unnecessary motions disappear and the typist uses only his fingers with an irreducible minimum of arm and shoulder action. This change is in accordance with our basic principle of homeostasis. The organism seeks to attain an equilibrium in which stimuli are dealt with by the use of minimum energy. It is wasteful to use adaptive techniques which require more than that amount, and all organisms seem to move in the direction of minimum energy cost. (Thus rats, given a choice of a long and a short pathway to food, will soon learn to take the shorter route.)

We can get a record which shows graphically the progress toward a least-action pattern of movement by the familiar mirror-drawing technique. In this case the subject sits facing a mirror, his hand under a screen so it is visible only in reflection. With a pencil he attempts to trace a star pattern. At choice points he finds that he must reverse his customary response to a visual cue. When his hand seems to be moving forward, it is actually moving backward. This creates a motor conflict which can readily be observed in the first tracing (Fig. 9:19). After several trials, however, we get the smooth, coordinated pattern of the later tracings. Most subjects learn this skill unconsciously by kinesthetic sensations; it is more efficient, however, to analyze the mirror distortion and verbalize self-instructions at the choice points.

Random choice vs. perceptual analysis. The importance of getting a clearly structured perception of the task, even in skilled movements, can be easily illustrated. A writer with a gift of fantasy has suggested that sheer blind trial and error, unguided by perceptual analysis, would have no survival value in this complex world of ours. He offers the instance of a turtle who is trying, on a typewriter, to write the word "nest":

Since there are 43 keys on Mr. Stone's typewriter, the turtle has one chance in 43 of hitting any one correctly. After he hits the first one correctly and sees the letter *n*, he has learned one thing. The motivational reinforcement connects that key with that letter. Then he has one chance in 42 of hitting *e* at random and learning the next key-letter combination. Then one out of 41 for *s*, and one out of 40 for *t*. There are $43 \times 42 \times 41 \times 40$ ways of doing all this, so in any attempt our energetic turtle has one chance in 3,361,840 of spelling out "nest." Though we may admire his patience we cannot say much for his method. It is quite likely that the turtle, or his motivation, will expire before his typing improves at all.[1]

Now let us contrast this pathetic victim of pure trial and error with the typical human subject. The classical study of learning to type was done by W. F. Book (1908). His subjects used the touch method and not only were constantly observed and timed but also kept extensive introspective reports on their progress. The subjects

[1] Johnson (1948), p. 144. Reprinted by permission.

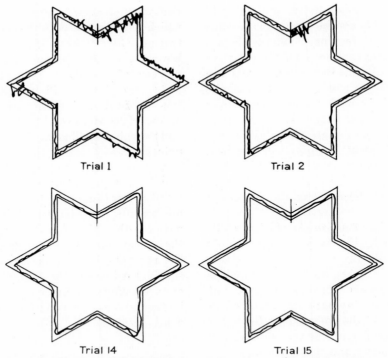

FIG. 9:19. The course of perfecting a skilled movement. The task is to trace a star pattern with a pencil, looking into a mirror rather than seeing the design directly. Note extreme irregularity of movement on trial 1, smooth, coordinated performance on trial 15. (*From Kingsley, 1946, p. 222. Reprinted by permission of Prentice-Hall, Inc.*)

first memorized the keyboard directly or by using a keyboard diagram. After a few hours of practice, the position of every letter was known. At this stage the subjects stated that they were responding letter by letter, *i.e.*, each letter was perceived and responded to before the next was in focus. Continued practice led to keeping a whole word in mind and striking the keys in sequence; gradually the anticipatory movements were tied together in such a way that the successive letters were struck without recognition as discrete responses. Later the subjects reported that they developed "phrase habits," such that visual recognition of a common phrase set off a whole series of finger movements without awareness of the individual words (note the curves in Fig. 7:9 for learning Morse

code). The difference between such a skilled performance and the turtle laboriously trying each key is, of course, a function of perceptual learning of the keyboard and of mechanical association of visual stimulus with finger response. The process would have been facilitated even more had the typewriter keyboard been designed with some meaningful arrangement of the letters.

The development of *higher order habits* (such as word and phrase habits) depends on *motivation*. The learner develops just enough skill to satisfy his existing needs. He then coasts along on a plateau of constant performance. Now if new motivation is introduced, pushing him to develop a new higher order habit, he moves off the plateau to a new level of speed and efficiency, and at this level a new pattern of least effort becomes standardized.

This problem has been the focus of violent controversy in industry. Workers in industrial establishments are motivated to learn job performance, but not enough, in many instances, to improve to high levels of speed and skill. Patterns of inefficient movement are formed and the worker stays on a plateau, perhaps for years. Managers have therefore hired psychologists or engineers who would study the job performance and seek to determine the maximum-efficiency pattern of movements and then teach the workers to use this procedure.

Such time-and-motion study often enough results in a pattern of movement which is essentially less fatiguing, requiring minimum energy output for a given total work load. One might expect, therefore, that the workers would be grateful for this assistance from management; but not so. The worker is quite likely to perceive the efficiency engineer as an enemy and to react with marked noncooperation in this situation. Many labor unions, in fact, have made one of their cardinal policies the elimination of such engineering activities.

The explanation of this is clear in the light of our prior analysis. Unless the worker is highly motivated, he will be unwilling to exert the additional energy required to form the new higher order habit, or to break his old movement patterns. The new proposed way of doing the job does not offer him, as an individual, a significant reward; sometimes there is included a modest pay increase, and sometimes nothing at all. Furthermore, the efficiency program may evoke negative motivations: fear of layoffs if the job is completed too fast, resentment at being compelled to abandon a familiar method at the command of a stranger, fear that the rate will be cut as soon as production has

been stabilized at the new high speed. In factories where these fears have been allayed and resentment eliminated, efficiency procedures operate successfully.[1]

Positive transfer. The extraordinary skills developed by human beings are based upon positive transfer from years of prior learning. A long infancy and childhood provide opportunity for acquisition of varied habits which aid tremendously in new tasks. A girl learning to type is capable not only of analyzing the printed page to pick out the letters which must be typed, but also of holding a word (several letters) in memory and striking each letter key in order of its memory image. Such a procedure obviously helps in the development of work habits, as it is unnecessary to look back at the copy for each consecutive letter. Many other aids come from her enormous background of prior learning. Typing would be far more cumbersome if it were not preceded by learning the alphabet and learning to read. Our hypothetical turtle who was going to learn to type did not possess these advantages. To every task of skill acquisition man brings both superior innate endowments, as compared with other species, and also this extensive background of useful prior learning.

Speech is a skilled performance of a high level of complexity. As we observe the process of speech acquisition in very young children, we see excellent illustrations of these integrations. The child learns to make specific sounds, but he has difficulty in putting them together in the proper order. Or he may omit some entirely,

[1] It is interesting to note, for example, that many companies such as Lincoln Electric in Cleveland guarantee that no improvement in performance by the workers will lead to a rate cut. At Oliver Iron and Steel (Pittsburgh), the union chooses the time-study man, although he works, of course, under the supervision of a company engineer. Such approaches remove the negative motivations and make possible the release of worker energies in higher levels of production.

especially from longer words. If, in trying to correct an error in pronunciation, we focus his attention on a specific sound, it may pop up earlier in the word than it should (thus resembling errors of anticipation in maze learning, etc.).

"One little boy was having trouble with the 'g' in 'Lone Ranger.' We gave him some drill on the 'zh' sound in isolation, then asked him to say the phrase again. It came out as 'Lone Razhner.' "

In some respects it is correct to say that, as skill improves, the role of the kinesthetic sensations from muscles becomes greater. In another way, however, it is the perceived pattern of movement which is becoming dominant. As the person gets a clearer picture of the movement pattern he really wants to produce, it seems easier to coordinate the specific responses into this smooth sequence. Attention should not be focused on the separate movements, but on the over-all action.

Imitation and skill learning. Developing a picture of the total action pattern, in a skilled performance or in ordinary goal-directed learning, is facilitated to some extent by observing another performer. Its usefulness is limited, however, by the fact that one cannot perceive all details of the skillful act, nor does one get the muscle sensations which must be closely integrated with the visual and auditory awareness of the outside situation. A judicious combination of self-practice, imitation, more practice, and more imitation seems to give the best results.

Discussion of this phase of the learning process has often been confused by differences in the meaning of terms. Some people (including nineteenth century psychologists) have spoken of an instinct of imitation. The existence of an inborn tendency to imitate others has been just about unanimously rejected by American psychologists. Further, it is clear the imitative behavior takes at least two different forms

when it does occur.[1] First we note *reflexive imitation*, mimicking the movements of others—smiling when others smile, yawning when they yawn, etc. This purely mechanical type of repetition is explained by the conditioned-response formula. The sight of this movement pattern is associated with the inner cues setting off the same muscle responses. A second type of imitation is an aspect of *goal-directed learning*. In such a case one person watches another who is engaged in some complex action and learns what points are crucial, what the completed performance should look like, and so on. Thus a piano teacher can help the student to a limited extent by showing him the correct performance of a Mozart sonata. The student learns the *kind of sound* to be produced rather than the specific finger movements involved. The latter type of learning must be done by trial and error, and imitation is of very little help. By getting a clearer picture of the goal, however, the student is aided in his total activity.

Rats can be trained to simple reflexive imitation, such as turning to the right or left in following a leader. Such acts must be reinforced by food if they are to be made dependable. Observation of complex goal-directed learning seems to be useless in species below the primates. Figure 9:20 shows the apparatus used in one experiment on this problem (Warden, 1935). There are two compartments in the cage; duplicate puzzle tasks are set up in parallel positions, one in each compartment. One monkey is allowed to work out the solution to the puzzle by repeated trials. He is then placed in one compartment and an inexperienced subject in the other. The crucial test is whether the second animal watches the

[1] We also observe situations in which one person seems to be imitating another, but in fact both are responding to the same stimulus (people running to catch a train, drivers stopping for traffic lights).

first and then shows superior performance in solving his own puzzle. The experiment is then repeated with a new task. One animal made successful use of imitative observation in 23 out of 24 puzzles, and for the over-all group, evidence for imitation was obtained in 46 per cent of the tests.

The significant question in these experiments, and also in imitation studies on humans, is this: how does the subject perceive the situation? Does he grasp the idea that he is to solve the same problem? How many of the essential cues can he get from direct observation? Did Warden's monkeys learn to perceive the actions of the "leader" as cues, or were they focused only on the reward? It seems clear that successful imitation of this type cannot take place unless the observer perceives the leader's acts as signposts directing his own actions. This is just as true of humans as it is of monkeys.

The successful use of imitation as a guide in learning depends also on the relations between leader and observer. A boy who is fond of his father will desire to be like the father and therefore will be motivated to imitate. If his dominant motivation is one of hostility to his father, imitation is likely to be in reverse—*i.e.*, negativism, rejection of the father's behavior. Teachers who fail to establish good personal relations with their classes cannot expect imitative behavior by students. Employers whose workers feel hostility toward the company will not be able to make effective use of imitation in guiding job behavior.

Reflexive imitation. Although reflexive imitation is not goal-directed in nature, it is socially important and of considerable significance for some of our theoretical problems. We can therefore pause to treat it at this time.

Reflexive imitation has the same basic character as classical conditioning or stimulus substitution. Whenever two stimuli are

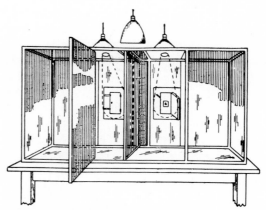

FIG. 9:20. Apparatus for studying imitative learning. Various puzzles suitable for monkeys can be inserted in the wall panel. One animal was allowed to solve the puzzle by trial and error, without the other animal watching. Then both animals were put in their respective cages; the question was: would the naïve monkey watch the experienced one solve the puzzle and profit from this observation? The answer was clearly that some monkeys did learn by imitating—at least to the extent of focusing attention on the significant parts of the puzzle. (*From Warden and Jackson, 1935, p. 106.*)

frequently paired, there is a tendency for an association to be established, without regard to our interest and with the involvement of only minimal motivational tension. The conditioned pupillary reflex is an illustration of one kind; the association of the sight of a man's face and the sound of his voice is another. The difference between these kinds of stimulus substitution and the process of goal-directed learning becomes important in connection with imitative behavior, for example, in the child's learning of language.

The acquisition of speech. We may start with E. B. Holt's concept of the "circular reflex." Holt has pointed out that the human infant shows no tendency to imitate adults. As adults become associated with good, comfort, and the gratification of tissue needs, the child reacts with pleasure to the perception of an adult. However, there is still no imitation of the adult's actions. First it is necessary for the child

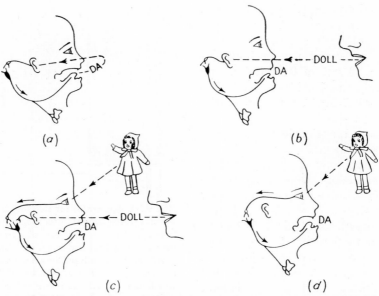

FIG. 9:21. Allport's theory of language acquisition. According to this view (modeled on Holt's circular reflex concept), the child must first make random sounds and hear himself (a). This establishes a circular CR, in which hearing the sound is a stimulus for making the appropriate speech movements. Now it is possible for him to imitate an adult (b); the adult makes a sound and the child gives the CR in his repertoire nearest to that he hears. After this, visual-auditory-motor connections (c) and the visual-motor connections (d) can be established. The theory assumes that, during the first year of life, when no apparent speech development occurs, these basic circular CRs are being established, so that rapid progress is possible after the age of twelve to eighteen months. (*Redrawn from Allport, 1924, by permission of Houghton Mifflin Company.*)

to establish some sensory controls over his own responses. Suppose that a child says "da." The muscles in the speech mechanism are innervated; while the muscle tension and kinesthetic sensations are still present, the auditory mechanism is stimulated by the sound "da." As our classical conditioning experiments show, there is a tendency for two cortical areas, activated simultaneously, to become associated. Thus hearing "da" comes to be linked with the muscular process of producing "da" (Fig. 9:21). We can confirm this assumption by listening to infantile babbling; often the child seems to become intoxicated with a particular sound and repeats it interminably with no apparent satiation.

Once the child has become conditioned so that the auditory stimulus "da" is firmly related to the muscle responses producing "da," it is possible for him to "imitate" adults (see Fig. 9:21). The fond mother hears the child babbling and attempts verbal play. She bends over the baby and says "da." This sets off the associated response and the child is said to be imitating. Probably the mother's enthusiasm over the verbalization, and the extra attention she gives the baby at this point, focus his attention on the speech mechanism. He begins to perceive the appropriate cues for behavior which will be goal satisfying. Thus, even with unmotivated reflexive imitation, it is impossible to

FIG. 9:22. A deaf child learning speech. It follows from the circular-reflex theory that, if a child cannot get any "feed-back" from producing sounds, no circular CR is established, and speech will not develop. The deaf child obviously cannot hear himself babbling; presumably this accounts for the very slow speech development of such cases. In this photograph an amplifying system is being used to help the child get feed-back cues; also, the speech correction st is providing a visual model to help induce the correct speech movements. Such methods have helped many deaf children to speak comprehensibly. (*Chicago Tribune photograph.*)

leave out of consideration the ever-present tendency to seek stimuli which will gratify the needs of the organism. The child will soon shift from automatic reflexive imitation to goal-directed imitation, *i.e.*, he will learn to attend to cues of adult speech and action patterns and attempt to control his own acts accordingly. Holt was concerned only to emphasize that the initial phase of this process is classical conditioning and is not a form of intentional imitation.

If the person gets no sensory feedback from his actions, reflexive imitation becomes impossible. Deaf children have great difficulty in learning speech because they have not learned the auditory-motor connections represented in Fig. 9:21. Current work with them uses sound amplifiers as well as visual cues to help them establish the appropriate controls over their speech movements (Fig. 9:22).

If the sensory feedback is tampered with, disruption of the skilled habit results. Dr. Grant Fairbanks of the University of Illinois has used a tape recorder with a movable head to show this effect for speech habits. The subject speaks into a microphone, and his words are played back to him through earphones, after a delay of perhaps 0.1 second (Fig. 9:23). The result is catastrophic; the subject stutters, stammers, or blocks completely. Some become violently emotional as a result of the disruption.

Reflexive imitation based on these sensory feedbacks is involved in many forms

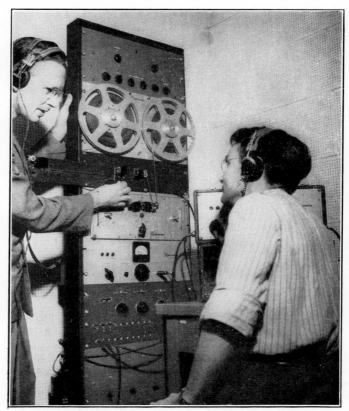

FIG. 9:23. The Fairbanks delayed-feed-back device. Dr. Grant Fairbanks demonstrates to an assistant his device for inducing speech blockages at will. The subject speaks into a microphone which feeds into the tape recorder. By means of a movable head, the playback to the subject's earphones can be delayed by a fraction of a second. This upsets the guide stimuli which normally control the smooth flow of speech; every person who has been tested has shown severe speech disturbance—stuttering, stammering, blocking—as a result. Some become highly emotional—presumably a reflection of low frustration tolerance. (Courtesy of Dr. Grant Fairbanks.)

of social interaction. Football fans push in the direction toward which their team is driving. A man who is in a group of excited, shouting, angry people will tend to develop similar feelings. He sees their facial expressions, hears their emotional voices, and reflexively begins to experience similar states himself. This is a key principle in the understanding of mob action, wildcat strikes, college-student riots, and the like. No group mind is involved; it is the mutual stimulation of circular reflexes which

explains the rising tension and emotional overflow in such situations.

From the point of view of skilled acts, one utility of the circular-reflex phenomenon lies in the perfection of isolated action units. Modern life presents many demands for new complex activities. But these can best be executed if the necessary component units have not only been learned, but also automatized. Typing is facilitated by prior automatic knowledge of the alphabet. It is also dependent upon the ability to move each finger independently. Driving a car requires prior automatization of movements of the hand, arm, and foot, in addition to the correct perception of the parts of the car and of the highway. Thus the circular reflex plays an important role in developing these isolated movements to such a level that, in complex task situations, attention can be focused on the overall problem and not on the control of fingers, hands, arms, and legs. The ability voluntarily to manipulate these parts of the body, and to achieve desired movement patterns, seems to be perfected by the circular-reflex mechanism. This, in turn, contributes materially to the homeostatic adjustment of the total organism, as it reduces the required expenditure of energy in adaptation to modern life.

Insight and Learning

We can think of learning tasks as varying in kind, according to the emphasis upon acquisition of skill, or upon understanding. The preceding pages have been devoted primarily to goal-directed learning in which skill elements were of major importance. The person knows what he must do, but he must develop the sensory-motor coordination needed to execute the task. At the other extreme, there are learning tasks in which skill is of no importance, but understanding what to do is difficult. Naturally there are all degrees between these two extremes; most learning problems involve some degree of perception of the total situation, not merely motor skill.

Consider the problem facing a boy on an iron grid in the sidewalk, chewing gum and looking at a dime inside the well, 4 feet below the sidewalk. The more he looks at it, the more fascinated he becomes. He tries to reach it with his fingers; no luck. He picks up a short stick and touches the dime with it; the coin slides on the floor but of course does not come closer to his grasping

hand. He becomes more tense and chews harder. If only the coin would cling to the stick! Suddenly the stick looks different. It has a piece of sticky stuff on the end. Quickly he places the gum on the stick and retrieves the coin. The success is due not to development of motor skill, but to a new perception of the situation. This form of problem solution is called *insight*.

Insight learning is characterized, first, by the fact that no new skill is involved, and secondly, by the fact that it is sudden. The change takes place at a cortical level, involving the perception of aspects of the situation in a new combination. While every insight is in some degree novel, we must not exaggerate this point. Memories of past experiences are always at hand to be rearranged in a new pattern. The boy cited above had undoubtedly got gum on his shoe and found that it picked up pebbles. He may have seen park workers picking up papers with a nail on the end of a stick. The essential feature of insight is that the *combination* is novel for *this person*.

Sudden solution in problem solving is nothing new. We have dealt with the same phenomenon in perception; many of Ruger's subjects showed sudden improvements in their puzzle solutions, and Adams' cats likewise often manifested a sudden drop in time required to open the puzzle box. As far as humans are concerned, it would be easy to say that the person has just "reasoned it out." But we are reluctant to use such an explanation for animal behavior; furthermore, it is an explanation which does not really explain. What processes underlie this answer?

We can get at the nature of insight more readily if we start with a purely perceptual task. Look at Fig. 9:24. You may say that this is a picture of an old lady wearing a bonnet. However, there can be a difference of opinion. I say it is a picture of a young lady. You are puzzled by my peculiar interpretation but start examining the

FIG. 9:24. Ambiguous figure. The restructuring of perception which occurs in this type of figure may be a simple example of what goes on when one achieves insight into a complex problem situation.

picture again to try to understand my remark. Suddenly you say "Oh, now I get it; she has her face turned so that only a little of her profile shows." Now it is certain that the drawing itself has not changed. The light rays striking your eye have not been altered. But you have suddenly restructured your perception—a cortical process— to get a new set of relationships. Probably, in some degree, all perceptions of the environment are in such a state of flux due to the constant shifting of attention, but most of them are sufficiently structured that a drastic reshuffling is impossible. On the other hand, if one gets a habit of seeing a situation in a certain way, that might block him from getting these other relationships (cf. Leeper, 1935, page 234).

If the solution to a problem depends on getting awareness of the young woman, this drawing provides us with a good illustration of insight on the purely perceptual level.

The boy with the chewing gum solved his problem, most likely on the perceptual level, but with some action involved. He did, however, have to evolve a new way of seeing relationships between gum, stick, and coin before he could satisfy his desire.

The study of this kind of problem solving in man is difficult. From early years children are taught all kinds of relationships; furthermore, they live in an adult world where they can see examples of recombinations which may affect the solution. It has seemed worth while, therefore, to turn to the study of animals even at this fairly complicated level.

Some of the most ingenious experiments of this type were done by Wolfgang Köhler, a German psychologist who found himself isolated on one of the Canary Islands during World War I, with his animal laboratory. Köhler was impressed with the importance of perception in problem solving and arranged his researches to test this hypothesis.

Chickens and dogs were tried in a very simple situation. The animal is in a U-shaped enclosure (Fig. 9:25). Food is placed beyond the barrier at F. A chicken will peck and scratch at the wire but will not perceive the possibility of going away from the food to reach it. The dog at first behaves just as the chicken does but suddenly turns and runs out of the enclosure, around to the food. This so-called "detour behavior" suggests that the animal has suddenly perceived the problem in a new way. Probably it was facilitated by shifting attention and random movements

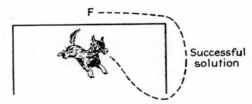

FIG. 9:25. The detour problem. Food is placed at F, and the animal inside the U-shaped enclosure. This problem is useful for adult animals below the primate level, and for young children and monkeys.

of body and head which brought other parts of the situation into the visual field; however, these movements also occurred with the chicken, without effect. The dog does not get the new solution at once; he also spends some time attacking the barrier. As long as a direct approach leads to tension reduction, new insights do not develop. *Frustration of a goal-directed activity favors restructuring of the field to produce insight.* It does not, of course, guarantee that insight will occur.

Experiments with tools. Animals normally use objects as tools to a minimal degree or not at all. However, Köhler decided to try some experiments which would indicate the animals' capacity to perceive the relationship between a tool object and a goal object. He placed an ape in a cage, and a banana outside the cage, beyond arm's length. Close by, within reach, were some sticks. The question was: could the animal perceive the stick as a tool for raking in the fruit?

Tschego first tries to reach the fruit with her hand; of course, in vain. She then moves back and lies down; then she makes another attempt, only to give it up again. This goes on for more than half an hour. Finally she lies down for good, and takes no further interest in the objective. The sticks might be non-existent as far as she is concerned, although they can hardly escape her attention as they are in her immediate neighborhood. But the younger animals, who are disporting themselves outside the stockade, begin to take notice, and approach the objective gradually. Suddenly Tschego leaps to her feet, and quite adroitly, pulls the bananas until they are within reach.[1]

This experiment illustrates the ape's capacity for developing insight into a new technique for obtaining food. The process seems dependent upon intensity of motivation; Tschego did not solve the problem of using the stick as a rake until the prospect

of losing the banana to one of the other animals appeared imminent.

Once the new insight has been developed, it functions independently of specific elements in the situation. Nueva, another ape, solved the stick problem. Then she was placed in the experimental cage without any sticks. She immediately began using other objects, even though they did not in the least resemble sticks.

When the objective was put down outside the cage, she at once tried to pull it towards her with rags lying in her cage, with straws, and finally with her tin drinking bowl which stood in front of the bars, or to beat it towards her— using the rags—and sometimes successfully.[1]

In other words, what was learned in the stick situation was not a specific habit of stick manipulation, but a new way of looking at the problem. Almost any movable object will now be perceived as a potential tool for raking in the food. Humans show the same behavior; in the experimental problem involving tying together two strings hanging from the ceiling (page 314), no subject who solved the problem ever had any difficulty repeating, even though all the "tools" were changed on the second trial. Any small object which could be used as a pendulum bob would serve his purpose. It is this *flexibility*, this independence of specific environmental resources, which marks the superiority of insight learning over trial and error.

Structure building. Another of Köhler's experiments involved the use of boxes to reach food suspended in the air. When Sultan first saw the cookie hanging from the ceiling, he kept leaping for it. Suddenly he seized the box, moved it under the objective, and in one movement sprang to the top of the box and grasped the cookie. Here, again, it seems that the box has been perceived in a new way. To make the task

---

[1] Köhler (1927), pp. 31–32. Reprinted by permission of Harcourt, Brace and Company, Inc.

[1] *Ibid.,* p. 34.

FIG. 9:26. The solution of the box-stacking problem. Although the ape had never piled boxes on top of one another, he devised this technique to reach the bananas suspended over his head. (*Lilo Hess, photographer. From Three Lions, Inc.*)

more difficult, Köhler then contrived a task requiring two boxes.

The objective is placed very high up, the two boxes not very far away from each other and about four meters away from the objective; all other means of reaching it have been taken away. Sultan drags the bigger of the two boxes towards the objective, puts it just underneath, gets up on it, and looking upwards, makes ready to jump, but does not jump; gets down, seizes the other box, and pulling it behind him, gallops about the room, making his usual noise, kicking against the walls and showing his uneasiness in every possible way. He certainly did not seize the second box to put it on the first; it merely helps to give vent to his anger. But all of a sudden his behavior changes completely; he stops making a noise, pulls his box from quite a distance right up to the other one, and stands it

upright upon it. He mounts the somewhat shaky construction.[1]

Here the basic insight is that into the piling up of objects (Fig. 9:26). Three- and four-box problems were successfully handled after the two-box solution was developed; also, the apes promptly transferred the technique to other objects. A table was used; one ape would climb on another's back to reach the food, and in one instance an ape tried to lift the keeper so he could reach the goal. These variations show the speed of *positive transfer* once insight has been achieved; it also warns us that past experience must be carefully controlled if we are trying to study the development of truly novel problem solutions.

Chance solutions. Were these chance solutions? In a realistic sense, this seems unlikely. Solutions were of course favored by random variation in location and posture. In the detour experiment, the animal was most likely to get a solution when, in his dashing about, he had reached a point near the end of the screen. (Note, nevertheless, that the chickens did not achieve this, although they showed such random behavior.) Similarly, some of the more complex problems were undoubtedly facilitated by chance fumbling. Köhler describes Sultan's solution of the jointed-stick problem (requiring a small stick to be fitted into a hole in the end of a larger), as follows:

Sultan first of all squats indifferently on the box, which has been left standing a little back from the railings; then he gets up, picks up the two sticks, sits down again on the box and plays carelessly with them. While doing this, it happens that he finds himself holding one rod in either hand in such a way that they lie in a straight line; he pushes the thinner one a little way into the opening of the thicker, jumps up and is already on the run toward the railings, to which he has up to now half turned his back, and begins to draw a banana towards him with the double stick. I call the master; meanwhile,

[1] *Ibid.*, pp. 135–136.

one of the animal's rods has fallen out of the other, as he has pushed one of them only a little way into the other; whereupon he connects them again.[1]

These experiments indicate the importance of perception in problem solving, and they probably identify the critical factor in perception which correlates with a sudden solution. The animal *sees the situation as a whole.* At first and for some time there is no progress toward a solution. Suddenly an object in the field is seen as functionally related to the goal. This is favored by a physical arrangement of the situation such that the organism perceives the tool in physical proximity to the goal. So, when Sultan "saw" the two sticks as one longer stick which would reach the banana, he solved the problem.

Köhler, in theorizing from his experiments, emphasized the present perceptual field and minimized the role of past experience. However, we have already seen (Chap. 6) that objects are always perceived with some modification due to prior experience. This can be illustrated neatly in relation to problem solving by Birch's (1945a) study of chimpanzees. His task was that of using a hoe to rake in food, thus closely resembling Köhler's pioneer research. Six animals, all of whom had been closely observed from birth, were used. Four of them failed to solve the hoe problem. These animals were now returned to their enclosure, where they found straight sticks varying from 16 to 30 inches in length. After three days of opportunity for stick play, they were retested on the hoe problem and immediately solved it without difficulty, *even though none of them used sticks to reach objects during the play interval.* In this case we are certainly justified in saying that learning the qualities of sticks contributed to insight problem solving, even though no trial-and-error use of sticks occurred. Con-

[1] *Ibid.*, p. 127.

FIG. 9:27. A simple perceptual problem for monkeys. Food is attached to the chain ending left foreground. The monkey must pick out the significant cues from the complex total situation (a much simplified version of the human task presented in Fig. 6:36, page 233). (*Courtesy of Dr. H. F. Harlow.*)

versely, we cannot expect children (or adults) to solve problems unless they have learned the properties of the materials essential to a solution.

Role of motivation. Birch (1945b) also used these six apes in a study of the effect of differential motivation upon problem solving. Motivation was varied by keeping the animal without food for 2, 6, 12, 24, 36, or 48 hours. Short deprivation presumably is related to low intensity of motivation (Chap. 2). On experiments with short periods without food, the animals tended to wander, ignore the food, and play with their neighbors. On the very long deprivations (high drive intensity), they tended to concentrate their attention and activity to the region of the food. Problem solving was interfered with because the perceptual field was limited to the food area (focusing). Under these conditions, the frustration of the barrier induced vigorous aggression and disturbed behavior. "A series of unsuccessful attempts to get the food would frequently be followed by disruptive behavior. This behavior would include screaming, temper tantrums, of marked violence and acts of aggression against the neighbors, the apparatus, and the experimenter." Thus an *intermediate* degree of motivation, neither too slight nor too intense, was found to be most efficient for problem solving.[1]

Adult Human Learning: A Synthesis

In the chapter on rote learning we were concerned about acquisition of knowledge, of the kind we expect our children to get in the early school years. A common example would be that of learning to read. The first step must be to learn the meanings of individual words, so that one may concentrate on the act of reading without dividing one's attention. In our primary schools, the child might be said to be learning the "vocabulary" of life; he memorizes certain fundamentals like recognition and spelling of a sufficient vocabulary, numbers and simple arithmetic, a few geographical facts, a limited awareness of history. With this minimal equipment it becomes possible for us to live, function, and solve simple problems in the normal cultural environment.

Association. Underlying the acquisition of these primitive facts is the process of association. Association has much of the externally controlled, mechanical character of classical conditioning. Two and two make four, not because of any quality of the natural situation or because of any property which can be insightfully perceived; the relationship is arbitrarily asserted by the society in which we live. Like

[1] *Cf.* Fig. 3:17, p. 105.

the experimenter who rings the bell and then feeds the dog, society coerces the child into becoming aware of certain properties, associating certain stimuli with each other and with responses, and so on.

Our analysis of learning by association involved an attempt to keep other variables constant. Motivation, for example, was given little attention; yet it is clear that the intensity of motivation does affect the speed of formation of associations. The structuring of the associative material by intelligent analysis of the meaning involved was also ignored. The principles of association, which were developed in that chapter, work fairly well if the subject takes a somewhat passive attitude and learns sheerly by rote—as, for example, a college student taking a subject which he finds uninteresting. In free-learning situations, adults rarely learn in this passive manner. A man will transform a series of nonsense syllables into abbreviations of railroad names, misspellings of familiar words, or even pretended samples from a foreign language. He will also cluster them in rhythmical units or in units to which he can attach some meaning. The principles of association, to be sure, are still doing their work, but the motivated learner does much more than mechanical association; he reconstructs the material in ways which facilitate its acquisition.

Transfer. When we talked about transfer of training, our experiments showed slight amounts of positive transfer—not enough, certainly, to justify the idea that sheer practice in learning gave one a superior mind. And yet, unless positive transfer is really a significant reality, no one could ever become "educated." Knowledge, after all, must transfer from book and classroom to daily living.

Efficient transfer probably depends upon two factors: the person's intellectual capacity (see Chap. 12), and the way in which learning is carried out. If the act of learning comes to be perceived as a "good" way to satisfy one's needs, then learning becomes perceived as "good" in itself. We develop an interest in learning, a "set" to learn more, a sensitivity to certain kinds of occurrences in our environment. Harlow (1949) has demonstrated that animals "learn how to learn." After solving five problems, his monkeys learned new tasks far more rapidly than after the first one. Humans also evidence this phenomenon.

Many college students fail in attaining maximum transfer and utilization of education because they focus too narrowly upon a practical goal. Like the animal who stays so close to the food that he cannot see the tool needed to reach it, these students demand an immediately "practical" kind of education and thus miss important kinds of learning. It will be recalled that principles transfer easily, whereas concrete facts transfer poorly. The student who misperceives principles and theory as "unimportant" is handicapped in his future learning.

In perception, as in goal-directed learning, the *development of a schema* is important. When we can arrange words in alphabetical order, numbers in a series, scientific facts in a general principle, we have greatly increased their chances of retention and utilization. Schema development is therefore homeostatic in character. Man is distinctively superior to all other animals in his capacity for schema development. When we compare people of different levels of competence, we find that superior performance goes with success at organizing specific facts into schemata.

Conditioning. Classical conditioning shows that man learns to perceive and behave in terms of the relation between recurring pairs of stimuli. The roar of the tiger reinstates the image of his appearance; and either the sound of his roar or the word *tiger* will set off the conditioned heartbeat, stomach constriction, and other visceral reactions. Like association of ideas, from which it is distinguished only formally, classical conditioning is primarily rote and mechanical in character.

The circular reflex was found to be a variety of conditioning which played a substantial role in human development. The child must first learn to control his own muscles before he can acquire adult behavior patterns. His vocal babbling sets up a circular reflex in which a sound is conditioned to muscular action; then when an adult speaks, this tends to set off the same muscle movements and "imitation" of the spoken word. Similarly the child must first be conditioned so that the sight of his moving arm is tied in with actual muscular contractions before he can imitate adult arm movements.[1]

Instrumental conditioning. Unlike classical conditioning, instrumental conditioning involves active effort by the organism to restore equilibrium. Because response variation—with selection of an efficient reaction—is a part of this process, the instrumental CR illustrates dynamic rather than static homeostasis. Instrumental conditioning provides an excellent model for understanding many kinds of reactions to simple threats and simple goal-directed problem situations. In both classical and instrumental conditioning, the learner must identify the significant stimulus, separating it from a background of other stimuli.

Goal-oriented learning. In this chapter we have been concerned with an analysis of learning which is more realistic, because it includes a wider array of determining factors. This is not to deny the reality of association and conditioning but to suggest that they do not have the distinctive quality of involving the total organism. In the type of learning which is goal-directed, we find the organism wanting something and embarking on a voyage of discovery.

[1] A deft literary production which gives a realistic picture of what life might be like, if conditioning were the sole principle of learning, is the novel by Aldous Huxley, *Brave New World*.

The motivation modifies the perceived situation; and objects related to the goal are especially perceived differently.

Even goal-directed learning, however, involves automatic, mechanized constituents. When a learned act is repeated, kinesthetic sensations begin to take over control —probably by way of conditioning—so that the cortical processes, perception and learning, can be focused on other aspects. Once we have learned to speak a foreign language, we can concentrate on better expression of ideas. In the early stages, we are focused on the mechanics and cannot attend to the ideas. Skilled habits may therefore be considered as aids to higher mental activity by freeing the organism of the necessity for attending to simple, mechanical activities. On the other hand, a habit can be a block to mental progress because, once a given skill is developed, it tends to run off automatically even when it is no longer truly appropriate. Similarly, if one gets fixed in a certain way of perceiving situations, he has trouble in developing new insights which would represent better adaptive solutions.

In drawing all these aspects of learning into a simple, comprehensive schema, we emphasize the role of motivation and adjustment. Man is constantly seeking satisfactions. In goal-oriented learning he makes use of associations of ideas and past conditionings, but he also actively puts together these past elements in new ways. He perceives familiar facts in new relationships, and in so doing he moves progressively toward a more successful adjustment.

Recommended Readings[1]

HOLT, E. B.: *Animal Drive and the Learning Process.* New York: Holt, 1931.

KATONA, G.: *Organizing and Remembering.* New York: Columbia University Press, 1940.

KÖHLER, W.: *Mentality of Apes.* New York: Harcourt, Brace, 1925.

SNYGG, D., and A. W. COMBS: *Individual Behavior.* New York: Harper, 1949.

TOLMAN, E. C.: *Purposive Behavior in Animals and Men.* New York: Appleton-Century-Crofts, 1932.

UNDERWOOD, B. J.: *Experimental Psychology.* New York: Appleton-Century-Crofts, 1949. Chaps. vi, vii, and viii.

WERTHEIMER, MAX: *Productive Thinking.* New York: Harper, 1945.

[1] See also p. 547.

CHAPTER 10

Remembering

The problem of memory has a variety of aspects. We have already noted that in certain respects memory cannot be separated from learning; if the effects of a learning experience were not retained over time (retention) and manifested in subsequent behavior (recall), no complex behavior could ever be developed. In Chap. 7 we presented some of the known facts with regard to quantitative aspects of remembering; the effectiveness of various conditions could be ascertained by measures of amount recalled.

In these quantitative studies the experimental model was: learning, time interval, memory testing. Variations were introduced in terms of the kind of stimulus material to be learned, the activity during the interval, and the conditions at the time of recall. But in all these studies the emphasis was upon rigid control of the situation and the quantitative measure of memory performance.

As an explanatory concept the term *memory trace* was introduced. Variations in the memory trace were ascribed to conditions at the time of learning, during the lapsed interval, or at recall. The curve of forgetting, for example, showed quantitative variations in memory traces with differing intervals of time. However, we did not attempt to explore the concept of memory trace as such or to consider the qualitative changes in the memory trace with time. It is now essential that we take up these problems, since they become basic aspects of the psychology of thinking.

The memory trace cannot be observed directly. It is an inference, a hypothetical construct, contrived to explain the fact that the effects of learning persist over time. Memory traces must be assumed in animals as well as in man. However, if we wish to study qualitative changes in memory, we can study only human beings, since some kind of symbolic report on what is recalled must furnish the data for that research. Furthermore, we shall have to forgo studies of infants, since they too cannot communicate the quality of their memories.

Infants are capable of learning, even prior to birth. During the first year of life sensory impressions have an effect, the CR can be established, simple goal-directed habits are learned. We cannot, however, investigate changes in the memory of these experiences. It may be—since there is little competition from other similar memories—that these experiences register almost photographically and are recalled precisely. Most parents who read stories to very young children know how promptly the child protests omission of a single word in a familiar passage. Primary-school children show much more vivid, even eidetic imagery (see page 359) than do adults. Thus we may infer, but on extremely limited evidence, that memory traces in the early years persist with little modification.

The acquisition of language. As the child becomes civilized, he acquires a language; indeed, the two processes are probably the same. It takes a whole year for him to learn a few words; but at the age of three he may understand as many as 1,000 verbal symbols. And at this early age he is no longer focused primarily on the physical stimuli around him. He is likely to be much more centered upon communicating with and receiving communications from the human environment in words. He asks for goal objects to satisfy his desires, and gets—or is denied—them. Adults impose requirements upon him. The distinction between "me" and "they" becomes sharper. The child becomes aware of himself as a separate personality; he comes to perceive himself as a distinctive part of the world. (The young infant apparently perceives parts of his own body— hands, legs, etc.—as objects, not as part of himself.) With language development he comes to perceive and label himself as a member of the Smith family, as a Presbyterian, as a first-grader, and so on. These "roles" exert an impressive influence upon the formation of personality; we shall discuss them in detail in a later chapter.

Philosophers once referred to the mind of the newborn human as a blank page, a *tabula rasa* upon which anything could be written by the external environment. That conception may be correct at birth, but it speedily becomes inaccurate, especially so when language is acquired. From that time on the external stimulus decreases in importance; the linguistic reaction, the evaluation of the stimulus, and its relation to past experience increase sharply in psychological significance. The organism must be thought

of as constantly trying to achieve some goal, to reduce tension. In this process the stimulus is taken and fitted into an ongoing pattern; it is less often that the stimulus molds the organism. To a man trying to drive a nail, a brick may be perceived as a substitute for a hammer; if he is disturbed by wind blowing his papers about, the brick becomes a paperweight; and if he is in the grip of intense anger, the object is now seen as a weapon. Such considerations suggest that it is most misleading to say that a stimulus initiates action. The stimulus is likely at best to be trigger, releasing action determined by inner forces.

The changing memory trace. When we think of memory traces within this dynamic pattern, it is difficult to suppose that the trace is merely a copy of the stimulus object or situation. We must expect that memory items will be exaggerated, suppressed, or distorted to fit into a pattern of need and adjustment. As later pages will show, this is precisely what does happen.[1]

There is one respect in which man attempts to resurrect the memory trace in its original form as a copy of the stimulus (although it is difficult to do this much of the time). When I am consciously trying to evaluate a past experience as a guide for future action, or when I am trying to imagine a future situation so that I can be prepared for it, I am likely to try to reinstate images exactly as they occur in experience. In this case, memory is like a new type of distance receptor; by it man can perceive the past and the future, as well as the physical present.

The importance of changes in the memory trace can best be evaluated by referring back to the summary of human learning at the close of the preceding chapter. The *identification of the significant stimulus* was stressed at that point. Pavlov's dogs had to salivate only to a particular stimulus, not to others. The student

[1] Look again at Fig. 1:4.

memorizing a foreign-language vocabu-
larly must correctly recall the English
words paired with these foreign words. A
physician must learn to recognize the symptoms calling for one treatment, distinguishing carefully those demanding a different procedure. In all these cases, changes
in the memory trace could conceivably
destroy the value of much training and
teaching.

The preceding paragraphs reveal the
scope of the problem of memory. In this
chapter we shall examine the data concerning memory in its broad interrelations with
perception, emotions, language, attitudes,
and social conditions. Psychoanalysis, for
example, has developed an elaborate technique for exploring infantile and repressed
memories; in many cases it is easy to show
the distortion which has affected the
memory material. In addition, there are
numerous objective types of research which
throw light upon the problem. Let us
now turn to a consideration of these
investigations.

The Memory Image

Every human being apparently has the
ability to reinstate past perceptions in the
form of images, although these range from
vague impressions, largely verbal in character, to vivid, sharply defined pictures almost photographic in nature. Because it is
impossible to communicate mental content
directly from one person to another, it is
difficult for people who differ markedly in
imagery to describe this difference. Both
must use language; but a verbal description
of an object is not the same as an image of
the object.

To clarify this point, particularly for
readers with poor imagery, it may be helpful to begin with a consideration of the *afterimage*. As has been noted in Chap. 5, all
receptors theoretically mediate both sensations and afterimages, but it is easiest to

observe the afterimage in certain special
cases.

The *positive afterimage* is a reproduction
or persistence of the original sensation. Swindle (1916) demonstrated the visual afterimage in this fashion: one enters a dark room,
waits a few minutes for adaptation, then
turns on a bright overhead light for a fraction of a second. After the light goes off,
there is a short *latent period* during which
nothing happens; then the room seems to
be illuminated, and one sees the image of
his own body, as well as the outstanding
objects in the room. This experience lasts
for a few seconds, but under special conditions of repeated stimulation with a strong
light, the effect may persist for hours.
Swindle states that he obtained a vivid
afterimage of his friend, then went to bed
and to sleep. Upon awakening, while his
eyes were still closed, he flashed a light
through the eyelids and again set off the
afterimage of the friend.

Recurrent afterimages are reported rather
commonly. People who experience a somewhat excessive sensitivity to light (photo-
phobia) often report that a long day's
fishing in bright light is followed by afterimages of the pools and foliage which are
so intense as to interfere with relaxation
and reading. Many persons are bothered by
sensations of continued movement after a
long car, ship, or train ride. Swindle (1917)
suggests that recurrent afterimages may
be the correct explanation for reports of
apparitions and ghosts.

Galton's study. The first attempt to gather
general data on the frequency and vividness of imagery was made by Sir Francis
Galton 70 years ago. This did not deal with
afterimages, but with memory images,
voluntarily recalled. (The true afterimage
does not depend on an effort to recall it.)
However, it is quite likely that the memory
image has the same ultimate basis as the
afterimage.

Galton asked hundreds of people to recall

5	3	9	1	4
2	7	3	9	8
4	2	6	5	9
3	5	2	8	1
8	3	4	7	2

FIG. 10:1. Block of numbers for testing eidetic imagery. Various blocks of random numbers were used in testing lightning calculators and persons with eidetic imagery. The block is exposed briefly, and then the person is required to give the diagonal figures, the second vertical column, etc. Obviously such answers can be given only if a kind of photographic image is retained. (*From Binet, 1894.*)

the appearance of "this morning's breakfast table" in order to obtain data about the "pictures in the mind's eye." A rough scale in degrees of vividness of the image was proposed. Zero indicated no image, 5 an image equal in clarity to the original percept. Galton was surprised at the wide range in the results. Many people reported no imagery at all. Others described images as vivid as hallucinations.

Here are some of the findings of Galton's and other studies of this type. Visual imagery is commonest and most vivid. Auditory, tactile, kinesthetic, gustatory, and olfactory are in that approximate order. Those who are high in one type of imagery tend also to be high in others. People working at jobs requiring abstract thinking are below average in imagery.

Binet (1894) reports an interesting difference between two professional calculators. He presented to each man a block of numbers such as that in Fig. 10:1. He found that both calculators were able to remember the digits in any order, but one of them invariably reached the solution more quickly. It turned out that the speedier individual used visual imagery and simply read off the digits, while the other used auditory images and was forced to repeat the numbers in their original order before he could rearrange them in the order demanded by the instructions. In this case visual imagery was more efficient; in other instances, of course, this would not be true. For instance, it has been shown that people using auditory imagery do better on a test involving finding rhymes for a given word and that musicians have more vivid auditory imagery than do psychologists.

Variation in imagery. There is considerable reason to think that children have, on the average, more vivid imagery than adults. As we get away from interest in the concrete, unique object, into concern with meaning and abstract ideas, imagery deteriorates. It is likely that fragmentary images or verbal cues (including speech movements) are more efficient in helping us to recall decisions, judgments, and logical deductions, even though these were originally based on concrete data.

Performance of routine activities may be associated with lack of imagery; the same person, when engaged in an unusual activity, may find himself employing images. Studies of thinking indicate that images are more likely to occur if something blocks the flow of thought; a person trying to solve a problem has more imagery when he finds himself stuck and unable to proceed. Fatigue also seems to favor the heightening of memory images; just before one goes to sleep he may find his imagery very intense, and of course dreams involve brilliant imagery for most people.

These observations suggest that the *threshold* for imaged experience changes from time to time. When one is at work on a task requiring attention, the threshold is high and images are shut out (focusing). Fatigue, relaxation, and daydreaming lower the threshold and permit images to appear. In problem solving the threshold may be high; but if additional energy is mobilized to deal with some blockage to a solution this may overpass the threshold and activate brain areas concerned with sensory experience. The images intensified in such instances would be those associated in some degree with the goal sought or the tension operating.

Training apparently can improve the quality of imagery. Terman (1926) reports a case of a boy who was strongly motivated to become a musician, who practiced a long time to improve his auditory imagery. He apparently was quite successful. But attempts to impose such training from the outside, in the absence of vigorous inner motivation, have not worked well.

Motivation affects both content and intensity of imagery. The subjects in the Minnesota starvation experiments (page 57) reported that they were constantly plagued by thoughts of food and that their imagery for foodstuffs was more vivid than normal. Clinical studies indicate that men with powerful sex drives find themselves preoccupied with visions of women and sexual embraces; the reverse, of course, is also true.

The imaginal processes, therefore, far from being simple, exact copies of past experience, are modified in various ways. The image which is evoked at any given time is subject to determination by the conditions of the whole organism. It is thus very difficult for one to be sure that he is recalling an incident exactly as it occurred; an unknown amount of *retrospective falsification* enters into most of our memories.

Image and percept. Since almost everyone occasionally has intense, clear imagery, there is a potentially serious problem of distinguishing the image from a realistic percept. How shall we know that a given visual experience is determined by an outside, physical stimulus? Can we distinguish it from an hallucination? If I should see an elephant strolling quietly down Main Street in Hanover without an attendant, I might well doubt the realistic basis of the sight. In such cases one looks for supporting cues from other senses: is the elephant walking with heavy, sinking steps, producing muffled sounds? One may also look for supporting meanings, probabilities that the elephant might be there: is there a circus in town? Is it an advertising stunt? Even with such additional data, the decision may be difficult.

Perky (1910) has illustrated well the confusion that may arise. College students in a dimly lighted room were asked to imagine certain common objects (banana, apple, etc.) pictured on a translucent screen. Without their knowledge a slide was projected onto the screen from behind, showing the object very faintly. If the illumination was gradually increased, the subjects could clearly see the pictured object, yet continued to think it was the inner image. In pathological states such as delirium tremens, the victim may have extraordinarily vivid experiences of animals, people, and objects which are not physically present. He perceives them as real; as far as his behavior is concerned, they *are* real.

Memory and percept. It is probable that only infants experience a simple, direct perception unmixed with memory images. Of adults it is clearly true that "we see more than we see, and hear more than we hear." An automobile, a dog, a man—all are perceived differently on successive occasions. If the dog bites you, you will never see him again without your percept being modified somewhat by this occurrence. A man who on first acquaintance is quite unattractive may—after he has helped you—be perceived as "interesting looking." Past experience and the resultant memory images induce some of the perceptual distortions illustrated on page 228.

It is not surprising, therefore, that under certain circumstances the image may actually dominate over the physically determined percept. Over 50 per cent of college students report that they have had the experience known as *déjà vu*—the illusion, upon looking at a new landscape, that they have already seen it. Analysis usually indicates that some element of the physically present percept is equivalent to some past stimulus; this arouses associated memory images and invests the whole scene with a feeling of familiarity. This memory error, or false recognition, is known as *paramnesia*.

Experimental paramnesia. In the nature of the situation, objective demonstration of *déjà vu* is difficult. People report dramatic instances of premonitions which have been verified; a driver comes to a fork in the road and feels that it will lead to a certain scene, even though he is sure he has never traversed the route before—and his expectation proves correct. We cannot, in such isolated instances, assay the role of factors such as similarity of landscape, the unconscious goal orientation described in the preceding chapter, wish (or fear) to reach a certain place, and so on.

One of the few experimental studies relevant is that by Banister and Zangwill (1941). They presented picture cards to their subjects for study. Each subject was then hypnotized and shown another series of cards, varying in resemblance to the previous days' series. Now he was instructed (hypnotically) to forget the cards—that he would be unable to recognize these pictures if they were seen again. On the following day the old cards and several new ones were presented. All six cards seen in the hypnotic session elicited the feeling of doubtful recognition, similar to paramnesia. Here is a typical protocol:

I have the impression . . . I have the impression that I have seen that before . . . . (pause) Do you remember where or anything about it? I have a feeling I should like to tell you but why can't I say it? I have the same feeling as I had . . . . I know exactly . . . . There is something in my mind which is making continual efforts to tell you but my tongue won't get on with the job. Now where did I? I am just saying to myself now: "Come, don't be so dumb! You know you have seen it before!" . . . . It's like making up one's mind to jump over one of those walls that give way under you . . . . I simply can't give the answer to you. It's a very tiring process too.[1]

This experiment illustrates the *feeling of familiarity* which is the hallmark of the memory image, the irreducible factor in ordinary recognition: *I have seen this before.* Often things are correctly recognized, yet the perceiver can give no evidence for the accuracy of his judgment except this feeling of recognition. No satisfactory analysis of this feeling has ever been made. We should be tempted to say that the feeling of familiarity is a judgment based on slight differences between a physically stimulated percept and a memory image—if it were not for the facts, stated above, which show that sometimes the two cannot be distinguished.

Another interesting outcome of the Banister-Zangwill study was the fact that subjects would invent nonexistent occurrences to explain the felt familiarity. Isolated memories, which do not fall into their proper place in the continuity of experience, are disturbing. If the person feels sure he has seen a picture, he will invent a fictitious incident to explain it (retrospective falsification). It makes him uncomfortable to recognize a scene without being able to anchor it properly to the rest of his experiences. Normal, well-behaved memories fit in with goal-directed action (I was on my

[1] Banister and Zangwill (1941), p. 42. Reprinted by permission of the British Psychological Society.

FIG. 10:2. A test picture for eidetic imagery. This is a picture used by G. W. Allport in a study of imagery of English school children. After only a 35-second exposure, those with eidetic imagery could give numerous details from the picture and could even spell the long German word over the doorway. (*Courtesy of Dr. G. W. Allport.*)

summer vacation; I was with my unit in southern Italy). Atypical situations, memories which cannot be anchored, percepts which do not harmonize with other cues (tactual, kinesthetic)—such experiences arouse insecurity. Because they are confused and ambiguous, it is easy for the person to project into them what he hopes or fears will happen (Chap. 6). Such is the origin of premonition. We need not add that no scientifically controlled evidence for the validity of such premonitions has been obtained.

Eidetic imagery. Many children and some adults have the capacity for developing images which are almost photographic in character. These images are called *eidetic* (virtually, identical) and persons having such experiences are often classified

by the German term *Eidetiker*. Children ten to fifteen years of age seem most frequently to show eidetic imagery. A typical test picture is shown in Fig. 10:2. This picture was exposed for 35 seconds, then covered by a gray screen on which the image was projected. Of 30 such children, several could spell the long German word, either forward or backward, by reading their own image. They could also give many more details than could have been noted in the exposure time.

Eidetic imagery has interested psychologists because it seemed to offer a way of studying phenomena closely related both to afterimages and to actual percepts. Meenes and Morton (1936) compared the afterimages of eidetic and noneidetic children. As might have been anticipated, the afterimages of the *Eidetikers* were more promptly aroused, lasted longer, were more often positive (same color as the stimulus), and were more detailed than the afterimages of the other group. Apparently in the eidetic cases, the threshold for imagery of all types is low. After a week's delay the eidetics were markedly superior in their ability to reactivate the image and to report details about the pictures.

The eidetic image, however, is not the same as the percept or the afterimage. It is less tied to the supporting framework in which the picture is set. The image can be projected to any location and can be seen with the eyes closed. (This is also true of afterimages, but not of percepts.) Some children can modify their eidetic images by voluntary effort; for instance, the monkey can be seen to jump. Afterimages cannot be so modified. This flexibility makes it seem that the eidetic image is a true memory image, but of uncommonly high vividness.

It has proved impossible to segregate *Eidetikers* as children who are unique in any respect. Furthermore, there are always borderline cases who might—or might not—have eidetic imagery. As we noted at the beginning of this chapter, people vary along a scale, from virtually no imagery whatever to very clear, brilliant imagery. The *Eidetiker* is apparently nothing more unique than the extreme case on this scale. He is unusual, but his images arise in the same way as yours and mine.

Associated imagery. Every image is likely to be associated, not only with other experiences in the same modality, but with images from other sense organs. If a person is asked to image the tone of an organ, he may also experience a visual image of the pipe organ in a familiar chapel, along with the auditory image. A "mental picture" of a chocolate cake may be accompanied by gustatory experiences. All normal incidents involve sensations from several receptors.

If one attempts to remember the occurrence, he gets a better reproduction if these various images "hang together." We have already noted (Chap. 8) that experimental evidence favors the view that one sensation can directly arouse an image from another modality as a result of conditioning. Students who have served in a bell-shock learning experiment often say that they hallucinate the shock even when it is not administered.

This type of association between sensory modalities is particularly common with regard to vision and hearing. Many people translate the sounds heard in program music into visual pictures which give their interpretation of the music in story form. A survey of 276 college students reveals that more than half showed some tendency to associate color with short musical selections (Karwoski and Odbert, 1938).

The tendency to make these cross-modality associations has evidently been present in our culture for a long time. Our language illustrates the phenomenon: we speak of "warm" and "cool" colors, of "rasping" sounds, of "sweet" voices, and so on. Some kinds of wine—and humor—are said to be "dry."

Early psychologists were so impressed with this phenomenon that a special vocabulary built up around it. *Synesthesia* is the general term used for situations in which a stimulus to one sense arouses a vivid image in a different modality. *Chromesthesia* is the occurrence of color in association with nonvisual stimulation. *Color hearing* is the special case of chromesthesia in which color is seen when sounds are presented. Color hearing is the most common form of synesthesia, but cases of colored tastes and odors, and other unusual combinations, have been recorded. Estimates of color hearing in the American population range from 1 to 10 per cent, depending on rigidity of classifications and the nature of the auditory stimulus used. Musical selections reveal more cases than the pure tones of tuning forks. As with other forms of imagery, synesthesia is most frequent among children, and such children are often *Eidetikers* (Argelander, 1927).

Some of the theories about synesthesia have proposed that the individual with such experiences is physiologically unique, having direct nervous connections between the related sense organs. These proposals have fallen foul of the same difficulties that we mentioned in connection with attempts to segregate eidetic images as unique phenomena. There are too many borderline cases. One may see colors and hear sounds when hit on the head with a club. A few people see a splash of color when a door is being slammed; others simply experience the jar as unpleasant and relate an unpleasant color to the sound. In some measure the sensory centers in the brain can be set off by strong stimulation even if it is inappropriate. And people differ markedly, of course, in their thresholds for different kinds of stimulation. However, it has so far proved impossible to demonstrate experimentally any kind of nerve connection which is different in synesthetic cases from that of normal subjects.

Another difficulty arises from the fact that synesthesia does not follow a constant pattern in different persons. People with colored hearing are likely to associate high treble tones with bright colors, and low tones with darker shades. But the specific hue (red, green, blue) differs widely from individual to individual.

What does seem to be a rather consistent finding about synesthetes is that *they have arranged two series of stimuli in parallel.* We can, for example, readily arrange visual experiences along a gradient from dark to light. In the same way we can arrange tones from bass to treble (Riggs and Karwoski, 1934). Synesthetes characteristically see bass tones as dark colors, treble as a lighter

hue. Similarly, some instances of synesthesia involve parallel gradients of weight (heavy—light) and tone or color. As we shall see later, there is considerable evidence in favor of the view that these parallel associations are influenced by the culture in which we live.

Some psychologists have proposed that creative artists possess synesthesia to an extent markedly greater than the average of the population. The evidence, however, is rather scanty. June Downey (1929) made a study of eight major English poets in quest of proof for the theory, analyzing the writings and also the biographies of Poe, Blake, Swinburne, Keats, Rossetti, Meredith, Browning, and Shelley. While she admits that there is not much proof for the existence of "true" synesthesia in these men, "there is sufficient justification for concluding that they enjoy, more than the ordinary reader, analogies between the senses. It may be stated as a principle that an analogy which the average reader finds forced and unmeaningful probably represents a peculiar but natural, rather than reflective, mode of thought for the poet." Thus it may be that the artistic mind is characterized especially by a greater facility in arranging these sensory experiences in parallels, and in sensing similarities which cannot be perceived by most of us.

Origin of synesthesia. The development of synesthesia has not been adequately studied; hence its origin is unknown. Some physiologists have speculated about "short-circuiting" between brain areas, but most of the evidence on brain function contradicts this view. An explanation which seems fairly plausible would run like this: The synesthete starts as a child with unusually vivid imagery. Because of association (or conditioning), he begins to see colors accompanied by certain tones or to have some other irrelevant sensory intrusion. This phenomenon is likely to be somewhat disturbing—it creates inner tension. The tension is reduced and equilibrium restored if the situation can be organized into a pattern. The colors are set into a series and arranged in an order correlating to the musical scale. This schema gives the child a feeling of control of the situation. It is perhaps analogous to the disturbance felt by the child who moves to a country where a new language is spoken. He can restore equilibrium and gain control of his environment only by learning the language and arranging it in relation to his prior speech. This relieves the insecurity felt while he is assailed by stimuli which he cannot understand.

The foregoing explanation is rather similar to that offered for the occurrence of paramnesia. A person goes into a new place and feels "this is familiar." This feeling, in the absence of a remembered experience, is upsetting. He restructures the situation by inventing a false memory to account for his "memory" of the novel stimulus.

Structuring a series of experiences by arranging them in an orderly sequence is likewise a property of human and animal organisms which we have already encountered. In Chap. 5 we noted that sensations are spontaneously classified and arranged. In Chap. 6 attention was called to the generalization of perceptions, in which we form classes of objects, animals, people, etc. Apparently this kind of device is commonly used to bring order into a confusing environment. Synesthesia, then, is not a unique phenomenon, but simply another illustration of man's attempt to keep control of his environment.

Imagery types. Before leaving the subject of imagery, we should mention briefly a concept once widely prevalent in psychology: the notion that people can be classified into imagery types, such as visual, auditory, and tactual. Occasionally we find a person who seems to have little imagery other than in one preferred modality. It is likely that he also will report that he learns best by having material presented to that sense; that is, an "auditory-minded" man would say that he learns best by listening rather than reading or watching. Some psychologists made a great deal of this scheme for classifying people; they worked on tests for identifying a person's imagery type, and so on. Unfortunately, the general result of these investigations was to show that people who have vivid imagery in one modality are usually gifted with good imagery in the others and that there is no tendency for people to group themselves as visiles, audiles, etc. When any considerable number of subjects have been examined, the "mixed types" always predominated; hence the type theory was abandoned.

It is, of course, worth while finding out what kinds of imagery a person has. If one were teaching a school child who had vivid visual imagery, this could certainly be utilized in helping him learn. Similarly, a boy very poor on auditory imagery might be advised against music. But it is wiser to think of a continuum, from persons with little imagery to those with rich, vivid images, rather than of groups having a predominance of one sensory mode or another. This rule holds for many other attempts to classify people into "personality types"—see Chap. 15.

The Memory Span

The span of memory is defined as the amount of material which can just be remembered perfectly, immediately after a single presentation. Measurement is usually accomplished by presenting a series of unfamiliar composition, although the separate elements are familiar; for example, a number series like the following:

$$7\ 1\ 4\ 9\ 2\ 8\ 5$$

If the individual succeeds on the first span presented, he is given another scrambled list with one more digit, and so on until he fails. If he fails the first, he is given lists of decreasing length until he succeeds. If careful measurement is desired, a variety of lists will be tried to be sure that he can normally succeed at one level and will fail at the next longer list.

The memory span tends to increase with age. Children four to six years old can hold about four digits in immediate memory; college students average about eight. This span can be improved by training, but few people are willing to do the work required; for most purposes, there is little advantage to such an extended memory span. "The lightning calculator" has a wide span; this is due to a variety of factors. Many number groups may be perceived as a unit (*e.g.*, 1492 in the above example), because of his constant manipulation of numbers and the numerous associations number groups have for him. He forms schemata based on relations within the list; *e.g.*, in the example above, each number above 5 is immediately followed by one below 5. These processes occur so rapidly that they make a 13-item series as easy for this specially trained person as a 7-item list would be for most of us. The "lightning calculator" may also have eidetic imagery, but most of them apparently rely heavily upon organizing the items into meaningful units (Bousfield and Barry, 1933).

The effect of *overloading* on memory span is interesting. If one can just handle eight digits and is presented with nine, he will successfully recall, not eight, but five or six. The attempt to "stretch" and encompass a series beyond the effective span results in breakdown of the whole process. Two factors are involved here: (1) the retroactive interference of later items in the series, blocking recall of the early items; and (2) the interference with discrimination when an excessively difficult task is presented (as in the case of Pavlov's dogs who became "neurotic" when the ellipse was made very similar to the circle). The first of these is obvious enough; experiments on association and retroactive inhibition show emphatically how later learning interferes with earlier learning. The second is not so obvious; however, anyone who tries the experiment will find that he does not first acquire six, then add a seventh and perhaps an eighth, but that he must grasp the entire group at a single perception. Apparently, then, the effort to encompass too much results in a real loss of efficiency in the perceptual function.

Memory span and delayed memory. In a sense, of course, memory as tested by memory span, and memory as tested by delayed recall must be the same basic process. I recall now what happened 5 seconds ago, and tomorrow I *may* still be able to recall that incident. Had it not been learned (perceived, attended to) in the first instance, it would not have been remembered at the later time.

Delay, however, sharply reduces the efficiency of memory for meaningless groups of items. Even a requirement of a 30-second delay can introduce significant errors into recalls of digit-span material (Maslow, 1934). The introduction of any kind of distracting activity requiring attention will also break down the memory span. A student may be able to handle seven digits with a 10-second delay as long as he sits quietly during that interval, but if he must also press a button when a bell sounds, he will drop to six or even to five. The performance seems to depend on a momentary persistence of the impression, and attention must be keyed to catch the persisting impression.

Rehearsal to obtain the benefits of repetition (see Chap. 7) is necessary if immediate memory is to be converted into durable memory. I forget the names of most people immediately after being introduced to them; but if I really want to remember the name, I repeat it several times in the conversation or to myself, note its distinctive characteristics, and tie it to the person's facial appearance, occupation, or some other significant feature.

Memories of the aged. It is a matter of common observation that the aged may have great difficulty recalling what happened an hour ago but can discourse fluently about events of 50 years past. This is due to a decline in the memory-span function with encroaching senility. That, in turn, may well depend upon loss of perceptual acuity. An item which was never clearly perceived can hardly produce a sharply defined memory impression and so can never be clearly recalled. Childhood and early adult memories, on the other hand, were clearly formed and moreover have probably been rehearsed many times during life. The *wish to be young again* may also motivate the older person to direct his attention to his youthful achievements and obtain gratification by talking about them. He may think that this will distract the listener's attention from the old man's inadequacy.

Effects of shock. The fragility of the memory trace when first established can also be verified by studying the effects of shock (page 272). A blow on the head often causes loss of memory for events immediately preceding the blow ("retrograde amnesia"). The opportunity to observe this process at close hand has occurred frequently since psychiatrists have begun to use electroconvulsive shock and insulin shock as forms of therapy for mental disorders. The following account is quite characteristic of these observations:

One patient, immediately after her seventh electro-convulsive treatment, was unable to recall that she was married. Actually she had been so for ten years. She could not remember her three children, the onset of the illness, coming to the hospital, nor could she recognize her physician. Within a few hours she was able to recall her marriage, her children and her ill-ness, but was still unable to remember coming to the hospital or to identify her doctor. By the end of the day these last major defects had vanished. It is of importance to note that this recovery adheres to a chronological order.[1]

According to a long-accepted principle in psychology (Jost's law), recent memories are more readily lost than those of long standing. This principle is based upon laboratory experiments, but the facts cited with regard to aging and shock suggest that it holds also for real-life occurrences.

Are memories ever forgotten? The studies of forgetting based on precise measurement of learning in the laboratory (see pages 269–275) raise an interesting point which should be considered here. Is *anything* ever completely forgotten? Measurements of the curve of forgetting using the most accurate methods led to the intriguing observation that the curve tends to approach, but not to reach, absolute zero (page 270).

From another angle, psychoanalysts raise the same question. In their incessant and constant probing of the memories of their patients, they often elicit recall of incidents in very early childhood. These incidents are likely to be highly emotional in character—fright, deprivation, joy, pain. Objective verification from adults has occasionally been obtained for these memories which go back into the first 2 years of life.[2]

In states of intense emotion, adults often swear or use other expressions from a

---

[1] Cameron (1947), p. 27. Reprinted by permission of Nervous and Mental Disease Monographs.

[2] It should also be noted, of course, that the analyst often gets a "pseudo memory"—the patient claims to recall something which adults insist did not occur. This is probably explicable in the same way as paramnesias; *i.e.*, the patient has a feeling—such as hostility—toward some person, and he unconsciously invents a "memory" to justify his feeling. This does not, of course, detract from the importance of valid early memories uncovered by analytic probing.

language unused since early childhood. People in delirium may babble of events long past. All these kinds of data confirm the view that memory may be surprisingly durable.

On the other hand, it is worth emphasizing that what is true in a microscopic sense may be so minute as to make no practical difference. Thousands of trivial events, occurring daily, are remembered so poorly that they might as well be lost; and indeed, it is best so. Facts and situations important to need satisfaction tend to be retained; those items which do not contribute to the gratification of motives are dropped by the wayside. The detective may remember isolated details of no apparent significance, but he has a motive for observing and recalling such materials. Most of us do not. Forgetting trivial data serves the purpose of conserving energy for more important functions.

The infantile memories resurrected by the psychoanalyst are not trivia. They represent motivational events of great significance to the child. Trivialities which have a *sign function* with reference to such satisfactions or frustrations may be recalled; probably, *only* such minor incidents are retained. For practical purposes it is correct to say that the memories never forgotten are those which have significance in relation to organismic needs and motives.

Pleasant and Unpleasant Memories

Psychoanalysts have called our attention to another important aspect of memory. They have proposed that memory acts selectively; that we tend to force out of consciousness, or *repress*, the constituents of painful happenings. Such selective forgetting would obviously contribute to mental peace, in the sense that constant rehearsal of frightening or shocking occurrences—about which nothing can be done— simply tends to keep one in a state of visceral disturbance. There are some long-range disadvantages to the process; we shall have a look at these in Chap. 14.

Experimental psychologists have attempted to verify the repression hypothesis by studying the comparative forgetting of pleasant and unpleasant materials.[1] These investigations have used words with pleasant or unpleasant connotations for the subject, as well as personal experiences. Most of the researches do in fact find that pleasant materials are remembered somewhat better than unpleasant, but the differences are slight.

An investigation by Stagner (1931) can be used to illustrate the problem. At the end of a college holiday, students were asked to write a concise description of some especially pleasant incident that had befallen them. Below the description were blank lines on which they wrote associated items related to this incident. Then they repeated the process, picking a very unpleasant occurrence. Two weeks later, they were supplied with sheets on which the description of the event had been copied; they were asked to write in the associated items. The average student recalled 54 per cent of his pleasant associations but only 43 per cent of the unpleasant items; this difference was well beyond chance expectations.[2]

Such data appear to confirm the repression hypothesis. Stagner suggested, however, that a simpler explanation might be available. He noted that the incidents reported as pleasant or unpleasant were rather different in kind. The pleasant events

[1] The analysts have pointed out, and rightly so, that this is not a satisfactory check of the repression hypothesis. Repression implies a *need* to get the material out of consciousness; certainly this is not true of words which at best are very mildly unpleasant.

[2] A few investigators using the recall of personal experiences have found no difference between pleasant and unpleasant incidents as to rate of forgetting. Most of these studies, however, agree that unpleasant occurrences are lost more rapidly.

included dates, concerts, seeing old friends, etc. By and large, these were memory impressions of completed events; the tendency was to keep them constant, rehearse them perhaps; they did not require further action. The unpleasant incidents, by contrast, represented tension situations—getting back a bad check, receiving a warning from the Dean—events which called for action and a desire to change the situation. Such memory traces might be modified as action is taken successfully to alleviate the tension. Retroactive inhibition is one mechanism by which this modification may have taken place. Another is simply the fact that the event may be recalled as a whole, including the final resolution of the tension; thus the intermediate stage (first recall) tends to get swallowed up in the final modified picture. We can observe such a phenomenon in memories of childhood pranks and punishments. A friend comments: "I can still remember stealing a watermelon from a neighbor's garden so we boys could eat it. My dad gave me quite a walloping when he found out about it. Yes, we had lots of fun in those days." If his memory had been checked just after the punishment, it might have been quite different from what it is today. Seen from a secure adult position, the punishment is no longer important; it fades out of the picture and only the humor of the situation is noted.

Pleasant and unpleasant words. Several investigators have asked subjects to rate words as pleasant, unpleasant, or neutral, and later used the words in learning experiments. Generally the order of efficiency in learning, and in memory tests, comes out with pleasant materials best, unpleasant next, and neutral terms least efficient for learning or for memory. In terms of motivation, the neutral terms have little significance either of satisfaction or of frustration to the individual; unpleasant terms are more important, since they symbolize

situations which may threaten the person's goals; and pleasant terms usually symbolize desired gratifications. The unpleasant words may suffer a memory loss because, by the time we reach maturity, we will have gone through the process of dealing with unpleasant situations many times; since unpleasant words symbolize unpleasant occurrences, they will be objects of a generalized tendency to avoid. This interpretation seems to be supported by studies of children (*e.g.*, Gilbert, 1937), in which it has been found that children recall pleasant and unpleasant words equally well. Whatever is happening at the adult level, then, may be a function of experience.

Frame of reference. A formulation of the problem which does not contradict the explanation above, but goes somewhat farther, uses the concept of "frame of reference." This view asserts that people develop certain generalized ways of looking at reality; they will then accept and remember what fits in with this framework but will reject and not remember things which are incompatible with the framework. This way of explaining the data from the pleasant-unpleasant experiments was developed by Edwards (1942) on the basis of his own interesting research. A brief sketch of one of his studies will clarify his interpretation.

Edwards (1941) prepared a speech which was carefully balanced so that it contained a number of statements favorable to the New Deal and an exactly equal number critical of the New Deal. This speech was memorized and presented to college students who had earlier been tested for New Deal attitudes. In his memory tests, Edwards found that pro–New Deal students remembered more favorable than unfavorable statements about the New Deal. Likewise, the anti–New Dealers conformed to the prediction; they forgot the favorable but remembered the unfavorable remarks. Thus we tend to go through life learning only what agrees with our prejudices; we refuse to learn, or to remember, items which might disturb our established ways of thinking.

The hypothesis regarding effect of frame of reference can be extended as follows: memory traces which conflict with the frame of reference will be distorted to fit. Edwards tested this point by administering a multiple-choice test in which a given item from the speech appeared in three forms: as it was stated, in reverse form, and in a distorted form which would tend to make it more acceptable to the group to whom it would be "unpleasant." The following example will make this clearer:

Many of the key positions of the New Deal (1) are under Civil Service which does not question one's political beliefs and therefore communists may be in governmental office as well as any one else; (2) are controlled directly or indirectly by the communists; (3) are not controlled directly or indirectly by the communists.

The speech as presented contained item 2. As communists were not very popular even prior to World War II, this allegation was unpleasant to the pro–New Dealers.[1] They might, on the memory test, reject this answer, in which case they could choose 1 or 3. Actually, the pro–New Deal group tended to choose 1. This kind of answer implicitly accepts the charge made in the speech but immediately cloaks it in a rationalization intended to make it less unpleasant. (The anti–New Dealers followed the same tactic in dealing with items friendly to the Roosevelt administration.)

The "frame of reference" interpretation deals successfully with other experimental data; that is, studies using other groups and other attitudes confirm the Edwards finding. Now how does this bear on the

student of pleasant and unpleasant memories? The answer is fairly obvious. Pleasant words, like pleasant occurrences, are "acceptable" to the individual. Unpleasant incidents and unpleasant words which symbolize such incidents are not acceptable. Most of us have established a way of looking at life and experience which is essentially optimistic; we expect to solve our problems; we expect satisfaction of our motives. Thus we have a mental framework into which pleasant items fit properly but from which unpleasant materials tend to be rejected.[1] Whenever a "pleasant" incident occurs, it is fitted into a schema, associated with related, well-learned items, so that it is readily available for recall. An unpleasant occurrence may be "glossed over" or "explained away" so effectively that it is remembered, if at all, only in a distorted form.

Modification of Memory Traces

The distortion of memory traces is a major theme of this chapter. Memory traces are first formed as images (sensory or verbal in nature) and are held in some manner so that on later occasions we can describe the item from memory or recognize it when it is presented with others. It is likely, however, that many memory traces are modified—by a frame of reference, as described above, or by other factors. How many of us have had the experience of revisiting a familiar place, after a lapse of years, and being astounded at the difference between the percept and our memory image? Perhaps distortion actually is the rule, not the exception.

Distortion of memory traces takes many

---

[1] We take no position as to whether this charge is true; Edwards asked his subjects to recall what was given in the speech, not to give their personal opinions.

[1] This statement clearly implies that a person who had a pessimistic, defeatist outlook on life might be expected to recall more unpleasant items. Werner Wolff (1943) found exactly that; in fact, he makes the assertion that such memory tests give us rather penetrating information about the subject's inner personality.

different forms: change in size, in shape, in color, and so on. Perhaps an illustration will show how even familiar items are modified and how behavior is affected by the change. The following is a personal experience:

We have a baby crib which is kept for occasional visitors with young children. The crib is usually taken apart after the departure of the guests, and in doing so, a number of bolts and screws have to be put in a bag for safe keeping. On one expected visit I could not find where the bag had been placed. I searched for hours without avail. Finally I sat down and said to myself, "Where do I put things for safe keeping?" The answer was: in the case of the clock. But this did not seem reasonable; the clock was not large, and only small objects could be put there. The bag of bolts was pictured as much too large. Nevertheless, I looked in the case, and there, to my amazement, was the neatly folded bag.

In this case, the memory image had become exaggerated in size (based on the extended paper bag, before it had been folded); and the apparent impossibility of placing such a large object within the clock case had inhibited correct recall of its hiding place. Many other such anecdotes could be cited. More instructive are the experimental studies of changes in the memory image. In the following pages some controlled studies will reveal how and why distortions occur.

Effect of verbal labels. We have already noted (Chap. 6) that an ambiguous figure can be perceived in one way with one set of instructions and in a quite different manner if the instructions are changed. This effect is even more clearly manifest if we direct our inquiry to the modification of the memory image.

An ingenious study of this problem made use of ambiguous drawings of simple forms, which the subjects were later asked to reproduce. Twelve drawings were used as stimulus figures; while none of them was an accurate representation of any object, each

was so prepared as to be plausibly related to at least two common objects. The figures were presented one by one in a memory drum (Fig. 7:1, page 252). Just before each presentation, the experimenter said, "The next figure resembles . . . " giving one of the two plausible names for that picture. The subjects were instructed to memorize the drawings and were tested by having them actually sketch the figure from memory (Carmichael, Hogan, and Walter, 1932).

Three groups of subjects were employed; for Group A, the suggestions in Word List I were used; Group B received suggestions in Word List II; and Group C, the controls, saw the figures without words. Immediately after a trial (series of the 12 figures), the subject drew as many of the figures as he could recall. Then another trial was run, followed by another recall, and so on until all 12 figures had been sketched from memory.

The influence of the verbal labels upon the memory images can readily be observed in Fig. 10:3. There is a consistent tendency to modify the drawing to make it resemble more closely the object suggested. Features may be exaggerated, minimized, or even eliminated to accomplish this modification.

This finding has significance far beyond the laboratory. Every new experience has some similarities to past occurrences. We tend to attach verbal labels to most, if not all, such observations. Subsequently we distort the remembered picture in order to make it conform with the descriptive label. Advertising makes successful use of this technique in many cases—for example, to counteract memories of throat irritation from smoking by using slogans such as "Easy on the throat," "Mild and soothing." Blindfold tests prove that smokers cannot discriminate among the popular cigarettes, yet most smokers believe that they can describe their favorite smoke as

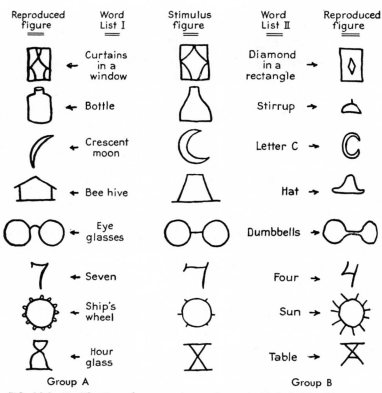

Reproduced figure	Word List I	Stimulus figure	Word List II	Reproduced figure
	← Curtains in a window		Diamond in a rectangle →	
	← Bottle		Stirrup →	
	← Crescent moon		Letter C →	
	← Bee hive		Hat →	
	← Eye glasses		Dumbbells →	
	← Seven		Four →	
	← Ship's wheel		Sun →	
	← Hour glass		Table →	
Group A				Group B

FIG. 10:3. Modification of memory image by verbal label. All subjects saw the center row of drawings. Group A was told that this represented the word on the left; Group B was given the word on the right. Approximately 75 per cent of all figures were modified in the direction of conformity with the label. (*Modified from Carmichael, Hogan, and Walter, 1932.*)

"somehow" different. Political propagandists likewise use the method: Hitler described the situation in Germany in 1918 in such vivid terms that many of his listeners changed their memories to agree with his suggestions. Nostalgic longings for "the good old days" are set off by memory images which bear little relation to reality; in considerable degree these are functions of the romantic words used to describe our early experiences.

Testimony and rumor. Distortion of memory images has a unique importance for the psychology of law. In the courtroom a skilled trial lawyer often can, by leading questions, elicit "memories" which can later be unquestionably proved false.

Psychologists often use the following type of experiment to illustrate this point:

The professor is lecturing to his class. An assistant (chosen to be unfamiliar to the students) comes rushing in, gesturing excitedly. He insists that the professor must "do something right now." The professor shouts back. The assistant draws a gun and fires in the air. Then he rushes from the room. The "witnesses to the crime" are now asked to give precise eyewitness reports.

The results of this experiment are most discouraging to those who hope for justice to be done in the courts. Details are added or subtracted freely. One or two extra men are included in the argument. Descriptions of clothing and of specific acts are hopelessly confused. The sequence of events, the length of time involved, and even the kind of weapon employed are variously reported by the members of the class. And these are college students, presumably fairly intelligent, and in an excellent position to see clearly what has happened!

Experiments of this type have shown that considerable distortion can be introduced by leading questions: *e.g.*, was the man's hat gray or brown? when in fact he wore none. Errors are maximized when the witness is emotionally disturbed or when he is completely uninterested. If the witness is allowed to "tell his story in his own way," fewer mistakes creep in; cross-examination elicits more correct facts, but it also evokes an even greater number of "incorrect facts." The typical courtroom situation, consequently, is admirably adapted for distortion of the witness' memory by shrewd lawyers. Whether it is so admirably conceived for achieving justice is another matter.

Blackburn (1945) reports some discouraging statistics on the accuracy of memory for such incidents. Without warning the members of the Cambridge Psychological Society, he arranged to have a stenographic record made of one of their meetings. Two weeks later each member was contacted individually and asked for a complete recall of what went on—the persons present, discussion, etc. He reports that the average memory score was only 8.4 per cent—*i.e.*, over 90 per cent of what happened had been forgotten. Furthermore, almost half the memories reported were substantially incorrect. In his analysis of the reports he mentions the following four types of errors: (1) inventions and importations (remarks reported which were not made); (2) muddles (confusion of different parts of the discussion, interchanging speakers, etc.); (3) emotional alterations (modifications to fit the views of the person

giving the memory account); and (4) elaboration and interpretation (expanding upon an incident which actually did occur). Another discouraging feature of his study is that there was no agreement whatever between a person's certainty that he remembered and his score based on a check with the stenographic record. Since many criminal trials revolve around exactly such recalls, we can only wonder that justice seems done most of the time.[1]

Rumor. The term *rumor* applies to descriptions of "fact" passed on by word of mouth from person to person. They become particularly frequent when communications are poor; *e.g.*, in a factory where management does not keep workers informed of developments, one hears rumors of shutdowns, new machinery, wage cuts, and so on. If the motives of many individuals are frustrated, rumors relevant to these motives spread widely. Battle-weary soldiers heard rumors that they were going to be replaced tomorrow. Pessimistic as well as optimistic rumors travel; we fear the worst while hoping for the best. During World War II many bizarre rumors circulated, giving gory details of American defeats which never occurred or which were grossly exaggerated. The armed services contributed to these rumors by the policy of refusing to release bad news promptly.

The processes involved in rumor distortion include at least two phases: selective learning, and modification of the memory image. In everyday life it is impossible to separate the two; in the laboratory this can be done, but of course it is difficult to get the kind of emotional involvement which features significant rumor circulation in the general population. The laboratory method (method of serial reproduction) involves presentation of a written account of some incident to individual A. He reads this and then reports it from memory to B. B later relays it verbally to C, and so on through

[1] Blackburn (1945), p. 48.

a "chain" of subjects. If recordings are made, the successive changes in the story can be identified and studied. We find the same exaggeration, elimination, and distortion of details which occurred in the drawings of remembered figures as described above.

Dreams. The most extreme distortions of memory images occur in dreams. Here a familiar figure, such as that of the person's father, may be twisted into a giant, a dwarf—may be represented as having characteristics which do not pertain at all to the physically real person. The dream material is drawn from the day's experiences, as well as from childhood memories. However, the nature of the modifications in these images can be traced to motives and attitudes within the dreamer, often unconscious in character. The changes resemble closely those which occur in eyewitness testimony and in rumor. The dynamic factors involved make it convenient to postpone a full examination of dreaming to Chap. 11.

Time and the Memory Trace

Much popular psychology equates forgetting to a process of decay. It is clear, on the contrary, that forgetting is an active process. Memory images are transformed by later experience, by verbal labels, by frames of reference, by emotion and desire. There remains the question: is this the whole story? Is every memory change simply the effect of these inner pressures, or does sheer lapse of time also modify memory traces?

So phrased, the question is difficult to answer. How can we be sure we have controlled all the pressures of experience, verbalization, emotion, and the like? Since the data just cited prove that these factors are significant, they must be eliminated before time can be isolated as a specific influence. On the other hand, we have also cited evidence (see page 272) that the memory trace needs time to become consolidated. The effects of retroactive inhibition, of shock, of sleep, and of other variables show that time is somehow a significant variable, since immediate memories are more disrupted than those which have had a time interval for consolidation. We may therefore rephrase our question and ask: what are the laws of consolidation of memory traces?

Wulf (1922) attempted to work out an answer to this question. There is room to doubt that his results are due to the time factor alone; nevertheless, they are highly significant for our analysis of memory and also for an understanding of the process of thinking. Wulf's method can be demonstrated in a classroom as follows: before the students assemble, the instructor draws four or five irregular geometrical patterns on the blackboard. During the class hour the patterns are erased; then the students are asked if they noticed the drawings. Most will say that they saw, but did not attend to, the figures. Now they are asked to sketch what they remember. A comparison of these with the original figures quickly shows that the reproductions change in the direction of symmetry and conventional form. An irregular triangle becomes equilateral; an egg shape becomes an oval. We may say then that memory changes tend toward making the image more symmetrical and toward representing a conventional figure.

Such modifications could be due to the subject's pinning a verbal label on the drawing; this interpretation might then effect the change in shape. Wulf holds that this is not a sound explanation. He attempted to control the interpretation factor by using the method of *successive reproduction.* This simply means that his subjects first sketched the figures immediately after Wulf presented them; then again after 24 hours (without advance warning) and again after some weeks, likewise without having any reason to expect that they would be asked to do so. Thus whatever effect was due to interpretation ought to appear in the first or second reproduction, and later changes might be ascribed to the consolidation process.

Wulf held that the fundamental law of memory change is the tendency toward *good form*. By good form is meant the simplest, most symmetrical, or most familiar form which is compatible with the actual outline as it was presented visually. (For example, Wulf presented a double figure, something like a dumbbell, but with unequal circles on the ends; in reproduction, the ends became equal.) It seems that the memory trace of an irregular, unfamiliar figure is unstable. Better equilibrium is attained when the irregularities are ironed out and the figure becomes more compact. Thus unbalanced patterns become symmetrical, and irregular waves become evenly spaced. (The principles of perception operate to favor symmetry and balance; cf. Chap. 6.)

Two superficially contradictory processes appear in the results. *Sharpening* refers to the exaggeration of a specific feature in the drawing; for example, a projection may be accentuated as time passes. *Leveling* involves the ironing out of unevenness. Minor irregularities tend to get lost as a result of leveling, but if they are of more than some threshold value in prominence, they are picked up and accentuated by the process of sharpening. In recalling a friend's face, for example, you may lose a tiny mole on his cheek but grossly exaggerate a larger one on his forehead. Cartoonists use these two techniques, especially sharpening, in caricatures of famous persons; Theodore Roosevelt's teeth, John L. Lewis's eyebrows, Truman's spectacles, are picked up and exaggerated, the rest of the face virtually disappearing;[1] most people neverthe-

less identify the person rather readily. This suggests that the cartoonist's rendition is in harmony with the memory image to a satisfactory extent.

Gibson (1929) repeated Wulf's experiment in part. His results could in many instances be phrased in terms of sharpening and leveling, as Wulf had done. However, Gibson states that the most common change of memory images was of a kind which could best be called *assimilation*. This term refers to a process of fitting the visually perceived outline into the store of past experiences, *i.e.*, assimilating the present percept to some remembered object having a similar outline. Thus a meaningless figure might be seen by one person as a schematic female torso, by another as a dumbbell, and by a third as a violin. In each case certain features have been emphasized and others leveled out. It immediately becomes apparent, therefore, that there is no contrast between the work of Wulf and of Gibson. Wulf has emphasized the changes in the figure itself, while Gibson has emphasized the object with which the image was associated or identified.

Throughout the study of psychology, we constantly encounter this feature of human behavior. A man is stimulated by some object or situation; immediately, he asks, What was that? Is it a threat to me? Is it useful in satisfying needs? What can I do with it? The percept is unconsciously compared with the multitude of memory images already available and tends to be identified with one of these. If a verbal label is attached to the percept, as in the experiment by Carmichael *et al.* (1932), this favors the selection of a particular item from past experience. Otherwise, the subject will pick some image from his own store, and the new item will be modified in recall to have a closer resemblance to this model.[1]

---

[1] Note the similarity to reduction of cues necessary for a skilled performance, p. 337.

[1] This is another reason why it is so hard to change the personality of the average adult; once

Closure. A concept closely related to the idea of "good form" is that known as *closure.* Closure literally refers to visually perceived outlines which are broken and incomplete; *e.g.,* the triangle with open apex (Fig. 10:4) lacks closure. A perfect circle has closure (as well as good form). However, closure does not depend exclusively upon having a completely bounded figure; if a familiar percept is broken up, the tendency to closure will simply involve closing the gaps, as in the letter E (Fig. 10:4).

Bobbitt (1942) did an extensive study of the closure phenomenon, making use of the broken triangle figure with very brief exposures (0.1 second). He found that, if less than two-thirds of the outline was presented, his subjects reported two angles rather than a triangle. The threshold value was about 68 to 72 per cent of the outline; with larger proportions, all subjects reported a triangle.

Gibson's results do not conform closely with Bobbitt's, as relatively few of his broken figures were "closed" when remembered. However, the time of exposure may account for this difference. Bobbitt gave his subjects only the briefest glimpse (0.1 second) of the drawings, while Gibson allowed 1.5 seconds. This is ample time to observe clearly and verbalize the fact that the figure is broken. We may infer that closure occurs in memory if the figure was originally perceived as a unit in spite of the gaps, but the figures remain separate if they were clearly perceived and labeled as two separate items. This, of course, is true of most of our everyday memories. We recall what was clearly perceived and noted, and make few errors; but, when attempting

FIG. 10:4. The process of closure. The broken triangle (left) tends to be perceived and remembered as a complete triangle. The broken letter E (right) is seen and recalled as a closed, complete figure.

to remember items which were briefly observed and perhaps out of focus, our images are distorted by these processes of leveling, sharpening, assimilation, and closure. It also follows, from this and numerous other experiments on memory, that we can never successfully separate memory from learning, attitude, set, and mode of perceiving. What happens to a memory trace will depend in large part upon the original material. Wulf has, on the other hand, called our attention to some fundamental processes in the modification of remembered material. If we examine the functioning of memory in everyday life, we shall see that a knowledge of these processes makes a real contribution to our understanding.

Memory Transformation in Complex Situations

Closure. The phenomenon of closure, or the filling in of gaps in incompleted figures, can be related to memory processes in complex relationships. Zeigarnik (1927) studied the effect of failure to complete an assigned task upon memory for the task. She gave a variety of simple problems to her subjects: writing favorite quotations from memory, solving simple arithmetic problems, naming 12 cities beginning with K, stringing beads, solving riddles, etc. Most of the tasks required 3 to 5 minutes for completion. In one-half the tasks, the experimenter permitted the job to be finished; in the other

---

he has a set of models for use in classifying his experiences, new incidents are simply fitted into the old frame of reference. Thus he fails to learn new ideas when new experiences would seem to force them upon him. We could call this a process of "leveling" in terms of expectancies and past experiences.

TABLE 10:1. Forgetting of Completed and Incomplete Tasks
(*Based on Zeigarnik, 1927*)

Group	Number of subjects	Average I/C ratio	Percentage of subjects recalling		
			More I	Equal	More C
A	32	1.9	80	10	10
B	14	2.0	78	7	15
C	47	1.9	77	7	16
D	45	2.1	79	9	12

half, she interrupted the subject and required that he go on to a new task. Memory was tested as soon as the series of problems had been completed.

The results in this investigation were quite striking. *Incomplete tasks* were recalled much more often than completed tasks. This was true even though more time had actually been spent on those which were finished. As can be seen in Table 10:1, the differences in correct memory recall are quite substantial. Zeigarnik proposed that "unfinished business" tends to be retained in memory because there is a *tension* to complete the task once begun. Thus a person who had started drawing a vase of flowers and been interrupted still had a certain "tension" in the direction of completing this assignment. The activities which did not benefit especially (as to memory score) by interruption were the routine tasks with no definite goal—*e.g.*, punching holes in a sheet of paper, or stringing beads.

Zeigarnik's experiment has been repeated many times, and it is now clear that certain limitations must be imposed upon her generalized principle. *Incomplete tasks are remembered better* if the subject interprets the interruption as an accident or if he feels *challenged* to finish the job. *Incomplete tasks are forgotten* if the subject feels that he was a *failure*, i.e., that he should have completed it within the time allowed. (In this

case the interruption operates like a threat —see page 494.)

Many examples occur in everyday life which illustrate these principles of memory. A student who is actively engaged in preparing for an examination may build up quite a stock of information on a certain course. When he takes the examination, he recalls very well. But the following week he has forgotten almost everything. What has happened? The task as perceived was that of taking the examination. Until the student took the examination, he was still under tension; the process was not complete. After the examination, the tension is discharged, the set has served its purpose, the assignment is finished. Now the material disappears from memory. It is easy to infer from this that learning which is focused directly on the passing of a specific examination is extremely inefficient. Learning which is tied in with long-time purposes will be remembered much more effectively.

Schematization and conventionalization. Since perception and learning both show the human tendency to develop an outline or *schema* within which specific materials can be classified, it is not surprising that memory processes also follow this form. Bartlett (1932) has demonstrated that recollection of a complex past event rarely takes the form of an exact reproduction of a series of impressions. On the contrary, the memory is likely first to come back as a kind of over-all impression of the event. Upon repeated questioning, details will be filled in, but the selection of these details is such as to conform to the general schema, not necessarily to the original experience.

Suppose, for example, that I am suddenly asked if I remember the story of Huckleberry Finn. Of course, I say—it was my favorite book when I was a boy. However, the strong feeling of familiarity is not backed up by recall of concrete episodes. The story was read long ago, and the memory is very hazy. In attempting to recall it,

Original drawing   Reproduction 1   Reproduction 2

Reproduction 3   Reproduction 4   Reproduction 5   Reproduction 6

Reproduction 7   Reproduction 8   Reproduction 9   Reproduction 10

FIG. 10:5. Drawings by a series of persons. Subject 1 sees the original drawing and later reproduces it from memory. Subject 2 sees only the drawing of Subject 1 and later reproduces it from memory; Subject 3 sees the drawing of Subject 2, and so on. By the time the drawing has been so treated ten times, the owl has changed into a cat. (*From Bartlett, 1932, p. 180, by permission of Cambridge University Press.*)

I first get a generalized schema which includes the locale—the Mississippi River; the topic—the ideal American boy; the moral—boys will be boys; action, adventure, the happy ending. With further effort, I can reconstruct more of the story and fill out the content. But the reconstruction is not a true remembering; it is a process of pulling out possible episodes or items from memory and seeing if they fit the schema. Falsification occurs without detection if it is in conformity with the general pattern. Thus an O. Henry story about a boy readily gets "assimilated" into *Huckleberry Finn* because it fits the schema. Crocodiles may be added by the unwary who have read

of alligators on the lower Mississippi, but it is inconceivable that anyone would garnish the tale with a rhinoceros or a hippopotamus.

Bartlett's experimental technique included having his subjects recall both stories and pictures, using both the method of *serial reproduction* (by a series of persons) and the method of *successive reproduction* (by a single person). Memory transformations occurred in very much the same way for both pictures and stories. There was a tendency to preserve a form or schema throughout the entire series of reproductions. There was an "effort after meaning" which is like Gibson's "assimilation"; *i.e.*, the subjects looked for some familiar pattern in their past experience to which they could relate this stimulus.

In Fig. 10:5 we show the changes by a series of subjects who drew from memory one of Bartlett's pictures (method of serial reproduction).

The elaboration of this series is obvious. The reversal of the wing curve by subject 3, and its doubling at once suggested a tail, and thereafter the tail drops lower and lower until it assumes its proper tail position, and is greatly emphasized, in which process it is reversed twice more. The apparently disconnected lines in the original drawing are all worked into the figure, and the original beak mark is elaborated into a ribbon with a bow. Whiskers are introduced in due course, and the small lines on the back are multiplied and become shading. A rather unusual figure, carrying a fairly strong suggestion of some realistic representation, becomes greatly elaborated into a familiar whole. Once this end has been achieved, simplification tends to set in again, and the whole progresses towards a truly conventionalized form.[1]

In this manner, the sketch of an owl becomes an outline of a cat.

Schema as economy. The term *schema* has been found useful in understanding the phenomena of perception and of learning. In connection with memory it serves approximately the same purpose. It can be summed up as an *economy measure;* people are simply exposed to such an extensive variety of experiences that it would be burdensome to attempt to retain each of them vividly in memory. Probably retroactive inhibition would intrude to cause loss of more items if they were held in this detailed form. The schema is a device by which a number of specifics can be held in memory as instances of a generalization. Students use this technique constantly by making outlines and subsuming specific experiments under general categories. Text-

book writers attempt to help them by introducing section headings and subheads which call attention to the general schema of the chapter. Thus the student can recall the various phenomena of classical conditioning easily if he once gets the general picture of this concept; but if he identifies problem solving with classical conditioning, he will forget almost everything about both processes.

The absolute ability to remember new material reaches its maximum at sixteen to twenty years of age and begins to decline after thirty. In terms of memory for details related to a familiar business enterprise, science, or profession, however, the man of forty will surpass the youngster of twenty. Why? Because he has a series of schemata into which new observations can be neatly fitted. The behavior of the market today resembles its action at some time in the past, and this has in turn been organized into some generalized principle (which may be wrong but helps memory nonetheless). For the professor, a new experiment in physiology may elicit startling conclusions, but all the results can be incorporated into familiar categories and easily filed for future reference. Of course, this carries with it the danger, to which reference has already been made, that the lessons of changing times will not be learned. The conservatism of people past fifty is in some respects due to the fact that their schemata now resist modification; contradictory facts are simply forgotten.

Let us refer briefly once more to the Allport-Postman investigations on rumor. They found the processes of sharpening and leveling in memory for stories, just as Wulf found for pictures. They used the concept of assimilation in a broader sense than Gibson did. It is defined as having "to do with the powerful attractive force exerted upon rumor by the intellectual and emotional context existing in the listener's mind." In concrete terms, this means that,

---

[1] Bartlett (1932), p. 181. Reprinted by permission of Cambridge University Press.

if an individual has a generalized pattern of classifying Negroes as criminals and hears a crime story in which one figure is a Negro, he tends to "remember" that the Negro was the criminal. We have used the term *schema* to identify the smaller patterns which unite a series of specific experiences (such as a stereotype of a Negro character) and the term *frame of reference* to comprehend the larger sets of relationships such as might be identified by adjectives like liberal, conservative, prejudiced, etc. Thus a specific incident may be "assimilated" to a limited schema, and this in turn is incorporated within a more comprehensive frame of reference. Distortions of memory may take place at each level.

The individual's concept of self (his self-image) is perhaps the most potent of all frames of reference (see page 525). Thus it is not surprising that Shaw (1944) found that people distorted remarks made about them to fit this framework. Shaw had college students check lists of adjectives to show which they considered desirable personality traits and then to show which each ascribed to himself. Later they were given sheets carrying bogus ratings which agreed with the self-rating in some respects and disagreed in others. These ratings, they were told, had been made by their classmates. Two weeks later they were asked to recall these classmate ratings. Forgetting was especially potent in eliminating those bogus ratings which ascribed to the person undesirable traits which, in his self-rating, he had denied possessing. Ratings got a high memory score when they ascribed to the person desirable traits which he had described himself as possessing.

Memory Research and Learning

Learning precedes memory chronologically, and we have therefore adopted the same sequence for this book. It should be obvious, however, that some of the facts revealed by these researches on the memory trace should be focused backward upon our analysis of learning. They should help the student to understand better some phases of the learning process.

We have presented two theories about the fate of memory traces. One theory suggested that a memory trace in the nervous tissue is at first in an unstable equilibrium, subject to various stresses; that with time the trace resolves into a "good figure" displaying symmetry and closure. This is an interesting idea, but it has not been demonstrated by sound empirical research.

The second theory was to the effect that the memory trace is subject to stress in the direction of readjustment to conform with past experience, the pressure of simultaneous stimuli, and needs of the organism. This theory is supported by ample evidence; it could be called one of the basic principles of memory. It has been referred to as the principle of assimilation, but it might equally well be labeled the principle of "effort after meaning."

The need for meaning is a cardinal fact of adult human psychology. Children may accept experience passively and unquestioningly (although even this may be doubted); but adults are characterized by a continuing effort to make experience meaningful by relating it to prior memories, present circumstances, and future eventualities. It is, after all, by way of meanings that communication takes place, and without communication man would simply be another species of ape. Everyone has his own private universe, composed of his impressions from vision, hearing, taste, and the multitude of other senses; but these must be reduced to some kind of common denominator in words or symbols before they can be communicated to others. Furthermore, the possibility that the new stimulus signals a threat (or goal achievement) depends upon its meaning. Thus tension is set up with every new experience;

when a meaning is identified for it, the tension is relieved.

In this connection, consequently, we must point to the importance of language as a determiner of learning and memory. We learn better those things which have verbal labels attached (page 369); recall is facilitated by finding a verbal label for the stimulus presented. However, we pay a price for this efficiency. Pinning a verbal label onto an experience modifies the learning and also the recalled memory trace. Thus "language begins by conventionalizing one's social behavior and then goes on to intrude upon one's private thought."[1] Language becomes a schema which is so ingrained that sense impressions are automatically and unconsciously translated into social meanings. All this is done so rapidly that it is independent of voluntary control. But nevertheless it shapes the kinds of things we can learn and remember into a stereotyped, conventional pattern.[2]

Where a convenient schema cannot be located in one's memory, there is an effort to develop one. The normal adult will not learn a list of nonsense syllables as an automatic series unless instructed to do so by the experimenter. He attempts to systematize the series, noting syllables which remind him of past items and welding these into a pattern, later fitting the other syllables somehow into this schema. This process is easier for lists of words, because it is not very difficult to make up an arbitary story or rhythmical pattern which contains and relates them to each other (see page 253).

Some practical implications. The great value of schemata and principles for learning and remembering has numerous obvious applications. To attain a better memory,

we do not simply practice memorizing; we practice developing schemata. Facts become manageable when they are seen in a larger pattern. All scientific effort starts with classification of things and events into categories. Similarly, anyone who begins collecting stamps, seashells, or butterflies must classify, consciously or unconsciously, in order to deal effectively with his varied material. The scientist is superior to the amateur only in his skill at classifying, not in the basic process.

Experiments have shown that students who were instructed to study for an essay examination succeeded equally well on essay and on objective questions, whereas those who studied for the objective type were handicapped if given essay questions. In preparing for essay examinations, the student tends to look for generalizations and relationships, and these in turn provide "anchors" for specific facts. Those who looked chiefly for specific facts failed to develop the generalizations which were necessary for dealing with the essay task.

The educational problem is not so much that the student is not interested in meanings. He actually strives constantly to achieve meaning in relation to his own felt needs. The problem is one of establishing a relationship between academic materials and the student's motives. In those activities where he can see this relationship (as in the involved interrelationships between fraternities, the intricacies of campus politics, the significant features of athletic competition), he learns rapidly and organizes well in terms of broad meanings. Such knowledge is directly related to his need satisfaction—his attempt to maintain a favorable equilibrium on the campus scale of status. Academic studies do not carry immediate and effective rewards and punishments in terms of present needs. The acquisition of knowledge in a liberal-arts curriculum thus exists for the student as a hazy and tenuous goal; it has little dynamic

---

[1] Norman Cameron (1947).

[2] So, for example, Westerners find it difficult to communicate with, or understand, people of certain cultures with a distinctly different language structure.

quality to mobilize energy on behalf of the effort to achieve meaning. To some extent the more intelligent students are superior in this respect; the ability to relate present learning to long-range future activities is one aspect of what we call *intelligence*. Many "inferior" students move up into the "superior" class as they succeed in perceiving the relationship of present knowledge to future goals.

The value of any education other than specific trade training must be found in its transfer to life situations. However, transfer is a function of stimulus generalization and stimulus equivalence (page 350). Consequently transfer of training will follow certain channels. There is more transfer from Latin to Italian than from Russian to English. There is more transfer from arithmetic to algebra than from civics to algebra, because the manipulation of quantities is similar in both mathematics courses. Learning, therefore, to be usable in later life must have some classes in common with the materials and problems to be encountered in the future.

It would be a mistake to leap from this point to the conclusion that only vocational education is functional. Many subjects involve learning to develop schemata, evolving generalizations, organizing and relating data. These skills can transfer over a wide area. It is possible that the teacher, his technique, and his example have more to do with transfer than does the subject matter of the course. Teachers who require the ingestion and regurgitation of vast quantities of specific factual material probably induce little schema formation and consequently little transfer to life situations. The liberal-arts college can thus be defended only if it focuses on training the student to develop broad skills in the development of general principles; and even the technical college will serve the needs of its students more effectively if it moves away from specifics toward generalizations.

Generalized principles can be developed by making cross linkages between almost any pair of subjects if the effort is made. One could, for example, teach Latin with the aim of bringing out the similarity of human nature today and in ancient times. This would involve linking Latin and psychology. The problem is one of motivation, because such a special goal orientation is complex and will be sought only if fairly strong, clearly defined tensions can be set up in that direction. To some extent the same problem exists with reference to modern survey courses cutting across chemistry, physics, and zoology, or economics, sociology, and psychology. The schemata involved are complicated, even for the expert; students often prefer the spuriously simple, clear-cut formulations of the separate disciplines.

We have noted in an earlier chapter the relation of *curiosity* to goal satisfaction. The organism behaves curiously, inspecting new situations carefully, because such situations may offer satisfactions or threats. In this sense, almost every human adult is curious. But some people become curious about intellectual affairs. They nose around, sniffing at philosophy, sociology, anthropology, ancient history, and other fields of knowledge. These persons have developed the kind of frame of reference into which new knowledge is readily accepted and is experienced as a source of satisfaction.

On the other hand, a rigid frame of reference can block further learning and use of knowledge. The fanatic distorts, by the processes of sharpening, leveling, and assimilation, so that all new material is forced to conform to his understanding. Thus a communist rides roughshod over the facts of heredity, biology, and psychology to compel a fitting of these items into his preconceived notions, using logic which appears to others to be mostly rationalization. He reduces tension by forcing all facts into his frame of reference. It is easy for him to achieve maximum transfer of his principles of Marxism from economics to psychology to genetics, but this achievement is won at the cost of complete inability to handle the facts which stubbornly do not conform.

Remembering and homeostasis. In conclusion, let us relate this analysis of memory to the principle of homeostasis. We have shown that perception and learning set up certain constant ways of looking at objects and certain constant habits of behaving. These uniformities are part of man's continuing effort to preserve and extend his basic biological equilibrium, by building an optimal environment for himself.

Recollection fits into this same scheme of organization. Events are experienced— seen, heard, smelled, touched. They may be novel at first, but soon the process of recollection functions to identify this new stimulus with past experience. If identification is made, the environmental constancy is preserved, or at least the nature of the disturbance is understood and methods for dealing with it can be initiated. If the event is not immediately absorbed into our scheme of things, it will probably be distorted in greater or less degree so that it can fit into the pattern.

When a new event refuses to be assimilated into a preexisting schema, we are forced to think. A new phenomenon, such as the explosion of the atomic bomb, disturbs our previous frame of reference. After some thinking, the framework may be modified to admit the new event, and equilibrium is again restored. (As a matter of fact, even a development of the magnitude of the A-bomb seems not to have forced any change in the frames of reference of many public figures; they go right on advocating the same policies in the same ways as they were prior to 1945.)

Learning and recollection, then, are essentially conservative forces. They tend to weight the past heavily, and this weighting increases with age, so that the elderly person is likely to be extremely conservative. He has an equilibrium which he desires to maintain, and he will deny the existence of new phenomena if they threaten his basic pattern of existence (cf. the traditional "Southern Aristocrat" living in a fictitious world long since dead as far as realities go). The new is modified to make it just an illustration of an old, familiar item. In some degree this conservative process is essential to survival; no one could mobilize the energy necessary to deal with every event as a totally new occurrence. But, if carried to an extreme, this kind of method for maintaining equilibrium is fallacious and self-destructive; it was ridiculous to characterize the Nazis as just a new group of conservative militarists, and the mistake was almost fatal to us. In individual as in social life, some flexibility of interpretation must be retained, so that new occurrences are not invariably identified with familiar memories. Reliance upon memory must at some point give way to reliance upon thinking, a process to which we turn in the following chapter.

SUMMARY

The purpose of learning is to remember. This chapter has been concerned with the intimate character of the process of remembering, modifications of memory traces, and some variables which can be shown to affect memory.

Remembering is manifested when a present process stands for or reinstates a past occurrence. The commonest basis for this seems to be imagery; that is, one may picture a past scene, "hear" a past conversation, and so on. The memory image has certain features in common with the sensory afterimage, but it is clearly different in some important respects. Many people remember without definite sensory content; they experience only words and abstract meanings. Some experiments suggest that these memories may be "carried" by minute electrical processes in muscles, or perhaps even by electrical states entirely within the brain.

The memory image does not simply copy the physical stimulus—indeed, even perception does not do this (Chap. 6). Rather, the perceived situation is modified; some parts are omitted, some exaggerated, and some distorted. The evidence indicates that memory images which do not "fit" with the rest of a person's experience are changed to conform. Thus the illusion of having seen something in the past which is objectively new (paramnesia) gives rise to false memories (retrospective falsification) which explain why this scene looks familiar. In synesthesia, series of sensations from two modalities are arranged in parallel so that order and security are maintained. The psychoanalytic concept of repression (active forgetting of painful material) seems somewhat similar. Each of us develops a personal frame of reference, and experiences which cannot be accepted into this framework are rejected from memory.

This process of arranging images in a pattern leads to the concept of the schema —a device by which many specific details can be remembered as parts of a totality. A simple schema involves alphabetical arrangement of materials to be remembered.

When looked at in this way, it becomes obvious that schema formation occurs in perception and in learning, as well as in remembering. There is a danger, of course, that, if an inappropriate schema is employed, the memory will be distorted to fit it; and the construction of a schema which will include a wide variety of experiences is quite difficult. Some instances of this will be examined in the succeeding chapter, which deals with the process of thinking.

Learning and remembering are inextricably linked to the homeostatic process of maintaining essential constancies. Indeed, after a sizable stock of memories has been accumulated, they evolve into a series of schemata, or a frame of reference, which tends to hold constant. The rigidity and conservatism of the aged appears to be a function of this type. New facts and new ideas are discarded because the weight of accumulated memories offers resistance too great to overcome. Within limits, however, it is obvious that man must behave in terms of his experiences, and that means clinging to the past as opposed to shifting with every new stimulus. The attainment of a nice balance between the rigidity of conservatism and the flexibility of adaptation to new conditions is a major problem for the human race in our atomic age.

Recommended Readings[1]

ALLPORT, G., and L. POSTMAN: *The Psychology of Rumor.* New York: Holt, 1947. Chaps. 4, 5, and 6.

BARTLETT, F. C.: *Remembering.* London: Cambridge, 1932.

CAMERON, D. E.: Remembering. *Nerv. ment. Dis. Monogr.*, No. 72. New York: 1947.

DOWNEY, J.: *Creative Imagination.* New York: Harcourt Brace, 1929.

FREUD, S.: *Psychopathology of Everyday Life.* New York: International University Press, 1904.

GRAVES, R.: The Vehicles of Thought. In *Poetic Unreason and Other Studies.* London: C. Palmer, 1925.

KATONA, GEORGE: *Organizing and Remembering.* New York: Columbia University Press, 1940.

KOFFKA, K.: *Principles of Gestalt Psychology.* New York: Harcourt, Brace, 1935.

[1] See also p. 547.

CHAPTER 11

Thinking

Man's eminence in the animal kingdom is commonly ascribed to his superior ability in thinking and reasoning. It should be apparent, however, from the facts of learning and memory, that the human species excels in a wide range of cognitive skills. Indeed, it is not easy to draw a line between learning and thinking so that attainment could be ascribed exclusively to the latter. All thinking depends upon prior learning, and much thinking, especially reasoning, is a form of abstract learning.

We have noted that remembering is essentially a search for identical stimuli. Is this the face I saw before? Is this date the correct one for the Declaration of Independence? Is this the S which signals food? Is this formula the one I learned last week? The search embodies a comparison of a memory image with a physical percept. This percept may be presented by someone else (as in case of recognition test) or it may be a matter of verbalizing and then questioning one's own recall.

Looked at in this way, it becomes obvious that much of what passes for thinking is in fact remembering. When one says, "I am trying to think of the answer," he is only attempting to reproduce past learning. What, then, is the criterion of *thinking?* The answer is, the *discovery of new relationships*. To get beyond the mere memory

level, the person must produce something new—an invention, a novel arrangement of remembered facts, a solution to a problem.

Memory, of course, provides the raw material for thought. If we are to differentiate problem solving from reasoning, it must be on the basis that the former deals with present material, the latter with situations which are present only as symbols. Thinking, therefore, must necessarily involve some manipulation of memory images. There is a whole range of "thinking" activities from the idle play of fancy, the free flow of images in reverie, to logically controlled manipulation of abstract symbols at the other extreme.

Symbols. Let us examine this concept of the symbol for a moment. When thinking occurs, there is a revival of a memory image, to be sure; but this is more than a mere kaleidoscopic picturing of the original perceptions. These images have *meaning;* they refer to or "stand for" objects. A picture of my dog may refer not only to that particular pet but also to a whole class of animals. The word *vertebrate* is an even more inclusive symbol. For one of the authors it frequently evokes an image of a diagrammatic tree, with the branches representing various species of vertebrates. One behaves toward a symbol as he does toward the real object. If I am thinking about dogs,

I might solve a problem involving canine diets, the use of animals in psychological research, or possible activities of the K-9 Corps. In any case, my responses to the symbol "dog" must be closely equivalent to that necessary with the living animal, or my problem solution will not carry over to a practical application.

Thought and percept. While a symbol is based upon perception, it should not be identified with perception. Percepts are anchored in space and time; thoughts have reference to near and far, past and future. Percepts are tied to the objective world; "people are seen upright and objects roll down hills." Thoughts transcend these objective limitations. We can imagine people floating in the air, and furniture which follows one around to be constantly available for use. We can, indeed, imagine centaurs and griffins and chimeras, which have no objective reality.

It is true, of course, that desire can distort perception; to some extent, one sees what he wants to see rather than the objective reality (page 240). But this manipulation of percepts is drastically limited as compared with the flexibility of imagination. For adaptive purposes we utilize thoughts to supplement perceptions by extending them in space and time, and by dislocating concrete percepts from their supporting frames of reference. In this way we can anticipate threats to homeostasis before they occur and provide the means for satisfying motives far in advance of any significant deprivation.

Thought and symbol. It is possible for thought to deal with past and future situations, objects which are not physically present, because thought operates through symbols. Man is the symbol-making and symbol-manipulating animal par excellence. But he is not entirely unique in this regard. Lower species of animals can also use symbols; they cannot use them so often or so effectively as we do.

A simple level of symbolization is found in the CR experiment. The bell rings; food is presented; after a few trials, the dog responds to the sound *as if* it were food. The bell has now become a symbol for the food itself. Man, however, can substitute many levels of symbols between his perception and the real goal; the quotations of shares on the stock exchange are far removed from the food, clothing, and commodities which they represent. Only with great difficulty do we get animals developing symbols for symbols (cf. the difficulty of obtaining higher order CRs).

Man is also markedly superior with regard to the length of time he can hold a symbol in mind and use it as a guide to action. In Pavlov's laboratory it was found that dogs would learn a *trace conditioned reflex* of this type: the bell rings, and 30 minutes later food is given. Eventually the animal comes to secrete saliva about 29 minutes after hearing the bell. This, however, is about his limit. Man is capable of very long delays; he can make an appointment during the winter for a Fourth of July picnic and respond appropriately when the time comes. This capacity for delayed response depends upon some persisting internal state which functions as a symbol. It will therefore help us in understanding the process of thinking if we examine such delaying mechanisms more closely.

The Delayed-reaction Experiment

Let us suppose that a dog is placed in the apparatus of Fig. 11:1, in the starting box. From this point he can see, but cannot approach, three doors behind which are food boxes. While he is held in the starting box, a light goes on over one door. He then is released and goes to the lighted door, where he finds food. So far this is a simple discrimination learning experiment. But if (after this habit is well established) we turn out the light and restrain the dog for 30

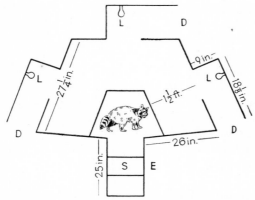

FIG. 11:1. Delayed-reaction box used by Hunter. The animal is placed in the starting box; then one of the three lights is turned on. After a delay of varying length, the box (made of wire mesh) is lifted and the animal can go look for food. Success on the delayed reaction is indicated by remembering which door was lighted, as the animals had learned that this signaled food. The above box was used for raccoons, who delayed considerably longer than rats and dogs. (*From Hunter, 1913.*)

seconds, a new problem is introduced. Can the dog retain a symbolic process which tells him to go to the same door? The delayed reaction thus becomes a crucial test of the animal's ability to use symbols on a very simple level.

Hunter (1913), who devised this technique, found that rats and dogs failed after even a few seconds delay, unless they were allowed to "point" in the direction of the light. When this set was disturbed, they could not direct their acts by any symbolic guide. Raccoons and young children (CA 2½ years) were able to delay for substantial periods of time even after the motor set was broken up; he therefore concluded that they were responding to a genuine symbolic process.

While Hunter's method has been accepted as a way of testing for ability to use symbols, his specific results have been discarded. Even the lowly rat has been shown capable of symbolic response. The rat, however, needs to be tested under conditions which ensure his attention to the symbol.

Thus McCord (1939) lowered his rats in a small cage into a square box. On each of the four walls was a door, distinctively marked. The experimenter thrust a food dish through one door and waved it until the rat looked at it. The rat was then allowed to jump to that door and get food. Delays were then introduced, and some rats proved capable of correct responses after 6 minutes. Obviously, some kind of symbol has been maintained during the interim. The difference between these responses and those obtained by Hunter is probably due to the fact that the animal can perceive sharper differences between the various response alternatives. His symbolic response might be "jump to the door with zebra stripes" rather than "jump to the door next to the right end." As we have noted in Chap. 6, the former type of discrimination is basically much easier for both animals and humans.

Adult humans use verbal responses to mediate such delays. If I say to myself, "My train leaves the LaSalle Street Station at 11:45 P.M." it becomes possible for me to delay for hours and still go to the right station when the time is suitable. Animals and young children cannot use such verbal cues. The growth of vocabulary parallels increasing complexity of thinking.

Motor set and symbol. Hunter's animals were able to give the correct response only so long as they kept a motor set toward the door. This is the way a hunting dog points to a bird. However, the pointer is helped in keeping his pose by the scent of the game. Hunter's apparatus was deliberately devised to eliminate such cues; it was thus far more difficult for his rats to find the correct door when the motor set had been disturbed. When McCord modified the experiment to provide some distinctive sensory cues on the doors, it was easier for the animals to use a symbolic representation of the correct door and dispense with the motor set. While we do not know what these rats experienced, it seems safe to assert that they were responding to a memory image of the design associated with food. This is much closer to true symbolic behavior than the mere maintenance of a muscular set pointed toward the goal.

Man, of course, can go much farther than this; he can deal with abstractions deprived of any sensory content, as when he discusses electron theory, hypothetical brain states, unconscious mental processes, and the like. There is little reason to supppose that any other animal species is capable of using symbols for symbols—to think about thinking. As noted in our analysis of conditioning, the substitution of one CS for another ("higher order conditioning") quickly runs into difficulties with lower animals. When we deal with human subjects, on the contrary, it is possible to establish third-order, fourth-order, and even higher CRs. *Man has the basic learning capacity for stimulus substitution which must provide the foundation of highly symbolic thinking.* Were we not capable of generalizing from "falling apples" to "falling bodies" to "mutual attraction of masses," Newton's law of gravitation could never have been formulated. Generalizations in psychology are even more subtle in the sense that symbols must be devised for symbols which are in themselves subjective and difficult for some people to grasp.

Motor set has its correlate in mental set. When McCord's rats were able to abandon a fixed pose and still orient to the correct door when released, they showed that a set of some kind had been maintained. As this is not muscular, we can call it a *mental set.* Man, of course, shows a multiplicity of mental sets. The student reading this book is set to learn about psychology, and if he were suddenly asked a question about history, even a familiar item, he might be momentarily blocked as to the correct answer. A child set for adding numbers is

confused if asked to subtract. Set is therefore a *control mechanism* for directing thinking.[1] As the Hunter-McCord type of experiment shows, the length of time a set can be maintained agrees roughly with the position of an animal in the phylogenetic scale—rats are poor, raccoons and dogs higher, chimpanzees still better, man at the top. Mental set is thus an important component of the complex pattern that makes up thinking.

Concept Formation

In its most primitive form, the symbol functions as a discrete sign or signal. The red traffic light signals me to stop; green serves as a symbol for free movement. Plus, minus, and other mathematical symbols "stand for" certain operations with numbers. The dinner bell signals the availability of food. At this very specific level the symbol is little—if any—more than a conditioned stimulus. In our analysis of learning we have spoken of signs or cues for action. In perception, part of a sensory pattern could serve as a sign for the entire pattern—thus the animal learned to perceive objects as having a certain color, size, and distance on the basis of limited cues. In all these usages, the sign has an immediate function in controlling experience and behavior.

But, as we have just seen, the response to a sign can be delayed. This makes possible certain operations on the sign, or symbol as it should be called when delay is involved. One can perceive, for example, a *relationship among symbols;* that is, one can generalize about symbols. Thus one does not have to be looking at a horse, a cow, a dog, and

[1] Actually, set is one of the *focusing* functions for the exclusion of irrelevant stimuli. In highly motivated behavior, stimuli not related to the motive are blocked out. Similarly, when one gets "set" for a task, he raises the threshold for unrelated stimuli, making it more likely that he will complete his assignment and reduce the tension involved.

a cat to note that all have four legs; one can compare the images of these experiences and develop the generalized idea of a quadruped.

In many respects this generalized symbol does not differ from the ordinary stimulus generalization which has been described in Chap. 6. The child learns that one specific object is called a "chair" when he perceives another, rather similar object, he generalizes and calls it a chair. Sometimes this is based on the wrong portion of the pattern; thus he may call a stool a chair, just as he may call all men "daddy," to his mother's marked embarrassment. When correct generalizations are developed, they are called *concepts;* and a definition of a concept is "the psychological process by which we perceive and react to similarities in the changing environment" (Humphrey, 1948). One develops a concept of a triangle by dealing with specific triangles and observing that all are closed rectilinear figures with three vertexes. One develops a concept of a chair by dealing with furniture and observing that all objects called chairs have a seat, legs, and a back.

Note how many generalized concepts we become adept at using. In defining a chair as suggested, we make use of generalized symbols for leg, seat, and back, as well as the higher order abstraction, furniture. Much of the process of learning to think is a process of acquiring these concepts. Intelligence tests (see Chap. 12) weight heavily the number of common concepts the person can use correctly—*i.e.*, as approved in our culture.

Concepts, however, break with the process of generalization at some point, or rather, they go beyond it. Stimulus equivalence can be stretched so far, but not infinitely. Let us consider a specific example. Here is Mr. Jones, a pedestrian who has been hit by a car as he stepped off a curb. Later Mr. Jones shows fear of bicycles, horses, motorcycles, trucks, and busses —all treated as equivalents for the moving object which injured him. This clearly illustrates stimulus generalization. But if Mr. Jones abstracts the quality of *force* and relates the motion of automobiles to the explosion of a cannon, the flow of an electric current, and the fission of the atom, he certainly cannot be said to be using stimulus generalization. He is now reacting to *similarities and relationships among symbols.*

The foregoing example suggests the crucial difference between stimulus generalization and concept formation. The former involves only *similarity;* the latter, *similarity and difference.* Mr. Jones's fear of objects in motion is based on pure perceptual similarity. The abstract concept of force is based on an awareness of likeness and difference. One must first eliminate certain differences between explosion and electricity before he comes to the underlying similarity. Often it is easiest to define a concept by first telling what it is *not.* Try defining "democracy," and you will see how this works.

Value of concepts. Without some ability to generalize, life would be far more hazardous. Events in life rarely repeat themselves in identical form. Man and animal need to be alert to meaningful similarities rather than to irrelevant differences. If the tiger you escaped yesterday had a black stripe across his right eye, this does not mean that you can ignore tigers lacking this stripe. Stimuli which threaten danger are quickly and widely generalized. Later (perhaps) we learn to differentiate those which are not real threats. This explains why young children generalize danger signals so extensively—why a conditioned fear may spread to many stimuli which seem quite different to the adult.

Furthermore, concepts greatly increase the efficiency of thinking. How easy would it be to solve an automobile problem if we had to itemize Fords, Chevrolets, Plymouths, Studebakers, etc., for each step in the solution? How much simpler to use a single generic concept and later insert corrections if the answer depends on features not common to all! If someone starts talking about internal-combustion engines, I do not have to identify the various types of carburetors and ignition systems; I can deal with concepts and later relate the solution to the specific engine I work with.

Concept and hypothesis. Every concept can be considered as an hypothesis or expectancy. If John says, "that girl is a golddigger," he is setting up an hypothesis as regards her behavior. He expects certain responses from her. When the psychiatrist says, "this is a paranoid schizophrenic," he sets up an hypothesis regarding his patient. He expects certain symptoms to show up, certain facts to be revealed in the life history, certain results in treatment.

It follows that every concept is subject to change with more precise differentiations. The child learns that only one man is to be called "daddy," and later, that some people wearing trousers are not "men." Newton's concept of gravitation was modified by Einstein, who showed that certain differences ignored by Newton were important. Your concept of "human nature" may be modified, and probably should be, by studying this book. You will find that processes appearing to be the same may, in fact, be quite different.

The higher order abstract concepts, such as time, inertia, gravitation, emotion, intelligence, and culture, represent hypotheses based on relations among symbols. They are subject to modification with additional data and with new insights into the relationships. They are based on delay in response to symbols and may be called logical abstractions rather than perceptual abstractions. Logical abstraction is a function which requires a wealth of symbols, plus the ability to delay, to note features of these symbols, to abstract a common element by noting differences and to generalize from it. It is not surprising to

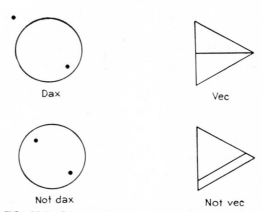

FIG. 11:2. Concept drawings of the type used by Smoke. Any circle with one dot inside and one outside was called "dax." Any equilateral triangle with a perpendicular bisector was called "vec." In the second version of the experiment, both "dax" and "non-dax," "vec" and "non-vec" figures were presented; the concepts were formed much faster under this condition. (*As described by Smoke, 1932.*)

learn that such a complex function developed late in the evolutionary sequence and that it is disrupted quite easily by brain injuries (Goldstein and Scheerer, 1941).

Study of concept formation. A typical laboratory procedure for studying concept formation is as follows: we present to the learner a series of specimens, all of which belong to a given class. We also present some which, he is told, do *not* belong to the class. He is required to differentiate and generalize the feature (or features) which identify the class, so that when he is presented with new cases, he can tell whether they do or do not belong to the class.

In one experiment (Smoke, 1932) subjects were shown figures consisting of a circle and two dots. They were told that this class of figures was called "dax" (see Fig. 11:2). The figures used varying sizes and colors of dots and circles. After they had studied the figures, one at a time, they were asked to give a definition, to draw a new "dax" and to draw a "non-dax." In repetition of the experiment, he presented both dax and non-dax figures to the subject for study. This variation speeded up concept formation. By seeing non-dax instances, the subject could reject erroneous hypotheses more rapidly.

It was interesting to note that many subjects could identify dax and non-dax without being able to give a definition. This apparently is a process closer to generalized percept than to a true concept. The individual had developed a mental image but could not respond to it, *i.e.*, could not describe its characteristics. Many garage mechanics seem to have a gift for perceiving the working characteristics of an engine but are completely incapable of verbalizing what they know.

Heidbreder's study. An experiment which illustrates the relative difficulty of different levels of concept formation was conducted by Edna Heidbreder (1946). The subjects were told that they were being studied for memory of various kinds. (Concepts do, of course, depend upon memory.) A series of nine figures was exposed on a memory drum, one at a time. At each exposure, the experimenter spoke a nonsense word. After one run through the list, the figure was exposed and the subject told to name it. If he failed, the experimenter named it and showed the next item. The subject kept going through the whole series until he named every figure correctly. (This is the "prompting method" for studying learning and memory—cf. page 251.)

Five of the series used are reproduced in Fig. 11:3. The subjects, of course, were not instructed to look for similarities (as, indeed, young children are not told to form concepts about squares, airplanes, or animals). But the names were so chosen that a picture always fell into a certain class. Thus *relk* always stood for a face; *mulp* for a tree. (These were examples of concrete concepts.) Spatial relations formed the basis for another series; *pran* always applied to a drawing of crossed objects—golf

clubs, streamers, canes, etc. A third series was based on variations in number; a particular word went with objects duplicated two, five, or six times in the sketch. There were three examples of each class (concrete, spatial, and numerical) in each series of nine drawings. Sixteen such series were learned.

Obviously the subject could not develop a concept on the first series, but on the second, he might note that the drawing of a face had the same name as a different face of series 1. Many subjects acquired the concrete concepts (face, tree, etc.) after studying only a few series. The spatial patterns were more difficult. A few subjects did not evolve the numerical concepts even after learning 16 variations with the same name.

Heidbreder was particularly interested in the "order of dominance" in concept formation. She found that concrete concepts form rather easily. Spatial form is almost as readily generalized. Lowest in dominance (greatest in difficulty) is numerical-concept formation—a fact which may have some connection with the difficulties many of us encounter in arithmetic. Heidbreder attributes this dominance order to functional characteristics of the material and of the human organism. Thought, after all, is related to motives, and motives are satisfied by manipulating concrete objects. The child has literally thousands of experiences handling and being satisfied by objects, to one of being satisfied by identifying a numerical relationship. Further, identification of a number concept seems inherently more complex than *identification of qualities*. The redness, shape, and taste of apples can be directly sensed, but the fact that five apples are in view depends on counting.

Induction vs. deduction. Both Smoke and Heidbreder used the inductive method of developing concepts. In teaching by this method, many examples are shown the

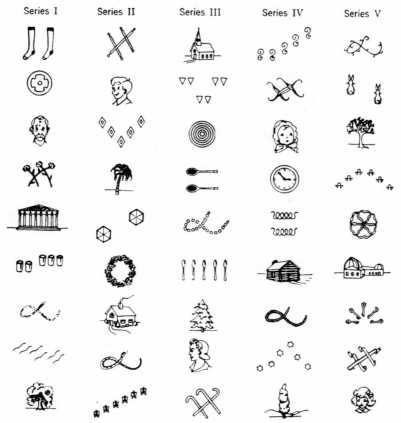

FIG. 11:3. Concept-forming series used by Heidbreder. The subject watched each of the figures in Series I appear on a memory drum (see Fig. 7:1, page 252) and the experimenter pronounced the name of the figure as it appeared. The subject repeated this name; on the second trial, S tried to name the figure, and was prompted by E if necessary. Series I was repeated until S had named every drawing correctly for two successive runs. Then S began learning Series II. At this point it became possible to transfer the names from Series I, *e.g.*, the face is always named *relk*, a tree is always *mulp*. This kind of concept formed quickly; but learning a concept name for objects in groups of five proved to be quite difficult. (*From Heidbreder, 1946, p. 182.*)

pupil, together with others which do not fit the concept. Thus a child can learn triangularity by seeing triangles of different sizes and proportions, and by contrasting not-triangles (circles, squares, rectangles). He will go through a period of trial and error but eventually will make the differentiation. Many of Heidbreder's subjects got the concept suddenly (insight).

In the *deductive method* the rule or principle is stated first and the subject is required to develop examples. Experimental research indicates that natural concept formation includes a mixture of both deduction and induction. The subject scrutinizes a series of samples and sets up an hypothesis (induction) which he proceeds to test on other samples (deduction). All scientific research advances in this manner. When an hypothesis has been

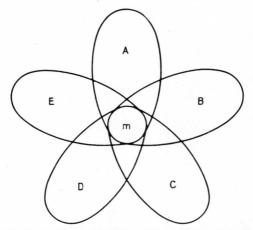

FIG. 11:4. James's illustration of varying concomitants. If one encounters situations A, B, C, D, E, all having characteristic *m* in common, the tendency is for *m* to "roll out" from its varying concomitants and stand out in the observer's field. Note how similar this is to the problem of stimulus equivalents (Chap. 9) and positive transfer (Chap. 7). (*From William James, 1892, p. 366, by permission of Henry Holt and Company.*)

verified in a variety of contexts, it is stated as a principle or law.

Varying concomitants. William James wrote of the principle of dissociation by varying concomitants: "What is associated now with one thing and now with another tends to become dissociated from either, and to grow into an object of abstract contemplation by the mind." If a child should ask you, "What is red?" it is unlikely that you would reply, "the visual sensation produced by a light wave of 700 millimicrons length." It is probable that you would point to various red objects, using the word "red," and also to others, stating that they were "not red." At some point the child suddenly grasps the concept, runs into the next room, and brings in his red ball, showing signs of elation. We can diagram this process as James did, in Fig. 11:4. If A, B, C, D, and E represent real percepts, all possessing characteristic *m*, there is a tendency for *m* to "roll out," *i.e.*, to be abstracted, as the child gets the quality "red."

Thinking and Goal Direction

In thinking, as in overt behavior, man's activities are motivated. Thinking is directed to the achievement of goals, and this means that the recall of images and concepts is not random but is controlled in some manner. There is available, in any situation, a tremendous variety of memories which might conceivably be serviceable. Only a few of these get through to conscious awareness. Some kind of screening process keeps most of them even from being recognized, and many others are rejected as soon as they reach awareness.

This idea is not new, for it played an important part in our discussion of problem solving. At that time we pointed out that the animal, in seeking a goal, does not move randomly; he makes movements which bring him nearer to the object which will satisfy his need. The same kind of goal orientation occurs in thinking, but it is even more important. In thinking there is truly an infinite number of combinations of images possible. In trying to solve my financial problem, I could dream up a fourth-dimensional traveler by which I loot bank vaults with impunity, or a new drug for which a grateful public would gladly make me wealthy. When the control mechanism breaks down, this is exactly the kind of thinking which goes on—in the psychotic personality.

Psychologists have long been interested in the process of directional control as it applies to thinking, but it would be an exaggeration to say that the control mechanism is clearly understood. The principle of *selective perception* is helpful. Remember that, when a motive is aroused, objects likely to satisfy that motive are perceived more readily. At the same time, other percepts tend to be suppressed. The principle of mental set is of the same type. When a person is "set" for a given stimulus, he senses it at a lower intensity—it is more quickly perceived—than when he is not set. Thinking operates on the principles of mental set and selective perception of images. When we are set to solve a given problem, images and concepts relevant to that problem are quickly observed, while those which seem irrelevant are screened out. Persons who have learned to do this selection efficiently are said to be "good at concentrating"; those who are poor at it may be called "scatterbrained." Children learn rather early to establish mental sets; adults punish lapses from the correct set and reward successes. Long before he goes to school, a little boy learns to disregard distracting stimuli and to concentrate on those related to the activity in progress. The delayed-reaction experiment, of course, illustrates ability to block out distractions and keep set toward a symbol which means satisfaction.

Experiments on mental set. Early experiments on this control phenomenon used the reaction-time technique, described on page 202. Figure 11:5 illustrates the usual reaction-time procedure: P represents a preparatory signal (get ready); S, the stimulus; R, the response. The interval from P to S is called the *foreperiod* during which the set is established and operating. It has therefore been a matter of particular interest.

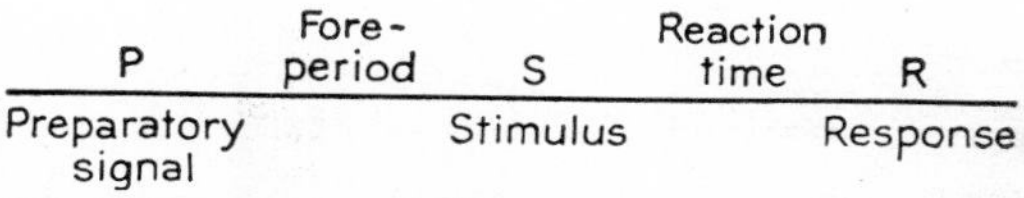

Watt (1905) asked his subjects to report what they experienced during the three phases outlined above. The reaction task was to give a certain type of controlled association; for instance, to name a whole of which the stimulus word is a part (wheel-automobile). Unfortunately, many of his subjects reported a complete blank for the foreperiod. Some of them were conscious of the task but not of associated ideas. *As a person became skilled at the task, consciousness decreased.* He might even report that he was not clearly conscious of the stimulus word until after he had responded! (This is like the skilled driver who compensates for

P	Fore- period	S	Reaction time	R
Preparatory signal		Stimulus		Response

FIG. 11:5. The reaction-time experiment. Students of the psychology of thinking have been particularly interested in trying to ascertain what goes on during the "foreperiod."

road conditions without even being conscious that they exist.)

Is set muscular? We noted, in connection with the delayed-reaction experiment, that some of the lower animals used fixed muscular tensions as guides to the correct response and were confused when this muscular set was disturbed. However, the higher animals tested seemed pretty clearly to be responding to a symbol which was held at the level of the CNS, not in a muscle.

The same conclusion derives from the reaction-time studies. Hathaway (1935) had his subjects making responses by moving the arm. He then recorded action currents from the arm muscles. He did not get any evidence of any muscular activity during the foreperiod. Mowrer (1940) used an indirect method. He trained his subjects to make the same response to two different signals. He assumed that the muscular set, if any, would be identical for both stimuli, since the response was identical. Then he presented signal A repeatedly, until the subject "expected" that signal. When signal B was presented, there was a marked delay, even though it called for the same response as A. Mowrer therefore concluded that the locus of set must be in the brain, not the muscles.

Shifting the mechanism from the muscles to the brain does not solve the problem. It does indicate, however, that set is primarily a matter of *selecting incoming stimuli*, rather than of getting the muscles prepared to respond. Set is mental, not muscular.

Mental set and shift. Set is productive of efficiency in thinking as long as the task

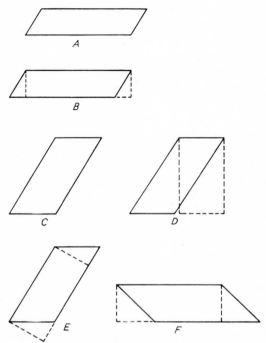

FIG. 11:6. A study of rigidity in thinking. Drawings *A* and *B* show the conventional parallelogram solution as presented by the geometry teacher. Wertheimer now drew *C* on the blackboard, and the children were confused. Some of them attempted to use the conventional solution rigidly, and drew *D*, which of course does not work. The superior students either drew *E*, or rotated the figure and drew *F*. (*As described by Wertheimer, 1945.*)

remains unchanged. Unfortunately, our world is constantly in flux, and if we are to satisfy our needs, we must shift from one set to another. History said of the Bourbon kings, "they learn nothing and forget nothing"; and eventually they were dethroned. A businessman who is set to make decisions in terms of conditions 20 years ago is doomed to failure. The neurotic who reacts to his wife as if she were his mother could be said to have a mental set which has been fixated; it remains unchanged and rigid while reality has changed. Such rigidity prevents adjustment.

An illustration of rigidity in set derives from a study by Wertheimer (1945). In a high-school geometry class the teacher first gives the usual proof of the theorem that the area of a parallelogram is equal to the product of base by the altitude (Fig. 11:6*A*, *B*). On the following day the children are tested with problems in which the parallelograms are of differing sizes; the results are excellent. Wertheimer then draws Fig. 11:6*C* on the board. Some of the pupils are taken aback. One raises his hand: "Teacher, we haven't had that yet." Others busily draw the auxiliary lines as they have been taught. Then they look puzzled, for what they get is Fig. 11:6*D*. The better students draw the auxiliary lines correctly, as in Fig. 11:6*E*, or turn the paper through 45 degrees and draw Fig. 11:6*F*. The teacher, seeing that only a minority of the class had solved the problem, said, "You certainly gave them a queer figure. Naturally they are unable to deal with it."

Wertheimer stresses the point that our methods of pedagogy are likely to encourage learning by rote memory rather than by understanding of the situation. The children applied the learned formula to situations where it did not make sense and were unable to see applications to a novel variation of the original example. A different mode of teaching would develop flexible mental sets in which this blocking would not occur.[1]

Silent assumptions. A logician has been defined as a man who can reason in a straight line from a false assumption to a preconceived conclusion. We are concerned here, not with the falsity of assumptions but simply with the fact that people do not know they are making assumptions. They are "set" for a certain conclusion and so it appears logical (and would be, if the silent assumptions were valid). For example, let

[1] It would be unfair to lay all the blame for this situation on the schools. There are many simple thinking problems which have no connection with schooling, yet which most people fail because they stick to a particular set in looking for a solution.

us consider a variation of the Sells atmosphere experiment. Several thousand college students were asked to judge this syllogism: "Pressure groups are dangerous to our democracy; the American Legion is a pressure group; therefore, the American Legion is dangerous to our democracy." The majority judged the syllogism false, although as stated it is logically sound. Then they were given this one: "Pressure groups are dangerous to our democracy; the CIO is a pressure group; therefore, the CIO is dangerous to our democracy." In this form a majority judged the syllogism sound. It now fitted with their silent assumptions about the CIO, whereas it clashed with their assumptions about the American Legion.

Unconscious biases dominate much of our lives. If we dislike Negroes or Jews, we can easily discover evidence which seems absolutely to justify our conclusions. The Russians have no problem in proving to themselves that the Americans are imperialistic warmongers. Because we are set for certain conclusions, we blindly ignore all the contradictory evidence and pass by new and fruitful solutions to our personal and social problems.

The Stream of Consciousness

So far we have pointed out that thinking requires the use of symbols; that these symbols are developed by noting likenesses and differences in experience; that we become set for certain kinds of symbols and may observe them, even when the real situation should lead us to a different concept. Basically, we have been analyzing man's quest for *identities:* "is this the same as . . . ?" Whenever we make a judgment that a certain concept applies, we are asserting an identity. When we say that the U.S.S.R. is totalitarian, we are saying that we identify certain features common to a variety of nations, although they differ in many other respects.

How do these symbols actually appear in experience? When man attempts such introspection, he observes a sequence of thought, a "stream of consciousness." William James wrote vividly of the "stream of consciousness," and recent novelists have attempted to reproduce this stream in words. When a sensitive person seeks methodically to picture *every* idea, without exception, which occurs to him, we get a chaotic, apparently lawless flow quite different from the orderly sequence of ideas involved in problem solving.

The majority of our thinking, as remembered, is controlled thinking. The stream of consciousness is directed by mental sets, oriented to one goal or another. However, when trained observers note their mental activities, it becomes clear that much of the day's thinking is an incessant flow of pictures, words, and relations, tenuously associated and in many cases perfectly fantastic in character. This kind of thinking with minimal control by set is called *reverie*. Because we would feel ridiculous, we rarely communicate our reveries to others—in fact, we quickly forget them. The technique of psychoanalysis places a good deal of stress on getting the person to talk about everything that occurs to him; it may take several weeks to get the patient to do this, so reluctant is he to verbalize these illogical associations of ideas. Once this freedom to communicate is established, the patient communicates much which is of value to the therapist, but which seems to the patient merely silly.

Still another device for getting at the uncensored flow of ideas is through the study of children and primitives. Children have not yet learned that they will sound foolish if they verbalize freely; hence Piaget and other psychologists have studied thinking in terms of childhood reports. Some of this work will be reviewed later.

The nature of mental symbols. Before we continue with the examination of the stream of consciousness, it will be worth while to ask: what makes up the stream? What is the nature of the symbols which are experienced by human adults and which seem to operate in young children and animals as thinking progresses?

Images. At the beginning of this chapter we suggested that symbols were primarily derived from perception and that they took the form of memory images. Much of our thinking depends on remembering how someone looked, the spatial arrangement of objects, the sound of a particular musical selection, the smell of hot apple pie, etc. The widespread role of the memory image in mental life has already been suggested (page 355).

In quest of satisfaction for motives, in search of restored equilibrium, the organism may manipulate real objects or symbols for them. If you are up a tree with a sabre-toothed tiger pacing hungrily below, it is much safer to picture different actions in the hope of perceiving an escape route than to rely on physical trial and error. Man's high status on the earth today is unquestionably due to his great capacity for holding onto symbols, recombining them in various ways, creating symbols for symbols, and so on.

Feelings. In the flow of consciousness one is aware not only of images, but also of feelings. The memory picture of a certain incident also evokes the feeling of pleasantness or unpleasantness which was present on the original occasion. Often one has feelings which seem not to be related to any memory that has been recalled; in such cases the feeling may have been set off by associated implicit movements or words (see below).

It may seem that feelings are not symbols in the usual sense, because they do not "stand for" a particular object or action. It should be clear, however, that they do symbolize inner needs and tensions (see page 113). Thus, in the thinking process,

their role as symbols may be as linkages to the basic human motives without which no thinking would occur. They symbolize tensions and tension reductions.

Implicit movements. It has been known for a long time that many people have little imagery and yet think very well. At one time, some fifty years ago, the controversy over images vs. imageless thought was a center of psychological research. Today it is accepted that both kinds are common and that thinking can go on without reproductions of past vision, hearing, taste, or other sensory experiences.

Some of these imageless thoughts probably are symbolized by minute movements or tendencies toward movement. Extensive research has been done on the problem. Jacobson (1932) for example, found that imagining a movement of the arm was accompanied by electrical action currents in the appropriate muscles, even though no detectable movement occurred (Fig. 11:7).

This is exceedingly important because of its bearing on the problem of meaning. As we shall develop more fully later, meaning is in part a question of how one responds to a stimulus. The meaning of the object "chair" is "something to sit on." The meaning of "knife" is "something to cut with," and so on. Try to define the word "spiral" to someone without using your hands, and you will become aware of the role of movement in thinking.

It seems likely, then, that part of the flow of consciousness is some kind of awareness of tentative muscular movements, symbolic movements which do not quite occur but which do have some physiological reality. These implicit movements may link images or other movements, as in a skilled habit; one might imagine walking down the street and seeing the shop windows; the images are interlinked by symbols of muscular action.

More difficult problems seem to involve more muscular action. In a study of deaf

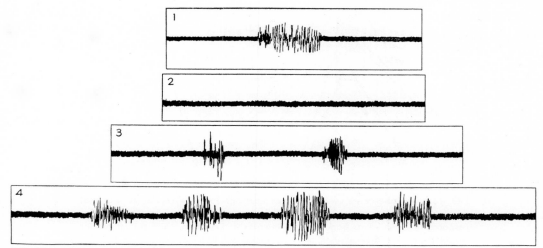

FIG. 11:7. Action currents without muscular movement. In his study of the physiological aspect of thinking, Jacobson placed electrodes on the skin just over the right biceps muscle, so that he could record nerve impulses to the muscle even when no physically discernible movement occurred. Each subject was trained in relaxation to eliminate random movements. Record 1 shows the result of instructions: "Imagine lifting a ten pound weight with your right arm." (Note volley of nerve impulses.) Record 2: "Imagine lifting a ten pound weight with your left arm." (No action currents in right arm.) Record 3: "Imagine hitting a nail twice with a hammer in your right hand." Record 4: "Imagine some rhythmical activity such as climbing a rope." Observe the close correspondence of the nerve activity to the imagined act. What relation does this have to the problem of muscular movement and learning? (Fig. 8:10, page 295.) (*Sketched from Jacobson, 1932.*)

mutes, Max (1935, 1937) found (as might be expected) more hand and arm action currents than in normal subjects; the deaf mute uses his hands in communicating and must therefore be expected to use them in thinking. When Max gave progressively more difficult mental problems to his deaf mutes, the amount of electrical activity increased proportionately. Difficult problems may also overflow into other muscle groups. When one is thinking on some tough problem, he is likely to furrow his brows, tense his shoulders, and so on. This may be a function of the increased tension which accompanies the need to solve the problem; or it may mean that, on difficult tasks, the organism has to mobilize more resources than for simple jobs. Tension does actually help to solve the problem, as is shown by experiments in which people combined support of a fairly heavy weight with solving arithmetic and other questions.

Brain waves. Considerable controversy has also centered around the question of the role of the brain in thinking. Some psychologists have gone to the extreme of saying that the muscles and sensory processes are the crucial elements in thought, the brain being primarily a giant switchboard and ammeter. Others have argued that the peripheral processes are just by-products of thinking, the significant elements being confined entirely within the brain itself. These two views are diagramed in Fig. 11:8.

At present the hope of resolving this conflict rests particularly on research with the electroencephalogram (EEG). The EEG is a recording of the changes in electrical action of the brain. If one electrode is placed over the occipital lobe (visual area) and another in a neutral area, the record will reflect effects of visual stimulation; similarly, the temporal area reflects auditory stimuli (cf. Fig. 5:12, page 154). There are several kinds of "waves" which are characterized chiefly by speed. The *alpha*

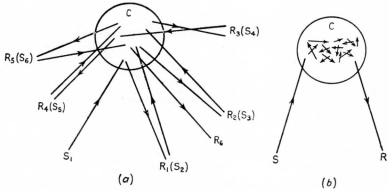

FIG. 11:8. Peripheral vs. central view of thinking. Some psychologists hold that thinking is a function of the whole body (a). Thus an outside stimulus (S₁) sets off a response (R₁); this sends back sensory impulses to the brain which set off further responses, more self-stimulation, more response, and so on until a final solution (R₆) is achieved. This corresponds to trial-and-error learning (Chap. 9). Others take the view that thinking is primarily, and can be exclusively, intracerebral (b). The stimulus sets off an impulse to the cerebral cortex, within which a variety of activities ensue, and these finally lead to a solution or response. This corresponds more to the "insight" emphasis in learning. (*From Dashiell, 1949, by permission of Houghton Mifflin Company.*)

rhythm has a frequency of about 10 per second. It is most noticeable during relaxation; concentration on a stimulus (or a problem) causes it to shrink or disappear (Fig. 11:9). The *kappa* wave has a frequency of about 8 to 12 per second; Kennedy (1948) and his collaborators thought they found evidence that it appears in records when the subject is doing mental work (Fig. 11:9).

Aside from its use in locating brain tumors (where it has been most valuable), the EEG has been used medically in diagnosing epilepsy and in some cases of brain injury. From the psychologist's side, it has been rather disappointing, but it may yet lead to significant discoveries about the brain function in thinking.

Most psychologists accept the view that thinking depends on the total organism. The brain plays a crucial role, but thinking could not occur without sense organs to provide information about the environment and very probably could not occur without muscles to execute actions on the environment. Thinking, in other words, is a *sym-*

bolic reproduction of everyday behavior. In our daily efforts to satisfy motives, we get sensory cues, use our muscles in attempting to adapt, correct our mistakes as we perceive them, and so on. These pictures of the environment and of one's responses to it are retained in the brain and are manipulated in thought.

The Nature of Meaning

The stream of consciousness is a flow of pictures, implicit movements, words, and perhaps brain states. Constant shifts of attention bring new symbols into awareness at intervals measured in fractions of a second. These symbols are effective devices for guiding human behavior because they possess *meaning*. This, however, is a much misunderstood term. The psychologist does not interpret meaning in terms of a dictionary definition. The meaning of a symbol is given by the object or action which it symbolizes; more specifically, meaning must be understood in terms of the *effects which are signaled* by a particular sensory cue. If a child has learned a bell-shock CR, it is correct to say that the bell "means" shock to him. Similarly, a delicious smell in the kitchen "means" delectable tastes in the mouth and a contented feeling in the stomach later on. The sight of mother means care, cuddling, and pleasant sensations. The one cue has become identified, in his mind, with the sensory consequences which have followed it. We can say, therefore, that meaning implies *partial identity* of the sign and the thing signified.

Contiguity obviously is a basic determinant of partial identity. The red traffic light and the act of stopping occur together; the first becomes identified with the second. The ringing of the dinner bell is followed by the taste of food; soon, the sound *means* food. Much of our thinking is determined by meanings based on contiguity of two experiences.

Stimulus equivalence also plays a role in determining meaning. Partial identity is often based on generalization of stimuli. In Watson's experiment it was found that fear of a white rat would generalize to a white fur muff and a Santa Claus mask. These were equivalent stimuli; the fear generalized to them. The identity elements are fairly obvious. Here we can say that the fur muff *means* the white rat which *means* danger to the child.

Verbal mediation is a third basis for meaning. Because words are so versatile and so readily linked to different cues, they provide connections between experiences which would never be associated by way of contiguity or equivalent stimuli. Suppose Johnny is spanked when he does something "bad." Later he learns that stealing is "bad." Stealing can mean that for which one is spanked, by way of the verbal mediation process, stealing—bad—spanked. Thus partial identities can be established on the basis of common verbal labels.

The process of "free association." Let us return now to our consideration of the

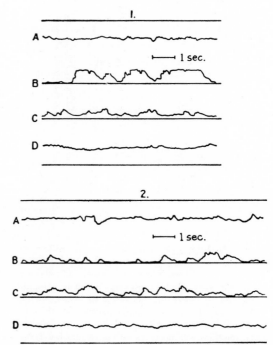

FIG. 11:9. Brain-wave records associated with "mental work" and with relaxation. (1) EEG records taken while subject is doing mental arithmetic. Line A gives the kappa waves, line D, alpha waves. Line B is the accumulation of kappa waves, C, of alpha. Note the great preponderance of kappa over alpha (B compared with C). (2) EEG records taken with "mind a blank." Note the relative preponderance of alpha over kappa waves (C compared with B). (*From Kennedy et al., 1948.*)

stream of consciousness. Thinking goes on as the individual experiences images of past experiences, implicit movements representing past actions, and words (which may take the form of images or minute speech movements). The content of this stream is determined by the meaning relationships existing among these elements. For example, as I sit here, I see some carpenters erecting a house across the street. This evokes a memory image of the house a friend is building elsewhere in the community. I am conscious of his name, of an image of the blueprints which I recently examined, and of some other people present at the same time. One of these men had just

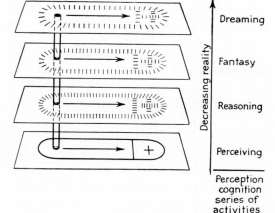

FIG. 11:10. Levels of reality in thinking. The level of perceiving is the level of physical reality. Above that we can recognize different levels of unrealistic thinking, from reasoning, which differs only slightly from physical reality, up to dreaming, which is quite different. As we move up this series of levels, we find that barriers become more penetrable; solutions can be found quickly to all our problems. However, if these solutions will not work on the reality level, they are not very satisfying; goals at the higher level are easier to achieve but much less apt to relieve tension and restore equilibrium. The insane person may have solutions to all his problems—and those of the world, too—but on a level of unreality which makes them quite useless. (*Modified from Brown, 1936, p. 285.*)

returned from Korea, and this evoked verbalizations (silent) about the Far Eastern situation. I was aware of muscular tensions, perhaps relating to my anger that this conflict had interfered with some personal plans. Then I was conscious of inflation in terms of my inability to build the house I had planned; this was followed by an image of a cartoon on inflation which had impressed me not long ago.

True "free association" would produce a sequence of ideas like this, only far more random and illogical if the time span were a little longer. But most "normal" people are unwilling to speak "off the top of the mind" in this unguarded manner. They are guided by mental sets, excluding irrelevant associations and seeking, among the many ideas present, those ideas which are logical

and "rational." Thus we do not get real "free association" in most cases.

This can readily be illustrated by reference to the "free-association" experiment. On page 74 we described this technique as a device for identifying persistent emotions, noting that the emotion guided the choice of associated words. Let us now consider it as a technique for studying meaning through association of ideas.

If the stimulus word "chair" is given, under instructions to reply with the first word that comes to mind, we do not get a random sample of the dictionary in responses. Of 927 college students tested in this manner, 297 replied "table"; an association based chiefly on contiguity. The next most common reply was "furniture" (159 cases), based on verbal mediation. The third association in frequency was "desk" (93 cases), again based on contiguity. Thus 549, or 60 per cent, of the replies used only three words. Plainly, this is not "free association"; it is association of ideas controlled by contiguity of experiences, by the fact that most of us live in a common environment where one perception is followed by another in a "logical" manner. Thus the free-association test is given in many cases to show whether the person is well socialized; if he has a high proportion of these common responses, it would appear that he is in close touch with his social milieu (Tinker and Baker, 1946).

Autistic thinking. Problem solving is controlled by a need to reduce tension. Indeed, all thinking is related to motives in some way. However, problem solving and reasoning differ from much everyday thinking in respect to the degree of realism involved. If I try to solve a problem involving a 23,000-volt current, I must adhere strictly to the conditions of the real situation or my "solution" may be fatal. However, much daily thinking is directly controlled by motive and relatively free from reality conditions (Fig. 11:10). Thus John may be bothered by a conflict with his girl friend. He may then fantasy joining the football team, becoming a star, and having many girls compete for his favor. His present sweetheart also comes begging for his affection, and he pictures himself graciously accepting her and ignoring their previous conflicts. Such a thought sequence ignores the fact that John doesn't like football and couldn't make the team if he did. The control of association in this case is determined purely by his personal needs.

This type of thinking is called *autistic* (as opposed to *realistic*) because it is dominated only by need and not by need plus real conditions. Obviously, autistic thinking is somewhere between free association and reasoning, since the motive exerts some control over the flow of images and ideas. A good way to organize these kinds of sequences might be thus:

Free association	Autistic thinking	Reasoning and problem solving

This diagram would suggest that any specific act of thinking might fall anywhere on this continuum. Observation of human activities indicates that most thinking is autistic rather than rational. Much of what passes for reasoning has a large autistic component.

Autistic thinking is very common among children. The child is prone to brush aside reality in favor of desire; in his games and even in talking with adults he treats reality as if it would bend to his needs. As he matures, he learns first about the unyielding character of physical objects, and second, that he cannot communicate successfully (hence satisfy his social needs) if he ignores logic and realism. Gradually, therefore, we get a transition from immature, predominantly autistic thinking to reasoning and problem-oriented thinking. Some special phases of this development will be examined later in this chapter.

Mature and Childish Thinking

All thinking makes use of symbols. But symbols may be treated in a very concrete, restricted sense; on the other hand, they may show a high level of abstraction. The word "cat" may be only a symbol for the black tabby who sleeps by the fireplace; or it may be a symbol for lions, tigers, leopards, jaguars, lynxes, and so on. Such scientific terms as "carnivorous" and "viviparous" are necessarily symbolic. And we get very far away from the concrete when we deal with symbols like

$$e = mc^2$$

Our analysis of the learning process can help us to understand the development of concrete symbols and their progress to abstract symbols. Liddell (1942) reports on the behavior of sheep used in a CR experiment. After a few sessions, the sheep puts up violent resistance to being led to the barn. As far as he is concerned, the barn door means pain, *i.e.*, it is perceived as identical with the electrodes used for shock. However, if he learns that by lifting his leg at the sound of a bell, he can avoid shock, his behavior changes. He no longer has a simple anxiety CR to the experimental situation; he now has an instrumental CR as well. Thus it becomes possible for him to progress past the crude identity of barn with shock; now barn is a signal of danger but is not itself the danger. When we get to the point that we can distinguish the sign from the thing signified, we are beginning to operate on an abstract level. Thus identity based on contiguity provides a basis for symbolic process.

Similarly we can analyze the role of stimulus generalization. At first little Albert identifies the white fur muff with the white rat. As he has more experience, finer discriminations can operate. He can observe that the muff is not accompanied by the terrifying noise. Thus the differentiation between the decisive sign qualities and irrelevant aspects of the sign is brought about. Mature thinking shows this accurate discrimination.

It would take too much time to analyze the learning process in detail as it leads to each successive stage in the development of symbolic thought. Let us simply sketch, in the next few paragraphs, some stages in the shift from infantile to adult thinking.

Egocentrism. Jean Piaget (1928, 1932), one of the great French psychologists, spent many years in studying the thought of children. One of his main conclusions was that the earliest phase of thinking seems to be primarily egocentric, or self-centered. The child does not clearly distinguish between himself and other people or objects. The baby's hand is perceived merely as another part of the environment; he may bite it, and cry, without realizing his own responsibility. Conversely, at a slightly later age, the external world comes to be perceived as alive. Chairs can be hurt, automobiles can feel cold, and so on. There is a partial identity of the self and the external object.

This use of the term *egocentrism* is of course slightly different from that in which it is applied to personality of adults. The egocentric adult is not lacking in discrimination; he knows self from not-self. He does, however, think of everything purely in terms of its utility for his own needs; he ignores the needs of other persons. In this respect he is still infantile.

Syncretism. Piaget coined the generic term *syncretism* to refer to the child's tendency to unite incompatible ideas in a single impression. Juxtaposition is one typical form. He asked his children "why does the sun not fall down?" The answers were things like, "because it is hot" or "because it is high in the sky." The child's thinking is very concrete; he does not have abstract symbols adequate to deal with this situation. He has not yet differentiated the

various aspects so that he knows what is relevant and what is not. In like fashion we get "The man fell off the bicycle because . . . " and the child says "He was ill afterward." These are pure contiguity associations; the concrete situation has not been differentiated so that true symbolic thinking is possible.

Animism. Animistic thinking is the tendency to personalize inanimate objects and to explain the behavior of objects as if they were human. Primitive peoples use this kind of thinking in relation to natural forces; the wind, the river, and the mountain are gods, animated by the same desires and impulses as man. Children in our society do a great deal of animistic thinking, but adults are prone to the same approach when dealing with complex, confusing materials. Thus the depression of 1929 was ascribed to Herbert Hoover, not to economic processes; Nazism, to Adolf Hitler, not to an authoritarian culture and economic frustration; and so on. This kind of thinking is no doubt simpler and easier to put across through propaganda; the communists build up a glorified picture of Stalin as the source of all blessings, instead of stressing the hard work and natural resources of the land and people.

Physiognomic thinking. We have noted in our discussion of perception (page 235) that children learn to identify certain features in persons—especially expressions of emotions—and that very minute cues can evoke the perception of an expression of anger, dislike, affection, kindness, etc. Children transfer this same tendency to their interpretations of objects, and perceive buildings, stones, trees, and furniture as good, bad, threatening, helpful, and the like. This reading of human attributes into nonhuman objects is of course a variety of animism. It is also tied in with another kind of illogical thinking which we call *identification by attributes*. The child perceives some part or quality of the object which looks to him like a part or quality of a person and thinks of them as identical. So a tree with an upraised branch is seen as about to strike; an old house may be seen as threatening. This process of identification by attributes is actually fairly common. We shall consider some experimental studies of attribute thinking in later pages of this chapter. When it involves emotional attributes for nonhuman objects, it is called physiognomic thinking.

Childish thinking among adults. It is clear from the foregoing that we cannot draw any sharp line between childish and adult thinking. Some people are always "young in spirit," and some are infantile in emotions. Likewise there is reason to suppose that some people never reach a truly mature way of thinking, involving the use of symbols clearly separated from the concrete situation, and without reading human characteristics into nonhuman material.

This is partly a function of our culture. We do not make much of an effort to encourage logical thought at an early age; we foster belief in magic and fairy tales; we talk animistically to children—about statues in the park getting frostbite, and about "the naughty chair that bumped Baby." Our language is full of similes and metaphors that fit in with this same pattern: we speak of the "table groaning with good food" and so on.

Adults also regress to more childish modes of thinking when pressed by strong needs. This is probably a function of the narrowing of the psychological field (see pages 39, 73) which is so characteristic of powerful motives and emotions. Only crude concrete situations are observed; the finer symbolic differentiations get lost. Thus, in a period of great alarm when communists are perceived as a serious threat, we regress to a crude form of partial identity called *guilt by association*. This kind of thinking is on the level of the sheep which behaved identically toward the barn and the elec-

trodes. The only association is one of contiguity.

Psychotic thinking shows this same tendency to establish partial identities on the basis of irrelevant factors. Von Doramus (1944) illustrates schizophrenic thinking with the case of a patient who believed that Jesus, a cigar box, and sex were identical. He explained his belief by saying that "the head of Jesus, as of a saint, is encircled by a halo, the package of cigars by a tax band, and the woman by the sex glance of the man." The common identity is based on the "attribute" of being encircled.

This kind of thinking, which Von Doramus calls *paralogical* (distorted logic), can be diagramed as in Fig. 11:12. If circle X identifies the statement, "Some Republican leaders believe in universal military training" and circle Z, "Russian communist leaders believe in universal military training," the paralogical thinker may conclude that "some Republican leaders are Russian communist leaders."

Adult thinking—defined as truly mature, realistic thinking about the environment—is characterized by differentiation of the significant attributes and use of these as symbols for the external object. The identification of the significant attributes is sometimes difficult. For this reason the study of semantics (see below) is one method of improving the clarity and maturity of our thinking.

Public and private thinking. In our private thinking we are especially likely to be guilty of childish thought, identifying by human analogies, by irrelevant attributes, by contiguity, and so on. It is possible to run though a problem situation hastily and reach some kind of practical conclusion without being careful as regards the errors noted above. If the conclusion appears ridiculous, we simply discard it and start over.

In public thinking—that is, thinking, the result of which is to be communicated to others—we are under pressure to be more careful. Symbols are screened more rigorously and identifications are scrutinized for irrelevant combinations. The rules of syllogistic logic and semantics help us in eliminating errors, and the rules of grammar and rhetoric help the communication process. Cameron (1944), who has done some of the most distinguished work on schizophrenic thinking, suggests that the schizophrenic has abandoned any effort to order his thinking for communication. He is simply thinking autistically, for his own pleasure.

The work of the psychoanalysts confirms the suggestion above that normal people think much of the time in the paralogical manner characteristic of schizophrenic patients and children. When the analyst's patient has really learned free association, he abandons the rules which govern public thinking for communicative purposes. He simply verbalizes all the associations of ideas in his stream of consciousness. In this way the analyst is enabled to spot childish thinking in his patient. This is of vital importance because, after all, *we act on the basis of these illogical thoughts.*

Dream analysis. The dream is particularly useful in the study of autistic thinking because it is not governed by the rules of communication. It occurs, of course, in response to a wish—as does all our thinking. But it is not subject to the conscious screening which selects associations of ideas for communicating logical meaning to others. Hence dreams usually seem illogical and ridiculous when we awaken. Actually, analytic studies indicate that they are even less logical than first appears.

The dream as reported upon awakening is called the *manifest content.* This is likely to have undergone considerable face lifting to prepare it for public statement, even in the very intimate rapport which develops between patient and analyst. Gaps are filled, and sequences arranged to give them an appearance of order. The analyst, however, does not accept this as the real dream. He subjects it to thorough dissection, using free association as the basic tool.

Free association reveals that behind the manifest content is a hidden or *latent content.* This is primarily a wish—a wish that something will happen, or, as in nightmares, a wish that it should not happen. The elements of the dream are disguised because the wish is one which the conscious personality would not accept—it may be immoral, destructive, or antisocial. (If it were not, one could think about it consciously and not need to dream of it at night.)

Symbolism. The symbolism observed in dreams is a private matter, a substitution of one item for another to conceal the forbidden wish. An item can serve as a symbol if it has partial identity with the element symbolized. Such partial identity may be based on contiguity, on common attributes, on stimulus generalization, or on verbal mediation. Thus dreaming is simply autistic thinking. In dreams one allows the wish to select the flow of ideas, without regard to the real situation or the social pressure for logical thought.[1]

All symbolism is strictly private and personal. The meaning of a dream must be determined in relation to the personality, problems, and experiences of the dreamer. Nevertheless, just as we found in the case of the free-association experiment (page 398) that common environment makes for common associations, so there is some justification for believing that certain symbols are quite common in our culture. Table 11:1 shows some of the dream symbols often reported in psychoanalysis.

Many of these symbols are based directly on partial identity. However, we get some interesting complications of simple association as a result of the *dream work,* which is

---

[1] It will be interesting at this point to look again at Fig. 1:5, p. 8, and identify the manifest content, latent content, and symbolism, indicated there.

the analytic label for the process of disguising the latent as the manifest dream. One of these processes is *condensation*. The symbol may represent several unconscious elements; *e.g.*, a woman reports a dream about a very striking man; analysis reveals that the man (manifest dream) symbolizes her father, her former husband, and her present husband (latent dream), all at the same time. Conversely, it is frequently noted that the same person is symbolized by two or three dream characters. Especially in dreams expressing hostility, the dreamer is split into a "bad" murderer and a "good" person who tries to prevent the murder but—significantly—fails to do so. Thus even in dreams social motives express themselves in opposition to antisocial impulses.

Another aspect of the dream work is called *displacement*. Displacement may be spatial or temporal; *i.e.*, we may displace an emotion to a different object or location, or we may juggle it in time. A dream about the sex organs may be symbolized by "displacement upward"; the genitals may be symbolized by the mouth, nose, or arm. Displacement can also be focused around attributes; the sex act may be thought to be "filthy" and a dream about physical filth results. Displacement to the opposite occurs when one attribute is replaced by its opposite; naked is the opposite of clothed; hence nakedness may be symbolized by elaborate costuming. All these, as was noted above, must be related to the personality of the dreamer; they are not valid generalizations for an individual, although they are for Westerners in general.

Still further changes are made in the dream to "make it sound good." Details are added and a story may be developed. This phase is called *secondary elaboration*.

Attribute Thinking

In our consideration of perception we noted that the perceived characteristics of objects

TABLE 11:1. Some Common Symbols in Dreams (*Based on Cole, 1939*)

Latent meaning	Manifest dream symbol
The dreamer's body....	A house
Parents..............	King and queen (or other respected persons)
Brothers, sisters.......	Little animals, vermin
Birth.................	Water, swimming, diving, rescuing someone, being rescued
Nakedness...........	Clothes, uniforms
Death................	Journey, riding on the train
Male genitals.........	Sticks, umbrellas, poles, trees, weapons, faucets, fountains, airplanes, snake
Female genitals........	Space-enclosing objects, pits, caves, pitchers, bottles, trunks, cases, pockets, churches, chapel, stove, room
Masturbation.........	Sliding, piano playing

tend to fall along dimensions and that we are likely to verbalize a given attribute in terms of a dichotomy. Thus we think of temperature as hot-cold, height as tall-short, brightness as black-white, and so on.

When people are asked to think about two objects, especially when they are not physically present, there is a tendency to exaggerate the differences between the objects. Apparently this is a function of the need to differentiate carefully between them. If you have two friends who are often together, you will probably find that you remember one as taller and the other as shorter than they really are—making the true difference greater. To some extent this may be a function of sharpening (see page 372). It will also be remembered that Carmichael (page 369) found that a word label influences the memory image, distorting it to fit the label more closely.

This tendency to dichotomize experience picks up relatively small differences and exaggerates them. Suppose I ask you to give me the opposite to the word "man."

The chances are very high that you will say "woman"—yet, in reality, man and woman have perhaps 99 per cent of their characteristics in common and differ only as to sex. A better opposite might be "stone," which differs from "man" in far more attributes. The tendency to dichotomize thus selects a single attribute and over-emphasizes it.

The basic dichotomy in thinking is probably "good-bad." As we suggested in the treatment of motivation, goal objects are treated as good if they satisfy needs and bad if they increase tension. People are labeled in the same way. My own acts will seem to me good if they reduce tension and bad if they increase it. So will the acts of other people. The good-bad dichotomy is fundamentally related to motives.

Parallel dichotomies. The formation of attribute dichotomies is important because one may think of two objects as identical on the basis of common attributes (see above). It plays an extensive role in shaping the thought process because dichotomies tend to become parallel to one another; thus ideas may become associated by virtue of some related attribute. Let us examine this process more carefully.

Suppose we take a simple dichotomy like large-small. This dimension of perceived objects necessarily crystallizes out of our day-to-day observations. We *must* classify events according to size if we are going to deal with them successfully. Now take another dichotomy, loud-soft. This is based on auditory experience and logically un-related. Yet, when several hundred college men were asked to make a choice, 92 per cent matched large with loud and small with soft. We could rationalize this finding by saying that large animals and people are likely to make loud noises; actually, observation would not bear this out a great deal of the time. However, it *seems* that these two dimensions ought to be parallel to each other, and when 92 per cent of the group agree as to direction, it is probable that some cultural influence has been at work making them uniform.

Table 11:2 shows the average agreement among 40 pairs of words (40 dichotomies) in a group of 100 college men. These are simply averages to show the cultural uniformity, and ignore specific figures. In some cases agreement was unanimous; for instance, 100 per cent of the group linked happy with good and sad with bad.

The table shows that good-bad has more agreement with the other pairs than any other dichotomy. This probably is due to the fact mentioned above, that good-bad identifies a basic need-satisfying quality and hence can be attributed to almost any percept or idea.

If these dichotomies were arranged in parallel by each man individually, there would be just as much chance that he would associate body with good and mind with bad as that he would follow the crowd. Then we would get a 50 per cent association between these dichotomies. Since the lowest figure is 66 per cent and the highest, 87 per cent, we infer that the arrangement of these attributes is guided by cultural pressure. Some of this is obvious; the association of up-down with good-bad is certainly fostered by tradition.

The writer and poet use similes, metaphors, and analogies to communicate experience. They not only must attempt to stay within the bounds of what can be understood by their readers (some modern poets perhaps excepted), but they also have a profound effect in perpetuating these parallels. The child's mind is sensitive to the analogies created by the poet and to the animistic phrases of popular speech. Popular speech is full of intersensory analogies; there is no particular reason why certain tastes should be called "sharp," but the parallel is now culturally established. Some sounds are also identified as "sharp," and so we have the possibility of new meanings

TABLE 11:2. Extent of Agreement on Various Attributes
(*Based on Sorlien, 1942*)

Pairs	Percentage	Pairs	Percentage
1. bad-good	87*	21. moving-stationary	78
2. happy-sad	85	22. male-female	77
3. alive-dead	85	23. bass-treble	77
4. depressing-inspiring	83	24. large-small	77
5. dark-light	83	25. far-near	76
6. friend-enemy	83	26. eat-drink	76
7. love-hate	82	27. loud-soft	76
8. heavy-light	82	28. fast-slow	76
9. laugh-weep	82	29. crooked-straight	76
10. war-peace	81	30. individual-society	76
11. praise-blame	80	31. thick-thin	74
12. pass-fail	80	32. animal-plant	74
13. accept-reject	80	33. relaxed-tense	74
14. awake-asleep	80	34. science-art	73
15. wiseman-fool	80	35. earth-water	73
16. blurred-distinct	80	36. plant-harvest	73
17. down-up	79	37. body-mind	70
18. rise-fall	79	38. background-figure	70
19. sink-swim	79	39. angular-rounded	69
20. preserve-destroy	78	40. harmony-melody	66

* This figure means that, when 100 college men matched "bad-good" with the other 39 pairs in this table, they showed the high degree of uniformity in associations indicated by 87 per cent agreement. If associations were made purely by chance, this figure would have been 50 per cent.

and communications of ideas. In our discussion of perception we noted that the term *anchorage* is used of those outstanding experiences which anchor our scales of judgment. Social and cultural traditions serve as anchorages, tying different scales together so that communication by analogies is possible.

There are, however, other kinds of experience which also anchor these dichotomies and influence the kinds of mental relationships in thinking. Powerful motives will affect the organization of attributes and ideas. Early childhood experiences are dominated by hunger; in later life we use, *e.g.*, in love, analogies based on hunger. The loved one is sweet, delicious, desirable enough to be "eaten up."

Partial identity and propaganda. Hitler's technique of the "big lie" was dependent not so much upon selling the Germans a direct lie, but rather on anchoring their

perceptions on a part truth by repetition and dramatic exaggeration of the partial identity, so that finally the whole percept would be dominated by the suggested identity. This technique was artfully tied in with powerful motives of the Germans— economic frustration, wish for restoration of national power, fear of attack. Hitler's craving for terrific personal power provided a convenient channel for the average German's desire for national grandeur. Under these conditions, Hitler found the following simple rules of propaganda to be effective in molding the thinking of the German people:

(1) Arguments must be directed to the "least intelligent" of the people; (2) avoid "scientific ballast" as much as possible; (3) give the simple points "thousandfold repetition"; (4) seek ever to hold the attention of the great masses; (5) seek not "the many-sidedness of scientific teaching"; (6) restate the main few points as

slogans; (7) never try to become versatile, altering the methods, for the masses will not retain the idea; (8) never permit the faintest suggestion that there is "right on the other side"; (9) no half-way urgings will do; things are either "positive or negative, love or hate, right or wrong, truth or lie"; and (10) regardless of all else, keep focused on the fundamental principle, limit the program, and repeat it eternally.[1]

From the point of view of our discussion of attributive thinking, it is significant that Hitler stressed that everything is either black or white. All the fundamental dichotomies: love and hate, right and wrong, truth and falsehood—are lined up in parallel. Our side is exclusively good; the enemy illimitably evil. From the point of view of technique, he proposes that strong anchorage be provided for these parallels by constant repetition.

Dangers of attribute thinking. In view of the examples cited, there is perhaps little need to call attention to the dangers of attribute thinking. Yet it cannot be eliminated. In the last analysis, all human knowledge comes through perception. We *must* think in terms of attributes. How difficult would it be to describe personalities if we had to abandon such adjectives as sour, cold, magnetic? All of these are analogies, and illegitimate at that, but they have become so culturally standardized that they aid communication greatly.

The use of these attributes is a part of what we call the *effort after meaning*. Unfortunately, the assistance they give us in one respect is often more than canceled by the detriment in other areas. Our civilization is complex and intricate. When we try to think about involved problems of business, labor, politics, and international affairs, using the simple terms of attribute and analogy, we inevitably oversimplify. Furthermore, we often drag in unintended

[1] Lee (1941), p. xviii. Reprinted by permission of Harper & Brothers.

meanings that are not truly a part of the picture. For example, we characterize capitalism as democratic, ignoring the fact that nothing is so undemocratic as a big corporation. Or we say that capitalism ignores human rights, forgetting that we have made tremendous progress on welfare measures in recent years. When a person tells a lie, he becomes a liar; liars are bad; therefore this person has all kinds of bad traits.

Whenever social conflicts become acute, thinking becomes more polarized. All attributes migrate to either the good pole or the bad pole. When management and unions clash, people take sides and perceive everything here as white, there as black. Such thinking is unrealistic and destructive of intelligent problem solving.

The extent to which polarized thinking becomes "all-or-none" in character can be illustrated by the extremes to which partial identities are carried. Hitler sends six million Jews to the gas chambers; southern whites lynch six Negroes. Under emotional pressure many people say both acts are bad and cruel; therefore both are the same. This ignores an enormous quantitative difference. Fifteen communists in American jails are equated to fifteen million slave laborers in Russia. Again, polarized thinking ignores the important question of numbers. This is not to say that injustice anywhere is to be condoned; but we should not allow thinking to be distorted to the extent of identifying phenomena so different in magnitude.

As has been noted earlier, some classification of people in terms of race, religion, politics, or vocation is not necessarily sloppy thinking. For economy in thinking we pick out minor attributes and focus on them for purposes of communication. However, when these symbols are treated as including *all* attributes of the persons labeled, and especially when they become polarized so that all the good attributes are segregated for one group and all the bad adjectives apply to another group, they are incredibly dangerous. It is particularly likely that these *stereotypes* of minority groups will become symbols of need, threat, and conflict. They may be used to relieve chronic anxieties ("it is the Jews who are threatening us"); they may be used to release aggression ("the Russians are about to attack us, so we must attack them first"). Since everyone is likely to have some insecurities, anxieties, and hostilities disturbing him, polarized stereotypes are constant threats to peace and social cooperation.

Logic, Semantics, and Clear Thinking

It should be clear from the foregoing analysis that clear thinking depends upon the kind of identities we use in approaching problems. How can we avoid the risk of treating things as identical when they are basically different? How can we be sure that we are using the correct attributes, not irrelevant characteristics, in relating one event to another?

Traditional philosophy offers the syllogism as the classic device for clarifying thinking. Modern research has developed semantics as a supplementary technique. Both have much to offer in improving man's thought processes. It will therefore be worth while to examine briefly how each relates to the psychology of thinking.

The syllogism. The syllogism is primarily a device for isolating and bringing into clear focus the unconscious assumptions which have been made in reaching a conclusion. It can therefore be helpful in exposing paralogical thinking which is based on unsound assumptions. Let us first consider a formula for the syllogism:

All X is Y (major premise)
All Z is X (minor premise)
　　Therefore, all Z is Y (conclusion)

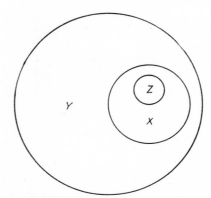

FIG. 11:11. Diagram of a syllogism.
If all X's are Y's
And if all Z's are X's
Then all Z's are Y's

This is a valid syllogism and can be illustrated by inserting concrete examples into the formula:

All women are human beings
All old maids are women
　　Therefore, all old maids are human beings

Suppose, however, that the basic syllogism is altered. Here is a common type of paralogical reasoning, converted into a symbolic formula:

All X is Y
All Z is Y
　　Therefore, all Z is X

This false syllogism is seductive in leading to an erroneous conclusion because of the "atmosphere effect." Actually, it induces a mental set favoring the conclusion but does not hold up under close examination. For example:

All Caucasians are white
All snow men are white
　　Therefore, all Caucasians are snow men

Diagrammatic analysis. It helps many people to reject invalid syllogisms if they make use of the diagrammatic representation of the problem situation. Look at Fig. 11:11, which illustrates the valid syllogism cited first. The large outer circle

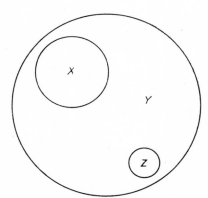

FIG. 11:12. Diagram of a syllogism.

If all X's are Y's

And if all Z's are Y's

Then all Z's are X's

Does the diagram help spot the fallacy in this syllogism?

represents class Y, the first inner circle, class X, and the smallest circle, class Z. Thus all Z must be X, which in turn must be Y; therefore all Z is Y. (You can fit the old-maid example into this diagram easily.)

Now suppose we try to use the diagrammatic solution on the snow-man syllogism. Its falsity becomes obvious (Fig. 11:12). The large circle represents white objects; one small circle, Caucasians, the other small circle, snow men. There is no identity here. Yet in many recent political campaigns, we have had this kind of argument:

Communists oppose military aid to Chiang Kai-shek

Candidate X opposes military aid to Chiang Kai-shek

Therefore, candidate X is a communist

If we let the large circle represent persons opposing aid, one small circle represent communists, and the other candidate X, the lack of identity is clear. The paralogical character of such thinking, unfortunately, may not have much to do with its success.

There is no question that breaking down problems into syllogistic form can make for more accurate thinking. However, as a technique it is subject to serious limitations.

In the first place, it is easily used only in cases which can be treated in all-or-none form. While many issues fit into this formula, others do not. Secondly, the syllogism depends upon the use of concepts which assign events to certain classes. This means that all terms must be strictly defined. If everyone agrees on the definitions, then syllogistic logic is unassailable. But when the definition is rejected, then the conclusion is rejected too. Can we, then, evolve a technique for improving thinking through the clarification of definitions?

Semantic analysis. It is out of the need for such tools of thought that semantics has developed. The basic principle of semantics is that a word is not the same as its object. Now this may seem too obvious to need repetition; but if it is pursued, the significance becomes apparent.

Suppose we consider the word "apple." This is a symbol for a real object, an edible fruit. However, as a symbol, it abstracts only a few attributes of the whole object. For example, "apple" to a cook may mean the raw material for a pie—until she finds a worm in the fruit. "Apple" to a hungry boy means something to munch on—until he finds that it is green. "Apple" has different meanings to farmer, broker, and grocer. Thus, if we start behaving toward symbols as if they were physically real objects, we are likely to make serious errors.

The abstraction process. The purpose of semantic analysis is to reveal the effects of different kinds of abstraction upon meaning. Ultimately, the purpose is to increase precision of thinking and communication by using symbols which identify exactly and solely those aspects of reality with which we are concerned. There are always similarities among things; semantics cautions us that there is always a difference too—and the difference is important.

Figure 11:13 shows one device in semantic analysis. This is an analysis of the class concept "cow" at different levels of ab-

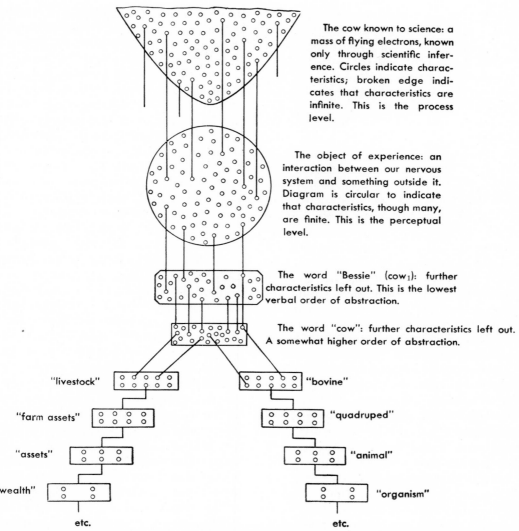

The cow known to science: a mass of flying electrons, known only through scientific inference. Circles indicate characteristics; broken edge indicates that characteristics are infinite. This is the process level.

The object of experience: an interaction between our nervous system and something outside it. Diagram is circular to indicate that characteristics, though many, are finite. This is the perceptual level.

The word "Bessie" (cow₁): further characteristics left out. This is the lowest verbal order of abstraction.

The word "cow": further characteristics left out. A somewhat higher order of abstraction.

"livestock"   "bovine"

"farm assets"   "quadruped"

"assets"   "animal"

"wealth"   "organism"

etc.   etc.

FIG. 11:13. A modification of the Korzybski Structural Differential. This semantic device is intended to emphasize the unitary nature of experienced reality and the fact that all abstractions involve the selection of some partial aspect of reality, ignoring the total experience. Whenever we employ words to symbolize events, much of reality is left out. Thus, when we treat a cow as a "quadruped," we are responding to only one aspect of reality, and must always be prepared to refer back to the real experience from which a partial identity has been abstracted. (*Based on A. Korzybski, Science and Sanity, 2d ed., 1941, Fig. 5, p. 398, by permission of the Alfred Korzybski estate. Labels from S. I. Hayakawa, Language in Action, Harcourt, Brace & Co., 1941.*)

straction. At the physical level, Bessie the cow is simply a mass of electrons and protons in rapid vibration. At the biological level she is a set of organ systems having certain structures and functions. At the perceptual level she is a brown-and-white cow with a pleasant disposition and good milk capacity. At higher orders of abstraction she becomes respectively a mammal, a vertebrate, an animal; or on a differing line, a domestic animal, a piece of farm equipment, or a capital asset. Now it can obviously lead to serious misunderstanding if the word "cow" is used without reference to the level of abstraction implied. The difficulty was once graphically presented by a cartoon showing two people, each saying "I like fish" but one is thinking of an aquarium and one of broiled filet.

It is necessary that symbols become abstract and generalized. This means that the symbol "cow" for example, loses the characteristics of Bessie the gentle Holstein and refers only to the attributes of the entire class. Unfortunately, in our day-to-day thinking, we need to use both kinds of symbols—those relating to concrete individual cases, and those relating to the class concept. Many errors in thinking result from the confusion of these two uses. It must be noted, nonetheless, that higher order generalizations are basic to our complex civilization. If we could not employ the abstract concepts of mass, force, and relativity, most of our prized technological achievements would never had developed.

High-level generalizations run the risk of ignoring facts on the physical level; on the other hand, a low level of abstraction may degenerate into citing specific examples but getting no broad guiding principles from them. At the one end of the scale we have high-minded discussions of democracy as dependent upon liberty, equality, and human rights, but ignoring economic handicaps, racial discrimination, and so on; at the other end of the scale people engage in the mechanical listing of endless observations without drawing conclusions. Efficient thinking in the service of human motives demands both kinds of symbolic process. The semanticists emphasize that we must indicate clearly at what level of abstraction we are operating. It is helpful to think of an abstract concept as an hypothesis, having some undefined probability of predicting real occurrences. The value of the concept increases as its probability in accurate prediction goes up.

Time indexes. Not only does semantics

lead us to recognize the dangers of different levels of abstraction; it has also focused attention on the time variable. Bessie the cow in 1940 is not the same as Bessie the cow in 1950. Neither the German government nor the German people as of 1939 should be identified with the German government and people of 1929. More important, perhaps, from the point of view of personality and immediate family adjustment, is the fact that individuals also need a time index. $Mother_{1930}$ is not the same person as $Mother_{1950}$. Incorrect identification on this level leads to many personal frustrations or family conflicts. We shall elaborate on this point in Chap. 13.

Et cetera. Finally, semanticists have emphasized the fact that a great many statements really should be followed by *etc.* The statement is inclusive but not exclusive. A cigarette advertisement, for example, says "Pall Malls are mild, easy on the throat." Implicitly this suggests exclusion—other cigarettes are not. The implied conclusion of course is false but intentional. If the statement were "Pall Malls and other cigarettes are mild" it would have less sales value but more validity.

When we use stereotypes or group labels the use of *etc.*, either explicitly or implicitly, is desirable. One may say "Negroes are dirty" and validate this for some members of the Negro race; but it would be more accurate to say "Negroes, etc., are dirty," thus clearly indicating that the generalization applies to other groups equally.

Every word in the English language has a history, and this means that it has a symbolic value including more than its dictionary definition. When the word "mind" is employed, it carries a whole series of metaphysical implications which may—or may not—be intended by the user. Thus if we make use of abstraction levels, time indexing, and the *etc.* device, we reduce the probabilities of error due to these unwanted implications. Words are major

TABLE 11:3. Terms Used by the Chicago Tribune and by the New York Times in References to the Same Event
(*Based on Sargent, 1939*)

New York Times	Emotional value*		Chicago Tribune
	Times	Tribune	
Progressive.....................	+92	−53	Radical
Senate investigation............	+57	−38	Government witch hunting†
Regulation.....................	+32	−53	Regimentation
Maritime leader................	+10	−68	Communist CIO leader
Labor organizer................	+12	−63	Labor agitator
Home relief....................	+27	−35	The dole
Crop control...................	−02	−55	Farm dictatorship
Nonstrikers....................	+08	+60	Loyal workers
Investigator...................	+23	−22	Inquisitor†
CIO Chieftain..................	−33	−72	CIO Dictator
Foreign........................	0	−35	Alien
Picketing......................	−50	−55	Mass picketing

* Sixty college students judged the words to be pleasant (+) or unpleasant (−) without any information as to the source of the terms.

† A recheck of the *Tribune's* pages during the days of Senator McCarthy's investigations of the State Department indicates that this term is not used when *Tribune* policy is friendly to the investigator.

tools of thought. But, like most tools, they may slip and cut us—or others. The techniques of semantic analysis clarify the relationship between stimulus and response so that such accidents are less probable.

Language and feeling. One of the reasons for the suggestion that nouns should be followed by *etc.* is that most words carry, in addition to factual reference, a certain quality of feeling or emotion. Semantic analysis seeks to eliminate this additional unwanted freight, so that words can be used as precise tools for thinking.

In many cases words are deliberately selected because of this additional, emotional value. Sargent (1939) did a study of the use of emotionally toned words by the Chicago *Tribune* in news stories about New Deal activities, labor unions, and other groups to which *Tribune* policy is violently opposed. For comparison he tallied the words used in the corresponding stories (describing the same "real" event) in the *New York Times*. Table 11:3 shows his major results. It is obvious at a glance that

the *Tribune* writers selected words which would adequately convey their feelings to the reader and could reasonably be expected to evoke the same hostility in him. We are not concerned with whether this is ethical journalism; from a psychologist's viewpoint, this illustrates how language can be systematically utilized to indoctrinate readers with a specific set of biases—to influence thinking.

Language, thought, and action. Any difference between feeling and action, in the present context, may be considered unimportant. The advertiser and the propagandist seek to evoke feelings as a preliminary to action. The advertiser wants people to have pleasant feelings toward his product but eventually to convert feeling into purchase. The propagandist will be seeking for votes, for mob action, for financial contributions, or for other tangible manifestations of approval.

It is true, of course, that language and thought also have a more immediate relation to action. In infancy one learns that crying is likely to lead to being picked up, caressed, and fed. In early childhood, the word "mama" has magical power to bring satisfying action from others. As he grows older, he acquires a wider vocabulary with which he can induce others to act in his behalf.

He must also learn the reverse of this relationship. Words are used as demands upon him to do certain things. In this reciprocal process of give and take, the child learns to distinguish himself as an individual from other individuals, and he should learn how to take the role of another toward himself. At this age we hear the child giving himself instructions, acting out the role of the parent and then his own response. Later this process of self-instruction reduces to a series of implicit activities —images, words, muscle tensions—by which he cues his own actions.

If the child is overprotected, if parents do too much for him and make too few demands in return, he remains selfish and egocentric. He has never learned to instruct himself, to take the role of others, to see himself as others see him. The thinking of such a child is distorted, and his ability at communication—especially in receiving messages from others—is seriously limited. His problem solutions will be relatively autistic; he will expect others to do things for him and will ignore their desires and wishes as relevant factors in a problem.

Most scientific psychologists would agree to the proposition that language is a tool of thought, recognizing that the word is an unusual tool. Perhaps the best analogy for communicating here would be to compare language with a map. The map is a guide to a territory, but it is not the territory. It would be virtually impossible, in many cases, to think without words, but this does not mean that the words constitute the total process of thinking. It is probable that much of thought never gets expressed in words; thought is so complex

and individualized that language gives only a simplified version of the part which can be communicated to others. Painting, music, and sculpture indicate that man can sometimes communicate meanings not capable of being wrapped in words.

Language and reasoning. The expression of feelings and the part of factual thinking that cannot be communicated are probably highly individual in character. When a man says, "that scene depresses me," he is not making a statement which can be validated by others. We have used the term *autistic thinking* to identify thinking which is not restricted by the requirements of "reality" and the agreement of other observers. Reasoning, by contrast, was thinking which eventuated in conclusions which could be checked by others.

Language and reasoning, then, must be very closely related, since reasoning must make use of the common attributes of reality. If we wish to have our conclusions validated by others, we must abandon our unique thoughts and communicate those aspects which can be formulated in words (including mathematical and other symbols). The artist may, of course, reject reasoning in favor of his private intuition; there is nothing wrong with this course except that it means cutting off communication with people around us.

In a sense, this is what has happened to the schizophrenic. As the quotation on page 401 indicates, the schizophrenic patient is using language to express his own autistic thoughts, without much regard for communication value. The words have been redefined to fit his unique system of meanings and so may be much more satisfying as a form of expression. But this distortion makes reasoning impossible.

The Psychology of Invention

So far we have traced the process of thinking by identifying symbols and examining their characteristics. Symbols may be memory images, words, or implicit movements. Their flow is determined by the principles of association—contiguity, frequency, similarity, etc. From this flow or stream of consciousness, motives impel the individual to select some and reject others. Since language makes such a large segment of our stock of symbols, we paid particular attention to the impact of language on thinking.

Let us now get down to the real nub of the matter. The purpose of thinking is need satisfaction. Thinking is therefore closely related to the type of learning we have described as problem solving. In that chapter we emphasized that man exerts himself to restructure his environment and perceive new relationships only under pressure from some inner tension. The same holds for reasoning, or problem solving by thinking.[1]

Stages in reasoning. It may help us to get a clear picture of the reasoning process if we break it up into stages. John Dewey (1933), the great American philosopher, has formalized reasoning as a five-step process: (1) awareness of a problem (and motive to solve it); (2) collection of facts needed to solve it; (3) formation of hypotheses or possible solutions; (4) evaluation of these hypotheses against the facts collected; and (5) verification, or actually trying out a solution which seems valid. He gives an example from one of his students, as follows:

Projecting nearly horizontally from the upper deck of the ferry boat on which I daily cross the river, is a long white pole, bearing a gilded ball at its tip. It suggested a flagpole when I

[1] In case there is any doubt, let it be stated clearly that the difference between problem solving and thinking is in the use of symbols. In Chap. 9 we analyzed instances of learning by the actual manipulation of objects. In the present context we are concerned with problem solving by the manipulation of symbols—words and images. Obviously the two frequently go on together.

first saw it; its color, shape, and gilded ball agreed with the idea, and these reasons seemed to justify me in this belief. But soon difficulties suggested themselves. The pole was nearly horizontal, an unusual position for the flagpole; in the next place, there was no pulley, ring or cord by which to attach a flag; finally, there were elsewhere two vertical staffs from which flags were occasionally flown. It seemed probable that the pole was not there for flagflying.

I then tried to imagine all possible purposes of such a pole, and consider for which of these it was best suited: (a) Possibly it was an ornament. But as all the ferryboats and even the tugboats carried like poles, this hypothesis was rejected. (b) Possibly it was the terminal of a wireless telegraph. But the same considerations made this improbable. Besides, the more natural place for such a terminal would be the highest part of the boat, on top of the pilot house. (c) Its purpose might be to point out the direction in which the boat is moving.

In support of this conclusion, I discovered that the pole was lower than the pilot house, so that the steerman could easily see it. Moreover, the tip was enough higher than the base, so that, from the pilot's position, it must appear to project far in front of the boat. Moreover, the pilot being near the front of the boat, he would need some such guide as to its direction. Tugboats would also need poles for such a purpose. This hypothesis was so much more probable than the others that I accepted it. I formed the conclusion that the pole was set up for the purpose of showing the pilot the direction in which the boat was pointed, to enable him to steer correctly.[1]

In this account it is easy to distinguish (1) the problem: what is the function of the pole? Stage 2 involves data as to its shape, position, location, absence of pulleys, etc., which are relevant to a solution. Stage 3 and stage 4 are mingled as he considers, evaluates, and rejects two hypotheses before accepting the third, to the effect that the pole served as a steering aid. Stage 5, verification, is not listed, but

[1] Dewey (1933), pp. 69–70. Reprinted by permission of D. C. Heath and Company.

it should be noted that the student inquired of the ferry captain and learned that he had reasoned correctly.

Improving reasoning. It would seem likely that a knowledge of Dewey's five stages, with some practice in applying them, would make for greater efficiency in reasoning. No experimental studies exactly of this type are available, but one by Marks (1951) is rather close. He taught some of his statistics students a formula for analyzing sources of error in a statistical computation. Then he deliberately contrived a situation in which they were caused to make errors, and observed them to see whether the training was of value.

The students were engaged in the use of computing machines for solving certain routine statistical problems. Marks provided them with conversion tables for certain functions which were beyond their training at that point. He deliberately inserted an error in one of these tables. The question was, would the student locate the source of his error?

In the lecture on problem solving, he had told half the subjects that there were four possible sources of error in such a situation: (1) the operator himself, (2) the machine, (3) the method, and (4) the tables. Since the students could systematically demonstrate that 1, 2, and 3 could not be the source of the error, they should have been led immediately to checking the tables (the error in which could be detected by successive inspection of entries). An interesting result emerged at this point: those students who worked on the problem with tables handed them by their professor had great difficulty locating the error, apparently because their confidence in him (or inability to suspect him) blocked critical examination of the tables! However, when similar students worked on the task as an *impersonal* problem (not related to their own instructor), they solved it much faster.

The lectures on problem solving by themselves did not seem to be of value. If, however, the student was reminded, during his search for the error, of the four elements to be inspected, the speed of solution mounted rapidly. One may suspect that most lecture notes likewise fail to function unless the student is reminded that they are relevant.

Finally, Marks noted a very high relationship ($r = .83$) between amount of vocalization and success. Those students who talked a lot to themselves or to others about the problem were most successful. Since the significant symbols here are verbal, and since talking gives an opportunity for recombination of words in new patterns, this makes very good sense.

The role of set. We noted at the beginning of this chapter that set can either facilitate or inhibit reasoning, depending on its appropriateness. Without set one could not keep focused on his task and hence would never solve a problem. But set can also block productive hypotheses. One may get set for a roundabout solution and thus overlook an obvious direct path to the goal. The study by Marks suggests that undue confidence in an authority can block a solution. Probably any strong motive, such as love, hate, fear, or patriotism, prevents us from observing certain problem solutions.

One of the major blocks to successful reasoning and creative thinking lies in this focusing function. Because the individual keeps producing hypotheses based on a single approach to the problem, he never backs off and gets a broader look, thus being able to see the appropriate technique. College professors do not make as many inventions as they should, because they teach the old, established solutions so often that the situation is rigidly perceived in terms of these patterns. One does not make an invention without a good set of data on the problem; but it may help not to be too firmly set in the orthodox pattern of solution of related problems.

Because of this blocking by inappropriate set, it is often good practice, when dealing with a tough problem, to drop it completely for a time. Coming back to it afresh, one may see a totally new approach which had simply been ignored before. Graham Wallas (1926) holds that an essential step in creative thinking is *incubation;* after you have steeped yourself in the facts, you must drop the problem and relax for a time. Presumably, during this interval, spontaneous recombinations of images will occur. Suddenly you get the new hypothesis which solves your problem, as in the tale of Archimedes leaping from his bath and rushing through the streets with his solution to the problem of the king's crown.

The solution of problems demands the invention of new gadgets, new techniques, and new operations. The term *invention* applies equally to the steam engine, the corporation, and the town meeting. If man is to satisfy his needs, he keeps running up against situations for which he has no ready-made solution. He must invent one.

The psychology of invention goes back to the problem of attributes and identities. We have stressed the principle that reasoning involves the "realistic" determination of identities and that autistic thinking involves identities based on irrelevant attributes. Semantics helps us to determine what is realistic in the way of symbols. Now it is possible to have realistic inventions and autistic inventions. A realistic invention is one which can be validated by other observers—*e.g.*, a steam engine. It consists of a set of parts brought together because someone first put these parts together as symbols. The accuracy of this new combination of ideas is shown by the fact that it works.

We can illustrate an autistic invention by the following anecdote.

I was visiting a mental hospital with a psychology class. One of the patients drew me aside and explained that he had been unjustly confined there on the complaint of relatives, and it was important for him to escape. He wanted me to help him get away. If I did so, he would reward me with a half-interest in a tree he possessed which grew Swift's Premium hams and bacon.

Luther Burbank invented various kinds of hybrid fruits and vegetables. But his inventions fitted generally accepted concepts and could be verified. This patient's invention was autistic; it could not be checked by other observers.

The process of invention. One way to describe the invention process is in terms of schema formation. When we establish certain kinds of relationships among observed events, we may come up with an invention. Spearman proposed that this be called the *eduction of relations.* In form it is like the simple analogies among attributes which were illustrated earlier in this chapter. Spearman starts his discussion with such an analogy:

Apple is to Apple Tree as Milk is to _____?

Having one pair of items for which a schema already has been learned, the observer then takes a third item and tries to fit it into a similar schema. In this case one comes out with cow as the fourth term.

One of Spearman's students (Cattell, 1941) illustrates this method of generalizing an analogy to produce an invention, as follows: Trevithick was an engineer in a mine, where he installed a steam engine, a thing of metal, to replace a donkey working the pumps which removed surplus water from the mine.

But he remembered also that a donkey can be used not only as a source of power, but also as a means of locomotion. He reasoned:

Donkey as   steam   donkey as
source of   is to   engine   as   means of
power   locomotion
                      is to   _____

In this way the first vague conception of the steam locomotive was born. The practical details were further eductions within the framework of this idea.

By this application of relationships, therefore, it is possible for us to have ideas of things which we have never actually known, or of purely fanciful things which we can never hope to meet. Somewhere in the depths of primitive life the longing for love and protection must have evoked in many early thinkers the process, "child is to father as father is to _____" and given rise to the conception of God.[1]

In such thinking we have a rearrangement of symbols of prior experiences, giving rise to a new perceptual pattern. It is theoretically possible that every experience be paired with every other experience. However, looking at these combinations, we see that the vast majority are meaningless and useless. Sometimes, though, we have the "insight" experience: "Ah ha! I see something important here!" The French mathematician, Jacques Hadamard, has written about the process of invention in his own field, and in science generally, as follows:

Indeed, it is obvious that invention or discovery, be it in mathematics or anywhere else, takes place by combining ideas. Now there is an extremely great number of such combinations, most of which are devoid of interest, while, on the contrary, very few of them can be fruitful. Which ones do our minds—I mean our conscious minds—perceive? Only fruitful ones, or exceptionally, some which could be fruitful.

However, to find these fruitful ones it has been necessary to construct the very numerous possible combinations among which the useful ones are to be found.

It cannot be avoided that this first operation takes place, to a certain extent, at random, so that the role of chance is hardly doubtful in the first step of the mental process. But we see that that intervention of chance occurs inside the unconscious; for most of these combinations—more exactly, all those which are useless—remain unknown to us. . . . This shows the manifold character of the unconscious, which is necessary to construct those numerous combinations and to compare them with each other.[1]

The concept of memory images, experiences, or ideas being linked at random to create new concepts must inevitably seem strange at first glance. And yet more careful consideration will suggest that this must be the correct interpretation. Every experience in man's life must be potentially available for linkage with any other. The striking, the impressive accomplishment of Albert Einstein in developing his generalized theory of relativity lies precisely in the fact that he so successfully linked observations from widely diverse fields, such as the movements of the planets, the changes in color of starlight, the falling of apples from their twigs, and the measurement of distances. Every child learns to identify as a "chair" a variety of objects having no particular visual similarity to one another (especially in this day of modern furniture design). All abstract concepts—democracy, charity, competition—tie together a variety of experiences which bear little or no superficial resemblance to each other.

In early years the child makes by analogy many random linkages which merely amuse adults. He learns that the table has legs, and so he speaks of the table's knee. All men are called "daddy," and anything that moves is said to be alive. (These are not truly random, but they approach that condition.) In his imaginative processes he hooks up human, animal, and object characteristics indiscriminately. Dreams

[1] Cattell (1941), pp. 427–428. Reprinted by permission of Sci-Art Publishers.

[1] Hadamard (1945), p. 29. Reprinted by permission of Princeton University Press.

and free fantasy, even in adults, show how wide a range of random linkages is possible.

But most of these do not, in adult life, succeed in reaching consciousness. We have shown, in connection with the perception of physical objects, that the mind is a "lightning calculator"; that it can add up cues and reach a conclusion as to the existence of a complex object, within a time span almost too brief to be measured. Experiments have shown that one can react to a stimulus without being aware of that stimulus. So it is no form of mysticism to assert that the organism can link up, randomly, experiences A and B, decide that the linkage is useless, and reject the whole idea, before consciousness develops. I could, for example, imagine that there is a lion in my bedroom closet. Such a random association of ideas would be screened out had I not deliberately set myself to look for one. But the thought of a moth in the closet not only gets through for conscious consideration; it may even lead to action (hunting for evidence, and installation of insecticides). The normal person acts on combinations which have a fair "probability value," while screening out those which are highly improbable. People whose selective mechanism breaks down are considered insane.

What are the principles governing this screening process? A moment's consideration will indicate that everything we have discussed in the area of psychology up to this point is relevant. Linkages get through to consciousness if they (1) have a bearing on need satisfaction, (2) correspond to perceptions which have seemed real, (3) fit in with past learning, or (4) suggest a path out of a problem situation. However, these factors do not determine whether this novel combination of symbols will work. That depends on the success with which the thinker has picked out significant attributes or identities.

The problem of creative thinking. Crea-

tive or original thinking has not been, as yet, successfully explored in the laboratory. The studies available indicate that the steps in creativity are essentially similar to those in problem solving (page 413). However, great inventions are not improvised in the laboratory. The most fruitful source of information is that obtained from the reports of the mental processes of great inventors, mathematicians, scientists, artists, and writers who have either written about their discoveries or have answered the questions of investigators. Great ideas are not readily come upon by sheer methodological analysis. It is true that great innovators usually have a rich background of knowledge and experience in their field, but their most significant ideas often come suddenly and unexpectedly after a logical appraisal of various hypotheses has led to nothing. A wellknown example is Poincaré's solution of a difficult mathematical problem suddenly while getting into a taxi to go to an opera. Such incidents, which are called *illuminations*, have been attributed to "unconscious cerebration."

It is unnecessary to place the burden of creativity on the unconscious. When we are tired of the problem and abandon it, we still tend to mull over it. The problem set tends to persist, as we saw in the studies on incomplete tasks. With a change of scene, the tendency to attack the problem from certain preferred orientations is broken down; the mind tolerates suggestions which in the working situation were not allowed central attention. In this less serious mood there is less rigorous rejection of what would have been considered improbable combinations of ideas. This playful tolerance of thoughts too bizarre to consider seriously may, in the tired or relaxed mood, permit them expression. Some of these "click."

The creative genius. Creative genius is rare. It is estimated that of all the people that have lived in historical times, only two in a million could be called *geniuses* (page 447). Psychologists have raised questions such as these: Why do so many geniuses spring from parents who are themselves far from distinguished? Why is there so little apparent correlation between education and creative productivity? Why do we not produce a greater number of creative geniuses than we do, under supposedly enlightened, modern educational practices? There is evidence that great men have had high IQ's; but Terman's 1,000 children of very high IQ's, who are now mature, have yet to produce a person of creative genius.

Such considerations lead to the assumption that genius is a special disposition in personality as well as ability. Recently Bluemel (1948), a psychiatrist, has speculated on the drives of great men. He distinguishes between dynamic and aggressive or belligerent people. His group of dynamic persons who are not belligerent produces the kind of accomplishments we are concerned with here. He attributes their success to a "tendency to obsessive compulsions." "An obsession is a thought which cannot be readily dismissed from the mind. The thought may dominate one's actions as well as one's thinking, and it then becomes a compulsion as well as an obsession."[1] Bluemel illustrates the obsessive trait in the Wright brothers, describing the extremes to which they went in attempting to build a heavier-than-air flying machine.

Persistence is certainly one of the personality traits of great minds. But an open mind, willingness to consider new possibilities, no matter how bizarre they may be on first impression, is probably the most important trait. A person who is too impressed by authoritative opinion and accepted beliefs and modes of thinking is too rigid mentally and too conventional emotionally to get new ideas. Inventiveness

[1] Bluemel (1948), pp. 29–30.

requires not so much the courage of one's convictions, but more the courage to take one's fancies seriously. We do not know the exact pattern of traits which constitutes creativity, but we offer these suggestions to show that personality traits (given certain abilities) are the determining factors in whether a person will or will not create.

Hutchinson recently published a book entitled *How to Think Creatively* which is based on firsthand materials such as letters, comments, interviews, and questionnaires obtained from about 250 famous contemporary thinkers of England and America. Hutchinson illustrates two types of creative thinkers: the expert craftsmen in ideas who systematically go through the formal stages in reasoning, on the one hand, and those who report solutions which seem to arise by accident. Edison worked largely by systematic analysis of hypotheses. He is quoted as saying: "But when it comes to problems of a mechanical nature, I want to tell you that all I have ever tackled and solved have been done by *hard logical thinking*. . . . I speak without exaggeration when I say that I have constructed three thousand different theories in connection with the electric light, each one of them reasonable and likely to be true. Yet in two cases only did my experiments prove the truth of my theory."[1] On the other hand, Rosanoff, long an associate of Edison, found success by studying a problem, then relaxing and waiting for an insight to develop. Apparently either technique may lead to the creation of new ideas or gadgets.

It is interesting to note that most of us feel quite a thrill of joy upon solving a difficult problem. This is a function of the *tension reduction* which is accomplished. During the quest for a solution, motivational tension has built up. Energy is mobilized in the attempt to overcome the obstacle. Then, suddenly, the goal is

[1] Hutchinson (1949), pp. 14–15. Reprinted by permission.

FIG. 11:14. The process of thinking. Thinking is homeostatic in character. We do not engage in reasoning unless something disturbs equilibrium. As tension develops, more of the organism's resources are mobilized, and action (either overt or implicit) increases. Several hypotheses may be considered, one of them leads to insight, the organism achieves the goal, and equilibrium is restored.

achieved; the tension is drained off in the exuberance of joyful emotion.

Creative Thinking and Identities

Reasoning goes on as we establish partial identities between different objects or classes of objects and draw conclusions from these identifications. The subtlety and complexity of thinking is directly a function of the kinds of identities set up by the thinker. Ordinary everyday thinking uses simple, obvious identities. When we say: "All men are mortal; Socrates is a man; therefore, Socrates is mortal," we are making a simple identification based on Socrates's physical characteristics. When we say: "Harder substances can be used to scratch softer materials; diamonds are harder than glass; therefore, diamonds can be used to scratch glass," we set up partial identities based on the attributes hard and soft.

Creative thinking, however, is distinguished by the very fact that the identities employed are unusual. When Trevithick invented the steam locomotive, he mentally identified the steam engine with the donkey pulling a cart. His creative act was the making of a novel identification, based on an attribute (transporting force) which had not previously been noted by other men. When Archimedes discovered the technique of measuring the gold content of the crown by displacement of water, he identified his own bulk displacing water with that of the crown. The technical details (getting equal weights of gold and silver to use as standards) came later. The basic phenomenon of invention, discovery, or creation of ideas seems to be that of perceiving *a novel basis upon which to assert a partial identity*.

In ordinary thinking such identification is usually based upon a directly observable feature of the stimulus, as in stimulus generalization. Similarity in color, sound, size, or shape will serve. At a slightly higher level similarities in function (edibility, power source, political institutions) can be employed. At the most complex level of thought, identities are based upon symbols and usually derive from some abstract schema (for instance, Einstein's "field" concept identifies as fundamentally similar many natural phenomena which do not look at all alike to the lay observer). But such identifications must not be made at random; at least, only the insane do so. Successful thinking occurs as we make novel identifications which are *related to the goal;* the new analogy must be one which will stand the test of verification. Hence autistic thinking cannot serve as a basis for invention; such thinking is too far divorced from real objects and conditions.

Some everyday thinking involves little more than putting familiar symbols together in an unfamiliar order. I come home and find the house locked; I have forgotten my key. However, I picture an unlocked upstairs window and a ladder in the garage. Soon I am comfortably at home. Creative reasoning may involve familiar steps in an unfamiliar order, but the relation to the goal is hidden and so there may be a long period of blockage, until the person happens to perceive an arrangement of these steps which will get him to the goal. This sudden awareness of a path to the goal gives the surprising quality to insight. As Fig. 11:14 suggests, it is the building up of tension, the search for paths (hypotheses), and finally, insight, with tension reduction, which sum up the process of thinking.

SUMMARY

In this chapter we have considered thinking within a broad frame of reference. Thought occurs wherever symbolic processes are essential to the activity. Much thinking, then, is a simple, routine matter of making judgments based on past experience. Also, much thinking is private and autistic in character—reminiscences, fantasies based on memory images, and so on. The psychological analysis of thinking must give an adequate account of such human activities, as well as of man's feats of complex reasoning, creative imagination, and invention.

We have shown how evidence from anthropology, psychoanalysis, and everyday observation can help us to understand man's thinking process. Dreams illustrate thought with little control from mental set. Motivation is important, but there is no selective mechanism operating to exclude the bizarre, the irrational, from coming through to awareness.

Problem solving has been more emphasized in most discussions of thinking because it can be dealt with experimentally. It can be observed, influenced from outside, and verified by reality testing. But most of man's everyday thinking does not really correspond to the problem-solving pattern. Even when we start out to solve a problem, if it is reasonably complex and has emotional significance, we are likely to reach an autistic solution based on prejudice and then accept it as a rational answer.

We have shown that there are common features running through autistic and logical thinking. Both make use of the process of observing partial identities based on attributes. In the dream, a tabooed sexual object may be symbolized by a neutral, nonsexual object which has some attribute perceivable as an identity (shape, for example). Reasoning progresses as one notes identities which can be manipulated on the reality level, as in the invention of the steam locomotive.

Thinking can be improved, made more efficient and thus more adaptive in obtaining need satisfactions. The syllogism compels us to make explicit unconscious assumptions of identity which, often enough, prove to be false. The diagramed syllogism has proved particularly useful in separating necessary from unnecessary conclusions about identities. Semantics gets at a problem even more fundamental: showing us how to analyze our percepts and concepts to determine if an attribute is available to be identified with one from another abstract symbol. Semantic analysis indicates that much paralogical thinking arises because we assume attributes to be present which are not there.

Underlying the whole process of thinking is motivation. Perhaps idle reminiscence might occur in a completely unmotivated individual—but, more likely, he would go to sleep. Certainly the active quest for a solution to a problem is always dependent upon some tension. In much everyday thinking the solution is found so rapidly, tension reduced so quickly, that this generalization seems questionable. But in fact, whenever we examine any kind of problem solving, from the simplest to the most abstract and complex, we find this to be true. In difficult instances, the building up of tension and the joy associated with insight are familiar to everyone.

Recommended Readings[1]

DEWEY, J.: *How We Think.* (rev. ed.) Boston: Heath, 1933.

DOWNEY, JUNE E.: *Creative Imagination.* New York: Harcourt, Brace, 1929.

HADAMARD, J.: *Psychology of Invention in the Mathematical Field.* Princeton, N.J.: Princeton University Press, 1945.

HUMPHREY, G.: *Directed Thinking.* New York: Dodd, Mead, 1948.

HUTCHINSON, E. D.: *How to Think Creatively.* Nashville: Abingdon-Cokesbury, 1949.

KASANIN, J. S. (Ed.): *Language and Thought in Schizophrenia.* Berkeley: University of California Press, 1944.

PIAGET, J.: *Judgment and Reasoning in the Child.* New York: Harcourt, Brace, 1928.

———: *The Language and Thought of the Child.* New York: Harcourt, Brace, 1932.

RIGNANO, E.: *The Psychology of Reasoning.* New York: Harcourt, Brace, 1923.

SPEARMAN, C.: *Creative Mind.* New York: Appleton-Century-Crofts, 1931.

THOULESS, R. H.: *How to Think Straight.* New York: Simon and Schuster, 1939.

TITCHENER, E. B.: *Experimental Psychology of Higher Thought Processes.* New York: Macmillan, 1909.

WALLAS, G.: *The Art of Thought.* New York: Harcourt, Brace, 1926.

WERTHEIMER, MAX: *Productive Thinking.* New York: Harper, 1945.

[1] See also p. 547.

CHAPTER 12

Intelligence

So far our discussion of psychology has centered around general laws of behavior and experience. We have been concerned first with the principles of motivation, the development of inner needs, the quest for homeostasis, the identification of goals. In a second series of chapters we have described how the individual explores his environment (sensation, perception) in search of gratification, and how he learns action patterns which will bring about tension reduction and satisfaction (learning, thinking).

An understanding of these basic laws is vital to the comprehension of human psychology. But they are not enough. You and I, as persons, deal with other human beings as specific individuals, and not as generalized abstractions. All individuals obey these laws, but they show wide variation with regard to such parameters as speed and complexity of functioning. It now becomes important, therefore, to deal with some of the scientific findings regarding *differences between individuals*.

Kinds of abilities. It may be worth noting at the outset that the term *ability* is a class term relating to many specific functions of the individual. Thus we can study individual differences in *visual* functioning, and we find that human beings differ as regards acuity of near vision, distance

vision, color vision, and so on. Wide differences occur in *auditory* sensitivity and in various other modalities.

In the *motor* sphere, people differ in speed and power of gross muscular actions (running, jumping) and in speed and coordination of fine movements of the fingers, lips, etc. To some extent variations may depend on sensitivity (of sense organs in muscles and joints), to heredity of muscular tissue, or to differences in the central nervous mechanisms controlling motor acts. Variations in musical and artistic performance are almost certainly complex combinations of all three of these possibilities.

Learning is a function which we find in all human beings, but there is an enormous range of speed and complexity of learning possible. At the lower extreme we have some feeble-minded cases who at maturity have not yet learned the acts normal to a child of two years. At the upper extreme we have persons who deal with fabulously complex abstract functions such as nuclear physics, biochemistry, or the philosophy of society. This dimension of ability, which corresponds more or less to what we call *intelligence*, is of especially great importance.

How the psychologist studies abilities. First, a word about the general problem of methodology in studying ability. Without being technical, we must explain a little about how the psychologist identifies a specific ability and separates it from the numerous other human abilities. The necessity for this can be quickly illustrated from the vocational field. The particular abilities which are predictive of success as a physician are not the same as those predictive of success as a lawyer. It might be colloquially correct to say that it takes "a lot of ability" to succeed in either field, but for purposes of advising young men about a career, this loose expression is not satisfactory. We must therefore identify fairly specific abilities and measure the extent to which they are present in a given individual.

Covariation. The key concept in identification of an ability is the concept of covariation. Suppose we find that little Johnny is the speediest runner in his gang and can also jump farthest. Tommy, on the other hand, is low man in both contests. We are immediately tempted to infer that we have here a general athletic ability dimension. If running and jumping vary together (relative standing on one predicts relative standing on the other), then we assume that there must be something (an ability) which determines both functions.

This is actually the way in which scientific psychology has gone about identifying groups of performances which lump together as "abilities," and about distinguishing one ability from another. Consider the following table:

	Scores on	
	Arithmetic	*Vocabulary*
John Jones..........	98	76
Bill Smith...........	93	74
Tom Fry.............	81	68
Henry Brown........	78	65
Sam Allen...........	71	62

In this case (with a very small sample, of course), covariation is perfect. Every man who exceeds Sam on arithmetic also exceeds him on vocabulary. And this is true of every other person in the table. If we found such data consistently for considerable numbers of subjects, we would be justified in inferring the presence of a single ability underlying both these tests.

Correlation coefficient. Because it will be necessary in the following pages to use and compare correlation coefficients, we pause for a moment to define and illustrate them. The correlation coefficient is a numerical measure of the extent of covariation of two measures. In the above example, arithmetic and vocabulary correlate perfectly, and this would be expressed by a coefficient of +1.00.

Most test data do not agree so beautifully. (In fact, arithmetic and vocabulary tests do not correlate that well; the sample was arbitrarily chosen to illustrate the point.) In the following example, we have merely ranked men in order of performance on two tests for speed of learning:

	Performance on		d	d^2
	Poetry	*Maze*		
John Jones.........	1	3	2	4
Bill Smith..........	2	1	1	1
Tom Fry...........	3	2	1	1
Henry Brown.......	4	5	1	1
Sam Allen..........	5	4	1	1
				8

If we have a small number of cases, we can compute the correlation coefficient rapidly by this formula:[1]

$$\rho = 1 - \frac{6(\Sigma d^2)}{n(n^2 - 1)}$$

in which d is the man's difference in rank on the two tests, and n is the number of

[1] Better formulas will be found in textbooks on statistics. See, *e.g.*, Edwards (1946).

men. Thus, in the example, d^2 adds up to 8, and n is 5.

$$\rho = 1 - \frac{6 \times 8}{5(25 - 1)} = 1 - \frac{48}{120} = +.60$$

The correlation coefficient of $+.60$ can thus be interpreted by saying that, in general, people superior on one test do better than average on the other, but there are frequent exceptions to this rule.

Suppose the order had been:

1	5
2	1
3	3
4	2
5	4

Anyone looking at this table would say that these two tests do not "go together," that is, the covariation is small or non-existent. Actually, the coefficient is $-.10$, very close to zero, or no correlation at all.

Take one more instance:

	Ranking on	
	Grade average	Dates per week
Mary..........	1	5
Betty..........	2	4
Norma.........	3	3
Ruth..........	4	2
Ann...........	5	1

Here we have another perfect correlation, but this time it is negative. The girl who ranks 1 in dates per week ranks 5 in grades, and vice versa. If you compute this coefficient, it comes out to -1.00. It means that there is perfect covariation, but in such a manner that high standing in one respect goes with low standing in another.

Let us summarize, then. We identify abilities by testing various performances of individuals, and finding how they covary. A large correlation coefficient (approaching 1.00) means close agreement of the two

tests; it is easy to predict one from the other. A low coefficient (approaching .00) means little or no covariation; even if you know a man's score on A, you can only guess at his score on B. A *positive* coefficient means that high scores on A tend to go with high scores on B. A *negative* coefficient means that high scores on A go with low scores on B.[1]

With this in mind, let us go on to a consideration of psychological studies on the most widely investigated human ability, intelligence.

Intelligence

What is intelligence? Jesting Pilate might have asked and not waited for an answer. The difficulty with the question is that it suggests a definition in terms of substance. And intelligence is not a physical object. Pilate might have asked, "What is speed?" In this case, we immediately realize that speed is not an object, but a function of performance—the rate of movement of an object in relation to a scale. If we stop the car and search it from stem to stern we never find its "speed." Speed is a performance variable.

Intelligence must be understood as a complex characteristic of human performance. Its two main dimensions are speed and power; how fast the person solves problems and how difficult the problems can be before he fails completely to solve them.

Psychologists have offered various definitions of intelligence. Generally, these have simply focused on different kinds of performance: learning ability, ability to manipulate abstract symbols, ability to use learning in new situations, ability to solve

[1] It should be recognized that a person varies in performance from time to time, and hence his obtained score should be considered as an approximation to his "true ability." This variation is indicated by the *probable error* in psychological measurement.

problems. These definitions simply point to some of the different manifestations; and, indeed, the easiest way to learn what psychologists mean by "intelligence" is to look at some of the devices used in its measurement.

How we measure intelligence. It would be possible to measure individual differences among college students in intelligence, by throwing together a variety of problem-solving and abstract-thinking situations as suggested by these definitions. The test so constructed could be given to many students and the number of right answers in a limited time counted. The person making the largest number of correct answers would be judged most intelligent, and so on. This (with great refinement of detail to eliminate chance errors) is about what is done in preparing tests to predict college success—and such tests do predict rather accurately how well a person will perform.

However, this procedure could not be utilized with young children. Furthermore, it depends upon our assumption that thinking and problem solving are the operations which reveal intelligence. There is no outside criterion against which we can check our tests to see if our assumption is correct. If we start with young children, we can develop such an outside criterion, and it will prove useful in connection with other psychological problems as well.

The concept of mental age. The great French psychologist, Alfred Binet, devised the best solution yet offered for this problem. He proposed this postulate: if there is anything we agree on, it is that intelligence tends to increase year by year, through childhood and adolescence. There are exceptions, *but on the average*, the five-year-old is more intelligent than the four-year-old; the twelve-year-old children are more intelligent than those of eleven, and so on. Hence tests of mental performance arranged in order of difficulty by age levels

should give us a mental age scale. This is precisely what Binet did, and his test of almost fifty years ago, revised and brought up to date by Lewis M. Terman and his students at Stanford University (hence the Stanford-Binet) is still the basic test for intelligence of children.

Here are some of the items indicative of successive mental age levels on the Stanford-Binet for American children (see Fig. 12:1 for materials used):

Mental Age III:

Form board with circle, square, and triangle.

Identifying parts of body (large paper doll, to indicate hair, mouth, ear, and hands).

Mental Age IV:

Naming objects from memory (toy automobile, dog, shoe, etc.; three are presented and named; then, while the child is not looking, one is covered and he is asked to name it from memory).

Pictorial identification (card with pictures of objects; child is asked to "show me what we cook on," "what we carry when it is raining," etc.).

Mental Age VII:

Similarities ("In what way are wood and coal alike?" "Ship and automobile?" etc.).

Copying a diamond (printed in the record booklet).

Mental Age IX:

Verbal absurdities ("I saw a well-dressed young man who was walking down the street with his hands in his pockets and twirling a brand-new cane." "What is foolish about that?")

Defining abstract words (compare, conquer, obedience, etc.).

Repeating five digits reversed.

FIG. 12:1. Stanford-Binet testing kit. The form board, blocks, and miniature objects are used for testing at the very early mental ages. Most of the tests beyond MA 7 use either words or pictures printed in the record booklet and do not involve manipulation of any objects. (*Courtesy of C. H. Stoelting Co., Chicago.*)

Average Adult:

Proverbs (person is asked to explain in his own words the meaning of two or more common proverbs).

Orientation (person is asked "Which direction would you have to face so your *right* hand would be toward the *north?*" etc.).

How is an item placed in the scale? Binet built his scale on the assumption that children vary, *i.e.*, that among six-year-old children there will be some less intelligent and some more intelligent than six years, but the majority will be of six years mental age (MA). Thus he expected a test item to be appropriate to MA 6 if about 75 per cent of six-year children passed it successfully (all the average children, plus those above average). If it were passed by less than 50 per cent, it was too difficult and was moved to a higher level; if it were passed by over 80 per cent, it was too easy and was tried out at a lower age level.

When we say, therefore, that a test item indicates a mental age of 8, we are saying that the typical, average child of eight can just pass it. Conversely, when we say that little Billy has an MA of 8, we mean that he can do those performances characteristic of eight-year-olds.

The concept of the IQ. The MA tells us nothing about relative brightness. Oscar, a bright boy, may have an MA of 8, while Archibald has an MA of 8 and is very dull. How is this? It follows because we have not indicated the chronological age (CA) of the boys. If Oscar is 6, and can do the tests for 8, he is one-third ahead of normal. If Archibald is 12, but passes tests only through 8, he is retarded by one-third.

The *intelligence quotient* converts the MA into an index of brightness. Simply divide MA by CA and multiply by 100. Thus Oscar would have an IQ of 133, but Archibald would rate an IQ of only 67.

The normal intelligence quotient is 100. It cannot be anything else. How did we determine the tests which define an MA of 12? By finding those which can just be passed by the average child of 12. Thus the definition of the MA guarantees that, unless some kind of selection of cases is operating, the average IQ will be 100.

The MA is determined by the number of tests actually passed. For example, consider the case of Sammy, who is six years and eight months old. He passes the following tests on the Binet, and receives mental age credits as shown:

Year		MA credit (months)*
V	All tests passed	60
VI	4 tests passed	8
VII	1 test passed	2
VIII	All tests failed	0
		70

* At most age levels there are six tests. Passing a single test thus earns 2 months' credit; the child must pass all six to get full credit for that year.

Thus Sammy has an MA of 70 months (5 years and 10 months). His CA is 80 months. Then:

$$IQ = {}^{70}\!/_{80} \times 100 = 87$$

Thus he is shown to be slightly retarded, as compared with the standard group of his own chronological age.

Criteria for item selection. We are interested in obtaining items for our tests which will measure the child's performance. That is, we want to include in our scale of mental age some tests which the average child of a stated age can perform successfully, and others which he cannot. But, at the same time, we must try to exclude from the scale the effects of specific training. Our test would measure only education, not basic ability, if we included questions like "When did Columbus cross the Atlantic Ocean?" or "What is the chemical composition of water?"

It will be noted, in conformity with this requirement, that virtually none of the Stanford-Binet items cited above, nor of the other tests cited later, depend on formal school training. Vocabulary items, it is true, depend to some degree on education; yet it is possible for an alert person to learn the definition of words, without attending school, and conversely, many college students do poorly on vocabulary tests. Hence the inclusion of vocabulary as an item in the mental-age scale does not weight education very heavily.

The basic rule which has been applied in devising new intelligence tests is this: *the material must have been equally available to all the persons for whom the test is intended.* This may mean that *all* persons have been exposed to the chance to learn this, or that *no one* is likely to have had such an opportunity. An example of the former is "show me what we cook on" (age IV); counting objects, indicating missing parts of pictures, and so on. Examples of the latter would be repeating digits reversed, verbal absurdities, letter-code substitutions, and other novel problems. (Note that a few children may have played games using "secret codes" and so have developed superior performance on this item; but as it is only one of six for a given age level, it does not offer much of an advantage.) It would, of course, be possible for a parent deliberately to coach a child to give correct answers on all the test items, even well above his age, and thus win a spuriously high IQ; interestingly enough, such coaching gives only a very temporary advantage, as the items above his proper level are forgotten rather quickly.

Obviously this approach to item selection means that tests must be appropriate to the culture in which the child lives. An environment without automobiles and airplanes would not provide the experience background appropriate to the Stanford-Binet. Tests using bow and arrow, identification of animal tracks, etc., might be fair for primitive children but unfair to the

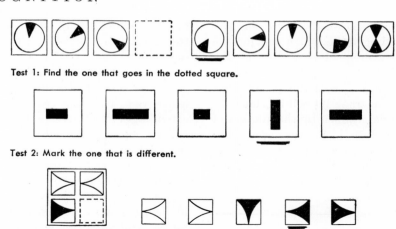

Test 1: Find the one that goes in the dotted square.

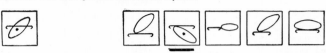

Test 2: Mark the one that is different.

Test 3: Find the one that goes in the dotted square.

Test 4: Find another figure where you can put a dot inside the oval and below the line.

FIG. 12:2. Items from a "culture-free" intelligence test. The test is divided into four parts; one of the demonstration items is shown for each part. Instructions can be given by pantomime, and there is no specific cultural content, but it is much more appropriate to Western culture than to many others. In each sample item, the correct answer has been underscored. (*Courtesy of Dr. R. B. Cattell.*)

city dweller. Some attempts have been made to devise "culture-free" intelligence tests, equally adaptable to all cultures; some items from one by Cattell are shown in Fig. 12:2. Actually, these may be suitable for comparing people of different languages within a highly civilized system such as western Europe; they would not be at all suited to testing preliterate individuals unaccustomed to perceiving minute differences in symbols. Another "culture-free" test is the Porteus maze test (Fig. 12:3) which has been used with a wide variety of primitive groups; it is likewise far from "culture-free."

At present most tests are constructed on the assumption that they are to be used within a definite language and cultural area; tests based on American children do not transfer unchanged even to England. Thus we must standardize the test and determine mental age levels by studying samples of children within the area where the test will be used. In this way we may identify those youngsters who are most alert, most efficient in picking up meanings and abstractions common to their environment.

The Intellectual Functions

It is useful for some purposes to think of intelligence as a general ability, a kind of all-around "goodness of the psychological apparatus." It is, however, productive of greater understanding if we break intelligence down into more specific intellectual functions, at least for examination. We can do that by considering some of the kinds of test items which are successful in differentiating successive levels of intelligence.

Look back at the samples of items from the Stanford-Binet which were reproduced on page 425. If we examine these, and other test items, we find it possible to identify various psychological functions which are

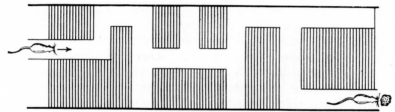

FIG. 12:3. Porteus maze test. This is another nonverbal test. The form illustrated is for MA 5; the rat is added to increase the child's interest. The mazes become very complex toward the adult level. Primarily a test of "foresight" or ability to look ahead for obstacles, the Porteus maze correlates fairly well with the Binet but often reflects personality factors of importance. (*Courtesy of Dr. S. D. Porteus.*)

involved in the increasing mental maturity of successive age levels on the test.

1. *Perception.* In a very real sense, perception is a basic function of the organism. Broadly conceived, intelligence is the capacity for adaptation to the requirements of the environment. Accurate perception of the environment, its characteristics and manipulative possibilities, must precede any adaptive action. Thus we find that early maturation of the ability to perceive forms is indicative of advanced performance (MA 3).

Early perceptions, as we have noted in Chap. 6, tend to be of wholes, total configurations, such as a person or an object. This ability progresses as the person becomes capable of analyzing the total pattern, differentiating parts, locating inappropriate details, etc. So at MA 4 the child is required to note missing details in a drawing of a man and to mark in with a pencil what should be there.

Finally, perception develops to the stage of perceiving similarities and differences among objects. It is difficult to be sure whether our tests get indications, at the early age levels, of differential perception or of differential naming. So, at MA 3½, the child is asked which of two sticks is longer. It may be that the test really measures vocabulary rather than perception. However, at MA 4½ a more clearly valid test of differentiation appears. Here the child is shown a series of forms which

are alike, with one which is not. He is asked only to point to the one which is not the same.

2. *Symbolization.* One definition of intelligence which had a wide acceptance in America years ago was the ability to delay a response or the ability to respond to a symbolic representation of an absent object. The delayed-reaction experiment (page 383) illustrates a manner of testing this function. In the Stanford-Binet it appears that early development of this kind of performance indicates superior intelligence. At MA 4 the child should be able to look at three toys, then, after a short delay, indicate which one has been taken away by the tester.

The memory-span test (repeating numbers or words) measures a performance closely related to symbolization, and the reversed memory test even more clearly requires response to symbols. The child must hear "2-7-4," remember the digits, and then say "4-7-2," indicating that he has mentally reversed the symbols (MA 7). At a more complex level the ability to move symbols about mentally is tested by the dissected-sentences test, such as "for the started an we country early at hour." The child of MA 13 is expected to rearrange this into a meaningful sentence in less than 1 minute.

3. *Verbalization.* Verbalizing ideas, relations, and situations is really a form of symbolizing, but it takes such a dominant

place in mental functioning under civilized conditions that we list it separately. The ability to comprehend words, and later to manipulate them, is a major factor in intelligence at all age levels (see below). Even at MA 2 the naming of common objects seems to be a test which identifies children making normal or superior progress. Naming pictures is even more discriminatory, involving as it does the drawing as symbol of object and the name as symbol of both. At MA 2 the child is expected to name 2 of 18 pictures; at MA 4, 16 of 18 should be correct.

Definition of words is first introduced at MA 6 and continues to be a valid test through the superior adult level. Naturally the terms and the type of definition expected change in the direction of greater abstraction. Similarities and differences are tested, beginning at MA 7. At the later ages, three words rather than two may be presented, thus making the symbolic comparison more difficult.

4. *Schema formation.* As would be expected from our discussions of perception, memory, and thinking, the ability to form abstract schemata, or patterns of relationships, is of great significance in the development of intellectual ability. This kind of performance grades into the perception of similarity and difference at the earlier years. However, when we ask the child to give the opposite of a word (as in "an inch is short; a mile is ____?") we are obviously looking for a controlled association of an abstract kind. This very simple use of relational thinking can be expected at MA 4½. At MA 6 the child must be able from memory to copy a bead chain alternating round and square beads. At MA 9 rhyming of words is required. At MA 14 he must formulate a general rule covering the increase in the number of holes torn in paper as it is folded. Various tests require performances such as completing a number series (1, 3, 6, 10, 15, —).

5. *Recombinations.* The child not only must be able to recall ideas and symbols from past experience, but must be able to put them together in new ways. Some of the mental-absurdities items call for judging whether a presented novel combination violates our standards of reason; explanation of proverbs may require a spontaneous putting together of ideas not formerly associated. The digit-symbol test measures speed of forming new associations. Many of the reasoning problems essentially call for new combinations of familiar data.

Assimilation of the culture. In addition to the mental functions listed above, which we can identify with some confidence and ascribe to certain kinds of psychological processes, there are many test items on the Binet and other recognized tests which involve many functions. They generally demand a knowledge of the child's culture and its requirements, rather than performance of any specific type of mental manipulation. For example, one question (MA 3½) asks, "What must you do when you are hungry?" The answer must indicate some understanding of the problem of getting food in our society: "My mommy cook," or "We buy bread." At MA 8 this statement is presented: "About two o'clock one afternoon a number of boys and girls, dressed in their best clothes, rang the bell at Alice's house. Alice opened the door. What was happening?" At MA 11 the child should be able to give two reasons why there should be plenty of railroads in the United States. Such test items involve perception, memory, abstraction, formation of schemata in some instances, but essentially they can be understood as tests of the extent to which the child has been alert to and profited by exposure to his culture.

Adaptive value. A way to pull together these various observations on the specific kinds of functions we include in our intelligence tests is this: intelligence is an attribute of the adaptive process: the efficiency of dynamic homeostasis.

From the very beginning of this volume, we have stressed that psychology is the science of adaptive human behavior. Physiological needs reflect demands for certain environmental goal objects, such as food and water. These dynamic states are mediated through the autonomic nervous system. But attaining the goal—finding the way past the barrier, resolving the difficulty, eliminating the obstacle—must be mediated through the central nervous system. The individual must perceive the problem, recall past experiences with similar situations, choose between possible courses of action. The ability to manipulate symbols, as opposed to real objects, has great survival value here. Overt trial-and-error learning is not adaptive if the first error means being eaten by a saber-toothed tiger. Mental trial and error is incalculably more suitable. And it should not be necessary to stress the biologically adaptive value of accurate generalization and differentiation. The individual must perceive details accurately and reach a correct interpretation of the object as goal satisfying or threatening. Correct differentiation of poisonous from nonpoisonous foods is a case in point.

Intelligence, then, is a judgment which we pass upon the level of homeostatic functioning of the organism. The child cannot show efficient adaptation unless he matures at a rate at least normal for his age, in the functions of perception, abstraction, visualization, practical judgment, and number manipulation. To some extent a child can be good at one of these and poor at others; but our correlations show that superiority on óne such test generally goes with superiority on others. So we come back to the thought that intelligence does represent a kind of "general goodness" of the organism in dealing with symbolically represented situations.

The Organization of Intelligence

It would be theoretically possible, of course, for each of these various functions to be entirely unrelated to one another. This is in fact true of many human abilities. The ability to run the 100-yard dash seems to correlate zero with ability in mathematics. A person who is superior in one may be high, low, or average in the other. The specific functions which have been grouped into the Stanford-Binet scale and similar tests of intelligence, however, do not vary independently of one another. Each of them correlates positively with the others, and in most cases these correlations are high. That means that human beings differ with regard to some generalized characteristic which corresponds to ability to manipulate symbols.

It was Professor Spearman of the University of London who first called attention to the significance of these positive correlations among intellectual tasks. He proposed a two-factor theory of intelligence, which is still widely espoused in Europe and to some extent in America, although the multifactor theory (see below) has more support here. Spearman suggested that there is a "hypothetical general and purely *quantitative* factor underlying all cognitive performances of any kind" for which he offered the simple, unambiguous label, g. He held that people differ as to g, just as they differ with regard to height and weight. A tall man necessarily has longer arms, legs, fingers, etc., than his short cousin. We relate these specific measures to his general quality of height. In the same way, Spearman said, we get specific measures of perception, abstraction, and judgment; from them we can infer g, or general intelligence.

Operationally, g refers to all-around mental performance. Some people are inferior at all kinds of thinking assignments (although they may do quite well on motor skills). Such individuals are said to be low in g. At the other end of the scale is the person who shows rapid learning and deft use of all kinds of symbolic materials; we would say that he is high on g as defined.

Now it is obvious that no person is absolutely uniform in his mental performances. Some people who are very good at natural science are poor in social science, and some who excel in mathematics are poor in language. Thus the theory proposes a second factor, or s, a specific factor for each task. Then performance in any given situation would be predicted by this formula:

$$P = g + s$$

However, this way of writing the formula implies that g and s participate equally in determining success. Actually, they vary in different activities. Vocabulary is very closely related to g; so performance on vocabulary tests ought to be written

$$P_v = G + s$$

whereas performance on a test of esthetic judgment may depend mostly on art training and some special ability; hence we would write

$$P_e = g + S$$

The exact nature of g is unknown. It might be a matter of the number of functioning nerve cells in the cortex of the cerebrum. At one time it was believed to be dependent on differences in speed of nerve conduction. Its physiological correlate is not known.

The nature of s can, of course, be various. For a numerical test, s may be a function of early pleasant experiences with numbers, or drill in counting at a tender age. For an art test, it may involve sensory acuity, emotional experience with art objects, training, etc. We do not, therefore, attempt to define s unless we are doing an intensive analysis of some special ability.

Thurstone's multifactor theory. No one questions the fact that persons superior on one "intelligence" test are generally superior on others. Whether we should interpret this as evidence for a basic general intelligence, or g, is more debatable. Dr. L. L. Thurstone has argued that g can be broken up into a cluster of related abilities, which he calls the *primary mental abilities*. Because the method of factor analysis is basic to his proof that such abilities exist, he refers to his theory as a multifactor theory of mental organization.

Factor analysis is a technique rather too complex to be treated in an introductory text. Let us just say that it is a mathematical device for isolating, from a mass of observed facts, the smallest number of variables which can adequately account for the observations. For example, Thurstone once measured hundreds of boxes, as to their volume, diagonal distance, cross-sectional area, and so on. All these measures, when intercorrelated and factored, reduced to three measures: length, width, and depth. Now no one was surprised by this finding; but if factor analysis can uncover known basic dimensions, perhaps it can also find fundamental variables in cases where we do not know the answer ahead of time. For instance, what factors determine performance as a concert pianist? We know that finger dexterity, auditory sensitivity, and motor rhythm are important. But there may be many other variables, and perhaps they can all be reduced to a simple set of factors. Thurstone set out to determine the basic dimensions along which intellectual performances differ.

In the Thurstone study, a wide variety of tests, calling for almost every kind of performance we could describe as intelligent, was administered to a large population of high-school and college students. As Spearman had predicted, all the correlations were positive. It was, however,

VERBAL MEANING

The first word in the following line is **ANCIENT**. Mark an ✗ in the
A, B, C, or **D** box of the word that means the *same* as **ANCIENT**

ANCIENT   A. Dry   B Long   C Happy   D Old ·········

You should have marked an ✗ in D̲. because **Old** means the
same as **ANCIENT**.

SPACE

Some of the figures in the next row are like the first figure. Some are made backward.

A   B   C   D   E   F

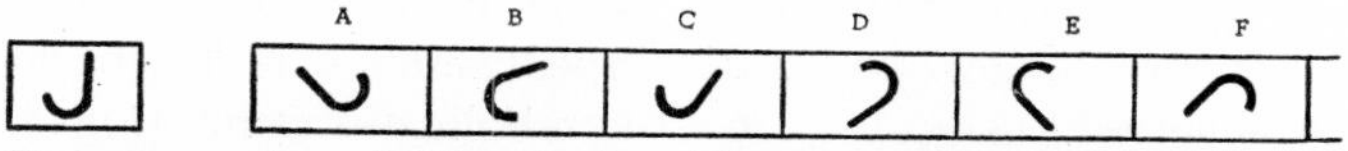

J | ∪ | ⊂ | ∪ | ⊃ | ⊂ | ∩

Figures C, E, and F are LIKE the first figure. ✗'s have been marked in C̲, E̲, and F̲
on the Answer Pad. Notice that ALL the figures which are LIKE the first figure have
been marked.

REASONING

Now study the series of letters below Decide what the NEXT letter should
be. Mark an ✗ in the box of the NEXT letter in this series.

c a d a e a f a

The series goes like this: **ca da ea fa.** You should have marked g̲

NUMBER   WORD FLUENCY

	A	B
At the right are two columns | 16 | 42 |
of numbers which have been | 38 | 61 |
added. Add the numbers for | 45 | 83 |
yourself to see if the answers | 99 | 176 |
are correct. | | |

Look at the words in the list below Each word
begins with *d*

doll

dinner

daisy

doughnut

The A answer is Right, so an ✗ has been marked
in R̲ on the Answer Pad.

The B answer is Wrong, so an ✗ has been marked
in W̲ on the Answer Pad.

FIG. 12:4. Thurstone primary-ability items. These are demonstration items from the
Thurstone "primary mental ability" test. The five subtests correspond to five factors iso-
lated by statistical analysis of about 60 standard intelligence tests. (*From SRA Primary
Mental Ability Test, by L. L. Thurstone and T. G. Thurstone. By permission of Science
Research Associates.*)

possible to show that some tests grouped
themselves together in clusters, seemingly
having something in common. The correlations within the cluster were higher than
with tests not in the cluster. Thurstone
suggested that each group of tests was
tapping some primary mental ability. He
eventually identified seven such abilities:
verbal comprehension, word fluency, ability
to handle spatial relations, number ability,
memorizing, reasoning, and perceptual
ability. The following sample items (Fig.

12:4) will give a clearer idea of what is
meant by each term.

There is some reason to believe that
Spearman's *g* is a more accurate description
of mental organization in young children,
and that the Thurstone multifactor description is more correct for adults. It would not
be surprising if the intelligence of the young
child were relatively undifferentiated; that
is, he would do either well or poorly on
almost any kind of task presented to him.
But as he grows, he acquires experience in

manipulating some symbols and has little contact (or success) with others. Some of us develop visual skills and judgment of spatial relations, others succeed in arithmetic and come to enjoy number work, others are clever with words, and so on. For whatever reason, it may well be that at sixteen, or eighteen, or twenty, the *g* concept is no longer appropriate; the general ability has now been channeled in a specialized pattern and is no longer equally available for all intellectual tasks. It also appears that we have to think of this specialization as permanent; the evidence suggests that this process cannot be reversed once it has occurred. Once a young man has become focused on such tasks as are identified above for abilities such as *P*, *R*, *N*, or *S*, it seems that he cannot go back and develop equal competence on *V* or *W*.

This means that, for practical purposes such as educational guidance, the Thurstone tests are quite useful. In early years, the Stanford-Binet gives us an IQ which is an estimate of *g*. From it we can predict the probability that this child will pass college entrance examinations, will drop out of high school early, and so on. But at the adolescent or adult level we may want

to advise him on such questions as: shop work or commercial course? engineering, law, or medicine? For these questions, an estimate of *g* is not enough. The Thurstone primary factors tell us in what specialized area our client has most potentiality. For this reason his tests are now widely used in counseling with young people.

On the question of theory, the following generalization seems best to fit the facts: Spearman's *g* is a general ability to make symbolic discriminations and to manipulate symbols in pursuit of goals. But there are many kinds of symbols in our complex civilization; by virtue of heredity or unidentified experiences, some people become more able at handling the verbal, others the numerical, others the spatial symbols. In the early years, or for gross predictions about the person, an estimate of *g* is enough; for more precise judgment we may want the scores on Thurstone's measures of *V*, *N*, *S*, and other "primary abilities."

Other Important Tests

Space obviously does not permit us to describe all the major tests which have been developed for the measurement of intelligence. We have given the Stanford-Binet in detail because it illustrates the basic theory of MA and IQ so well. The sample items in the preceding section on the Thurstone primary-ability theory will serve adequately to illustrate a totally different type of approach: one in which we ignore age entirely, and simply ask: how many of these problems can you solve? This approach is characteristic of pencil-and-paper group tests, used by the thousands for vocational guidance, student sectioning, college entrance, employment, and so on.

Another test so widely used as to merit brief mention here is the Wechsler-Bellevue Scale of Adult Intelligence. This test, like the Binet, combines both verbal and nonverbal items, and the author even advises computation of verbal and performance

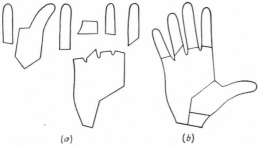

(*a*)   (*b*)

FIG. 12:5. Wechsler-Bellevue performance item. The Wechsler-Bellevue test of adult intelligence is equally divided between verbal and performance items, giving two measures of IQ. The subject is merely told, "If these pieces are put together correctly, they will form something. Go ahead and put them together just as quickly as you can." Scoring is for time and accuracy. (*Reprinted by permission of Dr. David Wechsler.*)

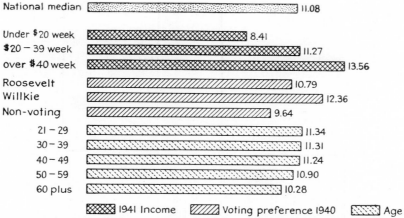

National median	11.08
Under $20 week	8.41
$20 – 39 week	11.27
over $40 week	13.56
Roosevelt	10.79
Willkie	12.36
Non-voting	9.64
21 – 29	11.34
30 – 39	11.31
40 – 49	11.24
50 – 59	10.90
60 plus	10.28

1941 Income   Voting preference 1940   Age

FIG. 12:6. Data on American national intelligence. The national median score of 11.08 on this vocabulary test is equivalent to an MA of about 16 years, 4 months. The score of 8.41 is about MA 14. (*Data from Thorndike and Gallup, 1944.*)

IQ's separately. This is useful with young children, as well as adults, particularly in cases of speech handicap and other problems. The Stanford-Binet, however, makes no provision for two measures of IQ; hence child psychologists customarily supplement the Binet with one or more nonverbal tests (see below).

The Bellevue test includes items of general information (*e.g.*, what is a thermometer?), general comprehension, arithmetical reasoning, repetition of digits forward and backward, and defining similarities. The performance items are: picture completion, arranging pictures to tell a story, assembling parts to form an object (see Fig. 12:5), making designs with blocks, and code substitution. Unlike the Binet, Wechsler's scale is standardized on a population ranging all the way up to sixty years of age. At the lower ages, IQ's based on his test agree well with those based on the Binet; extensive studies of the Binet at advanced ages are not available. Because of the tremendous increase in psychological work with adults, as in guidance, counseling, and psychotherapy, the Wechsler-Bellevue fills a major need in applied psychology.

Vocabulary tests. Because of the heavy

saturation of most general intelligence tests with the verbal factor, it is feasible to get a quick and fairly accurate estimate of the IQ by a vocabulary test alone. Thus, in both the Binet and the Wechsler scales, an IQ computed from a vocabulary score is commonly used when time for more thorough testing is not available.

Population surveys. This use of vocabulary tests has also suggested the possibility of doing a survey of the whole American population. In 1942 the Gallup opinion polling organization administered a 20-word vocabulary test to a scientifically selected sample of the voting population and came out with the conclusion that the average MA of our American adults was about 16 years, 4 months. (This is considerably better than the estimate based on draftees in World War I, which had been about 14 years.) Figure 12:6 gives some of the interesting comparisons among groups reported for this national survey.

Vocabulary-comprehension tests. The use of vocabulary tests to estimate general intelligence gives rise to another important problem. What can we do about getting a fair vocabulary score for children with speech defects, persons of limited education, bilinguals, and others who may be

FIG. 12:7. Vocabulary-comprehension test. (*Courtesy of Dr. R. B. Ammons.*) The examiner pronounces a word, and the subject points to the picture which illustrates that word. The words for this plate, with their estimated mental-age values, are:

pie (1.7)	transparent (13.3)	illumination (16.0)
window (1.7)	rectangular (14.7)	culinary (17.2)
seed (6.5)	sector (16.0)	egress (A6.3)
sill (6.7)		

handicapped in giving straightforward definitions of words? A rather ingenious solution has been developed by Ammons (1950). His scale for word comprehension consists of a series of 16 plates, each showing four pen-and-ink sketches. (One group is reproduced in Fig. 12:7.) The examiner reads a word and asks the child to point to the picture illustrating the word. Thus it is possible to get a relatively pure measure of comprehension, without any confusion due to handicaps in expression. Handicapped persons are likely to score substantially higher on this type of test than on the Binet or the usual group tests; normal children, on the other hand, make scores agreeing closely with Binet IQ's.

Nonverbal tests. The heavy weighting placed upon verbal aptitude would also

lead us to expect that devising good non-verbal tests of *g* will be difficult. Nevertheless, such tests have long been used, and some of them have proved consistently valuable, especially in work with children. In some cases a child will refuse to co-operate on a language test, answering questions, repeating numbers, and naming pictures; but he can be enticed into "playing a game" with jig-saw puzzles, colored blocks, and bits of string. *Form boards* usually present geometrical figures cut out of the board; blocks suitably shaped to fill the holes may be presented and the child must perceive the proper place and insert them. In more complex forms, the blocks have been cut into pieces which must be assembled to fill the hole properly (Fig. 12:8). Picture form boards have pictures

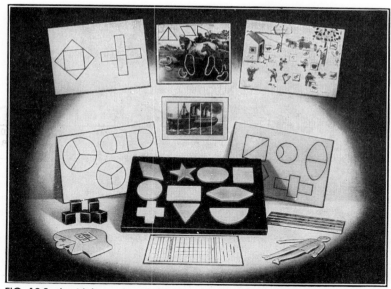

FIG. 12:8. A widely used performance scale. The Pintner-Paterson performance test includes picture form boards (parts of the picture are cut out and must be replaced by the child), geometric form boards, object assembly, and other items. (*Courtesy of C. H. Stoelting Co., Chicago.*)

from which parts have been cut out, as in a simple jig-saw puzzle.

The *Porteus maze tests* have been widely employed as a nonverbal test of mental ability. The task requires looking ahead to see a clear path in a rather confusing field (Fig. 12:3); as such, Porteus believes that it is a measure of planfulness and foresight. IQ's based on the test generally agree moderately well with the Binet; where the Porteus IQ is considerably lower, it is not uncommon to find a personality problem blocking the child from adequate use of his general intelligence. If the Porteus IQ is higher, a verbal handicap (deafness, speech trouble) is often uncovered.

Group tests. As can readily be inferred from an examination of the sample items shown, the Stanford-Binet, Wechsler-Bellevue, form board, and Porteus maze tests must be given individually. Such a procedure is necessary and valuable when the results will be used for a careful study of a

particular individual. The amount of time required is obviously too great for such individual tests to be used in the armed services, in college entrance examinations, in public-school testing programs, or in many employment situations. To get a rough indication of the person's ability, in these mass testing programs, we resort to group tests, where large numbers of people can be tested simultaneously.

The Thurstone primary-ability tests (Fig. 12:4) are excellent illustrations of group tests. Somewhat similar to them are the Army General Classification Test (AGCT) and the Navy GCT. The American Council on Education publishes a Scholastic Aptitude Test which is widely used as part of college entrance requirements, employing somewhat similar items. For obvious reasons, sample items from the armed services tests and college entrance tests are not reproduced in textbooks. IQ equivalents to different AGCT scores can be read from Fig. 12:9, or the AGCT and

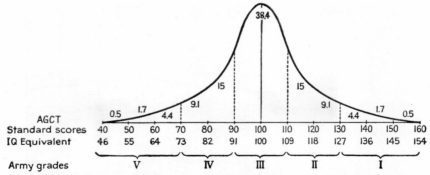

FIG. 12:9. Distribution of AGCT scores. This curve shows the distribution of several million soldiers on the Army General Classification Test. The figures along the curve show the percentage of men falling in a given bracket; thus 15 per cent of the men scored between 80 and 90. IQ equivalents are given below the AGCT standard scores, and the rough Army grades are at the bottom of the figure. (*Data from Bingham, 1946, and official sources.*)

NGCT scores can be converted into IQ's as follows:

(AGCT score minus 100)(times 0.9) plus 100
= IQ

(NGCT score minus 50)(times 1.8) plus 100
= IQ

Most group tests, using pencil-and-paper procedures, necessarily are influenced somewhat by education. Where they are used, as in college entrance, with persons of equal educational background, this is no problem. In the armed services, it was obvious that educational differences handicapped some men, although it was surprising to see how well some recruits of very limited schooling did on the tests.

The Growth of Intelligence

The mental-age placement of different kinds of tasks on the Stanford-Binet scale gives us some information on the growth of intelligence. We can visualize the kinds of performances indicative of average mental ability at each age, and when a younger child reaches these levels, we are aware that he is growing more rapidly than we would expect. Any IQ above 100 tends to indicate above-normal speed of development; an IQ less than 100 suggests some slowness of mental maturation. But there are numerous other questions that should be considered. When does intelligence begin? When does it stop growing? Does it grow at a uniform rate? These and many other problems have been objects of psychological research. In this book we can pick only the high lights of such investigations.

Does the newborn infant have an IQ? Since we have defined intelligence as a function, an aspect of the way in which the individual deals with his environment, we have difficulty in conceiving of the newborn as having any intelligence. The basic potentialities are there, but until the infant has some experiences, he cannot behave intelligently.

Baby tests have been standardized in much the same way as the mental-age scale of the Stanford-Binet. The normal ability of infants to follow a shiny moving object with the eyes, to brush away a stimulating object, to sit alone, to pick up a small cube, etc., can be determined for average babies at one month, two months, three months, and so on. Doctor Arnold Gesell and his students have published extensive tabulations showing just what kinds of motor performance can be expected at defined chronological ages. In general, these acts do not seem a function of intelligence; at least, *most of them do not predict the child's IQ at a later age.*[1] It is only when we begin to get some reactions to language that we begin to get tests which correlate well with later IQ. This seems plausible when we recall how outstanding the verbal factor was in the composition of intelligence.

Despite these difficulties in relating later performance to infant intelligence, psychologists have continued to speculate about the infant and his mental capacity. An especially interesting question has been, what is the zero point of intellectual development? The child might score zero on IQ tests until he was two years old, simply because the tests are not suited to his developmental level. Can we get any hunch on the true starting point for the growth curve of intelligence?

Thurstone (1928) tackled this problem mathematically. He devised methods of statistical analysis of intelligence test scores for later childhood such that he got absolute mathematical units of scores (instead of years of mental age, which is not a mathematically defensible unit). Then he plotted the growth curve of intelligence from 6 years back to 2 years, and found it to resemble a straight line. By projecting it still farther back, he found that it intersected the base line (zero level) at about 3 months prior to birth, or 6 months after conception (Fig. 12:10). It is interesting to note that this is about the time at which the infant first makes movements which

<hr/>

[1] Escalona (1950) has pointed out that the conditions of testing are especially important for infants. If these environmental circumstances are such that the baby does not cooperate fully with the examiner, a drastic interference with efficiency may result. Even if only one or two test items are failed as a consequence of this disturbance, the IQ may be sizably in error; the infant does not have a wide enough repertoire of responses that we can neglect chance successes or failures as we can with older children.

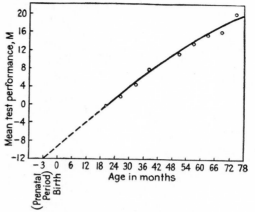

FIG. 12:10. Estimating the absolute zero of intelligence. This is a statistical attempt to estimate when intelligence actually begins to develop. Obviously the child at birth has some mental ability, but it cannot be tested by our present methods with any accuracy. Thurstone therefore took the data on older children (18 to 78 months), scaled the results, and plotted the curve (solid line). He then assumed that this curve had been continuing at the same rate, and projected it backward (dotted line). This gives an absolute zero at about minus three months, that is, three months before birth or six months after conception. Studies of the central nervous system suggest that this is a rather reasonable date for the beginning of the total organismic functions which we later call intelligence. (*Modified from Thurstone, 1928.*)

can be noticed by the mother; presumably, therefore, the age at which the central nervous system matures to the point of setting off muscular responses.

If Thurstone's reasoning is sound, we should have to conclude that the neonate is intelligent; that intellectual growth has been going on for about 3 months. This growth, however, has not reached the point such that it can be measured with the crude devices now at our disposal. With more refined testing techniques, it may some day be possible to ascertain the IQ of the newborn before he leaves the maternity hospital. But as yet, this cannot be done.

The progress of intellectual growth. Thurstone's growth curve shows that intellectual development is a more or less continuous process as far as a theoretical

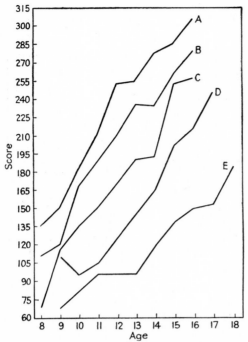

FIG. 12:11. Individual-mental-growth curves. These are the growth curves for five boys who were first tested at the age of eight or nine years and annually thereafter until seventeen or eighteen. While each shows some irregularity, there is no crossing of the curves; an inferior boy does not become superior, or vice versa. The tendency is for relative differences to persist throughout life. Obviously, in a larger group there would be exceptions to this. (*From Freeman and Flory, 1937.*)

average child is concerned. We should expect this, because the concept of mental age assumes that mental growth parallels physical maturation up to the adolescent level. It is assumed that there will be a steady progression from MA 5 to 6 to 7, and so on. Thus, as noted earlier, the average IQ of a group of children will always be about 100.

How does this work out for specific individuals? We could have a function which gave a smooth line of progression for groups, but specific children might be growing faster at one time and more slowly at another. Or it might be that some children seem very bright (develop faster) in

early years, but stop growing, while others seem retarded in the first few years, only to come from behind at a later date. Some well-meaning physicians, for example, have been known to encourage the parents of dull children by suggesting that the child will eventually catch up with his fellows. What are the facts in the case?

The evidence seems pretty clear that, although there are numerous exceptions, children tend to remain in their relative IQ position from age five to age sixteen (after which time we stop using the IQ as a measure of intellectual status). For example, Fig. 12:11 shows the mental growth curves for five boys who were retested annually between the ages of eight and seventeen. While there are variations in the rate of growth, each tends to keep his own speed fairly uniform through the 10-year period.

Individual-growth curves are subject to chance fluctuations due to illness, school conditions, and so on. What would happen if we compared the growth of bright, average, and dull children when they are grouped together? Figure 12:12 indicates that each group keeps its relative position throughout a 10-year study. The only interesting feature of this figure is the tapering off for the bright group at about seventeen years. Two reasons may explain this: (1) many tests have a maximum score which bright children at this age begin to approach; hence they may not have had "room to grow" on the test used; and (2) the very brightest children graduated from high school before age seventeen and hence were not included in the last testing. The conclusion seems to be that bright children are not only ahead of, but also grow faster than, dull children throughout most of these years. There is no indication that the duller child will "catch up" with his more fortunate playmate.

Another approach shows that we must, in any sizable group, expect substantial changes in IQ for some children. Cattell (1937) found that, of 1,300 children she studied, 10 per cent gained as much as 10 or more IQ points, while another 10 per cent lost 10 or more points at retest. Thus we cannot expect all children to maintain a constant IQ.

Furthermore, it is true that an occasional child will start off slowly and later improve in rate. Lowell (1941) mentions a boy who on successive tests earned IQ's of 82, 98, 111, and 132. This often happens if a mild birth injury, emotional problem, nutritional handicap, thyroid deficiency, or other temporary source of retardation is involved. At the very least, we certainly would take the position that every child should have the benefit of the best training he can get; no human being should be relegated to the scrap heap simply because an early intelligence test indicates him to be handicapped. As we shall show in later pages, a superior educational environment can improve the *effective* intelligence, if not abstract ability. Thus we do not want to seem defeatist about the possibility of helping the slow child.

When does mental growth stop? It is easy to understand, in an abstract way, that people stop growing physically in their late teens (except for some lateral expansion in middle age) and that mental age likewise must be assumed to stop growing. Practically, however, there is much resistance to accepting this idea. It seems offhand to imply that, just as the young man is physically superior to his middle-aged father, he is likewise capable of greater mental feats.

The confusion here is due to failure to distinguish *capacity* from *achievement*. The young man may have reached a peak in terms of potential, but until he has wide experience, he cannot use this capacity to best advantage. In fairly simple sports, such as the 100-yard dash, only young contenders set records; but in the complex

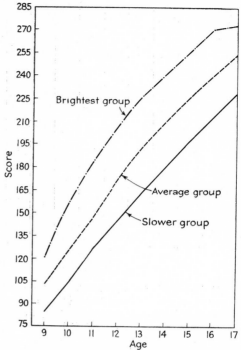

FIG. 12:12. Group-mental-growth curves. When a large number of pupils are grouped together in three brackets, and average-growth curves are plotted, we get smooth, almost straight lines. The irregularities in Fig. 12:11 are ironed out. Again we note that the groups stay about the same distance apart through the years. (*From Freeman and Flory, 1937, p. 65.*)

games involving experience and judgment (golf, baseball), the oldster may achieve more despite his slight physical decline. In mental tasks this is even more true. If mental growth stops at sixteen, as some say, this does not mean that a lad of sixteen is qualified for the presidency of the United States. To use his capacity effectively, he needs breadth of experience with people, facts and relationships which may not be achieved until he is fifty. Thus there is no contradiction between the idea of an early ceiling on growth, and advanced age requirements for responsible offices.

The exact age at which people reach their peak in terms of MA is not fixed. It used to be said that MA 16 was the maxi-

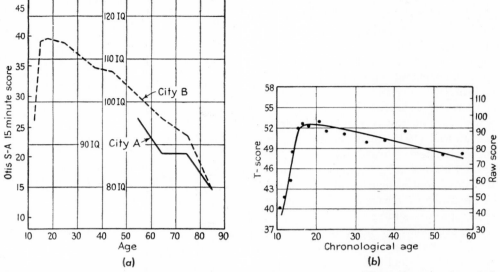

FIG. 12:13. Effect of aging on the IQ. Curve *a* is for the Otis examination, which is almost purely verbal, and curve *b* is for Army Alpha (Army test from World War I), which includes a few nonverbal items. Both show substantial declines in ability from the twenties onward. (*From Miles and Miles, 1932, p. 51. Jones and Conrad, 1933, p. 241.*)

mum. This does not seem entirely correct; in fact, some people probably stop growing before others. Trying to determine it for the general population is not easy, as the following quotation from Terman and Merrill shows:

The correct placement (of this maximum) must take into account of the age at which unselected subjects cease to improve in mean score (on a test like the Binet). Unfortunately, the precise determination of this terminal age is complicated by the fact that it is extremely difficult to secure truly unselected test-populations above the age of fourteen or fifteen. . . . For our data, the yearly gain begins to decrease after the age of thirteen and by the age of sixteen it has become approximately zero. Chronological age beyond sixteen has therefore been entirely disregarded in computing the I.Q.[1]

According to this view, general intelligence (as indicated by MA) does not increase beyond the age of sixteen. This is

[1] Terman and Merrill (1937), pp. 29–30. Reprinted by permission of Houghton Mifflin Co.

not the same as saying that there are no mental ages above sixteen. On the Stanford-Binet one can get an MA as high as 22 years 10 months. This is attained only by persons with IQ's above 150, as they must reach it by the time they are sixteen years old.

Effects of aging. With a population rapidly shifting toward a large percentage of persons over sixty, the effects of aging on intelligence have great practical significance today. This problem has proved more than a little complicated. In the first place, it is hard to find a representative sample of people after high-school age. Secondly, it is difficult to find items which are equally fair, in terms of our criteria (page 427), to persons who have specialized in different occupational fields. Third, at the upper age levels physical deterioration may affect test performance even if inner intelligence is not lessened. (For example, loss of visual acuity may affect test results, while the ability to manipulate abstract

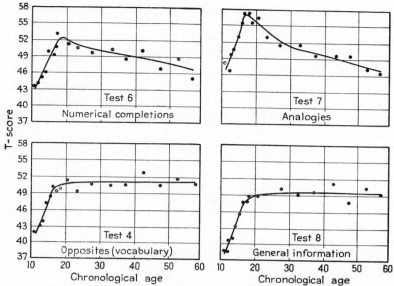

FIG. 12:14. Effect of aging on specific tasks. When the Army Alpha subtests are plotted against age, the results are less gloomy than suggested by Fig. 12:13. Some performances (numerical completions, analogies) show a sharp decline with age. These are kinds of activities which may encounter negative transfer from long-practiced habits. Other tasks (vocabulary opposites, general information) show little or no loss up to age 60. Here the repeated use of certain habits may cause them to be remembered well and executed efficiently on the test. (*From Jones and Conrad, 1933.*)

ideas is unchanged.) Fourth, older people are not readily motivated to work hard at a test and so may make scores somewhat below their capacities.

Despite these difficulties, numerous investigators have tackled the problem. In Fig. 12:13 we summarize the results of studies using standard intelligence tests, covering a variety of functions. Here it will be noted that the curves slope steadily downward from a peak at twenty, with a rapid decline after seventy. That this decrease in ability may be exaggerated by such data is suggested in Fig. 12:14. When we separate out different kinds of tasks, it appears that some functions persist with little loss until a comparatively late date. Others fall off rapidly from the early peak. Some of the latter may be those which are particularly affected by declining physical efficiency, as sensory acuity. But another

group of items seems to be suffering chiefly from the effects of *negative transfer*. The poor performance of older folk on some test items may result from the fact that these items demand *flexibility* in breaking old habits and establishing new ways of grouping associations or looking at situations. With each successive decade of practicing the old ways, these items may become constantly more troublesome.

The Distribution of Intelligence

It is common to think of people as being divided into sharply different classes, such as feeble-minded, normal, and genius. Actually, as the student should readily see on the basis of the foregoing illustrations of mental tests, we do not have any method for separating people into types or classes of intelligence. What we do is measure them

TABLE 12:1. Intelligence Quotients and Mental Ability Classifications (Stanford-Binet and Wechsler-Bellevue Tests)
(From Wechsler, 1944)

Classification	Percentage of population	Bellevue IQ	Stanford IQ	
			Age 8–12	*Age 14–18*
Mental defective...........	2.2	67–below	70–below	68–below
Borderline................	6.7	68–79	71–79	69–79
Dull normal..............	16.1	79–90	80–91	81–91
Average.................	50.0	91–110	92–115	92–115
High average............	16.1	111–119	116–125	116–126
Superior................	6.7	120–127	126–137	127–136
Very superior............	2.2	128–over	138–over	137–over

and then apply descriptive labels for shorthand convenience. But it is important to recognize the basic measurements and ignore, for the most part, the class labels. This can be illustrated quickly if we take an example from physical measures such as height. It would be possible to work out a scheme by which men under 5 feet tall would be labeled "pygmies," those over 6 feet 6 inches as "giants." But all of us would still recognize that there is only a shade of difference between a man 6 feet 5 inches and one 6 feet 7 inches, despite the difference in classification.

This is equally true, but easier to forget, as regards intelligence. For arbitrary convenience, we speak of children below IQ 70 as feeble-minded (see Table 12:1). But in the everyday realities of the schoolroom and the factory, some people with IQ's of 66 adapt more successfully than those of IQ's of 71. There are even some children with IQ's in the high sixties who profit from academic school work, if well taught; and there are some in the seventies who have to be institutionalized. Thus it should be emphasized vigorously that the classifications we employ are merely matters of convenience and that the numerical differences in IQ may represent very slight variations in adaptability, which can be canceled by personality and training factors.

With this caution in mind, let us consider the actual distribution of intelligence in the population. The figures given here are for the United States, but similar data could be presented for England, France, Sweden, etc. Because the theoretical approach throughout the world to this problem is very much the same, all the figures look quite similar.

Table 12:1 gives figures based on the Wechsler-Bellevue Scale of Adult Intelligence, and the Stanford-Binet 1937 Scale for children. Another way of presenting the material is by way of a distribution curve, as in Fig. 12:9. It will be noted in both instances that people of average intelligence predominate. Wechsler sets his scoring limits in such a way that the middle 20 points of his scale (91 to 110) take in about 50 per cent of the adult population. The Stanford-Binet scale puts 38 per cent of children in this middle group, called the *normal* or *average* level of intelligence. For both tests, half the population falls below IQ 100 and half above that point; and the IQ's taper off in frequency as we depart from 100 up or down. Between IQ 81 and 90 we expect to find about 16 per cent of children or adults; between 71 and 80, about 8 per cent; and only 2 per cent below 70.

It is important to remember two points

about the distribution curve for intelligence: (1) The center is arbitrarily set at IQ 100, so that in any large sample of persons, the average will be around 100. Let us not, therefore, be alarmed when someone announces that the average IQ is only 100. (2) Frequencies decrease rapidly as we move away from 100, so that the chance of finding a given child with an IQ of 70 is only 1 in 50, and for an IQ of 130, the same. This, of course, is no more than a statistical way of making the obvious point that it is unusual to find a person of unusually high or low mental ability.

The Feeble-minded

Suppose we shorten the focus a little and examine more carefully the nature of this unfortunate group, the lowest 2 per cent of the population, which is referred to as *mentally defective* or *feeble-minded*. It may be encouraging to some to learn that this proportion is only 2 per cent, if they have read the alarmist statements of those eugenicists who foresee the swamping of Western civilization by a flood tide of mentally deficient children. However, we should not underestimate the magnitude of the problem either. Two per cent of the present American population is roughly three million persons. Such a group certainly cannot be ignored.

The definition of feeble-mindedness is in fact a social definition. As far as commitment to a state institution is concerned, this definition is usually couched in such terms as "unable to handle himself or his affairs with ordinary prudence." Such an approach recognizes the practical reality that there are some individuals who cannot care for themselves and may in fact be dangerous to others because of their inability to exercise good judgment. To a scientific psychologist, on the other hand, the practical definition is hopelessly fuzzy. How much is "ordinary prudence"? In

TABLE 12:2. Customary MA and IQ Equivalents for Feeble-minded Groups

	MA range at maturity	IQ range
Moron................	7–10 years	51–70
Imbecile..............	3–7	26–50
Idiot.................	0–3	0–25

what kind of environment is the person living? A person who is perfectly safe on the farm may be a terrific hazard in a nitroglycerin factory. Thus the psychologists have preferred to move away from the social definition into a mental age or intelligence quotient definition of the feeble-minded.

As was shown in Table 12:1, it is customary to define persons below an IQ of about 70 as feeble-minded. This means, in terms of mental-age development, that the individual never progresses beyond the level of performance which has been attained by an average child at the age of eleven years.

It is common to break down the feeble-minded category into three subgroups: idiots, imbeciles, and morons. Table 12:2 shows the IQ and MA equivalents which psychological custom ascribes to these terms. Again, it may be worth while to remind the student that there is no significance to be attached to the difference between an IQ of 48 and an IQ of 52; the labels are descriptive and convenient only.

Idiots. The term *idiot* is applied to a human organism which has failed at maturity to achieve abilities equal to the normal child of three. Obviously such an individual cannot care for himself; he is permanently dependent on others in virtually every respect. He will never learn to read, may learn a few or no spoken words, may not even be able to be toilet-trained. A most extreme form is the "vegetative" case, which can be described as living, but little else.

Imbeciles. The next higher category of mental defect is labeled *imbecile.* In such cases self-care is usually developed, and they may learn to sign their names, to do simple work under supervision, and to avoid "the common dangers" of life. Many become self-supporting and make an adequate adjustment as long as the environment is simple; on a farm they may seem only simple and single-minded, rather than defective. In the city, especially if they have poor family supervision, they are likely to get into trouble. The girls become prostitutes, the boys tools for more intelligent criminals. Such undesirable outcomes are made more probable by two factors: (1) lacking general ability, they have trouble getting jobs and thus earning money in a socially approved fashion, so they are forced into disapproved channels; and (2) lacking symbolic grasp of situations, they cannot foresee the trouble their actions may bring upon them.

Morons. The most numerous category of mental defect is that called *moron.* Children in this group mature to a maximum MA of 7 to 10 years (which they reach only at 13 to 16 years). They can thus profit from some academic work, although they will experience many failures and thus are likely to stop trying at the third- or fourth-grade level. They can benefit more extensively from an educational program focused around manual work, or concrete materials, where their symbolic and verbal handicap is less significant. In a study of 256 morons in a Connecticut town, Kennedy (1948) found that only one completed high school (less than 10 per cent even entered high school).

The occupational adjustment of the moron, however, may be more encouraging than this would suggest. At the time of his follow-up, when the average age of his group was twenty-four years, Kennedy found three-fourths of them to be wholly self-supporting. Most of them, naturally, go into laboring jobs, but a fair proportion develop enough skill to get into the higher wage-worker brackets.

Importance of careful testing. There has never been any difficulty, of course, in identifying extremes of feeble-mindedness, such as the first and second cases cited above. Such unfortunate children are so clearly retarded by the time they reach school age that they can only be helped to acquire a few routine skills, under supervision, and care for themselves to some extent. They must always live in a protected environment.

It is the borderline group, with 20 to 40 per cent retardation (IQ's 60 to 80) who represent the major problem. They are of course more numerous, and potentially they can become useful, self-supporting citizens. But if treated unwisely they become hopeless institutional charges. They do not, for example, profit from a college-preparatory program.

Unfortunately, many schoolteachers mistakenly diagnose a variety of other handicaps as feeble-mindedness. A dull child with a hearing difficulty, for example, may miss what goes on in the classroom, give foolish or irrelevant answers to questions he misunderstands, and so be labeled as a hopeless case. Personality problems, particularly those of stubborn and rebellious attitudes toward school discipline, may cause a similar misclassification. Careful testing of such children will often reveal that they possess normal (even superior!) mental ability, which can be directed into useful channels by proper educational procedures.

Conversely, it is important that a truly serious mental handicap be recognized early, at least to the extent of removing excessive pressure from parents and school for types of achievement the child cannot reach. This may be just as important around the average range of intelligence as in the lower brackets. Parent or school pressure on the child in the IQ 70 to 80 range will not make him capable of average performance; but it may, as a consequence of the frustrations imposed, release so much aggression that he becomes a serious behavior problem.

The emphasis here is not on accepting the verdict of an intelligence test as a final diagnosis of the child's ability. All psychological measurements are subject to error, and no one has yet developed a foolproof test of mental capacity. Adults would be wise, however, to accept the test result as an indication of what can reasonably be expected *at this time*. It is possible by wisely chosen methods to raise the effective intelligence of some children by a substantial proportion. Until we know more about the factors involved in such cases, the IQ of a carefully administered Stanford-Binet is still the best prediction as to a given child's true ability.

The Gifted

We avoid here the widely misused term *genius* as applied to children of very high IQ. Terman set an unfortunate precedent, in his early work *Genetic Studies of Genius*, by arbitrarily defining a genius as anyone with an IQ in excess of 140. This was particularly painful to later generations of psychologists, who occasionally have a student walk into the office and casually announce, "I am a genius" meaning, in fact, "I have been told that I have an IQ over 140."

It is probable that genius, like feeble-mindedness, needs to be referred to a social criterion (page 445). To merit this classification, a person probably should possess not only superior mental talents, but also a drive to create and an unusual flexibility in some respect (musical, artistic, ideational, etc.). In other words, it seems wise to consider high intelligence as only one aspect of genius. In this sense, children

above IQ 140 might be "potential geniuses" but only a limited percentage of them will achieve such status.

Children above 180 *IQ*. When we move up into even higher IQ levels, we get amazing reports of precocious early development. Dr. Leta Hollingworth spent years searching New York City for children with IQ's above 180, and located 12. Such children can be expected to occur, in our population, about once in a million. Here is an excerpt from her description of one of the gifted children she discovered:

He began to articulate words at 10 months, and at 14 months could pick out letters on the typewriter at command. At 12 months he could say the alphabet forward, and at 16 months he could say it backward as well. His parents had no idea that he could reverse the alphabet until one day he announced that he was "tired of saying the letters forward" and guessed he would "say them backward." The concepts of "forward" and "backward" had thus been developed by the age of 16 months. At 12 months he began spontaneously to classify his blocks according to the shape of the letters on them, putting V A M W N together, O P Q G D together, and so on. This love of classifying has remained one of his outstanding characteristics. . . . By the time A was 30 months old he could copy all the colored designs possible with his kindergarten blocks . . . before the age of 3 years A objected to stories containing gross absurdities. For instance, he rejected the story of the gingham dog and the calico cat who "ate each other up." A learned to read for himself during the third year of life, and read fluently before he entered school.[1]

This boy, when tested at CA 6 years 6 months, obtained a Binet MA of 12 years 2 months and an IQ of 187. A year later he was retested and earned an IQ of 191. At 8 years 8 months he took Army Alpha and made 95 points, equal to an MA of 16 years or an IQ of 184.

[1] Hollingworth (1942), pp. 72–73. Reprinted by permission.

TABLE 12:3. Economic Achievement of Terman's "Gifted Children"
(*Based on Terman and Oden, 1947*)

	Men	Women
Mean annual income from wages and salaries, general population, 1939..........	$1,389	$ 916
Mean earnings, gifted group, 1939.....................	2,373	1,660

Later accomplishments of gifted children. These rare cases of IQ above 180 have not been studied long enough to know how they will perform as adults. Terman has recently published some follow-up data on his group of 1,300 children above IQ 140, and these are suggestive of the social values to be expected from children in the upper ranges of intelligence. These children were surveyed in 1940 and again in 1946 (they were first identified in 1922), after most of them were well established in adult roles.

On the whole, the results were convincing evidence that gifted children make superior adults. At age thirty, they were averaging an earned income of $200 a month, almost twice the national average at that time (Table 12:3). The concentration in professional fields was very great. Ninety per cent of them went to college, and over 80 per cent graduated, earning grades and honors far above the average. The statistics on death, suicide, insanity, and divorce rates all indicated that the gifted group was superior to the general average of the population.

Value of early recognition. Like the feeble-minded or dull child, the superior youngster encounters various hazards in adjustment. Our schools are geared to the IQ 100 child and the adjacent range which includes two-thirds of the population. Parental expectations, too, are more appropriate for the average youngster. The very bright child may encounter resistance when he wishes to read rather than play outside, and he may be ostracized by his peers because his thought processes are so different from theirs. He often upsets teachers by his inquiring mind and perhaps humiliates them by knowing more in a specific field than they do. If the teacher has a strong need to feel superior, this may provoke hostility which handicaps the child's later adaptation to the educational system.

The unrecognized brilliant boy or girl may become a maladjusted personality, a behavior problem, or an inefficient performer. Emotional maladjustment coupled to intellectual superiority is a threat to all of us. The gifted child who becomes antisocial can do far more damage than an aggressive moron. The leaders of Nazi Germany were generally of superior mentality (Table 12:4), but their attitudes toward the rest of humanity were an essential link in the chain of events setting off World War II. If we examine their intelligence-test results (based on examinations at Nuremberg during the war crimes trials), we see that most of them were well above average in mental ability, even though few of them could be called "geniuses." The destructive use to which they put these superior talents should make us vividly aware of the importance of proper educational programs for exceptionally gifted children.

Emotional Difficulties and Test Intelligence

Some people do very poorly on tests because they become anxious, tense, and rigid. Sarason (1949) reports on a girl who at 16 years of age received a Binet IQ of 70 and Arthur (performance) IQ of 73, thus being in the borderline zone. During a year in the institution she learned to do preparations of bacterial media, urinalyses (except microscopic), staining of slides, blood typing, and keeping laboratory

TABLE 12:4. Wechsler-Bellevue Intelligence Quotients of Nazi Leaders
(*From Gilbert, 1947*)

Name	IQ	Name	IQ
Hjalmar Schacht................	143	Albert Speer..................	128
Seyss-Inquart..................	141	Alfred Jodl..................	127
Herman Goering................	138	Alfred Rosenberg.............	127
Karl Doenitz..................	138	Constantin von Neurath.......	125
Franz von Papen...............	134	Walther Funk................	124
Erich Raeder..................	134	Wilhelm Frick...............	124
Dr. Hans Frank................	130	Rudolf Hess (estimated)......	120
Hans Fritsche.................	130	Fritz Sauckel................	118
Baldur von Schirach...........	130	Ernst Kaltenbrunner..........	113
Joachim von Ribbentrop........	129	Julius Streicher..............	106
Wilhelm Keitel................	129		

records. Most of these tasks, it is commonly assumed, require an IQ above 100. Yet she was entirely successful at these jobs.

Sarason suggests that past learning may be the decisive factor in explaining the contradiction between her test and job performance.

It may be assumed that her previous experiences in (the IQ test) situation were not of a kind to arouse feelings of adequacy or self-confidence. The nature of the situation—its teacher-pupil, question-answer quality—was one in which she had experienced failure and one on which unpleasant consequences were based. . . . This girl knew that she was being tested by a person whose opinions were important to her future. Another factor . . . was the inordinate strength of her desire to do well at the same time that she fearfully anticipated failure.[1]

In contrast, her job relationship was happy, she became emotionally attached to her supervisor, and new duties were presented so gradually that she never felt threatened by failure.

Further reference to this problem will be made in later chapters. At this point we wish to emphasize that fears, tensions, and anxieties about verbal tasks may account for a significant number of cases diagnosed

[1] Sarason (1949), pp. 105–106. Reprinted by permission of Harper & Brothers.

as feeble-minded, and some of these will perform well in adult life because they are less anxious when dealing with concrete tasks. Conversely, it is probable that many persons of normal test intelligence are job failures because they have the misfortune to encounter jobs and bosses to which they react with tension and disturbance. They cannot use their ability because of emotional blockage.

Nature and Nurture Again

Psychology is the science of human behavior, and its immediate aim is the understanding of human characteristics. But we can never divorce ourselves from the practical demands of the world about us, and thus we find constantly hovering, somewhere on the edge of consciousness, the question: what can we do about it? This question comes up again as we deal with the problem of intelligence. Is the child's intellectual level fixed by heredity? Or is it subject to improvement (or damage) from environmental influences?

This matter is of particularly grave importance in the field of intelligence because of the broad social implications. The progress, if not the very survival, of civilization depends upon human intelligence. Methods which can lead to an increase in the average intellectual level can potentially mean the widening of security and opportunity for all of us, just as an increase in the IQ of a specific man would widen his chances of achievement in our society.

We must therefore ask, How is the intellectual level of an individual determined? Is it definitely fixed by heredity, in the way that height, for example, seems to be determined and unmodifiable except by marked pathological conditions? Or is the IQ a function of environment, which can be raised by good home and school stimulation, or depressed by inadequate surroundings? Would a program for improving the environment result in a higher population IQ, or can such advances be achieved only by steps to get more babies from intelligent parents, fewer from the duller adults?

As has been noted regarding other psychological functions, it is futile to ask, which determines intelligence, heredity *or* environment? In every case, the IQ is a function of *both* heredity and environment. Without heredity there would be no organism to be acted upon by external stimulation; without environment, the organism would die. It is foolish to ascribe everything to nature (genes and chromosomes) or to nurture (home, school, etc.). Always the two are in interaction.

It is especially important to remember this as we examine some of the evidence which has received wide consideration during debates on this question. Many observers "view with alarm" the large number of children produced by adults of low mental ability, and the small families from parents who are college graduates. It is suggested that this foretells a nation of morons in the not too distant future. Is this gloomy prediction justified by the facts?

Pedigree studies. The earliest type of evidence gathered to evaluate the role of heredity used the pedigree method, or the study of all persons directly related within a given family. Thus Galton (1869) reported that geniuses tended to have in their families many other eminent persons and that undistinguished "average" men had very few relatives who achieved eminence. Goddard (1914) published a now famous study on a family he called the Kallikaks, which showed a heavy concentration of feeble-minded, dependent, and criminal cases in the family of a feeble-minded girl. Goddard's data have been criticized on the ground that his data were impressionistic, and many of the people reported as subnormal may not have been so. This defect seems not to be important, as more recent studies, using mental tests, confirm his observation. Consider the case of the "Hominy" family reported by McPherson (1936):

The father of this family was a laborer, very deaf. Accused by wife of having relations with daughter. He was said to be alcoholic. The mother, 48, admitted to Belchertown in 1932, with an IQ of 68. Attempts were made to improve her care of the family under the supervision of the S.P.C.C. for eleven years but she did not improve. She kept a filthy home, was sexually promiscuous, and had incestuous relations with son, who may be father of twins born in 1930. Her own husband requested her commitment to this institution following her arrest for neglect of home. This family has been known to welfare departments for years. Children of this family, Louise, Harry, and Ruby, were committed in 1930 to the Division of Child Guardianship. Louis, age 23, IQ 70, was committed to Belchertown State School in 1934. In 1930, he was in court charged with incest with mother and sister, charge later changed to assault and battery. In court in 1933 for abuse of a female child, committed to County Jail and then to Belchertown. He escaped in 1934. Louise, 20, IQ 69. Was committed to Belchertown in 1934. She was in Juvenile Court as delinquent child, admitted having relations with father and brother. Had been in care of Social Service Division of Department of Mental Diseases where she was found to be childish and incompetent and she was returned to aunt who found her unmanageable and requested her removal. Harry, age 18, IQ 47. Sent to this school in 1930. He was suspected of imitating incestuous acts he had seen at home. Has defective speech. Ruby—no information. Earl, 14, IQ 52, speech defect. Admitted to State School, in 1931. Margaret, 9 years old, in care of Division of Child Guardianship. Said to be very backward. Her paternity is denied by father of this family. Winifred, age 7, IQ 63. Admitted in 1933. It is suspected that her own brother is the father.[1]

Unquestionably, such a case history as this makes gloomy reading. Of the seven children mentioned, five have intelligence test scores below IQ 70, hence are technically feeble-minded. On the other two no test information is available, but unfavorable descriptions are given by neighbors. The mother is reported as having an IQ of 68; the father, not tested but obviously handicapped. Such families represent a tremendous social cost in terms of welfare loads, jail and institution costs, and potential damage to other citizens.

But does such an investigation—even if repeated and confirmed many times over—prove that intelligence is determined by heredity? Obviously not. We can well ask, what would have been the effect upon a normal child of living in such a home? Clearly, it would not have been such as to stimulate awareness of the outside environment, in observing similarities and differences, in abstract ideas, in the development of an extensive vocabulary. Yet it is exactly such performances which are demanded of the child in the intelligence testing situation.

As will be set forth in a later section, the evidence today indicates that, if we take a child out of such unfavorable environment and place him in a more stimulating situation, his test performance improves mate-

[1] McPherson (1936). Reprinted by permission.

rially. It is certainly likely that, at the same time, his ability to fit into society expands rapidly. A boy living with the Hominy family is certainly not going to develop habits of honesty, dependability, and industry, such as most employers demand. Thus he will be a vocational as well as a test failure. In a different home he may acquire, not only the skills called for by tests, but also the behavior patterns demanded by the larger social order.

At best we can interpret such family studies as proving only the importance of an unknown mixture of hereditary and environmental factors. This does not lead us to ignore their importance in terms of social problems, but to search for more dependable evidence as to the relative significance of heredity and environment as regards intelligence.

Terman's "gifted" group. Mention has been made of 1,300 children, identified by Terman in 1922 as "gifted" (IQ's above 140). When they were followed up in 1946, it was found that they had 1,551 offspring. The mean IQ of these children was 128, as compared with approximately 155 for the gifted parents. (However, it must be noted that the other parent contributes 50 per cent of hereditary determinants; and while the gifted tend to marry other bright people, the mean IQ of spouses was not up to the level of the Terman group.)

Something over 400 of the offspring have been tested. The average, as noted above, was IQ 128. However, five cases (1.3 per cent) fell below IQ 70, hence were technically feeble-minded. Twenty-eight cases (7.3 per cent) were below 100; compare this with the expected 50 per cent below 100 (Fig. 12:9). Conversely, 59 (15.4 per cent) were above IQ 150; in a random group the percentage would be less than one.

But, when we attempt to generalize from these data to the nature-nurture problem, we get little assistance. These gifted parents

FIG. 12:15. Identical twins show physical and mental similarities. A pair of identical twins at 1½ years and 11 years of age. The similarities cannot be attributed exclusively to heredity, since they also have very similar environmental conditions.

brought to their children not only excellent heredity, but also a stimulating, healthful, and nourishing environment. The IQ's of the children are substantially higher than even those of the highest economic status (see Table 12:7); hence heredity is clearly one factor. But their environment is also better than average.

Note also that 1.3 per cent of the children were feeble-minded. All humans carry a highly mixed heredity. Even the ablest of us carries genes determinative of low men-

tal status. Selective sterilization can never eliminate feeble-mindedness from the population.

We can, of course, make good use of the above data as reflecting the need to encourage superior adults to have more children, and as far as possible, to discourage reproduction at the lower levels. This social interpretation is not dependent upon proof of the decisive role of heredity.

Twin studies. The trouble with family studies in this area is obvious. We cannot

TABLE 12:5. Resemblances between Pairs of Identical Twins Reared Together, Fraternal Twins Reared Together, and Identical Twins Reared Apart
(*Based on Newman, Freeman, and Holzinger, 1937*)

Traits	Identicals unseparated	Fraternals unseparated	Identicals separated
Height...................	.98	.93	.97
Weight...................	.97	.90	.89
Head length..............	.91	.69	.92
Binet IQ.................	.91	.64	.67
Educational age...........	.96	.88	.51
Personality..............	.56	.37	.58

make accurate inferences as to the roles of heredity and environment unless we can hold one constant and let the other vary. In cases like the Hominy family, both heredity* and environment vary simultaneously.

Nature has provided us with the most satisfactory technique for resolving this dilemma in the form of twins. Twins usually grow up together and are treated in a rather uniform manner; their environments are about as constant as one can hope for, without putting children into cages. If twins also had identical heredities, we would be back in our dilemma, as we would then have constant environment and constant heredity. But fortunately, some twins are identical and some are not. Identical twins develop from a single fertilized ovum, which somehow splits and gives rise to two babies with exactly the same gene patterns. They are thus called *monozygotic.* Fraternal twins, on the other hand, result from the accidental presence of two egg cells in the Fallopian tubes at conception. Each is fertilized by a different sperm; they thus have the same degree of hereditary similarity (and difference) as brothers and sisters born at different times. Deriving from two fertilized ova, they are referred to as *dizygotic.*

Identical twins are so much alike as to confuse even their relatives (Fig. 12:15). Often they seem to be mirror images of

each other; one may have hair which whorls to the right, the other to the left, and so on. In physical measurements and in psychological tests of ability, their scores are almost as much alike as those of a single person measured on different occasions. Fraternal twins, by contrast, are likely to differ considerably in both physical and psychological characteristics. Table 12:5 gives correlation coefficients which show strikingly how much higher is the similarity of identical twins. Comparison of unseparated identicals with unseparated fraternals shows the identical twins to be more closely alike in every respect.[1]

A few cases have been discovered of identical twins who were separated at an early age and reared in quite different environments. Here we have the test situation of heredity constant, environment varying. The correlations shown in Table 12:5 suggest that heredity triumphs over environment, in that the identicals reared apart resemble each other more closely than fraternal twins reared together.

It is worth while to remind the student at this point that neither fraternal nor identical twins have exactly identical environments. By accident, some stimuli will affect one and not the other; friends and associates can never treat them with exact equality. Furthermore, we must remember that the effective environment

[1] See also Fig. 15:7, p. 533.

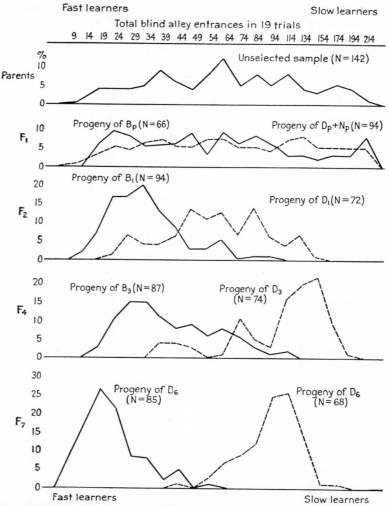

FIG. 12:16. Selection of hereditary strains of "bright" and "dull" rats. The uppermost graph shows the distribution of maze-learning scores for 142 unselected rats. The fastest learning rats were mated to give a bright strain, the slowest being mated to give a dull group. There is little difference in the curves for F_1. When, however, the fastest of the bright group were bred, and the dullest of the dull group, we begin to get decided differences (F_2). By F_4 the difference is clear, and by F_7 there is virtually no overlap in learning speed for the two strains. (*From Tryon, Thirty-ninth Yearbook, National Society for Study of Education, 1940, I, p. 113, Fig. 4. Reproduced by permission of the Society.*)

(in determination of behavior) is not the physical milieu, but the environment as perceived. One twin may feel threatened or frustrated by stimuli which do not appear so to the other. Hence, at best, we can only approximate a constant environment even for twins, and much less, therefore,

for siblings (brothers or sisters of different ages).

Animal research. Twin studies, and particularly the cases of identical twins reared apart, give us a fairly high degree of confidence that heredity contributes more to IQ differences than does environment. The final confirmation of this hypothesis would demand controlled breeding experiments, in which the children of superior parents were mated, and in a separate group, children of inferior parents likewise, with environment constant for both groups. After several generations, we could expect a family strain of decided mental superiority or inferiority to appear, if heredity were truly decisive. Such experiments, of course, are forbidden by our social code.

It is possible, on the other hand, to do such research with animals. Tryon (1940) had white rats learn a maze. He took males and females who learned rapidly (Group B) and bred them; also bred were males and females who had learned poorly (Group D). Their offspring then learned the same maze; as can be seen in Fig. 12:16, there was a slight superiority for the bright group. However, Tryon further selected those doing best, from Group B, and bred them; selected those doing worst, among Group D, and bred them. After this process had continued for seven generations, there was a clean separation of the offspring in terms of learning scores; only one or two of the dull group learned as fast as the poorest animal in the bright group.

Since all these animals lived in a standard laboratory environment, we can say that this experiment demonstrates the fact that learning speed depends markedly upon heredity; the environment remained constant while heredity varied, and variations in learning speed were found. Naturally there are many obstacles to a direct translation of this study to the human realm; nevertheless, it seems to reinforce the twin studies in emphasizing the role of heredity in human intelligence.

Studies of Environmental Influence

Experimental studies directly bearing on the role of heredity in human ability cannot be performed, because such crucial steps as family inbreeding or the arbitrary separation of identical twins are forbidden by social taboo. We do have a few accidental cases of twin separation, but the number of cases involved is too small for us to be very confident as to the results.

On the other hand, children are constantly being shifted from one environment to another. The effects of variations in the environment can therefore be estimated from a number of different bases. Children placed in foster homes, children sent to nursery school, children given special training—such instances provide a wealth of material for studying the impact of environment on the IQ.

Foster-home studies. It would be quite helpful if children's IQ's could be determined prior to placement in a foster home and then measured again after specified intervals of time. This is made difficult by the tendency toward early placement for adoption and the fact that infant tests do not predict later IQ with any precision. However, certain facts stand out in all the studies of foster children.

Poor heredity. If heredity were a direct determinant of IQ, in the sense that the child resembled the parents closely, large proportions of foster children would be feeble-minded. Skodak (1939) reports on a group of 154 babies placed for adoption in Iowa. The IQ's of 80 of the mothers were known; they averaged 88, significantly below average. The children were mostly illegitimate; where the father's occupation was known, it was usually very low in the economic scale, which suggests low intellectual level. Thus, at best, we should predict for these children average IQ's below 100.

The facts obtained do not bear out this prediction. When the children were first tested, at about two years of age, the average IQ was 116, distinctly above average; a second testing at four years four months of age gave an average IQ of 112, still above the average range. (Most of them had been placed in the foster home before age six months; so their effective environment had been chiefly in the new home.)

These homes were not uniformly superior in quality, although there is no question that they were more favorable than the homes the true parents could have given the children. Furthermore, the IQ dropped slightly rather than rising, on the second test; hence we are not dealing with a cumulative effect of learning from a superior environment. About all we can conclude with certainty from the Skodak data is that, in a good environment, children of poor heredity are found to have average or superior IQ's; the common belief that "bad blood will show" is certainly not confirmed by these findings. Only five children, on the first test, and seven, on the second, scored below 90; about two-thirds of the group scored above 110. When we compare these figures with the average maternal IQ of 88, we see that environment must be quite significant.

Poor true-home environment. The children in Skodak's study were placed in foster homes very early in life. What would have been the effect of leaving them in an undesirable home environment for some longer time interval? An answer is provided by data gathered by Speer (1940) on a group of 184 children who were declared dependent by the courts and placed in foster

TABLE 12:6. Children of Feeble-minded and Normal Mothers Placed at Differing Ages *(From Speer, 1940)*

Years' residence in own home	Children of feeble-minded mothers, median IQ	Children of normal mothers, median IQ
0–2	101	100
3–5	84	91
6–8	75	91
9–11	72	92
12–15	53	81

homes as a result of death, desertion, or incompetence of the true parents. The home environments, in these cases, resembled that of the "Hominy" family described above (page 450). The mothers of 68 children were feeble-minded and confined in state institutions. The other mothers were at least ostensibly normal.

The effect of remaining in this inferior environment for varying lengths of time is shown in Table 12:6. We are immediately struck by the fact that there is no difference in the average IQ of children of feeble-minded and of normal mothers during the first 2 years. Both groups come out just at the expected IQ of 100. However, the inferior environment begins to take its toll after age two (perhaps because language stimulation now becomes important). For the group of feeble-minded mothers, the decline is continuous and severe; for the other group there is no further drop except at the oldest age level, which may be a statistical accident.

If the inheritance from the mother were decisive, we should not get this steady decline, but a uniformly low level at all ages. It would seem, from Speer's data, that the poor environment provided by feeble-minded parents is a cumulative retarding factor which ultimately pulls all the children down to a dull or defective level of mental functioning.

Institutional environments. If we consider the types of performances which are required by intelligence tests, we can readily see the importance of a stimulating environment. The child needs to have opportunities for perceiving varied situations, for having similarities and differences pointed out, for learning symbols, especially words, relating to varied activities and objects. He is much more likely to get such stimulation in a home than in an institution and is more likely to get it from some institutions than from others.

Crissey (1937) compared children from

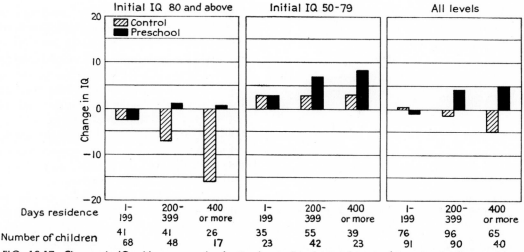

FIG. 12:17. Change in IQ with nursery-school attendance. For the total group (chart on right), attendance beyond 200 days serves to produce a net gain in IQ as compared with the group not attending preschool. However, as the left and center charts show, this gain is chiefly confined to the duller group (IQ 50 to 79). Such findings suggest that the positive values of preschool attendance may be limited or that the brighter children had already passed the point at which they would have benefited by these specific conditions. (It is, of course, true that the preschool group of IQ above 80 made a considerable net gain, since their controls lost 5 to 15 IQ points during the study.) (*From Skeels et al., 1938.*)

four Iowa institutions: an orphans' home, a juvenile home, and two schools for the feeble-minded. He tested the children at the beginning of his work and retested the same cases after specified time intervals, thus getting the amount of change in specific individuals (as most of the foster-home studies could not do). He found that the children in the feeble-minded schools lost more, and continued to lose IQ longer, than in the other institutions. He interpreted this as evidence that the feeble-minded environment was more detrimental to normal mental growth than the others.

Nursery school. If we grant, as the studies of Crissey and others seem to indicate, that an orphanage is a poor environment for child development, we may then ask, how can we improve it? What would be the effect of adding nursery school, with deliberately calculated experiences to stimulate the children's growth? Skeels *et al.* (1938) have described such an experi-

ment. The staff of the Iowa Child Welfare Research Station organized a nursery school at the Iowa Soldiers Orphans Home. The children were carefully divided into equal groups, one group receiving the nursery-school training, the other continuing the established orphanage routine.

Because there was some changing of children into and out of the home, and because some children seemed to profit more than others by the nursery school, the data have been broken down in various ways. A quick summary of the major findings is given in Fig. 12:17, which shows the amount of IQ change for different groups. It will be noted that among the duller children (IQ 50 to 79), all groups improved during the experiment, but the nursery-school group improved more. For the average group (IQ 80 and above), the non-nursery-school children steadily lost in mental performance, while the nursery school group held its own. On the whole, it appeared that a year made a difference of

TABLE 12:7. Relation of Occupational Status to Intelligence of Children and of Adults
(*From Johnson, 1948*)

Occupational group	Average IQ	
	Children (Terman and Merrill)	Adults* (Harrell and Harrell)
I. Professional..........	116	120
II. Semiprofessional and managerial..........	112	113
III. Clerical, skilled trades, retail business....... .	107	108
IV. Rural owners, farmers.	95	94
V. Semiskilled, minor clerical, minor business....	105	104
VI. Slightly skilled........	98	96
VII. Day laborers, rural and urban...............	96	95

* Based on incoming selectees, World War II, hence no officers and no rejectees. Had these groups been included, the spread of scores would have been greater and the difference between high and low occupational groups substantially larger.

about 10 IQ points, favoring the nursery school.

Isolated communities. It is possible to locate not only specific institutions which give poor stimulation to children, but whole communities as well. Sherman and Key (1932) visited isolated mountain villages of the "Dogpatch" variety in the Appalachians. Some of these were so remote from what we call "civilization" that they were practically vestiges from the Revolutionary period when these settlements were established.

The investigators found that there was a decided tendency for the average IQ of children to decline as they got back farther into the mountains. Furthermore, this tendency is cumulative—it appears more sharply in the older children, thus resembling Speer's data (see above). Thus, even though the hereditary stock has not deteriorated (as the IQ's of the youngest

children are not markedly subnormal), by the time they reach maturity these youngsters are quite handicapped. In turn, they pass this handicap on to their own offspring in terms of poor environment.

Social and economic status. Another line of evidence which has some value in this connection derives from the study of adults and children at different social and economic levels of our culture. We know, of course, that the individual's ability is one of the factors influencing his type of work, earning capacity, and community standing. (It is obviously not the only factor; educational opportunities, family "pull," and other considerations confuse the issue. Generally, however, we would expect enough mobility in our society that superior persons tend to move up and inferior persons downward in the status scale.)

When we study the mental performances of persons from different socioeconomic groupings, we confirm this expectation. The data from selectees in World War II (Table 12:7) show that occupational groups I and II (professional and managerial) include men who are, mostly, above average IQ. The unskilled and farm groups tend toward below average intelligence. These differences would have been materially larger had officers and rejectees been included, since we know that officers are somewhat likely to come from the upper economic groups and rejectees from the lower.

On the other hand, the overlap between these groups is very great. Some of the men in the laboring group have higher IQ's than many men in the professional category. A convenient way to represent this overlap graphically is shown in Fig. 12:18, where AGCT scores for several common occupations have been tallied. The black dot shows the average score, the gray line the range covering the middle 50 per cent of men from that occupation.

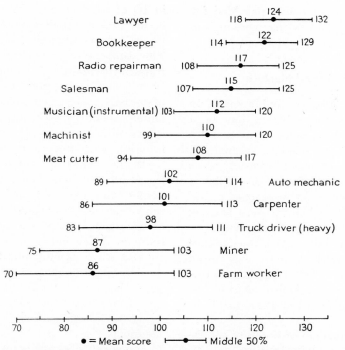

FIG. 12:18. Overlap in occupational intelligence. While it is true that there are substantial (and significant) differences in the intellectual level of men in different occupations, we must keep in mind the degree of overlapping of these distributions. The average lawyer scores above the average salesman, but some salesmen are more intelligent than many lawyers. In this chart the round dot shows the mean AGCT score for men in the defined occupational group, and the middle 50 per cent of the group is marked off by the line. Thus 25 per cent score above the highest figure shown, and 25 per cent below the lowest; one-fourth of the lawyers scored below 118, and one-fourth of the meatcutters scored above 117. These data are based on a sample of 83,618 white enlisted men. This means that some of the higher scores were lost, as officers score, on the average, higher than the ranks. (*Based on data in Stewart, 1947.*)

It is immediately apparent that there is substantial overlapping at almost every job level.

The general trend for superior occupational status to go with higher test performance holds also for the children. As inspection of Table 12:7 shows, when children are classified by father's job standing, the groups average out so that the ranks are identical with those based on the Army data. "Like father, like son" is still a pretty dependable psychological generalization.

But let us emphasize, once again, that such data prove nothing about the role of heredity. They prove only that, with an unknown mixture of hereditary and environmental influences, children tend toward the same mean intelligence level as their parents. In the light of the series of studies on environment just cited, we should certainly be as justified in emphasizing the kind of home a man provided for his children as in stressing heredity in itself.

Summary on Nature and Nurture

It is impossible, in a reasonable space, to cover all the evidence which has been accumulated on this problem. In the foregoing pages we have tried to summarize, selectively, some of the significant *kinds* of investigations, as well as to give a flavor of the field. Many more researches would need to be considered if we were to seek comprehensive knowledge of the area.

Instead, let us simply cast a quick glance at the conclusions reached by experts on this problem. First, what is the relative impact of heredity and environment on the IQ? When we consider the wide variations

TABLE 12:8. Contributions of Heredity and Environment to Various Characteristics*
(From Newman, 1940)

Characteristic	Percentage of variance due to heredity	Percentage of variance due to environment
Physical characters:		
Standing height........	81	19
Weight..............	78	22
Total finger ridges......	90	10
Ability tests:		
Binet MA............	65	35
Binet IQ.............	68	32
Educational tests:		
Word meaning........	68	32
Arithmetic...........	12	88
Science..............	34	66
Personality:		
Woodworth-Mathews..	30	70
Motor performance:		
Tapping test—wrist....	27	63
Tapping test—finger...	46	54

* Based upon correlations of performance by 50 pairs of identical twins reared together and 50 pairs of fraternal twins reared together.

in IQ of children growing up in the same home, under rather similar environments, we are led to realize the weight of heredity. The studies on identical as compared with fraternal twins, and especially of identical twins reared apart, point to the importance of heredity. Selective breeding studies in animals confirm the view that relatively enormous differences in ability can be a function of differences in inheritance.

On the side of environment we can cite the studies of poor home and good foster home conditions, the effects of nursery school on IQ of orphans, the study of mountain communities, and similar researches which indicate that variations in the IQ of a specific individual are often due to environment. Particularly it appears that a poor environment at about the age of two to four years, when language is being acquired, can be a very severe handicap.

The conclusion was reached by Newman (1940) after some complex calculations, that variations in IQ were determined about 68 per cent (on the average) by heredity, 32 per cent by environment (Table 12:8). This is another way of saying that, when we compare any two children, about twice as much of their difference is due to heredity as is due to environment. There is no evidence to date which would justify rejecting that conclusion. But this is a statistical, on-the-average statement. Under selected circumstances *all* of the difference can be due to environment or to heredity.

Furthermore, as far as any specific child is concerned, all the variation in his own IQ must be due to environment. His heredity never changes. Any rise or fall of IQ must be a function of his stimulus situation. Thus, as a practical matter, the environment looms very large. We have cited studies which show changes of 10 to 20 IQ points as a result of home conditions. In terms of everyday living, such differences are very significant. A rise from IQ 70 to 90 brings the child from borderline feeble-mindedness to low normal. It changes our prediction of his adult adjustment from economically depressed, inferior, to economically average.

What about the eugenics-euthenics controversy? Our data clearly show little support for the eugenicists. Young children, both of whose parents are feeble-minded, average well up toward IQ 100. The decline in IQ is associated with years of living in a depressed environment. Less drastic measures than sterilization can reach this factor. The great majority of the feeble-minded children today have parents who would have tested well within the normal range. If all feeble-minded adults were sterilized, the reduction in below 70 IQ's in the next generation might run around 10 to 20 per cent. While this would be a social gain, it is certainly no panacea for our social ills. Better homes, better schools, better medical care for children, and less economic discrimination will be a quicker, surer path to a mentally abler population.

Sex Differences

One possible approach to the question of hereditary influences upon intelligence might seem to be by way of the study of differences between males and females. We know that there are various hereditary differences between the sexes—not only in the sex organs themselves, but in endocrine glands, in size, and in external appearance. It might be thought, therefore, that differences between boys and girls would give us some clues to the role of heredity in determining variations.

Unfortunately, we run into difficulties as soon as we attempt to study this question. One of the criteria of a good intelligence-test item (see page 427) is that it shall have been equally available to all the persons taking the test. Now we know

perfectly well that the sex roles are different in our society; from early years little girls are led toward housework, interest in clothes, manipulation of people to achieve their goals, and so on. Boys are influenced toward manipulation of tools and physical objects, outdoor sports, and "manly" activities. Thus many kinds of problems and symbols will not have been objects of equal attention for the two sexes. Many test constructors (notably Terman and Merrill, in the 1937 revision of the Stanford-Binet) have deliberately thrown out test items which showed substantial sex differences, because they wished to construct a scale which could be used without alteration for all children. Now it is obvious that you cannot in the first instance throw out items revealing sex differences, and then use the final scale to measure sex differences!

Where data have been collected on reasonably representative samples of boys and girls, the female of the species has usually scored slightly higher. This is particularly true at the preschool and primary levels, and is widely held to be a function of earlier maturation by the girls. It is more noticeable with regard to verbal than to nonverbal tests. (Whether this has any relationship to the alleged verbosity of the female is not clear.) By the time first-year high-school students are being tested, the boys have forged ahead, and this lead is held through high school. At this point, however, we run into a sampling problem. Dull boys will drop out of school at the eighth grade and go to work. This is much less true of girls. Hence the average score for boys will rise during the high-school period.

As a result of these two difficulties—the cultural influences which make for differential interests and practice, and the sampling problems after the compulsory school age is passed—it is almost impossible to reach a defensible conclusion with regard to the inheritance of sex differences in intelligence. Certainly there are some differences; and, if the early maturation hypothesis is accepted to explain the primary-test results, this in itself proves that heredity is a significant factor. The tendency to mature more rapidly, after all, must be inherited. But it has not been possible to go beyond this and estimate the relative force of nature and nurture in modifying the IQ for boys and girls.

Racial Differences in Intelligence

In the foregoing discussion of heredity and environment as factors determining intellectual level, the topic of race was deliberately omitted. This was done because, to date, no convincing evidence on this problem has been obtained.

It is easy enough, of course, to give tests to children of different national origins or different racial background. But, when we have shown that differences between families are largely environmental in character, how much more must this be true of racial and national groups? An illustration, extreme to be true, but none the less suggestive of the problem, comes from the work of Porteus (1937). Porteus was attempting to use his pencil mazes as intellectual tests with the Australian aborigines, to compare them with American and other groups. But he found that it was virtually impossible to get them to work as individuals. In their culture, all problems were solved cooperatively, and it was, to them, obviously stupid for a man to work alone on a task when his neighbor could help him do it. When the psychologist finally got them to work alone, it was apparent that the test situation was abnormal for them and did not represent their usual level of functioning.

This is true, even if less apparent, for subgroups within the American population. There is no question, for example, that on the average, Negroes make lower scores on

tests than do whites. About the interpretation of this there is a great deal of doubt. Beckham (1933) found, for example, that Negro children in New York City made approximately the same scores on tests as white children of the same socioeconomic level. Southern-born Negro children, however, scored substantially below the white norms. This suggests a difference in attitude toward speed of work, toward the significance of symbols, or toward the test situation in itself, which was cultural in nature.

As we noted earlier, there have been many efforts to devise "culture-free" tests of mental ability. It is, however, manifestly impossible to avoid cultural differences if they determine the child's attitude toward the situation of being tested. Among some Indian tribes, testers were baffled by the fact that boys would not compete with each other. The desire not to humiliate one's tribal brother by surpassing him made the testing procedure unacceptable. The value placed by the culture upon the type of activity required (manual, verbal, numerical, pictorial, etc.) is an unmeasurable variable. The rewards and punishments for success or failure in such activities will weigh heavily in these comparisons.

These difficulties in testing and in interpretation offer massive roadblocks to any investigator interested in the problem of racial differences. At best we can state, today, that such differences represent an unknown mixture of hereditary and environmental influences. When we consider the heights of culture which have been achieved by examples of each racial group, we are inclined to doubt the role of heredity and accept the data as evidence of environmental, mainly cultural, influences upon test functioning.[1]

---

[1] Some psychologists hold that, while cultural factors account for most of the differences in intelligence-test performance among the varying racial groups, the consistency of results from such

Health and Intelligence Quotient

The problem of health is of course, from our view, purely environmental in form. Nothing can change the child's heredity, once the ovum has been fertilized. His functioning, however, can be modified by his physical health; necessarily, then, this must be classed as an environmental influence even if inside the organism.

The consensus is that health has surprisingly little effect on intellectual performance. Even fairly severe malnutrition does not seem to lower the IQ, nor does rehabilitation increase it. In their extensive study of semistarvation during World War II, described on page 57, Keys *et al.* (1950) found that there was some loss on tests requiring physical speed and coordination, but virtually none on the purely "mental" tasks.

Vitamins, especially B-complex vitamins, have been thought to have some significance for intelligence because of their intimate relationship with the functioning of the nervous system. It has been found that small supplements of vitamin B do bring about slight improvements in some types of mental-test data, but they are usually not statistically significant. In a very careful study, Bernhardt (1948) and his coworkers took 36 pairs of identical

---

investigations justifies a belief in true inherited racial differences in ability. Whether one accepts or rejects this view is a matter of faith. The importance of the cultural factor is demonstrated; the alleged residue of innate differences cannot be demonstrated. The intricacy of the problem can be illustrated by a simple example: Northern whites in the United States consistently score above Southern whites. Since they are racially similar, the result must be culturally determined. Can we argue that any differences greater than this (*e.g.*, the white-Negro difference) must be partly hereditary? The argument is not convincing, because Negro culture is not identical with Southern white culture. At present, therefore, those who cling to a belief in innate race differences do so on faith; our techniques are not sufficiently developed to solve the problem factually.

twins and gave one the vitamin and the other a sugar pill (identical in appearance). Over an 18-week period the vitamin group gained slightly in certain mental test scores, but the differences were not reliable; the IQ average remained unchanged.

A similar conclusion seems to hold for glutamic acid. This substance is unique in that it seems to be the only amino acid capable of being metabolized directly by nerve cells. Zimmerman and coworkers (1947) reported some startling increases in IQ when it was given to subnormal children; unfortunately, the cases selected were complicated by various factors (*e.g.*, convulsive seizures), and the controls were not good. Later work indicates that some children profit by glutamic acid treatments and others do not. It may be supposed that those who benefit may have had a mild deficiency of this substance and that the supplemental doses were enough to restore them to normal. Those not improved may have been getting their normal requirement; an overdose would presumably be of no value.

We have, then, no royal road to intellectual superiority by way of physiology. No one doubts that intelligence is in some way dependent upon the cortex of the cerebrum. But the nature of this relationship is shrouded in mystery, and we shall only store up disappointments for people if we give them hope that vitamins, amino acids, hormones, or miracle drugs will raise the intelligence level. Our knowledge today suggests that only a very few will be benefited by these treatments.

SUMMARY

The human being, in search of goals and satisfactions, must perceive his environment, learn about it, and think about it. Previous chapters have dealt with these functions as general features of human psychology.

Some individuals, however, are more perceptive than others. Some learn faster; some think more effectively. Intelligence is the term used to identify the ability to perceive, think, and learn.

Studies of young children indicate that intelligence is rather general, showing up equally well in tests using words, numbers, and pictures; that is, the child tends to be superior, average, or inferior on all test situations. At later ages, more specialization seems the rule. A boy may be superior on numbers but only average on verbal and spatial material. Thurstone's primary mental abilities scales help us to identify individuals who are especially good at specific kinds of performances. These tests can be used to locate causes of trouble and to help the person choose an occupation in which he can be most efficient.

Heredity contributes more to individual differences in intelligence than does environment. However, there appears to be little cause for alarm as to a possible lowering of the national intelligence as a result of excessive reproduction by parents of low mental level. So far, favorable education and other influences seem to be raising the intellectual average more than this alleged hereditary differential is lowering it.

Differences of intelligence performance among "racial" and national groups have been ascribed to both heredity and environment. At present the evidence favors the position that such differences are mainly environmental in origin.

Emotional factors can affect intelligence level as measured by tests. Persons suffering fear, anger, anxiety, and similar tension states are underrated by the usual procedure. Many of the increases in IQ attributed to better environment may be due chiefly to reduction of frustrations and improved emotional adjustment of the child.

Recommended Readings[1]

ANASTASI, ANNE, and J. P. FOLEY, JR.: *Differential Psychology.* (rev. ed.) New York: Macmillan, 1949.

FLETCHER, J. M.: *Psychology in Education.* New York: Doubleday, 1934.

HOLLINGWORTH, LETA S.: *Children above 180 IQ.* Yonkers, New York: World, 1942.

STODDARD, G. D.: *Meaning of Intelligence.* New York: Macmillan, 1943.

TERMAN, L. M. (Ed.): *Genetic Studies of Genius.* Stanford University, Calif.: Stanford University Press, 1926.

—— and M. A. MERRILL: *Measuring Intelligence.* Boston: Houghton, 1937.

—— and M. H. ODEN: *The Gifted Child Grows Up.* Stanford University, Calif.: Stanford University Press, 1947.

[1] See also p. 547.

PART THREE

Personality

So far we have proceeded with our study of psychology in a purely analytical fashion, by dividing man up into parts, or separate functions, for detailed study. While this is unavoidable—it is impossible to study everything simultaneously—we have inserted occasional reminders to the effect that these functions are interacting, not independent.

We have now reached a point, in our survey of the science of psychology, at which we can have a try at putting man back together again. Psychology, as we noted in the very beginning of this volume, is the study of the organism as a whole. Dynamics, or wanting, and cognition, or knowing, are of course functions of the total individual, but our treatment has tended to keep each in isolation. In real life, dynamic and cognitive processes are combined into a higher level integration which makes up the unique individual as we know him in his daily actions.

For this integrated person, who has his own distinctive pattern of desires and ways of satisfying them, psychologists employ the term *personality*. Thus the study of personality calls for putting together all the knowledge presented in the preceding chapters, into an organized pattern.

Since the human personality is, in many respects, the most complex unitary event ever studied by scientists, we make no apologies for the fact that the psychology of personality cannot be reduced to a simple formula. Even in streamlining it for inclusion in this introductory textbook we have found it necessary to omit many important points. We have attempted to maintain a feeling for the rich variety and uniqueness of individuals, while getting down to penetrating general principles. This is, while the most complex phase of psychology, also the most fascinating.

CHAPTER 13

Foundations

Psychology is the study of man's intellectual processes and also of his dynamics: the study of perceiving, learning, and thinking, as well as of desiring, fearing, and hating. We opened this introduction to psychological science with an analysis of man's basic motivations, because these give us an insight into the pressures which drive man along paths of action. From this we turned to a consideration of man's cognitive life—how he comprehends his environment, learns to deal with it, thinks and reasons about it. As the data in the last few chapters have amply shown, man has some claim to being a rational animal. At least part of the time his actions are such as to verify the presence of intelligence and other special abilities.

To round out this picture of human psychology, however, we must now return to a consideration of dynamics. If there is anything clear, as far as man is concerned, it is that he is not a reasoning machine. His abilities are integrated into a complex pattern of loves, fears, ambitions, and prejudices which we call his *personality*. In most instances this personality is so constructed that his abilities are used inefficiently a great deal of the time; or, to put it differently, the irrational elements often dominate over the rational aspects of behavior.

By personality we mean the particular, unique pattern of traits and attitudes characterizing any specific person. Thus we are continuing with our study of the individual as opposed to general laws of behavior. It must be noted, however, that all personalities obey certain principles and are unique in outcome, not in process. These general processes will be the subject matter of this chapter.

Definitions of personality. Let us sharpen the focus a bit and clear up the definition of personality before going farther. In popular speech, personality is often used rather loosely and in a variety of meanings. Scientific psychology might do better to discard the term entirely; as we are trying to retain it, we must define it with precision while keeping as much as possible of the popular significance.

1. *Personality as stimulus.* Popular usage often identifies the term *personality* with one's impact upon others. "She has a lot of personality" equals "she has a pronounced effect upon people who meet her." Leadership personality means qualities which effectively influence the behavior of followers. "Sales personality," "executive personality," and similar phrases illustrate the same kind of approach.

We could sum up such uses of the term by saying that one common definition of personality is "social stimulus value." In what ways does my personality affect others? Several psychologists like to employ this kind of definition of personality.

The chief difficulty which appears when we consider the scientific use of this definition is the following: social stimulus value is never the same for two different observers. My personality does not affect my students as it does my wife, my children, or my colleagues. A boy is not seen as the same by his teacher, his gang members, his girl friend, and his employer. Just which one of these various stimulus values shall we pick as being his personality? Obviously, we are not justified in picking any single observer to use as the standard. We must say that John's personality is different for each of these people. Then, how can we ever define "John's personality"? This approach may be useful in special cases, but it does not provide us with a general scientific approach to personality.

2. *Personality as response.* To get away from the difficulties just cited, it has been proposed that we study John and learn which patterns of response affect others. Then we can define his personality as this unique set of response patterns—facial expressions, gestures, ways of saying things, habits of emotional reaction, and so on. Such a definition is much more objective and thus more adaptable to scientific research. Once we agree on the response patterns to be included, we can set up careful observations and experiments to investigate the individual personality. For this reason, the definition of personality as a unique pattern of responses characterizing a specific person has been accepted by a large number of psychologists.

Many adjectives descriptive of such differences between individuals have crept into common speech. We speak of people as "explosive," "changeable," "talkative," "brusque." When I say that "John has an explosive disposition," I am more likely to be describing his actions than my feelings about them.

Many investigations of personality are based on this definition. Studies of facial expression, of emotional outbursts, of social interaction, of visceral responses to emotional stimuli, for example, follow this line.

Even here one important difficulty arises. This stems from the fact that a specific response may be evoked by a variety of perceptions and emotions. For example: an item on a widely used personality test asks, "have you ever crossed the street to avoid meeting someone?" Now my crossing the street to avoid someone may be a symptom of shyness; or it may indicate that I owe this person some money; or it may reflect the fact that I have been gossiping about him and am now embarrassed to see him; or it may be only that I have a lot of work to do and don't want to stop and chat.

3. *Personality as intervening variable.* The kind of example just cited is used to suggest that the real personality is not to be ascertained simply by observing what the individual does; rather, it must be *inferred* as some kind of inner state underlying the external action. Thus a man may be shy with strangers, afraid of taking chances, and avoid leadership positions in groups; all these may point to an inner *feeling of inferiority* which affects a wide variety of responses. In this case we could well argue that understanding of the personality advances much more rapidly if we concentrate our attention on the inner state, not on the outer behavior.

A definition of personality as an inner state, intervening between stimulus and response, would be something like this: Personality is the unique pattern of perceptions and motivations which characterizes a specific individual. Such an approach puts the emphasis upon what a person desires and upon how he looks at ways of satisfying these desires. An ambitious personality is motivated in the direction of prestige or power; a ruthless personality is one who looks upon other people as mere tools to be used for his own purposes. According to this definition, the real personality is neither the external response pattern (which is easily changed) nor the impact upon others. It is the *inner organization* of motives, emotions, perceptions, and memories which determine a way of behaving.

The phrase "real personality," however, should not be interpreted as denying validity to other aspects of the individual. Sometimes we see a man under the influence of alcohol and say, "Now I know what he is *really* like." This is not scientifically sound procedure. This is only his real personality under alcohol; what he does when sober is just as real.

Some individuals develop a "mask" or superficial appearance with which to meet other human beings—all of us do, to some extent. Yet it is just as "real" as the deeper patterns of motive, emotion, and value; the mask is easier to change and may not predict behavior in an emergency, but it is a significant feature of this personality.

The components of personality. In describing any personality, the psychologist has to make certain judgments as to what items are important. A complete description of any one individual would make an encyclopedia. What are the components which must be included to give a worth-while summary of any personality? The list will sound like a résumé of the preceding chapters of this textbook:

1. *Dynamic patterns.* The motives and emotions which impel this person to act in significant ways are obviously important. Not only biogenic drives but also social values and emotional reactions to other people must be studied and evaluated. The first and prime element in an understanding of any personality is this: what is he striving to accomplish? What are his goals?

2. *Perceptions.* In everyday life it often becomes difficult to distinguish perceptions from dynamic impulses, since the latter are related to objects and people. The essential distinction should, however, be clear. In discussing motives we concern ourselves with the inner state desired by the organism; in discussing perception we attend to the objects and actions which look as if they can be utilized to obtain these satisfactions. The child in infancy may perceive strangers as threats but perceive members of her family as sources of pleasure. On this basis are developed such very important perceptions as "mother" and "father," which transfer to guide the individual's reactions to many people in later years. The child's perception of self—as attractive, intelligent, "good," or "bad" is also formed in the family.

3. *Learning.* Each of us learns certain response patterns in the nature of talking, smiling, gesturing, entertaining people, taking responsibilities, inhibiting our own selfish impulses, and working with other people. These responses provide the basis for our "social stimulus value" to friends, teachers, and others.

Learning also leads to the establishment of conditioned responses to external stimuli —visceral changes, muscular and glandular activities. These CRs provide bases for fears, annoyances, and preferences. The average person also acquires a wide variety of skills and interests, which help in social adjustment. Finally, we learn a general way of looking at life—a frame of reference —which gives a broad underlying unity to the personality.

4. *Intelligence.* It is apparent that the individual's level of g, and the degree to which this is specialized along numerical and spatial factors, has an impact upon personality, although it is not usually considered a personality trait. Obviously the ability to think and generalize about one's experiences will determine the extent

to which he is integrated and organized, although other factors are also important.

Comparisons with other people. Implicit in the preparation of personality sketches is the notion of a comparison with specific people or with a hypothetical average. As we observed in connection with concept formation (page 387), the contrast between two examples can help us to identify the specific item we want. When, in everyday speech, we say, "John is aggressive," we imply but leave unsaid, "as compared with other boys" or some other norm group. If we desire to identify a particular trait more carefully, we may add, "It isn't like Sam; Sam is so smooth and pleasant that people don't mind, but John makes them angry."

Comparisons may be made on a variety of bases. We may be looking at the *frequency* of a response, such as smiling, or at the *intensity* of response, such as loving or fearing. The focus may be on an intervening variable which must be inferred from responses, such as a desire to be loved; it may be on a generalized trait which is also inferred in one way or another.

At the beginning of this chapter we suggested that different psychologists had defined personality in terms of a pattern of responses, as one's social stimulus value, and as a system of intervening variables which cannot be directly observed. It would be nice if we could point to certain processes in the development from infancy to maturity and say that these give us the foundations for personality conceived in each of these different ways. Unfortunately, human behavior does not organize itself so neatly.

In the earlier parts of this volume (especially Chap. 3), we have described certain events such as love, fear, valuing people, perceiving the self, and so on. At that time we were trying to give a picture of what people in general are like; we ignored the problem of differences between individuals, and the unique pattern of liking, disliking, loving, and hating which makes up a specific personality. We are now concerned with the way in which these elements are put together to form a personality pattern.

It will be convenient to arrange the material on basic development of personality according to the kind of phenomenon being studied. First, we can examine studies of *temperament*, which deals with the drives and emotions characterizing a person. This provides a kind of inner core, the dynamic side of the individual. Around this is built a *social personality* (the personality as a mask which we show to others, or the pattern of responses which determines how others will like us). Facial expressions and gestures should be considered here. However, the social personality also includes many inner processes not directly observable; it includes the question of how we perceive other people, how we expect to treat them and them to treat us. Obviously temperament affects the social personality; however, for purposes of convenience we can treat them separately.

Temperament

When we study any individual closely, we observe a kind of core, a broad underlying structure of dynamic trends which is close to the physiological level and relatively resistant to change. This is contrasted with the social exterior of personality, which is more a product of learning and thus more modifiable. For this underlying dynamic organization we use the term *temperament*. Adjectives such as energetic, lazy, explosive, anxious, irritable, cheerful, depressed, and exuberant may help to identify it for you. Obviously temperament is the *characteristic pattern of energy mobilization* of the individual.

Freeman (1948) holds that temperament is the consistent way in which the person mobilizes and discharges energy to satisfy his needs and maintain psychological equilibrium. Max responds quickly to stimuli and builds up tension rapidly. He explodes into vigorous, well-directed action and then relaxes into normal status promptly. Bill gets going slowly and builds up a "full head of steam" only if given plenty of time. He may (or may not) control this energy well in dealing with problems. He may mutter and reverberate for some time before cooling off, or he may recover quickly.

Temperament, then, is diagnosed primarily by the frequency and intensity of energy mobilization. Anger, fear, love, hate, joy, and the like fit into the common notion of temperament, but the psychologist adds strength of biological drives, ability to delay immediate satisfaction of needs, intensity of energy arousal, and so on. Burt (1948) has demonstrated that there is a general emotionality factor or temperament factor running through the individual's performances in a wide variety of situations—all of those listed in the preceding sentence. Persons high on this factor have many and intense fears, loves, irritations, tantrums, and so forth. At the opposite pole we find individuals who have few emotions and those tend to be of low intensity. The majority, of course, are in between.

This general factor looks rather like *g* in our discussion of intelligence, in the sense that it shows up in a wide variety of specific performances. Burt therefore christened it *e* to suggest that it played a role in temperament comparable with that of *g* in intelligence.

Burt also found other generalized factors in temperament, the main two being: (1) introversion-extraversion, or a tendency to focus attention and activity upon external stimuli or upon inner states; and (2) a relative predominance of pleasant or of unpleasant experiences (see Fig. 13:1).

It is obvious that we would have a good deal of information about a person if we knew that his standing on *e* (general emotionality) was average, that he tended to react outwardly, and that he showed a preponderance of pleasant emotions.

Heredity and environment. Is personality determined more by heredity, or more by environment? This question may be one which cannot be answered. If we confine ourselves to temperament, it seems safe to say that these individual differences seem due more to heredity. Let us consider some of the evidence.

1. *Physiological foundations.* While it does not "explain" temperament to say that it has a physiological foundation, this statement does point to a fairly close relationship with heredity. We know that our glands, ANS, visceral musculature, etc., are inherited. Since our emotions are closely involved with these structures, the presumption of hereditary determination is increased.

Jost (1941) showed that children having many personal problems were physiologically different from those who were personally well adjusted. He tested 18 children from the Orthogenic School of the University of Chicago (which specializes in emotionally disturbed cases) and 20 of the same age from the University Elementary School. The former group would be described as high on Burt's *e* (very temperamental, explosive, erratic); the latter were chosen by teachers as emotionally well balanced. The disturbed children were markedly higher in visceral responses, both in normal situations and in an emotionally frustrating situation (the experimenter gave them a problem to solve which looked easy but was actually insoluble). The emotional children showed wider blood pressure changes, more GSR (electrical skin conductivity) changes, more variable respiration, wider change in pulse rate, etc.

Similar differences between personalities

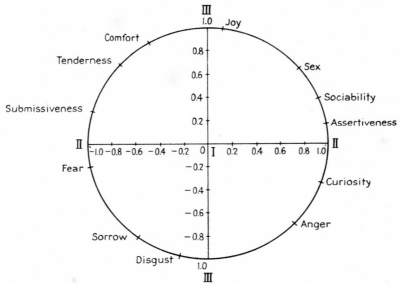

FIG. 13:1. Organization of emotions in temperament. This sketch is intended to represent a three-dimensional plot of the relations among temperamental qualities. The vertical axis of a sphere going directly away from the reader is indicated by I. This axis is the dimension of "general emotionality" or e. Persons high on this have many emotions of all kinds; those scoring low have few emotions. II-II is the axis from "low-activity" to "high-activity" emotions; note that submissiveness and tenderness are at the left ("asthenic" emotions), while assertiveness and anger are at the right ("sthenic" emotions). Fear seems somewhat misplaced on this scale. III-III is the pleasant-unpleasant or "euthymic-dysthymic" axis. Comfort, joy, and sex are at the upper end; sorrow, anger, and fear at the lower. This chart can be interpreted to mean that, while a major dimension of temperament is simply the person's general level of emotionality, people also differ with regard to the predominance of sthenic-asthenic and euthymic-dysthymic emotions; or, in other words, that some lean toward an excess of one or more of these, as compared with the other emotional patterns. (*From Burt, 1948.*)

can be demonstrated with adults. Cattell (1950) presents data on the varying physiological reactivity of three adults. Individual A was rated high, relative to others in the group, on general vigor, sociability, and persistence. He also shows large physiological changes (in this case, the GSR) to energy-mobilizing stimuli (a task to be performed, a symbol likely to evoke love or sex impulse, and a physical threat stimulus). Persons B and C are rated lower on the personality variables, and they have correspondingly lower physiological reactivity.[1]

[1] These data should not be taken as highly

It will be recalled that Hall's study of rats (page 86) proved emotionality in that animal to be determined at least in part by heredity. The kind of functions tested by Jost and Cattell would seem to fall in the same category. Certainly the physiological data support the notion that heredity has a decided influence on temperament.

significant. The three cases were selected to show a relationship, but the actual agreement of personality estimates with physiological responses is not very high. It is only with a large number of subjects that we can be sure of getting differences such as Cattell reports. For any specific person we would not be at all sure that the personality rating and the physical data would agree.

2. *Resemblances of twins.* In Chap. 12 we cited Newman's study on identical and fraternal twins, from which it was inferred that both physical and intellectual characteristics had a heavy component of hereditary determination—perhaps as much as 80 per cent of the differences between individuals being due to heredity, 20 per cent to environment. In that table (page 460) it was noted that for differences on the Woodworth-Mathews questionnaire of emotional maladjustment, the proportions were reversed: 30 per cent of the variance was judged due to heredity, 70 per cent to environment.

It is easy for us to overestimate the contributions of heredity. When a boy grows up in the household with his father, his behavior will reflect not only what he has inherited from the father but also imitation of the father. A group of brothers may all show certain traits, but they may have learned these traits in their play together.

3. *Role of physical constitution.* A third line of evidence, considerably more debatable, as to the importance of heredity in temperament comes from the study of body build. Various investigators have claimed that patterns of personality are related to patterns of physique. As far back as the ancient Greeks we have had theories about the temperament of the fat man, the thin man, the muscular man, etc. Shakespeare has his Julius Caesar saying:

Yond Cassius has a lean and hungry look;
He thinks too much; such men are dangerous.

It is impossible, in this text, to go into much of the evidence on this problem. We shall mention only one of the most controversial studies, the elaborate work by W. H. Sheldon and the Harvard Laboratory. This is one of the most pretentious theories on the problem, and it has aroused a great deal of debate among American psychologists.

Sheldon (1942) has proposed that there are three components of physical build and three corresponding patterns of temperament. Here are the basic ideas of his theory, arranged in parallel columns:

Physical components	*Temperamental components*
Endomorphy	*Viscerotonia*
Large viscera	Love of comfort, gluttony
Soft body contours	Sociability, affection
Mesomorphy	*Somatotonia*
Heavy muscular development	Vigorous, self-assertive
Hard body contours	Ambitious, ruthless
Ectomorphy	*Cerebrotonia*
Long, slender extremities	Restrained, inhibited
Poor muscular development	Withdrawn socially, thoughtful

Sheldon supports his views with elaborate data on physical measurements of young men studied in the Harvard Laboratory, and with ratings of temperament made by himself and his collaborators. While the physical components can be identified by actual measurements, Sheldon generally uses a 7-point rating scale to describe a particular physique. Any individual can be identified or described by the combination of his ratings on the three components: thus a 7-1-1 would be an extreme endomorph, with very little mesomorphy or ectomorphy (see Fig. 13:2). A 4-4-4 would be just an average figure with no particular trend toward the overdevelopment of any of the three components. Other examples of the physical types are shown in Fig. 13:2.

Sheldon reports some amazingly high correlations between his ratings of somatotypes (body build) and his ratings of temperament. For example, in one of his groups he finds the following correlations:

Endomorphy with viscerotonia 79
Mesomorphy with somatotonia 82
Ectomorphy with cerebrotonia 83

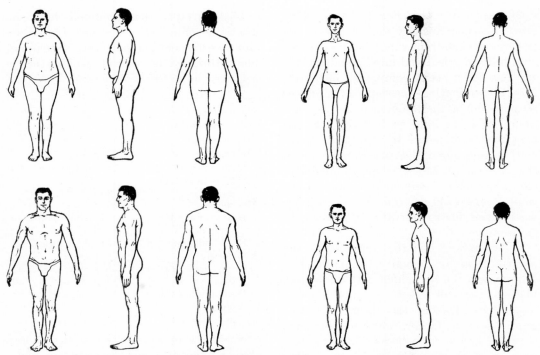

FIG. 13:2. Sheldon's system of body types. At the upper left is shown the extreme of endomorphy; lower left, decided mesomorphy; upper right, predominant ectomorphy; and lower right, an average individual with equal components of all three trends. If Sheldon's results prove correct, physical types leaning toward one of the extremes will have temperamental traits in the corresponding direction. (*Drawn from Sheldon and Stevens, 1942.*)

If these close relationships are confirmed by other investigators, it will be very convincing proof of the role of physique in determining temperament.

The studies on Sheldon's somatotypes in relation to personality are unsatisfactory because no one has devised a way of judging the three temperamental components without studying and observing the individual to be rated. Since such observation means becoming aware of the physical type, there is the possibility that the judge will be influenced one way or another by his knowledge. Studies using objective tests of personality show very poor agreement with the Sheldon body types, but people who approve of the theory can always claim that these are not good tests of the three temperament components. Consequently, for the present we must let the matter rest. Probably heredity is a major determinant of body build, and perhaps body build is a determinant of temperament.

Environment and temperament. If we define temperament as the person's characteristic pattern of energy mobilization, we stack the cards to some extent in favor of heredity as the main influence. Human energy, after all, is physiological, and certain broad lines of energy expenditure are laid down by the biogenic drives which are the basis of man's motivation.

Environment and learning, however, can have an influence even on temperament. The child's experiences will have an impact upon his demands for satisfaction, upon the frequency and intensity of emotions, and upon speed and vigor of response.

The child's capacity to experience love, fear, anger, and the like is definitely inherited. The frequency with which these patterns are exercised will depend on his environment. If he lives in a warm, friendly atmosphere where most adults provide him with need satisfactions, he will come to love a variety of people and he will perceive many kinds of persons as lovable. If, on the contrary, he encounters many frustrations which make him angry, he will perceive many people as signs of frustration, and his temperamental pattern in later life will be irritable and belligerent. Or a surplus of fears will presumably set up many conditioned fear reactions, and he will perceive people as threatening, to be avoided.[1]

The Social Personality

After we abstract the dynamic features of personality—motives, emotions, energy level, etc.—which we have called *temperament*, there is still a great deal left over. This is primarily the social aspect of the individual, his ways of interacting with other people. Its importance is suggested by the frequency with which we use such terms as friendly, irritating, attractive, cold, quarrelsome. It will be important for us to examine the foundations of the social personality.

This should not lead to the conclusion that, in a real person, temperament and social traits are cleanly separated. On the contrary, in the total personality, all these characteristics are closely intertwined. A boy's energy level determines how active he will be, and this activity will affect his social interactions. At least we can predict that he will bump into more people and probably make more of an impression on them. However, some active individuals have many contacts and are mostly liked; others literally crash into their fellows and antagonize them. Thus we cannot predict

[1] Consider in this connection the relative importance of deprivation, satiation, and habit in determining intensity of emotion (pp. 83–85).

from the temperamental level to the social level. The positive or negative emotional quality of the interaction depends on environment.

Personality as mask. By a devious route, the word personality is linked to the masks worn by the players in a Greek drama. These masks were stylized and were put on to show the audience what kind of person was being represented. Some of personality in everyday life is unquestionably a mask; we are trained from early childhood to be polite when we wish to be rude, to wait when we want to rush, to give in to others when our real preference is to be selfish. As we become adults and learn something about the psychology of influencing others, we act parts calculated to help us gain our own ends. The salesman laughs at the customer's joke and cultivates a genial front which may have little connection with his inner feelings. Most business executives find that they have to cultivate a "hard-boiled" exterior to avoid being imposed upon. Columns of advice to wives urge them to act a part with their husbands, to pretend emotions they do not feel, and so on.

Probably these masks are, to some extent, necessary. Certainly the social taboos against violence help to preserve civilization. If no one disguised his feelings to avoid hurting others, life could become much more unpleasant. However, a psychologically intriguing aspect of this phenomenon is that the mask becomes an integral part of the personality. La Rochefoucauld is quoted as saying that "We become so accustomed to disguise ourselves to others, that at last we are disguised to ourselves." More accurately—habits practiced to achieve certain ends become established as permanent parts of us and may even be valued in and for themselves (cf. Chap. 4).

Personality as perception. If we look at the social personality from the outside, we may find the conception of a mask to be useful. The individual has learned a set of habits and ways of doing things which will make predictable impressions on others. However, if we look at this same phenomenon from the inside, from the subjective approach, we find that the individual has learned certain ways of perceiving reality. The timid person sees many frightening people and events around him; the bold person sees no threats nearby. The optimist looks upon the world as "his oyster"; the pessimist feels more that the world is about to devour him. The behavior of each person is appropriate to what he sees around him.

In Chap. 6 we noted that what a person perceives is only in part a function of physical reality. To some extent each of us constructs his own private universe. The psychotic lives in a world in which pink elephants carry trombones, and trees grow hams and bacon. The neurotic seems to be in a strange unstable universe full of vaguely defined dangers. The communist lives in a world threatened by capitalist imperialism, and the capitalist perceives himself in peril from the red terror. The analysis of any perceptual process, then, calls for an attempt to find out how much is structural (determined by factors outside the person) and how much is behavioral (determined by his own inner needs and past experiences). To the extent that personality is *an individual's unique way of looking at himself and his environment,* it is an organized pattern of behavioral influences on perception.

We can distinguish, then, two aspects of the social personality. One, the response side, is composed of actions, habits, gestures, facial expressions, and the like. The other, the perceptual side, is made up of stereotypes, perceptual constancies, positive and negative valences. In the following pages we shall say a little about the foundations of each aspect.

The Expressive Aspect of Personality

When the term *personality* is used in the popular sense mentioned at the beginning of this chapter, it includes the characteristic gestures and facial expressions of the person. Our first impressions—which determine our liking or disliking the newcomer—depend substantially upon his way of smiling, talking, walking, gesturing.

The origins of these features of personality go back to the expressions of emotion in early infancy. We noted (Chap. 3) that young children do not have any set patterns for expressing such states as fear, anger, love, etc., in such a way that judges can easily identify them. The facial and bodily activities, at least for all the unpleasant states, looked alike to these observers; and there is at least some evidence to suggest that the visceral phases of the emotional response are also alike. The two parts of the ANS—the sympathetic and parasympathetic systems—seem to correspond roughly to tension-arousing and tension-reducing states, and there is a clear distinction between these two patterns, but none within each category.

This undifferentiated manner of expression begins to be modified by learning at an early age. Perhaps little Johnny is punished for crying and stamping his feet; hence when he starts making these responses he feels anxious and inhibits them. Percy, on the other hand, may find that making enough noise leads to satisfaction of his physical desires; he becomes more and more expressive and responds to ever slighter frustrations. Mary is praised and cuddled for climbing on an adult's lap, while Betty finds herself shoved off and scolded.

Lorge (1936) showed that it is possible to teach a white rat certain habits which resemble some of our social gestures. He placed a rat in a small box and watched him closely. As soon as the rat assumed a kind of "begging" crouch, Lorge pressed a button, opening the door to the food box. In a few trials the rat seemed to have "caught on" to the movement he must make and began giving it dependably within a few seconds. At the end of a hundred trials the rat was "begging" within 2 seconds after being dropped into the box—about as fast as he could get into position.

Much child training is like this. We reward the child for certain behavior in social situations and punish or ignore other actions. The child may try conformity and submission, or he may behave in a rebellious, negativistic manner. He may show some active, aggressive, outgoing responses, and also some which are quite and seclusive. Which of these were rewarded and which ignored? If we had this information for a given child, we could probably explain why the adolescent personality retained certain patterns from childhood and dropped out others.

Cultural differences. The wide range of expressiveness of children reared in different families within American culture may be impressive, but it is even more startling to see the extent to which cultures vary in this regard. Children can be trained to use almost any muscular pattern to communicate an emotional state. Blackburn (1945) comments:

In Western culture it is conventional to stand up in the presence of a superior as a mark of respect. But the inhabitants of Fiji or the Tonga Islands sit down in those circumstances. The inhabitants of the Friendly Islands take off their clothes as a mark of respect, and the Todas raise the open right hand to the face, resting the thumb on the bridge of the nose. To us it means something rather different from respect.

Tears, too, do not always imply sorrow . . . and even when they are used to imply grief there is often a conventional pattern—thus in China it is reported that the amount of emo-

tional display permitted on a sorrowful occasion depended on a person's social class. A nobleman showed less emotion than a commoner, and for the latter to be restrained implied that he was presuming beyond his class.[1]

Experimental studies of facial expression. The observations of emotional expression from different cultures do not rule out the possibility that certain emotions may innately pattern specific responses, and the culture simply determines the situations in which that emotion is to be shown. If this were true, facial expressions of persons within a single culture should agree reasonably well when these people are subjected to the same emotion-arousing situation. Unfortunately, this is not verified by experiment.

One of the most convincing studies, because of its realism, is that of Landis (1924). By getting college students firmly strapped in a chair (on the pretext of taking blood pressure and similar readings), he made it impossible for them to leave the laboratory. Then they were subjected to some rather drastic situations. For example, they were handed a live white rat and directed to cut off its head with a knife. If the subject refused, the experimenter cut off the animal's head on the arm of the experimental chair. They were asked to write out an account of some humiliating experience, being assured that they could tear it up when it was written. Then the experimenter snatched the paper away and read the account aloud. Pictures of loathsome diseases were used as stimuli, as were some pornographic poses. Both still and motion pictures were taken of the subjects in these situations.

Landis analyzed his results in two ways: (1) he attempted to identify the use of particular facial muscles in responding to specified situations; and (2) he asked

[1] Blackburn (1945), pp. 151–152. Reprinted by permission of Routledge and Kegan Paul, Ltd.

the subjects to look at their own photographs and identify the emotion they were feeling at the time. Then he looked for similarities in photographs given the same label. Both procedures led to very little agreement. Different subjects did not use the same muscles in the same situation, and the same subject did not use the same muscles in different pictures which he labeled as the same emotion. About the only agreement in the findings was the very general one that pleasant situations could be distinguished from unpleasant stimulation. This is in harmony with what has been said about the visceral reactions.

These observations suggest that, while temperament may have a firm basis in heredity, by the time these emotional states have been subjected to socialization for several years, they do not reflect any common core of inherited expression of emotions. To the extent that a person has any consistent kind of facial expression, it arises from learning.

Gestures and handwriting. What about the movements of the hands and arms? We know that there are group differences in manual gesturing, the "volatile" Mediterranean people being distinguished by a great deal of gesticulation, the "inhibited" northerners being quite chary of such movements. It is fairly easy to relate these differences to culture, the best evidence being that children transferred from one country to another imitate the gestural style of their surroundings unless trained not to do so. Parents, of course, act as "agents of the culture" in this training.

The gestures and expressive movements about which we are concerned find their origin in the energy-mobilization phenomena of drives and emotions. The more vigorous of these states, hunger, anger, and so on, lead to high energy activity with many muscles tense. These muscles are likely to respond more vigorously than normal; for example, a man who is angry

about conditions at the office slams doors at home. On the other hand, depression, which is generally associated with failing to achieve the desired goal, is characterized by a very low energy level. The depressed person goes about drooping, with slow and weak responses to stimulation. It is plausible to suppose that, if certain motive states occur often, a person will begin to show consistent patterns of expression.

There is also the probability that conditioned responses and habits will be developed. A person who is very timid and anxious will form CRs to various stimuli in his daily environment. Even when he is not specifically anxious, he may show the facial and manual patterns appropriate to anxiety, simply because these ways of responding have become habitual. Tension, tremor, jerky movements, and inhibited verbalization may thus appear in his characteristic daily activities.

Gestures as communication. Many expressive movements probably find their origin not in a specific emotional state, but in the need to communicate to others. By facial expressions and gestures we can tell others (1) how we feel, or (2) how we want them to think we feel, or (3) how we want them to feel. This is probably achieved by differentiating out certain elements of the pattern aroused by motive states. Thus little Johnny may both laugh and cry when he is upset, but he finds that adults point to his laughter and do not believe that he is really sad. He thus learns to eliminate that part of the response. Children also become marvelously adept at producing tears to order, or pretending fear, anger, or distress, in order to get certain results from adults, when the inner feeling is absent.

Because of the failure of the experiments on facial expression, and the wide variation that we get between different cultures, most psychologists today are highly skeptical of any theory that expressive movements derive directly from motives and emotions. There is undoubtedly a general phenomenon of heightened or lowered activity which contributes something, but most of the patterning of facial and similar expressions depends upon learning to communicate inner emotions to others.

This does not mean that expressive movements are useless in the study of personality. Some worth-while data have been gathered from the observation of gestures and from analysis of handwriting and drawings. But these must be interpreted in the light of the kind of family, the nationality culture, schooling, and such influences to which the child has been exposed. They do not show hereditary factors in personality. At most they indicate that inherited temperamental traits, such as vigor, speed of response, and persistence, will modify the social side of the personality. Training must operate on inherent raw material, and the final result, the adult personality, will reflect both factors.

Personality as social stimulus value. At the beginning of this chapter, we noted that in popular speech personality is often considered to be the social stimulus value of the individual. Expressive movements provide us with a base for understanding this phenomenon. If a person has developed an expressive face, a pleasant smile and tone of voice, ways of behaving which will effectively arouse in others the kinds of emotions he wishes to evoke, then we can say that he has a socially desirable personality. If, on the other hand, his voice is rasping, his facial mannerisms unpleasant, his gestures irritating, it is unlikely that he will be able to "win friends and influence people." People who register amusement where they should look sad, or fear where others find it inappropriate, will at the very least be considered queer and perhaps may evoke active hostility.

The process of socialization is a process of molding the child into a culturally approved pattern. The parents, as agents of society, must teach the child the right ways of behaving, or they also are subject to reproof and punishment. Thus the child must acquire the approved attitudes toward death, misfortune, power, and other social realities. If he smiles, laughs, weeps, bows, and salutes at the proper times, he is accepted as a member of society. If he fails to show these approved expressions, he may wind up in jail or in a mental hospital.

This process of socialization follows a fairly well defined plan. Temperamental traits, expressive patterns, and inner perceptual systems develop in a continuous interaction between the child and his environment. Different psychologists have written about this developmental process; the most influential analysis of the unfolding of personality has been that of Sigmund Freud, the famous Viennese physician who founded the psychoanalytic school. As a means of bringing a consistent interpretation to bear upon these observations, let us briefly summarize Freud's theory of personality development.

The Freudian Theory of Personality Development

Freud's writings seem to assume, not always explicitly, a kind of inevitable unfolding of a hereditary pattern in personality. Freud treated environment largely as something which could disrupt the smooth flow of the developmental process, giving rise to various personality traits, neuroses, and breakdowns. This, of course, is contradictory to the tenor of most of this book, where emphasis has been placed on perception, learning, and thinking as means by which we guide our behavior, shaped by our environment.

Freud's theory is primarily dynamic. It focuses on the motives and desires of children and adults, along with the techniques they develop for obtaining satisfaction. While sex is treated as the major motive in life, sex is defined in such a broad way that it is approximately equal to pleasure. Further, in many respects gratification is a matter of restoring equilibrium. Hence it is not so far from the homeostatic theory which has been the basis for this book.

Stages in personality development. Freud proposed that personality development should be considered as a matter of going through a series of stages from infancy to complete maturity. At times he seems to consider these stages as determined by heredity, although on other occasions he writes as if they were simply a natural consequence of the environment in which the child lives. (Most American psychologists seem to incline to the latter view.) People differ with respect to the success with which they resolve these various stages. A maladjusted or neurotic adult can be thought of as having got "stuck" at one of these points and failed to progress beyond it; or he may still carry unresolved vestiges of it about, in a manner inappropriate to an adult. We shall note examples of such occurrences as we sketch the theory.

1. *The infantile passive stage.* Freud assumes that the infant is desirous of sexual pleasure from birth, but sexual pleasure in this context means any bodily pleasure. The quest for pleasure in different parts of the body begins with the intense enjoyment of sucking, during the first months of life when the baby is necessarily passive and dependent. This stage, consequently, is often referred to as the *oral sucking* stage.

During this period the infant is completely narcissistic, loving only himself. For some time there is doubt that he has any awareness of an environment or other people—he has only his sensations, particularly somesthetic, although he gradually comes to respond to light, sound, etc. All

need satisfactions come to him without effort on his part, except occasionally to cry. If, for any reason, he fails to evolve satisfactorily out of this stage, therefore, he becomes an adult who is completely dependent upon others; he thinks "the world owes him a living" and he is going to lie around waiting for it to be placed in his mouth.

All adults, of course, in our culture show some oral eroticism: kissing, for example, is a vestige from the oral passive stage. Many cultures do not include kissing as a form of adult love-making, but there are other forms of oral play which may have a similar function.

Gradually the child learns that his body is something uniquely attached to his sensations, that there is at least one other person (the mother or her surrogate), and that there is "something out there" (the environment) from which sensations and pleasures seem to arise. As he becomes conscious of his mother as a separate individual, he loves her as a source of gratification and comes to imitate her in many ways (smiles, gestures, babbling, etc.). This seems to be the earliest phase of the process we shall call *identification*, which is most important in the molding of personality.

2. *The oral sadistic stage.* There is no sharp border line between these stages. Gradually, however, we get the development of more active effort on the child's part. Instead of passively waiting for pleasure, he begins to seek it and demand it. Pleasure is still derived from the mouth, but biting rather than sucking is the preferred activity.

This phenomenon of enjoying the act of biting probably coincides with the age of weaning for most breast-fed babies, the reason being obvious. However, it seems to occur also in bottle-fed babies, so that no interpretation of a desire to hurt the mother is plausible. Rather, it seems to coincide with the development of capacity for *aggression*—for actively wresting satisfaction from the environment against opposition (see Fig. 13:3).

Id and Ego. During the passive stage the child's personality is said to be purely "Id." The term *Id* was coined by Freud to refer to the sum total of biological drives or pleasure-seeking demands of the person. Thus hunger, thirst, sex, comfort, escape from pain, etc., were all considered Id demands. The Id, of course, was said to be entirely innate.

The *Ego* was defined as that part of the personality which attempts to attain satisfaction for Id impulses. Thus there is very little Ego at birth, and it is gradually developed by the organism as sensory and muscular capacities mature and knowledge increases as to how satisfactions can be achieved. It follows that Ego development coincides more or less with the onset of the oral sadistic stage, with active self-assertion and seizing of satisfactions.

Sadism. The term *sadism* refers to a tendency to get pleasure out of inflicting pain upon others. Freud did not, of course, assert that the infant consciously intends to inflict pain by biting, or that there is any conscious anticipation of pleasure if something is bitten. Rather, these are merely consequences of the way the infant is organized at this time. He has a few teeth (plus, probably, some itching gums which are soothed by biting against objects not too rough); also, he has more muscular strength. These factors influence the development of the biting pattern.

On the other hand, we must recognize that the obtaining of pleasure through biting can lead to learning, and so the expectation is established that biting others will be pleasurable. In later years (at least as early as the age of two) biting can be replaced by pinching and other forms of aggressive play; as language improves, "biting" remarks can also serve. Many conversational interchanges between

FIG. 13:3. A picture for eliciting oral sadism. In the "Blacky" test, cartoons show the little black puppy engaged in activities which may be assumed to represent the various stages of psychosexual development identified by Freud. The theory is that younger people will find it easier to write or talk about emotional problems with the puppy as the center of attention rather than a human figure. Blum, who devised the test, finds substantial evidence to indicate that the comments written by subjects about each picture conform to Freudian theory. (*From Blum, 1949.*)

people come under the heading of vestiges of oral sadism. Actual fusion of sexual pleasure with the infliction of physical pain upon another person is, fortunately, rare; Freud would claim that this, too, occurs in a person who has inadequately worked through his oral sadistic phase.

3. *The anal stage.* Some time during the first year, the child also finds that pleasurable sensations can derive from the anus. Particularly if toilet training is started early, and a great deal of fussing over bowel movements results, attention may be focused on this area. Freud believed that a period of anal eroticism was inevitable in any event, but that excessive severity in training for cleanliness, having a movement on schedule, etc., could cause *fixation* at this level, with consequent failure to mature normally.

Toilet training represents a real crisis in the life of the child. It is the first of many encounters he will have with social rules and regulations. Up to this time he has been completely selfish and self-centered, and while his parents may have refused to cater to some of his whims, they probably have not actually tried to impose any behavior patterns. Socialization begins with the control of excretory impulses.[1]

Rebellion, submission to adult control, and other patterns find their initiation at this stage. Since the attempt to train the child for sphincter control is the first real effort to impose a new behavior pattern, it is the first opportunity for a head-on collision between child and parent over the matter of authority. Negativistic behavior ("I won't!") becomes noticeable. On the other hand, the child learns that he can please the mother by using the toilet rather than soiling his clothes; thus, we have a whole complex series of social interactions developing for the first time. Giving in to the mother, doing something to make her happy, or rebelliously withholding, refusing to submit—these are some of the basic patterns of relating oneself to other people.

Adult manifestations. Fixation at the anal level may give rise to excessive cleanliness, orderliness, and fussiness about details, if the child accepts parental control. If he refuses to submit to the parents' demands, he grows up to be bohemian, sloppy, and careless.

Concern about odors is said to be a vestige of the anal stage. Some people enjoy odd, even foul-smelling odors; others find any putrid smell extremely repulsive. Presumably these reactions are traces of the emotional relationship which characterized the toilet-training period. Concern about money is also alleged to be an anal trait; miserliness is related to withholding, unwillingness to "give up" anything. On the other hand, irrational generosity, inability to use normal caution in financial matters, is presumed to be an outgrowth of "giving" to please the mother.

The Superego. It is now necessary to introduce Freud's concept of the superego. We have mentioned the Id, the raw animal demands for gratification, and the Ego, the portion of the personality concerned with trying to get satisfaction for Id drives. During the anal stage we begin to observe some behavior of the type which gave rise to Freud's conception of the *Superego.* In brief, the Superego is the *conscience* of the child; it is his feeling that he *must* do certain things and *must not* do others. Clearly, this kind of feeling must first be implanted from outside. Toilet training is one of the first situations in which this kind of indoctrination occurs. The relations of Id, Ego, and Superego are sketched in Fig. 13:4.

Pleasure principle vs. reality principle. Another point about Freudian theory ought to be introduced at this point. The Id, we noted, is completely selfish.[1] Furthermore, it has no regard for consequences. Behavior at these early stages follows the *pleasure principle;* namely, grasp the maximum of immediate pleasure or avoid immediate pain, regardless of the future.

Gradually the child comes to realize that this policy is not too good. He may eat too much and get a bellyache, or he may continue playing in defiance of orders and get a spanking. There is a slow tendency for a new pattern to show in his behavior, the *reality principle:* try to get the maxi-

---

[1] Here, for example, we find clear-cut differences between various cultures. Some primitive groups are as rigorous about excretory cleanliness as we are. Others are not; generally, we find that they do not show some of the patterns of behavior said to be associated with the anal stage. This confirms Freud's idea about the relationship but indicates again that environment, not heredity, is the factor responsible.

[1] This manner of speaking is metaphorical; it should not be interpreted as meaning that "the Id" is a little man in a red suit, up inside your head, directing your behavior. Freud used this way of saying things as a short cut for the more devious expressions, such as "At the stage when Id motivations are uninhibited, behavior is completely selfish." Likewise, the student should avoid thinking of Ego and Superego as persons; they are simply convenient ways of talking about *a set of habits, motives, and expectations.*

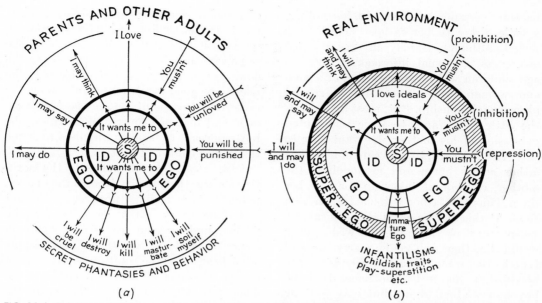

FIG. 13:4. Relations of Id, Ego, and Superego. In the infantile stage (a), the Id is constantly demanding satisfaction, and the immature Ego is constantly trying to obtain the goal objects demanded. The environment, however, is beginning to impose restrictions in the form of punishment and threat (negative valences). The Ego develops in the process of learning to deal with the problems so presented.

In the mature stage (b), the environmental controls have mostly been accepted into the personality, and inhibitions of Id impulses are now imposed by the self without the necessity of outside threat. Of course, there is always an awareness of the possibility of outside punishment. The Ego habit systems develop in such a way that socially acceptable solutions are found for most Id-Superego conflicts; however, most of us have a few areas of immaturity in which we act childishly, evade social controls, demand infantile gratifications from others, and so on. *(From Hendrick, Facts and Theories of Psychoanalysis, 1934. By permission of Alfred A. Knopf, Inc.)*

mum of pleasure and minimum of pain in the long run, not just the immediate situation. This means the evaluation of an immediate pleasure as against a possible future pain; it means considering an immediate discomfort in the light of the possibility that it might have a big reward hiding behind it. (We have sketched the elements of this process on page 112.)

By the time a person reaches maturity, he should have abandoned the pleasure principle and be living by the reality principle. Unfortunately, many people do not. They buy things they can't afford, because they can't forgo immediate gratification; they miss out on long-term pleasures, because they are unwilling to accept a little present inconvenience. When we say that "so-and-so is infantile," we

usually mean that he just can't restrain himself and gets into trouble because of his failure adequately to consider reality.

4. *The Oedipus complex.* You will note that most of the phenomena we have cited so far do not involve the sex organs at all. While Freud based his theory on a sexual motive, he did not base it on sex in the adult sense, but on a quest for pleasure through stimulating parts of the body. The oral and anal stages represent periods during which the child allegedly gets most of his pleasures from sensations from these organs. These early stages are thus sometimes identified as "pregenital."

The first explicitly sexual phenomena Freud reports involve what he called the *Oedipus complex.* At about the age of four or five years, he asserts, the little boy becomes very much in love with his mother, a little girl with her father. This love is sexual, although it may involve no real awareness of sexual intercourse. By this age, children will have learned that a man and woman have some kind of special pleasure relationship. But, most important, the little boy wants to have undisputed possession of his mother; he wants her to cater to his desires, to take care of him. The father comes home and monopolizes the mother, or at least takes up some of her time. Thus the father is looked upon as a rival. At this age we get little boys saying, as so many of them do, "I wish daddy would die; then you could marry me and keep house for me." Mother often is unduly horrified at this; it does not mean that the boy knows about dying but only that he wants competition out of the way. Little girls often make similar remarks to their fathers.

However, it is important to recognize that the child's reaction here is *ambivalent*. To the boy, father has negative valence (threat, frustration) because he competes for mother's attention. But father also has positive valence; he is a source of play, of money, of fun in various ways. At this age the child comes face to face with one of the grim realities of life; lots of goals are both attractive and threatening.

The normal resolution of the Oedipus complex is worked out in this manner (we use the boy as an example): "I can't compete with father; he is too big and strong. Besides, mother seems fond of the big lug. She doesn't like me to fight him. Maybe the best thing I can do is to act the way he does, and she might love me more." In other words, the child solves his problem by *identifying himself* with the parent of the same sex.

The *Superego* is greatly strengthened by this identification; in fact, Freud treats this as the true foundation of the Superego, since the process of learning to be "good" at the toilet-training stage is more a matter of pleasing mother or of avoiding punishment. If the Oedipus complex is resolved by identification with the parent of the same sex, then the child really accepts the adult personality as a part of his own; he tries to be good because he wants to be like father. At this point we see the first signs of a real internal control of motives; the boy can react to his own impulses with the thought, "I mustn't do that."

Repression. What happens to the negative feeling, the hostility toward the like-sex parent? Such feelings apparently do not just fade away. They may be forcibly pushed underground, to pop up again in some other form. If the child accepts identification as the solution to his conflict in the Oedipus situation, then he must dispose of the hostility he feels toward the parent with whom he identifies. *Repression* is the common technique for accomplishing this. The boy denies that he has ever felt any hostility toward his father. He refuses to remember it.

Repression is a solution for ambivalence, but it often runs into difficulties. The negative feeling may be *displaced* (see page 97) onto some other adult, as witness the irrational hostilities children sometimes develop toward particular relatives or acquaintances. Or it may be associated with policemen, with foreigners, or with members of some minority group.

If, on the other hand, the child fails to solve his ambivalent dilemma, he can be expected to have inconsistent feelings about people, to love and also hate them, to help and then hurt his friends. He will probably fail to take any consistent course of action, because this basic ambivalence will always be cropping up, causing him to feel paralyzed with indecision.

5. *The latency period.* Repression involves giving up the sexual desire for the opposite-sex parent. The girl can identify with her mother, she can want to win her father's love by indirection, but she must stop talking—even thinking—about push-

ing her mother out. The easiest way to accomplish this is to *forget the whole thing;* in other words, to repress sexual desire along with felt hostility toward the same-sex parent. Characteristically, therefore, adults will vehemently reject the notion that they ever went through a period of sexual desire prior to puberty. Sometimes the very violence of this denial suggests its falsity. At any rate, observation of young children, as well as memories of patients under analysis when their barriers are down, confirm the notion of early sexuality as propounded by Freud.[1]

When early sexuality is repressed at the close of the Oedipus period, the child then is said to move into a *latency* period. Sex is taboo; sexual desires are denied and are completely unconscious; playmates are selected exclusively from the same sex; love-making and romantic movies are disgusting. This period is sometimes referred to as the *normal homosexual stage,* since it is normal at this time to get all one's pleasure from contacts with people of the same sex. Gang formation is common. The latency period is likely to extend from the age of five to twelve or fourteen.

6. *The genital stage; maturity.* At puberty, the physiological promptings from the sex glands so strengthen the sexual impulse that it breaks down the barriers of repression. The person again looks toward the opposite sex for pleasure but now, of course, within a new perception of the situation. He wants a mate of his own age, not the parent. There is, however, evidence that the boy tends to fall in love with girls who resemble his mother (as the boy remembers her), and conversely, the girl prefers a man resembling her father.

The genital stage is the first one with the characteristics of true maturity: abandonment of the pleasure principle; full development of the Superego, and so on. Sex at this period involves the notion of

[1] The denial of early sexuality is a form of *perceptual defense* (see p. 243).

getting pleasure for oneself by giving it to another—that is, abandonment of the purely selfish, egocentric approach characteristic of earlier stages. It must be recognized that few people achieve such maturity in all their interpersonal relationships. Most of us have many hangovers in the form of infantile mannerisms. We demand that things be done exactly our way, in an irrational manner. We have superstitions, fixed ideas, prejudices. As was intimated in Chap. 11, much of our thinking is autistic and immature. The goal of scientific psychology is to help us understand our own irrationality; the goal of applied psychology is to help us reach full maturity and the maximum of personality development.

Development as conflict. The recurring theme in Freudian personality theory is conflict. The Id demands sexual and comfort gratifications when society says they are forbidden. The Id lashes out in violent aggression against people when society says such behavior will be punished. Society demands actions which will impose inconvenience or pain upon the person. Early stages of personality growth consequently are battlegrounds between the raw biology of man and his social surroundings.

With increasing development, the conflict simply shifts inside the person. As the Superego develops, it denies satisfactions to the Id, just as the parents had done. Maturity implies, not that one suppresses the Id, but that Id satisfactions are obtained under conditions approved by our social code. The mature personality is one which maximizes personal satisfaction without hurting others and without arousing anxiety regarding social punishment.

Psychological Processes in Personality Development

The Freudian writings about personality, summarized so arbitrarily in the preceding pages, include a great deal of fact and a considerable amount of hypothesis. This is necessary; facts without theory become meaningless. However, it will probably advance our understanding of personality substantially if we skim through the same facts, using the concepts of psychological process which have been elaborated in the earlier chapters. What we propose is to outline in more precise, operational terms what happens during the early stages of personality development, without the assumptions which are so prominent in the psychoanalytic interpretation.

1. *Motivation.* In infancy, the biogenic drives are very powerful. The baby operates on a kind of all-or-none law as regards energy mobilization. Every disturbance of homeostasis is probably experienced as a severe threat; all gratifications give rise to intense pleasure. Only after much experience does the individual become capable of evaluating the degree of threat really involved and of controlling his intensity of effort accordingly.

The capacity to inhibit demands for immediate satisfaction may depend to some extent on physical maturation of muscles, glands, and nervous system. To that degree it is based on heredity. But much more seems to depend on experience. If the child learns that yelling gets results, he learns to yell louder and longer. It is probably true, also, that there are hereditary differences in what Freud would call Id-strength; some people have stronger drives than others. They would have more trouble developing frustration tolerance.

The specific goals are probably far more flexible than the theory proposes. Who cares for the child: father or mother? Who does the disciplining? The direction of affection, and of hostility, can be related to environment more readily than to an innate tendency to prefer the opposite sex.

2. *Sensation.* We do not know much about the extent to which differences in sensory processes may contribute to per-

sonality formation. An obvious possibility is that differences in pain threshold would be important. A child who is extremely sensitive to pain would have more anxiety CRs, would fear more objects and people, and hence would adjust by trying to escape or trying to destroy those he perceived as sources of danger. Another possibility is the threshold for organic sensitivity. In emotion we get a great deal of organic reverberation. The child with a great deal of sensitivity in his viscera would be more profoundly disturbed, would develop fixations, etc., more readily.

3. *Perception.* Freud wrote extensively about the role of the father image, the mother image, and similar pictures of people in relationship to the child's personality. If a boy pictures his father as stern, forbidding, unyielding, and punitive, this will provide a different guide to behavior from that if the father is seen as jolly, generous, forgiving, and helpful. This perception of the father may determine the boy's reaction to bosses, to government, and to leaders in every kind of social group. Stimulus generalization operates to attach this percept to all kinds of related adult figures. Furthermore, the constancy tendency makes it very difficult to change such a percept, once it has become well established.

The child's perception of his environment as warm and friendly, or as cold and hostile, is one of the fundamentals of personality. Security is built into the personality and becomes a strong protection against later disturbance, if the child in the first year of life learns that he will be loved, comforted, fed, and protected. An insecure period at this time can lay a shaky foundation upon which no habit structure is ever really firm.

Note was made in the chapter on perception of the fact that behavior is determined by how we perceive a situation, not by the physical situation. Freud illustrates this at many points. For example, the mother may be trying to protect the child from harm, but if the child perceives this as restraint and interference, his response is one of anger. To a person who has become fixated on the oral sadistic level, any denial of friendship may be seen as an outrageous insult, calling for vicious retaliation.

4. *Learning.* The point at which Freud's theory is really weakest is in the area of learning. Whether because the scientific study of learning had not proceeded far in his day, or because he was more interested in the dynamic side of the picture, he paid very little attention to this process. The result is sometimes confusing. For instance, fixation (his main concept for these phenomena) may result from too much gratification, from not enough gratification, or from some frightening, traumatic experience at a given stage in development. Obviously such an explanation explains too much.

It seems reasonably certain that the effects of too much gratification will be different from those when too little satisfaction is obtained. Suppose we take the oral stages as an example. If the child gets the breast freely, is generously indulged, and is not weaned at the usual time, he feels no motivation to develop to a later stage. He can just lie passively and wait for pleasure to drop in his mouth. He will acquire an *expectancy* that everything will work out with no effort on his part. Conversely, the child with too little oral pleasure will acquire an expectancy that people will deprive him, and he must fight for everything he wants.

The results of frightening experiences, on the other hand, probably have the character of *conditioned responses*. We have noted that fear gives rise to anxiety. If the child discovers a way of reducing his anxiety, that method will be learned (instrumental CR) and will be very hard to extinguish. Now the methods developed

by a child are likely to be very inappropriate for an adult, yet, because they do not extinguish, they become a permanent part of the mental apparatus and show up whenever anxiety is aroused (cf. combat fatigue, page 511). If, on the other hand, the child does not figure out a way of reducing the anxiety, we get a classical CR—heart palpitations, visceral disturbance, and so on. These likewise hang on long after they should have disappeared.

Imitation. Learning by imitation was mentioned briefly in Chap. 9. It should be observed that in Freudian theory there are two kinds of phenomena which involve learning by imitation; both of them are called *identification* by Freud, but it seems likely that they are different.[1] In the early oral stage, the child learns that his mother is a separate person. He also learns to love her. Apparently quite spontaneously he comes to imitate some of her movements and vocalizations (after he has acquired some motor control via the circular reflex route, page 342). Since the mother praises and rewards such imitation, it becomes fixed as a habit pattern.

The other kind of identification is that which first appears at the Oedipus complex stage as a device for reducing anxiety. The child feels anxious because of his aggressive behavior toward the same-sex parent, and also because of the disapproval he gets from his love object, the opposite-sex parent. To reduce this anxiety he tries imitation of the same-sex parent. This is a form of power identification, as opposed to the earlier type, which is a love identification. So the boy imitates his father in an attempt to placate him and also to be like someone the mother loves. He learns, consequently, that the way to be praised and rewarded is to be a "good" boy, *i.e.*, to act out the pattern set by the culture and the parents. At this stage the boy and girl

[1] Dr. O. H. Mowrer first called our attention to this difference.

suddenly differentiate very sharply, developing activities and preferences appropriate to their sex roles in our society.

Associations. Association and conditioning are, of course, rather similar. It is obvious, however, that we can correctly speak of association when the child learns to love or fear one person, then responds similarly to another because of a purely verbal relationship. The major psychoanalytic technique, as a matter of fact, is asking the person to start with some idea and give all the verbal associations he can think of. So, for example, a child patient with a phobia for horses, when asked to tell what he thought of, spoke of size, strength, and finally, of his father. The real source of his anxiety, it developed, was his fear of his father because of sins the boy imagined he had committed; he did not wish to express fear of his father, and it had got associated with horses as an indirect expression.

Verbal associations with powerful emotional coloring can crowd out other ideas. All strong motives have a focusing effect; attention is concentrated on this goal or threat, and other items are excluded. *Obsessions* develop when the person cannot get his mind off a certain idea. Any irrational association, firmly held, is almost certain to be emotionally determined. Jung tells of a poet walking near a village who commented vehemently about the extremely unpleasant tone of the nearby church bells. Since there was nothing unusual about the sound of the bells, this seemed irrational. Shortly it developed that the clergyman of that church wrote poetry, some of which had been praised as superior to the products of the man criticizing the bells. The antagonism to a rival poet had been displaced to the church bells which were associated with him.

5. *Remembering.* Freud placed a great deal of stress on repression as a device for dealing with anxiety. Apparently a rather spontaneous technique for getting rid of an unpleasant memory is just to bury it. However, some people use this method much more often than others. Repression may be a function of retroactive inhibition; if I think of X, and X disturbs me, I quickly start thinking of something else. In this way I may gradually succeed in blocking out the thought of X entirely. Or I may jump from X to Y so rapidly that X never becomes clearly conscious.

Memory images are also subject to distortion (Chap. 10). Emotion and desire are the most potent forces making for such transformations. One may develop a dislike for John, and afterward "remember" that he has done things to justify this dislike, even though such events did not objectively happen. We have discussed this matter of inventing fictitious memories in connection with the problem of paramnesia (page 358), which is closely related to this type of memory distortion (cf. Fig. 13:5).

This is a serious problem in research on the role of childhood events as determinants of adult personality traits. Suppose we study a group of very infantile, passive, dependent adults. In their memories we find reports of long-continued indulgence by parents. Is this fact, or is it what they wish to remember? Conversely, persons who are hostile to their parents claim that they recall excessive severity by parents. Much of this may be retrospective falsification to confirm the present emotional feeling.

The Decisive Role of Early Childhood

Scattered throughout this book have been casual references to the great importance of early infancy and childhood in shaping the personality of the individual. Our discussion of Freudian theory has simply brought this into focus; however, most psychologists hold this is simply a fact, no question of theory at all. What are the

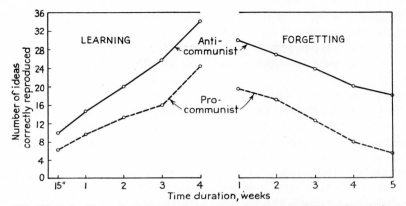

FIG. 13:5. An illustration of selective learning and remembering. Personality develops as the individual learns certain ways of perceiving situations. Furthermore, as he gets slanted in a given direction, he learns more readily items which fit into that frame of reference, and forgets more readily those which do not (cf. Edwards, page 366). In the experiment illustrated above, subjects were asked to memorize a paragraph of violently anticommunist material. Those subjects who were themselves anticommunist learned this passage more rapidly, and retained it longer, than subjects who were procommunist. When the content of the passage was reversed (procommunist), the relative efficiency of learning and remembering was higher for procommunist subjects. Thus personality tends to become more consistent as we learn what fits our prejudices, ignore or forget that which does not. (*From Levine and Murphy, 1943.*)

reasons for this extraordinary significance being attached to early experiences?

1. *The first experience defines a pattern of perception.* If the parents are kind, the child expects others to be kind and perceives them as kind (unless they are definitely unpleasant). Within fairly wide limits, the child will see what he expects to see. The first few experiences with people, then, may be crucial for the interpretation of a far greater number in later years. The greater intensity of infantile emotions and motives probably contributes to this effect.

2. *The first experience biases future learning.* You avoid situations which are perceived as negative; hence you may never learn your error—if there is one. Furthermore, by acting in a negative or antagonistic way, you may evoke rejection or dislike from others and hence conclude that you were right.

You acquire a certain frame of reference, based on these early experiences, and then

ignore evidence which does not fit this framework, or distort the facts to fit it.

3. *The first experience sets up standards of value.* Whether a particular object shall be positive or negative in valence may be determined by the first contact with it. An object associated with need satisfaction is perceived as positive and sought after in future, and these values may persist indefinitely. The objects which are assigned positive values by the parents also come to be perceived as positive, and sought after. The infantile need satisfactions and frustrations seem to be more intense (see above) and consequently will be more potent in determining valences than will later incidents.

4. *The young child lacks critical evaluation.* When one has had experience with one hundred people, he has data in terms of which comparison, criticism, and evaluation are possible. When he has met only three people, and all happen to be unpleasant,

he must inevitably conclude that all people are bad. He lacks the breadth of experience to criticize his conclusions; and, once established, these become set and resist criticism.

5. *The young child lacks symbols for experiences.* In Chap. 11 we laid great stress on the role of manipulation of symbols. Man thinks by putting symbols together in new combinations, by perceiving relationships among symbols, and so on. But such thinking presupposes that the relevant objective material has symbolic representation. Experiences in the first year of life are prelinguistic. Conditioned responses, habits, perceptual patterns are formed but not attached to suitable verbal symbols. This means that thinking about these events and attempting a reevaluation of them is most difficult.

These generalizations suggest that the child's personality is most plastic at birth but soon begins to set. Rigidity steadily increases throughout life, with older people especially difficult to change. However, personality modification at any age is quite a task; this is why psychotherapy may be a matter of months and years. It takes a lot of work to break down these patterns which have become so firmly rooted.

The Role of Conflict

The great importance of conflict in shaping personality is another Freudian contribution which is now generally accepted as fact rather than theory. Personality, according to our summary of Freud, is largely a matter of the way the person now solves his conflicts of motives, or the way he has solved conflicts in the past. Each individual has his own unique pattern of goals toward which he is striving, threats he is avoiding, and devices for achieving these purposes.

This means that the question of conflict needs to be explored more thoroughly than we have so far. Freud has called our attention to at least two kinds of conflicts which have far-reaching implications for adult personality. One of these is the ambivalent conflict toward the parents: the feeling of love and hate, liking and disliking, for the parents who both satisfy and punish. Another is the Id-Superego conflict, between crude selfish impulses and the socialized motives which we acquire through group living. We shall therefore devote the following chapter to an analysis of conflicts, how they arise, and how they are resolved.

SUMMARY

Personality is defined as the unique pattern of perceptions and motivations which characterizes a specific individual. Personality is expressed, however, through facial expressions, gestures, and complex social habits. The early foundation of personality is ascribed to motives and emotions; children differ in their ways of responding to tension situations, and the sum total of these characteristic ways of mobilizing energy is called *temperament.*

Temperament provides only an inherited core for the development of personality. Social rewards and punishments reinforce certain ways of behaving and inhibit others. Identical twins appear to resemble each other highly on temperamental traits but to differ more on traits involving social interactions. Comparisons of people in different cultures show that there is little evidence favoring the inheritance of any specific facial expressions or expressive patterns for emotional states. All these seem to be learned under the need to communicate to others and to avoid social disapproval.

The social aspects of personality include habitual ways of interacting with other people. These patterns are first laid down in the child-parent relationship but are modified by play situations, school, and later experiences. Temperamental traits, of course, affect this development; a child with a high energy level is necessarily going to have a large number of interactions, but whether these will be predominantly pleasant or unpleasant seems to depend upon the social situation.

The most stimulating and comprehensive theory of personality development was proposed by Sigmund Freud. Even though it is still questioned at many points, it has had a profound influence upon psychological thinking. Freud showed that the child goes through a complex series of stages in quest of pleasure (satisfaction of motives). In this developmental sequence he acquires his preferences for certain kinds of people, for playing certain roles in relationship to people, for living a specific kind of existence.

Freud is doubted particularly on two points. One is that he places an emphasis on sex which, even though he defines sex very broadly, still seems unrealistic. The other biogenic drives, hunger, thirst, etc., are important, and so are the emotions (love, anger, fear, anxiety) and the social motives (security, dominance, group identifications and values). A second point of objection stems from the suggested emphasis on heredity. Freud treats personality development too much as an inevitable progress through certain stages, without regard to the importance of environment.

Freudian theory can be modified by tying the facts of childhood emotionality and adult personality to the realities of perception, motivation, learning, and memory. If we look upon the child as an organism in quest of need satisfaction and the restoration of a favorable equilibrium, we can understand the various stages through which he goes. Cultural evidence suggests that some of these stages drop out when the environment does not offer the appropriate rewards or obstacles.

Freud placed emphasis on two points which have great significance for modern psychology of personality. One is the extreme importance of the first few years of life; the foundations of personality are probably set to a major extent before the age of six. The second is the significance of conflict situations in molding personality. This will be the topic of the following chapter.

Recommended Readings[1]

ALLPORT, G. W.: *Personality: A Psychological Interpretation*. New York: Holt, 1937.

BURT, CYRIL: *Factors of the Mind*. New York: Macmillan, 1941.

CATTELL, R. B.: *Personality*. New York: McGraw-Hill, 1950.

HARSH, C. M., and H. G. SCHRICKEL: *Personality: Development and Assessment*. New York: Ronald, 1950.

HUNT, J. McV.: *Personality and the Behavior Disorders*. (2 vols.) New York: Ronald, 1944.

MURPHY, GARDNER: *Personality*. New York: Harper, 1947.

SHELDON, W. H., and S. S. STEVENS: *Varieties of Temperament*. New York: Harper, 1942.

STAGNER, ROSS: *Psychology of Personality*. (rev. ed.) New York: McGraw-Hill, 1948.

[1] See also p. 547.

CHAPTER 14

Conflict

Our development of the subject matter of scientific psychology has so far stressed the desire for a single goal and the learning of a behavior pattern adequate to achieving that goal. In the process we found it necessary to note the perception of environmental objects, as well as thinking, recalling, and imagining, in the search for goal achievement. If human beings manifested only the psychological functions so far examined, life would go on—but people would be not so interesting, or so complex, or so queer.

The decisive difference between the simplified psychology with which we have dealt and the realities of everyday life is the phenomenon of conflict. Man does not —alas—desire only one single goal at any given time. He is quite likely to find himself, like the gallant knight in the fable, attempting to leap on his horse and gallop in all directions. He wants conflicting and incompatible goals. Worst of all, he both wants and fears certain goal objects.

In the preceding chapter we began exploring the phenomena of personality development. A careful inspection of the area indicated that we needed to examine the various kinds of conflict and the way people resolve their conflicts, if we were to understand their personalities. Indeed, some psychologists have proposed that personality could be defined as the individual's customary pattern of conflict solution.

Taken literally, the term *conflict* refers to situations in which opposing motives press the person toward opposite or incompatible actions. Thus the child who wants to pat the dog and is afraid he will bite is in a simple conflict situation; and the adolescent boy who wants to ask a girl for a date and is afraid to lift the telephone and call her is in another. However, there are some situations which belong here even though it is difficult to identify a conflicting motive; the person may have an impulse which encounters a *frustration*, and this creates a problem which he must solve. In Chap. 3 we passed off the topic of frustration very briefly, noting that one of its consequences commonly was the arousal of aggression and the emotion of anger. At this time we shall examine frustration more closely and see that it also has other consequences for personality development. Finally, we have certain phenomena which perhaps should be grouped under the term *threat*, which belong here. If the individual feels his security or his power threatened by some outside influence, this will evoke the same kind of conflict-solving behavior.

Perhaps we can make this clearer by saying that the phenomena of conflict solution are simply applications of the techniques of problem solving which we discussed in Chap. 9. At that point we noted that problem solving occurred when we have (1) a goal desired by the organism, plus (2) a barrier which prevents the goal from being achieved until the organism develops some skill or insight into the situation. Conflict of motives, frustration, and threat are alike in that all pose a problem for the organism. Some solution must be devised. The solution may partake of the character of trial-and-error activity, as in maze learning, or insight, as in the two-rope problem. The person must perceive the essential aspects of the situation and perhaps must attend to certain stimuli within himself in order to reach the goal. The method adopted by the person may include the manipulation of physical objects, but it is more often a matter of manipulating symbols (thinking). The kind of solution achieved will obviously be a function of intelligence level, although many intelligent people fail to achieve satisfactory solutions to their conflicts.

Types of Conflict

Throughout this book we have made use of the topological diagrams first introduced into psychology by Kurt Lewin, as ways of representing dynamic situations. These are particularly useful in dealing with conflict, and we shall classify the different types of conflict in terms of this topological arrangement.

The simplest dynamic situation, of course, is that of the individual motivated toward a goal (Fig. 14:1). This kind of representation is useful because it applies equally to a hungry man wanting food, a college student aiming for a medical degree, and a politician seeking the presidency of the United States. It focuses on the essential elements in the situation.

Now, if the line dividing the person from

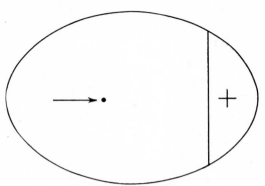

FIG. 14:1. Positive valence. We represent thus any goal object toward which the individual strives.

the goal in Fig. 14:1 is used to represent a barrier, we have a frustration situation. The individual is blocked from immediate attainment of the goal. How will he deal with this situation? There are several alternative ways, which we shall discuss later in this chapter. In many cases, the barrier has the qualities of a threat, so that it actually becomes one of our basic conflict situations. Let us see how these line up.

Three basic conflicts. Valences can be either positive or negative. We can be attracted to an outside goal, or we can be repelled by it. From this twofold classification of valences we can derive three basic types of conflicts, as follows:

1. *Approach-approach conflicts.* Suppose the dynamic situation is that represented in Fig. 14:2. The person finds himself faced with two attractive but mutually exclusive goals. So a child may have only one nickel and want both an ice-cream cone and popcorn. A man may wish to marry a beautiful blonde, and also a lovely brunette. In a complex world like ours, we must often expect to encounter such incompatible choices.

The fable of Burian's ass recounts that he starved to death because he was exactly halfway between two attractive piles of hay. Unable to choose, he stood rooted to the spot until he collapsed. Fortunately,

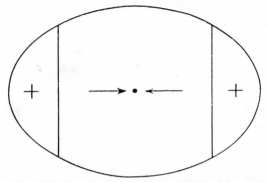

FIG. 14:2. Approach-approach conflict. The individual is impelled toward incompatible goals, each having a positive valence.

neither donkeys nor human beings are this stupid. A chance stimulus will start the donkey moving toward one goal; as he gets closer, it looks larger and more attractive, so the choice is quickly made. Approach-approach, or Type I, conflicts, then, are usually solved quickly and with little evidence of damage to the personality.

2. *Avoidance-avoidance conflicts.* Sometimes the individual finds himself between two threatening valences. The little boy must do his arithmetic or face the prospect of a spanking. The draftee must become a soldier or go to jail. Social pressure compels us to carry out many unpleasant tasks.

What happens in the case of avoidance-avoidance conflicts? If the individual starts toward one negative valence, it begins to appear larger and more threatening. If then he turns back toward the second, it seems more alarming in turn. Thus this Type II conflict gives rise to great vacillation of behavior.

When there is pressure on the individual to go away from each of these conflicting valences, the resultant is likely to be a force out of the field. If the person can travel along the dotted line shown in Fig. 14:3, he will escape from the unpleasant situation without embracing either alternative. It is usually necessary, therefore, to put restraints around the edges of such a

situation, to prevent this kind of escape.

While Type II conflicts undoubtedly cause some distress, they are usually resolved without any substantial damage to the personality. There is some reason to believe that they are associated more with delinquent and criminal behavior, running away from home, and similar responses which might be considered "going out of the field" than with disturbance of inner response systems.

3. *Approach-avoidance conflicts.* The third type of conflict seems to be the one which is most serious in relation to personality. This is the kind presented by a goal which is both attractive and threatening (Fig. 14:4). It is typified by the child's ambivalence toward his parents, *e.g.*, in the Oedipus complex situation the boy may feel both affection and rivalry toward his father. It is also characteristic of Id-Super-ego conflicts, as in the case of a selfish impulse to do something immoral and the socialized desire to avoid such acts.

Both the Type II and Type III conflicts create a great deal of inner tension. It is, however, possible to escape from an avoidance-avoidance conflict if one can get out of the field. This is impossible with the

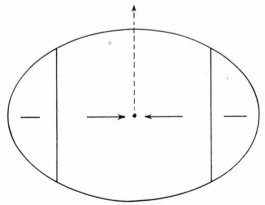

FIG. 14:3. Avoidance-avoidance conflict. The individual is between two threats or dangers. Unless restrained by barriers of some kind, he is likely to take the course represented by the dotted line, and "go out of the field."

Type III conflict because the person carries the conflict with him wherever he goes. If you have a strong desire to love someone and also are intensely afraid of loving anyone because that exposes you to the possibility of being hurt, you cannot run away from your conflict. It is for this reason that the Type III conflicts cause the greatest personality problems.

It is worth while noting here that some situations which superficially are Type I (plus-plus) dynamically fall in this group. Suppose a college man has a desire to make high grades and also to excel in athletics. He knows the time spent on the latter will endanger the former. Some men can make the choice without disturbance, as suggested above. But others will find the idea of giving up either goal quite threatening. If he interprets low grades as a serious threat and failure to make the team as a serious threat, then he is in a *double approach-avoidance* situation; both courses of action carry both positive and negative valences. Such conflicts have the disturbing quality of the other Type III examples.

There is one other Type I situation which dynamically belongs with Type III. Consider the case of the young man who wants both the blonde and the brunette. Perhaps he marries the blonde. If his interest in her was pretty much limited to the physical sex impulse, then this will be weakened by satiation. Should the other goal (the brunette) still be available, the impulse to move in that direction may now be quite strong, opposed only by the Superego restrictions on socially disapproved behavior. (If the marriage is based also on symbolic desires—*e.g.*, for companionship, tender affection, common interests, which are not weakened by satiation, this is less likely to occur.)

There is one important feature which all conflict situations have in common. This is the high level of tension arousal. We know that the presence of a single strong

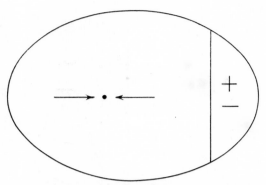

FIG. 14:4. Approach-avoidance conflict. The individual is attracted toward a goal, which also signals danger; or he is attracted toward a goal and must undergo a painful or threatening experience to achieve it.

positive or negative valence in the field can cause the person to mobilize energy and get ready for vigorous action. Conflicts are characterized by the presence of two valences, both of which may be quite strong. Thus tension is generated to an unusually high degree. Unless the person devises some solution for his conflict, the tension persists; this is physiologically somewhat analogous to letting an automobile engine run at high speed with the gear shift in neutral. The machine seems to be shaking itself to pieces. As will appear in this chapter, the human machine can do likewise.

Barriers and valence. We have noted in other chapters that, when a positive valence is behind a barrier, it seems somehow more attractive. Thus children rated a toy behind a wire cage as more desirable than the same toy when it was within reach. This apparently is tied in with the extra energy mobilization which goes with deprivation and frustration. When a goal is behind a barrier, there is a possibility of deprivation, of being prevented from reaching it. This presumably evokes a more vigorous energy mobilization, and this in turn would be reflected in perception of the goal as more desirable. Thus "distant pastures look greenest" and a sex object

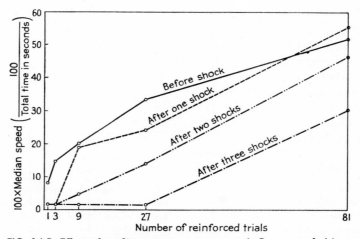

FIG. 14:5. Effect of conflict upon response strength. Rats were fed in a goal box 1, 3, 9, 27, or 81 times. The speed of running to the goal box for these animals is shown in the "before shock" curve. Now they received one, two, or three shocks in the goal box. The marked decrease in speed of response as conflict is introduced can be noted by these curves. (*From Kaufman and Miller, 1949.*)

which is forbidden by a taboo may therefore seem more attractive.

It is probable that this holds, not only for a simple barrier in front of the goal, but also for threat or negative valence, as in the Type III conflicts. There is danger in seeking a certain goal, but that just makes it all the more interesting. So the individual starts toward it, but as he gets closer, the threat seems more alarming. This may cause him to stop or even retreat. Then the positive valence looks more attractive, and he starts approaching the goal again. In a conflict situation involving strong positive and strong negative valences, as in sex vs. social taboo, this can lead to long-continued oscillation, indecision, and confusion.

Experiments on conflict. It is difficult to study the very personal types of conflict in human subjects except by clinical means, which prevent any direct comparison of people subjected to exactly the same stimuli. It would also be difficult to measure the results of the conflict. For these reasons, psychologists have recourse to experiments on conflict. N. E. Miller of Yale University has devised some ingenious studies which

support very nicely the generalizations in the preceding pages based on complex human problems.

One of Miller's investigations (Kaufman and Miller, 1949) had white rats trained to run down an alley for food. With repetition, the rats ran faster and faster until they approached their physiological limit. This curve is shown in Fig. 14:5 as the "before-shock" series. Then the animals were divided into groups and given one, two, or three electric shocks in the food box. The results are shown in the other curves in Fig. 14:5. Animals which had had only one rewarded trial simply did not go to the food box after even one shock. The same was true of those receiving only three rewarded trials. Rats who had had nine rewarded trials and one shock went fairly quickly to the food box; those with nine rewards and two shocks went very slowly; with nine rewards and three shocks, they did not go. Only when we get to animals which had experienced 81 food rewards before shock do we get enough habit strength to overcome three shocks.

Another way of arranging the data is

shown in Fig. 14:6. Will the rat actually enter the food box after two electric shocks there? About 30 per cent of the animals fed once finally ventured into the box; but there is a gradual increase until with 81 feedings, about 90 per cent still enter the box after two shocks.

This type of experiment directly opposes a positive valence, food, to a negative valence, threat of shock. The results show that the positive valence must be strengthened by many rewards before it will overcome a small number of punishments. The more rewarded experiences, the stronger the approaching tendency; the more punished runs, the stronger the avoidance tendency. Miller also found evidence that, at a distance, the positive goal had more pull; but as the rat approached the food box, the negative tendency became stronger. Thus the rat would start toward the box, slow up, and finally stop.

Our main interest in this chapter is in the devices by which human beings resolve conflicts, and the subsequent personality developments. These features cannot be studied with animals. The animal researches are interesting chiefly because they verify some of our deductions regarding behavior in a conflict situation and regarding the strength of tendencies to approach and avoid particular stimuli.

Common sources of conflict. Our culture tends to present young people with many conflicts. In a simple, primitive society, there may be only a few goals, well defined as to when and how they are available. The parents and other adults have clear expectancies as to how young men and women should act, and they communicate their beliefs directly to the younger generation. This tends to eliminate Type I conflicts almost completely. The lack of ways of escape, plus the potency of social pressure, means that Type II situations are usually solved by doing the unpleasant task which is demanded. The relative acceptance of

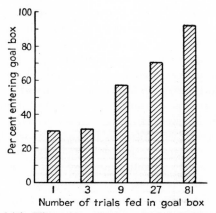

FIG. 14:6. Effect of two shocks upon entering the goal box. When 1 positive reinforcement (food in goal box) is balanced against 2 negatives (shock in goal box), only about 30 per cent of the rats would again enter the goal box. If, however, 81 positive experiences are balanced against 2 negatives, about 90 per cent of the animals will continue to enter the box. (*From Kaufman and Miller, 1949.*)

impulses, with fewer taboos on gratification and less anxiety about punishment, would decrease the frequency of Type III conflicts.[1]

In the United States, certain kinds of conflicts are practically universal. We have tried a little experiment in class of handing out a fake "personality diagnosis." One of the sentences reads: "You have experienced considerable difficulty with your sexual adjustment." About 95 per cent of college students agree that this "diagnosis" is correct. Similarly, 70 per cent or more are likely to say that they have been bothered by feelings of inferiority—which connotes a conflict between a positive desire for achievement or dominance, and a fear of failure.

Conflicts between biogenic drives are rare, and usually easy to solve. If I am both hungry and sleepy, I will act on the stronger impulse—probably eat first and then sleep.

[1] There are, of course, primitive societies with numerous taboos on impulse gratification; as might be expected, they show numerous conflict and personality problems resembling those in our own culture.

Difficulties arise, however, as soon as we get conflicts between the biogenic drives and emotions or social motives. Thus it is possible to have conflicts between hunger and either anger or fear; indeed, many maladjusted children have difficulties in this area as a result of nagging and fighting at mealtimes. However, those drives which represent constancies necessary for life— food, water, etc.—will usually become sufficiently potent that they will overcome any but the most extreme opposition. Sex, on the contrary, does not represent any vital constancy. When it conflicts with anger, fear, ambition, or ethical values, the result may be a deadlock, with sexual gratification indefinitely postponed.

Most of the biogenic drives consequently can be subject to only a few social restrictions. A society which imposed excessively stringent taboos on eating would simply disintegrate. Its members would leave or die. Sex, on the other hand, can be subjected to numerous and severe restrictions; small groups of people can abandon sexual gratification permanently with no mental or physical damage. Thus it is hardly surprising that sex carries more restrictions

and hence is involved in more conflicts than the other drives.

Sex also conflicts with various social motives. An ambitious man may avoid sexual involvements which would interfere with achieving his status goal. A woman may have a picture of a wife's role as inferior and hence reject sex to avoid feeling inferior when she is married. Sex may come into conflict with group identifications and with social values of various kinds. Thus it is hardly surprising that Freud, working as he did primarily with disturbed, unhappy people, found sexual problems in a prominent position. Our culture offers numerous occasions for this to happen.

But there are many other conflicts too. Second in frequency, probably, is the power or dominance motive. In Western civilization exaggerated expectancies are built up as to possible status achievement. Boys are told that, if they work hard they can be president, general, financial magnate, etc. The opportunities for achievement are microscopic relative to the number of aspirants. Thus frustration, guilt feelings, etc., are common. At the opposite pole we have many individuals whose basic desire is to be passive and dependent on someone else. They live in a culture which exaggerates the importance of active, aggressive striving, of standing on your own feet. This creates many problems for them.

Parent-child relationships provide many situations involving conflict over dependence and independence, especially with adolescents striving to assert themselves against what they perceive as excessive parental control. The Oedipus period involves conflict over affection and monopoly of one parent's attentions. If a child feels unloved by his parents, he may punish them by being bad; they attempt to discipline him, and this leads to further friction. Husband-wife relationships offer numerous conflicts based on sexual motives. Terman found that the happiest marriages are those in which sex drive is equal in

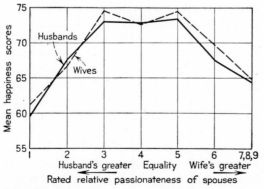

FIG. 14:7. Sex drive and marital happiness. When sex drive is judged to be relatively equal, happiness is at its maximum; a slightly greater drive on the part of the male is not much of a handicap. If, however, there is a marked disparity in sex demand by either partner, happiness scores go down. (*From Terman, 1938.*)

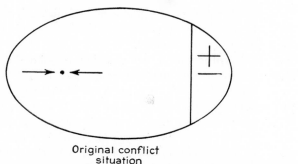
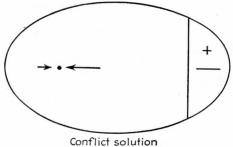

Original conflict   Conflict solution
situation

FIG. 14:8. Conflict solution by diminishing one valence. If the person can redefine the situation so as to convince himself "I don't really want that," then the conflict weakens. Repression can cause the positive valence to disappear completely. (Or he may structure the situation so that he does not perceive the probability of punishment; in this case he suppresses the negative valence. This weakens the conflict but of course does not avoid the later unpleasantness.)

strength (Fig. 14:7). If the drive is still strong in one, and satiated in the other partner, this may easily lead to friction. But many marital difficulties arise from conflicts over dominance (who is boss), from conflicts over expectancies (I want my wife to make a fuss over me and she doesn't want to be bothered), and from differences in values and interests. All other forms of interpersonal relations—boss-worker, teacher-student, and so on—can also lead to conflicts of motives or frustrations of one person's motives by the other.

It is literally impossible to give any satisfactory statement as to the specific impulses which give rise to our personality problems and conflicts, because virtually every motive can, under appropriate conditions, come into conflict with some other impulse. This means that it will be more constructive for us to think in terms of the schematic analysis of positive and negative valences given earlier, rather than trying to pin down each conflict to some specific motivation.

Mechanisms of Conflict Adjustment

The person who finds himself in a conflict situation experiences a disturbance of equilibrium. In accordance with the general principle of homeostasis, he attempts to

restore either the prior equilibrium or a new one. All the resources of the organism can be drawn into this effort. Perception, association, remembering, problem solving, and thinking are particularly involved in significant conflicts.

It is possible, broadly speaking, to classify conflict adjustments into two groups. One group is composed of those techniques developed by the organism primarily through a modification of the stimulus. If one can look at things differently, perhaps the conflict will disappear. If the positive valence can be made to seem much smaller (Fig. 14:8), then the

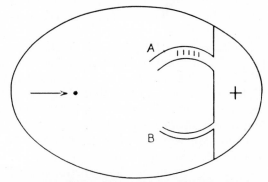

FIG. 14:9. Shifting response. Some conflict solutions are simply matters of varying the response. If one course of action (A), which is easy to begin, leads to pain and punishment, the person may shift to B even though it is less accessible and perhaps requires more effort.

conflict is decidedly less severe, and a decision can be made. A second type of adjustment emphasizes modification of the response. The person may first take the obvious pathway A to a goal (Fig. 14:9), but as he encounters a conflict, he may shift to the less available but safer pathway B. These two classes of adjustment are not, of course, mutually exclusive. They do give the main emphasis in these efforts at equilibrium.

Modification of the Stimulus

Throughout this volume we have shown how man, by learning to focus attention on certain stimuli, comes to deal adaptively with his environment. He learns to pick out the goal object when it is hidden in the total psychological field. He learns to attach positive and negative valences to perceptions as they lead to satisfaction or deprivation. He learns to observe minute changes in the facial expressions and voices of other people and guide his behavior accordingly. We suggested in Chap. 6 that no two of us live in identical worlds, that each has his own "private universe" constructed out of his motives and his experiences. With this background it should occasion no bewilderment when we describe a conflict solution as involving a change in the characteristics of the perceived situation.

Another way of saying this is that the person in a conflict is at a *choice point* (Chap. 9). This may lead to a restructuring of the environment. The individual may perceive things differently and thus may find a way out of his problem.

There are several ways in which this modification of the situation can occur. One simply involves the substitution of equivalent stimuli—displacing one by another. Another involves refusal to see certain aspects of the situation, with, perhaps, exaggeration of other aspects. A third involves various kinds of distortions of the perceived situation. We shall examine each of these briefly.

Displacement. An emotion can be displaced from one object to another. We illustrated this (Chap. 3) with examples such as the businessman who is angry at his wife and bawls out his secretary. A woman who has no children of her own to love may lavish a lot of affection on some cats. Displacement, of course, extends to the biogenic drives and social motives. We may crave tenderloin steak but can displace this appetite onto hamburger if necessary. A man who had set his ambitions toward becoming president of a big corporation may have to settle for becoming president of a big union.

Displacement tends to operate along the lines of equivalent stimuli. It is a case of positive transfer. Note that the response remains substantially unchanged; it is simply directed upon a new stimulus other than that which triggered the conflict.

Displacements occur when the avoidance aspect (negative valence or threat) of a situation is too potent for the approach tendency; as, for example, a man who would like to attack the policeman who gives him a ticket for speeding may fear the consequences of such aggression. He inhibits this action but comes home and kicks the dog. Displacement also occurs if the barrier in a frustration situation is impenetrable. When additional energy is mobilized against the barrier without success, this tension has to go somewhere; it frequently is drained off in displacements, such as attacks on minority groups.

Repression. One of the commonest types of conflict solution is repression. This takes the form of denying the existence of one horn of the dilemma, of *refusing to see* one of the conflicting valences. It is interesting to note that repression usually affects the positive valence; negative valences, by virtue of the powerful visceral tensions they arouse, are usually prepotent. However, repression of the negative valence can also occur.

A boy who has been reared in a strongly Victorian tradition that "sex is shameful" may find himself in a severe conflict between his sex drive and his anxieties about such behavior. In this case one of the simplest solutions is to deny that he has a sex drive. He represses the attraction value of sexual objects (Fig. 14:8), and withdraws completely from situations which might arouse his sexual impulse.

In the case of repression of a negative valence, we get the kind of blind grasping after pleasure which is sometimes called *psychopathic behavior*. In the foregoing illustration, the person might deny that he felt any anxiety. By refusing to see the dangers in the situation, he can engage in uninhibited sexual gratification (for a time).

Repression has the unfortunate implication that tension is not reduced. Whereas displacement leads to some degree of release through action against a substitute stimulus, repression simply bottles up the tension and denies it an outlet. Since tensions tend to persist under such conditions, various unfortunate consequences are likely to result. We shall mention some of these in later parts of this chapter.

Repression, like its political analogue of killing off the people who threaten the stability of the ruling class, operates in an ever-widening circle. First one may deny that he is motivated toward a certain stimulus. Then he has to drive out of consciousness certain memories which would contradict this basis for a new equilibrium. After this he must repress associated ideas which would tend to recall these rejected memories, and so on. It is this aspect of repression which we discussed in Chap. 10.—the phenomemon of selective forgetting of items which might tend to arouse anxiety.

Perceptual vigilance and perceptual defense. This is a good point at which to bring together certain ideas which have been developed in earlier chapters. Motives, we noted, have the result of bringing certain aspects of the environment into focus and shutting out other stimuli. The frightened person is unaware of everything around him except the object of his fear.

Attending is another function which operates in the same way; indeed, it may only be the same function described differently. Apparently we can learn to keep certain stimuli in the area of maximum clarity and, to some extent, keep others in obscurity by refusing to observe them. Similarly, in the chapter on memory we cited a study (Belmont and Birch, 1951) which indicated that a painful shock causes some subjects to forget the associated material, while the same shock caused others to remember it better than usual.

These various observations lead to this conclusion: there are two different processes here, both of them homeostatic in character. *Vigilance* involves increased sensitivity, a readiness to observe, remember, and respond to stimuli related to certain motives. This could help in restoring equilibrium in many cases, as in locating food. *Defense* is the converse of vigilance; it is a process of protecting equilibrium by refusing to be aware of disturbing elements in the environment. So, if a person has had some humiliating experience which would conflict with his desire for dominance, he represses it, tries to forget all about it.

Perceptual vigilance seems to relate to situations where the environment offers satisfaction to some motive which is strong and where the satisfaction will not be followed by anxiety. It also appears in contexts where an outside stimulus tends to arouse the anxiety. Defense is manifest in situations where anxiety is related to the inner state; doing something to satisfy the impulse would set off anxiety. In that case the individual protects himself by refusing to see the stimulus as long as possible.

So, for instance, Freud pointed out that, at the resolution of the Oedipus complex, the child normally represses any memory of hostility toward one parent; and indeed, it is common in counseling work with college students to find this repression very effective. A young man comes in for aid because he can't concentrate on his studies. He says his father is a wonderful man, and he and the father have fine times together. Later it appears that he is constantly frustrating the father by obstructing the latter's plans; and specifically, in refusing to do well in college, he is asserting his unwillingness to obey the father's desires. Conscious recognition of this hostility would give rise to anxiety. After this antagonism is uncovered and cleared up, the student's grade record improves sharply.

Perceptual defense, then, is particularly important because what starts as a purely protective device may turn into a stumbling block. Refusing to see disturbing stimuli (like the child who is not allowed to eat candy, and eventually comes to ignore it completely) may help to maintain equilibrium under certain conditions. But if this extends to the point of being blind to objects which are essential to survival, it creates a serious problem. Adjustment devices which are homeostatic in their *origin* may actually work against survival if carried to extremes.

Logic-tight compartments. When repression and perceptual defense operate not to block out a certain topic of thought, but simply to prevent the awareness of certain relationships, it is common to speak of logic-tight compartments in thinking. We noted in Chap. 11 that logic is the device by which we clarify relationships between ideas. When ideas are blocked off from one another so that relations cannot be observed, thinking is nullified.

A few years ago, in the city of Akron, an ex-mayor attempted to organize a "Law and Order League" with the avowed purpose of "driving these labor organizers out of town." We are probably safe in assuming that he and his supporters did not see the inconsistency involved in the use of the appeal to law and order as part of a plan for illegal violence. Fortunately, both local newspapers spotted the inconsistency promptly and opposed the idea vigorously. The followers of Hitler found it necessary to use logic-tight compartments, as Hitler promised contradictory policies to different people. On June 21, 1941, the American communists were denouncing the war against Germany as an imperialist exploit; on June 23, the war had become a crusade for democracy. Only people who have well-developed logic-tight compartments can tolerate such inconsistencies.

In interpersonal relationships we often observe a man who keeps his business tactics and his religious ethics in separate compartments; and a woman who is very scrupulous about her behavior in other ways may abandon all Superego standards when it comes to "getting her man." Logic-tight compartments, then, are devices to aid in the toleration of efforts toward incompatible goals. Using this method, one avoids the anxiety which would be aroused by his own actions.

Unconscious visceral responses. Repression does not completely resolve any conflict because it affects mainly the conscious component of the total response. If one has, for example, an arousal of anger as a result of a certain stimulus, the total pattern includes visceral changes, striped muscle activities (readiness to strike, etc.), and conscious feelings. Let us say that a CR of anger has been established; a man becomes angry whenever his wife mentions the fact that her family was socially and intellectually superior to his. The emotion is repressed (to avoid his own Ego injury, to avoid quarreling, etc.). This eliminates the conscious feeling of anger and the motor tendency to engage in fisticuffs. But it cannot wipe out the visceral mobilization. Unconscious visceral CRs thus persist and cause trouble, even when the significant stimulus is no longer observed. Thus, in the preceding example, arterial hypertension can become established and be a grave threat to the man's health. Figure 3:6 (page 82) shows the gastric secretion set off by feelings of hostility in a psychiatric interview.

Repression, therefore, tends in the short run to be protective and in the long run to be destructive. Unless we can look coolly at threatening stimuli, evaluate them, and work out constructive solutions for dealing with them, we fall into these techniques which make us victims of irrational, unconscious processes. Psychotherapy consequently consists, in large part, of uncovering repressed material and learning how to deal with it on a rational basis.

Rationalization. It is possible for a person to distort a perceived situation in such a way as to make it appear that the conflict does not exist. This is achieved by misperceiving one or more parts of the situation (Fig. 14:8).

Freudian theory states that Id impulses demanding selfish gratifications come into conflict with Superego impulses forbidding such behavior. The area of conflict between the two desires is the area in which the Ego functions. We have proposed, in Fig. 14:10, a way of understanding how the Ego may achieve satisfaction for an Id impulse by avoiding a head-on collision between it and the Superego requirements. Here is an amusing example: Little Johnny's mother had baked some cookies. As she left the house, she said, "Johnny, you must not take any of the cookies." So Johnny went next door and got his playmate. They went to the cookie jar and Johnny said, "Eddie, you take two cookies and give me one." Thus he obeyed the letter of his

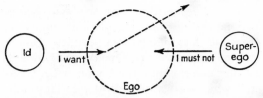

FIG. 14:10. Ego function in rationalization and displacement. Faced with a conflict between his desire and his fear, the person may try to devise an excuse for going ahead with the desired act, e.g., "this isn't really stealing," or he may substitute a new object to which the taboo does not apply.

mother's command, while still getting what he wanted.

Rationalization is thus a process of redefining a situation, of changing the nature of the external world so that laws and other restraining influences are said not to apply to this instance. Adults are more devious and ingenious than children in working out rationalizations, but all of them follow this same pattern. There are a variety of standard rationalizations which most of us use at regular intervals. Perhaps it will be of some value to mention them individually.

"Sour grapes." When the fox failed to reach the grapes, he decided that he didn't really want them, as they were probably sour. When a high-school boy tries to make the football team and fails, he may adopt a sneering attitude toward athletes with strong backs and weak brains. A businessman who misses out on a big contract may say, "Well, I was probably lucky. I might have lost money in it." In all such cases, the individual is trying to deny the existence of a frustration or a sense of failure. It is not only unpleasant to be deprived of a desired object; it is doubly unpleasant if the failure looks like an insult to one's Ego. Since the desire for achievement is rather strong in most Westerners, a failure may carry a decided negative valence. Rationalization tries to restore equilibrium by trying to make it look positive, **or at** least neutral.

"*Sweet lemons.*" Since the sour-grapes rationalization has an obvious opposite, someone has coined the phrase "sweet lemon" to describe it. This type of rationalization asserts that the lemon we got was just what we wanted all along. Thus it is basically the same as the sour-grapes example, although superficially different; in both cases we try to make a negative situation look positive.

So, for instance, the girl who doesn't catch the football hero and finally marries a less spectacular man will exaggerate his good points to show that she really got what she was after. (This is fortunate, if the marriage is to last.) A professor who attempts to get a deanship and fails may develop rationalizations about how much more valuable work he can do when not snowed under by administrative routine. If these remarks are coupled with derogatory jokes about deans, the rationalization becomes a combination of sour grapes and sweet lemons.

Blaming circumstances. "Alibi Ike" was a character who always failed in what he was trying to do; but the blame always rested on circumstances, not on Ike. "Dust got in my eyes." "There must have been a hole in the pavement." "I couldn't study that night because I had a headache." The common factor in all these excuses is that the blame should not rest upon me; I was blocked by circumstances beyond my control.

It is worth noting, of course, that a person will, occasionally, be blocked by some barrier he cannot overcome. No psychologist is going to maintain that it is rational behavior to try to knock over a brick wall with your head. On the other hand, we sometimes observe a particular person who oozes these rationalizations at every pore. Sometimes he even presents his excuses ahead of time, to ward off even the expectation that he might fail. These individuals reduce the amount of energy

they could apply to the task in hand, diverting too much of it to the creation of these excuses.

Blaming people. A variant on the foregoing is to blame someone else for your shortcomings. Adam said of Eve, "The woman tempted me." Women today are more likely to lay the blame on a man for their errors. Americans today are prone to blame the communists for the deplorable state of the world, declining to carry their obvious share of the responsibility. Southern whites even go so far in many cases as to blame the Negro for the practices of discrimination and persecution.

Blaming people has strong elements of the process of *projection* (see below). However, we are interested here only in the rather simple case in which a person wants to avoid anxiety cued by recognition of his own failure to meet moral standards or to achieve up to his level of aspiration. It is usually fairly easy to blame somebody else for starting the fight, for initiating the seduction, or for planning a robbery.

Blaming human nature. A form of rationalization which is particularly exasperating to psychologists is that which rationalizes an antisocial act by an appeal to human nature. Hitler expounded the philosophy that man was inherently aggressive and warlike. War, then, was not due to the Nazis' mad drive for power, but was just "human nature." Apologists for the "robber barons" of our nineteenth century lay their grasping exploitation of others to an "instinct of acquisitiveness." Men even rationalize their marital infidelities by appealing to some myth about the male of the species being inherently polygamous.

The common core of all these and many other rationalizations is an attempt to distort the perceived situation so as to evade the conflict. "I'm not really stealing the money from the church; I'm just borrowing it." "This is a strictly business transaction; these people are so foolish as to buy stock I know to be worthless, that's their lookout." Social situations are never quite so clear-cut, quite so objective, as physical situations. Hamlet could tell a hawk from a handsaw, and so can most of the rest of us. But if we come to a problem of distinguishing between situations where our ethical values demand one kind of behavior, and situations where the ethical values do not apply, we become alarmingly weak on discrimination. This is an illustration of what, in Chap. 6, we called *behavioral factors* affecting perceptions. The percept is only determined in part by the external reality; some determination is from within the organism. If strong motives operate in favor of a certain view, that is the one which is likely to prevail, even if it means ignoring many features of the "structural" external situation.

Introjection. Let us now consider certain manifestations of conflict which are somewhat more complex. Displacement, repression, and rationalization involve fairly simple dealings between the organism and the environment. The process of distortion of percepts is capable of much more extensive operations than we have so far mentioned.

The phenomenon of introjection is a complicated method by which the child takes into and makes a part of himself that which is originally in the external world. The mother is the first object of introjection. Because she is close, because she is the source of need satisfaction, because she is loved, the child wants to be like her. He finds certain respects in which they are similar (generalization of stimuli) and probably exaggerates these. Then, on the basis of these similarities, he attempts to act like her. This is the early or primitive form of identification mentioned in Chap. 13.

As the child attempts to introject the mother and make her characteristics part of his own personality, he begins to act toward himself as she acts toward him. That is to say, he gives himself instructions, he forbids certain of his own actions, he expresses value judgments of good and bad about his behavior. Gradually these are incorporated into a systematic habit structure and become what Freud called the *Superego*.

Introjection extends far beyond the family circle in relatively short order. Again on the basis of similarities perceived, the child begins to take on features of his playmates, teachers, and other adults. Introjection applies also to groups; the college man says "We won the game," even though he is not on the team; labor unionists feel enraged by an attack on a distant union local; patriots are sensitive to insults to "our national honor." In all these cases the person is taking something which really exists out in the external world and is treating it as part of himself.

Introjection as conflict adjustment. But how, the student may be asking, does this help to resolve conflicts? There are several ways in which introjection is related to conflict solution. To take the first example we started with, the child probably avoids pain by introjecting the mother. Especially when he begins to give himself instructions as she would, he is learning to inhibit actions which would lead to punishment. Thus he is learning to *interpose his own barriers* where moving toward a goal would result in pain and anxiety.

However, there are many other advantages to introjection. When the child incorporates his mother as a part of himself, he undoubtedly feels stronger and more secure. Mowrer has proposed that infantile babbling when the mother is out of the room may be a device for warding off insecurity. The child tries to reinstate the mother's presence vocally as a reassurance that she has not left permanently. Many mothers keep up a chatter with the child while they are in another room and hence not visible. Perhaps the child simply tries to maintain this on his own.

Introjection of a group also can lead to feelings of security, power, and achievement. If the group is part of me, and if the group is powerful, then I am powerful. I am not the weak, frustrated character that I appear, but a member of a master race. So negative valences (failure, cues for anxiety) can be replaced by positive symbols through introjection.

Many psychologists have used the term *identification* to refer to this same kind of phenomenon—that is, the child is said to identify itself with the parent, the patriot with the nation, the follower with the leader. While there are shadings of difference in the use of introjection and identification by clinical psychologists, we shall for purposes of this text treat the two terms as equivalent.

Projection. Projection is the opposite of introjection and differs from it in many ways. Basically, projection is a process of denying the existence of certain traits within the self but perceiving them in others. Since the kind of trait one wants to ignore himself is an undesirable one, projection is largely a matter of seeing our own sins in other people. In this respect it may bear a superficial similarity to rationalization by blaming others.

If we are to use the term precisely, however, projection always implies at least some vague awareness of a certain characteristic within the self. Thus a man may become aware that he has a strong sex drive, an impulse to steal some money, or a desire to shirk responsibility and behave childishly. He is unwilling to entertain these thoughts; they arouse anxiety, and he deals with them by the method of perceptual defense. This, of course, does not eliminate the presence of the impulse mentioned, nor does it prevent him from being reminded of it occasionally, though he may successfully block it out most of the time. Never-

theless, this percept lurks on the edge of consciousness. Now he sees another person, and some element in his behavior, or even in his appearance, may set off an association of ideas. *The other* is really the man who is oversexed, or dishonest, or infantile. By perceiving these undesired qualities in another (and by judiciously exaggerating them there), I can make myself seem quite pure by comparison.

Selective vigilance is obviously a part of this process. The presence of the antisocial impulse within the self makes one excessively sensitive to manifestations of the same kind in others. In an annoymous study of cheating, Katz and Allport (1931) found that college students who admitted cheating also claimed that they saw a great deal of cheating around them. Non-cheaters reported much less. To claim that one saw a lot of cheating is, of course, a kind of rationalization (if everyone else does it, why shouldn't I?). But it is also suggestive of the vigilance phenomenon; because the student is aware of his activity and its implications, he is excessively sensitive to any suggestion of the same impulse in others. Thus, strongly sexed individuals see a lot of sexual misbehavior where others see very little; this, as we noted earlier, is the basis for self-appointed censors. The censor, of course, gets a double gratification out of his solution; he accuses others of being oversexed, thus alleviating his own guilt feelings, and he sees all the sexy shows, thus satisfying his Id impulses. There is a striking quotation from the diary of Anthony Comstock which is apt here: "It has pleased the Lord to place me at the mouth of a sewer. I am happy in the work of the Lord."

Modification of the Response

Adjustment is a process of trying to maintain or restore a desired equilibrium, or to achieve a new one which seems more attractive. The mechanisms which we have described in the foregoing pages (modifications of the stimulus) operate mainly to protect an existing equilibrium. Furthermore, they are often—not always—defective in that they do not provide for any release of the tension which has been built up, and this tension can precipitate other disturbances of importance. The mechanisms to which we now turn are in some respects more desirable, in that most of them do provide an outlet for tension.

Compensation. Some realist once suggested that the best solution for many conflicts was just plain hard work. The prescription, while unpopular with many, has its points. Psychologists, of course, feel the need for a technical name to cover this kind of adjustment; they call it *compensation.*

Whenever a person is blocked from a positive goal, either by a barrier or by a negative valence, additional energy tends to be mobilized. This may be due to the fact that the person anticipates deprivation and thus raises the tension level; or it may be that the goal now looks more attractive. At any rate, one of the common results of such a situation is that the person does try harder. The angry knocking aside of an obstacle is a case in point. This is fine if there is no punishment in store for breaking the barrier.

We mentioned the phenomenon of compensation briefly in Chap. 4, as an auxiliary of Adler's will to power. However, compensation is not limited to the dominance motive. A girl who feels herself to be sexually unattractive may engage in frantic efforts at self-beautification, using paint, hair-dos, clothing, and other weapons. Several million-dollar industries in this country flourish on such compensatory activities.

History abounds with illustrations of men who, starting under handicaps, attained exceptionally high status. Theodore Roosevelt, a weak, sickly youngster, compensated by becoming a rough rider and big-game hunter; his philosophy of force also expressed itself in his use of governmental power, *e.g.*, in Central America. Abraham Lincoln's energy pushed through amazing obstacles to achieve education as a lawyer and eventually the Presidency.

Overcompensation. The term *overcompensation* has been used by some psychologists to apply to compensations which are carried to a pathological extreme. Unfortunately, it is difficult to decide about such extremes, so that about all we can say is this: a person is overcompensating when his efforts to restore equilibrium go too far and cause another kind of disturbance. Thus some people would classify Theodore Roosevelt's obsession with physical vigor as an overcompensation; it became, at the very least, something of a social problem for him and perhaps for the people of various nations to the south. Bender (1942) has described an interesting case of a college boy who felt inferior to his classmates. This lad developed certain traits to an extreme: a kind of Oscar Wilde literary foppery, talking in languages unknown to the person with whom he was conversing, a contemptuous attitude toward the customary college activities, and so on. These traits may have served as compensations of sorts for his felt inadequacy, but they got him into greater social difficulties and hence caused more tension than they released.

Substitution. The kind of case just described involves both some modification of the stimulus and increased vigor of response. It might be better, therefore, not to include it in the class with compensations. If the individual changes the type of goal toward which he is striving but drains off into it the surplus energy from his compensatory effort toward a blocked goal, we may speak of *substitution.* Thus, a girl who is sexually unattractive may decide to become a brilliant scholar and thus compensate for her deprivation in the sexual field. The boy who failed to make the football team may, in addition to developing rationalizations, also direct his frustrated energies into writing and obtain prestige in this manner. In these cases we can think of the person as having substituted a new goal for that which was unattainable. (In compensation he strove onward to attain a goal in the same class.)

Delinquent behavior has sometimes been classified as substitution. Here is Sam, a big, energetic youngster who happens to have been endowed with an IQ of 75. For some years he continues striving to satisfy the demands of teachers and parents in the school system. With continued failure he is likely to decide to look for other satisfactions, and so he raises a disturbance in class (thus forcing the teacher to pay attention to him) or he engages in criminal activities to get prestige with the other children.

Sublimation. A special case of substitution is that which is commonly considered to involve moving to a higher moral or ethical plane. So, a woman who wants children of her own, but cannot have any, may sublimate by going into kindergarten or orphanage work. A man who cannot lavish sweet phrases upon his love because she will have nothing to do with him, may use this energy in writing lovely poetry or fine music. In these cases there is still a recognizable relationship between the original and the substitute goal, but the new one is more highly approved by society.

How far substitution and sublimation can go and still adequately reduce tension is a moot question in psychology today. Attempts to study sublimation clinically have not been very productive. Some young men who are highly productive in science or literature were found not to be leading active sex lives and hence might be said to be sublimating this energy. But an equal number, of just as high productivity,

were found to be getting complete sexual release through intercourse.

On the basis of the facts developed earlier in this volume, the following conclusions would seem justified: (1) The more similar a new goal is to the original goal, the easier it is to deflect energy toward the new goal, and—probably—the more satisfying this substitution will be. (2) With the exception of biogenic drives, for which the adequate goals are fairly restricted, there is a wide range of activities which can reduce tension to some extent. Just sheer physical exercise can get rid of a good deal of tension. This is not exactly what we call substitution or sublimation; it is more in the nature of a safety valve to get rid of surplus energy which might otherwise damge the organism.

Reaction formation. One type of psychological phenomenon seems particularly disturbing to lay observers. This is the fact that psychologists sometimes explain a given action in terms of its polar opposite. So, for example, we sometimes find bravery which is basically a manifestation of fear, puritanism which derives its energy from a strong sex drive, and so on. At this point critics sometimes throw up their hands and talk about sheer mysticism.

Unfortunately, as regards the critics, the facts are quite impressive. A soldier, for example, finds himself terrified of the enemy and ashamed to let his fellows see it. Between these two negative valences, some men will run away (escape from the field). But others, fearing the physical threat less than the opinion of their fellows, will rush into danger, perhaps getting killed or perhaps emerging as heroes.

More commonly, the term *reaction formation* is used to describe certain reversals of impulse direction of less extreme character. Here is little Sammy, for example, who has a lot of hostility and aggression within him. Perhaps he has lost his temper, with considerable violence, and been punished, or threatened with the loss of his

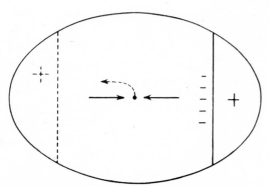

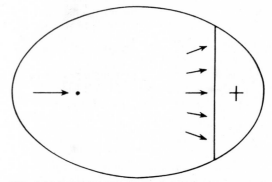

FIG. 14:11. Reaction formation. The individual, drawn toward a positive goal but facing a terrifying array of threats and dangers, may resolve his problem by picturing to himself an exactly opposite goal and directing his efforts in that direction. Since this is reinforced by the negative valences of the original situation, it may be successful even though the original positive goal is still exerting a pull on the personality.

FIG. 14:12. Trial and error under frustration. When progress toward a goal is impeded by a barrier, the person will first try his more recent successful techniques; if these fail, he will begin to dig back into his memory for earlier habits—hence, he is said to "regress" to more infantile patterns if the blockage persists and the tension also continues.

mother's love. At any rate, the mere stirrings of aggression within him are enough to set off conditioned anxiety. How can he protect himself against his temper? Perhaps, by acting very meek, mild, and submissive. To take an adult example: here is a man who has been on the verge of becoming an alcoholic. He is staying sober but is being strongly tempted. How can he reinforce the motives making for sobriety? By becoming a temperance lecturer, among other things (hence the success of Alcoholics Anonymous).

Reaction formation, then, involves picturing to oneself the exact opposite of the impulse gratification which also carries a threat (Fig. 14:11). This opposite goal will be something highly socially approved, somewhat like a sublimation. It will obviously have no negative valence attached. Thus the individual protects himself against this antisocial impulse which would expose him to punishment or misfortune.

Regression. Most of you will have noted that other people often behave childishly when emotionally perturbed. (It is much more difficult to observe this in oneself.) The term *regression* is used to identify

instances in which an individual behaves on a level which is less mature than his normal pattern. We do not, therefore, consider regression as including those cases of people who never "grow up." As noted in the preceding chapter, a person tends to develop through various phases from infancy to maturity. If he reaches a higher level and then slips backward to a less adult type of behavior, he has regressed.

Regression is rather easy to understand, at least in its simpler forms. Most of us remember childhood as a time when we had no problems, no responsibilities; parents took care of us, protected us from harm, saw to it that our needs were met. Hence, when we find ourselves faced with difficult and threatening situations, it is very easy to wish to be back in the childish state.

There is another reason why regression is common. When one is faced with a difficult, frustrating, or threatening environment, he will try various activities in quest of a solution (Fig. 14:12). After he has attempted those skills which he has recently acquired, and which are appropriate to his age level, what shall he do? If these devices have failed, and he is still motivated to keep trying, he will fall back on devices he used in earlier years. Memory dredges up forgotten habits, old techniques for influencing parents and playmates. Then we see adults wheedling, crying, stamping their feet, and otherwise behaving in manners appropriate to children.

The classic experiment on this problem is by Barker, Dembo, and Lewin (1941). They took nursery-school children into a playroom where they were allowed to play with some ordinary toys for a time, and their maturity of play estimated. Now a partition was raised and some unusually attractive toys (a dollhouse large enough for the children to enter, and scaled furniture, etc.) were exhibited. The children played a little while with these, after which they were required to return to the original toys. The special equipment remained visible, but behind a wire netting. In this situation the typical child became angry, fretful, and peevish; to the extent that he played with the ordinary toys, his play was at a much lower level of maturity than before. From this experiment it was concluded that frustration leads to regression in many cases.[1]

Like frustration, conflicts of motives can lead to regression. If the conflict is carried internally (e.g., a person reacts to the same object as both positive and negative valence), then the disturbance is chronic and the regression may be relatively more severe. One illustrative case is that of a young woman about to enter upon a marriage which was distasteful to her, but which she felt she had to accept. A few

---

[1] It was pointed out in Chap. 3 that frustration leads to aggression. Actually, the behavior of the children in this toy situation could just as well be called *aggressive*. Regression is demonstrated by the fact that the play with the ordinary toys was relatively infantile. Adults also are likely to do childish things when angry, such as breaking dishes, ripping up papers, and kicking furniture. In other words, whether we use aggression, regression, or perhaps some other term, in describing a specific action depends on what aspect we are emphasizing.

days before the scheduled wedding, she suddenly began acting very childish, did her hair in pigtails, skipped about, and talked in baby talk. She had apparently regressed to about twelve years of age, and her conversation, dress, and behavior were appropriate to that age. This is a device for escaping from a conflict by "going out of the field" mentally. If she were twelve years old, this painful dilemma would not confront her. So she escaped into childhood.

This kind of breakdown is characterized as *psychotic*, i.e., a major breakdown of personality. This person had lost touch with reality; her actions were not geared to the real situation about her. In other cases we get *neurotic* breakdowns, which are less severe in character. The individual keeps in touch with reality, although he may become incapable of functioning; for instance, he may have to be told by someone else what he is to do. He is so torn by indecision that he cannot act on his own initiative. The married woman who is always "running home to mama" when she quarrels with her husband is using a neurotic form of regression.

Phobia. Some regressions are accompanied by phobias. A phobia is an exaggerated fear of something which most adults find quite innocuous. Let us use as an illustration the case cited on page 99 of the married woman who developed a fear of going on the street alone. This kind of fear may be appropriate to a child. He perceives the street as a strange place, full of dangers, where he should go only if accompanied by an adult. But for this grown woman, such a perception is not appropriate. It becomes understandable when we learn that she is sexually dissatisfied and fears that she might be tempted to do something immoral if she went into the night-club area alone. She has a conflict between her Id and Superego—between her conscience and her sex impulse. The phobia provides her with a protective mechanism; if she

TABLE 14:1. Percentage of Men with Combat Fatigue Showing Certain Symptoms
(*Based on Gramlich, 1949*)

	Percentage showing this group of symptoms
Respiratory (choking, chest complaints)..	3
Cardiac (heartburn, palpitation).........	10
Gastric (poor appetite, nausea, discomfort)	62
Vasomotor (sweating, cold extremities, weak and dizzy, blackout, fainting).....	40
Stammer or stutter....................	13
Back and joint pains..................	14
Tremors............................	57
Headaches..........................	56
Fatigue............................	33
Nail biting.........................	18
Sleep disturbance (nightmares, insomnia).	62
Anxiety............................	84
Depression.........................	57
Irritability.........................	57
Confusion..........................	21
Withdrawn.........................	19

does not go out alone, there is no danger that she will do anything forbidden.

Momentary regression, such as that shown by the golfer who breaks his club after making a bad shot, is very common. It is not a sign of personality disturbance unless it becomes habitual and appears in a wide variety of situations. Chronic, persistent regression, as in the phobias and breakdowns, is a sign of serious personality difficulty and calls for psychotherapy by a psychiatrist or clinical psychologist.

Hysterical illness. Somewhat similar to regression in some respects is the mechanism of apparent illness. This varies in severity from the "social headache" which develops just before a tea one prefers not to attend, all the way to partial paralysis, blindness, or deafness. We exclude, of course, any illness which has a physical basis. The term *hysterical illness* applies to those cases in which the organic condition is normal but the person still feels ill.

Hysterical illness was a not unusual form of response to the conflict situation induced by combat conditions in World War I. The soldier, having a healthy desire to avoid pain and injury, not to mention death, would like to run away from the front lines. Against this tendency are such motivational pressures as patriotism, loyalty to one's unit and friends, fear of being called a deserter (and punished), and a code of social values. The soldier is thus in a severe positive-negative conflict situation. One day he sees a wounded friend being carried out, helpless on a stretcher; if he is not too seriously injured, the boys say he is "lucky." The thought occurs, "if I were paralyzed, I would be carried away from all this, and not be ashamed." Perhaps he is knocked over by a shell concussion; he finds himself paralyzed and unable to move. The nerves and reflexes are tested, found to be normal. *The soldier is ill,* but his sickness is mental. Literally hundreds of such cases recovered spontaneously on Nov. 12, 1918, a day after the cessation of hostilities from World War I.

Combat fatigue. For some reason, straightforward paralysis, blindness, and deafness were much less common in World War II than in its predecessor. These relatively gross illnesses were replaced by a state of general disorganization known as combat fatigue. Table 14:1 shows the percentages of a group of combat-fatigue cases showing the symptoms listed. Commonest is a feeling of anxiety; close behind are nightmares and insomnia, nausea and stomach upset, headaches, depression, and irritability. Men beset by such symptoms are no good in combat; they have to be shipped back to a hospital for rest and recovery. Thus combat fatigue served unconsciously the purpose of removing the person from the danger zone. We say unconsciously because it was fairly easy to prove that *these men were not malingering*—they were not pretending sickness just to get away.

Many of them refused to report to medical officers, hoping to "get control" and stay where they felt themselves needed.

The symptoms listed in this table for combat fatigue should be compared with those reported for fear during actual combat (Table 3:1, page 79). It will be noticed at once that there is a high degree of overlap. Disturbances of breathing, circulation, digestion, and muscular control were reported by most of the men in the study of fear, and they are again prominent in the symptoms of combat fatigue—as though the latter were simply victims of chronic conditioned fear. This viewpoint is graphically stated in the following quotation from a study of neurotic breakdowns in service:[1]

"The ones we are talking about, the psychoneurotics, *are* sick. They have functional disorders induced by nervous strain under stress. . . . They lose their appetites, develop headaches, or are constantly tired and depressed. Some of them have insomnia, or, when they do go to sleep, they have terrible nightmares. They get jittery and are too sick to carry on."

"What are you trying to give me?" George snorted in disgust. "Who doesn't lose his appetite just before going into a scrap? And who isn't jittery and who doesn't have nightmares after being in one?"

"The difference is, George, that you get over it in a very short time and are back to normal again. Some of the others don't. They're the same a month after a scrap as the day after."

The current interpretation of combat fatigue is that these men are unfortunate in that their viscera condition very readily to fear situations. They establish classical CRs such that heart, lungs, blood vessels, digestive tract, and other organs give the typical emergency response to all the stimuli which remind them of the combat situation. Since an army camp will be full of such reminders, these soldiers are constantly kept in a visceral uproar. Eventually, no matter how strong the man's positive motivation to stay on duty, he will break down and have to be removed. Thus these reactions serve a purpose, albeit unconscious, in terms of the total personality.

In a follow-up study of combat-fatigue cases after they left service, Carlson (1949) found that the longer a man stayed at the front after symptoms developed, the more difficult it was to effect a cure. Repetition is a factor in learning; the more often these visceral reactions were set off by danger, the longer the symptoms persisted after a man had been discharged from the services.

Alcoholism. A device for alleviating the tension of conflict and gaining a temporary escape from unpleasantness is the excessive use of alcohol. Alcohol is a depressant and acts to lower the activity of the cerebral cortex. This tends to interfere with fine discriminations and apparently therefore to reduce the individual's awareness of anxiety-arousing stimuli. Thus a few drinks may convert a very gloomy view of the universe into a glowing prospect.[1] (The next morning, things may be even gloomier, of course.)

It is difficult to offer any precise definition of the point at which a person becomes an alcoholic. We can say easily enough that any person who drinks to the point that he injures his economic, social, and family life has gone too far, but who is to say just when this injury begins? The alcoholic himself will be the first to protest any such accusation. He just takes a friendly drink, or one to help him relax after a hard day.

Alcoholism, like repression and hysterical illness, can easily become incapacitating. Indeed, most of these mechanisms of conflict adjustment represent personality disorders if carried to an extreme. Alcoholism prevents the individual from working up a realistic solution to his problems and so,

---

[1] Cooke, E. D. (1946), p. 134. Reprinted by permission of *The Infantry Journal.*

[1] Masserman (1946) has shown that alcohol has a similar effect on conflict behavior in cats.

frequently, makes them worse. Furthermore, by damaging the liver and the arteries, it may contribute to serious organic illness.

Autistic thinking. We have discussed autistic thinking at some length in Chap. 11. At that point we were interested in the general problem of symbol manipulation and pointed out the differences between reasoning and autistic thinking. Our interest here is rather different. We are concerned with the manner in which autistic thinking serves as a substitute response in conflict situations.

In Chap. 11 we noted that problems can be solved more readily on the autistic than on the realistic level but that, unfortunately, such solutions generally would not work. Nevertheless, it must be recognized that, when a person is under great tension because he is subject to conflicting motivational pressures, autistic thinking is an attractive substitute activity. By shifting levels (cf. Fig. 11:10, page 398) the individual gets away from impenetrable barriers and threatening valences. It is easy to reach his (fantasied) goal. Temporarily, then, he achieves tension reduction. Of course, if he returns to the real world, his tension is rearoused. (If he does not so return, he is classified as psychotic and put in an institution.)

Thus it appears that autistic thinking has in it elements both of substituting another response for that which failed to resolve the conflict, and of modifying the perceived situation to eliminate the conflict.

We have mentioned here only the two extremes, of acting on the physically real level, or of getting substitute satisfaction through daydreaming. Actually, there is an intermediate step, which is reasoning or realistic thinking. The person may first try to think through his conflict in terms of real rewards and punishments, and reach a choice. If the positive and negative elements still seem pretty much in balance,

so that he cannot make a choice, then he resorts to fantasy to get some tension reduction.

Some common fantasies. Since certain kinds of conflicts are common in our culture, it is not surprising that there are also certain common solutions—well exploited in popular fiction, movies, and radio programs. The fantasy of being a foster child, for example, is reported by well over half of American adolescents as something they have toyed with at one time or another. This kind of daydream seems to serve a dual purpose: it removes the child from the parents who at the moment seem cold and cruel (because they discipline him or interfere with his infantile pleasure seeking); and it offers him positive rewards, money, fame, status, and security (his "real parents" being wealthy, of course).

The "conquering-hero" fantasy is quite common and obvious. It is simply the daydream of achieving great success as a football star, a military hero, a scientist, or whatever the current interest happens to be. Then the dreamer imagines himself returning to his home town, where he was unappreciated, and receiving the plaudits of all. The "suffering-hero" daydream is simply a variant of this; the individual does something noble for his country or for humanity and is killed in the process. He dreams of his funeral, with all the people who have ignored him bewailing their lack of understanding. Thus these varieties of autistic thinking are simply fancied activities which lead to positive goals without the interference of barriers and dangers which exist in real life.

Social autisms. Problems and conflicts on the social level are also likely to give rise to autistic thinking. The phenomena of racial superiority, as dreamed up by Nazi theorists and Southern planters, are forms of autistic escapes from a real situation. Communist apologists for the use of military force to impose their ideology develop some remarkable autisms, such as the notion that "we must do good for the people even if they do not appreciate it at first."

Social problems, like personal problems, call for realistic thinking, hard work, and some acceptance of discomfort. Solutions worked out on an autistic level, ignoring the real barriers and pains involved, cannot alleviate real social tensions. Persons who believe in them resemble the psychotic in his refusal to abandon his daydreams for concrete reality.

Experimental Neurosis

Most of our discussion so far has been based on observation and clinical case material. Perhaps it will throw a little additional light on the problem of the effects of conflict if we cite some of the experimental studies in this area.

Pavlov's experiments. We have described in some detail the work of the Russian physiologist, Pavlov, on the conditioned salivary response. In addition to the important investigations which were summarized in Chap. 8, Pavlov deserves credit for the first observations on experimental neurosis. His procedure was fairly simple. The dog was first trained to give a salivary CR to a circle of light. Then he was given a series to discriminate an ellipse as a negative stimulus (when the ellipse appeared, no food was given). This differential CR was firmly established; then the ellipse was made more and more like a circle, until discrimination became impossible. The animal is now faced with two possible responses, but he cannot make both. When the stimulus is flashed on the screen, he cannot make a choice as to whether he should respond or not. At this point the animal is likely to develop the symptoms of a "nervous breakdown"—somewhat like the combat-fatigue symptoms mentioned above.

The differentiation proceeded—until the ellipse with a ratio of semi-axes 9:8 was reached. In this case, although a considerable degree of discrimination did develop, it was far from being complete. After three weeks of work upon this differentiation not only did the discrimination fail to improve, but it became considerably worse, and finally disappeared altogether. At the same time the whole behaviour of the animal underwent an abrupt change. The hitherto quiet dog began to squeal in its stand, kept wriggling about, tore off with its teeth the apparatus for mechanical stimulation of the skin, and bit through the tubes connecting the animal's room with the observer . . . . On being taken into the experimental room the dog now barked violently, which was contrary to its usual custom.[1]

Liddell's work. H. S. Liddell (1944) has described his work at Cornell in establishing experimental neuroses in sheep, pigs, and other animals. He holds that an essential part of the development of the neurosis is the restraint of free movement which is part of the laboratory situation. When animals are left relatively free, they are much less likely to develop neurosis. He relates this in an interesting way to the position of the human being in society. All of us are subject to a considerable variety of social controls, necessary for the maintenance of organized group living. If we are then faced with difficult choice situations, as in the types of conflict which we have been describing, we may break down and lose our ability to behave adaptively.

Symptoms in experimental neurosis. Depending on the design of the experiment and the animal studied, almost every symptom of human personality crack-ups has been duplicated in laboratory experimentation. Masserman (1946) developed a group of masochistic cats, who would apparently enjoy stimuli which, prior to the experiment, seemed quite painful to them. Gantt (1942) states that the dog

[1] Pavlov, I. P. (1927). Reprinted by permission of Oxford University Press.

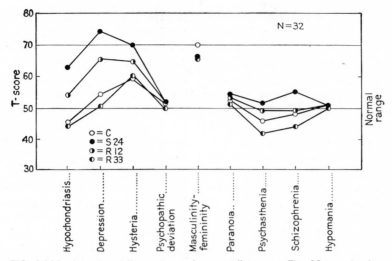

FIG. 14:13. A study of "experimental neurosis" in man. The 32 conscientious objectors who were subjects for the Minnesota starvation experiments filled out the Minnesota Multiphasic Personality Inventory prior to the starvation period. Their scores were about normal (50 is the exact normal; scores above 70 are considered pathological). After 24 weeks of the 1,500-calorie diet, they again took the test; now their scores were neurotic for depressive and hysterical tendencies, close to the border line for hypochondriasis. After 33 weeks of normal feeding, they were back to their former status. Hence there was no permanent damage from the experience. The conflict here was between the food drive and the idealistic motives which led them to volunteer for the experiment. It was ended when the experiment was completed and uninhibited enjoyment of food became permissible. To what extent can we assume that this would apply to other forms of conflict? (*From Biology of Human Starvation, by Ancel Keys et al., University of Minnesota Press, 1950.*)

suffering from an experimental neurosis "exhibits all the symptoms to a former signal for food that an ordinary dog does for actual pain, *viz.*, whimpering, howling, retreating, rapid panting, tachycardia." One of these dogs, with an unusually severe breakdown, showed pathological sexual erections and even spontaneous ejaculations to the experimental situation, and at times to the presence of the experimenter outside the laboratory. Masserman's cats developed phobias—*e.g.*, even the feeding signal became a stimulus for fear—and also showed regressive behavior, acting like kittens in many ways. Dworkin states that his cats sometimes vomited when confined to the conditioning apparatus (see Dworkin *et al.*, 1942).

Human neuroses, of course, include all these disturbances of function. Sexual symptoms are quite common, but disorders of digestion, respiration, and circulation are even more often noticed. Phobias and regressions are characteristic symptoms of the neurotic personality. There seems ample evidence, therefore, for interpreting the animal experiments as a laboratory model of the human neurosis.

Prolonged hunger and experimental neurosis. Keys (1950) and his coworkers have suggested that the conscientious objectors who spent 24 weeks on a semi-starvation diet developed an experimental neurosis. We have noted earlier (page 57) the disturbances these men experienced— in work, in sex life, in ordinary personal relations. Certainly there is some justification for saying that they have become "neurotic." Support for this view comes from the use of the Minnesota Multiphasic Personality Inventory, which measures the tendency of the person to show certain neurotic patterns. The men took this test before going on the restricted diet, and again at the end of the 24-week period. As Fig. 14:13 indicates, there was a decided increase in the number of neurotic symptoms shown by the men. A few really came close to a complete breakdown.

The conflict in this case was between a biogenic drive (hunger) and the social motives which had impelled the men to participate in the experiment (particularly, the wish to prove that it was not fear of hardship which caused them to refuse military service). The diaries and spontaneous remarks of the men show that this conflict was severe. With food available nearby, the temptation to take some secretly was very strong.

Some psychologists have questioned the idea of calling this an "experimental neurosis" because, as the figure shows, the men recovered spontaneously when put back on normal rations. However, it might be that other neurotics would also recover if we could eliminate the basic conflict which caused them to break down.

Frustration Tolerance

Not all animals break down in the experimental neurosis setup. Furthermore, they develop different symptoms—some become overexcitable, noisy, aggressive, while others withdraw, sleep most of the time, and sullenly refuse to cooperate with the experimenter. These differences conform to the notion that differences in *temperament* become involved in reactions to conflict.

The evidence indicates that human beings also differ with regard to the threshold for frustration and conflict. Some have

a high threshold; they can take a lot of punishment without breaking down. Others are easily put out of commission by relatively minor conflicts. This difference in ability to tolerate excessive tension is referred to as frustration tolerance.

We have already referred to frustration tolerance (Chap. 3) as the ability to take a high degree of overload in energy mobilization before organized activities are disrupted. Obviously we are still dealing with the same problem. In a conflict situation, high tension levels develop easily because of the effective presence of two or more strong valences. A person with low frustration tolerance will be unable to handle this tension; it will overflow into all kinds of random action, or into excessive daydreams, rationalizations, or physical symptoms.

The study of differences in frustration tolerance can be illustrated by a recent study by Hybl (1951). To patients in a hospital for mental disorders, he submitted such varied tasks as fitting the pieces into a form board (see Fig. 14:14), picking up little disks and replacing them, and substituting symbols for digits (a simple learning task). The person was encouraged and allowed to succeed on the first trial. Then he was given a second form, but this time it was impossible for him to succeed (pieces missing from the form board, impossible time limits on the other tests). The examiner made mildly disappointed comments during this trial. Then a third form was presented, and the person was allowed to succeed. The disturbance in relative performance on test 3 was the measure of frustration tolerance. Normals (patients with only a physical condition of some kind) had the highest frustration tolerance. Those with least tolerance included alcoholics and psychoneurotics. Psychopaths were very similar to the alcoholics, and schizophrenic (psychotic) patients resembled the normals, *i.e.*, failure did not disturb them much.

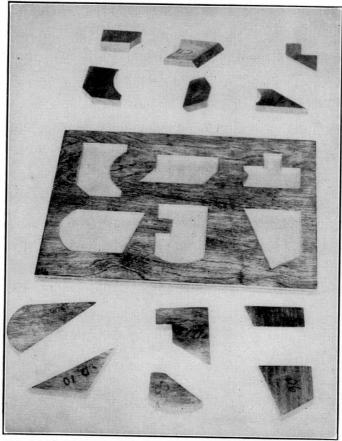

FIG. 14:14. Form board used in frustration-tolerance experiment. In studying frustration tolerance experimentally, the experimenter allows the subject to succeed on a task; then he presents a second, on which failure is inevitable; and then a third, on which success is again possible. The loss in efficiency from 1 to 3 is considered evidence of the disturbance induced by the frustration; some individuals have little tolerance; others can take quite a great deal. In Hybl's study, subjects were forced to fail on this form board by switching pieces so that a perfect fit was impossible. Neurotic personalities were found to have much less frustration tolerance than normals. (*Courtesy of Dr. A. R. Hybl.*)

These findings make good sense in that we interpret alcoholism and neurosis as indications that the person is running away from an intolerable conflict situation. There is an apparent problem with the schizophrenics, who have also run away from conflict. The answer seems to be this: the neurotics perceived failure on the test as a threat to status, security, and self-enhancement. The schizophrenics, on the other hand, had left reality so far behind that failure on the test simply did not bother them. The psychotic protects himself by simply ignoring the whole conflict situation.

Frustration tolerance seems to be a basic feature of personality. Certainly we observe wide difference in presumably normal people, with regard to their ability to accept delay in reward, ability to keep control of behavior in a frustrating situation, and so on. Frustration tolerance is probably linked to the sensitivity and stability of the autonomic nervous system, since research indicates that persons low in tolerance have highly reactive ANS reflexes.

SUMMARY

There are three basic types of conflict: situations which present a choice between two positive valences, situations which present two negative valences, and situations which present a positive valence closely associated with a negative valence. All these have in common the fact that the person must make a choice between incompatible responses.

Approach-approach conflicts rarely have serious impact upon personality organization. Usually a choice is made and accepted. The only exception occurs when giving up one positive goal is itself perceived as threatening to the self.

Avoidance-avoidance conflicts are likely to lead to delinquent behavior or some similar device for escaping from the situation. Approach-avoidance conflicts have the greatest tendency to produce serious personality disturbances. This is probably due to the fact that the person carries the conflict around with him, and it becomes intensified whenever he approaches the positive goal.

Conflicts may be resolved by modifying the stimulus (perceptual distortion) or by modifying the response (change in behavior). The first category includes refusing to recognize one of the valences (repression), redefining the situation so that no conflict exists (rationalization), introjection, projection, and identification. Modification of response includes such devices for reducing tension as compensation, sublimation, reaction formation, regression, hysterical illness, and autistic thinking.

Conflict adjustment mechanisms and frustration tolerance make up an important segment of personality. In the following chapter we shall consider how they are integrated with the patterns described earlier and are related to the person's social context, in the adult personality.

Recommended Readings[1]

GUTHRIE, E. R.: *Psychology of Human Conflict*. New York: Harper, 1938.
HENDRICK, I.: *Facts and Theories of Psychoanalysis*. (rev. ed.) New York: Knopf, 1950.
HORNEY, KAREN: *Neurotic Personality of Our Time*. New York: Norton, 1937.
O'KELLY, L. I.: *Introduction to Psychopathology*. New York: Prentice-Hall, 1949.
SHAFFER, L. F.: *Psychology of Adjustment*. Boston: Houghton, 1936.
STAGNER, ROSS: *Psychology of Personality*. (rev. ed.) New York: McGraw-Hill, 1948.

[1] See also p. 547.

CHAPTER 15

Maturity

In the two preceding chapters we have examined some of the raw materials out of which the adult personality is constructed: temperament, childhood experiences, modes of responding to conflict. We have seen, in these chapters, how all our preceding study of psychology is important for keen insights into personality. The strength and kind of motivation, patterns of perception, learning, and thinking are all significant aspects of the unique individual.

In the present chapter we wish to take a look at the adult personality: how psychologists study it, how they describe it and measure it, how it is related to the person's social environment, and so on. We are dealing here with an object of study which is tremendously complex; because it is so very familiar—as you observe other people's personalities every day—you may not realize just how complicated it is.

We have defined personality as *the unique pattern of motivations and perceptions* which characterizes a particular individual. A man's personality is the integration of his various desires, fears, ambitions, and anxieties with his characteristic ways of responding to these impulses. Thus his patterns of resolving conflicts make up an especially important part of his personality.

The Description of Personality

How can we describe anything as complex as this? It is a task which taxes the skill of the novelist, the dramatist, the poet. By and large, the psychologist does not attempt to compete with them. Artists seek to evoke the rich variety, the delicate nuances of the personality they are describing. The psychologist is concerned more with getting some kind of a practical system which can be communicated to his colleagues. It is not quite like describing the Venus de Milo vs. measuring her for a shipping crate; but necessarily, scientific descriptions of personality are likely to seem somewhat bleak and bare as compared with literary efforts. They are made in a different frame of reference, for a different purpose.

Typology. One of the favorite ways by which people deal with the problem of personality description is to invent a system of types. So we run into phrases like "the executive type," "the hard-boiled type," "the traveling salesman type," and so on. Since such typologies are limited only by the user's imagination, they have little scientific value. Essentially, they are useful if the speaker and the listener have a set of common stereotypes (cf. page 236). If the phrase "traveling salesman" evokes in

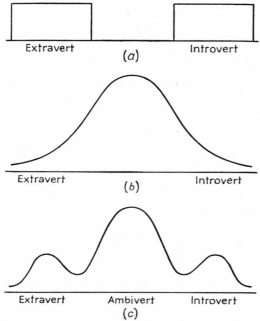

Extravert   (a)   Introvert

Extravert   (b)   Introvert

Extravert   Ambivert   Introvert
(c)

FIG. 15:1. Three conceptions of type theory. The early conception of types was that people could be cleanly separated into different categories, as at a. This has broken down because all studies show that people vary by degrees in personality traits. b represents the trait approach, which denies the existence of types, using them as descriptions of extreme degrees of a trait. c represents a modified type approach, which holds that people do tend to cluster at certain points, which can be called types, but there is no clean break between one type grouping and another. (*From Stagner, 1948.*)

both an image of a back-slapping, jovial, aggressive, talkative individual, they can use this term to describe other personalities. But if the phrase has different meanings for different people, then it is not a good descriptive device.

There are, however, scientific typologies which are based upon a more careful analysis of psychological characteristics and well-chosen terms. Some psychologists have even invented new terms, as Sheldon did with his somatotonic, viscerotonic, and cerebrotonic types (cf. page 473). Freud and his students have developed a typology based on the characteristic stage of devel-

opment at which a person seems to have become fixated: oral passive, oral sadistic, anal, etc. (cf. page 480). These typologies are really methodical scientific attempts to develop a system for personality description; it is thus worth while for us to consider them briefly.

Introversion and extraversion. One of the most widely used classifications in terms of types is that of Carl Jung (1923). Jung coined the terms introversion and extraversion to identify what he considered basic types of personal orientation. The introverted reaction is always directed inward; the individual reacts to a stimulus in terms of its significance to him; he is reflective, introspective, inclined to be self-conscious. Attention, interests, and thoughts are primarily oriented to the self. Extraversion is of course the opposite reaction. The person is oriented to objects; his interest and attention are directed outward. While he may be intelligent, he is not inclined to be thoughtful; he is more a man of action. His behavior is guided by the outer situation, much less by subjective considerations.

Jung, it should be emphasized, described these patterns as types of reaction, taking the position that a person may react in an introverted way today, extraverted tomorrow. He does say that, if a person comes to use one of these patterns habitually, he can be called an *introverted type* or an *extraverted type*. Other people, using Jung's terminology, have tried to classify the whole population into introverts and extraverts. This attempt necessarily fails, because most of us are not consistently one way or the other. Where we feel safe and secure, we may act in an extraverted manner; where we are in danger and under pressure, we become more introverted. To try to maintain the fiction of types, someone invented the term *ambivert* to describe this great middle group of people who were not consistent. A much more realistic way of meeting the problem is to give up the idea of types and treat introversion and extraversion as simply extremes on a scale (as in Fig. 15:1b).

Freud's typology. Freud assumed that some individuals become fixated at specific levels of the developmental sequence described in Chap. 13. Such a fixation would cause the person to acquire a certain pattern of motives, which he chose to call a *character type.* Thus, the *oral passive* type would be characterized particularly by a desire for dependency, for someone to mother him. He is essentially optimistic and passive; he thinks the world owes him a living but thinks, too, that it will drop in his lap without any effort. The *oral sadistic* type is assumed to have become fixated at the biting stage and to have developed appropriate traits. He sees evidence of malice on all sides; he thinks the world owes him a living, but he will have to fight for it. Since this stage precedes the development of the Superego, such an individual will generally use whatever tactics promise success, without regard to ethics and morals. His basic motive is aggression.

The *anal* type is characterized by parsimony, often to the point of miserliness, meticulous attention to details, stubbornness, and obstinacy. Such persons are also likely to be aggressive, although not in the same way as the oral sadistic character. The *phallic* type is exhibitionistic, adolescent, ego-centered, indifferent to others.

Most Freudian psychologists concede that these types, as described, are rare. It is common, however, to find a person who has some of the features of one of these type patterns, along with a mixture of other traits. Thus the scheme is defended as a good way to think about personalities, even though it would not be particularly useful if we were trying to classify the population into categories.

Fromm's revision of Freud. Erich Fromm,

TABLE 15:1. Character Types as Described by Freud and by Fromm

Freud	Traits	Fromm
Oral passive	Parasitic Optimistic Passive Dependent	Receptive (accepting)
Oral sadistic	Aggressive Malicious Slanderous Pessimistic	Exploitative (taking)
Anal	Stingy Obstinate Pedantic Belittling	Hoarding (keeping)
	Opportunistic Inconsistent Without principles Superficial	Marketing (exchanging)
Genital	Productive Adaptable Dependable Cooperative	Productive

another psychoanalyst, has proposed a revision of Freud's typology which many psychologists find valuable. Fromm (1947) emphasizes the functional relationship of the person to his environment as the basis for his types. Thus he describes the receptive, the exploitative, the hoarding, the marketing, and the productive type (see Table 15:1). The first three of these have a notable resemblance to Freud's oral passive, oral sadistic, and anal types; however, Fromm is disinclined to emphasize the notion that the type arises because of events during the corresponding stage of development. He notes that people necessarily have certain relations to one another; and, if a person learns to adopt an exploitative technique and gets results with it, he will continue to use that device in more and more situations. Thus the type gets organized as a result of learning.

Fromm introduces one type, the marketing type, which does not correspond to Freudian classifications. He holds that the marketing type is a product of our civilization, with its emphasis upon trade. Even people are valued in economic terms, and one is advised to change his personality so that he can command a higher price in the market. This, Fromm believes, leads to shallowness and superficiality, with an emphasis on grasping opportunities for self-advancement without regard to principles.

True emotional maturity is exemplified by Fromm's productive type, or Freud's genital type. These individuals have learned to value people as ends in themselves, not as objects to be manipulated for selfish goals. The truly mature personality can take pleasure in doing something for others, he can be tolerant of their failings, he can love another person and not just himself. This is the goal toward which man should develop, although relatively few, perhaps, could be called good examples of this level of maturity.

Is typology useful? The prevalence of typologies of all sorts testifies to the popularity of this way of thinking about personality. That does not, however, prove that typologies are useful or scientifically defensible.

The main defect of typologies is that they imply, if they do not assert, that all people can be separated into types. Thus any book which is written in a typological framework devotes itself to enumerating the criteria by which you can decide which of these various types fits a certain individual. The fact is that it is relatively rare to find a person who exactly fits any of these hypothetical descriptions. Real live people are hard to shove into pigeonholes.

Research studies on personality usually lead to the conclusion that the normal curve (Fig. 15:1*b*) gives the best indication of the way people vary. There is no dividing line at which we can say, "Everyone beyond this point is extraverted" or "All these individuals are anal erotics." There is a series of gradual variations from one ex-

treme to another. Thus this distribution exactly resembles that obtained for intelligence (see Fig. 12:9, page 438), as well as for height, weight, and other characteristics.

Traits vs. types. The modern trend in personality description is therefore away from typology and toward a different approach. This can be called *trait theory*, and the essence of it is that the functional units for describing personality are generalized patterns which can be called *traits*. Traits are conceived as varying by degrees, whereas types seem to follow the all-or-none principle (you are either in this type, or in that one). Suppose, for example, we take the introversion-extraversion aspect of personality which Jung described. Instead of postulating types, we might assume that this is a tendency in behavior which can vary by degrees. An extreme person might be one with ten introverted reactions, but we find others with nine, eight, and so on down to none. We would find similar degrees of extraversion. When we actually try this out on a normal population, we find that it is possible to locate people who vary in this fashion; furthermore, they fit the normal curve (Fig. 15:1). Thus this seems to be a more realistic approach to personality description than is typology.

The problem of dimensions. The question of what the basic dimensions should be, and how many are necessary, occurs in connection with many psychological problems. In studying sensations, for example, we had to classify them with regard to such attributes as intensity, pitch, and timbre (audition) before we could arrange the multitude of specific experiences in a meaningful way.

In the same fashion, we must determine what are the relevant dimensions, and how many of them there are, for describing personality. This is not so simple as for physical objects, where long experience has shown us that length, width, and depth

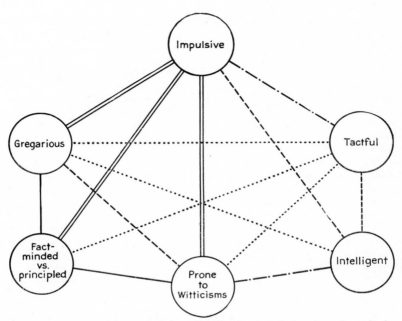

FIG. 15:2. A personality-trait cluster identified by covariation. A number of subjects were rated on the traits listed in the figure. When these ratings were correlated, it was found that variation in impulsive ratings agreed closely with ratings on gregarious, witty, and fact-minded. These form a "trait cluster" of the type used by Cattell in locating his basic dimensions of personality, as listed in Table 15:2. Note that tactful and intelligent drop out of the cluster, as they do not covary with the other items. (*Modified from Cattell, 1950.*)

give us data from which all other spatial characteristics can be computed.

We could start with the assumption that our language tells us how many different features of personality can be identified. Unfortunately, the language is too rich. Allport and Odbert (1936) counted no less than 17,953 trait names in English; and, while there was a considerable amount of duplication, it was obvious that no scientific system could ever use so many. Furthermore, it was clear from inspection that many of these names referred to related phenomena. For instance, integrity, altruism, conscientiousness, and honesty can hardly be considered independent of each other; there must be some basic dimension which all of them reflect. Similarly, emotional, tense, high-strung, unstable are all terms which seem to have much in common.

The quest for basic dimensions in personality has taken the same path as in intelligence. We noted in Chap. 12 that Spearman had looked for a *g* or general intelligence, with specific factors accounting for particular aptitudes, and later Thurstone had expanded this mode of analysis to find by factor analysis a group of fundamental dimensions along which intelligence can vary. Cattell (1945) applied the same procedure to personality description. He started with the Allport-Odbert list, boiled it down to characteristics which could be rated. When he correlated these ratings, he found a total of 131 clusters which he thought corresponded to common personality traits. These clusters could be grouped by factor analysis into 50 "nuclear clusters" of related traits, and these nuclear clusters could in turn be arranged in 20 "sectors of the personality sphere." These

TABLE 15:2. Chart of Principal "Surface-trait" Sectors
(*From Cattell, 1945*)

1. Fineness of character	vs. Moral defect, nonpersistence
a. Integrity, altruism	**vs.** Dishonesty, undependability
b. Conscientious effort	**vs.** Quitting, incoherence
2. Realism, emotional integration	vs. Neuroticism, evasion, infantilism
a. Realism, reliability	vs. Neuroticism, changeability
b. Practicalness, determination	vs. Daydreaming, evasiveness
c. Neuroticism, self-deception, emotional intemperateness	vs. Opposites of these
d. Infantile, demanding self-centeredness	vs. Emotional maturity, frustration tolerance
3. Balance, frankness, optimism	vs. Melancholy, agitation
a. Placidity, social interest	vs. Agitation, melancholy, obstinacy
b. Balance, frankness, sportsmanship	vs. Pessimism, secretiveness, immoderateness
4. Intelligence, disciplined mind, independence	vs. Foolish, undependable unreflectiveness
a. Emotional maturity, clarity of mind	vs. Infantilism, dependence
b. Gentlemanly, disciplined thoughtfulness	vs. Extraverted, foolish lack of will
c. Creativity, self-determination, intelligence	vs. Narrowness of interests, fogginess
d. Intelligence, penetration, general talent	vs. Lack of general ability
5. Egotism, assertion, stubbornness	vs. Modesty, self-effacement, adaptability
6. Boldness, independence, toughness	vs. Timidity, inhibition, sensitivity
7. Sociability	vs. Timidity, hostility, gloominess
8. General emotionality, high-strungness, instability	vs. Placidity, deliberateness, reserve
9. Gratefulness, friendliness, idealism	vs. Sadism, slanderousness, suspiciousness
10. Liveliness, instability, verbal expressiveness	vs. Reserve, quiescence, naturalness
11. Imaginative intuition, curiosity, carelessness	vs. Thrift, inflexible habits, smugness
12. Bohemian, disorderly	vs. Persevering, pedantic
13. Aesthetic, thoughtfulness, constructiveness	vs. Absence of these
14. Physical strength, endurance, courage	vs. Physical inactivity, avoidance of danger
15. Amorousness, playfulness	vs. Propriety
16. Alcoholism, rebelliousness, carelessness	vs. Piety, reverence, thrift
17. Curiosity, wide interests	vs. Limited interests
18. Hypochondriacal, taciturn retroversion	vs. Eloquence, interest in future
19. Asceticism, eccentricity	vs. Comfort-loving conventionality
20. Inflexibility, wandering	vs. Adaptableness, ease of settling down

20 sectors represent the best approach we have at present to a set of basic dimensions for the description of personality. While it is obvious that we lose something of the richness of individual description when we change from 17,000 adjectives to 20, we also get to a point where we can work scientifically with our research data, instead of treating each unique personality as a work of art, completely different from all others. As Table 15:2 shows, Cattell's 20 sectors or dimensions of personality give us quite a sampling of different aspects; if we knew how John Jones stood on all of these, we would feel that we had rather extensive information about him.

What is the nature of these dimensions? The first is obviously dynamic, an organization of motives. The individual perceives altruistic, honest, socially approved behavior as desirable and exerts effort to behave accordingly. The second is largely a matter of conflict solution mechanisms. The third emphasizes temperament, and the fourth, intelligence. Beyond this they are mostly generalized ways of perceiving the self or the social environment, plus appropriate ways of expressing these percepts.

Surface and source traits. It will be noted that Cattell refers to these as "surface traits" of personality. By this he means that they are manifested directly in action;

their expressions can be observed immediately. "Source traits" he considers to be deeper lying organizations which may be expressed indirectly through different surface traits; for instance, insecurity might be expressed through general emotionality, through rebelliousness, or through timidity and inhibition. The relation of surface to source traits, in this usage of terms, can be diagramed as in Fig. 15:3.

The self-image. The nucleus of the personality, it is suggested in Fig. 15:3, is the self. It is easy to see that a person who has a picture of himself as intelligent, capable, and attractive to others will have little occasion to feel threatened, anxious, and emotionally disturbed. Conversely, the boy who feels himself to be stupid, physically weak, or sexually unattractive will undoubtedly have many emotional disturbances and upsets. Remember that behavior is determined by what is perceived, not necessarily by physical reality. A man who thinks of himself as physically inferior will act accordingly, even though tests may show that he is bigger, stronger, and more agile than the average man.

We have noted on several occasions that the infant has no awareness of self and, indeed, may react to parts of his body as objects in the environment. The self-image seems to originate as a body image; that is, the somesthetic sensations derived from muscular movements, contact with objects, and organic processes build up a picture of the body as a continuing event which is always with the child. There is nothing about experience which says it has to be connected with a body; as the ancient Greeks indicate, it is easy to imagine that experience could go on in the absence of a physical organism. However, the child gradually builds up a picture of himself as a bodily unit having certain recognizable characteristics. Differences in temperament (cf. page 470) will play an important part in this development.

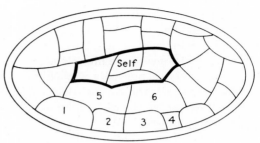

1, 2, 3, 4—Surface traits
5, 6 —Source traits

FIG. 15:3. A cross-sectional view of personality. The self is considered to be the central nucleus around which the rest of the personality is organized. Outer ellipse—facial expressions, gestures, etc., directly observable by others. 1, 2, 3, 4, "surface traits" which are directly expressed in action and words. 5, 6, "source traits," hidden from direct observation but manifested through modification of surface traits. (*From Stagner, 1948.*)

This process is speeded up as language is acquired. The child learns that he has a name which is unique to him and that it is used by others under conditions in which he is experiencing various sensations. For instance, he cries, and mother says, "Jimmy hurt himself." Or, on another occasion, "Jimmy is hungry." So, by the passive process of classical conditioning, the name Jimmy becomes tied in with these organic sensations.

Later on, the self-image is expanded and delineated for the child by still more verbal stimulation. If parents frequently say, "You are a bad boy," this is likely to be incorporated into the image. If he is scolded for being clumsy and stupid, he will picture himself accordingly. After all, his parents are always right, so if they say he has these traits, he must really have them. Playmates and other adults have some effect; not so great as the parents in the early years, although apparently the peer group (same age as himself) become very effective after the age of six—in what Freud called the *latency period* and sociologists have identified as the *gang-forming stage.*

Comparisons with others also have a part in shaping the self-image. A child of average intelligence, in a school for bright children, will come to see himself as stupid, and conversely, a boy only slightly above average may get the notion that he is a genius if he associates with children somewhat below average. When two children in the same family differ with regard to such a trait, both may suffer; the superior one becomes excessively egotistical, and the inferior one feels hopelessly defeated. Parents can improve this situation by stressing the good traits of the slower child and occasionally pointing out that he excels his brother in some regards.

Cultural ideals and personal ambitions also shape the self-image to some extent. If the child identifies himself with some prominent figure, which may be a military hero, a gangster, a scientist, or simply a teacher, he desires to be like that person and will exaggerate those aspects of similarity in himself. If he develops an ambition to become a writer or an actor, he will similarly build up a suitable self-image. Because inner needs can distort perception, it is possible for him to see himself as possessing these traits when outside observers see little evidence of their presence.

These four elements, then: bodily sensations, verbal descriptions, comparisons with others, and inner pressures contribute to the formation of the self-image. However, it is worth mentioning that not all of this process is positive. *Repression* also plays its part by driving out of conscious awareness those features of the picture which are distasteful. The development of a frame of reference always includes both the selection of elements which fit together, and the rejection of items which conflict with the picture. So the person, as his self-image becomes organized, will begin ejecting certain memories, certain pictures of his own activities, which do not harmonize with this image. If I think of myself

as a very intelligent individual, but on a specific occasion did something outstandingly stupid, I shall try to forget this incident. Similarly, a person who pictures himself as rigidly upright and moral will repress any memory of deviation from this code. So the self-image becomes highly consistent, as positive elements are exaggerated and items that do not conform are tossed out.

The nature of traits. Let us now revert to our consideration of traits. We have used this term to refer to the organized functional units of personality. They are usually designated by adjectives; we say that this person is calm, helpful, self-confident, quiet. The manner in which we apply these terms implies that these are not specific responses to specific situations; rather, they are *generalized ways of perceiving and responding to the environment.* We assume that he will be helpful, not only with his brother, but also with other people. The essence of the trait, then, is that it functions in a variety of situations, being thus differentiated from a conditioned response, a habit, or a simple association of responses.

Traits as mental sets. One way of describing traits is in terms of the concept of mental set. This concept has been employed to identify a persisting tendency to respond in a certain way when an appropriate stimulus occurs. Thus we spoke of a person getting "set" for arithmetic problems; and, on a more complex level, the architect is "set" to perceive differences in houses which the layman does not observe.

Let us now apply this concept of set to personality. Here is an individual who anticipates frustration. He expects people to try to take advantage of him (cf. Freud's oral sadistic pattern). He is thus set to respond with anger and aggression when even minute evidence of such behavior is observable. In his perceptions he magnifies these fragments because he is set for them. Cason (1930) found that there are wide individual differences in response to annoyances; some people get annoyed very easily to almost any stimulus, whereas others have a high threshold and are rarely angered by trivial frustrations. In Cattell's list (Table 15:2) we note several traits which fit this concept very well: (6) boldness, (7) sociability, (9) gratefulness, (15) amorousness, and (17) curiosity are obvious examples. The trait illustrates a generalized, persistent mental set to respond in a given way whenever the appropriate class of stimuli appears.

Traits as frames of reference. Another way of defining a trait is to call it *a way of looking at situations.* A frame of reference is an inner pattern for judging situations. Basically it is likely to be a matter of scaling an experience somewhere between good and bad on a dimension or continuum. How, for example, does the individual react to an offer of assistance on a job he is doing? Sam perceives this as an intrusion, a threat to his own ego, and so he responds with annoyance. Joe perceives the same offer as helpful and responds with friendliness. The point here is that we can best understand the contradictory behavior of the two men if we ask the question: how was the stimulus perceived by each? In one case the stimulus was seen as bad and threatening; in the other, as good and helpful. The difference between the two personalities, then, can be described as a difference in a generalized way of perceiving social situations.

Traits such as thrift, conventionality, radicalism, and sociability lend themselves easily to this kind of description. The thrifty person values highly the accumulation of property, and he judges situations in terms of whether they contribute to such accumulation. The radical perceives the existing order of things as bad; his evaluation of situations will lead to a preference for activities which move to-

ward new social organizations. The shy individual perceives close contact with people as dangerous; he tends to stay by himself in order to avoid tension.

There is no contradiction between the view of traits as generalized mental sets, and traits as frames of reference. One approach emphasizes the response tendency, whereas the other emphasizes the perceptual side of the relationship. Because it fits in better with certain points we shall introduce later in this chapter, we prefer the definition as frame of reference, but the alternative view is widely held also.

Traits and the self-image. Many of the traits we have mentioned involve a perception not only of the environmental situation but also of the self. When we speak of boldness, we speak primarily of the individual's perception of the environment as one with which he can deal effectively; thus he is not threatened by it. This implies an evaluation not only of the external situation but also of the self. Actually this is true of most traits. A dominant person is one who perceives himself as capable of being the leader, and also is one who perceives others as people to be bossed around. The exploitative personality (Fromm, page 521) sees people as objects to be manipulated for his own purposes.

In general, the self-image is an influence upon all traits. This leads to a higher degree of *consistency* within the personality than might otherwise hold. Because the person wants to behave in a manner which is appropriate to his perception of himself, he will perform in a more uniform fashion than if he were at the mercy of his environment. In connection with such phenomena as size constancy (Chap. 6), we noted that it is helpful to homeostatic adjustment if the person perceives an object as constant even though the retinal image is in continuous change. Similarly, there seems to be some advantage in maintaining a constant self-image. The facts show that the average person's picture of himself changes very slowly; psychotherapy, which has as its aim the improvement of personality, often involves modifying the self-image (see below), and this may take months or even years to achieve.

Character, "will power," and motivation. When we say that a person has a strong character, or a lot of will power, we are likely to be referring to the fact that he persists in self-initiated activities despite opposition from the environment. There is no evidence that people differ by heredity in any trait which could be called "will power." It is obvious, on the other hand, that if a person develops a picture of himself as strong, intelligent, capable of dealing with threats, he will be more likely to persist in the face of obstacles. Further, if he has a strong Superego (as a result of identification with parents, etc.), he will be strongly motivated to behave in accordance with social *mores*. Socially disapproved behavior will arouse anxiety, and he will avoid it.

The concept of character, then, is a fairly complex one including the person's self-image, his frame of reference for evaluating social situations (honesty, truthfulness, ethics), and his motivation to conform to socially approved standards. We observe all kinds of combinations of these elements, and consequently get all kinds of "character structures"; some people are meticulously honest in one phase of their behavior and not at all trustworthy in another area.

Despite the fact that the law divides us into "good" and "bad" characters, this is a psychologically unrealistic position. The psychologist finds "so much good in the worst of us, and so much bad in the best of us" that he rejects the notion of a sharp dichotomy between good citizens and criminals. Instead, he takes the position that honesty and similar traits follow the normal curve, which means that most of us fall in the center, being sometimes

honest and sometimes not, depending on the situation. Delinquent behavior often arises out of traits which have much good in them; for instance, a boy's loyalty to his gang may cause him to do things which are dishonest, or it may be a factor in his being very helpful to gang members who are having trouble.

Society has to have a system of controls in order that people can live together in groups. Unfortunately, social control relies almost exclusively on punishment, which has relatively little value in learning (Chap. 9), and not enough on reward, which seems to be a far more potent influence in the acquisition of behavior patterns. A social system which gave rewards for "good" behavior and treated "bad" behavior as symptoms of illness would undoubtedly turn out better adjusted personalities with far less social conflict.

The Measurement of Personality

Science inevitably moves from description to measurement of any event. Description of electricity and its phenomena was followed by efforts to quantify and measure this phenomenon. The description of personality is only a step in the scientific procedure; for deeper understanding, for verification of hypotheses about origins, and for the study of personality change, we must have devices for measurement.

Psychologists have experimented with many different techniques for reducing personality manifestations to an orderly sequence which can be counted, scaled for intensity, or treated in some other numerical manner. Which of these we use depends on our purpose. All of them have some value, although they are by no means equal in this respect. We shall give only a brief sketch of some of the commoner techniques.[1]

[1] A more detailed treatment of personality measurement is given in Stagner (1948), Chaps. 2–3.

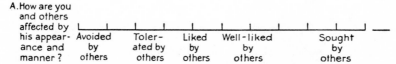

A. How are you and others affected by his appearance and manner?

Avoided by others — Tolerated by others — Liked by others — Well-liked by others — Sought by others

FIG. 15:4. A sample of a graphic rating scale. The rater is supposed to observe his subject and then indicate his impression by checking a point on the scale. The dash on the end is checked for "no opportunity to observe."

Personality as stimulus. Personality is often treated in terms of the individual's social stimulus value, or his effect upon others. While this is not a scientifically useful definition, it represents a real practical problem. Business enterprises want salesmen who have a pleasant personality as viewed by customers, and the military services want officers who are perceived as leaders by the rank and file. Thus there has been a good deal of work done on personality-measuring devices which attempt to reduce social stimulus value to easily observable units and get judgments on these scales from the people likely to be concerned.

Rating scales. The term *rating scale* is applied to any instrument which defines certain qualities of the ratee and asks raters to judge whether this quality is present or absent, or the degree to which it is manifest. Teachers use a simple A, B, C, D, E rating scale for estimating the quality of student's performance in most institutions. One of the more useful devices in this area is the *graphic rating scale* illustrated in Fig. 15:4. It calls for a judgment in terms of the degree of presence of a certain trait; a "measurement" attitude is suggested by the linear scale, marked off into equal units like a foot rule; objectivity of judgment is presumably aided by the descriptive phrases underneath. This scale is used by the American Council on Education as part of a standard recommendation form for college entrance. Many industries use a graphic rating scale in estimating the efficiency of performance of employees; these data are used for pay raises, for promotions, and so on.

The forced-choice rating form. Many difficulties arise in the use of simple rating scales such as those mentioned. If the rater likes the ratee, he may give him excessively high ratings. Or, if he is influenced by some specific trait (such as high intelligence), he may give high ratings on other unrelated characteristics. Such errors are sometimes called by the term *halo effect*—an unrelated item radiates out to influence judgments on other points. Halo can be negative as well as positive; the rater may underestimate and be too severe instead of too generous.

To avoid some of these problems, there has been a good deal of effort to devise a rating scale which would reduce halo and focus the rater on judging the presence or absence of specific traits. The *forced-choice scale* was devised in the Army to improve officer ratings for promotion. It consists of a series of groups of items, in which the rater picks one "most characteristic of this officer" and one which is "least characteristic of him." Since all the items in a group may be good, he is forced to try to identify the best feature; conversely, all four may be bad, and he is forced to name the ratee's defects.

It might still be possible for the rater to exaggerate the good points of his friends and the defects of those he disliked. To make this more difficult, the scale items are pretested and matched for emotional tone; that is, in a pair of items, each sounds equally good, but one corresponds to efficient performance as an officer, while the other does not. To use a different example, Staugas and McQuitty (1950) developed a forced-choice scale for judging

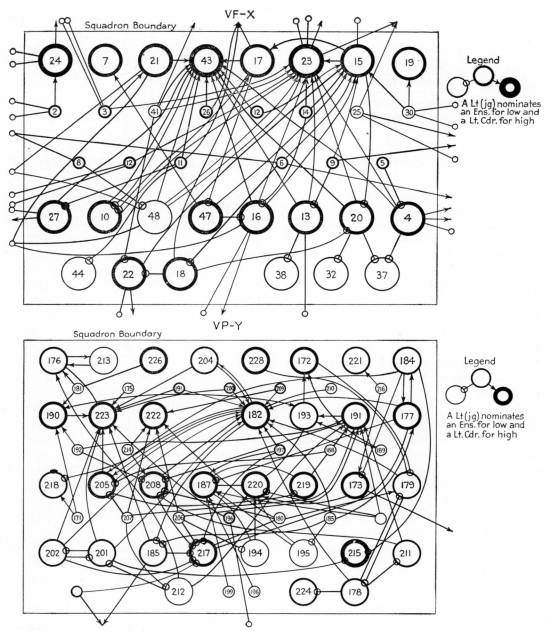

FIG. 15:5. A sociometric study in relation to air-group morale. These charts represent the morale situation in two Navy air groups. An arrow pointing to a number means that this person is chosen as "a man I would like to have alongside during combat" and similar choices. A line ending in a small circle by a man's number indicates a negative choice. In VF-X the ranking officers (23, 43) receive a high percentage of positive choices and no negative choices. Many of the rejections are of men outside the squadron; the men could not think of anyone inside the squadron they would give a low rating.

In VP-Y the situation is quite different. The ranking officers (215, 217) received only negative choices. There are accepted leaders (182, 191) but they are not the official leaders of the squadron. Only one negative choice goes outside the squadron, as compared with 22 outside VF-X.

The value of these sociometric charts is not only in estimating the morale of the group, but especially in locating men to move up to leadership positions. If a man's personality so impresses his fellows that he gets a large number of positive choices, he will usually make a suitable leader for that group. (*From Jenkins, 1948.*)

dormitory counselors. One pair of items reads:

_____ Even-tempered
_____ Cooperative

These items were matched for preference value, so that all judges thought both sounded equally good. But the second was found consistently to be applied to the most successful counselors, while the first was ascribed equally often to good and poor counselors. In the forced-choice rating situation, then, the judge can mark a "good-sounding" item for his friend, and yet it does not artificially raise his rating. Most psychologists in military and industrial work seem to feel that the forced-choice type of rating represents a real advance; however, critics have pointed out that a shrewd judge can still over-inflate his ratings if he attempts to do so.

Sociometry. Strictly speaking, it is not necessary to ask the rater to judge a series of separate traits. We can ask him simply to give an over-all judgment, to vote for or against the person. Thus, in a study of leadership in the Navy air force, pilots were asked to name the man they would most like to have flying alongside during combat. Good morale units were characterized by the fact that these choices (which were secret) piled up on the officer in command. Poor morale units showed a lot of choices of other men, even men outside the unit (see Fig. 15:5).

The term *sociometry* has been applied to such studies of social position. Sociometric work with young children and adolescents has shown that individuals who get many choices have socially desirable traits (which is fairly obvious). They have also shown that "isolates"—persons who are neglected in such choices—have a much higher score on general emotionality and symptoms of poor conflict adjustment than do the preferred individuals. We do not know, of course, which comes first—social isolation or emotional adjustment. Probably each reinforces the other.

Interviews. Another common way of assessing social stimulus value is by interview. Untrained interviewers have been shown to make many serious errors in their judgments of personality; however, with training, the reliability and validity of their judgments can be markedly improved.

The *stress interview* is another technique which is still an object of experimentation. The theory here is that a person who is interviewed in a calm, peaceful setting may give quite a different impression than when "the heat is on." Hence interviews have been held under distracting conditions, with one or more interviewers making sarcastic remarks, implying that the subject is stupid, and so on. The ability to maintain self-control here is probably a good estimate of frustration tolerance. Some studies suggest that ratings made in a stress interview situation are much better for picking men for tension-arousing jobs (*e.g.*, traffic policemen) than are ordinary interviews.

Limitations. The study of personality as social stimulus value is inevitably complicated by the fact that no one has exactly the same stimulus value for two other people. So, if one of my students rates me "A" on teaching, and another rates me "B," both may be right. My personality may be such that I am much more effective with one than with the other. The girl who would make a marvelous wife for Harry might be completely unsuited to Frank. Two interviewers may meet the same candidate for a job and give him different ratings; he is pleasing to one, and not to the other. Despite these limitations, some form of rating technique often proves necessary, and if its weaknesses are understood, it can be quite valuable.[1]

Personality as response. If we define personality as "whatever the individual

---

[1] Industrial psychology includes an extensive literature on the rating of employees and consequently makes a good place to read further about the errors and strong points of various rating methods. See, *e.g.*, Harrell, T. W., *Industrial Psychology*, Chap. 3, New York, Prentice-Hall, 1950.

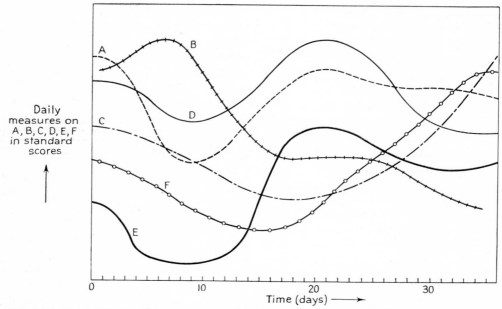

FIG. 15:6. Determining traits by covariation of responses. The same individual was measured on a number of physiological responses over a 35-day period. When these are plotted, it becomes clear that A, D, and E vary together, suggesting that they are aspects of a single trait. C and F also seem to vary together but are quite independent of the A-D-E cluster. (From Cattell, 1950.)

does," then our approach to measurement should be to find out exactly what he does. So, in nursery-school children, we have studies of frequency of nail biting, number of quarrels per hour, amount of smiling, talking, and so on. In adults, investigations of handwriting, drawing, and gestures, as well as visceral responses, come in this category (Fig. 15:6).

Unfortunately, we must not only find out what the person does; we must also find out whether what he does is important. In many cases it is not. Many studies which have involved laborious hours of observation and statistics have come up with the report that people do these things, yet it does not seem to help us in understanding them.

Handwriting and drawing are perhaps exceptions to this generalization. As noted in Chap. 13, muscular movements are readily influenced by mental states, as well as by symbolic processes; thus it may

be hoped that such fine movements as these will reflect variations in temperament and also in other personality traits.

Handwriting. Many extravagant claims have been put forth as to the identification of personality traits, honesty, ambition, and similar characteristics from handwriting. Most of these have been discarded because no evidence supported them. A small core of evidence remains to indicate that handwriting is of some value in the study of personality.

Handwriting is subject to so many variations that it readily becomes almost unique for adults in our culture. People are likely to develop little personal peculiarities in script and to change these to conform with emotional states. In Fig. 15:7 we show handwriting samples from a pair of identical twins who were studied for personality resemblances. It is interesting to observe how similar are the changes which occur between twelve and eighteen years. This

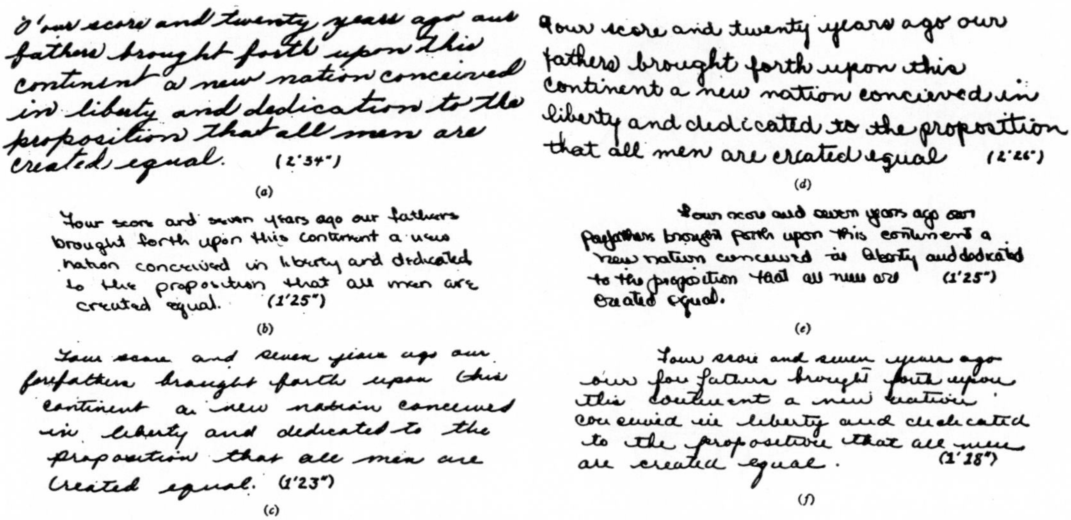

FIG. 15:7. Parallel changes in handwriting of identical twins. This pair of identical twins was reared apart, although they did correspond with each other; so some opportunity for imitation is present. Nevertheless, it seems surprising that relatively different writing patterns at age twelve (a, d) should become so much alike at age eighteen (b, e) and nineteen (c, f). (*From Burks, 1942.*)

would be even more striking if we did not know that the girls exchanged letters once or twice a month during this period, so that chances for imitation were present.

At present there are two schools of thought with regard to the interpretation of personality from handwriting. One group of investigators attempts to make judgments from the whole script, getting a general impression of style, evenness, pressure, originality in letter form, etc., and trying to relate these to the personality of the writer. Another group makes very detailed measures of letters and spaces, and relates these to personality traits. Both results have led to a few encouraging findings but nothing very exciting. For instance, handwriting pressure correlates fairly well with ratings of dominance in a study by Pascal (1942). This may be a temperamental characteristic of vigor showing up in a social situation.

Drawings. Even persons without artistic skill may convey a great deal of interesting information by their drawings. Figure 15:8 shows the drawings produced by a man when asked to draw pictures of a person of each sex. It is not difficult to infer that his picture of women is that they are strong, vigorous, protective; men are weaker, more idealistic, more retiring and thoughtful. These inferences can be made from the relative size of the pictures, the firmness of outlines, the position of hands and arms, relative amount of care given to the two drawings. They are confirmed by intimate clinical study.[1]

Personality as intervening variable. As the preceding comments about drawings should indicate, most psychologists who study responses are really concerned with assessing the inner states which are reflected in this behavior. In other words, they are interested primarily in the inner organization of percepts and motives, and only secondarily in the specific response forms. This is what we mean by the phrase

[1] Abt, L. E., and Bellak, L. (Eds.) (1950) contains interesting chapters on the interpretation of drawings by Levy and by Kadis. Krout (1950) has published an interesting drawing test, based on psychoanalytic symbols (see p. 402), which seems to be quite valuable.

FIG. 15:8. Drawings can reflect inner personality patterns. The subject was asked only to draw a figure of a male, and a figure of a female. Note the differences in size, in emphasis of line, in concern for detail, and in expressive position of arms. For discussion see text. (*Reprinted from Projective Psychology, by Abt and Bellak, by permission of Alfred A. Knopf, Inc.*)

"intervening variable." When we say, with regard to the person who drew Fig. 15:8, that he has a certain attitude toward women, we are talking about an inner state which determines how the person will respond to certain kinds of situations. Many devices for studying personality began as attempts to study actual responses but have been found to be more useful when treated as approaches to these intervening variables.

Inventories and questionnaires. This point is particularly true of those "personality tests" which consist of lists of questions to be answered "yes" or "no" (cf. Table 15:3) or lists of adjectives to be checked to describe oneself. When this kind of test was first developed during World War I, it consisted of a list of neurotic symptoms, and the theory was that, by counting the number of such responses, the psychologist could predict the soldier's chances of breaking down in combat. Later experience

showed that the answers to these questions did not necessarily agree with direct observation by a psychiatrist; a man might say he had a symptom and yet it could not be found, or he might deny one and the psychiatrist spotted it immediately. At first this led to a tendency to reject pencil-and-paper tests of personality entirely. Later the point of view developed that the person's answers are important because they reflect his picture of himself, and on this basis they have been useful in many situations such as counseling and guidance.

Table 15:3 shows a few questions from a scale developed by Guilford on the basis of extensive studies of introversion-extraversion. Jung, it will be recalled, thought he could use these terms to identify types of personalities. Later work showed that they should be used merely as extremes of a trait which varies by degrees. Guilford cut this still finer; he found that there were several kinds of introversion, social introversion, thinking introversion, low general activity level, and so on, all of which Jung had lumped together, but which were by no means equally present in a given person. In this table we show some of the items which Guilford found diagnostic of *rhathymia*, a kind of impulsive, happy-go-lucky etndency which would be high for the "typical extravert" and low for the "typical introvert." There is some evidence that people high on this trait do well at selling, advertising, and public relations, but poorly on accounting, production control, and other detail jobs.

TABLE 15:3. Sample Items from Guilford's Rhathymia Scale

Are you ordinarily a carefree individual?
Are you inclined to act on the spur of the moment without thinking things over?
Do you subscribe to the philosophy of "Eat, drink, and be merry, for tomorrow we die"?
Do you often crave excitement?
Do you often feel restless while listening to a lecture?

The usefulness of any such tests clearly depends on our assumption that we are measuring some kind of inner tendency. It makes little difference in a salesman's work whether he does (or does not) say "yes" to "Are you ordinarily a carefree individual?" but it makes a great deal of difference whether he has the kind of mental attitude which is probably reflected in a "yes" answer.

Such questionnaire inventories have been prepared for a great many traits. Neurotic tendency, ascendance, self-sufficiency, introversion, seclusiveness, insecurity, and inferiority feeling are some of the trait names attached to these lists of questions. Most of them are valuable if used under proper precautions.

Projective tests. Questionnaires attempt to get at the self-image by direct questioning. Perhaps the person will have repressed some items about himself as too painful; or he may refuse to tell the truth for reasons of the moment—*e.g.*, if he is applying for a job, he is prone to say what he thinks the company wants and can probably rationalize that this is true. To get beyond self-protective and repressive barriers, projective tests have been devised.

The projective test is based on the phenomena of projection (page 506) and autistic distortion of perceptions (page 243). People are prone to read themselves into external situations. They see as objective reality a tendency which is really within themselves. So, if I ask you to complete the sentence,

Professors are . . .

and you write in the word "dull," you are projecting some of your own ideas about professors into the external reality. If I ask you to look at an ink blot (Fig. 15:9) and tell me what you see, you cannot find much in the real stimulus to help you answer, so you must project some idea of your own into the blot. For these reasons

it is most difficult to fake on projective tests. The answer comes from within you, and almost any choice you make may give away significant information.[1]

The ink-blot test. The first test of this type to receive methodical development was the ink-blot test evolved by Hermann Rorschach (1921). Rorschach had been interested in the study of associations of ideas as clues to the inner states of the individual. However, he was dissatisfied with the use of verbal stimuli, as in the free-association test (page 74), because a word tends to set off associations which are logically or culturally determined (page 398) and not necessarily indicative of emotion. He sought for stimulus material which would initiate associations but would not have these limitations. His trial of ink blots seems to have been a fortunate choice.

The Rorschach blots are symmetrical but irregular in outline (Fig. 15:9), varied in shading, and susceptible of various interpretations. Five of them include color, while five are only in shades of gray. These 10 blots were retained out of literally hundreds which were tried. Each of these 10 has been found to evoke a wide variety of responses from different persons. So, to the same blot, one response is: "This is a wolf's head. Here are the eyes, here is the nose, mouth, and chin." Another person says: "This is a Halloween mask." A third says: "This is an X-ray photograph of a pelvis."

The interpretations of personality traits from Rorschach protocols are complex. Not too much attention is paid to the actual object seen, although some use is made of psychoanalytic symbolism. Weight is placed on the location of the object on the card,

[1] Any such test can be faked, of course, by a person who knows the scoring procedure and principles of interpretation. That is one reason why the widely used projective tests are not allowed to circulate freely and why the techniques of scoring and interpretation are not taught except at professional levels.

FIG. 15:9. An ink blot similar to those in the Rorschach test. "What might this be?" One subject says, "Here are two eyes staring at me; they look cold and suspicious." (Two small gray spots in lower center.) Another subject says: "This is a bear on his hind legs, facing away from me, batting playfully at something with his front paws." (Whole blot.) Is it apparent that personality differences may be reflected in such reports?

the clarity of form perception, the use of color or shading, the perception of movement in the figure, and numerous other details.

The Rorschach test has become a standard item of equipment in all psychiatric hospitals and clinics, in most counseling work with personality problems, and in a wide variety of other situations where personality diagnosis is important. The test has been compared with "psychological X ray" because it permits a glimpse of the interior without damage to the individual. It leads to judgments of introversion, creative ability, emotional balance, impulsiveness, and other important characteristics.

Despite its wide acceptance, the Rorschach is not thoroughly validated, and its use is still something of an art as well as a science. Some examiners get better results with it than do others. In clinical work, its diagnosis is always checked against other indications; there is no personality test which is considered absolutely dependable.

Thematic Apperception Test. The Rorschach is probably the most used projective test. Second in frequency is the Thematic Apperception Test (TAT) developed by H. A. Murray (1938). This material is somewhat more structured than the ink blots; each card presents a picture, to which the person is asked to make up a story. Like the Rorschach, its value comes from projection. There is no story suggested plainly by the picture; hence the individual must project something of himself into the situation and thereby reveals his own habitual patterns of desire and perception. For instance, one young man told a series of stories (one to each picture), all of which involved falling in love and then losing the wife or sweetheart through death, divorce, or accident. It was not difficult to infer his feeling of insecurity about his love life, which actually stemmed from the early death of his mother but which had transferred to a fear of loving any woman because she too might be lost to him.

The Rorschach test gets at deep, enduring traits (often, the kind referred to on page 525 as "source traits.") The TAT is more useful in identifying temporary trends, strong motives, moods, and so on. The Rorschach may give us an indication that the person has experienced an emotional shock; the TAT can often identify the kind of shock and thus help the therapist in alleviating the emotional disturbance. Thus both tests are widely used, generally as a team, in helping the clinical psychologist with his study of personality.

Tests resembling the TAT have also been developed for the study of more superficial features of personality, *e.g.*, social attitudes. In the field of race prejudice, it has been noted that people who insist that they are liberal and tolerant often give away concealed prejudices by the kind of stories they invent. Henry (1949) has shown that the TAT picks out differences in motivation between successful and unsuccessful business executives; we shall discuss this study a little later (page 540). Tests of the same type have been employed in studies of cultural differences; obviously the content a person projects into a picture will depend in large part upon the cultural background from which he comes.

The Total Personality

Ratings, questionnaires, ink blots, picture-interpretation tests—all these and many more devices are used to get at parts of the personality for description and measurement. The Rorschach and TAT lay some claim to getting the total personality, but even here it is to be observed that there is a lot of additional information about the personality which they do not pick up.

To understand an individual, we must have not only his present status but also his history. We must know something of his socioeconomic background, the kind of culture in which he grew up, the painful experiences and satisfying experiences of his early childhood. We need his intelligence, his job history, his relations with superiors and subordinates, his family life and school experiences. Thus the study of any one individual as a total personality is an extensive endeavor.

The most detailed information ever obtained by one person about another probably comes out of the therapy relationship. In psychotherapy the clinician works with his patient for perhaps an hour a day over a period of months. The patient recounts his life history, discusses his relationships with his family, reveals his emotional problems and conflicts, and soon becomes almost an open book to the therapist.

The tools of the clinician for understanding the personality of his client are introjection and empathy. Introjection, it will be remembered, is the response to something outside yourself as though it were part of yourself. Hence the clinician feels the experiences of his patient as if they were his own, but of course much less intensely. He must have more than a purely intellectual understanding of the conflicts and problems his patient has encountered. Knowledge of a wide variety of personality difficulties is, of course, a help; but some psychologists have this extensive information without ever getting a deep insight into the person with whom they are dealing.

Personality in its social setting. Traits of personality are chiefly outcomes of learning. It must therefore be expected that personality will always have to be interpreted relative to a social frame of reference and that a real understanding of the individual requires some understanding of his culture. We would certainly misinterpret the Plains Indian who describes his visions as real experiences, if we did not know that in his culture such hallucinations are not only considered normal, but actually desirable.

One of the factors shaping the self-image is one's *social status*. Ideas about social status are transmitted from parents to children from birth onward; "we are this kind of people, we don't do things that way." Proper ideas of dress, of recreation, even of morals, vary substantially as we move from one level to another of American culture. Before deciding whether a given form of behavior is maladjusted or not, we must learn how it fits into this person's social situation.

The concept of *social role* applies to the immediate social function of the person. When a young man gets married, he takes on a new role: as husband and head of a household. Because he will have acquired from his own parents certain notions as to the proper behavior for a person in this role, his "personality" may seem to change quite markedly on assuming the new role. For example, he may have courted his fiancée assiduously, been very courteous, thoughtful, and gentle; now he ignores her and drops all forms of romance. This does not mean—as she may conclude—that his former behavior was all pretense. It was a part of a social role, and his new behavior reflects his conception of his new role.

The concepts and ideas regarding personality which we have presented in the last three chapters have broad implications for human behavior in everyday life.[1] It is impossible for us to do more than touch upon some of these applications. To indicate something of what is possible, we shall take up briefly the work of psychologists regarding personality and marriage, and personality in vocational choice.

Personality and Marriage

Marriage, as we noted in Chap. 14, is a prolific source of conflicts of motives. The reverse, in a way, is also true: personality differences account for many marital conflicts.

What are the personality traits associated with happiness in marriage? Terman (1938) and his students have done extensive research on this problem, starting with the development of a "happiness scale" and going on to compare happily married couples with others who reported themselves not at all happy. Fortunately, the study indicates that happy marriages outnumber the others by a healthy majority.

Individual traits. The unhappily married person was characterized in these studies

as being grouchy, irritable, critical of others resentful of discipline, dominative in relation to members of the opposite sex; having periods of excitement; and alternating between elation and depression. One is tempted to wonder which is cause and which effect; such a person would certainly not be a pleasant marital partner! On the other hand, the frustrations and conflicts of a bad marriage would induce such reactions from the average person. Happily married persons were found to be kindly and cooperative, emotionally stable and secure.

Similarity of couples. In general, happily married people resemble each other. Some items on which similarity went with happy marital status were: being sensitive to praise and criticism, wanting someone to be around when you get bad news, taking the lead to enliven a dull party. It has also been found that happy couples are more likely to resemble each other in intelligence, education, religion, cultural background, recreational interests, social values, and introvert-extravert tendencies.

A momentary thought will show that these findings are obvious. A man and woman who differ markedly on any of these will find things to argue about. He will want to do things one way, she, another. Their preferred goals and their perceptions of proper ways to achieve these goals will differ. If the husband is extravagant and the wife thrifty, there is trouble ahead. If she likes to sit, read, and think, while he wants constant action, this likewise leads to difficulty. We noted in Chap. 14 that similarity in sex drive made for fewer marital conflicts.

On the other hand, there are a few traits on which the happy couples were less alike than the unhappy. One of these was dominance. Liking public speaking, for example, was all right for one member of a couple but not for both. We can readily understand that having two high-domi-

---

[1] See, *e.g.*, Harsh and Schrickel, *Personality: Development and Assessment*, which treats personality in terms of childhood, adolescence, love and marriage, maturity and old age; or Stagner, *Psychology of Personality*, which discusses personality in the family, in school, in occupations, and in relation to social values.

nance people living together might lead to disagreement over "who is boss"; apparently it is better for one to like leadership and the other to prefer having someone else take the lead.

Background factors. The background factors which make for happy marriages are the same as those which make for well-adjusted personalities in general. Happy couples had parents who were happily married; they reported that they had predominantly pleasant experiences in childhood; discipline in the family was described as neither lax nor excessively strict. Age at marriage, premarital sex experience, frequency of intercourse, and contraceptive procedures seemed to have no relation to marital happiness.

Choice of a mate. These findings suggest that we might raise the percentage of happy marriages still higher if young people would consider the personality factor before getting married. Generally speaking, it seems that your chances of success will be substantially greater if you find someone who resembles you in the ways noted above and differs in regard to dominance. Most colleges and universities now have counseling services where young people can take personality tests and get advice about themselves. Counseling for marriage is often a part of such a program. It can be a valuable contribution to one's future happiness.

Personality and Occupation

As we noted in Chap. 12, intelligence level is one of the determinants of occupational choice. Some jobs also require various special aptitudes, such as mechanical dexterity, visual acuity, and the like. On the personality side there is also a need to consider job requirements in relation to personal characteristics. It is as foolish to put an active extravert on a solitary office job as it is to put a moron on a task requiring an IQ of 110. Neither will be happy, and the work will suffer too.

Many of the relations between personality and occupation are obvious. Salesmen who do not worry too much have the best chance of success (see Table 15:3), and timidity would certainly be a handicap in this occupation. The aggressive, independent, dominant individual will not do well on a job where he must take orders all day long. Every person must act out a social role which fits to some degree with his temperamental and social traits. Every job carries with it certain kinds of relations to other people (working in groups or alone, giving orders or taking them, etc.). By the time a man is twenty-one years old, his way of perceiving and reacting to such situations is likely to be pretty well set. It is usually easier to find a job that will fit him than to change him to suit the job.

The interests and values of the person are also important to his success. E. K. Strong has published a Vocational Interest Inventory which calls for 400 reactions to items about preferred working conditions, people, activities, reading, and recreation. There is extensive evidence to the effect that a boy is well advised to choose a job for which he makes a fairly high score on this test—if he has the ability and training, of course. The Allport-Vernon Study of Values (see page 124) has also been used in this way. A person with a high theoretical and low practical score is unlikely to succeed in business—he will make all the wrong decisions. Figure 15:10 shows the values profile of a group of professors of psychology, compared with several hundred college men. The professors conform to the popular stereotype in being less concerned about practicality (economic scale) and power (political scale), more interested in theory, humanitarian, and aesthetic considerations.

Questionnaire tests like these are not satisfactory for selection of employees,

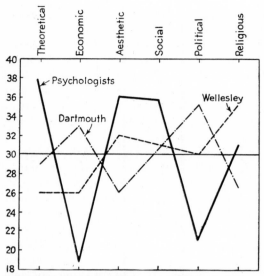

FIG. 15:10. Values profile for psychology professors. The composite values profile of six professors of psychology at Dartmouth College is plotted alongside the profile for several hundred men at Dartmouth and women at Wellesley. In some respects the professors confirm the popular stereotype as to their characteristics. (*From Stagner, 1948.*)

since it is fairly easy to fake them. They are useful in vocational guidance, where there is little motivation to give a false picture of oneself. The projective tests would be preferable for industrial purposes, since they are not so easily distorted. However, they are so time-consuming and expensive to use that they are rarely employed by industry.

One of the exceptions is a study by Henry (1949) of industrial executives. Using a projective test (TAT), he investigated the personalities of executives in six large corporations. The men were from the middle level in the organization; some of them were judged by their superiors as high quality, likely to go to top-executive posts, the others being relatively unsuccessful. The significant differences between the groups seemed to be in the personality area. He reports that characteristics of the successful group include: a need for achievement, not just for glory; a need to

move up the scale, to accumulate property and status in the eyes of associates; perception of superiors as helpful, not threatening; aggression channeled into work, not into personal hostility; emancipation from parents (neither dependence nor rebellion). Since the test can be used to check new prospects for such characteristics, it is to be presumed that many corporations will be looking for men with these traits in the future.

Influence of occupation on personality. Just as marriage may have an impact on personality, so can occupation. The accountant is interested in detail, but was he that way prior to his training? Perhaps he was the kind of person who liked detail, but on the other hand, he may have been successful at accounting and so came to like detail. After all, we learn those responses which are associated with tension reduction, and if a job leads to substantial rewards, we shall develop personality traits compatible with that situation.

What we want to emphasize, in closing this brief comment on personality and the environment, is that there is always a two-way relationship. The external situation has a selective effect: certain people are attracted to this role. It also has a coercive effect: once in the situation, the person is molded to fit his task. Another way of putting the same idea emphasizes the inner personality. I may seek a situation where I will feel comfortable and happy; but once there, I will modify my actions to conform even more closely to the situational requirements. This is the kind of dynamic interaction between person and environment which has been stressed in our entire account of psychology.

Normal and Abnormal Personalities

Psychology deals with all kinds of personalities, normal and abnormal. All human beings obey the same psychological laws;

there is no separate psychology for the abnormal. There is, however, a problem for the student: what is the dividing line between the normal and the abnormal? How do we define a normal personality?

The problem is even more difficult than it sounds. We have abandoned the typological approach to personality, and similarly we reject the notion that abnormal people are in any qualitative respect different from the general population. We assume that personality traits differ by degrees, in accordance with the normal curve (Fig. 15:1), and consequently that the abnormal is simply the normal carried to an extreme.

Let us see how this would work out in practice. Consider autistic thinking, which has been described in some detail, as an example. The normal person engages in some daydreaming. If he is faced with a tough problem, he will probably fantasy all kinds of solutions which are hopelessly unrealistic. However, he recognizes them as unrealistic; he keeps his feet on the ground. The person who begins to believe in his autisms—who thinks he owns a tree producing ham and bacon, or that he really is Napoleon, or that he possesses the power to destroy the earth—is abnormal. The problem is quantitative. How much does the person fantasy, and how far does he go in confusing the fantasy with reality? Similarly, a person may solve the conflicts induced by his own failure by developing delusions of persecution. He may rationalize his own shortcomings by saying, "Somebody did me a dirty trick." But if he begins to accept this as a true statement, and especially if he picks out some person or group and begins to attack them, he has slipped over the border line between the normal and the abnormal. A certain amount of egotism is our culturally approved norm; but when the person boasts that he invented radar, developed the atomic bomb, painted the Mona Lisa, and made millions

of dollars in the stock market, we are likely to classify him outside the normal group.

In previous chapters we have commented on particular forms of behavior as symptoms of *neurotic* or *psychotic* breakdowns. In psychological usage, a neurosis is a form of personality disturbance serious enough to make it difficult for the person to carry on his usual activities but not serious enough to require institutionalization. A psychosis is a breakdown which involves loss of contact with reality, and consequently the possibility of behavior harmful to the individual himself, or to others, hence usually requiring care in a hospital. For a long time it was customary to speak of the neurotic as somewhere between the normal and the psychotic personality; recently, evidence has been accumulating that the neurotic and the psychotic deviate in different directions from the normal. There may be a hereditary factor which predisposes some people to develop a psychosis when exposed to severe conflicts, while persons not possessing this factor would develop a neurosis.

The neurotic and the psychotic respond differently to personality tests. On questionnaire scales for general emotionality, symptoms of maladjustment, etc., the neurotic makes worse scores than the normal, whereas the psychotic may make what seems a perfectly normal score. Similarly, on frustration tolerance the psychotic may seem normal. In both cases this appears to be due to the fact that the psychotic has repressed his troubles so deeply that they no longer bother him; another way of putting this is that he has cut himself off from reality and no longer pays any attention to it. On motor tests, such as delicate coordinations and control tests, psychotics usually do much worse than neurotics; this may again be due to the fact that they simply do not care about accuracy on the test.

There are, of course, a variety of different

personality patterns within the general concept of neurosis, and a number within the category of psychosis. As suggested above, these constitute exaggerations of characteristics which would be considered normal if present to only a slight extent. For instance, all of us have had the experience of having some idea run through our minds repeatedly, so that we cannot seem to shake it off. When this becomes so pronounced that it interferes with the person's thinking about immediate problems, we refer to it as an *obsession* and the patient is diagnosed as obsessive neurotic. Similarly, most people have some ups and downs in mood, feeling cheerful one day and a bit gloomy on another. When these swings go to such an extreme that the person is now exuberant, euphoric, and uncontrollably excited, later so depressed that he cannot move or eat, we label his case as a manic-depressive psychosis.

We have hinted in Chap. 14 at some of the explanatory principles which must be invoked to explain the development of neurosis and psychosis. They result from conflicts of motives which are perceived as very important and also as insoluble. They develop on a background of childhood frustration. Physiology may be a factor (page 471). Often we find two individuals subjected to what look like the same conflicts, but one breaks down and the other does not. Preference at present goes to the explanation that an adult conflict on top of infantile frustration leads to breakdown, whereas an adult conflict striking a person with a relatively secure early childhood is less destructive.[1]

Readjustment of Personality

Personality difficulties, of course, are for the most part far less severe than those just

[1] For further treatments of this problem see some of the standard texts in abnormal psychology, such as Maslow and Mittelman (1951) or N. Cameron (1947).

mentioned. They involve CRs of anxiety to stimuli which objectively seem harmless, hostilities toward people who are not frustrating, love attachments to inappropriate persons or objects, exaggerated needs for dominance, dependency, security, and so on. People have problems in adjusting to work, school, parents, children, husbands, and wives. Few of these are major personality disturbances, but in a certain percentage of cases the chronic irritation will lead to breakdown if it is not corrected.

Personality can be improved. Some of the modifications, proposed by the "success schools" which will teach you how to make a lot of money, marry a beautiful woman, and get elected president, for only $50 a session, are relatively superficial. They seek to induce modifications of surface traits—what we called the "mask" of personality in Chap. 13—by practice and repetition. So far as we know, little harm is done by these schools, although the benefits are not, as a rule, proportional to the cost.

At a somewhat deeper level, personality changes can be induced by *counseling*. Often the person is so close to his conflict, and so focused upon it, that he cannot see alternative courses of action. Strong motives bind the attention so firmly that only the immediate goal or threat is perceived. Talking the problem over with a competent psychologist—or even a minister or physician—often leads the person himself to see the problem in a new light and to observe pathways which had been overlooked. Furthermore, the counselor, out of his experience, can point to possible solutions. Many educational, vocational, and marital problems can be handled on this level.

Finally, deep and disturbing personality problems call for the type of modification which we call *psychotherapy*. There has been an unfortunate reluctance on the part of many people to accept the suggestion that they seek therapy, because they felt that this was somehow insulting—that one was admitting that he was "crazy" by so doing. The psychological frame of reference leads one to see this as nothing different from seeking medical aid for a broken arm or a streptococcus infection. Some people break down with obvious physical symptoms; others break down with symptoms apparent only in thought and interpersonal relations. Since we believe in a monistic solution of the body-mind problem, we cannot consider these as different in kind. All illnesses are the result of some interference with organismic functioning. They should be treated by specialists who are trained to deal with this particular kind of malfunction.

It is out of place for us to discuss techniques of therapy in this book. We wish only to note that therapy seeks to change the individual's *perception* of his problem, so that he is no longer obsessed by an unattainable goal or an unrealistic threat. Therapy must penetrate *repressions* and bring out buried memories of painful experiences, where persisting emotional disturbances may have originated. Often therapy involves *modifying the self-image*, as where a girl has developed a picture of herself as stupid, unattractive, and unloved, but actually has many positive assets, including good looks and intelligence. Therapy leads to *choosing new goals, learning new techniques* for achieving goals, and looking at the self and the environment in new ways.

Homeostasis and Personality

At numerous points throughout this book, we have laid considerable stress on the equilibrium-maintaining tendency of the human organism. Under the principle of homeostasis we gathered those forms of behavior calculated to keep or to restore a favorable physical balance—oxygen, food, water, and so on. In later passages evidence was presented to show the same tendency in connection with many emotional patterns, and in those complex motivations designated as values.

Maintenance of a constant environment was also shown to be a characteristic of perception. The infant learns to identify objects as *the same*, and the perceptual process then tends to exaggerate the constancy and identity of these objects—thus, we have size constancy, brightness constancy, color constancy, in our visual perceptions, under circumstances such that constancy is physically impossible. Here we find the human artificially maintaining a constant environment by the way in which he sees it.

Let us now extend this conception to a consideration of personality patterns. It is a matter of common knowledge, as well as statistical evidence, that individual personalities tend toward constancy. John does not suddenly change from a shy, awkward boy into a poised, aggressive, self-confident man. Such transformations may occur, over a sizable time, but in general we are safe in assuming that the personality tomorrow will resemble what it is today.

One of the mechanisms by which this constancy evolves actually is the constancy of the environment. Let us see how this works out in a simple example and then derive a more generalized statement. Assume that John had a deep attachment for his mother but that, when a new baby was born, she neglected John for the younger brother. Later John developed a strong affection for a teacher, but because he did poorly in some schoolwork, she expressed strong disappointment and stopped giving him personal attention. As an adolescent John falls in love with a high-school girl, who for a time seems to reciprocate and then jilts him for a football star. At this point we shall probably find that John fears and distrusts females, especially as love objects; he sees them as fickle, untrustworthy. Whenever he meets a new woman, no matter how attractive, he will perceive her as having these same characteristics (perceptual constancy).

It is doubly unfortunate that this constancy phenomenon occurs, even though we grant that it is necessary for survival. John's perception of all women as fickle tends to set off behavior appropriate to that situation (keeping his distance, refusing to trust, making accusations of fickleness) because that is the only way he can behave, given his view of females. This is another illustration of behavior constancy. But this, in turn, tends to stimulate the other person and to evoke behavior which confirms John in his ideas. If he does become friendly with a girl but always acts as if he expects her to hurt him, to lead him on and then drop him with a thud, his behavior will irritate her and she will leave him. Thus he will be convinced that he was right in the first place.

This is the basic problem in the modification and improvement of personality. The individual has his present personality, primarily, because it is appropriate to the world as he sees it. The timid, fearful person lives in a world full of dangers. The cheerful man lives in a world full of satisfaction and promise. From the same physical event Tom can get evidence to support his pessimism, Harry can get proof to justify his optimism. Thus, by maintaining a constant environment, the individual keeps in equilibrium, even though, for the neurotic, this equilibrium is painful. To him it seems less painful than the alternative.

Furthermore, we must recognize that, within his own personal framework, the maladjusted person may be acting in a rational, intelligent fashion. Only a fool is brave in the face of overpowering threat. Primitive man had to cower in a cave by night in order to survive. To deny the reality of danger was to invite destruction. The neurotic personality lives in just such a world. It is thus entirely rational for him to be fearful, tense, apprehensive; he must protect himself by avoiding people or by setting up defenses of various kinds.

Psychotherapy, in its many forms, aims particularly to modify this way of perceiving the self and other people. It is necessary to induce a perception of the self as adequate, capable of dealing with threat; and part of this process is changing the picture of the environment so that it does not appear so dangerous.

The potency of this tendency to keep a constant inner psychic equilibrium is testified to by the great difficulty in much therapy. We noted in Chap. 3 that a child may learn fear in a single episode and unlearn it only in thirty. Personality maladjustments may be founded on childhood frustrations and may be practiced for many years before being brought to a psychologist or psychiatrist for modification. It is hardly surprising that the process is usually long and painful.

Stable and unstable equilibrium. Every adult personality represents an equilibrium of sorts between the pressures of the environment and the demands of the organism. The equilibrium of the normal personality appears to be relatively stable and secure; additional energy can be mobilized to meet threats, but threatening stimuli are perceived as neither overly frequent nor excessively intense. The neurotic often impresses us as balanced precariously upon a conflict solution which may continue to work, or may not.

Once the person has achieved this equilibrium, he attempts to maintain it. While it may be a painful state, it is less painful than the alternatives he can see. Consider the case of a neurotic phobia. This is uncomfortable, even distressing. *But it is less painful than the alternatives*, such as yielding to temptation and then suffering guilt feelings. People do things which look foolish, painful, even self-destructive; but in a psychological frame of reference they are less disturbing than other actions. Hence even the unhappy neurotic may resist efforts to change his personality, because this balance—uncomfortable and precarious as it is—seems better than the dangerous condition of change.

We are simply saying, in effect, that the principle which governs the simple needs of the body also applies to this complex psychological organization. The person seeks to maintain those constant states which are essential to life; and so, by an ever-spreading process of dynamic adjustment to the environment, he attempts to maintain his physical surroundings, his social situation, and his inner organization.

SUMMARY

We end our study of psychology as we began it, with a consideration of the constancy functions of the organism. We began with simple illustrations of homeostasis, as in the quest for food and water, escape from pain, and other essentials of biological equilibrium. We conclude with illustrations of homeostasis based on the maintenance of an elaborate system of traits and attitudes, organized around a self-image. The various traits of personality are themselves developments from the efforts of the individual to maintain equilibrium, using his resources of sensation, perception, learning, and thinking.

The exact minimum number of dimensions needed to give a scientifically adequate description of personality is not known. Cattell's proposed list of 20 is considered an approximation. Each of these 20 dimensions can be considered as an organized aspect of the behavior or experience of any individual. The unique personality is defined by the particular combination of these 20 traits, for this particular person.

There are many methods for the study of personality traits. We have given examples of ratings, questionnaires, experiments, and projective tests. Questionnaires are quite useful under favorable conditions, but they are easily faked. Projective tests are considerably better, but since they can be used only by experts, they are not available for extensive studies of large groups of people.

The core of personality is the individual's self-image or perception of himself. This is always perceived relative to the environment—that is, the evaluation of the self as adequate depends on how threatening the environment seems to be. Each person has his own private universe, as no two of us see the world exactly alike; and in some respects, this is an excellent key to the individual's personality. Similarly, the person's self-image may be quite different from an objective appraisal of his assets and liabilities.

Since the personality, once formed, tends to remain constant, it is necessary for adults to seek an environment into which they fit, rather than trying to make major changes to fit the environment. Thus marriage is more likely to be a success if the two personalities are harmonious; neither is likely to make many changes to conform to the other. Choice of a vocation should also include a consideration of the personality requirements of the job.

Since people do learn, both marriage and vocation can modify the personality slowly to fit into a pattern. It is also possible, by deliberate practice, to put on a better "mask" or set of surface traits, for the sake of "winning friends and influencing people." It is extraordinarily difficult to modify deeper traits in this manner; highly specialized techniques, lumped together under the general label "psychotherapy," are required for this. Psychotherapy should never be attempted by amateurs.

Abnormal personalities are considered

in modern psychology to be different quantitatively, not qualitatively, from the normal. If a specific trait is exaggerated, lacking, or distorted beyond a certain range, the person is labeled as abnormal. Such disturbances usually develop from a combination of infantile deprivation and adult conflict. Therapy is necessary to help the person learn new ways of perceiving himself and his world, if the abnormality is to be corrected.

Psychologists are still faced by vast areas of ignorance in the field of personality. We are confident, however, that continued naturalistic observation and experiment, combined with reflective theorizing, will lead to more penetrating and extensive insights into this fascinating problem.

Recommended Readings[1]

CATTELL, R. B.: *Personality.* New York: McGraw-Hill, 1950.

DOLLARD, J., and N. E. MILLER: *Personality and Psychotherapy.* New York: McGraw-Hill, 1950.

FROMM, E.: *Man for Himself.* New York: Rinehart, 1947.

GILBERT, G. M.: *Psychology of Dictatorship.* New York: Ronald, 1950.

HARSH, C. M., and H. G. SCHRICKEL: *Personality: Development and Assessment.* New York: Ronald, 1950.

KLUCKHOHN, CLYDE, and H. A. MURRAY: *Personality in Nature, Society and Culture.* New York, Knopf, 1948.

McCLELLAND, D. C.: *Personality.* New York: William Sloane Associates, 1951.

MENNINGER, K. A.: *The Human Mind.* (rev. ed.) New York: Knopf, 1937.

MURPHY, G.: *Personality.* New York: Harper, 1947.

STAGNER, ROSS: *Psychology of Personality.* (rev. ed.) New York: McGraw-Hill, 1948.

[1] See also p. 547.

Supplementary Readings

Chapter	Hartley et al.*	Dennis†	Crafts et al.‡	Garrett§	Valentine and Wickens¶
1	2–4				1–3
2	51–52	5(1–2)			10
3	56–59	4	6	7, 8	12–13
4		5(3–6), 9(1–2)	4	10	11
5	25–28	1 (1, 2, 4, 5) 2	8	14, 16	
6	17, 18, 21, 30–32, 70	1 (3), 3, 9 (4)	9, 13, 21	4, 15	15
7	44, 47–49		16	5, 6	17
8	6, 34, 40	6 (4)	15	1	16
9	37, 73	6 (2, 5)		3, 4	
10	41, 43, 46	6 (1, 3, 6, 7)	5, 18, 22	6	18
11	10, 33, 69, 70, 76, 79	7	23, 24		19, 20
12	11, 12, 42	8, 11 (3, 5, 6)	14	11–13	4–8
13	8, 9, 86		7		
14	19, 53, 61, 62, 89, 90		20		
15	29, 54, 83, 91, 97	10	25	9	21

* Hartley, E. L., H. G. Birch, and Ruth E. Hartley, *Outside Readings in Psychology*. New York: Crowell, 1950.

† Dennis, Wayne, *Readings in General Psychology*. New York: Prentice-Hall, 1949.

‡ Crafts, L. W., T. C. Schneirla, E. E. Robinson, and R. W. Gilbert, *Recent Experiments in Psychology*. (2d ed.) New York: McGraw-Hill, 1950.

§ Garrett, H. E., *Great Experiments in Psychology*. (3d ed.) New York: Appleton-Century-Crofts, 1949.

¶ Valentine, W. L., and D. D. Wickens, *Experimental Foundations of General Psychology*. (rev. ed.) New York: Rinehart, 1949.

Bibliography

ABERNETHY, ETHEL M. 1940. The effect of changed environmental conditions upon the results of college examinations. *J. Psychol.*, **10**, 293–301.

ABNEY, SIR W. 1913. *Researches in Colour Vision*. London: Longmans, Roberts and Green.

ABT, L. E., and L. BELLAK. (Eds.) 1950. *Projective Psychology*. New York: Alfred A. Knopf, Inc.

ACH, N. 1905. *Ueber die Willenstätigkeit und das Denken*. Göttingen: Vandenhoeck & Ruprecht.

ADAMS, D. K. 1929. Experimental studies of adaptive behavior in cats. *Comp. Psychol. Monogr.*, **6**, No. 1.

ADAMS, GRACE K. 1923. An experimental study of memory color and related phenomena. *Amer. J. Psychol.*, **34**, 359–407.

ADES, H. W., and D. H. RAAB. 1946. Recovery of motor function after two-stage extirpation of area 4 in monkeys (Macaca Mulatta). *J. Neurophysiol.*, **9**, 55–60.

ADOLPH, E. F. 1941. The internal environment and behavior: water content. *Amer. J. Psychiat.*, **97**, 1365–1373.

ADRIAN, E. D. 1947. *Physical Background of Perception*. New York: Oxford University Press.

ALEXANDER, FRANZ. 1948. *Fundamentals of Psychoanalysis*. New York: W. W. Norton & Company.

ALLPORT, G. W. 1924. Eidetic imagery. *Brit. J. Psychol.*, **15**, 99–120.

———— and H. S. ODBERT. 1936. Trait-names: a psycho-lexical study. *Psychol. Monogr.*, **47**, No. 211.

ALONZO, A. S. 1926. The influence of manual guidance on maze learning. *J. comp. Psychol.*, **6**, 143–157.

ALPER, THELMA G. 1946. Memory for completed and incompleted tasks as a function of personality. *J. abnorm. soc. Psychol.*, **41**, 403–420.

AMES, A. 1951. Visual perception and the rotating window. *Psychol. Monogr.*, **65**, No. 7.

AMMONS, R. B. 1950. The full-range vocabulary test: V. Results for an adult population. *J. consult. Psychol.*, **14**, 150–155.

ANDERSON, E. E. 1941. The externalization of drive: III. Maze learning by non-rewarded and by satiated rats. *J. genet. Psychol.*, **59**, 397–426.

ANDERSON, R. C. 1947. Motivation of flyer and his reactions to stress of flight. *J. Aviat. Med.*, **18**, 18–30.

ARGELANDER, A. 1927. *Das Farbenhören und der Synästhetische Factor der Wahrnehmung*. Jena: Carl Fischer.

ATKINSON, J. W., and D. C. McCLELLAND. 1948. Projective expressions of needs. II. Effect of different intensities of hunger drive on thematic apperception. *J. exp. Psychol.*, **38**, 643–658.

BAGBY, E. 1928. *Psychology of Personality*. New York: Henry Holt and Company, Inc.

BAKER, L. E. 1938. The pupillary response conditioned to subliminal auditory stimuli. *Psychol. Monogr.*, **50**, No. 3.

BALLARD, P. B. 1913. Obliviscence and reminiscence. *Brit. J. Psychol.*, Monogr. Suppl., **1**, No. 2.

BANISTER, H., and O. L. ZANGWILL. 1941. Experimentally induced visual paramnesia. *Brit. J. Psychol.*, **32**, 30–51.

BARE, JOHN K. 1949. The specific hunger for sodium chloride in normal and adrenalectomized white rats. *J. comp. Psychol.*, **42**, 242–253.

BARKER, R. G., TAMARA DEMBO, and KURT LEWIN. 1941. Frustration and regression. *Univ. Ia. Stud. Child Welf.*, **18**, No. 1.

BARTLETT, F. C. 1932. *Remembering*. New York: Cambridge University Press.

BAYLEY, NANCY. 1932. A study of the crying of infants during mental and physical tests. *J. genet. Psychol.*, **40**, 306–329.

BEACH, FRANK A. 1947. Payday for primates. *Nat. Hist., N.Y.*, **56**, 448–451.

BECKHAM, A. S. 1933. Study of intelligence of colored adolescents of different social-economic status in typical metropolitan areas. *J. soc. Psychol.*, **4**, 70–91.

BELMONT, LILLIAN, and H. G. BIRCH. 1951. Re-individualizing the repression hypothesis. *J. abnorm. soc. Psychol.*, **46**, 226–235.

BENDER, I. E. 1942. *Motivation and Visual Factors*. Hanover, N. H.: Dartmouth College Press.

———— and A. H. HASTORF. 1950. The perception of persons. *J. abnorm. soc. Phychol.*, **45**, 556–561.

BENEDEK, T., and B. B. RUBENSTEIN. 1939. Correlations between ovarian activity and psycho-dynamic processes. I. The ovulative phase. *Psychosom. Med.*, **1**, 245–270.

BENEDICT, RUTH. 1934. *Patterns of Culture*. Boston: Houghton Mifflin Company.

BERNHARDT, KARL S., MARY L. NORTHWAY, and CATHERINE M. TATHAM. 1948. The effect of added thiamine on intelligence and learning with identical twins. *Canad. J. Psychol.*, **2**, 58–61.

BINET, A. 1894. Psychologie des grands calculateurs et joueurs d'echecs. Paris: Librairie Hachette.

BINGHAM, W. V. 1946. Inequalities in adult capacity from military data. *Science*, **104**, 147–152.

BIRCH, H. G. 1945a. The relation of past experience to insightful problem-solving. *J. comp. Psychol.*, **38**, 367–383.

————. 1945b. The role of motivational factors in insightful problem-solving. *J. comp. Psychol.*, **38**, 295–317.

———— and M. E. BITTERMAN. 1949. Reinforcement and learning: The process of sensory integration. *Psychol. Rev.*, **56**, 292–308.

BLACKBURN, JULIAN. 1945. *Psychology and the Social Pattern*. London: Kegan Paul, Trench, Trubner & Co.

BLAKE, R., and W. DENNIS. 1943. Development of stereotypes concerning the Negro. *J. abnorm. soc. Psychol.*, **38**, 525–531.

BLUEMEL, C. S. 1948. *War, Politics and Insanity*. Denver: The World Press, Inc.

BLUM, GERALD S. 1949. A study of the psychoanalytic theory of psychosexual development. *Genet. Psychol. Monogr.*, **39**, 3–99.

BOBBITT, J. M. 1942. The experimental study of the phenomenon of closure as a threshold function. *J. exp. Psychol.*, **30**, 273–294.

BOOK, W. F. 1908. *The Psychology of Skill*. Missoula, Mont.: University of Montana.

BORING, E. G., H. S. LANGFELD, and H. P. WELD. 1935. *Psychology: A Factual Textbook*. New York: John Wiley & Sons, Inc.

————, ————, and ————. 1939. *Introduction to Psychology*. New York: John Wiley & Sons, Inc.

————, ————, and ————. 1948. *Foundations of Psychology*. New York: John Wiley & Sons, Inc.

BOUSFIELD, W. A., and H. BARRY, JR. 1933. The visual imagery of a lightning calculator. *Amer. J. Psychol.*, **45**, 353–358.

BREESE, B. B. 1899. On inhibition. *Psychol. Monogr.*, No. 11.

BRIDGES, KATHERINE M. B. 1932. Emotional development in early infancy. *Child Develpm.*, **3**, 324–341.

BROGDEN, W. J. 1939. Sensory pre-conditioning. *J. exp. Psychol.*, **25**, 323–332.

BROWN, J. F. 1936. *Psychology and the Social Order*. New York: McGraw-Hill Book Company, Inc.

BROZEK, JOSEF, and BURTRUM C. SCHIELE. 1948. Clinical significance of the Minnesota multiphasic F scale evaluated in experimental neurosis. *Amer. J. Psychiat.*, **105**, 259–266.

BRUCE, R. W. 1933. Conditions of transfer of training. *J. exp. Psychol.*, **16**, 343–361.

BRUNER, J. S., and C. C. GOODMAN. 1947. Value and need as organizing factors in perception. *J. abnorm. soc. Psychol.*, **42**, 33–43.

———— and L. POSTMAN. 1947. Emotional selectivity in perception and reaction. *J. Personality*, **16**, 69–77.

———— and ————. 1948. Symbolic value as an organizing factor in perception. *J. soc. Psychol.*, **27**, 203–208.

BRYAN, W. L., and N. HARTER. 1899. Studies in the telegraphic language: Acquisition of a hierarchy of habits. *Psychol. Rev.*, **6**, 346–376.

BUNCH, M. E., and W. K. MAGDSICK. 1938. A study of electric shock motivation in maze learning. *J. comp. Psychol.*, **25**, 496–506.

BURKS, BARBARA S. 1942. A study of identical twins reared apart under differing types of family relationships. In McNemar, Quinn, and Maud A. Merrill (Eds.), 1942. *Studies in Personality*. New York: McGraw-Hill Book Company, Inc.

BURT, CYRIL. 1948. The factorial study of temperamental traits. *Brit. J. Psychol., Statist. Sect.*, **1**, 178–203.

BURTT, H. E. 1932. An experimental study of early childhood memory. *J. genet. Psychol.*, **40**, 287–295.

BUSWELL, G. T. 1935. *How People Look at Pictures*. Chicago: University of Chicago Press.

BUTLER, J. R., and T. F. KARWOSKI. 1936. *Human Psychology*. New York: Pitman Publishing Co.

CAMERON, D. E. 1947. Remembering. *Nerv. ment. Dis. Monogr.*, No. 72.

CAMERON, NORMAN. 1944. Experimental analysis of schizophrenic thinking. In Kasanin, J. S. (Ed.), 1944. *Language and Thought in Schizophrenia*. Berkeley: University of California Press.

———. 1947. *Psychology of Behavior Disorders*. Boston: Houghton Mifflin Company.

CANFIELD, A. A., A. L. COMREY, and R. C. WILSON. 1949. A study of reaction time to light and sound as related to increased positive radial acceleration. *J. Aviat. Med.*, **20**, 350–355.

CANNON, W. B. 1933. *The Wisdom of the Body*. New York: W. W. Norton & Company.

CARLSON, A. J., and V. JOHNSON. 1937. *Machinery of the Body*. Chicago: University of Chicago Press.

CARLSON, W. A. 1949. Follow-up study of psychiatric cases which occurred in AAF combat personnel. *J. Aviat. Med.*, **20**, 459–468.

CARMICHAEL, L., H. P. HOGAN, and A. A. WALTER. 1932. An experimental study of the effect of language on the reproduction of visually perceived forms. *J. exp. Psychol.*, **15**, 73–86.

CARR, H. A. 1925. *Psychology: A Study of Mental Activity*. New York: Longmans, Green & Co., Inc.

——— and J. B. WATSON. 1908. Orientation in the white rat. *J. comp. Neurol. Psychol.*, **18**, 27–44.

CASON, H. 1930. Common annoyances. *Psychol. Monogr.*, **40**, No. 182.

CATTELL, PSYCHE. 1937. Stanford-Binet IQ variations. *Sch. & Soc.*, **45**, 615–618.

CATTELL, R. B. 1941. *General Psychology*. Cambridge, Mass.: Sci-Art Publishers.

———. 1945. Principal trait clusters for describing personality. *Psychol. Bull.*, **42**, 129–161.

———. 1950. *Personality: A Systematic Theoretical and Factual Study*. New York: McGraw-Hill Book Company, Inc.

CHISHOLM, F. P. 1944. *Introductory Lectures in General Semantics*. Chicago: Institute of General Semantics.

CIVILIAN DEFENSE: March, 1942. *Protective Concealment*. Washington, D.C.: Office of Civilian Defense.

COLE, L. E. 1939. *General Psychology*. New York: McGraw-Hill Book Company, Inc.

COOKE, E. D. 1946. *All but Me and Thee*. Washington, D.C.: Infantry Journal Press.

COWLES, J. T. 1937. Food tokens as incentives for learning by chimpanzees. *Comp. Psychol. Monogr.*, **14**, No. 71.

CRAFTS, L. W., T. C. SCHNEIRLA, E. E. ROBINSON, and L. W. GILBERT. 1950. *Recent Experiments in Psychology*. (2d ed.) New York: McGraw-Hill Book Company, Inc.

CRISSEY, ORLO L. 1937. Mental development as related to institutional residence and educational achievement. *Univ. Ia. Stud. Child Welf.*, **13**, No. 1.

CRUZE, WENDELL W. 1951. *General Psychology for College Students*. New York: Prentice-Hall, Inc.

CULLER, E. A. 1938. Recent advances in some concepts of conditioning. *Psychol. Rev.*, **45**, 134–153.

DASHIELL, J. F. 1949. *Fundamentals of General Psychology*. (3d ed.) Boston: Houghton Mifflin Company.

DAVIS, C. M. 1928. Self-selection of diet by newly weaned infants. *Amer. J. Dis. Child.*, **36**, 651–679.

DAVIS, H. (Ed.). 1947. *Hearing and Deafness*. New York: Murray Hill Books, Inc.

————. 1951. Psychophysiology of hearing and deafness. In Stevens, S. S. (Ed.), 1951. *Handbook of Experimental Psychology*. New York: John Wiley & Sons, Inc.

DAVIS, R. C. 1935. The muscular tension reflex and three of its modifying conditions. *Indiana Univ. Publ., Sci. Series*, No. 3.

————. 1940. Set and muscular tension. *Indiana Univ. Publ., Sci. Series*, No. 10.

DENNIS, W. 1941. Infant development under conditions of restricted practice and of minimum social stimulation. *Genet. Psychol. Monogr.*, **23**, 143–189.

DESCARTES, R. 1892. *The Philosophy of Descartes*. (Selec. and tr. by Henry A. A. Torrey.) New York: Henry Holt and Company, Inc.

DEWEY, J. 1933. *How We Think*. Boston: D. C. Heath and Company.

DICE, L. R. 1935. Inheritance of waltzing and epilepsy in mice of the genus Peromyscus. *J. Mammal.*, **16**, 25–35.

DINSMOOR, J. A. 1950. A quantitative comparison of the discriminative and reinforcing functions of a stimulus. *J. exp. Psychol.*, **40**, 458–472.

DIVEN, K. 1937. Certain determinants in conditioning of anxiety reactions. *J. Psychol.*, **3**, 291–308.

DOWNEY, JUNE. 1929. *Creative Imagination*. New York: Harcourt, Brace and Company, Inc.

DULSKY, S. G. 1935. The effect of a change of background on recall and relearning. *J. exp. Psychol.*, **18**, 725–740.

DUNCAN, C. P. 1949. Retroactive effect of electroshock on learning. *J. comp. physiol. Psychol.*, **42**, 32–44.

DWORKIN, S., J. O. BAXT, and E. DWORKIN. 1942. Behavioral disturbances of vomiting and micturition in conditioned cats. *Psychosom. Med.*, **4**, 75–81.

DYMOND, R. F. 1949. A scale for the measurement of empathic ability. *J. consult. Psychol.*, **13**, 127–133.

EASTMAN, MAX. 1917. The will to live. *J. Philos.*, **14**, 102–107.

EBBINGHAUS, H. 1913. *Memory: A Contribution to Experimental Psychology*. (Tr. by H. A. Ruger and C. E. Bussenius.) New York: Bureau of Publications, Teachers College, Columbia University.

EDWARDS, A. L. 1941. Political frames of reference as a factor influencing recognition. *J. abnorm. soc. Psychol.*, **36**, 34–50.

————. 1942. The retention of affective experiences: A criticism and restatement of the problem. *Psychol. Rev.*, **49**, 43–53.

————. 1946. *Statistical Analysis*. New York: The Ronald Press Company.

EDWARDS, A. S., and L. JONES. 1938. An experimental and field study of North Georgia mountaineers. *J. soc. Psychol.*, **9**, 317–333.

ELLIOT, M. H. 1928. The effect of change of reward on the maze performance of rats. *Univ. Calif. Publ. Psychol.*, **4**, 19–30.

————. 1929. Effect of appropriateness of reward and of complex incentives on maze performance. *Univ. Calif. Publ. Psychol.*, **4**, 91–98.

ELLIS, ALBERT. 1949. A study of human love relationships. *J. genet. Psychol.*, **75**, 61–71.

ELLIS, W. D. 1938. *A Source Book of Gestalt Psychology*. New York: Harcourt, Brace and Company, Inc.

ELLSON, D. G. 1941. Hallucinations produced by sensory conditioning. *J. exp. Psychol.*, **28**, 1–20.

ESCALONA, SIBYLLE. 1950. Use of infant tests for predictive purposes. *Bull. Menninger Clin.*, **14**, 117–128.

ESTES, S. G. 1938. Judging personality from expressive behavior. *J. abnorm. soc. Psychol.*, **33**, 217–236.

ESTES, W. K. 1944. An experimental study of punishment. *Psychol. Monogr.*, **57**, No. 3.

EWERT, P. H. 1930. Study of effect of inverted retinal stimulation upon spatially coordinated behavior. *Genet. Psychol. Monogr.*, **7**, 177–361.

FERNBERGER, S. W. 1950. An early example of a "hidden figure" picture. *Amer. J. Psychol.*, **67**, 448.

FINCH, G. 1938. Salivary conditioning in atropinized dogs. *Amer. J. Physiol.*, **124**, 136–141.

——— and CULLER, E. A. 1934. Higher-order conditioning with constant motivation. *Amer. J. Psychol.*, **46**, 596–602.

FINLEY, C. S. 1921. Endocrine stimulation as affecting dream content. *Arch. Neurol. Psychiat., Chicago*, **5**, 177–181.

FLETCHER, J. M. 1942. Homeostasis as an explanatory principle in psychology. *Psychol. Rev.*, **49**, 80–87.

FLUGEL, J. C. 1948. "L'appetit vient en mangeant:" Some reflections on the self-sustaining tendencies. *Brit. J. Psychol.*, **38**, 171–190.

FOSTER, W. S. 1911. The effect of practise upon visualizing and upon the reproduction of visual impressions. *J. educ. Psychoi.*, **2**, 11–22.

FRASER, J. 1908. A new illusion of direction. *Brit. J. Psychol.* **2**, 307–320.

FREEMAN, ELLIS. 1936. *Social Psychology.* New York: Henry Holt and Company, Inc.

FREEMAN, F. N., and C. D. FLORY. 1937. Growth in intellectual ability as measured by repeated tests. *Soc. Res. Child Dev. Mongr.*, **2**, No. 2.

FREEMAN, G. L. 1939. Changes in tension-pattern and total energy expenditure during adaptation to "distracting" stimuli. *Amer. J. Psychol.*, **52**, 354–360.

———. 1940. The field of "field" psychology. *Psychol. Rev.*, **47**, 416–424.

———. 1948. *Energetics of Human Behavior.* Ithaca, New York: Cornell University Press.

FREUD, S. 1904. *The Psychopathology of Everyday Life.* New York: International University Press.

FROMM, ERICH. 1947. *Man for Himself.* New York: Farrar & Rinehart, Inc.

FROMM-REICHMANN, FRIEDA. 1950. *Principles of Intensive Psychotherapy.* Chicago: University of Chicago Press.

GALLOWAY, D. 1946. Experimental investigation of structural lag in perception. *Amer. Psychologist*, **1**, 447.

GALTON, F. 1869. *Hereditary Genius.* London: Macmillan & Co., Ltd.

GANTT, W. H. 1942. Origin and development of nervous disturbances experimentally produced. *Amer. J. Psychiat.*, **98**, 475–481.

GARDNER, E. 1947. *Fundamentals of Neurology.* Philadelphia: W. B. Saunders Company.

GATES, A. I. 1917. Recitation as a factor in memorizing. *Arch. Psychol.*, **6**, No. 40.

GEBHARD, MILDRED E. 1948. The effect of success and failure upon the attractiveness of activities as a function of experience, expectation, and need. *J. exp. Psychol.*, **38**, 371–388.

GELB, A. 1929. Die "Farbenkonstanz" der Sehdinge. *Handb. norm. path. Physiol.*, **12**, 594–678.

GELDARD, F. A. 1948. Somesthesis. In Boring, E. G., H. S. Langfeld, and H. P. Weld. 1948. *Foundations of Psychology.* New York: John Wiley & Sons, Inc.

GERARD, R. W. 1941. *The Body Functions.* New York: John Wiley & Sons, Inc.

GIBSON, J. J. 1929. The reproduction of visually perceived forms. *J. exp. Psychol.*, **12**, 1–39.

———. 1950. *The Perception of the Visual World.* Boston: Houghton Mifflin Company.

———, E. G. JACK, and G. RAFFEL. 1932. Bilateral transfer of the conditioned response in the human subject. *J. exp. Psychol.*, **15**, 416–421.

GIDDINGS, F. H. 1907. *Elements of Sociology.* New York: The Macmillan Company.

GILBERT, G. M. 1937. The age difference in the hedonistic tendency in memory. *J. exp. Psychol.*, **21**, 433–441.

———. 1947. *Nuremberg Diary.* New York: Farrar, Straus & Young.

———. 1950. *Psychology of Dictatorship.* New York: The Ronald Press Company.

GILLILAND, A. R. 1948. Measurement of the mentality of infants. *Child Develpm.*, **19**, 155–158.

GLAZE, J. A. 1928. Psychological effects of fasting. *Amer. J. Psychol.*, **40**, 236–253.

———. 1928. Sensitivity to odors and other phenomena during a fast. *Amer. J. Psychol.*, **40**, 569–575.

GODDARD, H. H. 1914. *Feeblemindedness: Its causes and consequences.* New York: The Macmillan Company.

GOLDFARB, W. 1944. Effects of early institutional care on adolescent personality: Rorschach data. *Amer. J. Orthopsychiat.*, **14**, 441–447.

GOLDSTEIN, KURT. 1944. Methodological approach to the study of schizophrenic thought disturbances. In Kasanin, J. 1944. *Language and Thought in Schizophrenia.* Berkeley: University of California Press.

———— and M. SCHEERER. 1941. Abstract and concrete behavior. *Psychol. Monogr.,* **52,** No. 239.

GOTTSCHALDT, K. 1929. Uber den Einfluss der Erfahrung und die Wahrnehmung von Figuren. II. *Psychol. Forsch.,* **12,** 1–87. (Tr. and condensed as Gestalt factors and repetition, in Ellis, W. D. 1938. *A Source Book of Gestalt Psychology.* pp. 123–135. New York: Harcourt, Brace and Company, Inc.)

GRAMLICH, F. W. 1949. A psychological study of stress in service. *J. gen. Psychol.,* **41,** 273–296.

GRICE, G. ROBERT. 1949. Visual discrimination learning with simultaneous and successive presentation of stimuli. *J. comp. physiol. Psychol.,* **42,** 365–373.

GUETZKOW, H. S., and P. H. BOWMAN. 1946. *Men and Hunger.* Elgin, Ill.: Brethren Publ. Co.

GUILFORD, J. P. 1950. Creativity. *Amer. Psychol.,* **5,** 444–456.

GURNEE, H. 1938. Effect of electric shock for right responses on maze learning in human subjects. *J. exp. Psychol.,* **22,** 354–364.

GUTHRIE, E. R. 1935. *Psychology of Learning.* New York: Harper & Brothers.

HADAMARD, J. 1945. *The Psychology of Invention in the Mathematical Field.* Princeton, N.J.: Princeton University Press.

HALL, CALVIN S. 1941. Temperament: A survey of animal studies. *Psychol. Bull.,* **38,** 909–943.

———— and P. H. WHITEMAN. 1951. Effects of infantile stimulation upon later emotional stability in the mouse. *J. comp. physiol. Psychol.,* **44,** 61–66.

HANFMANN, E., and J. KASANIN. 1942. Conceptual thinking in schizophrenia. *Nerv. ment. Dis Monogr.,* No. 67.

HARLOW, H. F. 1932. Social facilitation of feeding in the albino rat. *J. genet. Psychol.,* **41,** 211–221.

————. 1949. The formation of learning sets. *Psychol. Rev.,* **56,** 51–65.

———— and R. STAGNER. 1933. Effect of complete striate muscle paralysis upon the learning process. *J. exp. Psychol.,* **16,** 283–394.

———— and ————. 1933a. Psychology of feelings and emotions. II. Theory of emotions. *Psychol. Rev.,* **40,** 184–195.

HARRELL, T. W., and MARGARET S. HARRELL. 1945. Army general classification test scores for civilian occupations. *Educ. Psychol. Meas.,* **5,** 229–239.

HASTORF, A. H. 1950. The influence of suggestion on the relationship between stimulus size and perceived size. *J. Psychol.,* **50,** 195–217.

———— and K. S. WAY. 1952. Apparent size with and without distance cues. *J. gen. Psychol.* (in press).

HATHAWAY, S. R. 1935. An action potential study of neuro-muscular relations. *J. exp. Psychol.,* **18,** 285–298.

HEIDBREDER, E. 1946. The attainment of concepts. *J. gen. Psychol.,* **35,** 173–223.

HELSON, H., and E. V. FEHRER. 1932. The role of form in perception. *Amer. J. Psychol.,* **44,** 79–102.

HENDRICK, IVES. 1934. *Facts and Theories of Psychoanalysis.* New York: Alfred A. Knopf, Inc.

HENMON, V. A. C. 1917. The relation between learning and retention and amount to be learned. *J. exp. Psychol.,* **2,** 476–484.

HENNEMAN, R. H. 1935. A photometric study of the perception of object color. *Arch. Psychol.,* No. 179.

HENRY, W. E. 1949. The business executive: The psychodynamics of a social role. *Amer. J. Sociol.,* **54,** 286–291.

HERON, W. T., and EMILY PEAKE. 1949. Qualitative food deficiency as a drive in a discrimination problem. *J. comp. physiol. Psychol.,* **42,** 143–147.

HILGARD, E. R. 1936. The nature of the conditioned response. I. The case for and against stimulus-substitution. *Psychol. Rev.,* **43,** 366–385.

————. 1948. *Theories of Learning.* New York: Appleton-Century-Crofts, Inc.

HOCH, PAUL, and JOSEPH ZUBIN. (Eds.) 1950. *Anxiety.* New York: Grune & Stratton.

HOELZEL, F. 1942. Fear and gastric acidity. *Amer. J. Digest. Dis.,* **9,** 188.

HOLLINGWORTH, LETA S. 1942. *Children above 180 IQ.* Yonkers, New York: World Book Company.

HOLMBERG, ALLAN R. 1950. *Nomads of the Long Bow.* Smithsonian Institution. Inst. of Social Anthropology, Publ. No. 10. Washington: U.S. Government Printing Office.

HOLMES, T. H., HELEN GOODELL, S. WOLF, and H. G. WOLFF. 1950. *The Nose.* Springfield, Ill.: Charles C. Thomas, Publisher.

HOLT, E. B. 1931. *Animal Drive and the Learning Process.* New York: Henry Holt and Company, Inc.

HONZIK, C. H. 1936. The sensory basis of maze learning in rats. *Comp. Psychol. Monogr.,* **13,** No. 64.

HOROWITZ, E. L. 1936. The development of attitude toward the Negro. *Arch. Psychol.,* **28,** No. 194.

HOVLAND, C. I. 1937. The generalization of conditioned responses. I. The sensory generalization of conditioned responses with varying frequencies of tone. *J. gen. Psychol.,* **17,** 125–148.

HUDGINS, C. V. 1933. Conditioning and the voluntary control of the pupillary light reflex. *J. gen. Psychol.,* **8,** 3–51.

HUDSON, B. B. 1950. One-trial learning in the domestic rat. *Genet. Psychol. Monogr.,* **41,** 99–146.

HULL, C. L. 1943. *Principles of Behavior.* New York: Appleton-Century-Crofts, Inc.

HUMPHREY, G. 1948. *Directed Thinking.* New York: Dodd, Mead & Company, Inc.

HUNT, J. McV. 1941. Effects of infant feeding-frustration upon adult hoarding in the albino rat. *J. abnorm. soc. Psychol.,* **36,** 338–360.

———— (Ed.). 1944. *Personality and the Behavior Disorders.* (2 vols.) New York: The Ronald Press Company.

HUNTER, W. S. 1913. The delayed reaction in animals and children. *Behav. Monogr.,* **2,** No. 6.

————. 1932. Effect of inactivity produced by cold upon learning and retention in the cockroach. *J. genet. Psychol.,* **41,** 253–256.

HUSBAND, R. W. 1931. Comparative behavior on different types of mazes. *J. gen. Psychol.,* **5,** 234–244.

HUSTON, P. E., D. SHAKOW, and M. H. ERICKSON. 1934. A study of hypnotically induced complexes by means of the Luria technique. *J. gen. Psychol.,* **11,** 65–97.

HUTCHINSON, E. D. 1949. *How to Think Creatively.* Nashville, Tenn.: Abingdon-Cokesbury Press.

HYBL, A. R. 1951. *Frustration Tolerance in Relation to Diagnosis and Therapy.* Urbana, Ill.: University of Illinois Library.

INBAU, F. E. 1942. *Lie Detection and Criminal Investigation.* Baltimore: The Williams & Wilkins Company.

IRWIN, O. C. 1930. Amount and nature of activities of newborn infants under constant external conditions during the first ten days of life. *Genet. Psychol. Monogr.,* **8,** No. 1, 1–92.

ITTELSON, W. H., and F. P. KILPATRICK. 1951. Perception. *Sci. Amer.* **185,** No. 2, 50–55.

JACOBSON, E. 1932. The electrophysiology of mental activities. *Amer. J. Psychol.,* **44,** 677–694.

JENKINS, J. G. 1948. The nominating technique as a method of evaluating air group morale. *J. Aviat. Med.,* **19,** 12–19.

———— and K. M. DALLENBACH. 1924. Obliviscence during sleep and waking. *Amer. J. Psychol.,* **35,** 605–612.

JESSE, F. T. 1924. *Murder and Its Motives.* London: William Heinemann, Ltd.

JOHNSON, D. M. 1948. *Essentials of Psychology.* New York: McGraw-Hill Book Company, Inc.

JOLLES, I. A. 1947. Study of mental deficiency by Rorschach technique. *Amer. J. ment. Def.,* **52,** 37–42.

JONES, H. E. 1930. The retention of conditioned emotional reactions in infancy. *J. genet. Psychol.,* **37,** 485–498.

———— and H. S. CONRAD. 1933. Growth and decline of intelligence. *Genet. Psychol. Monogr.,* **13,** 223–298.

JONES, MARY C. 1924a. The elimination of children's fears. *J. exp. Psychol.,* **7,** 382–390.

————. 1924b. A laboratory study of fear: The case of Peter. *J. genet. Psychol.,* **31,** 308–315.

————. 1926. The development of early behavior patterns in young children. *J. genet. Psychol.*, **33**, 537–585.

JUNG, C. G. 1918. *Studies in Word Association.* New York: Dodd, Mead & Company, Inc.

————. 1923. *Psychological Types.* New York: Harcourt, Brace and Company, Inc.

KARWOSKI, T. F., and H. S. ODBERT. 1938. Color-music. *Psychol. Monogr.*, **50**, No. 2.

————, ————, and C. E. OSGOOD. 1942. Studies in synaesthetic thinking. II. The role of form in visual responses to music. *J. gen. Psychol.*, **26**, 199–222.

KASANIN, J. S. (Ed.). 1944. *Language and Thought in Schizophrenia.* Berkeley: University of California Press.

KATONA, G. 1940. *Organizing and Memorizing: Studies in the Psychology of Learning and Teaching.* New York: Columbia University Press.

KATZ, D., and F. H. ALLPORT. 1931. *Students' Attitudes.* Syracuse, N.Y.: Craftsman Press.

KAUFMAN, EDNA L., and NEAL E. MILLER. 1949. Effect of number of reinforcements on strength of approach in an approach-avoidance conflict. *J. comp. physiol. Psychol.*, **42**, 65–74.

KELLEY, H. H. 1949. Effects of expectations upon first impressions of persons. *Amer. Psychologist*, **4**, 252.

KENNEDY, J. L., R. M. GOTTSDANKER, J. C. ARMINGTON, and F. E. GRAY. 1948. A new electroencephalogram associated with thinking. *Science*, **108**, 527–529.

KENNEDY, R. J. R. 1948. *Social Adjustment of Morons in a Connecticut City.* Hartford: Mansfield-Southbury Training Schools (Social Service Dept., State Office Bldg.).

KEPES, G. 1944. *Language of Vision.* Chicago: Paul Theobald.

KEYS, ANCEL, JOSEF BROZEK, AUSTIN HENSCHEL, OLAF MICKELSEN, and H. L. TAYLOR. 1950. *The Biology of Human Starvation.* (2 vols.) Minneapolis: University of Minnesota Press.

KIMBLE, G. A. 1947. Conditioning as a function of the time between conditioned and unconditioned stimuli. *J. exp. Psychol.*, **37**, 1–15.

KINGSLEY, H. L. 1946. *Nature and Conditions of Learning.* New York: Prentice-Hall, Inc.

KINSEY, A. C., W. B. POMEROY, and C. E. MARTIN. 1948. *Sexual Behavior in the Human Male.* Philadelphia: W. B. Saunders Company.

KITSON, H. D. 1922. A study of the output of workers under particular wage incentive. *Univ. J. Bus.*, **1**, 54–68.

KLINEBERG, OTTO. 1940. *Social Psychology.* New York: Henry Holt and Company, Inc.

KLÜVER, H. 1933. *Behavior Mechanisms in Monkeys.* Chicago: University of Chicago Press.

KÖHLER, W. 1925. *Mentality of Apes.* (Tr. by E. Winter) New York: Harcourt, Brace and Company, Inc.

————. 1938. Simple structural functions in the chimpanzee and in the chicken. In Ellis, W. D. 1938. *A Source Book of Gestalt Psychology.* New York: Harcourt, Brace and Company, Inc.

KORZYBSKI, A. 1941. *Science and Sanity.* (2nd ed.) Lancaster, Pa.: International Non-Aristotelian Library Publishing Co.

KRIEG, W. J. S. 1942. *Functional Neuro-anatomy.* Philadelphia: The Blakiston Company.

KROUT, JOHANNA. 1950. Symbol elaboration test. *Psychol. Monogr.*, **64**, No. 4 (whole No. 310).

LAIRD, D. A. 1928. Experiments on the physiological cost of noise. *J. Nat. Inst. Indus. Psychol.*, **4**, 251–258.

————. 1932. How the consumer estimates quality by subconscious sensory impressions. *J. appl. Psychol.*, **11**, 244–246.

LAMBERT, W. W., R. L. SOLOMON, and P. D. WATSON. 1949. Reinforcement and extinction as factors in size estimation. *J. exp. Psychol.*, **39**, 637–641.

LANDIS, C. 1924. Studies in emotional reactions. II. General behavior and facial expression. *J. comp. Psychol.*, **4**, 447–509.

LANIER, L. H. 1934. The interrelations of speed of reaction measurements. *J. exp. Psychol.*, **17**, 371–399.

LARSELL, O. 1942. *Anatomy of Nervous System.* New York: Appleton-Century-Crofts, Inc.

LASHLEY, K. S. 1929. *Brain Mechanisms and Intelligence.* Chicago: University of Chicago Press.

————. 1938. The mechanism of vision. XV. Preliminary studies of the rat's capacity for detailed vision. *J. gen. Psychol.*, **18**, 123–193.

———— and J. BALL. 1929. Spinal conduction and kinaesthetic sensitivity in the maze habit. *J. comp. Psychol.*, **9**, 71–106.

———— and J. T. RUSSELL. 1934. The mechanism of vision. XI. A preliminary test of innate organization. *J. genet. Psychol.*, **45**, 136–144.

LEE, I. J. 1941. *Language Habits in Human Affairs.* New York: Harper & Brothers.

LEEPER, R. 1935. A study of a neglected portion of the field of learning—The development of sensory organization. *J. genet. Psychol.*, **46**, 41–75.

LEVINE, J. M., and G. MURPHY. 1943. Learning and forgetting of controversial material. *J. abnorm. soc. Psychol.*, **38**, 507–517.

LIDDELL, H. S. 1942. The conditioned reflex. In Moss, F. A. (Ed.), 1942. *Comparative Psychology.* New York: Prentice-Hall, Inc.

————. 1944. Conditioned reflex method and experimental neurosis. In Hunt, J. McV. (Ed.), 1944. *Personality and the Behavior Disorders.* (2 vols.) New York: The Ronald Press Company.

LIGHT, J. S., and W. H. GANTT. 1936. Essential parts of reflex arc for establishment of conditioned reflex. Formation of conditioned reflex after exclusion of motor peripheral end. *J. comp. Psychol.*, **21**, 19–36.

LINDAHL, L. G. 1945. Movement analysis as an industrial training method. *J. appl. Psychol.*, **29**, 420–436.

LOEMAKER, K. K. 1930. Certain factors determining the accuracy of a response to the direction of a visual object. *J. exp. Psychol.*, **13**, 500–518.

LORGE, I. 1930. Influence of regularly interpolated time intervals upon subsequent learning. *Teach. Coll. Contr. Educ.*, No. 438.

————. 1936. Irrelevant needs in learning. *J. comp. Psychol.*, **21**, 105–128.

LOUCKS, R. B. 1938. Studies of neural structures essential for learning. II. *J. comp. Psychol.*, **25**, 315–332.

LOWELL, FRANCIS E. 1941. A study of the variability of IQ's in retests. *J. appl. Psychol.*, **25**, 341–356.

LUCAS, D. B., and S. H. BRITT. 1950. *Advertising Psychology and Research.* New York: McGraw-Hill Book Company, Inc.

LUCHINS, A. S. 1942. Mechanization in problem solving. The effect of einstellung. *Psychol. Monogr.*, **54**, No. 248.

McALLISTER, W. G. 1932. Further study of delayed reaction in albino rat. *Comp. Psychol. Monogr.*, **8**, No. 37.

McCLEARY, R. A., and R. S. LAZARUS. 1949. Autonomic discrimination without awareness. An interim report. *J. Personality*, **18**, 171–179.

McCLELLAND, D. C., and J. W. ATKINSON. 1948. Projective expression of needs: I. The effect of different intensities of the hunger drive on perception. *J. Psychol.*, **25**, 205–222.

————, ————, and R. A. CLARK. 1949. The projective expression of needs: III. The effect of ego-involvement, success, and failure on perception. *J. Psychol.*, **27**, 311–330.

————, RUSSELL A. CLARK, THORNTON B. ROBY, and JOHN W. ATKINSON. 1949. The projective expression of needs. IV. The effect of the need for achievement on thematic apperception. *J. exp. Psychol.*, **39**, 242–255.

McCORD, F. 1939. The delayed reaction and memory in rats. I. Length of delay. *J. comp. Psychol.*, **27**, 1–37.

MACDUFF, MARY M. 1946. Effect on retention of varying degrees of motivation during learning in rats. *J. comp. Psychol.*, **39**, 207–240.

MacFARLANE, D. A. 1930. The role of kinaesthesis in maze learning. *Univ. Calif. Publ. Psychol.*, **4**, 277–305.

McGEOCH, J. A. 1942. *Psychology of Human Learning.* New York: Longmans, Green & Co., Inc.

———— and W. T. McDonald. 1931. Meaningful relation and retroactive inhibition. *Amer. J. Psychol.*, **43**, 579–588.

McGinnies, E. 1949. Emotionality and perceptual defense. *Psychol. Rev.*, **56**, 244–251.

McGranahan, D. V. 1940. Critical and experimental study of repression. *J. abnorm. soc. Psychol.*, **35**, 212–225.

McPherson, G. 1936. Preliminary considerations of heredity in mental deficiency. In *Proc. Amer. Ass. Stud. ment. Def.*

Maier, N. R. F., and T. C. Schneirla. 1942. Mechanisms in conditioning. *Psychol. Rev.*, **49**, 117–134.

Marks, M. R. 1951. Problem solving as function of situation. *J. exp. Psychol.*, **41**, 74–80.

Maslow, A. H. 1934. Effect of varying external conditions on learning, retention and reproduction. *J. exp. Psychol.*, **17**, 36–47.

————. 1943. A theory of human motivation. *Psychol. Rev.*, **50**, 370–396.

———— and B. Mittelman. 1951. *Principles of Abnormal Psychology.* New York: Harper & Brothers.

Masserman, Jules. 1946. *Principles of Dynamic Psychiatry.* Philadelphia: W. B. Saunders Company.

Max, L. W., 1935. An experimental study of the motor theory of consciousness: III. Action-current responses in deaf mutes during sleep, sensory stimulation and dreams. *J. comp. Psychol.*, **19**, 469–486.

————. 1937. An experimental study of the motor theory of consciousness. IV. Action-current responses in the deaf during awakening, kinaesthetic imagery and abstract thinking. *J. comp. Psychol.*, **24**, 301–344.

May, M. A. 1948. Experimentally acquired drives. *J. exp. Psychol.*, **38**, 66–77.

Mead, Margaret. 1935. *Sex and Temperament.* New York: William Morrow & Company, Inc.

Meenes, M., and M. A. Morton. 1936. Characteristics of the eidetic phenomenon. *J. gen. Psychol.*, **14**, 370–391.

Melton, A. W. 1944. Selection of pilots by means of psychomotor tests. *J. Aviat. Med.*, **15**, 116–123.

Meltzer, H. 1933. Student's adjustments in anger. *J. soc. Psychol.*, **4**, 285–309.

Menzies, R. 1937. Conditioned vasomotor responses in human subjects. *J. Psychol.*, **4**, 75–120.

Miles, Catharine C., and Walter R. Miles. 1932. Correlation of intelligence scores and chronological age from early to late maturity. *Amer. J. Psychol.*, **44**, 44–78.

Miller, D. C. 1916. *Science of Musical Sounds.* New York: The Macmillan Company.

————. 1937. *Sound Waves.* New York: The Macmillan Company.

Miller, N. E. 1948. Studies of fear as an acquirable drive: I. Fear as motivation and fear-reduction as reinforcement in the learning of new responses. *J. exp. Psychol.*, **38**, 89–101.

————. 1948. Theory and experiment relating psychoanalytic displacement to stimulus-response generalization. *J. abnorm. soc. Psychol.*, **43**, 155–178.

Minami, H., and K. M. Dallenbach. 1946. The effect of activity upon learning and retention in the cockroach. *Amer. J. Psychol.*, **59**, 1–58.

Montgomery, M. F. 1931. The role of the salivary glands in the thirst mechanism. *Amer. J. Physiol.*, **96**, 221–227.

Morgan, C. L. 1894. *Introduction to Comparative Psychology.* New York: William R. Scott, Inc.

Morgan, C. T., and J. D. Morgan. 1940. Studies in hunger. II. The relation of gastric denervation and dietary sugar to the effect of insulin upon food intake in the rat. *J. genet. Psychol.*, **57**, 153–163.

———— and Eliot Stellar. 1950. *Physiological Psychology.* (2d ed.) New York: McGraw-Hill Book Company, Inc.

Mowrer, O. H. 1940. Anxiety-reduction and learning. *J. exp. Psychol.*, **27**, 497–516.

————. 1947. On the dual nature of learning—A re-interpretation of "conditioning" and "problem-solving." *Harv. educ. Rev.*, **17**, 102–148.

————. 1950. Pain, punishment, guilt and anxiety. In Hoch, P., and J. Zubin (Eds.), 1950. *Anxiety.* New York: Grune & Stratton.

————, N. N. Rayman, and E. L. Bliss. 1940. Preparatory set (expectancy). An experimental demonstration of its "central" locus. *J. exp. Psychol.*, **26**, 357–372.

———— and A. D. ULLMAN. 1945. Time as a determinant in integrative learning. *Psychol. Rev.*, **52**, 61–90.

MUENZINGER, K. F. 1934. Motivation in learning. I. Electric shock for correct responses in the visual discrimination habit. *J. comp. Psychol.*, **17**, 267–277.

MÜLLER-FREIENFELS, R. 1935. (Tr. by W. Beran Wolfe) *Evolution of Modern Psychology*. New Haven: Yale University Press.

MURRAY, H. A. 1938. *Explorations in Personality*. New York: Oxford University Press.

NEILON, PATRICIA. 1948. Shirley's babies after fifteen years: A personality study. *J. genet. Psychol.*, **73**, 175–186.

NEWMAN, H. H. (Ed.). 1926. *Nature of the World and of Man.* Chicago: University of Chicago Press.

————. 1940. *Multiple Human Births*. New York: Doubleday & Company, Inc.

————, F. N. FREEMAN, and K. J. HOLZINGER. 1937. *Twins: A Study of Heredity and Environment*. Chicago: University of Chicago Press.

NOBLE, C. E. 1950. Conditioned generalization of the galvanic skin response to a subvocal stimulus. *J. exp. Psychol.*, **40**, 15–25.

ORLANSKY, H. 1949. Infant care and personality. *Psychol. Bull.*, **46**, 1–48.

OSGOOD, C. E. 1949. The similarity paradox in human learning: A resolution. *Psychol. Rev.*, **56**, 132–143.

OSTROM, S. R. 1949. The O. L. key of the Strong test and drive at the 12th grade level. *J. appl. Psychol.*, **33**, 240–248.

PASCAL, G. R. 1942. Handwriting pressure: Its measurement and significance. *Character & Pers.*, **11**, 235–254.

PASSEY, G. E., and F. E. GUEDRY. 1949. The perception of the vertical: adaptation effects in four planes. *J. exp. Psychol.*, **39**, 700–707.

PAVLOV, I. P. 1927. *Conditioned Reflexes*. (Tr. by G. V. Anrep) New York: Oxford University Press.

————. 1928. *Lectures on Conditioned Reflexes*. New York: International Publishers Co.

PENFIELD, W., and T. RASMUSSEN. 1950. *The Cerebral Cortex of Man*. New York: The Macmillan Company.

PERKY, C. W. 1910. An experimental study of imagination. *Amer. J. Psychol.*, **21**, 422–452.

PERRIN, F. A. C. 1914. An experimental and introspective study of the human learning process in the maze. *Psychol. Monogr.*, **16**, No. 10.

PIAGET, J. 1928. *Judgment and Reasoning in the Child*. New York: Harcourt, Brace and Company, Inc.

————. 1932. *The Language and Thought of the Child*. New York: Harcourt, Brace and Company, Inc.

PIRENNE, M. H. 1948. *Vision and the Eye*. London: Chapman & Hall, Ltd.

POLYAK, S. I. 1941. *The Retina*. Chicago: University of Chicago Press.

PORTEUS, S. D. 1937. *Primitive Intelligence and Environment*. New York: The Macmillan Company.

POSTMAN, LEO. 1947. History and present status of the law of effect. *Psychol. Bull.*, **44**, 489–563.

————, J. S. BRUNER, and E. M. McGINNIES. 1948. Personal values as selective factors in perception. *J. abnorm. soc. Psychol.*, **43**, 142–154.

PRATT, K. C., A. K. NELSON, and K. H. SUN. 1930. The behavior of the newborn infant. *Ohio State Univ. Cont. Psychol.*, No. 10.

PRENTICE, W. C. H. 1948. New observations of "binocular yellow." *J. exp. Psychol.*, **38**, 284–288.

RASMUSSEN, T. A. 1943. *Outlines of Neuroanatomy*. Dubuque, Iowa: William C. Brown Co.

RAZRAN, G. H. S. 1933. Conditioned responses in children. *Arch. Psychol.*, **23**, No. 148.

————. 1935. Conditioned responses: An experimental study and a theoretical analysis. *Arch. Psychol.*, No. 191.

————. 1949a. Semantic and phonetographic generalizations of salivary conditioning to verbal stimuli. *J. exp. Psychol.*, **39**, 642–652.

————. 1949b. Some psychological factors in the generalization of salivary conditioning to verbal stimuli. *Amer. J. Psychol.*, **62**, 247–256.

————. 1949c. Stimulus generalization of conditioned responses. *Psychol. Bull.*, **46**, 337–365.

RIBBLE, MARGARET. 1944. Infantile experience in relation to personality development. In Hunt, J. McV. (Ed.), 1944. *Personality and the Behavior Disorders.* (2 vols.) New York: The Ronald Press Company.

RICE, S. A. 1926. Stereotypes. *J. Person. Res.*, **5**, 267–276.

RICHTER, C. P. 1927. Animal behavior and internal drives. *Quart. Rev. Biol.*, **2**, 307–343.

————. 1937. Hypophyseal control of behavior. *Cold Spr. Harbor Sympos. quant. Biol.*, **5**, 258–268.

————. 1939. Transmission of taste sensations in animals. *Trans. Amer. neurol. Ass.*, **65**, 49–50.

————. 1942. Total self-regulatory functions in animals and human beings. *Harvey Lect. Ser.*, **38**, 63–103.

————. 1947. Biology of drives. *J. comp. physiol. Psychol.*, **40**, 129–134.

RIESEN, A. H. 1947. The development of visual perception in man and chimpanzee. *Science*, **106**, 107–108.

RIGGS, L. A., and T. F. KARWOSKI. 1934. Synaesthesia. *Brit. J. Psychol.*, **25**, 29–41.

ROBERTS, J. A. F. 1947. High grade mental deficiency in relation to differential fertility. *J. ment. Sci.*, **93**, 289–302.

ROBINSON, E. A., and E. F. ADOLPH. 1943. Pattern of normal water drinking in dogs. *Amer. J. Physiol.*, **139**, 39–44.

RORSCHACH, H. 1921. *Psychodiagnostik.* Leipzig: Ernst Bircher Verlag.

ROSENZWEIG, SAUL. 1944. An outline of frustration theory. In Hunt, J. McV. (Ed.), 1944. *Personality and the Behavior Disorders.* (2 vols.) New York: The Ronald Press Company.

ROSS, SHERMAN, and JEAN GOODWIN ROSS. 1949. Social facilitation of feeding behavior in dogs: I. Group and solitary feeding. *J. genet. Psychol.*, **74**, 97–108.

———— and ————. 1949. Social facilitation of feeding behavior in dogs: II. Feeding after satiation. *J. genet. Psychol.*, **74**, 293–304.

RUGER, H. A. 1910. The psychology of efficiency. *Arch. Psychol.*, **2**, No. 15.

SANTEE, H. E. 1907. *Anatomy of Brain and Spinal Cord.* Philadelphia: The Blakiston Company.

SARASON, SEYMOUR B. 1949. *Psychological Problems in Mental Deficiency.* New York: Harper & Brothers.

SARGENT, S. S. 1939. Emotional stereotypes in the Chicago Tribune. *Sociometry*, **2**, 69–75.

SCHAFER, R., and G. MURPHY. 1943. The role of autism in visual figure-ground relationship. *J. exp. Psychol.*, **32**, 335–343.

SCHEERER, M., E. ROTHMAN, and K. GOLDSTEIN. 1945. A case of "idiot savant." An experimental study of personality organization. *Psychol. Monogr.*, **58**, No. 269.

SCHILLING, ROBERT F., and MARC J. MUSSER. 1949. Pain reaction thresholds in patients with peptic ulcer. *Amer. J. med. Sci.*, **218**, 207–208.

SELYE, H. 1946. The general adaptation syndrome and the diseases of adaptation. *J. clin. Endocrin.*, **2**, 117–230.

SENDEN, M. VON. 1932. *Raum und Gestalt-Auffassung bei operierten Blindgeborenen vor und nach der Operation.* Leipzig: J. A. Barth.

SHAFFER, L. F. 1947. Fear and courage in aerial combat. *J. consult. Psychol.*, **11**, 137–143.

SHAW, F. J. 1944. Two determinants of selective forgetting. *J. abnorm. soc. Psychol.*, **39**, 434–445.

SHELDON, W. H., and S. S. STEVENS. 1942. *Varieties of Temperament.* New York: Harper & Brothers.

SHERIF, M. 1935. A study of some social factors in perception. *Arch. Psychol.*, No. 187.

SHERMAN, M. 1927. Differentiation of emotional responses in infants. *J. comp. Psychol.*, **7**, 265–284, 335–351.

————. 1945. *Intelligence and Its Deviations.* New York: The Ronald Press Company.

————. 1947. The frustration threshold. *Amer. J. Psychiat.*, **104**, 242–246.

———— and CORA B. KEY. 1932. Intelligence of isolated mountain children. *Child Develpm.*, **3**, 279–290.

SHIRLEY, MARY M. 1933. *The First Two Years.* (Vol. 3) Minneapolis: University of Minnesota Press.

SHOCK, N. W. 1944. Physiological factors in behavior. In Hunt, J. McV. (Ed.), 1944. *Personality and the Behavior Disorders.* (2 vols.) New York: The Ronald Press Company.

SHURRAGER, P. S., and E. A. CULLER. 1940. Conditioning in the spinal dog. *J. exp. Psychol.,* **26,** 133–159.

SILLECK, S. B., JR., and C. W. LAPHA. 1937. The relative effectiveness of emphasis upon right and wrong responses in human maze learning. *J. exp. Psychol.,* **20,** 195–201.

SKEELS, H. M., RUTH UPDEGRAFF, BETH WELLMAN, and H. M. WILLIAMS. 1938. A study of environmental stimulation: An orphanage pre-school project. *Univ. Ia. Stud. Child Welf.,* **15,** No. 4.

SKINNER, B. F. 1938. *The Behavior of Organisms.* New York: Appleton-Century-Crofts, Inc.

SKODAK, MARIE. 1939. Children in foster homes. *Univ. Ia. Stud. Child Welf.,* **16,** No. 1.

SMOKE, K. L. 1932. An objective study of concept formation. *Psychol. Monogr.,* **42,** No. 191.

SNYGG, D. 1935. The relative difficulty of mechanically equivalent tasks. II. Animal learning. *J. genet. Psychol.,* **47,** 321–336.

SORLIEN, K. E. 1942. The Polarity Capacity of Nouns and Verbs. Unpublished B. A. Thesis, Dartmouth College.

SPEER, G. S. 1940. Intelligence of foster children. *J. genet. Psychol.,* **57,** 49–55.

SPITZ, R. A., and K. M. WOLFE. 1946. The smiling response. *Genet. Psychol. Monogr.,* **34,** 57–125.

STAGNER, ROSS. 1931. The redintegration of pleasant and unpleasant experiences. *Amer. J. Psychol.,* **43,** 463–468.

———. 1944. Studies in aggressive social attitudes. III. Role of personal and family scores. *J. soc. Psychol.,* **20,** 129–140.

———. 1948. *Psychology of Personality.* (2d ed.) New York: McGraw-Hill Book Company, Inc.

———. 1951. Homeostasis as a unifying concept in personality theory. *Psychol. Rev.,* **58,** 5–17.

——— and R. H. BRITTON. 1949. The conditioning technique applied to a public opinion problem. *J. soc. Psychol.,* **29,** 103–111.

——— and C. E. OSGOOD. 1946. Impact of war on a nationalistic frame of reference. *J. soc. Psychol.,* **24,** 187–216.

STAUGAS, LEONARD, and L. L. McQUITTY. 1950. A new application of forced-choice ratings. *Pers. Psychol.,* **3,** 413–424.

STEWART, NAOMI G. 1947. AGCT scores of army personnel grouped by occupation. *Occupations,* **26,** 5–41.

STOCKARD, CHARLES R. 1941. Genetic and endocrinic bases for differences in form and behavior as elucidated by studies of contrasted pure-line dog breeds and their hybrids. *Amer. anat. Mem.,* No. 19.

STONE, C. P. 1932. Wildness and savageness in rats of different strains. In Lashley, K. S. 1932. *Studies in the Dynamics of Behavior.* Chicago: University of Chicago Press.

STRATTON, G. M. 1896. Some preliminary experiments on vision without inversion of the retinal image. *Psychol. Rev.,* **3,** 611–617.

STREET, R. F. 1931. A Gestalt completion test: A study of a cross-section of intellect. *Columbia Univ., Teach. Coil. Contr. Educ.,* No. 481.

STRUGHOLD, HUBERTUS. 1949. The human time factor in flight; the latent period of optical perception and its significance in high speed flying. *J. Aviat. Med.,* **20,** 300–307.

SUPA, M., M. COTZIN, and K. M. DALLENBACH. 1944. "Facial vision": The perception of obstacles by the blind. *Amer. J. Psychol.,* **57,** 133–183.

SWIFT, E. J. 1903. Studies in the psychology and physiology of learning. *Amer. J. Psychol.,* **14,** 201–251.

SWINDLE, P. F. 1916. Positive after-images of long duration. *Amer. J. Psychol.,* **27,** 324–334.

———. 1917. Visual, cutaneous and kinaesthetic ghosts. *Amer. J. Psychol.,* **28,** 349–373.

SZASZ, T. S., E. LEVIN, J. B. KIRSNER, and W. L. PALMER. 1947. Role of hostility in the pathogenesis of peptic ulcer. *Psychosom. Med.,* **9,** 331–336.

TERMAN, L. M. (Ed.). 1925. *Genetic Studies of Genius.* (Vol. 1) Stanford University, Calif.: Stanford University Press.

——. 1926. (Reported by L. M. Terman, *Amer. J. Psychol.*, **37**, 233–236.)

——. 1938. *Psychological Factors in Marital Happiness.* New York: McGraw-Hill Book Company, Inc.

—— and MAUD A. MERRILL. 1937. *Measuring Intelligence.* Boston: Houghton Mifflin Company.

—— and M. H. ODEN. 1947. *The Gifted Child Grows Up.* Stanford University, Calif.: Stanford University Press.

THORNDIKE, E. L. 1898. Animal intelligence: An experimental study of the associative processes in animals. *Psychol. Rev. Monogr. Suppl.*, **2**, No. 8.

——. 1932. *Fundamentals of Learning.* New York: Teachers College, Columbia University.

——. 1933. An experimental study of rewards. *Teach. Coll. Contr. Educ.*, No. 580.

——. 1935. *The Psychology of Wants, Interests and Attitudes.* New York: Appleton-Century-Crofts, Inc.

THORNDIKE, R. L., and GEORGE H. GALLUP. 1944. Verbal intelligence of the American adult. *J. gen. Psychol.*, **30**, 75–85.

THOULESS, R. H. 1931. Phenomenal regression to the real object. *Brit. J. Psychol.*, **21**, 339–359.

THURSTONE, L. L. 1928. Absolute zero in intelligence measurement. *Psychol. Rev.*, **35**, 175–197.

TINKER, M. A., and K. H. BAKER. 1946. *Introduction to Methods in Experimental Psychology.* New York: Appleton-Century-Crofts, Inc.

TINKLEPAUGH, O. L. 1928. An experimental study of representative factors in monkeys. *J. comp. Psychol.*, **8**, 197–236.

TOLMAN, E. C. 1948. Cognitive maps in rats and men. *Psychol. Rev.*, **55**, 189–208.

——, C. S. HALL, and E. P. BRETNALL. 1932. A disproof of the law of effect and a substitution of the laws of emphasis, motivation and disruption. *J. exp. Psychol.*, **15**, 601–614.

——, B. F. RITCHIE, and D. KALISH. 1946. Studies in spatial learning. I. Orientation and the short cut. *J. exp. Psychol.*, **36**, 13–24.

TRYON, R. C. 1940. Genetic differences in maze-learning ability in rats. *39th Yearb. nat. Soc. Stud. Educ.*, **1**, 111–119.

TSANG, Y. C. 1938. Hunger motivation in gastrectomized rats. *J. comp. Psychol.*, **26**, 1–17.

TUNTURI, A. R. 1944. Audio frequency localization in the acoustic cortex of the dog. *Amer. J. Physiol.*, **141**, 397–403.

VALENTINE, C. W. 1930. The innate bases of fear. *J. genet. Psychol.*, **37**, 394–420.

VANDERPLAS, J. M., and R. R. BLAKE. 1949. Selective sensitization in auditory perception. *J. Personality*, **18**, 252–266.

VARNUM, W. C. 1942. *Psychology in Everyday Life.* (2d ed.) New York: McGraw-Hill Book Company, Inc.

VERNON, P. E., and G. W. ALLPORT. 1931. *A Study of Values.* Boston: Houghton Mifflin Company.

VON DORAMUS, E. 1944. The specific laws of logic in schizophrenia. In Kasanin, J. S. (Ed.), 1944. *Language and Thought in Schizophrenia.* Berkeley: University of California Press.

WADA, T. 1922. Experimental study of hunger in its relation to activity. *Arch. Psychol.*, **8**, 1–65.

WALLAS, G. 1926. *The Art of Thought.* New York: Harcourt, Brace and Company, Inc.

WALLEN, R. 1942. Ego-involvement as a determinant of selective forgetting. *J. abnorm. soc. Psychol.*, **37**, 20–40.

WANG, G. H. 1923. Relation between "spontaneous" activity and oestrus cycle in the white rat. *Comp. Psychol. Monogr.*, **2**, No. 6.

WARD, L. B. 1937. Reminiscence and rote learning. *Psychol. Monogr.*, **49**, No. 220.

WARDEN, C. J. 1931. *Animal Motivation Studies: The Albino Rat.* New York: Columbia University Press.

——. 1934. The relative economy of various modes of attack in the mastery of a stylus maze. *J. exp. Psychol.*, **7**, 243–275.

———— and T. A. JACKSON. 1935. Imitative behavior in the Rhesus monkey. *J. genet. Psychol.*, **46**, 103–125.

WARREN, H. C., and L. CARMICHAEL. 1930. *Elements of Human Psychology.* Boston: Houghton Mifflin Company.

WATSON, J. B. 1907. Kinaesthetic and organic sensations: Their role in the reactions of the white rat. *Psychol. Rev., Monogr.*, **8**, No. 2.

————. 1924. *Psychology from the Standpoint of a Behaviorist.* (2d ed.) Philadelphia: J. B. Lippincott Company.

WATT, H. J. 1905. Experimentelle Beiträge zu einer Theorie des Denkens. *Arch. ges. Psychol.*, **5**, 289–436.

WEBER, R. L., M. W. WHITE, and K. V. MANNING. 1952. *College Physics.* (2d ed.) New York: McGraw-Hill Book Company, Inc.

WECHSLER, D. 1944. *The Measurement of Adult Intelligence.* (3d. ed.) Baltimore: The Williams & Wilkins Company.

WEINGARTEN, ERICA M. 1948. Study of selective perception in clinical judgment. *J. Personality,* **17**, 370–406.

WELCH, L., and J. KUBIS. 1947. Effect of anxiety on conditioning rate and stability of PGR. *J. Psychol.*, **23**, 83–91.

WERTHEIMER, MAX. 1912. Experimentelle Studien über das Sehen von Bewegung. *Z. Psychol.*, **61**, 161–265.

————. 1945. *Productive Thinking.* New York: Harper & Brothers.

WEVER, E. G. 1932. Water temperature as an incentive to swimming activity in the rat. *J. comp. Psychol.*, **14**, 219–224.

WHITEHEAD, A. N. 1925. *Science and the Modern World.* New York: The Macmillan Company.

WICKES, FRANCES G. 1938. *The Inner World of Man.* New York: Rinehart & Company, Inc.

WIENER, NORBERT. 1948. *Cybernetics.* Cambridge, Mass.: Technology Press.

WILKINS, L., and C. P. RICHTER. 1940. A great craving for salt by a child with cortico-adrenal insufficiency. *J. Amer. med. Assn.*, **114**, 866–868.

WITKIN, H. A. 1949. Perception of body position and of the position of the visual field. *Psychol. Monogr.*, **63**, No. 302.

———— and S. E. ASCH. 1948a. Studies in space perception. II. Perception of the upright with displaced visual fields and with body tilted. *J. exp. Psychol.*, **38**, 455–477.

———— and ————. 1948b. Studies in space perception. III. Perception of the upright in the absence of a visual field. *J. exp. Psychol.*, **38**, 603–614.

———— and ————. 1948c. IV. Further experiments on the upright with displaced visual fields. *J. exp. Psychol.*, **38**, 762–782.

WITTENBORN, J. R. 1943. Factorial equations for tests of attention. *Psychometrika*, **8**, 19–35.

WITTY, P. A., and M. D. JENKINS. 1935. The case of "B"—A gifted Negro girl. *J. soc. Psychol.*, **6**, 117–124.

WOLF, S. G., and H. G. WOLFF. 1943. *Human Gastric Function.* New York: Oxford University Press.

WOLFF, W. 1943. *Expression of Personality: Experimental Depth Psychology.* New York: Harper & Brothers.

WOODWORTH, R. S. 1938. *Experimental Psychology.* New York: Henry Holt and Company, Inc.

WOOSTER, M. 1923. Certain factors in the development of a new spatial co-ordination. *Psychol. Monogr.*, **32**, No. 4.

WULF, F. 1922. Über die Veränderung von Vorstellungen (Gedächtnis und Gestalt). *Psychol. Forsch.*, **1**, 333–373. (Tr. and condensed as Tendencies in figural variation, in Ellis, W. D. 1938. *A Source Book of Gestalt Psychology.* New York: Harcourt, Brace and Company, Inc.)

YEAKEL, E. H., and R. P. RHOADES. 1941. Comparison of body and endocrine gland weights of emotional and non-emotional rats. *Endocrinology*, **28**, 337–340.

YERKES, R. M. 1912. The intelligence of earthworms. *J. Anim. Behav.*, **2**, 332–352.

———— and J. D. Dodson. 1908. Relation of strength of stimulus to rapidity of habit-formation. *J. comp. neurol. Psychol.*, **18**, 459–482.

Young, P. T. 1928. Auditory localization with acoustical transposition of the ears. *J. exp. Psychol.*, **11**, 399–429.

————. 1936. *Motivation of Behavior*. New York: John Wiley & Sons, Inc.

————. 1940. Reversal of food preferences of the white rat through controlled pre-feeding. *J. gen. Psychol.*, **22**, 33–66.

————. 1943. *Emotion in Man and Animal*. New York: John Wiley & Sons, Inc.

————. 1948. Appetite, palatability and feeding habit: A critical review. *Psychol. Bull.*, **45**, 289–320.

———— and J. P. Chaplin. 1945. Studies of food preference, appetite and dietary habit. III. Palatability and appetite in relation to dietary need. *Comp. Psychol. Monogr.*, **18**, 1–45.

———— and ————. 1949. Studies of food preference, appetite and dietary habit. X. Preferences of adrenalectomized rats for salt solutions of different concentrations. *Comp. Psychol. Monogr.*, **19**, No. 5. (Whole No. 102.)

Zeaman, David. 1949. Response latency as a function of the amount of reinforcement. *J. exp. Psychol.*, **39**, 466–483.

Zeigarnik, B. 1927. Das Behalten erledigter und unerledigter Handlungen. *Psychol. Forsch.*, **9**, 1–85. (Tr. and condensed as On finished and unfinished tasks, in Ellis, W. D. 1938. *A Source Book of Gestalt Psychology*. New York: Harcourt, Brace and Company, Inc.)

Zimmerman, F. T., B. B. Burgemeister, and T. J. Putnam. 1947. Group study of effect of glutamic acid upon mental functioning in children and adolescents. *Psychosom. Med.*, **9**, 175–183.

Name Index

Subject Index

571